FROM A BOROUGH TO A CITY

A HISTORY OF CHELMSFORD

1888 – 2012

STEPHEN NORRIS

A Bright Pen Book

Text Copyright © Stephen Norris 2014

Front cover image courtesy of Chelmsford Museums

All rights reserved. No part of this publication may be reproduced, stored in a retrieval system, or transmitted in any form or by any means, electronic, mechanical, photocopy, recording or otherwise, without prior written permission of the copyright owner. Nor can it be circulated in any form of binding or cover other than that in which it is published and without similar condition including this condition being imposed on a subsequent purchaser.

British Library Cataloguing Publication Data.
A catalogue record for this book is available from the British Library

ISBN 978-0-7552-1669-7

Authors OnLine Ltd
19 The Cinques
Gamlingay, Sandy
Bedfordshire SG19 3NU
England

This book is also available in e-book format,
details of which are available at www.authorsonline.co.uk

For Christine

Chapters

Preface 1

Introduction 3

1) Agriculture 5

2) Early industry 30

3) The Christy Group 51

4) Crompton 64

5) Marconi before 1945 83

6) Marconi after 1945 103

7) Hoffmann 120

8) EEV, Britvic and other post war industries 138

9) Trade unions, the Chelmsford Star Co-operative and Employment 151

10) Transport 168

11) The Development of the Town before 1945 190

12) The Development of the Town and Planning after 1945 209

13) Politics before 1945 225

14) Politics after 1945 255

15) Chelmsford during the First World War 276

16) Health 295

17) Sanitation 316

18) Housing 329

19) The Chelmsford Union Poor Law 349

20) Education before 1945 366

21) Education after 1945 389

22) Faith 405

23) The Police, the Prison and Crime in the Chelmsford area 428

24) Chelmsford during the Second World War 456

25) Sport before 1945 485

26) Sport after 1945 500

27) Leisure and Entertainment before 1945 514

28) Leisure and Entertainment after 1945 532

Conclusion 553

Index 554

Preface

This history of Chelmsford's recent past has been nine years in the making and a considerable number of thanks are in order. It could not have been written without the help of the members of the Essex Local History Writers group. Their positive criticism of both the research and my attempts at writing has been invaluable. I am also deeply indebted to Dot Bedenham, the retired social history curator of the Chelmsford Museums and Geoff Bowles, the present curator of the science and industrial heritage section of the Museum at Sandford Mill. Their detailed vetting has led to many improvements. My wife, Christine, has also made an enormous contribution by carrying out a good deal of proof reading. It goes without saying that any errors that remain are solely my responsibility.

The book is based on nearly five years of research from a wide variety of sources. References to a vast amount of notes were used to build up a large data base. This research started with a great deal of information gathered from the two local newspapers, the Weekly News and the Essex Chronicle. The minutes of both the borough council and rural district council have been extensively sourced as have those of the Essex County Council. I have also have also relied on a wide variety of local and business histories. Extensive use has also been made of the archives at the Essex Record Office, including their oral records. Much information was gathered from the Chelmsford and Essex Museum, from both its central headquarters in Moulsham Street and its industrial base at Sandford Mill.

After some considerable thought the decision was made to use a topic approach rather than a general chronological one. At the same time the text does make an attempt to make links between chapters. Each chapter starts with an introduction which sets out a few of the main themes covered.

It seems obvious to say but this book centres on the history of the town of

Chelmsford. There is a great deal of reference to the villages around Chelmsford, but in the main only where this develops an important thread in the text. These villages are well served by their own local histories. I decided not to give figures adjusted for inflation. Such figures tend to give distorted values because of the changing importance of different types of goods. My official starting point for the book is the incorporation of Chelmsford as a borough in 1888. The importance of various themes, however have necessitated the inclusion of material which is earlier than that date. Chelmsford's acquisition of city status in 2012 gave the book a natural finishing date, although a number of events in 2013 have been included. I decided to put all the material on the Hylands estate into the Leisure and Entertainment chapters rather than divide it between those chapters and the Development of the Town chapters.

Introduction

This book attempts to cover a broad history of Chelmsford since it became a borough in 1888. To think of Chelmsford as an industrial county town probably appears absurd anyone who has only known the new city since the new millennium. In the late nineteenth and early twentieth century Chelmsford however underwent a transformation from a small market town, largely dependent on the surrounding agriculture for its prosperity, to one where the rapidly expanding population was, directly or indirectly, reliant on the employment of the big three firms. During the second war up to thirty thousand people were employed in the main works and satellite factories and laboratories. Quite apart from Marconi, the Hoffmann and Crompton companies became national and internationally known concerns. The influence of the big firms on the lives of most of the town's population extended to their participation in sport and the types of entertainment they enjoyed. There is only one chapter in this book where the influence of industry does not play a significant part in the story. The history of the town in the second half of the twentieth century is to a considerable extent one of the decline and final demise of the big three firms. It is difficult to escape the conclusion that Marconi should still be a going concern in the city. After a rocky period in the 1980s the town re-invented itself with employment in county and local administration, the judiciary and financial services.

The development of Chelmsford as a town and now a city has not been a smooth one. Major mistakes were made in the 1960s and 1970s. Once landmarks and interesting features are removed they cannot be restored. Although the new city still has buildings of historical and architectural merit, recent criticisms of the blandness of the town in the twenty first century are perhaps not without some justification. If one looks above the normal eye line however, in the High Street and Moulsham Street, many buildings of interest are revealed.

When the borough achieved cathedral town status before the First World War it was generally felt to be only a matter of time before city status was conferred. It came as a surprise to many when almost a century later, after several failed attempts Chelmsford finally became a city in 2012.

1

The development of agriculture in the Mid Essex area

"The prospect of earning 10 to 12 shillings a week and ending up in the workhouse is not particularly exhilarating"

This chapter is not just concerned with agriculture in the rural area around Chelmsford and the market which so long served as a focal point; it also looks at the profound changes that have come about in the rural community. Moreover there are major links between this chapter and succeeding ones; nearly all Chelmsford's late Victorian industries were tied in some way to agriculture and later Chelmsford's rapidly expanding new firms were able to use surplus farming labour from the surrounding area that was no longer needed. The Mid Essex area had played its part in Essex's leading role in the period of 'High Farming' which characterized the county's agriculture up to 1873. After this the area was deeply affected by the agricultural depression which was well under way by 1880. This was instigated by the high imports of food, particularly from North America. Not all farmers in the Chelmsford rural district reacted in the same way; they were affected by their particular soil and access to transport facilities. The last one hundred and thirty years have seen a great reduction in the amount of employment connected with agriculture in the Mid Essex region. This does not mean however that agriculture was adversely affected throughout the twentieth century. Indeed agriculture is only judged to have had 30 'bad years' in the last century, whereas the nineteenth century only had 35 'good ones'. (1) The reduction in agricultural employment in mid Essex was primarily caused by the relentless march of mechanisation; by the late twentieth century the large farm with one and a half workers was the norm.

In terms of its physical features the Mid Essex area is made up of a trough from the North East of Brentwood, following the valley of the Wid until "it merges with the depression at the foot of the gently tilted boulder clay and Tiptree Heath". (2) The area is also dominated by a wide west to east valley of the River Chelmer leading to the Blackwater valley. In terms of soil there are two types of boulder clay in the region; one to the west of the Chelmer where gravel is mixed with the clay and one to the east where it is "heavier and more impermeable". The post glacial drift deposits are small but have been important to farming in the area. Alluvial deposits in the wide flood plain of the Chelmer and its tributaries have produced fertile soil suitable for market gardening. The soils are mainly loam. "Where the loam is free from any drift covering, the soil is very heavy, sticky and brownish in colour, very difficult to work in wet weather". (3)) Whilst the Mid Essex region, like much of the Eastern counties, has a generally dry climate there is the danger of thunderstorms at harvest time. (4)

By 1880 the agricultural depression had already been affecting the area for seven years. 1873 was the start of twenty years of falling wheat prices and falling rents for landowners. (5) In 1880 the Chelmsford Poor Law Union guardians were complaining about the depressed state of agriculture. (6) Farmers felt the burden of the Poor Law rate and church tithes even more than usual. Four years later the Essex Chamber of Commerce met at the Shire Hall to discuss 'The agricultural crisis and remedial action'. A motion on the imposition of a tax on imported corn was discussed. Major Carne Rasch (See chapter 13) was one who sided with free trade. Another said "free trade was taxing ourselves and letting the foreigner go free". The trade of the United States had increased by 80% in the previous twenty years but that of Great Britain only 20%. Another speaker bemoaned the burden of the tithe on tenant farmers. Chamber of Agriculture meetings repeatedly asked for this burden to be lifted. Another said "Farmers could not afford to farm high" (i.e. invest in fertilisers and mechanisation). (7) One factor which often added to the problems of the local agriculture was animal disease. There was a prevalence of sheep rot in 1880. (8) Three years later foot and mouth was widespread amongst cattle; Chelmsford market was blamed. The newly formed Essex Agricultural Labourers Union blamed bad farming for the depression. (9) Even in 1894 wheat prices were continuing to fall. In the Chelmsford Corn Exchange English wheat could be bought for 24 to 26 shillings a quarter, when foreign wheat could be obtained for 19 shillings a quarter. (10) In the same year there were 36 petitions by farmers in the Chelmsford Bankruptcy Court. (11) During 1891 the area was visited by a Commissioner investigating the depression. The Essex Chronicle thought that the amount of uncultivated land was very small but that many people had left the rural districts because of the increased use of agricultural machinery. (12)

Although there was a marked shift in the area from wheat growing to pasture during the depression this was by no means uniform. The effect of the depression depended on the types of soil mentioned earlier. In the Chelmsford area the parishes of the North West, the Chignalls, Good Easter, Pleshey and Great Waltham tended to have chalky clay. (13) The parishes with mixed soils covered those of the Chelmer valley including Broomfield, Springfield, Little Waltham and Great Waltham. Danbury, the Baddows and the Leighs could also be included. Heavy clay soils were found in the South East of the area including the Hanningfields, Rettendon Runwell and Woodham Ferrers. (14) In the area the three types of farming were arable, dairying and livestock farming, and horticulture. Arable farming included the growing of wheat, barley, bare or fallow, and fodder crops. Livestock included horses for agricultural purposes, permanent pasture and cows for milk. Horticulture included nursery and market gardening, orchards and soft fruit. (15) In 1874 25% of land in the whole area was under wheat production, by 1901 this was down to 15%. (16) There was a similar decline in barley production. Farmers in parishes in the north west of the area with lighter soil persevered with wheat even though the price had fallen. In parishes like Pleshey there was a lack of good transport for the new alternative cash crops so farmers stayed with wheat and barley. In Runwell, Rettendon, and Woodham Ferrers the heavy clay required labour intensive farming and as a consequence wheat production halved during the years of the agricultural depression. (17) Similarly barley production was less than 5% of total production in these three south eastern parishes by 1901. (18) Putting land down to permanent pasture or letting it become fallow cut costs for the beleaguered farmer. Farmers in the area could only respond to the pull of the huge London market for cash crops if they had access to railways. Great Eastern Railways were often criticised for not helping such farmers. Crops such as peas, soft fruit, and of course milk were transported on the railway at their own risk. The growth of Chelmsford by the turn of the century also produced a small but significant market for such crops.

Farmers turned to dairying only where they could get their milk and butter to the market. Beef prices remained low and did not encourage the switch to pasture, and sheep farming declined steeply. Again dairy farmers depended on the nearness to a railway station. There was a lot of support, including from Major Carne Rasch, for a light railway from Chelmsford to Braintree, which would have benefited the farmers of Broomfield, the Walthams and Great Leighs. (19)

Good transport did not always ensure the success of the market gardeners. In 1890 the mid Essex cucumber crop failed. The Weekly News reported "The large market gardeners of mid Essex have sustained a heavy loss by the bulk of their cucumber plants dying off just at the time when they should have been coming into full bearing". (20) By this time the G.E.R. were becoming more efficient in helping the producers of products like peas. The G.E.R. " have recently shown remarkable powers of dispatch". "The green pea traffic, now practically concluded, has displayed remarkable activity this season, the growers whose districts converge at the stations of Kelvedon, Witham and Chelmsford". One weekend saw the stations between Colchester and Chelmsford deliver 732 tons of peas to London. This involved 237 trucks and eight heavily laden trains. (21)

By the end of the Great Depression the local papers were bemoaning "the process of transforming Essex from a wheat growing to a grazing and milk producing county". In 1892 the agricultural returns showed a loss of 3,376 acres of wheat production in the county. (22) This was dwarfed by a loss of more than 23 thousand acres the following year. (23) Meetings on the depressed state of agriculture continued at Chelmsford. Carne Rasch noted that farmers and their landlords were always represented, but not the farm labourer, even though they had been equally badly affected and now had the vote. (24) Wages were often dropping as low as nine shillings a week in the area and in 1894 a large number of local farm labourers were unemployed. (25) By the mid 1890s alternative occupations were beginning to appear for the local agricultural labourer in Chelmsford itself. "Besides the prospect of earning from ten to twelve shillings a week and ending up in the workhouse is not particularly exhilarating". (26) Meanwhile the local papers continued to criticise the endless stream of investigations and reports both nationally and locally which did nothing to ease the pain of landowners and farmers.

One of the most interesting aspects of the agricultural depression was that it marked the beginning of the influx into the county, and Mid Essex in particular, of Scottish farmers. They were attracted by the availability of farms and the fact that they were cheap. The drier weather was more attractive than the inclement weather in their homeland. (27) By the third decade of the new century they were still arriving in the area and joining several generations of such farmers. The original Scottish arrivals put their survival down to the fact that they were prepared to work twice as hard as their fellow farmers in the county. It was a common occurrence for these farmers to work alongside the labourers they had hired and look little different from them in their clothes when working in the fields.

Chelmsford partly owed its existence to its market. By 1880 however the shopkeepers and the people who still lived in the High Street had become dissatisfied with it taking place there. By this time the impressive Corn Exchange building had already existed for 25 years. Nearby land for the new market site was bought for £3,460 and Charles Pertwee was engaged by the borough to design the new market. It was to accommodate 1,100 cattle, 300 pigs and 70 horses. Young beef animals were in the centre, sheep and pig pens on the east side and horses and fat stock on the west side. Farm machinery and other related businesses could use the space on either side of the market road. (28) The new market cost £15,000 and was opened in April 1881. All the Board of Health members were present at the inauguration which was followed by a dinner at the White Hart Hotel. (29) The opening had been delayed by a severe outbreak of foot and mouth disease. Petty sessions had been naming the farms affected which were not allowed to move stock and most markets in the county, including Chelmsford's, had been closed. The market expanded rapidly during the 1880s, despite the depression in farming and a physical expansion was carried out. In the Weekly News it was noted "the Market is developing in importance week by week, and the large and increasing numbers of cattle, sheep and pigs more than fill the pens which were amply sufficient to meet all requirements when the new area was laid out". (30) The Government insisted that a machine for weighing the cattle was installed but it was rarely used. In 1898 there was a proposal for a covered market but there was little enthusiasm for the suggestion. (31) Interestingly Joseph Brittain Pash's agricultural equipment business sold the town's first milk float in 1884. (32) A vetinary surgeon was regularly attending the market by 1912. His services were well needed because a severe foot and mouth outbreak in Ireland necessitated restrictions on the movement of cattle in the same year. (33) A local man, Harold Orrin, remembered the cattle drovers who used his father's boot shop. They drove cattle up the High Street. The metal posts were still there after the building of the new market and used with rope to make a cordon to prevent cattle from going into the shop windows (see chapter 11). This was not always successful and Orrin recalled one occasion when the cattle ran amok and one went into a china shop.

The Essex Agricultural Show had been founded in 1858 and held its first show in Chelmsford in 1860. It was intended to highlight Essex farming, its farmers, produce and equipment at their best. On average in the nineteenth century the Essex Show was held in Chelmsford area every nine years. (34) The town put the Show on in 1887 at no little expense as the local papers pointed out. "A large sum of money is being contributed to the prize list by the town. The general committee is offering £1,260 in prizes." (35) The showground was at the junction of Goldlay Road with Baddow Road. On one side was Goldlay House. The town was decked out in flags and bunting. In 1890 the Royal Show was held at Chelmsford resulting in the Prince of Wales visiting the town by rail. (36) "An enormous number of people lined the route from the railway station to the showground at Springfield Place." (37) The Chronicle complained about filthy songs sung in the street and indecent advertisings! It urged the police to do something about both. It was again held in the grounds of Goldlay House in 1897 and on the estate of T.D. Ridley the brewer in 1904. This was after Witham dropped out because of the financial outlay that was needed. (38) The Chronicle thought Witham should help Chelmsford with the cost of putting the show on.

Essex County Council was one of the first counties to make use of the so called 'whisky money' to make tentative steps into agricultural education. The amount of money available each year depended on the amount collected of whisky and spirits but in general was substantial during the 1890s. In 1891 the Essex Agricultural Society received £250 from the E.C.C. to enable them to continue their field experiments and their dairy classes. It wanted to establish "a permanent dairy in the town, where pupils could be taught the improved systems of dairying and butter making and initiated into the mysteries of manufacturing soft cheeses from both cream and skimmed milk". (39) An office was established in King Edward Avenue and the old Grammar school buildings had been bought by 1894. The building contained two lecture rooms, three biology laboratories, three chemical laboratories and a dairy. (40) David Houghton and Tom Dymond were the first full time appointments for biology and chemistry respectively. (41) By 1896 there were two horticulture classes. (42) In 1899 an inspection by the E.C.C. Technical Instruction Committee resulted in an excellent report, followed by a commitment to establish several scholarships. The early lecturers often felt hindered however by what they saw as the poor level of elementary education that the young farmers who took their courses had received. All the pupils were normally between 14 and 25 years of age. As well as horticulture there were also classes in fruit culture, bee keeping, dairy work, poultry, blacksmith work, the practice of agriculture, livestock keeping and agricultural machinery. (43) Amongst the 13 students who took a course in practical agriculture in 1900 were two members of the Marriage family (see later) (44) Meanwhile three acres had been acquired at Rainsford End along with two cottages to establish a school garden. A further four acres were added later. There was now a site for practical work for horticulture students but still no farm for agriculture students. By 1909 the work of the Winter School of Agriculture was being assessed by the Cambridge University Department of Agriculture and the school was beginning to carry out experiments in the field. (45) In 1912 the laboratories were renamed the East Anglian Institute of Agriculture. (46) Courses were taken to the villages e.g. a 12 week evening course on 'How plants grow'. In 1896 the buildings had been divided into three separate schools, the Winter School of Agriculture, the School of Horticulture and the Dairy School. (47) Apart from the courses a weed, pest and disease identifying service was established and Dymond set up a soil testing laboratory. (48) In 1913 Brittons Hall at Chignal St James was bought for the purpose of establishing an educational farm outside the town for four and a half thousand pounds. The war meant that it was never fully converted and it was sold six years later. It was intended to acquire a new site quickly.

By 1880 the Marriage family were already the leading farmers and millers in the region. They were a Quaker family whose roots could be traced back to the seventeenth century and had Huguenot roots. The Marriages had mills and farms in Broomfield, Chelmsford, Springfield and Little Waltham by 1865. In the same year William Marriage had started a partnership with his three sons William, Sampson and Philip, and with Phillip's son Henry. Henry was apparently bargaining with a butcher over the sale of some cattle when the butcher swore. He stopped negotiations immediately and sent the butcher to wash his mouth out before the negotiations could be finished. (49) By 1884 other farms had been acquired; Bedford's at Good Easter, Parsonage at Broomfield, Gardners and Woolpits at Springfield and Hayrons at High Easter. By then the family were farming over 2,000 acres. (50) Although the family records tend to mention only the bad years during the depression the partnership stayed mainly with wheat and barley production. They had already diversified into coal as early as 1855, bringing it up the Chelmer and Blackwater canal to be used at their Broomfield and Chelmer Mills. Later, early in the twentieth century, they supplied coal to the Essex Education Authority. William and Henry Marriage had introduced steam power to the mill at Broomfield. This gave production in all weathers. Their mill on the Chelmer was the only one of six on the river to have steam power by 1880. (51) From 1856 the family had also leased Bishops Hall mill from the Mildmay family.

A great deal is known about the Marriage family's farming because of their Cropping Book which dates from 1868. This shows the crop rotations used. For example one field on Brick Barns between 1878 and 1891 was sowed with wheat, clover, wheat, barley, mangold, wheat, triffolium, which was a type of clover, wheat, barley and beans. There was also an Agreements Book which showed the negotiations involved in selling the crops of the farms and the flour of the mills. The Cropping Book shows the way the family was affected by the depression. "We have had a very close trade all year, (1887) and a good many bad debts, also a very considerable drop in the value of horses and other stock. In January we had a bad case of anthrax at Brick Farms, about 40 cows and beasts died. The remainder were killed and got rid of at great sacrifice losing one thousand pounds by the outbreak." In 1891 a writer from the Miller magazine visited the Marriages' Moulsham Mill and noted the improvements they had made. "The roller plant has been fitted up in a new brick building of three stories built on the old premises at the back, and when the foundations were being excavated the remains of an ancient water mill were unearthed. Besides this roller mill Messrs W. and H. Marriage have three other mills working on the millstone system, namely the Broomfield Mills, which contain ten pairs of millstones worked by water and steam, the Bishop Hall Mills, having eight pairs of millstones and the Croxton Water Mill with five pairs of millstones." In 1898 the family had a new mill built with its own railway siding which was called Chelmer Mill. When the Hoffmann Manufacturing Company wanted to expand their site in 1910 they had to pay the Marriages £400 for land near the mill.

By 1901 conditions had improved for most farmers in the area with wheat prices for farmers 14% higher. (52) The agricultural labourer did not benefit a great deal. A small increase in wages was insufficient to prevent a large number moving from the surrounding rural districts to the town attracted by sufficiently higher wages in the new engineering firms. In 1914 there was a thirteen week strike in the county by the local branch of the National Union of Agricultural Labourers. (53) Although it was ultimately unsuccessful it did ensure that more notice was taken of farm workers, who did well in general during the war.

The role of the farm labourer in Mid Essex was little different in 1900 from centuries before. "Growing crops and tending livestock still employed the same techniques that had been used in Tudor times." (54) Farm workers had always lived in cottages but increasingly came to resent the fact that these were 'tied' to their job. This meant that there was always the threat of homelessness in retirement. The Workers Union used this to mobilise support in the county. (55)

The natural order of rural society remained largely untouched in the years leading up to the first war despite the partial unionisation of the farm labourer. Although Mid Essex, like the county as a whole, was never noted for a predominance of big landowners, the local landowner or 'squire' always had a pre-eminent position in the local village community. A number of the villagers would work at his house or in his gardens. He was usually a magistrate or justice of the peace. The first five or six rows of pews would be reserved for family members in the local parish church. Improving and repairing the latter was often one way the owner could carry out 'good works' in his community. In 1900, four of the eight Essex M.P.s were Essex landowners. (56)

Colonel Tufnell lived in Howe Street in the Walthams and owned almost half of the cottages: of 57 households when Edward the Seventh died, Tufnell owned 25. "Edwardian Howe Street would have been very much a working place with three farms, a mill, a malting, a smithy, businesses in the building and allied trades, market gardening, timber sawing, shops and a post office."There was no publicly provided water and of course no electricity. It had no cases of divorce and it was rare for a baby to be born out of wedlock. (57)

The Tritton family dominated Great Leighs as Andrew Clark noted in his diaries (See chapter 15). Herbert Tritton was Lord of the Manor and his country seat was Lyon Hall. He was a partner in Barclays Bank, which had once been Barclay, Tritton, Bevan and Co. "The Trittons had done much for the village: the sick were taken to hospital in one of their cars, food was distributed and help given when babies arrived." They had a village pump built and a clock put on the church tower. His four daughters were always doing 'good works'. Clark appreciated Tritton's support of the parish but found his evangelical fervour difficult to stomach. Although he filled the front rows of the parish church with family and staff he also supported nonconformity. He had a parish hall built which was also used for nonconformist services. (58)

Villagers in Great Leighs, such as Herbert Rolley, could not rely on just their wages for survival. He recalled that in 1904 "I lived in a cottage in School Lane and I rented it for one shilling and six pence a week. There were 18 fruit trees and a huge walnut. These incidentally provided the greater part of our subsistence for my wages at the time were 10 shillings a week which I earned by working at a nursery from 6.0 a.m. to 6.0 p.m." Another villager Alfred Green said "My parents were very poor. My father worked on a farm and his wages were 13 shillings for 54 hours. Our rent was about one shilling and sixpence a week and after buying a little coal and an ounce of 'baccy' for the old man 3d, and a pint of beer, 3d, it did not leave much for food and clothes." (59)

Before the first war most of the villagers in Great Baddow and Sandon still worked in local farms. As elsewhere in the rural districts they were housed in low cost cottages "often sharing a wash house with an earth toilet at the bottom of the garden". Les Sparrow's grandparents had an arable farm. "We had two horses, a cow and loads of chickens. It was mainly a two man farm. My grandparents got in extra labour at harvest time. All Essex farm houses had a brew house." (60) Fred Spalding senior bought Meadgate farm in Great Baddow, near where the Army and Navy roundabout is today, when he retired from his shop. He used a steam plough when these were beginning to be used more before the outbreak of the first war. Spalding remembered extreme poverty in the village. There was a man in the village known as 'Donkey'. This was because when his family was starving he cut up a dead donkey and used it for meat and soup. (61)

In every village the Great War resulted in a decisive change in attitudes within the community. As a member of Little Baddow parish council said "Never again would the schoolmaster cane a boy because a gentleman had complained that he had not doffed his cap to him". (62)

By 1900 the Darby Digger had a national reputation. Thomas Churchman Darby was born in Little Waltham in 1840. At 18 he invented a horse hoe and established a small engineering works for its production. He was scornful of the plough because it made the soil 'sour'. Darby moved to Pleshey where he worked on his digging machine. Initially he sought help from Eddingtons, the Chelmsford engineering firm (See chapter 2) which had developed a machine for laying land drains. Darby's machine had mechanical digging forks driven by means of an ordinary single cylinder steam engine. His first machine, introduced around 1876, walked on six steam operated legs. This encountered severe problems, not the least being that it cost £1,600. A second prototype with eight legs and a double boiler was no more satisfactory costing £1,800. He then set up his own firm, Darby Diggers which produced a more successful third digger. The boiler was retained but the legs removed. Its engine drove both the wheels and the digging forks. In 1880 it was shown at the Royal Show at Carlisle. One significant problem that remained was the time that it took to get the machine back on the road after digging because the wheels had to be changed. In 1900 Darby moved the works to Wickford and formed a new company, the Darby Land Digger Syndicate, to market a rotary digger. One of these was inspected by King George V in 1913 shortly before production was discontinued. The new digger had cost the company the enormous sum of £100,000. "Had he had the advantage of the internal combustion engine his story might well have been different." (63) In reality he was unlucky to have developed his expensive machine at the time of the agricultural depression. Darby's son Sydney later perfected the Darby 'All Weather' wheels to fit tractors. (64)

The agricultural machinery firm of Joseph Brittain Pash advertised "the largest stock of agricultural machinery, dairy goods and spare parts in Essex". He had started his workshop on his farm in Galleywood as early as 1866. (65) By 1900 he was producing comparatively few goods himself. He was the sole agent for Massey Harris, who claimed to have introduced reaping machines to Essex in 1866, sheaf binders in 1892 and tractors in 1915. Pash's workers were prepared to travel 100 miles to erect fences. (66) Tom Turner remembered his warehouses at the rear of the Corn Exchange; "the pioneer of selling, servicing and repairing agricultural machinery". (67)

The first war brought about a big change in farming conditions. By this time Britain was largely dependent on imported food. The attacks by German U boats on international mercantile shipping seriously disrupted these imports. This led to wheat production in the county increasing, in part ordered by the War Agricultural Committee. The shortage of labour changed the position of the remaining farm labourers decisively. Wages on average more than doubled to 30 shillings a week. (68) The war saw the first significant use of tractors in the area.

The end of the war brought about a short lived boom in food prices. Moves to control labourers' wages caused sporadic trouble and strikes in the county. (69) The Workers Union handed out strike notices for ten thousand members in Essex, but the Chelmsford district organiser said he had not been consulted. In Essex the Agricultural Labourers Union had eight thousand members. The new Government Wages Board was proposing to offer four shillings more than many current rates. (70) Part of the problem was that wage rates varied between different types of agriculture in the region. The market gardeners in mid Essex, for example, were already paying higher than the average rate. (71)

The boom proved short lived and in 1921 food prices fell sharply. Many, mostly small farms in the county, failed. (72) The National Union of Agricultural Labourers came out on strike in the country in 1923, but although it now had eight thousand members in the county the strike failed to materialise in Essex. Farmers were able to make individual deals with their groups of workers.

The Essex Farmers Union had been formed immediately prior to the war in 1913 after a meeting at the Saracens Head Hotel. It was meant to advise individual members and promote their interests. It didn't get involved with commercial activities but there was disguised support for buying groups. (73) The E.F.U. emerged from the war far stronger with a much increased membership. This was partly because of the increased number of small and medium sized farmers buying their own farms and ceasing to be in the relatively weaker position of tenants. Its first county secretary was George Knowles, who farmed at Lordship farm, later to be part of Writtle College. The Union's office was in Duke Street. Early meetings were in the boardroom of the Corn Exchange. The E.F.U. moved in 1936 to 1 Edward Avenue, now part of County Hall, and then to 'Agriculture House' at Brierly Place, New London Road. This building was eventually sold in the 1990s for just under a million pounds. (74)

In 1922, despite the depressed nature of local farming, the Chelmsford branch of the E.F.U. voted against a motion for protection. (75) They did not want to see the price of bread increase. Taxes and the tithe were still a bone of contention however. Pretyman, the Chelmsford M.P. said "Landlords do not even have sufficient income to pay the taxes levied on them: farmers cannot get as much for their products, as it costs them to produce it, and labour cannot get a living wage." (76) By 1925 the local branch of the Farmer's Union said regarding protection and subsidies "the country refuses to have one and pay for the other". (77) In 1927 the union was continuing to apply for state help because beef and milk couldn't be sold to cover their costs. (78) Wheat production continued to decline in the county until 1934. By 1932 however, after the belated adoption of protection under the Ottowa agreement, the Chronicle reported that the wheat quota was helping farmers. (79) The amount of land under wheat was still decreasing but would have decreased more without the quotas. During the 1930s there was also a belated attempt to help dairy farmers both nationally and locally. In 1932 an Eastern Area Milk Organisation was formed which met at Chelmsford to fix milk prices. (80) This was not however, completely effective. Six months later milk was being sold in Chelmsford at 2d a quart less than official prices. (81) Despite these government policies times were extremely difficult for Essex farmers. The E.F.U. reported a big fall in subscriptions in the early 1930s. (82) In the 1920s and 1930s however, a further migration of Scottish farmers into the area occurred, attracted by low land prices and the work of the Milk Marketing Board. (83)

Despite the depression, by the 1930s mechanisation was beginning to make serious inroads on the farm. Immediately after the war farmers had needed a lot of convincing to change age old methods. The unreliability of tractors, even those of Henry Ford, meant that most farmers stood by the horse. (84) The number of horses had even increased during the first war.

One of the biggest firms associated with Essex agriculture in the late 19th and through most of the 20th century was Cramphorns. Although they had a substantial farming operation until 1963, they were principally corn and seed merchants. They had two head offices, in Chelmsford and Brentwood. (85) By the 1960s the firm had over 70 shops after their retail operations had expanded three times as fast as their farming. Cramphorns ran a mill at Springfield and had granaries at Brentwood and Halstead as well as at Chelmsford. (86)

Marriages continued to expand during and after the first war. They bought Barnes Farm and Mousham Mills from the Mildmay estate. The family had been long term tenants of both farms. In 1926 the General Strike cost the business £700 because of the extra price of coal. The Marriage farms grew an increasing amount of potatoes. Although sugar beet production started in earnest during the first war, due to the shortage of sugar, Marriages didn't start producing it until 1926. They used steam cultivators extensively between the wars, but didn't own them. Marriages were one of the last farmers in Essex to use steam ploughs up to 1956. (87) They did own an early electric threshing machine and bought a Marshall tractor in 1934. (88) The family kept two herds of pigs, one at Chignal and another at Good Easter. They were sent by the firm on the flour wagons to London. "These pigs ran with the fattening bullocks and were supposed to live and thrive on the food the bullocks wasted!" Two flocks of sheep were kept for lamb at Easter. This meant lambing in mid winter and building straw yards every year. Another notebook of the family showed that man and horse were still the mainstays of work on the family's farms. In 1928 the family used a blacksmith, G. Mansfield and son, of Dolphin Yard, off Tindal Street and also had their own blacksmith who did all the shoeing and repairs to farm implements. The family's farms kept many horses for farm work and transport. A wheelwright, Mansfield's, was employed full time at their shop in Springfield, working on carts, wagons etc. All timber was home grown on the farms and transported by wagon to saw mills in Chelmsford. It was brought back the same day, stored and then sawed by for the purpose it was needed for. All wheels were repaired at the blacksmith's shop at Broomfield mill.

The introduction of roller milling had largely made stone grounding obsolete but a few people still preferred the quality of stone ground flour and the old stones still turned at Marriages' Moulsham Mill until well after the second war. Roller milling however brought spectacular improvements to the output of flour. Even by 1900 millstones were mainly being used for 'gristing' for animal feeds and a little wholemeal for brown bread. (89)

The work of the Agricultural Institute had been considerably disrupted by the first war. The teaching programme was abandoned as some staff left to join the armed forces and others were seconded to the War Agricultural Committee which took control of the Institute. A great deal of work was carried out advising farmers how to increase production. After the war normal courses resumed but out of 80 students on a market garden course, for example, there was only one female. (90) By this time some students were entered for external University of London degrees. (91) A review of the Institute heralded a move from advisory work to more education. The increased importance of poultry farming led the Institute to establish a poultry station in Beehive Lane, Galleywood.

The depression, of course, affected the Institute and by the 1930s it was having problems paying its staff. A report of 1934 emphasised the increasing lack of space at the Institute's old buildings and the difficulty of working from a site in the centre of town. (92) In a little over 30 years Essex had gone from being a leader in agricultural education to be being left behind. An out of town site was first proposed in 1935. Early possible sites included Hylands House, Boreham House and Margaretting Hall but eventually a 550 acre site was bought at Writtle including Lordship farm. Four farms were bought in all from Mr George Knowles at a cost of £25,000. The first design was turned down because of the estimated £250,000 cost. Money rapidly ran out for the approved design because of the shortage of labour and materials caused by the outbreak of the second war. "The Institute began work (in 1940) without any ceremony but with two full hostels of students and a full complement of staff." (93) In 1930 Henry Ford had established the Henry Ford Institute of Agriculture at Boreham to teach British farm workers the use of tractors and other innovations. It was later used for the training of Land Army girls before being cleared to make way for the American airfield (see chapter 24).

During the inter war period the Essex Show had difficulty in maintaining its importance but still survived. The 1922 show was held at Chelmsford. Each year the show was built from nothing on a different site. In 1927 it was held again in Chelmsford, this time at Hylands, but attendances were hit by the weather. Despite £1,500 being raised by donations, a loss of £600 had to be carried forward. Hylands however, was seen as the ideal site because of the ample facilities for parking. (94) By the 1930s each show had an enormous range of machinery which the typical farm labourer would never have seen before. By 1938 attendances were reaching almost 40,000, many were brought by motor buses from all over the county. (95)

With regard to fruit growing in the Mid Essex area in the interwar period, the

Chelmsford cattle market in the 1930s (Courtesy of Essex Record Office)

major firm was Seabrooks, which started in Boreham, but had also established itself in Great Leighs. William Seabrook had turned to fruit growing in the 1880s because of the depression in mainstream farming. Due to the cheapness of land compared with America, costs were considerably below those in the U.S. Seabrook himself designed a fruit farm plough. By the 1920s he was conscious of the need to spray the crops. The first grading and sizing machine to be used anywhere in Britain was erected at Seabrook's Chantry farm. Later the larger packing shed at Little Leighs Hall was the largest anywhere in Europe at the time. "In 1934 the first automatic one man sprayer came on to the scene." (96) Seabrook introduced bee houses because bees were needed to pollinate the crops. Boreham was the centre for fruit tree raising. Trees were lifted and sent to all parts of the country. His first book 'Modern fruit growing' went through nine editions. Seabrooks became particularly well known for its variety of blackcurrants. The firm was a large employer in Boreham and the Leighs. In Boreham between the wars about thirty families lived in houses owned by the firm but many also came from Chelmsford to work on the fruit farms.

The inter war period saw labourers continue to leave farm work in all the local villages. In many cases they just went to work in the now sizeable engineering firms in the town. Traditional craftsmen were also often under pressure. In Great and Little Leighs for example these craftsmen were still functioning but as in other villages the blacksmith was finding it a struggle to survive. The depression hit the village hard and as elsewhere there was a big increase in poaching. (97)

The second war gave a massive boost to farmers but farm workers were not reserved from call up and there was an immediate shortage of workers. Five thousand farm workers left the county as a whole for the war. School boys on their holidays and Italian prisoners of war helped locally but this was not enough. Boys from the grammar school worked at harvest time. The Women's Land Army were drafted in large numbers. In the county this was organised from the new Writtle Institute. All derelict land was commandeered by the War Agricultural Executive Committee. It was not handed back immediately after the war. Land Tribunals had to establish who owned what. The Chelmsford area was one of 13 established in the County. (98) Every farm was visited by the Ministry to gauge their potential. The War Agricultural Executive used its powers to reclaim over a thousand acres from building estates in the Chelmsford area for growing. (99) Around Boreham airfield, (see chapter 24) like other airfields in the county, the land was intensively farmed. The Executive directed the digging of four thousand miles of ditches in the county as a whole. As elsewhere the Chelmsford public made a valuable contribution by growing vegetables.

Pasture was halved in favour of arable farming. The war saw 144 thousand tons of wheat produced per year in the county compared with a peak of 162 thousand in the first war. The second war saw a big decline in the number of horses and an increasing move towards mechanisation. The new Writtle Institute played a major role in 'Dig for Victory' advising on soils, cultivation, cropping and pests. Women came to the Institute for short three week courses. As in the first war most staff were seconded to the War Agricultural Executive. (100)

In the immediate post war period agriculture was very prosperous with increasing guaranteed prices. The relative wages of those workers who remained improved. Working hours that had often been above 60 hours in the inter war period were reduced to 39 by 1990. (101) By the end of the twentieth century the practice of tied cottages had ended but the arrival of commuters to the villages around Chelmsford raised rents way above what farm workers could afford. In general however the later part of the century was a good one for farm workers. During the 1980s farm workers received a wage increase twice the rate of inflation. This didn't prevent local farm workers following up the increasing trend of protest. In 1975 farm workers from all over the county marched through the town to the Shire Hall. (102) In the later years of the century the membership of the E.F.U. drastically declined as the size of farms increased and the number of farmers fell. (103)

Amalgamations of farms were led by orders for large quantities of high quality food. Vertical integration also occurred where big commercial concerns took over contract farmers. (104) The war had seen a decline of 5,000 horses in the county but there were still 3,000 in 1960. It took another twenty years for tractors and combine harvesters to fully take over. Crops like sugar beet declined quickly in the Chelmsford area after the 1970s, because they remained expensive to produce. (105) Massive tractors increasingly crossed the fields. Combines took time to become popular requiring fields to be enlarged and the countryside stripped of many of its hedges. By the 1960s the self propelled harvester was taking over. (106) Marconi Instruments produced a moisture meter which both farmers and farm workers used. It became an essential piece of equipment.

After the war the Chelmsford area continued to be well known for market gardening, although it was generally on a smaller scale compared with the southern part of Essex. The region specialised in forced crops including onions, brussels, early greens, radishes, carrots, celery, runner beans, asparagus and the first early potatoes. (107) There was a big increase in local turkey production after the war. Pig rearing, after previously being popular, decreased towards the end of the twentieth century. (108)

Marriages' mills escaped damage during the second war, even though the Chelmer Mill was in real danger because it was so close to the Hoffmann factory. Henry Marriage died in 1938 and Croxtons Mill at Little Waltham was sold along with other parts of the estate. In the 1950s the Marriages had to expand their silos at Chelmer Mill to hold much more grain. By 1971 1200 tons could be held at the mill. Most of the flour went to master bakers, usually family businesses. Marriages were successful in the packeted, domestic, white flour trade where there were still many small grocers to sell to. When the supermarkets took over the firm concentrated on producing specialised flours for the 'more discriminating housewife'. In 1970 a new animal feed mill was built replacing the old one at Moulsham Mill. It used a Christy and Norris hammer mill but by the end of the century the firm was using computers to calculate the amounts of different raw materials needed for the feed. The Marriages separated the farming business from milling in 1960. Its farms later became known as Brick Farms Limited but the two businesses remained closely intertwined. Towards the end of the century 'Cash and Carry' warehouses were opened at Colchester as well as Chelmsford for orders of animal feeds and pet foods. (109) In the early 1980s Marriages closed Moulsham Mill and it was refurbished to be used by a charity operating small businesses, mainly arts and crafts. (110) Forty jobless people worked to restore the building, which is still owned by Marriages. (111) Despite deaths of three family directors, three young Marriages became the sixth generation of the family to become involved with the business. In 2012 the firm bought a second feed mill this time in Lincolnshire. Hannah Marriage featured on one of Michael Portillo's programmes on British railway journeys because of the historic importance of railway links to the firm, particularly Chelmer Mill.

By 1999 Chelmsford had one of only two animal markets left in the county. In 1945 the cattle market was being criticised by farmers and the public for its position and lack of space. It added to the traffic congestion in the town. Initially a move to a site on the Victoria Road was vetoed by the government even though it was agreed that Chelmsford was one of the worst markets for 'attested cattle'. The market was not actually built until 1961. (112) No longer did the cattle come to market come on foot but in single or double-decker lorries. "The cattle drovers are the same rough long coated unshaven noisy lot their fathers were." (113) In the late 1980s a major facelift was planned for the covered market which caused considerable opposition. The modernisation was not finally carried out until 1993. (114) Later the livestock market was moved again to a five million pound out of town site on the Boreham interchange. It however was smaller than the Victoria Road site and shared facilities with a car auction. (115) In 1996 the cattle trade collapsed after the onset of mad cow disease. As a result cattle prices at the livestock market dropped by a third. (116) This proved the final straw for the market and it ceased trading in June 1999. (117)

The first Essex Show after the Second World War was held at Hylands. Despite rain and mud 20,000 people turned up causing traffic jams for miles around. (118) In 1952 the show was also held at Chelmsford and 35 thousand people turned up on the first day. (119) The 1953 show was held at Springfield but crowds were again reduced because of bad weather. (120) Consideration was given to making Springfield the permanent site for the show but the town council refused to recommend to the E.C.C. that the Essex Agricultural Society be allowed to use the site because it was needed for housing. (121) Boreham airfield was also considered as a permanent site. (122) After the show made a big loss in 1955 at Halstead, the search continued for a permanent site in the area of the County town. (123) The show still retained its popularity among farm workers of which there were still 30 thousand in the county. Every year the machinery agents and corn merchants were generous with their hospitality. This was not limited to trial rides on tractors, and free three and four course lunches were not uncommon.

The Show finally found a permanent home on a 158 acre site at Great Leighs. (124) It was bought in 1956 and the first show was held there in 1958. Unfortunately the curse of the show, bad weather struck again, and the crowd was limited to 15,000 on the first day. (125) By 1962 the crowds had reached 50,000, the best since 1949. For 1966 the show was switched to weekends to attract more non-farming people. (126) In 1988 the addition of a Sunday meant that attendances topped 100 thousand for the first time, but the show still lost money. (127) The Essex Agricultural Society decided to mortgage the showground after bankers demanded action on a quarter of a million pound overdraft. (128) The site was bought by the E.F.U. with half the proceeds of the sale of their New London Road premises. (129) Unfortunately the show was again hit by bad weather in 1994 and 1995, resulting in the site being put up for sale for the second time in five years. (130) Thirty thousand pounds had to be advanced by E.C.C. to ensure the 1996 show went ahead. During 1997 John Holmes, an equestrian eventer, bought the site and in 1999 took over the running of the show. (131) In 2002 the show was finally axed after 134 years. The building of the racecourse, which it had been hoped would provide a lifeline to the show, had fallen behind schedule. Attendances at the show had fallen since the 1960s and 70s and many people in the society had lost their enthusiasm for the event. (132) Throughout the 2000s John Holmes made positive noises about reviving the show, but this looked increasingly unlikely until a return to the Great Leighs site was announced in January 2012. (133)

After the second war the War Agricultural Executive didn't move out of the Institute at Writtle until 1948, by which time one hundred and five students had enrolled. The farm was started with field trials of the main crops. (134) A dairy herd of fifty five Friesian cows was established and a new turkey farm built. (135) Commercial fruit farming was started and a vineyard planted in 1959. Despite extra hostels and halls of residence shortage of space was an increasing problem at the college in the 1950s. The 1960s saw further expansion and a four storey block built to accommodate the now two hundred and fifty students. The Hubert Ashton Recreation Centre was named after the Chelmsford M.P. because of his support for the college. (136) In the 1960s all the students were finding employment. The Institute was renamed the Agricultural College in the 1970s. An increase in degree courses and the expansion of research by contract, involving increasing links with industry, occurred during the later part of the century. (137) The gardens were developed as a teaching resource and in 1986 the staff began working on an arboretum at Hylands. (138) When the college started a farm shop, local nurserymen complained of unfair competition. (139) In 2006 it was announced that the college was in serious financial difficulties despite being rated third out of seventeen agricultural colleges nationwide. (140) Fears were voiced regarding the likely effect on the village if the College were to close. In 2009 however, multimillion pound plans were announced for the college including a new sports hall to be built on green belt land. (141)

The new millennium saw agriculture in the county once again affected by depression. The E.F.U. complained in 2011 that arable farmers could not make money even with their subsidies. Livestock farmers were however doing a little better in general. (142) Their situation was not helped by a virulent outbreak of foot and mouth disease. Beef farmer John Little of Runwell Hall Farm, near Rettendon said he and his son Richard could "only take precautions and cross their fingers". (143) The Ministry of Agriculture used statutory powers to close footpaths in the area. It was four months before they were re-opened. Two thousand and seven saw an outbreak of bluetongue disease in the county with cases amongst cattle at Great Leighs and Woodham Ferrers. Writtle College carried out a study of the disease. (144)

Agriculture in the area continues to change with the times. The owner of a thirteen acre vineyard in Galleywood announced 'Chateau Chelmsford 2012', claiming its soil and height above sea level was similar to the Champagne region! (145)

At the start of the new millennium rural areas bore no resemblance to the tight knit communities of a hundred years before. Commuters with their ability to pay hitherto astronomic prices for village cottages sounded the death knell for many rural institutions such as the village shop. The green belt meant however, that although villages such as Great Baddow and Danbury became absorbed into the urban spread of Chelmsford, others such as Writtle have managed to retain their identity (See chapter 12).

1)   Essex Farming 1900 – 2000 Wormell p. 14
2)   The Chelmsford region Walters p.1 – Essex record Office T/Z 561/7/2
3)   Walters p.15

4) Walters p.13
5) Wormell p.14
6) Essex Weekly News 7 5 1880
7) E.W.N. 5 12 1884 p.2
8) Essex Chronicle 9 1 1880 p.3
9) E.C. 4 1 1894 p.4
10) E.C. 25 5 1894
11) E.C. 4 1 1895 p.5
12) E.C. 22 9 1891
13) 'Hard Slogging Work' 'How did agricultural Depression affect land use between the parishes of the Chelmsford Union between 1870 and 1901' p.13 Neil Wiffen – E. R.O.
14) Wiffen p. 14
15) Wiffen p. 22
16) Wiffen p.25
17) Wiffen p. 34
18) Wiffen p. 41
19) E.W.N. 6 12 1895 p.4
20) E.W.N. 4 7 1890 p.4
21) E.W.N. 2 8 1890
22) E.W.N. 11 11 1892 p.4
23) E.W.N. 25 3 1894 p.2
24) E.W.N. 23 12 1892 p.4
25) E.W.N. 20 9 1894 p.4
26) E.W.N. 19 10 1894 p.4
27) Wormell p.266
28) 'Gone but not forgotten' Friends of Chelmsford Museum (Jane Beardsley – The Market)
29) E.W.N. 22 4 1881 p.5
30) E.W.N. 27 4 1884 p.5
31) E.W.N. 28 10 1898
32) Oral history records Harold Orrin – Essex Record Office
33) Essex County Council minutes 1912
34) E.W.N. 10 6 1887 p.6
35) Essex Chronicle 30 5 1890

36) E.C. 13 6 1890 p.8
37) E.C. 20 6 1890
38) E.C. 29 1 1904
39) E.W.N. 27 2 1891 p.4
40) Essex Institute of Agriculture 1893 – 1952 p.3
41) Writtle College: The first hundred years p.4
42) E.C.C. minutes April 1896
43) Writtle College: The first hundred years p.4
44) E.C.C. minutes p.32 1900
45) E.C.C. minutes 1909 p.206
46) E.C.C. minutes 1912 p.751
47) Writtle College: The First Hundred Years p.7
48) Writtle College: The first hundred years p.8
49) http://www.marriagefeeds.co.uk/about-us/history
50) William and Henry Marriage and Sons Limited 1824 – 1974 150 years of farming Stan Jarvis
51) http://www.marriage feeds.co.uk/about-us/history
52) Wormell p.20
53) E.C. 24 7 1914
54) Wormell p.155
55) Wormell p.156
56) Wormell p.96
57) 'An Edwardian Hamlet' 'Howe Street in Great Waltham 1901 – 1910 Alan Maddock
58) 'Echoes of the Great War' The diary of Reverend Andrew Clark 1914 – 1919 Introduction James Munson p.xviii
59) Great and Little Leighs Edited by Pat Watkinson
60) Great Baddow Oral history p.87
61) Chelmsford Museums Oral history records
62) Little Badow Part 3 Sheila Rowley p.60
63) Essex Countryside 1963-4 Vol. 12 p.210-11
64) Wormell p.268-9
65) Wormell p.263
66) Wormell p.264
67) Chelmsford Museums Oral history records Tom Turner

68) Wormell p.156
69) E.W.N. 18 8 1919 p.5
70) E.W.N. 22 10 1920 p.3
71) E.W.N. 20 1 1922 p.4
72) Wormell p.39
73) Wormell p.134
74) Wormell p.138-9
75) E.W.N. 20 10 1922 p.2
76) E.W.N. 15 12 1922 p.4
77) E.W.N. 6 3 1925 p.4
78) E.W.N. 20 5 1927 p.4
79) E.C. 12 8 1932 p.7
80) E.W.N. 2 12 1932 p.5
81) E.W.N. 26 5 1933 p.7
82) E.C. 20 1 1933
83) Wormell p.49
84) E.C. 20 1 1933
85) Wormell p.243
86) Wormell p.252
87) http://www.marriagefeeds.co.uk/about-us/history
88) Stan Jarvis p.24
89) http://wwwmarriagefeeds.co.uk/about-us/history
90) Writtle College: The first hundred years p.21
91) Writtle College: The first hundred years p.22
92) Writtle College: The first hundred years p.25
93) Writtle college: The first hundred years p.31
94) Wormell p.204
95) Wormell p.124
96) Boreham Burgess p.98- 107
97) Great and Little Leighs Watkinson
98) Wormell p.69-71
99) Wormell p.89
100) Writtle College: The first Hundred Years p.34
101) Wormell p.157
102) Wormell p.158

103) E.W.N. 8 7 1962 p.5
104) E.W.N. 8 1 1960 p.5
105) Wormell p.161
106) Wormell p.162
107) Wormell p.217
108) Wormell p.229
109) http://www.marriagefeeds.co.uk/about-us/history
110) E.C. 26 6 1981 p.1
111) E.C. 22 7 1983 p.1
112) E.W.N. 14 4 1961 p.6
113) E.C. 27 1 1978 p.3
114) E.C. 8 7 1993 p.7
115) E.C. 28 10 1988 p.14
116) E.C. 29 3 1996 p.1
117) E.C. 4 6 1999 p.1
118) E.W.N. 14 6 1946 p.2
119) E.W.N. 13 6 1952
120) E.W.N. 12 6 1953 p.1
121) E.W.N. 20 11 1953 p.1
122) E.W.N. 18 12 1953 p.10
123) E.W.N. 23 11 1955 p.4
124) E.W.N. 26 10 1956 p.3
125) E.W.N. 15 6 1962 p.2
126) E.W.N. 29 7 1966 p.1
127) E.W.N. 24 6 1988 p.7
128) E.W.N. 26 5 1988 p.2
129) Wormell p.132
130) E.W.N. 17 11 1995 p.2
131) Wormell p.132
132) E.C. 8 11 2002 p.1
133) E.C. 18 11 2004 p.6
134) Writtle College: The first hundred years p.38
135) Writtle College p.41
136) Writtle College p.47-52
137) Writtle College p.62

138) Writtle College p.64
139) Writtle College p.67
140) E.C. 13 7 2006 p.1
141) E.C. 8 1 2009 p.7
142) E.C. 12 1 2001 p.5
143) E.C. 2 3 2001 p.3
144) E.C. 18 10 2007 p.13
145) E.C. 26 5 2011 p.3

2

Beginnings – Industry in a sleepy late Victorian and Edwardian market town

*"Its steadiness reliability and comfort in all weathers,
make it far superior to all others"*

This chapter deals with .in the main, the less well known industrial firms in the town. Chelmsford was an unlikely town to become a centre for what been called the second British industrial revolution. This is especially so as now there is little to remind newcomers to the town of its recent industrial heritage with the exception of the empty Marconi factory in New Street, the still thriving electronics company e2v and a number of blue plaques. The chapter and the following six deal with this industrial transformation and the town's subsequent de-industrialisation. Taken together the chapters reveal an absence of an answer to the question of why the town became a major centre for industry in the first half of the twentieth century. In general there was a dearth of the location factors which economists look for in determining the location of industries. By the 1930s however the existence of a large pool of labour with various degrees of skill in the town was certainly an advantage to the firms concerned. This is shown by the extent to which workers moved between the town's big firms. Thomas Clarkson, who is heavily featured in this chapter, was probably guided to Chelmsford by Colonel R.E. Crompton. What Clarkson does have in common with Hoffmann and Crompton is that in all three cases the inventor was marginalised and then eventually eased out by those seeking to run the business at a profit.

The presence of fast flowing water in the Chelmsford area had long meant that the town was an important centre for milling and brewing. Chelmsford had always been known for its watermills rather than its windmills, because of the Chelmer and the Can. The Rainsford windmill, only a few yards from T.D. Ridley's steam mill, was dismantled in 1875, the last of six windmills in the area to close. (1) It is possible that there had been a mill at Moulsham even before the Romans; certainly there had been one in Saxon times. There is little doubt that the Tudor mill was on the same site as the current one. In 1839 the Marriage family had gained the tenancy of the mill. This was quickly converted to steam power to make it less susceptible to variations in the weather. Despite no longer being dependent on water the mill remained where it was because it now needed coal brought by barge from the Heybridge Basin. Eventually in the 1960s even the river bed was moved, as part of the attempts to solve the perennial flooding problem. By the 1970s the mill ceased to have a commercial use and fell into decay (see chapter 1).

Apart from the water mills on the Chelmer, mainly owned by the Marriage family, there was a major mill at Writtle, which in 1877 Andrew Southgate had rebuilt and was leasing from Arthur Prior of Hylands. There had been a mill on this site as far back as Domesday. Southgate bought the mill in 1923 when Prior died. The mill continued in use until 1957 despite being damaged in the second war. When it ceased working, the Essex Rivers Authority diverted the River Wid away from the road and mill, to try to ease the recurrent flooding problems frequently caused by that small but powerful river.

Fast flowing water also ensured that Chelmsford had a number of maltings and full scale breweries, although the scale and number of the former never matched the west of the county. Malting is the process of germinating grain by soaking it in water and then drying the grain to prevent it from germinating it further. Malt from a number of maltings in the Chelmsford area, including one off the Baddow Road, was primarily used for three main breweries. These were Wells and Perry, Gray and Sons and Ridley's.

The Wells and Perry brewery had originally been founded in 1793 at number 26 Duke Street under the name Bird, Hawkes and Woodcock. This was opposite the Friends Meeting House. The brewery was bought by Charles Wells in 1875. In the 1890s the daughter of Frederick Wells, the owner of Oaklands House, married William Perry Newport Ridley. During 1890 the business was made into a limited company with a share capital of £30,000 and a share issue of £295,000 debenture stock. Wells and Perry also used their Springfield wharf on the Chelmer and Blackwater Navigation to trade in coal, timber, stone, lime and tar. In 1906 they were acting as coal merchants at Ingatestone railway station. Like the other brewery companies in the area they used barley grown in the county. It was a successful business judging by the opulence of life at Oaklands House. In 1915 there was a serious fire at the brewery and the company complained about the delay in the fire service dealing with it. Faulty fire hydrants were blamed. (2) In 1934 the company was taken over by Taylor Walker of London. At that time it had 72 public houses including the Lion and Lamb, a small tap house on the site of what was Duke's nightclub in the 2,000s. (3) Taylor Walker itself went back to its origins in 1730 in Stepney as Salmon and Hare. Long after the brewery had been demolished in 1936, when the area was being re- developed at the end of the 1970s, an extremely large and deep well was discovered.

The Gray and Sons brewery was founded in 1828 on the Springfield Road. Brewing may have taken place at the Black Boy Inn on the corner of the High Street and the Springfield Road and it was this that became the brewery. It became a limited company in 1858 trading as Gray and Son (Brewers) Limited. (4) The brewery took over a number of public houses and this led the family firm to take over the Maldon brewery. This was closed in 1954 after which the tied houses were supplied from the Springfield Road brewery. The death of Thomas Raymond Gray led to heavy estate duties which forced the closure of the brewery in 1973 and the sale of the brewery followed the following year. In 1966 the River Chelmer had to be partly diverted as part of the alterations to the river in the centre of the town. This led to some of the wooden foundations drying out and the original house, in which Herbert Gray had lived in, had to be demolished. After the closure of the brewery a well was found on the site 122 feet deep. Following protests "part of the site was demolished but most of it was sympathetically converted to shops". Gray's moved its offices and warehouse to Rignals Lane in Galleywood. The Phoenix stands out at the depot. It originally came from the Phoenix Fire Insurance Company who rented part of the Chelmsford brewery site in the early nineteenth century. (5) In 1982 the firm still had 40 public houses in the Mid Essex Area. It now operates as Gray and Sons (Chelmsford) Limited.

There were other smaller brewing businesses in the town usually connected with public houses. The biggest of these Bilton and Durrant's which were linked by marriage but had separate breweries. They were linked to the White Hart in Tindal Street and were also wine, spirit and hop merchants. In 1897 Ind Coope of Romford bought the White Hart and brewing ceased. (6)

During the early 1800s Thomas Dixon Ridley was a miller in the Chelmsford area. By 1861 he had had a steam driven stone mill built at Chelmsford. At the end of the century this was changed over to roller milling. In 1840 the family branched out into brewing although they continued corn milling at Chelmsford and Felsted. T.D. Ridley was the son of William Ridley and Maria Dixon, who inherited a mill at Hartford, which was close to Felsted. During 1841 he married Lydia Wells, who was from the Chelmsford brewing family, and within a year he had built his own brewery downstream from the mill on the River Chelmer. During the later nineteenth century Ridley's had a number of maltings at Writtle, Broomfield, Baddow Road and Townfield Street, Chelmsford. These were gradually closed in favour of the largest one at Townfield Street. By the end of the century the family had acquired 47 inns including the Bird in Hand Moulsham. (7) The Sun at Saffron Walden was their most northerly inn and the Wheatsheaf at Rettendon the most southern. In the early 1970s Ridley's

Baddow Road Brewery 1930
(Courtesy of Essex Record Office)

had just over 60 tied houses, mostly in central and north west Essex. (8) Towards the end of the century the company began to brew a number of real ales. The firm bought out the Tolly Cobbold Brewery in August 2005. Three years later Ridley's itself was bought by Greene King and the company was dismantled. At the time it employed 160 people, had a turnover of £17 million and was the largest independent brewer and pub operator in Essex. According to Nelion Ridley, "We had a brewery with high overheads. Demand for traditional brewed English beer had declined over 30 years and our brewery was obviously built many years before that, when that was all people were drinking." The brewery at Hartford End was immediately closed. In 2012 it was scheduled to be redeveloped as flats and offices. (9) An application for listed building status failed in 2013.

There was also a brewery at Great Baddow, which was started by a Mr Crabb in 1798. His son, Richard carried on the business but was also a farmer and a breeder of shorthorn cattle. The brewery had been rebuilt in 1868 by Crabb, Veley and Smee to a design by Frederick Chancellor. It was a tall eleven bay building, gothic in style. Richard Crabb's three sisters took over the business because he died a bachelor. Ironically they became leading lights in the local temperance movement and were prone to giving out leaflets on the evils of drink outside the brewery! The last of the family Miss Louisa Crabb died in 1929 and the brewery was sold at auction in 1930. Since then the building has been used by a number of businesses.

Writtle brewery was a sizeable business by 1882 with its own gasworks. It was then listed in Kelly's Directory as 'Pattison, W.H.L. and Co. brewery, maltsters and wine and spirit merchants and owners of gasworks'. By 1894 the business was known as the Writtle Brewery Co. Ltd with W.H.L. as managing director. In 1906 Charles Russell was running the firm for the Russell family, which had taken over the brewery. Writtle brewery closed in 1920.

In 2013 the Round Tower Brewery started the first brewing in Chelmsford for almost 40 years. The chairman of the local branch of CAMRA said in the Chronicle "Now we are a city it seems fitting that we should have our own brewery." (10)

One firm that was inextricably connected with the Chelmer and Blackwater Navigation for 150 years was Brown and Son, the timber merchants. The opening of the Navigation in 1798 had transformed the economic possibilities at Chelmsford. Owing to the lack of water facilities at Chelmsford the cost of transporting coal from Maldon, where it arrived by sea, had been high. The opening of the navigation made it possible to get coal to Chelmsford cheaply. The Brown family bought Coates' yard at

Interior of Brown and Sons, Navigation Road (Courtesy of E.R.O.)

Springfield which Richard Coates had opened as a coal yard. Early in the nineteenth century the firm had been slaters and tilers but when they purchased Coates' business they installed machinery to cut timber, which had previously been cut by hand over pits. Several of these early pits were uncovered in 1922. In 1891 Brown and Sons was incorporated as a limited company. J.S. Brown, the grandson of the first owner, was a councillor and alderman in the first borough council. During the nineteenth century the firm maintained its business as coal as well as timber merchants. (11) After the first war, mechanisation of the saw mills was necessary but during it a fire completely destroyed the mills. The influence of the Brown family in the firm gradually waned. By the 1920s the firm was importing timber from the Baltic. "Steamers from the Baltic and White Sea ports bring their timber cargoes into the Blackwater estuary, at Heybridge Basin, where the Company's yard covers the whole of one side and extensive sheds provide ample storage for timber while awaiting shipment to Chelmsford." At the Chelmsford end of the canal additional land was bought in 1925 and the whole of the waterfront became one unit belonging to the company. The English timber department was separated from the softwood branch and new mills were provided for each branch of the trade.

John Woods was born at number 1 Navigation Road in 1934. This was the end terrace of a number of old weather boarded cottages. "We were surrounded by Brown's the timber merchants. On the Springfield Road side were the offices and some storage areas. Behind I believe were the stables for the horses. Across the road was the lorry depot, and extending along Navigation Road to the East was the timber yard." He remembered seeing a huge crane. "This crane was mounted on a gantry composed of two overhead rails twenty or thirty feet high. Spanning these rails was a large crossbeam on wheels at each end, which travelled along the rails. The crane itself was mounted on the cross beam, again on wheels, and could traverse from one side of the beam to the other. So the crane driver went up the fixed ladder to enter the crane and then could travel parallel to the road and from side to side. He could pick up a tree trunk from a lorry and then stack it wherever in the English timber yard it was required. He could later retrieve the log for debarking and sawing." Most of the logs remained in the stack for many years; the old saying for hard wood to mature was "seven years in log and seven years in plank". Later after going to the Grammar School John Woods worked in the yard in the years immediately following the second war. "The softwood arrived by barge along the canal and I'm fairly sure the barges were motorised." The wood was already in planks when it came up the canal. The saw mill was powered by electricity but the firm had to use an old gas engine when it failed, as it did several times each winter. (12)

By the 1960s the original premises were supported by five branches and showrooms. In 1932 Brown's had acquired Wray and Fullers, who were builders merchants and stone masons and who themselves dated back to 1700 in Chelmsford. The original Mr Brown had worked as a slater and tiler for the Wray family and the builder's merchants and monumental department was in Springfield Road. Heavy building materials were kept at New Street. Brown's became involved in church restoration. An ironmongery department was also started. From a staff of six in 1920 the firm expanded to a staff of 60, with a total number of employees of 300 by the early 1970s. By this time the business covered 15-16 acres more than five times the acreage covered in 1921. (13) Brown's stopped barge traffic in 1972 and the site became disused and was vandalised. The firm who took over Brown's demolished the quayside timber sheds. (14)

Another local timber firm, L.P. Foreman, was founded by Luther Foreman in 1886 on the Roxwell Road. Initially they supplied willow blanks to cricket bat makers including

Slazenger. During the second war they were timber stockists for the Ministry of Supply. After 1945 the firm started making packing cases. They made special protective cases for both Marconi and EEV. After becoming part of GEC Marconi in 1970 the firm was bought out by its management. In 1999 it moved to the Widford industrial estate. It makes composite, plastic, aluminium and foam packaging as well as plywood and softwood cases. (15)

Most of the industry in late Victorian Chelmsford was related to agriculture. Eddington's was one such firm. In the second half of the nineteenth century it became a nationally known engineering business. By 1859 it had moved from the Springfield Road to New street operating as W. and S. Eddington (father and son). This is now the site of Chelmsford police station. The business made traction engines and contractor's machinery and were pioneers in the development of steam engines and boilers for agriculture. Their involvement with the making of the famous Darby Digger was dealt with in the previous chapter. By 1881 it was employing 40 workers with two partners Silvanus and William Eddington. The firm became Eddington and Stevenson in 1886. They also made brickyard machinery. The firm took out a patent in 1888 for "The means of adapting traction engines for use as a road roller." "In 1890 two of Eddington's largest engines were used to test the new iron bridge on New London Road" but the firm was in decline and appears to have gone out of business soon afterwards. (16) James Alfred Norris left the company in 1880 to join Christy's. His knowledge of agricultural steam engines and boilers opened up new commercial areas for that business (see chapter 3). (17)

Coleman and Morton established their foundry on New London Road as early as 1848 after Richard Coleman came from Colchester. The original foundry was built by Frederick Greenwood. During 1875 the firm had 14 forges in use and by 1890 the firm had produced 25 thousand cultivators. (18) In 1862 it had exhibited a portable engine with a single cylinder at the Great Exhibition. It was used in a self moving machine. "This layout was quite satisfactory as the little engine worked for many years in and around Chelmsford in gravel pits and similar haulage". (19) In 1866 Richard's son Henry took over the business in partnership with Alfred Morton. During 1881 the firm won a number of prizes, including four first class entries at the Melbourne exhibition. These were for a patent cultivator, a patent corn screen, a water and liquid manure cart, a hand water-cart and a garden engine. (20) The firm's water pumps were used in villages throughout Essex. They also produced iron castings for iron bridges. Like Eddingtons, the foundry regularly invoked the ire of the council because of the nuisance its smoke provided. Employing 95 men the firm was also big enough to put out sports teams, alongside Eddington's and the Arc Works (See chapter 25). J.H.S. Coleman and G.E.M. Morton stopped trading in 1895 and G.H. Coleman and A.R. Morton took over the business. Afterwards the business declined and the whole site was put up for sale in 1907. (21) The firm, like Eddington's, was adversely affected by the agricultural depression, which meant that farmers couldn't afford its products. One part of the site was used as a roller skating rink after 1910.

For a period in the early twentieth century Thomas Clarkson's steam buses made him a nationally known business figure but he didn't come to Chelmsford until 1902. When he did it is highly likely that Colonel Crompton played a role (See chapter 6). Crompton would have known of Clarkson through his interest in cars and in particular steam transport from his days experimenting on the roads in India. He probably informed Clarkson of the availability of his old Anchor Works in Moulsham. "Clarkson was firmly of the opinion that the steam engine was capable of much further refinement, which would make it the pre-eminent power system for the motor bus: a belief that he held consistently through his career". (22)

Clarkson was born in September 1863 in Yorkshire. He spent his early life in Manchester. At college he gained a reputation as a 'gifted experimentalist' winning the Whitworth scholar award at the young age of 21, which carried an entitlement to £200 guineas, no small sum at the time. By all accounts "he was tall, had sandy hair and a beard, giving him a rather striking appearance, and he was possessed of a persuasive charm and eloquence combined with a sense of showmanship". He then went to the School of Mines and at twenty four had his first patent accepted for a centrifugal separator for mineral substances. Clarkson moved to London, where he lectured at Kings College after qualifying in Metallurgy at the Royal College of Sciences. He soon established patents for a condenser to a steam car. Clarkson decided he needed better facilities and a full time involvement in designing steam cars. For this reason he went into business with Herbert C. Capel to manufacture gas engines at the latter's works in Dalston. Six patents were taken out in their joint names in 1896 and more the following year. The Clarkson and Capel Steam Car Syndicate was then formed with a works off the Old Kent Road. Whilst other steam engineers felt that steam was only suitable for heavy traction engines, he thought light steam propelled cars were perfectly practical using high pressure generators with flash or semi flash, liquid burners or condensers. (23) In 1898 the Syndicate showed a steam powered landau at an exhibition of horseless carriages in Richmond Park. The vehicle had a small compound engine which drove it using a mixture of vaporised oil mixed with steam. (24)

Clarkson kept the Syndicate's name for a number of years but decided to move to Crompton's old works in 1902. The works had been established as the Moulsham Iron Foundry as early as 1815; it had been owned by first Christy's then T.H.P. Dennis, a hydraulics engineer before the latter went into partnership with Crompton (see chapter 4). After Crompton established his new works in Writtle Road, Dennis kept the foundry part of the works going until he retired in 1902. Following the move Clarkson changed the name of the business to Clarkson Limited.

In 1903 the firm exhibited a chassis called the 'Chelmsford' at the Automobile Show. The vehicle was described as a "substantial roomy steam brougham (bus) suitable for the conveyance of eight passengers." Clarkson had switched the multi tubular boiler to the front. In an advert he described the car as "safe, strong, speedy and simple". Almost all cars at the exhibition were petrol driven and there were few buyers. As usual however Clarkson didn't give up and after adapting the single decker bus so that it could take fourteen passengers interest came from the Torquay Bus Company. (25) "Of all the motors they seem the best." "The vehicles are particularly well suited for holiday and health resorts like Torquay". (26) An order was secured for eight buses and six months later the Chronicle reported "The people of Torquay are evidently delighted with the running of the Chelmsford Motor Bus". Two more buses were ordered. Clarkson's buses "did not miss a single journey when the waves beat with a relentless fury on the Torquay roads". (27) The first of the new buses had been driven to Exeter. "The buses coped very well in the Torquay area.... coping very well with the severe gradients and the poor quality roads". (28) This resulted in considerable positive publicity in the trade press. In turn this was followed by two buses being supplied to the North Eastern Railway Company, two to the Eastbourne Company and others for the Sussex Road Motor Company and the Maidstone Motor Omnibus Company.

It was London however that offered Clarkson the biggest potential market. The largest bus companies in the capital city were the London General Omnibus Company (L.G.O.C.) and the London Road Car Company (L.R.C.). Both were still operating horse drawn carriages. (29) The 'Chelmsford' was put through three days of trials with the L.G.O.C. which lasted eight hours each day, after which the Essex Chronicle reported "its steadiness, reliability and comfort in all weathers make it seem far superior to all other". (30) Clarkson built the L.G.O.C. a steam bus chassis at a cost of £605.The 14 seater entered service in October 1904. (31) By February 1905 Clarkson had designed a new double decker for the L.R.C. and this was displayed at Olympia. (32) The new steam bus was also sold to the London and South West Railway. (33) Later in the year 12 double decker chassis were supplied to the L.G.O.C. for its Canning Town to Oxford Street route at a cost of £7,200. Clarkson took the 14 seater back. (34) Following the Olympia show the L.R.C. ordered 20 and then 5 more. (35) In July 1905 Clarkson buses were operating in many districts including Sussex, Yorkshire, Kent, Gloucestershire, Westmoreland, Lancashire, North Wales, Cheshire, Devon and Scotland, as well as London. Overseas orders were sent to India, Ceylon, Barbados, New Zealand, Tasmania and New South Wales in Australia. Exports quickly reached £20,000. (36) The Institute of Mechanical Engineers praised Clarkson's steam buses. By 1906 for a company formed only four years previously with as little as £5,000 capital Clarkson's had done extremely well to have achieved a seven and a half percent dividend in each of the previous three years. (37) The Anchor Works needed new equipment and the factory was reorganised. W.J. Morrison was promoted to works manager and the financial side of the business was given over to Bert Smith but the staff still didn't exceed fifty. (38) Frank Searle was appointed chief engineer in 1907. At this time Clarkson still thought steam had a future as "petrol was notoriously unreliable and expensive to maintain". (39)

After such rapid expansion a downturn was perhaps inevitable. Railway companies like the Great Western and the N.E.R. showed their faith in steam buses, but some of those who had ordered them were finding operating costs excessive. In February 1907 the Chronicle asked why staff at the company had been reduced. This was due to poor business. One reason for this was that Scotland Yard were taking action against the London bus companies and they in turn were not buying buses. (40) By 1908 the L.G.O.C. was also using petrol buses. Clarkson actually converted one of these De Dions to a steam bus at Chelmsford. In 1909 however, the L.G.O.C. went completely over to petrol buses. (41)

Clarkson was however, by no means finished. He decided to make a new lightweight chassis which would operate at a competitive running cost but it had to meet stringent running conditions laid down by Scotland Yard to get a licence. A condenser was fitted at the front of the tank and the lightweight boiler contained a small amount of water. He was able to produce a steam chassis that was a lot quieter and more reliable than any of his petrol driven competitors. All of the other companies' steam buses were off the road by the first war. The new Clarkson steam buses were driven from Chelmsford to their destination, as before, but the driver stayed with the bus until the buyer was used to it. "After dark an approaching Clarkson steamer bus was easily recognisable in advance by the blue glow from the burner jets." (42)

In 1908 the War Department took an interest in Clarkson's new bus as a possible means of transport for troops. A Captain Wenley issued a challenge to Clarkson; he had to get an advance guard down to the River Crouch from Chelmsford in an hour and a half. Four buses each took 41 men. This resulted in an order from the Territorial Army. In this successful venture Clarkson used the name' National' for the first time. During the same year Clarkson allowed the bus to be used by 'Captain Drummond' and her fellow suffragettes. (See chapter 13) He drove the bus which was covered with 'Votes for Women' posters and the town band played on the top deck. It went through the town and around the villages. Although controversial he evidently felt, rightly that the resulting publicity would be worth it. Photos duly appeared in national as well as local papers, with the suffragettes dressed in prison uniforms in front of the bus. (43)

Despite this, Clarkson couldn't sell his new bus and decided he would use them in London himself. In June 1909 with financial backing from a Colonel Colvin he formed the National Steam Car Co. He took over the rest of the Moulsham works and garages were established in Putney and Peckham. (44) The directors of the new company were Clarkson, William Lewis Gray, J.W. Davidson and Aylmer Maude. Five new vehicles were built and four existing cars used. The Company had a dual role being both a manufacturer and an operator of a public transport service. Clarkson's new buses weighed one ton less than the majority of buses in London and had a superior interior finish. (45) The small boiler was fired by paraffin. A small steam engine drove a dynamo for electricity on Clarkson's patent lighting scheme. "At times the burners would go out or light back and clouds of vapour would pour from the bonnet grill'. The driver would then throw lighted matches on to the grill whereupon the burner would start again with a mild explosion! (46) For the driver the buses were very hot, especially in the summer. (47) The first service started in November 1911 and ran from Shepherds Bush to Regent Street. A second service went from Camberwell Green to Peckham. Clarkson soon found that his buses were less used on Sundays but came up with the idea of Sunday specials. The works department soon found it difficult to produce enough chassis to keep pace with the demand for new routes and buses. (48) By 1910 they were producing a new chassis every three weeks and by the end of that year 20 were in service. A new route was started from Victoria Street to Liverpool Street. Extra garaging was obtained in the North Kent Road and the company was showing good profits. New directors were brought in and Clarkson became managing director. In 1912 the National opened its last two new routes including one from Camden to Peckham. By this time the firm was operating 100 buses. In the same year the Essex Chronicle reported that the National Steam Car Company was in a strong financial position. (49) The following year the company acquired the buses operated by the G.E.R., including those to and from Chelmsford (see chapter 10). By the end of 1913 the size of the 'National's fleet had almost doubled again to 193 with 10 of them operating at Chelmsford. Clarkson's Moulsham works were now turning out one finished unit a week. The new bodies were obtained from an outside contractor and delivered, by rail, although a body shop was obtained at Wandsworth. The 'National's passengers went up from 6 million in 1911, to 15 million in 1912 and 24 million in 1913. This was the equivalent of 71 thousand journeys a day. (50)

As early as 1913 however, the Weekly News was reporting that the other directors were not satisfied with the company's profits. In addition the war posed a number of problems for Clarkson's firm. Firstly most of the Moulsham works had to be given over to producing munitions. Secondly, almost immediately there was a shortage of workers after many volunteered for the war. Women had to be brought in. Thirdly, paraffin rose sharply in price and became uneconomic. Coke was cheap and Clarkson experimented with using this fuel. (51) In 1914 Clarkson won the R.A.C.'s annual prize, the Dewar trophy, for "the most meritorious performance in automobile engineering', with his National coke motor", which he used in a truck. It was the first time the award had been awarded to a steam driven vehicle. (52) His new 'thimble boilers' were fitted to troop carriers and Clarkson demonstrated one of these at Buckingham Palace, but few of the buses adapted to use coke were sold. The coke fumes had an adverse affect on passengers on the upper deck. (53)

After George Clare resigned as Chairman, Clarkson became both Chairman and Managing Director. He was able to run the Moulsham works virtually as he pleased. Clarkson wrongly thought that the coke burner would quickly become a profitable product but very few chassis could be built because of the munitions production. Nevertheless Clarkson continued to experiment. It was said that no two buses coming out of the Moulsham works were identical. Despite the difficult wartime conditions an extension was built at the Moulsham works which included a steel foundry. In 1915 profits fell again at a time when many other firms were doing well out of the war. "Shareholders were now definitely forming the opinion that all was not well within the company. The absence of standardisation in particular led to excessive amounts of parts having to be stockpiled." (54) Clarkson's other directors elected a Mr Hawksley in Clarkson's place as Chairman in 1917. This in turn led to the appointment of W.J. Iden as executive in charge of the omnibus business. Later he became chief executive of the whole business. Iden had worked with the L.G.O.C. Company. From the outset there was a clash of personalities with Clarkson. As far as the other directors were concerned Clarkson was too wrapped up in development work. Iden reported back to the directors in favour of the petrol driven bus; a recommendation which they quickly accepted. (55) Clarkson had just finished the first chassis of his latest design for his steam car as well as a new design for a three or four seater commercial vehicle. The latter was apparently a clever design that he had managed to develop despite wartime conditions. Only a few of the former were built and, after the Board had accepted Iden's recommendation, none went into service for the bus company. Hawksely proved himself an able Chairman and the Company recovered quickly from a loss of £19,000 in 1919. This was despite a lightning strike at the Chelmsford depot after a Christmas box had not been distributed. The directors then decided to withdraw from their London routes under an agreement with the L.G.O.C. Company. (56) Clarkson's last National bus ran in London in November 1919.

Meanwhile Clarkson remained totally immersed in new steam chassis and other developments. (57) He started producing steam driven lorries using compound engines and his 'thimble' boiler. In February 1920 when the last of these had been produced he sold his interest in what became the National Omnibus Company (See chapter 10) He went on to sell his 'thimble' boilers for industrial and other uses. Clarkson then moved to St Leonards on Sea, near Hastings, where he continued to experiment in a workshop he set up there. (58) He died in April 1933, a comparatively poor man. Clarkson was never fully recognised, possibly because his perfectionism wouldn't allow him to have his vehicles mass produced.

Another manufacturing business in Moulsham, which was well established by the late 19th century, was H. and T. Godfrey, the rope makers. Fred Spalding junior remembered them as tent and sack makers as well. (59) During the 1880s they added a shop at 54 the High Street selling ropes, wagon covers, marquees and tents. By 1911 they had another shop in Tindal Square. (60) Fumes from the actual works frequently caused a nuisance. In 1902 the Nuisance Inspector warned the firm, one of several such warnings. (61) In 1906 the Weekly News reported a "destructive fire" at the firm's works. Unfortunately the building was full of flammable materials. Two thousand feet of fire hose were used when the fire brigade dealt with the inferno because of the extensive nature of the works. One hundred thousand gallons of water was used. The paper reported that the "whole of the contents of the store and the factory were destroyed". (62) Even after over 80 years, local man, Harold Orrin remembered the fire. (63) After the first war the Moulsham works was mainly given over to tent manufacture. Before the war the firm had a sports shop at 87 Duke Street. This continued after the war and was joined by another shop at 5 Tindal Square, which concentrated on saddler and leather goods. These closed in the early 1960s, after which the firm sold its wares from the Moulsham works. The firm ceased manufacturing in the early 1970s but was still advertising marquees for hire.

A business which started in Chelmsford well before the first war was Hawkes the sweet manufacturer. Albert William Hawkes was born in 1866 in Great Baddow. Originally he was a carrier for the Lee brothers who made confectionery at Thaxted and Chelmsford. By the 1891 census he was shown as a sweet boiler. In 1900 the three Hawkes brothers and their brother in law bought out the Lee brothers. Their shop in Chelmsford soon got into difficulties as one of the brothers drank too much. In addition, their horses, which were essential for deliveries, all succumbed to anthrax and had to be destroyed. Hawkes' business had to be rebuilt. The wives worked in the factory, while the men delivered. Hawkes' factory was on the corner of New Street and Victoria Road. The business had taken over the old Eddington site in 1907, which in time was enlarged. They also had a warehouse in Roseberry Yard behind the shop. This was opposite the Empire cinema. After his first wife died in 1912, Albert married Alice Green from Witham in 1917. She then managed their shop in Duke Street. When he died in 1922 she was joined by a distant relative to help run the shop.

The Hawkes factory was hit by a bomb in the second war, as was the shop near the railway station, next to Cannons restaurant. At the start of the war if you took in two pounds of sugar into the factory you got a considerable amount of sweets in return. (64) After the war the firm's problems continued when it was hit by the national cuts in fuel, even though the firm thought initially they would be exempt from the cuts because sweets were a rationed good. (65) By the 1950s Hawkes had a shop in the High Street, as well as their one in Duke Street.

Workers at the factory remembered the sickly smells of sweets. Muriel Carston, who worked as a bottle filler for nine years from 1930, recalled there being two boilers, with two or three men working on them, mixing two or three tons of sweets at a time. Later on she also wrapped seaside rock. Hawkes also bought in sweets from several other factories to sell, using several lorries. At this time Charles Hawkes was the owner and his son Bernard also worked at the business.

Mary Scott worked at the factory in the 1950s. There were, she said, 40 people working at the factory. You could eat as many sweets as you liked. She remembered the day a pregnant girl flung herself down the stairs to get rid of her baby. Mary had joined Hawkes straight from school and received £2 - 12 s - 2d. Workers were given 3d extra for every 50 pounds they were over target. Heather Case remembered the firm making peanut brittle in the 1960s. Joy Baker worked in the factory from the age of fifteen. In 1961 at the age of 18 she lost part of a finger at the factory. Gepp's, the solicitors (See chapter 23) got her £600 in compensation. She remembered rats running through the factory under the workers feet. There was no canteen. Sugar was stored in a shed which attracted thousands of wasps in the summer. David Johnson worked at Hawkes between 1958 and 1963. He helped stack orders in the loading bay. David was taught to drive in the Hawkes' yard and the transport manager then took him out to train him to use one of the four works lorries.

In the 1960s and 1970s the firm was sold several times. It was first bought by Mackintosh, who then sold it to Rowntrees, who then sold it to Palmer and Harvey. Arthur Brittain worked at the firm's Broomfield road office from 1963 to 1973. He was happy there until the firm was taken over and was no longer a family business. Palmer and Harvey closed the Broomfield Road office in 1975. (66)

County Linen is a business which still exists today, after being originally founded in the late Victorian period as a carting business by Edward Moore. Before 1914 it had bus and taxi interests and it was not until after the Great War that the laundry was born, initially at Coggleshall. The first laundry in Chelmsford was opened in Springfield in 1930. After 1963 the business concentrated on laundry and included the Hilton and Intercontinental hotels amongst its clients. In 2009 the firm had 550 staff operating at Chelmsford and Clacton with offices still in Coggleshall. "We launder a million items a week serving London, the Home Counties and Heathrow, Gatwick and Stansted." The seventh generation of the Moores family were about to see the rebuilding of the firm's premises on the Widford business park. (67)

Pinkhams was a glove making business that started in Devon in 1884. It is still based in Witham but during the early part of the interwar period also had a factory in Chelmsford. This closed in the early1930s when the firm was badly affected by the slump when cheap foreign imports undercut the firm's gloves. (68)

Gas manufacture had started in Chelmsford in the early nineteenth century when Coates, the engineer of the Chelmer and Blackwater Navigation, built a small gasworks at the head of the Springfield Basin. It was in a good location to supply residents in the better streets with gas through pipes. Chelmsford was one of the first towns to be lit by gas. (69) By the late nineteenth century the Chelmsford, Gas, Light and Coke Co. was an important company in the town, with most of the leading townsfolk having shares in the company. W.W. Duffield (see chapter 13) was a leading director who was seemingly obsessed with the fortunes of the company and frequently a zealot with regard to its interests. The fact that the 'great and the good' of the town had such a big stake in the company was probably the reason why the council initially spurned Crompton's offer to light the town by electricity (See chapter 6). The company was continually trying to gain more customers in the town and to get existing ones to use more gas. In May 1881 it held an exhibition of gas cooking apparatus and this event was combined with a dinner cooked by gas at the Corn Exchange. (70) By the early twentieth century although the borough had gone over to electric lighting, villages like Widford and Springfield then became lit by gas supplied by the Chelmsford Gas Company. (71) At the end of the century the borough showed no desire to go back to gas lighting, although the Gas Company regularly put in tenders for the contract. The situation changed however, with the municipalisation of the company. In 1913 the passing of the national Gas Act gave the council the option of buying the company. (72) The first moves were made to municipalise the company in 1914. (73) Remarkably the municipal gas company regained the contract to light the borough in 1920 (See chapters 6 and 13) The town was not fully lit by electricity again until 1938. When the council took over the company it built a large plant close to the later distribution centre and the two gasometers, which still stand, were constructed. "Gas making was carried out in large corrugated iron structures which contained the retorts and furnaces." (74) In the 1920s the transport of coal by barge along the Chelmer and Blackwater Navigation was abandoned. A firm called Dykes bought the coal from the railway goods yard in New Street in carts drawn by horses. After the furnaces were emptied the coke residue was sold to local coal firms to be used in domestic boilers. The ash and clinker were spread haphazardly around the site and its toxity became a problem in later decades. Surprisingly there were no special measures taken to protect the gasworks during the second war. One shell passed right through a gasometer, causing no damage apart from the loss of gas, which rapidly deflated the gasometer. Gas from the works was used not only to inflate the town's barrage balloons but those of other towns as well. After the war gas production was concentrated at Chelmsford and Colchester with a pipeline along the A12 connecting the two towns. A new brick built works was built and in the 1960s another followed, which converted oil to gas.

To get the oil a pipeline was built from Shell Haven. It had just started operating when North Sea Gas came 'on stream'. (75) The works became redundant and closed apart from the gasworks and the gas distribution area. Its oil buildings were all demolished. Since then the site has been described as an eyesore. Attempts to develop it as a hotel and other leisure activities have always come to nothing. (76) In 2008 the Essex Chronicle commented "the gasworks still linger after 192 years". (77)

Another firm established before the first war was Crown Windley Bros Limited. After being founded in 1906 as the Crown works on part of the old Coleman and Morton site, the firm became well known for precision engineering, making engineers plane tables and measuring equipment. After the Second World War the firm moved to Beach's Drive off Roxwell Road. In 1966 the firm started making granite tables and components after acquiring Robert Gibbs and Sons of Aberdeen. It then transferred to Ripley in Derbyshire in the 1970s. The Crown logo became an identifiable mark in most laboratories and industrial standards rooms. It still produces layout machines, surface tables and Metrology standards. In March 2001 the firm was taken over by Eley Metrology (Sales Services) Ltd.

Robinson King and Company (Chelmsford) Ltd was formed in 1926 manufacturing glass and operated from the New London Road. Its parent company was based in Stratford. The firm was taken over by Pillar Limited in 1968 and the following year the specialist silvering department was transferred from Stratford to Chelmsford. In 1970 Pillar Limited was itself taken over by Rio Tinto Zinc Corporation. The company played its part in distributing the group's aluminium products.

As the county town Chelmsford developed a number of service industries in the nineteenth century. Administrative employment had grown slowly with the old Board of Health, but the formation of the borough Council and the Essex County Council led to the first real expansion of clerical employment. This eventually led to thousands being employed by the end of the twentieth century. The existence of the courts at Shire Hall also created some employment.

Another source of service employment was banking. There had been one bank, Crickitt and Co, in Chelmsford as early as 1784. They also had branches in Maldon and Colchester. In Chelmsford the office was known as Crickitt, Menish and Crickitt and for a while as the Chelmsford Bank. During 2007 a bank note of the latter turned up. The bank had been started in Colchester by a Huguenot family. Several banking firms in Essex failed during the national crisis of 1825 - 6. Before this, Crickitt's business was taken over by Sparrow and Co. By 1830 this was trading as the Essex Bank. During the previous crisis it had to temporarily suspend payments and a meeting of creditors was held at the Shire Hall. In 1838 W.M. Tufnell of Langleys, Great Waltham (see chapter 1) joined the firm and was connected to it until his death in 1905. It had become the Sparrow and Tufnell Bank in 1881. (78) In 1839 the London and County bank had opened a branch in Chelmsford, one of a number established in the three East Anglian Counties. (79) In 1896 Barclays absorbed the Sparrow, Tufnell and Co .branch in Chelmsford. By 1900 the London and Counties Bank had a branch in Chelmsford and this was taken over by the National Westminster Bank.

A number of the firms we have looked at in this chapter had disappeared by the first war. All the businesses we will look at in the succeeding chapters had their origins in the late Victorian period. Christy's was already a substantial business by the time our period starts. Crompton was also beginning the town in partnership initially with T.H.P. Dennis. Guglielmo Marconi came to the town in 1897. His Hall Street factory was the same premises that Fred Spalding regretted Courtaulds had not stayed manufacturing in. The Barrett cousins already had a small works in Chelmsford at the end of the century before they got hold of Hoffmann's patents (see chapter 7). Today's e2v was a post Second World War offshoot of Marconi. Even Britvic had its origins in a small lemonade business above a chemist shop in the Tindal Square.

1) Essex Windmills, Millers and Millwrights K.G. Farries
2) Chelmsford Borough Council minutes 25 8 1915
3) Essex Brewers: A Brewers History Society publication p.25
4) Essex Brewers p.21
5) http:www.grayandson.co.uk/history.htm
6) 'Ale and Hearty' Friends of Chelmsford Museums and the Campaign for Real Ale 2013 p.13
7) Essex Countryside Vol. 17 1968/9 The Ridley Family of Essex David L Tyler
8) The Beer Drinker's Companion Frank Baillie p.210-13
9) EADT24 Website 28 9 2011 Steven Russell
10) 'Ale and Hearty' p.13
11) Brown's Through the Centuries
12) The Chelmer Canal Trust' Newsletter August 2003 Issue 23 –Reflections on Brown's Timber Merchants by John Woods
13) Brown's Through the Centuries.
14) The Chelmer and Blackwater Navigation Industry – article by John Marriage

1997 The Chelmer Canal Trust
15) 'Chelmsford firms' Chelmsford Museums records Sandford Mill
16) 'Gone but not Forgotten' Chelmsford Museums pamphlet
17) Christy and Norris 75th anniversary pamphlet
18) G.B.N.F. pamphlet
19) Steam Engine Builders of Suffolk, Essex and Cambridgeshire Ronald H. Clark
20) E.W.N. 6 5 1881 p.3
21) G.B.N.F. pamphlet
22) 'The National' RJ Crawley etc p.4
23) 'The National p.6
24) Thomas Clarkson Blue Plaque pamphlet Chelmsford Museums
25) The National p.8
26) Essex Chronicle 5 6 1903 p.5
27) E.C. 8 1 1904 p.4
28) 'The National' p.8
29) 'When steam buses were made at Chelmsford' G. Woodstock Essex Countryside Vol. 12 1963/4
30) E.C. 30 9 1904 p.3
31) The 'National' p.8
32) 'When steam.....'
33) E.C. 3 2 1905 p.4
34) 'When steam....'
35) The 'National' p.9
36) E.C. 10 2 1905 p.4
37) Essex Weekly News 27 12 1906 p.5
38) The 'National' P.8
39) The National' p.11
40) E.C. 8 2 1907
41) 'When steam...'
42) The 'National p.12
43) The 'National p. 14
44) 'When steam....'
45) The 'National' p.15
46) 'When steam...'
47) Thomas Clarkson Blue Plaque pamphlet

48) The 'National' p.19
49) E.C. 27 12 1912 p.3
50) The 'National' p.22
51) 'When steam....'
52) Thomas Clarkson Blue Plaque pamphlet
53) 'When steam...'
54) The 'National' p.30
55) The 'National' p.31
56) Essex Countryside Vol.38 Jan John Marriage
57) The National' p.33
58) 'When steam.....'
59) 'Chelmsford in my younger days' Fred Spalding p.14
60) Hilda Grieve Vol.2 p.381
61) C.B.C. minutes 24 9 1902
62) E.W.N. 13 7 1906 p.2
63) Harold Orrin Oral history records –Essex Record Office
64) Chelmsford Museums records
65) E.W.N. 14 2 1947 p.8
66) C. Museums Records
67) E.C. 4 6 2009 p.2
68) E.C. 6 10 2012 p.30
69) E.C. 25 4 2003 Article by John Marriage
70) E.W.N. 13 5 1881 p.5
71) C.B.C. minutes 25 3 1908
72) C.B.C. minutes 3 3 1913
73) E.W.N. 17 7 1914
74) E.C. 25 4 2003 John Marriage
75) E.W.N. 17 8 1972
76) E.C. 25 4 2003 John Marriage
77) E.C. 21 2 2008
78) A History of Banking in Essex Miller Christy p.14
79) Early East Anglian Banks and Bankers Harold Preston

3

The Christy Group

"A firm so steeped in the family traditions of caring and benevolence"

The Christy group of companies may have been the smallest of Chelmsford's big companies but it was internationally known for much of the twentieth century. In the 19th century the Quaker Christy family controlled a strictly run business but their very benevolent attitude to those who stuck to the rules, led to many families working for the firm for several generations. The distinction that it was a family firm with a paternalistic attitude towards its employees worked in its favour until after the second war. After 1945 this way of running a business, although still not without merits in many respects, became outdated. The way to survival and further prosperity was pointed out to the firm but unwillingness to take on new management techniques played a big part in its eventual demise. All the big three Chelmsford firms, received early support from the Christy Company. The Barrett cousins received a lot of help and advice from the company in the early days of the Hoffmann Company. Early contacts with the Crompton Company resulted in Frank Christy being apprenticed to the Colonel's business. This resulted in a second branch of the business being established revolving around electrical engineering. Marconi himself carried out testing on the firm's premises at Broomfield when he was just beginning to get established. The fact that Christy and Norris' disintegrator was used in non agricultural industries enabled them to survive the depression in farming in the late nineteenth century when a number of the other local engineers didn't.

The Christy family tree goes back to the seventeenth century. Fell Christy, who started the engineering firm, was the youngest son of James Christy and Charlotte Fell. (1) James Christy was a farmer but did a certain amount of clay digging and brick making in 'Pottery field' near Patching Hall off the Broomfield Road. He is known to have established a Temperance Council in Chelmsford. Fell Christy "an engineer by intuition" was apprenticed by his father to Whitmore and Binyon, well known millwrights and agricultural engineers at Wickham Market. In 1858 Fell was allowed to buy Browning's farm, which included a house off the Broomfield Road. This became the site for the family business when Fell went into partnership with his father. By 1859 the partnership had works in Broomfield and Moulsham but the family were still manufacturing pots. (2) The site at Broomfield became known at the Broomfield Ironworks. Fell spent much of his time servicing and repairing wind and water mills. He went all over the country, even as far as Ireland. (3) During this time he gained "a reputation for meticulous care and attention to detail" and business was good from the start. (4) In the 1860s he was also producing brick making equipment, as well as horticultural and heating apparatus, steam engines and grinding machinery. He did not make his own iron castings until the end of the 1860s when he had an iron and brass foundry built at the Broomfield Road site. Although there was another foundry in Chelmsford at Coleman and Morton, such foundries were still comparatively rare in the county. He made sure that the latest iron making techniques of Naysmyth were incorporated into the new foundry. In about 1872 the firm started to make the beater type of disintegrator which had previously only been used in the United States. After this the disintegrator, with many developments and improvements, became the centre of what became Christy and Norris. It was used to reduce a variety of materials into powder very efficiently. Eventually it was employed not only in agriculture but also milling, food manufacture and other industries. (5) The resulting rapid growth of the firm meant that much of Fell Christy's time was being taken up with the engineering side of the business and he had little time left for the equally essential commercial side of a business. For this reason he approached James Alfred Norris in 1880. As we have seen Norris worked for Eddington's. His financial acumen was vital but also his knowledge of agricultural engineering opened up further business for the company. In 1885 he became a full partner of the business. (6) The Essex Chronicle in 1884 reported on a dinner to celebrate Fell Christy's silver wedding at which all the seventy workmen employed at the iron and brass foundry and milling works on the Broomfield Road site attended. Richenda Christy said "Now the works cover half an acre. 14 years ago there were only six workers." (7) In 1890 a serious fire occurred at the Broomfield works. At the time it was common for workmen to supply their own tools and many of these were destroyed in the fire. Subscriptions raised by councillor Whitmore amounted to over £39 and were used to replace these tools. As with the fire at Crompton's Arc Works the previous year, Christy's responded to the blaze positively. Rebuilding was done on modern lines enabling them to experiment further in methods of grinding, sifting and conveying. The firm benefited from the rapidly expanding demand for both feeding stuffs and fertilisers. Its disintegrator and the connected equipment were recognised as the leader for these types of products.

The two partners were certainly hard task masters. Work began at 6.0. a.m. and the gates were then locked. They were re-opened to latecomers at 6.25 a.m.. After that nobody was let in until breakfast. No overtime was given until it was considered essential. Smoking and swearing were banned. Rule 13 included the sentence "we look to the men to see that the lads do no mischief". The fines system included 6d for leaving work before the horn blew, 6d for being absent without reason and one shilling for wasting materials. All the fines went towards the employees' sick club. (8)

In 1897 William Christy, Fell's son, was taken on to concentrate on millwright activities. He was responsible for improving the windmill at Stock. Meanwhile as the disintegrator progressed it was used for grinding limestone, hooves, horns, bones and phosphate rock for the fertiliser industry. (9) Well before the end of the century Christy and Norris were becoming well known in the British Empire and South America. (10)

Frank Christy, another son of Fell Christy, was born in 1865. He was educated at the Friends School in Croydon. (11) After being apprenticed to Colonel Crompton's Arc Works he set up a business in the Broomfield Road in 1883. In 1887 he went into business with another brother Leonard Fell Christy to form Christy Brothers. Initially they carried out electric lighting installations in mills, factories and farms. An Irish bacon factory was their first contract. This involved installing 200 lights. (12) It was followed by installations in a number of flour mills at Bristol, Tewkesbury, Bedford and Nuneaton. In 1889 the Chronicle reported "Messrs Christy's firm appears to be making rapid progress in the electrical world." The new venture was only 18 months old but had already lit 30 flour mills including Ridley's at Chelmsford. (13) In 1891 the Weekly News reported that electric lighting was making steady progress in the shops and houses in Chelmsford according to a pamphlet produced by the firm. (14) During the 1890s installations were made in worsted mills, hosiery and boot factories, silk mills, paper mills, dye works and foundries. Electric installations were also carried out in a number of country houses beginning with Lord Rayleigh's house at Terling.

Before the end of the century much of the Christy Brothers' business became the provision of public electricity supply undertakings. At the same time the use of water power to produce electricity began to fascinate Frank Christy. The firm produced a small scheme for a country house in Aberdeenshire in 1897 and a larger scheme at Fine. (15) At the turn of the century the firm became one of the pioneers of the electrification of small towns and villages. In 1900 the firm produced the lighting for the town of Yarmouth on the Isle of Wight and in 1903 they lit Midford on Sea, Hampshire. This was followed by contracts for towns and villages in Yorkshire, Wiltshire, Essex, Cornwall, Devon and Suffolk. (16) The firm also lit the Chelmsford and Essex Hospital as well as the hospital at Colchester. (17)

Frank Christy was also interested in the motor car and in 1907 the firm took the agency for the Adam Hewitt car. This didn't last long but the car was popular with the medical profession. For some time the firm serviced both cars and electric accumulators. At this time the firm also had the first motorised taxi cab rank in the town. Christy Brothers also invented and patented an electric oven for the baking of flour samples. It was an interesting example of the two sides of the business converging. This electric oven became widely used in mills across the country. Christy's also patented an electric magnetic separator for separating iron ore. (18) The Christy Brothers arm of the family business was converted into a private limited company, Christy Brothers and Company Ltd in 1883. (19)

The large Christy family played a wide ranging part in Chelmsford life in the late nineteenth and early twentieth century. Miller Christy was an extensive writer on natural history and county history. He was a member of the Essex Field Club and of the Council of the Essex Archaeological Society. Richenda Christy belonged to the Chelmsford Women's Liberal Association. She was also Honorary Secretary of the Chelmsford branch of the National Union of Women's Suffrage Societies, the moderate wing of the women's suffrage movement (See chapter 13). In 1888 she passed the Cambridge University External Exam. James Christy junior was the eldest son of James Christy senior. He lived all his life in the Chelmsford area and was a well known farmer and breeder of horses. James was a member of the Council of the Essex Agricultural Society and a keen hunter, especially with the Essex Staghounds. He was a member of both the Chelmsford Poor Law Guardians and the Chelmsford Rural District Council. In 1905 he became a Justice of the Peace. James was also churchwarden at Writtle parish church. (20) Much later Leonard Fell Christy was a borough councillor and in 1930 he was the Mayor. The firm was always an enthusiastic participant in the Chelmsford works' sports day.

In 1918 two years after the death of the founder Fell Christy, the original partnership was converted into a private limited company with five directors. H.B. Norris the son in law of James Norris, and F.B. Wiseman, who had started at the company as an apprentice, were both invited to be directors. (21) William Christy was responsible for a new range of machines for milling and millwrighting after the first war.

In 1929 William introduced a non contributory pension scheme covering every employee. The firm also started a co-partnership scheme. Employees could buy vouchers which received a dividend at a similar rate to the ordinary shareholders. In addition a profit sharing scheme was drawn up covering all employees of the firm. Christy's wasn't large enough to run an apprenticeship school of their own so apprentices were released one day a week at the local technical school.

The 1930s saw a further extension of the firm's buildings with the erection of a modern steel fabrication workshop. A new iron foundry was opened in 1938. Nineteen forty two saw the first production of the Essex Mill, which was redesigned six years later. This was the ideal grinder for all types of farm material and was a major success. In 1933 the firm became a public limited company.

Christy and Norris Grinding machinery
(Courtesy of E.R.O.)

At this time the Essex Chronicle recorded that Christy Brothers were the oldest firm of electrical contractors in the country (although Crompton had in fact started earlier). It made steady progress in the 1930s. In 1930 Frank Christy formed the West Devon Electric Supply Company, which covered 830 miles. A hydro electric power scheme was started there in 1931. This wasn't completed until 1937. (22) At the time it was the largest H.E.P. scheme in Britain. (23) The Devon Company performed well, as did one established in North Somerset. Christy Brothers regularly issued dividends of 10% on their ordinary shares before the war and their total sales reached over a third of a million pounds a year. A new share issue for the North Somerset Company was oversubscribed. All Christy Brothers employees were given a minimum bonus of two weeks wages. The Company had also established a successful radio relay service in Chelmsford and at the home of their other works at St Neots. This brought radio programmes to homes, schools and hospitals. (24) It was needed because ironically radio reception was often poor in the town that was the 'Home of Radio'.

During the war Frank Christy refused to let the Christy Group of companies be directly involved with war production and he went into farming. Christy Brothers did however design a vast underground factory at Corsham. This was a high production aircraft unit and amounted to a virtual underground city. They also designed factories at Riseley and Wolverhampton and played a part in the construction of the Mulberry Harbour for the D-Day invasion. (25)

William Christy died in 1947 and F.F. Christy was appointed managing director of Christy and Norris. He had joined the company in 1927 and was appointed to the board in 1934. (26) Christy Brothers had opposed the idea of nationalisation of the electricity supply industry before the war but in 1948 it was introduced. Christy Brothers Limited immediately lost 80% of its business. (27) This forced a merger of the two separate Christy companies into Christy Brothers (Chelmsford) Limited, a holding company. The financial interests of the two companies were merged by an exchange of shares between Christy and Norris and the new company. Frank Christy became chairman of the Christy group. This was not the end of the electrical side of the business. The British Electricity Authority allowed the new company to buy back the premises at Broomfield Road together with a number of uncompleted electrical contracts. (28)

In 1958 the group celebrated the centenary of the foundation of the original firm. One family had worked at the Broomfield Road works for all but 20 of the 100 years. R.J. Smith worked at Christy and Norris, as did his father and grandfather. J.F. Mayall, then works director, had been with the firm for more than 50 years; with his father, they had between them also completed over 80 years service. Marking the occasion the Essex Chronicle commented "Nowadays Christy and Norris will build you a milling plant, complete with elevator, conveyors, sifters and separators, which will grind to powder anything but anything." This could range from pepper to Perspex and cardboard to coconut shells. (29)

The nationalisation of the electricity industry was without doubt a blow to the electrical wing of the group but it was able to put its efforts into general contracting work. It did a wide variety of overhead line and underground cable work. The fact that an increasing number of colonies were getting independence enabled the firm to get a number of electricity supply installation orders abroad. At home the firm became well known for producing and installing floodlights, being responsible for those at almost 200 football clubs, including Chelmsford City. The company lit Southend and Luton Airports and Lowestoft, Felixstowe, Ipswich and Tilbury Docks. (30) It also made and erected the lighting systems for a number of cathedrals, including Westminster, Canterbury and Chelmsford. Similar work was carried out at various British Steel and British Coal sites. (31) In 1952 Christy's took on the responsibility for the electricity supply of Alderney: the island, not being part of the United Kingdom, was not supplied by the nationalised concern. (32)

In 1957 the Playle Company of Maldon became a wholly owned subsidiary of Christy Brothers. The company specialised in refrigeration and produced display cabinets and manufactured and installed cold rooms. It also serviced and maintained refrigeration equipment. Seven years earlier Christy Brothers had started a retail shop at 95 the High Street. It sold electrical goods including sets and radios. Repairs were carried out at the back. (33) The motor trade division was also carried on after the second war. It supplied garages with a wide range of accessories and also included a brake lining service. (34) Although much of this diversification was successful for a while, it made the group more difficult to manage.

By the 1960s it was obvious that the company was doing less well than previously. Dividends were down and in some years absent. It was probably dissatisfaction amongst shareholders that prompted the group to commission a thorough going investigation into the running of the company. The resulting report must have made difficult reading for the company's directors. It was produced by the management consultants H. Whitehead and Partners and should have resulted in a much leaner and more efficient group of companies.

A major fault identified in all parts of the company was a lack of standardisation.

Individual draughtsmen worked to their own ideas rather than a basic plan. With the exception of the 'X' mill no new designs had been produced in recent years. "The lack of anything which looks new must have made the work of the sales team more difficult." This may have been partly caused by friction between the chief draughtsman and his deputy. To remedy this, the report recommended the appointment of a new Chief Designer.

It would have also helped the sales department if it had standardized products to sell. Greater sales would have helped fill the one third of capacity that was unused. The sales staff were also underpaid, which must have been de-motivating. Although sales was one of the best organized departments, it didn't feed information on future sales through to the manufacturing departments.

The Report said the Christy and Norris electrical part of the works was of modern design, with high quality machine tools, but could still be more efficient. Christy and Norris' output had declined over the previous three years and there had been a big and unnecessary increase in the sub-contracting out of work. This was apparently the only way it could meet delivery dates.

The Report was most vicious in its assessment of managerial ability in the Group. "We consider that with the exception of the foundry, there is a complete lack of managerial ability from the top to the bottom." There were for example personality differences between the works manager and the managing director. The Group had Process Planning and Production Control Departments which sounded advanced, but the report commented "It is sufficient to say at this point that in our opinion they are a mess and virtually useless."

The foremen were old and loyal servants but "Unfortunately the foreman is an important link in the management chain and this link is very weak indeed." All three foremen would need to be replaced if the works were to be placed on a really efficient basis. (36) The status of the shop floor supervisor had to be raised if higher standards were to be set.

No studies were carried out of the methods of production used. The foremen attempted to load the machine shop which should have been the function of Production Control. Vital job cards for individual operations were often lost. "A considerable proportion of raw stock and materials is uncontrolled." The stock figures on records were known to be wrong and there was no list of shortages. (37) The Production Controller needed replacing. There was no system of pre-allocation of work and materials which was essential in a business where small batch production was mixed with special contracts. The large amount of overtime done did not match the amount of extra work completed. (38) Even the foundry, where the manager was effective, was probably overstaffed.

The electrical wing of the Group came out better in the report. Its workshop was fully competitive, with the switchgear and electrical control panel activities doing well and being capable of expansion. This indeed was part of the problem because the Group should have been concentrating more on these activities, which would require greater space and resources. For this to happen it was recommended that the Manufacturing and Sales departments of Christy Brothers and Christy and Norris should be merged and that all of the present workshop building should be given over to switchgear and control panels. These changes would necessitate a sales plan with targets, dates and sale cost budgets. (39)

The report recommended a streamlining of most of the other diverse elements of the Group, in particular the refrigeration business, should be sold unless profits improved within two years. It was doubted whether the shop was of much value to the firm. Its sale would release cash for other activities. (40) Whitehead was impressed by the running of the motor trade division but thought it should have been made into a separate company. (41)

Despite these swingeing criticisms the report was still enthusiastic about the future of the company if its weaknesses were overcome. A fifty percent increase in production should have been possible with only a small increase in costs. (42) Such a wide ranging conglomerate needed overall co-ordination. There was a desperate need for new expertise to be brought in. At that time directors and management had no idea how their responsibilities had done until four months after the end of the financial year. A 'root and branch' change of management was probably needed from the managing director down.

Many of the recommendations of the report were ignored. A friendly atmosphere existed in the business between senior employees who were co-operative and hard working but this continued to mask a serious lack of competition between the units. The Group seemed to still be run on the basis of 'you keep off my back and I'll keep off yours'. The fact that the report had indicated that the group was vulnerable to a take-over unless there was a fundamental change to its approach to profitability and the return on its capital, still failed to force the directors hand. (43)

Some of the easier changes were carried out. The refrigeration business was sold but at too low a price and the shop property was sold to Pope and Smith for £90,000.

Six years later it would have fetched six times the price. (44)(45) The successful motor trades division was also sold off in the later 1960s despite the report's recommendations.

In 1967 however Christy's obtained its largest ever contract from a Liverpool Company for an automatic feed plant. The order benefited both Christy and Norris and Christy Brothers. (46) Three months later however it was decided to close the iron foundry; it was maintained that it had become uneconomic and that castings could be obtained cheaper from reliable suppliers. (47)

August 1973 saw the death of Frank Fell Christy. During the second war after leaving the engineering industry, because of its association with armaments, he had worked long hours on his Great Baddow farm. This farm also provided employment for others who objected to violence. After the war he was managing director of Christy and Norris for many years and Chairman of the Christy Group until 1960. He was a keen President of the Christy Sports and Social Club and edited the works magazine the Christy News. Frank Fell Christy was also President of the Chelmsford Engineering Society for over ten years. He was a prison visitor for thirty years and served on the Free Church Council. (48)

Occasional big orders couldn't mask the group's underlying problems. In 1970 Christy and Norris produced 76 giant hoppers for a Unilever subsidiary and in 1972 the Group were carrying out floodlighting projects for British Rail. (49) They lit up Parkeston Quay, Harwich for the new Sealink passenger terminal. (50) Christy and Norris hit a new export record in 1973 and landed a £500,000 order to supply machinery and electrical control equipment for nine new feed mills in Turkey. (51) The following year they clinched a one million pound order for seven animal feed plants in Iraq.

There were however, redundancies as the firm's difficulties grew. In 1975 alone, 66 were released. (52) There was an attempt not to affect production staff. In 1974 the firm had to give assurances they were not considering pulling out of the town after a dispute over insufficient parking for employees around the Broomfield works. (53)

A possible takeover had already come to nothing in 1973 when a firm called Byrne Brothers had purchased a significant number of Christy shares. This came after electrical contracting had had two good years. (54) Christy's bought Byrne Investment Management to regain complete control but B.I.M.'s losses wiped £157,000 off the group's £202,000 profit in March 1974. (55) In 1977 both Christy Electrical and Christy and Norris enjoyed a short lived boom with each taking on skilled workers. Christy and Norris received a £825,000 order for a feed mill in Stroud. Christy Electrical put their electronic equipment into one of the largest cargo handling systems in the world at

Taiwan's Keeling Harbour. A belated attempt was made to make the wage structure at the group more competitive with the big three firms in the town. (56)

By 1980 a major shake up at the firm had become inevitable. The Group had 350 workers but had lost £119,000 in the last nine months of 1979. There had been no dividend since 1978. Losses were blamed on recent industrial disputes (See chapter 9) (57).The Board of Directors recommended to shareholders that they accept the offer of Jim Dyer on behalf of a consortium. When this went through Dyer said that the company had to be made profitable. (58) Before the end of the year workers at the Group were on a three day week because of the recession. They had already lost 80 further workers and the order book was continuing to fall. (59) It was rumoured the consortium was looking for a new buyer. (60) The following year however, with the upturn in economic conditions, Christy's returned to full time working. There were still 24 redundancies however. The firm had received a government subsidy for short time working for the previous eight and a half months. In July 1981 order books were still not back to the level of 18 months previously. (61) A number of orders from Africa however, safeguarded jobs. The largest of these was for the supply of hammer mills for grinding maize and was worth £60,000. Another order was for a tea processor in Zambia worth £50,000. As a result the company announced a profit for the first time in years. (62) In the following two years however the company had shrunk further and the 350 employees of 1980 had fallen to just 121. The group's operations were moved to the back of the factory and four of twelve units were leased to small companies. (63)

In 1985 following an amalgamation with R. Hunt and Co., Christy's left their Broomfield Road site. (64) Production was moved to Christy Hunt Engineering Ltd at Earls Colne. This was also closed in 1988 after a takeover by Bentall-Simplex of Scunthorpe. (65) A small part of the original business moved to Scunthorpe. (66) The Broomfield Road site quickly became derelict but eventually was converted into a pleasant housing development, Broomfield Court. In the new millennium the name Christy and Norris could still be found on manholes and grates.

This sad end to a once proud company, after a history going back almost 130 years, was perhaps inevitable. The radical changes needed for the firm to progress further in the harsh business environment of the late twentieth century were never likely to come from within a firm so steeped in the family traditions of caring and benevolence.

1) A History of the Christy Group 1858-1985 Bill Tincknell p.2
2) Fell Christy Blue Plaque pamphlet Chelmsford Museums.
3) Christy and Norris 75th Anniversary pamphlet
4) Tincknell p.3
5) Fell Christy pamphlet
6) A Century of Progress 'Expansion by Reduction' Christy and Norris
7) Essex Chronicle 7 3 1894 p.5
8) Essex Weekly News 18 7 1958 '100 years at Christy's' p.9
9) Tincknell p.4
10) Tincknell p.22
11) Tincknell p.94
12) Fell Christy Blue Plaque pamphlet
13) E.C. 5 4 1889 p.5
14) E.W.N. 20 11 1891 p.4
15) Tincknell p.98
16) Tincknell p.99
17) Tincknell p.100
18) Tincknell p.114
19) E.C. 4 5 1934 p.2
20) Chelmsford Museums Records – Chelmsford people
21) A Century of Progress
22) Tincknell p.101
23) 'Two pioneers of Chelmsford' by Fred Roberts Essex Countryside Vol.28
24) E.S.W. 10 3 1943 p.3
25) Tincknell p.103
26) Tinchnell p.28
27) Tincknell p.133
28) Tincknell p.138
29) E.W.N. 18 7 1958 p.9
30) Tincknell p.139
31) Tincknell p.465
32) Tincknell p.485
33) Tincknell p.450
34) Tincknell p.460
35) Tincknell p.49

36) Tincknell p.51
37) Tincknell p.54
38) Tincknell p.56
39) Tincknell p.280
40) Tincknell p.455
41) Tincknell p.462
42) Tincknell p.50
43) Tincknell p.515
44) Tincknell p.439
45) Tincknell p.455
46) E.W.N. 3 12 1967 p.16
47) E.W.N. 19 5 1967 p.20
48) E.W.N. 9 8 1973 p.7
49) E.W.N. 21 3 1970
50) E.W.N. 18 5 1972 p.5
51) E.W.N. 6 9 1973 p.7
52) E.C. 17 10 1975 p.1
53) E.W.N. 19 12 1974 p.8
54) Tincknell p.518
55) E.W.N. 16 10 1975 p.1
56) E.W.N. 21 7 1977 p.3
57) E.C. 6 6 1980 p.1
58) E.C. 13 6 1980 p.1
59) E.C. 10 10 1980
60) E.W.N. 19 10 1980 p.1
61) E.C. 17 7 1981 p.3
62) E.C. 27 11 1981 p.1
63) E.C. 11 3 1983 p.1
64) Tincknell p.59
65) Fell Christy Blue Plaque Pamphlet
66) Tincknell p.518

4

R.E. Crompton and the Crompton Company in Chelmsford

"Circumstances directed his attention to electric lighting"

Colonel R.E.B. Crompton (1845 -1940) was not only an internationally known electrical engineer but his company was closely interwoven with the industrial development of Chelmsford. He was responsible, according to the Essex Chronicle, for Chelmsford becoming the first town in England to be solely lit by electricity. Although he, like Marconi, was more an adaptor of inventions than an inventor per se, Crompton's contribution to the new fields of electric lighting and electricity generation was immense. Although they were not financially a success, he developed and patented a wide range of electric domestic appliances. His stress on the need for standardisation in industry and transport unfortunately fell on deaf ears. Although by the time of his death the company (then Crompton Parkinson) had a number of factories, Crompton himself always said the one at the original Arc Works was closest to his heart. The firm itself was, like many electrical engineering concerns at the time, never wildly successful financially. This often led to a good deal of tension between the directors of the company and those responsible for technical progress. Although not the size of Hoffmann's or Marconi in Chelmsford, the Crompton factory still employed 2,300 people in the 1950s. Its importance to the town was still sufficient for Stevas, the Chelmsford M.P., to lead a delegation to the House of Commons when the factory in Writtle Road closed in the 1960s. In its early days the Crompton Company played an important role in creating a pool of skilled engineering labour in the town. Crompton himself also significantly encouraged the development of the other works in the town, especially Clarkson and Marconi. Although in certain respects he was very paternal towards his employees and this led him to provide good working conditions for them compared with many late Victorian employees, his anti trade union stance was the cause of some degree of industrial unrest at the factory which continued after he retired from the company in 1912.

Rookes Evelyn Crompton was born at Thirsk in North Yorkshire. His parents were cultured and widely travelled. He was the fifth son. His father was a country squire, who was interested in engineering and his mother was a good musician, who was descended from the diarist John Evelyn. (1) Crompton senior received a commission from the army during the Crimean War and took the 11 year old Rookes to Gibraltar. R.E. actually went to Sebastopol and received a medal and a Sebastopol clasp. From 1854 until 1864 he went to Harrow, where he was assessed as only 'fair' at Science, although in his holidays he built a steam road engine called 'Bluebell' (2) After going to Paris to learn the language he joined the Rifle Brigade. This led to a period of military service in India. Crompton sent home for his tools and the incomplete engine and set up a mobile workshop in which he made dog carts. He was soon put in charge of the regimental workshop, where he met R.W. Thompson, the inventor of the pneumatic tyre. Together they worked on a steam engine to replace the bullock trains. The new engines enabled the mechanical transport of supplies, tents and the heavy baggage of the regiment. (3) Twenty years later Lord Roberts remembered this contract when he put Crompton in charge of transport in the South African conflict. (4)

Crompton however, was disappointed that his superiors didn't show more interest in steam road transport. When he returned to England he decided however, to go into business to develop further his steam road engine. This led him to buy a third of T.H.P. Dennis' firm in Anchor Street, Chelmsford after he had married. (5)

An ironworks had been first opened in Anchor Street in 1815 by a John Bewley. This was taken over by his son in 1843 and was later called the Anchor Street Works. T.H.P. Dennis, an ironmonger in Chelmsford High Street took over the site of the ironworks to manufacture high pressure steam valves and hydraulic equipment. It was this that attracted Crompton. (6) Dennis continued in business after his partnership with Crompton was dissolved, becoming a limited business in 1904 and still carrying out general engineering as well as decorating. The firm was responsible for the first telephone installation in Chelmsford. (7)

Initially road transport was uppermost in Crompton's thoughts, although he had conducted some electrical experiments at school. At this time steam was the only type of power on the road. The internal combustion engine wouldn't be developed for another 20 years. He introduced new methods of moulding in the ironworks using semi automatic machine tools. "Circumstances directed his attention to electric lighting instead." (8) Crompton had relatives who ran an ironworks in Derbyshire. He designed a mechanised foundry but it needed to operate on three shifts and therefore through the night. To light the mine he initially imported Serrin Arc Lamps and Gramme Generators but he found these unsatisfactory. He then decided to start the production of electric lighting equipment at the Chelmsford works. Arc lamps produced light from an electric arc struck between two carbon rods. Crompton designed a new improved lamp which he patented in 1879. He met Emile Burgin, a Swiss engineer, and they worked on a new type of generator. The first Burgin generator was produced at the Chelmsford works in 1880. Crompton took over the whole of the works for the manufacture of electrical plant. (9) In March 1879 he had employed A.P. Lundberg, a Swedish engineer who was married to an English woman, to be his first foreman of the electrical apparatus shops in part of the Anchor Ironworks. It was soon renamed the Arc Works. Crompton then worked to improve the Gramme generator. The compound windings could provide constant voltage without needing continuous attention. These were patented by Crompton and Gisbert Kapp, an employee in 1882. They disagreed about the size of castings and armature needed for the generators. Crompton used laminated conductors in the rotating armature and compound windings to strengthen the magnetic field which surrounded it. Despite the opposition of Kapp, the generator was successful and this was the beginning of the Crompton dynamo. (11) Kapp went on to design dynamos for other companies. Crompton based his first arc lamps on Serrin's. He improved the mechanism which kept the gap between the carbon rods constant and placed it above the lamp so that it cast no shadow downwards.(12) The principal problem with these lamps was that they could not operate in a series and initially every lamp had to be supplied with its own generator. Crompton and Kapp also patented voltmeters and ammeters to measure the flow of electricity. Colonel Crompton later played a leading role in the introduction of international standard measurements of electric currents.

In 1880 Crompton met Joseph Wilson Swan, originally a chemist, who had developed an incandescent filament lamp, the forerunner of the electric light bulb. Crompton immediately saw the potential of his rival's invention but rather than be intimidated he went into business with him, becoming a director of the Swan United Electric Co. This was founded in 1882 because the demand for lighting needed more working capital than the first Swan Company and Crompton's own company could provide. Crompton and Co. started producing lamp fittings and generators for Swan's lamps. Many of Crompton's first installations included both arc and filament lighting. (13)

By June 1881 the Essex Chronicle was reporting that a new electric light shop was being erected in Anchor Street. The work was progressing day and night, using Crompton's own lamps. (14) In September of the same year Norwich City Council accepted Crompton's tender to light some of the city's streets. The contract for £400 was less than half of some experiments elsewhere. (15) Six months later it was reported that the scheme had been a great success. (16) In October 1882 the Chronicle contained a detailed article on the firm. "These works promise to add materially to the prosperity of the town." Orders were increasingly rapidly. "One of the commissions is to light the Guildhall with electric lamps." The company was about to light the Mansion House. It had won two gold medals at the Paris exhibition, one for the Crompton lamp and one for his adaptation of the Burgin machine. He had lit Kings Cross station and made mining lamps using Swan's incandescent design. The Kings Cross installation was the first in which one generator supplied more than one arc lamp. Twelve four thousand candle power, lamps were suspended ten metres above the platforms. Four Crompton - Burgin engines each supplied three lamps. A fifth engine supplied two large lamps in the station forecourt. Crompton also supplied lamps for the terminal stations in Glasgow. He had already taken out a patent for a solid system of underground mains with tubular conductors. The Chronicle noted as early as October 1881"It is rumoured that four or five residents of Chelmsford have a scheme under consideration for establishing electric lighting with the Crompton Lamp." (17) Before the end of 1881 Crompton had lit football matches at Kings Meadow, Chelmsford. This involved 1,200 yards of wire. (18) In 1881 he had also lit the Crystal Palace exhibition with arc lamps and produced a paper on how it was done. Crompton also lit the Law Courts, the first really large installation with incandescent lamps. Windsor Castle was lit by electricity in April 1882. In later years Crompton used to relate the story that Queen Victoria slapped his face for saying that electric lighting was better than gas. Berechurch Hall, near Colchester, was the first time a private house had been lit throughout with electric light. Building workers, who were working on the house at the time, eventually went into business as master contractors for the wiring of houses.

In 1882 an Essex Chronicle reporter was given a guided tour of the factory. There were 70 or 80 "hands at the works". There was however a shortage of skilled workers and because of this, new men were drafted in from, Leeds, Ipswich, Colchester, Woolwich and Silvertown. Crompton was certainly worried by this shortage and started an apprenticeship scheme. "Besides the workmen there were several young gentlemen, whose parents, believing in the future of electric light have gladly availed themselves of the opportunity of apprenticing themselves for a term of three years to this new profession, with the understanding that they shall doff their coats to it, and master it from top to bottom in a thoroughly practical manner." "As time goes on it may be supposed that native talent will make itself of more value in the more technical branches of the work that is carried on." (19) In an interview to commemorate his 90th birthday Crompton recalled that he had tried importing a few Yorkshire men, because the local workmen were not easy to train but he found that these soon got a bad name because they were in the habit of getting drunk on a Saturday. For this reason Crompton set about securing young men in the immediate neighbourhood.

Apart from his apprenticeship scheme, Crompton was also interested in the welfare of his workers. He was one of the first employers to provide a well furnished factory canteen, as well as baths and wash houses and a social and recreational centre for his employees. (20) The Crompton sports ground in Wood Street was regularly used for the United Works Sports days in the Edwardian period (See chapter 25)

By this time there were sixteen lathes at the works driven by steam and six worked by treadle. Gun-metal castings were obtained from the Dennis part of the works. These castings were used in the lamps and the fittings. Iron castings were also obtained from Coleman and Morton.

The first proposal to light Chelmsford by electricity, intriguingly, didn't come from the Crompton Company at all. A proposal by the Brush Electric Company was referred to the lighting committee by the Board of Health in 1882. (21) The Board replied saying it would oppose any application by the company to the Board of Trade. A number of those on the Board of Health were major shareholders in the local gas company. (See chapter 2) Two months later Crompton sent a letter to the Board of Health saying he had applied for a licence for lighting from the Board of Trade but his offer was turned down. (22)

After members of the Leeds Corporation visited Chelmsford it was announced that the Crompton-Burgin engine was to be used to light parts of Leeds. (23) December of 1883 saw the manufacture of lights for the King of Siam. (24)The following year saw Crompton installing electric lights in a number of collieries, including some in South Wales. This was the first time the bottom of a pit had been lit in this way. (25) Crompton's agent in the north carried out several installations for the Company in woollen mills. (26) Also in 1884 the company lit Paddington station and a Brazilian 'ironclad' ship that was being built in England. "Three Crompton dynamos, each capable of driving three hundred lights, will be placed in the vessels and three powerful searchlights for naval purposes giving a light of almost ten thousand candles will be provided." (27) Probably as a result of this the firm received an order to light the training ship, the Lynmouth, lying off Grays and also led the Admiralty to become interested in Crompton's searchlight. (28) In previous tests Danbury church spire and the building next to it facing Chelmsford were sufficiently illuminated to be seen in detail from a distance although they were close on five miles away in a direct line from the searchlight. (29) Later tests resulted in searchlights being supplied for five Admiralty ships. (30) Commercial shipping companies also became interested. In 1887 two Peninsular and Oriental steamships were fitted with searchlights and internal lights.

Meanwhile, Crompton having been rebuffed in his first attempt to light the town made an offer to light the Agricultural Show for free. Doubtless he saw this as worthwhile publicity. December 1887 saw a small fire at the Arc Works. Prompt action using a recently purchased hose prevented any serious damage but this was a foretaste of what was to happen eight years later. (31)

The year of the Borough's Incorporation saw the Company being converted into a limited company. It initially had a capital of £140,000 in 28,000 shares of £5 each. Lord Torrington was the first chairman of the new company. Crompton and Albright, two directors of the previous partnership retained a substantial interest in the company. During the previous five years average profits had averaged seven thousand pounds per annum. (32) Necessary heavy investment saw the company make reasonable profits in the 1890s but as with other electrical engineering companies, heavy capital outlays often reduced profits and were frequently the cause of conflict between directors and those involved with the technical side.

Crompton pushed for the passing of the 1888 Electric Lighting Act, which superseded the 1882 Act and meant that the period in which the local authorities had the right to purchase electricity supply companies doubled from 21 to 42 years. (33) This he correctly thought would make councils much more likely to allow companies to develop lighting and generating schemes. The Act and the Borough's Incorporation also meant that he was more likely to get his wish, namely to light his adopted home town. In a special meeting of the town council in March 1889 the proposed lighting of the town by electricity was discussed. The lighting committee recommended that the council accept Crompton's tender to light the town for five years. Albright, a councillor, and Crompton, claimed that the lamps were 50% more brilliant than those under the gas system. The Clerk insisted that "the interest of certain councillors in the electricity and gas concerns was too remote to disqualify them"! The meeting was adjourned. (34) Such was the interest in the town in the issue that a public meeting was held. Most of those who attended were in favour of electric lighting but would have preferred incandescent lamps to arc ones. After the gas directors on the council abstained from voting, electric lighting was finally adopted by the council at their next meeting. (35) The Chronicle reported in May "Chelmsford will become the first town in the United Kingdom to be fully lighted by electricity."(36) At first it was hoped that the town would be lit by the end of 1889 but Crompton had to reposition the lamps. Even after the new lighting system had started there were a number of problems, with the public and the council complaining about defective lamps. (37) Eventually the Council instituted a system of fines on the company which were taken from the payments they received. In 1892 Crompton created a subsidiary, the Chelmsford Electric Lighting Company, for contractual purposes. As early as 1893 Crompton said he was providing lighting for Chelmsford at a loss but the editor of the Chronicle was certainly not convinced. (38) A further difficulty was that the company was coming under pressure from the Board of Trade to put their cables underground. The company's lighting contract was renewed for a further five years but a clause was inserted in the new contract allowing for a council buyout of the lighting concern during the next 21 years. (39) In 1896 Crompton wrote to the council offering to sell them the electric station and plant. This was probably triggered by the recent fire (See later). (40) The Weekly News thought that the offer had come too soon. "We have heard it hinted that Crompton and Co's obligations in regard to the public and private lighting in the town are the only effective ties that bind them to Chelmsford." The paper argued that such was the importance of the firm to the town already, that the council should bear this in mind. Crompton's proposal was not taken up by the council and a new lighting station for the town was erected in Anchor Street later in the year. In 1898 the Chelmsford Electric Lighting Company laid about five and a half miles of underground cable. "These will be much larger than the present overhead cables, and will practically, bear all the high tension pressure. A large gang of men has already been set on, digging out the necessary trenches: and another one is to be employed almost immediately, the object being to have all the work completed within a month." By 1899 the Weekly News had changed its mind on the municipal ownership of the town's lighting. "We believe there is a strong feeling both inside and outside the council that it would be a good thing to have control of the town's lighting." A report valued the subsidiary at £24,000 but the parent company wanted £41,000. (42) Even if the valuation by the company had been lower it is extremely doubtful whether the council, with its extremely cautious approach to spending, would have opted for municipalisation. Despite Crompton's previous utterances the Chelmsford Lighting Company continued to be profitable in the Edwardian period, making a profit of £3,817 for example in 1906. (43)

The 1880s had seen Crompton work to improve his company's ability to produce generating equipment. He had formed the Kensington Court Company to supply a number of private houses in that area, where he happened to live. Here he developed the system which went on to be used in many other towns in some cases for over 50 years. This consisted of bare copper conductors carried on porcelain insulators, based in conduits beneath pavements, with access through manholes. (44) He had to reduce the cost of generating electricity. There was also the problem of the maintenance of an uninterrupted supply and levelling out the difference between peak load lighting in the evenings and the relatively small day load. Electric domestic appliances were only used on an extremely small scale. The central station at Victoria, London used a new type of generator. Crompton had improved Edison's machine by strengthening the magnetic field. His generating stations used a group of accumulators to store energy. The high reputation of Crompton's generating equipment led to requests to advise on or submit schemes for power from all over the world. Crompton sent senior engineers to examine, report and usually carry out these schemes. The provision of a public power station in Pretoria, South Africa led to a number of other power stations being built in other towns. Crompton's installation of power stations and H.E.P. stations in India led to similar installations in Burma and the Malay states, as well as Australia and New Zealand. These orders for generating equipment complemented similar ones in the early 1890s from English towns and cities such as Northampton, Southampton and Birmingham. The proven reliability of Crompton's equipment resulted in cities like Birmingham putting in repeat orders for generating equipment.

Crompton was a leading inventor of electric domestic appliances, although in the main these were a generation too early for the company to make financial gains out of these developments because too few houses were supplied with electricity. He developed a wide range of cooking appliances including cookers, toasters, hot plates and hot cupboards. By 1894 the firm had won five diplomas and four gold medals in this field. (45)

From the mid 1890s Crompton designed and built many electric traction engines for tramcars and locomotion. During 1890 the world's first underground tube train ran on the City and South London line, driven by a Crompton locomotive. Locomotives were to remain part of the Company's production for well over half a century. In 1885 he had built a double decker electric tram car. By 1890 his motors were driving the electric trams up and down the tramway on Southend pier. (46) "The tram runs without a hitch and the light is beautiful." (47)

In addition to all these developments Crompton also worked on furnaces. He took out patents for electric furnaces using a new dynamo and produced electric welding equipment, which foreshadowed the later dominance of electric tools in industry. In his leading role in the Institute of Electrical Engineers, of which he became president in 1895, he continually stressed the usefulness and cheapness of electric motors in small industrial workshops. (48)

In Chelmsford the progress of the works was not without problems. During October 1889 there was another fire in which the roof of the foundry was discovered to be ablaze. Again the hose ensured that it was put out before any real damage was done. (49) The following year part of the works was moved to new premises on Lower Anchor Street. In 1895 a serious fire engulfed the main works. The entire engine room was destroyed. In the immediate aftermath of the fire 167 workmen had to be laid off by the firm. Ever mindful of the importance of the firm to the town, the council set up a relief fund for those left unemployed by the blaze. (50) By the time the fund committee finally met all but 32 had found jobs or had been re-employed by the firm. (51) Only three months after the fire Crompton bought a site on Writtle Road for a completely new works. The local papers were not slow to realise and be pleased that this meant the firm was going to stay in Chelmsford for the foreseeable future. At the time the new works was being built he also showed his commitment to the town by introducing a new bonus scheme at the Arc works. Ten shillings were given to men and five shillings to boys who lost no time during a quarter of the year. (52)

The firm experienced a particularly bad year financially in 1896 when it made a loss of £10,000. (53) Although this was largely due to the fire even before this the firm was struggling to get a return on its capital investment. In 1898 Crompton commented "two years ago the demand for small generating plant closed up.... consequently all the machinery that we used for manufacturing the smaller class of generating plant seemed likely to remain idle". (54) Some of the directors were evidently worried. Crompton argued that the move would save on transport costs, because the new works would be nearer the railway line. The new works were being built using non-flammable materials but other economies had to be made. A works at Hove had to be sold because this was making the domestic appliances that were not selling in any appreciable quantities. Other subsidiaries were sold in the following few years. Competition was increasingly fierce. Crompton tried to get an agreement with his fellow manufacturers to try to get better terms from their municipal buyers. During March 1898 an agreement to strengthen the position of the manufacturers was agreed. In practice this attempt at oligopoly control had little effect. A new attempt in 1902 floundered because firms like British Westinghouse, that were bigger than the Crompton Company, were not party to the agreement. (55) For several years in the early 1890s the Crompton Company found it difficult to borrow money. In 1888/9 £25,000 was raised on 5% debenture shares but an attempt to raise another £25,000 later in 1890 was less successful. By March 1891 only £10,800 of them had been sold. In the autumn of 1891 the company attempted to sell £50,000 of preference shares but they sold badly, forcing the company a year later to try to sell £100,000 of ordinary shares. Another £100,000 debenture issue was never completely sold. Crompton's like other firms in the industry had to borrow to finance stock, work in progress and loans to purchasing companies. The company was hampered by the period of production being long and by the fact that payments were never made until the plant had been working some time. (56) These were the reasons that potential shareholders didn't always see the company as a gold plated investment. Crompton didn't have the access to the type of industrial banks that were prevalent in Germany or the patronage of a financial powerhouse like the Morgan interests which supported General Electric in the United States. These financial difficulties caused a deterioration of the relations between the old partners in the original firm, Crompton and Albright, and the new commercial directors. These disagreements caused Albright to resign in 1898. Crompton stayed to look after the technical side but took progressively less part in the commercial affairs of the company. There was a massive shift in the running of the company as engineers ceased to manage it; this was carried out by businessmen who saw management of the company as their function. This change was illustrated by a speech by Lord Emlyn, who by 1898 was chairman of the company. "In the early days, there was a great deal of experimental work to be carried out.... it required a great deal of application and attention on the part of those who were responsible for technical details and there is no doubt that while the technical side of your business has been developed to the very highest state of efficiency, the business side got into a somewhat confused condition." The Board resolved to appoint a General Manager "who would not be a member of the Board but open to every possible criticism". Doubtless Emlyn was right to a considerable extent and mistakes had been made. Some technical developments had been followed by the company without consideration of profit and loss. The establishment of an electric cooking and heating department was an example of this. Crompton thought this department was going to be more important than electric power. Emlyn thought the answer was a rigid separation between the two sides of the business, the technical and the commercial, not the development of commercial engineers. (57)

Undoubtedly business problems played a part in Crompton getting involved with the Army again. He was asked to lead a corps of electrical engineers to South Africa in the Boer War. (See chapter 15) Many of the men in the corps came from Chelmsford with a recruitment office established in the town. Crompton was responsible for some good bridge building, lighting and telegraph repairs. The company's searchlights were extensively used and Crompton's involvement in the war led him to design wagons for the transport of supplies and lightweight engines for hauling guns (58). All this meant he spent less time on electrical work for his company.

While he was away an extension of the new Writtle Road Arc Works was carried out. The main area of the works was increased by 50%. (59) The following year the Board bought an additional ten and a half acres adjoining the works. Part of the old Anchor works was still being used by the Chelmsford Electrical Lighting Co, with their generating station positioned there. (60) By this time over one thousand workers were employed at the Writtle Road works, having doubled in the previous decade. The depression of 1904 led to the works laying off a number of workers but a £40,000 order from Calcutta and a new contract with the Admiralty saved the firm from serious difficulties. This didn't prevent the company from posting a low dividend of two and a half percent. (61) Despite its overall expansion the company, like the rest of the electrical engineering industry, was affected by the trade cycle. Two years after this business low the company's order books were full. (62)

During the Edwardian period Crompton's reduced involvement with the company led to him extending his other interests. He had been one of the founders of the Royal Automobile Club. Crompton was a judge at the first motor show in 1903 and the first President of the Institute of Automobile Engineers in 1907. He was an adviser to the Ministry of Transport from its inception. Crompton also developed a fully electric omnibus. His technically inquisitive nature never left him and he investigated the problem of road surfaces. Before 1914 he was busy establishing an international consulting practice on road construction; unfortunately the war put an end to this venture. (63) Crompton's concern at the lack of standardisation in British industry led to his involvement with the establishment of the Engineers Standardisation Association.

During the first war the Chelmsford works was a controlled establishment under the Munitions of War Act but still produced some electrical equipment for use in the war. During the first war the firm increased its output by 96%. (64) The company exploited its position to the full and was subjected to the excess profits tax. (65) Like the other major works, the company was threatened by an acute labour shortage as workers joined the army. By the end of the war there were hundreds of women working at the factory. As in Chelmsford's other big firms all the workers who went off to war were promised that their jobs would be given back to them when they returned. As a result of this most of the women lost their jobs after the war. As with Marconi however, their manual dexterity meant that they retained a foothold at the works. By the 1930s a third of all workers at the main works were women.

While Crompton ran the company he had taken a strong anti union stance and had done his utmost to prevent the Amalgamated Society of Engineers from getting a foothold at the Chelmsford works. After he left, the company's increased unionisation was accompanied by several instances of industrial unrest as workers in the major works in the town were increasingly affected by the vagaries of cyclical economic activity. A strike of moulders at the works in 1920 disrupted production for some months afterwards. (66) Nineteen twenty saw the short lived post war economic boom which led the company not being able to meet all the demand for its products. September of that year saw a dispute between the Electrical Trades Union and the National Employers Federation. Crompton had hundreds of E.T.U members and although some workers left the union, the firm made it clear that they would impose a lock-out if a dispute started. (67) In the event the national dispute was settled. Two years later however, the deep recession which affected electrical engineering as much as other industries, led to a real dispute. This led to a lock out of workers at the Arc Works as well as at Marconi. (68) During the General Strike the firm managed to carry on comparatively unaffected despite restrictions on the supply of coal for the foundry used by the firm.

The merger of the firm with F. and A. Parkinson Limited of Guisely, Yorkshire occurred in 1927. An amalgamation of some type was well overdue. The first two decades of the century had seen a strong movement towards concentration in the electrical engineering industry. By this time the Crompton Company was a fairly small and uncompetitive concern. In 1919 the Armstrong Whitworth Company had proposed a limited merger with the firm but although they bought some shares in the Crompton Company this came to nothing. Parkinson was a fairly new company concentrating on the manufacture of alternating current motors. In terms of capital assets Crompton was by far the bigger company with shares worth almost half a million pounds. Parkinson's shares, in contrast, were worth only £83,000. The latter however, was the more profitable company, with profits averaging almost £33,000 in the previous two and a half years. Crompton's profits had averaged just over £21,000 over the three previous years. (69) The company's shareholders accepted the deal immediately. It was agreed that what was needed was a stable board of directors although Crompton returned to the Board in 1928.

The merger was followed by an increase in exports but competition was intense and prices low. (70) Despite this, the year after the merger the new firm's profits were £70,000, which compared favourably with the previous year's total profits of the two separate companies combined. The years following the merger saw the company expand their Chelmsford works considerably so that by the time of their diamond jubilee in 1938 it covered fourteen and a half acres. In total 1,400 men and women were employed at the works. The firm also had works at Guisely, plus the British Electric Transformer Company at Hayes and the Derby Cable Works. Nationwide the firm employed 5,000 people. By this time the firm was producing A.C. and D.C. motors and generators, auto synchronous machines, switchgear instruments, ceiling fans, transformers and lamps. The firm had increased standardisation and there was an increased use of conveyors in production at Chelmsford. (71)

Despite the depression the company generally performed well in the 1930s. In 1936 profits rose by £110,000 to £353,000. The dividend rose to twelve and a half percent. All its factories, including Chelmsford, were operating at full capacity. In 1938 there was a link-up between Callender's Cables and Construction Co. Limited, which fell some way short of a merger. This made sense because there had been a good deal of competition between Callender and Derby Cables, a subsidiary of Crompton Parkinson. (72)

By the 1930s every male worker could qualify for a pension at 60 instead of, as previously, at 65. This could be up to half his salary. Female workers were also being admitted to the scheme. (73) One of the other features of employment at the Arc Works was that, although there were numerous examples of long service, many workers had spells at the other major works in the town. Philip Bartlett for example worked for the company in the 1930s, but after a spell unemployed, he went to work for Hoffmann during the war. Cliff Bohannon worked for over twenty years at different times at both Crompton Parkinson and Marconi. Many however, worked their way up the company's employment ladder. Vic Hales first got a job with the company as an office boy but his parents paid for him to go to evening classes four nights a week to train as a draughtsman and he was then assigned to a drawing board. Mrs Sybil Olive worked for the firm when it was taken over by the government in the second war. She helped make winding gear for planes. It was purely manual work. There were a wide variety of women on the production lines. Olive had a 'posh' lady on one side of her and a country girl on the other. Before the war the T.G.W.U. did not allow female members but Olive became a shop steward during it. She had to work one month day shifts and then one month nights. Conditions were poor and the pay low, lower than the men. The men were not helpful to the women when they were new to the work. (74) Crompton's Arc Works was bombed many times during the war but no serious damage was done. (See chapter 24) Crompton had moved from London at the start of the war back to his native Yorkshire. He died in February 1940.

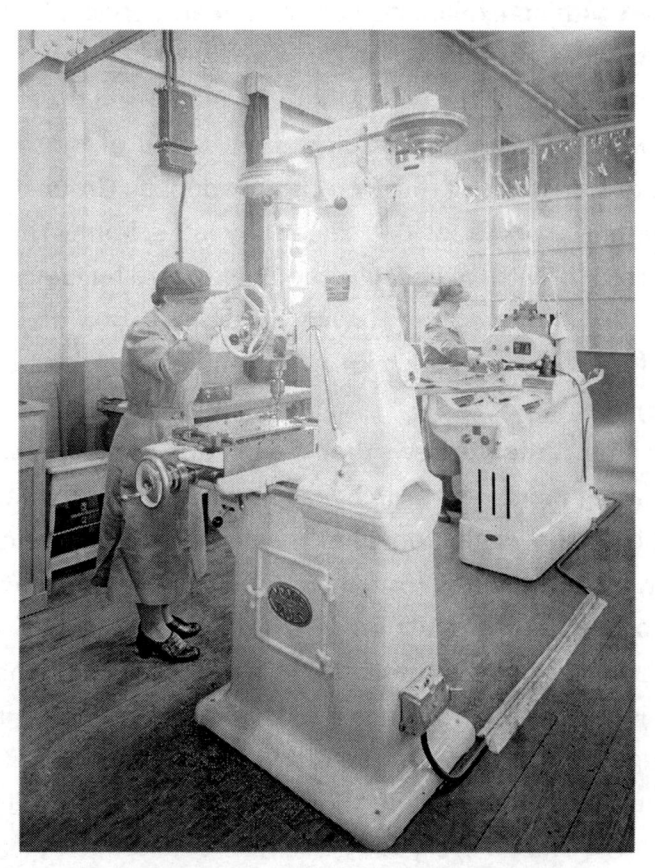

Two ladies using machines at Crompton - Parkinson 1940 (Courtesy of E.R.O.)

The early post war period saw the company expand the Writtle Road works yet again. This was needed to produce the large electrical switchgear equipment that the company manufactured, mainly for the export market. Switchgear comprises the combination of electrical disconnect switches, fuses or circuit breakers, used to control, protect and isolate electrical equipment. In 1957 a large 3 year contract for Russia was completed. (75) The order had come about because of a government trade mission. This equipment was for small electrical stations for Soviet farms and hamlets. The firm was also still producing locomotives. In 1959 it received a £10 million order from British Rail for 137 powerful diesel line locomotives. "It means continuity of employment for three years to come". "£2 million will come to the Chelmsford factory."(76)

During the 1950s and early 1960s industrial relations were often bumpy at the Chelmsford works. In 1958 the managing director said that 22 shop stewards were enough and the company did not need any more. (77) These shop stewards called the men out on a short unofficial stoppage in 1960. (78) In 1963 600 men struck over the dismissal of one man with no explanation after 34 years service. (79)

Drastic staff cuts were announced at the works in 1966. Two hundred and fifty workers lost their jobs, 1 in 10 of the workforce. The Board said the changes were being made to turn the works into a more efficient unit. Some of those made redundant were relocated to other sections of the Crompton Parkinson Group. It was "a new start for many men who have worked for C.P. since they left school". The instrumentation section was transferred to Witham because the Chelmsford buildings were unsuitable. (80) At the end of 1966 however, the Hawker Siddeley Group made a successful 25 million pound bid for Crompton Parkinson. The unions were disgruntled "to be the last to be told". (81)

Just over a year later came the news that the historic Arc Works were to close. The manufacture of rotating machines, switchgear and distribution transformers, was to be concentrated at Loughborough. Convenor Haydn Edwards, a Chelmsford councillor, said "It's a sad day for the town". Norman St John Stevas, the M.P. tried to get the parent company to continue production in a reduced form, but Hawker Siddeley rejected these proposals as uneconomic. (82) Charlie Osborne, who was 59, said "I can't find another job at my age: there is a nasty feeling generally in my family." Bill Ward of Upper Bridge Road, a turner at the works for 44 years said "The management have been a damned long time making their mind up. To top it all they go and tell the press and we're not told till everybody else has read it in the local papers." (83) A few of the workers were able to get jobs with Marconi in the town. One unanswered question was why the Chelmsford traction division was sold at the last moment to Brush Electrics when it had just received the order to build the finest traction motor of its type which was to be used for the new Victoria Tube. This would have produced three years work for the Chelmsford works. (84)

Today most of the site is used for housing, although in the mid 2,000s e2v were still using part of the site. There is little besides the blue plaque in Anchor Street to show that a once great electrical engineering firm was in the town. In 1966 the company had donated its collection of historical electric equipment to the Science Museum. (85) Two years before an original Crompton-Pochin Arc Lamp, which still worked, had been donated to the Ontario Museum. More recently the new extension to the Chelmsford and Essex Museum included a working Arc Lamp as well as other original equipment.

The Crompton name still exists in a number of other related factories elsewhere in the country. Crompton Lighting is still manufacturing in Doncaster and has offices at Waltham Abbey. Brookes Crompton, a manufacturer of electric motors, is based at Huddersfield and Crompton Controls manufactures switchgear at Wakefield. Crompton Greaves is the modern descendant of Crompton and Co's Indian operations with headquarters in Mumbai. It was recently involved with the electrification of the Indian railways. Tyco Electronics of Witham sells a variety of digital metering systems under its Crompton Instruments brand which it acquired in 2002. According to Tyco's brochure "The Crompton range offers one of the largest product offerings of power measurement, control and protection, for switchgear and generation set manufacturers and panel builders".

1) Essex Countryside 1958/9 Vol. 8 p.87
2) A History of Electrical Engineering P. Duncheath p.135
3) Colonel Crompton J.H. Johnson and W.L. Randall p.4
4) Essex Countryside 1958/9 Vol. 8 p.87
5) Colonel R.E.B. Crompton Blue Plaque Pamphlet Chelmsford and Essex Museum
6) Frederick Roberts Archive of Industrial Archaeology
7) Essex Chronicle 8 7 1904 p.8
8) A History of Light and Power Bowers p.81
9) Johnson and Randall p.6-7
10) Bowers p. 93
11) Bowers p.98

12) Bowers p.103
13) Bowers p.110
14) E.C. 7 7 1881 p.5
15) E.W.N. 23 9 1881 p.5
16) E.C. 7 3 1882 p.5
17) E.C. 25 10 1881 p.5
18) E.C. 11 11 1885 p.5
19) E.C. 6 1882
20) Johnson and Randall p.9
21) E.C. 1 12 1882 p.7
22) E.C. 1 12 1882 p.7
23) E.C. 25 5 1883 p.5
24) E.C. 14 12 1883 p.5
25) E.C. 9 5 1884 p.5
26) E.W.N. 29 2 1885 p.2
27) E.C. 12 12 1884 p.5
28) E.C. 29 5 1885 p.5
29) E.C. 4 12 1885 p.5
30) E.W.N. 10 4 1885 p.5
31) E.W.N. 9 12 1887
32) E.W.N. 10 8 1888 p.5
33) Johnson and Randall p.11
34) E.W.N. 22 3 1889 p.5
35) E.W.N. 29 3 1889 p.6
36) E.C. 10 5 1889 p.5
37) E.W.N. 26 8 1892 p.5
38) E.W.N. 28 7 1893 p.4
39) E.W.N. 1 12 1893 p.4
40) E.W.N. 31 1 1896 p.4
41) E.W.N. 25 11 1898 p.5
42) E.W.N. 31 1 1899 p.4
43) E.W.N. 11 5 1906 p.4
44) Johnson and Randall p.10 -11
45) Johnson and Randall p.14 -15
46) Essex Countryside 1958/9 Vol. 8 p.87

47) E.W.N. 8 5 1890 p.4
48) Johnson and Randall p.17
49) E.W.N. 4 10 1899 p.8
50) E.W.N. 29 11 185 p.6
51) E.W.N. 13 6 1895 p.4
52) E.W.N. 3 7 1896 p.7
53) E.W.N. 31 7 1896 p.3
54) The British Electrical Industry I.C.R. Byatt p.148-9
55) Byatt p.172 -3
56) Byatt p.181
57) Byatt p.190 – 1
58) Johnson and Randall p.19
59) E.W.N. 15 9 1899
60) E.W.N. 27 7 1900 p.2
61) E.W.N. 12 8 1904 p.2
62) Johnson and Randall p.22
63) Essex Countryside 1958/9 Vol. 8 p.87
64) E.W.N. 14 7 1918 p.4
65) E.W.N. 21 7 1916 p.4
66) E.W.N. 16 7 1920 p.2
67) E.C. 17 9 1920 p.6
68) E.C. 3 3 1922 p.7
69) E.W.N. 29 7 1927 p.7
70) E.W.N. 29 7 1927 p.7
71) E.W.N. 31 5 1935 p.6
72) E.C. 27 7 1938 p.7
73) E.C. 4 12 1936 p.4
74) Essex Records Office Oral history records
75) E.W.N. 27 12 1975 p.1
76) E.W.N. 27 2 1959 p.1
77) E.C. 28 11 1958 p.6
78) E.C. 6 5 1960 p.9
79) E.C. 1 1 1963 p.1
80) E.C. 27 5 1966
81) E.W.N. 14 10 1966

82) E.W.N. 19 1 1968 p.1
83) E.C. 9 2 1968 p.1
84) E.W.N. 16 2 1968 p.1
85) E.C. 12 8 1966 p.1

5

Marconi and Chelmsford before 1945

"Young man if you think I am going to climb up there at my time of life,
you are very much mistaken"

For nearly all of the twentieth century Chelmsford was known as the 'Home of Radio'. This chapter looks at how that reputation became established: why Guglielmo Marconi came to Chelmsford and his early links with the other firms in the town. It looks at the research completed at the Hall Street and New Street works, as well as some of the famous engineers associated with the firm such as Round, Eckersley and Franklin. Marconi was responsible for both the world's first factory producing radio equipment and later the first purpose built factory manufacturing radio equipment. By 1945 the company had a number of research sites in the area as well as the Marconi College. Many of the early developments in both television and radar were made in Chelmsford. The early progress of the Marconi Company before the first war was not without its problems. Its factory in Hall Street was actually closed for four years when production moved to North London. Once Godfrey Isaacs was brought in to run the company he played a vital role it getting it properly established financially: this involved fighting for the firms' patents in the courts and getting the New Street factory built in record time. The company made an enormous contribution to Britain winning both wars. It suffered to a considerable extent when as a result of the conflicts patents and research were opened to others. A large number of engineers devoted themselves to the company for decades and felt a strong affinity to Guglielmo himself. Their 'model shop' techniques lent themselves to the production of capital equipment in their field rather than consumer goods. These engineers did not want to use standardised mass production techniques. Marconi certainly did not invent radio on his own. His contribution was however, sufficient for him to share a Nobel physics prize with a Telefunken engineer. Marconi's perceived mistreatment by the British authorities over the 'Marconi Scandal' led him to stay away from Britain for long periods and after the first war he hardly ever visited Chelmsford.

Marconi was born in Italy but his mother had Scottish and Irish ancestry. Building on the experiments of Hertz, Marconi was sending 'wireless' messages more than a mile by 1895. (1)The Italian authorities showed little interest and the family made arrangements to send Guglielmo and his equipment to England. His mother's contacts were sufficient to get him an immediate meeting with the General Post Office. This was followed by trials on the roof of the General Post Office building in St Martin's and on Salisbury plain. (2) In July 1897 the Wireless Telegraphy and Signal Company was formed, which was soon changed to Marconi's Wireless Telegraph Company Limited. The new company then set out to get control of all Marconi's patents in all countries apart from Italy and her colonies. (3) He was by this time certainly already familiar with Chelmsford.

Why did Marconi choose Chelmsford? Mid Essex was flat and therefore suitable for sending messages. Property was fairly cheap. It is possible that Colonel Crompton made Marconi aware of the Hall Street premises. Although it was currently used by Wenley's as a store, it had previously been a silk factory run by Samuel Courtauld and, crucially, was equipped for steam power. In December 1898 it became the world's first radio factory. Before this it is possible Marconi conducted experiments in the town. In 1963 a memo from F.F. Christy of Christy and Norris to the Marconi Company included the following comments. "My father told me during the 1930s that an old black shed which stood on the side of our present roadway to Kings Road was in fact the shed where Signor Marconi did his first transmission tests in England. Marconi had come to Colonel Crompton as the best electrical engineering works and it was through the acquaintance of Colonel Crompton with my father that his shed was the first place loaned to Marconi." "The second shed was 300 yards away." Charlie Jarvis a Christy man at the time remembered Marconi being "rather short with a limp." (4)This would have been caused by an accident that only occurred in 1899, two years after he probably came to Chelmsford. Marconi was probably checking on the reception of signals on Christy's land. It is more likely that Marconi originally came to Chelmsford because of the connection with the Jameson business empire, which Marconi's mother was related to, and therefore with the grain trade. Several of the directors of the first Marconi Company were corn merchants.

In April 1899 the Weekly News interviewed Marconi's assistant George Kemp when a 150 foot 'pole' was about to be erected on the corner of Hall Street and Hamlet Road. Kemp talked about possible transmissions from Chelmsford to Harwich. He enthused about the success of cross channel experiments. "This is going to be our works it will also be our experimental station." Two further experimental stations were also being established in Alum Bay and Poole Harbour. "Vertical wire enables messages to be sent long distances." "The message is sent by long and short taps or long and short air waves, which answer the same purpose as dots and dashes in ordinary telegraphy." "Wireless telegraphy will be simply invaluable where ordinary telegraphy between telegraph or telephone cannot take place, from lighthouse to shore, between ships at sea and on land where a wire cannot be laid." (5)

In 1901 the Essex Chronicle reported that the company had erected a 160 foot mast at Frinton where half a dozen students were being instructed in the use of Marconi apparatus. (6) The Boer War was the first conflict to use wireless telegraphy in the field, although its use and effectiveness were limited. Orders were few with the exception of the Royal Navy. To develop demand from commercial shipping companies, a subsidiary, the Marconi International Marine Communication Company, was set up. (7) The new medium obviously had great potential for the safety of international shipping. The company offered both the equipment and the operators to use it. Marconi installed his wireless equipment in the Royal Yacht, so that Queen Victoria at Osborne House on the Isle of Wight might send messages to the Prince of Wales. (8) The company needed to be able to transmit much longer distances if it was to compete with the powerful cable companies. To the general horror of his Board of Directors, Marconi spent £50,000 on huge transmitting equipment to send messages across the Atlantic. After the celebrated three clicks were heard in Newfoundland having been sent from Poldhu in Cornwall in 1901 the cable companies and the newspapers sought to discredit his achievement. They immediately saw the competition Marconi could represent. (9) Progress however, was slow. In 1907 only 139 ships of all flags used Marconi's system which had a range of 150 – 300 miles. Most of these ships had only one Marconi man on board. These wireless operators were paid £4 a month, but were not expected to pay anything for their board and lodging at sea. Ashore they were given two shillings and six pence a day. These skilled men were prepared to put up with these comparatively low wages and were immensely proud of their new messaging service. (10) Despite owning most of the world's master patents for radio and the fact that the use of wireless was becoming essential for shipping companies to get insurance, the Marconi Company was having financial problems. The Hall Street factory was closed down for four years, starting in 1903, and the company moved to bigger premises in Dalston. (11) In 1904 the Wireless Telegraphy Act, by granting licenses to transmit and receive messages bought a temporary stability to the company. Shipping companies were finding that the promise of communication ashore to their better off customers, as well as messages to other vessels if anything went wrong, was proving a major attraction. The development of the 'Bent aerial' made transatlantic transmissions much more feasible. Marconi's engineers also experimented with wireless direction finding, which was to prove important in the first war and was eventually to prove the forerunner of radar. (12) In 1906 however, the company was hit by an international conference which said that all coastal wireless stations should receive from and transmit to all shipping regardless of type of apparatus. (13) The decision was taken on the grounds of safety, but Marconi had easily the largest number of radio stations, many more than its competitors such as Telefunken. This had been a strong inducement to use Marconi equipment and engineers. For this reason Marconi had previously refused to allow their shore stations to accept messages from their competitors. The vote was a major boost for Telefunken in particular. In contrast a transatlantic messaging service finally started in 1907.

One of the company's great engineers, Henry Round, joined the company in 1906. He experimented with transmitting intelligible speech. In 1908 speech was transmitted over thirty miles but the quality was not good. (14)

The huge works at Dalston was not a success, with the company forced to produce products other than radio equipment, including ignition coils. It closed in 1907 and the Hall Street works were re-opened. A new 200 foot tall mast was erected at the Moulsham works in 1909. Godfrey Isaacs, who had been brought in to run the business side of the company, so that Marconi could concentrate on research, thought that Hall Street was too small and soon began looking for a larger works.

In 1911 the company bought land on New Street. (15) The New street works was completed in 17 weeks, despite a strike. In June 1912 the Chronicle reported "Six months ago the site was a cricket ground. Two new roads are being constructed and cottages built for the 'denizens' of the new works. The ground was pegged out on February the 10th and bricklaying began on February the 26th. The buildings, floor and piping were completed in early May. Two a quarter million bricks were laid, 400 tons of steelwork erected and 9,000 cartloads of earth carted. Fronting New Street is a two storey block comprising general offices, show rooms and a drawing office, 200 foot long by 40 foot wide." The paper mentioned the "handsome entrance with its inside hall "of noble dimensions, paved with marble." A reporter was shown around the new works.

The mounting shop was the first department. Here army carts were fitted with wireless telegraphy. Many were to be used by the Italian army. In the next girls were engaged winding miles of wire. They were employed because the work required lightness of touch. Like Hoffmann, Marconi employed significant numbers of female workers before the first war. The assembly shop had transmitters and receivers in various stages of completion. These were the same as the one used to send the fateful messages from the Titanic. New Street had its own power house and water supply; water sprinklers were fitted in all rooms in case of fire. For this, a water tower held 8,000 gallons. (16) The official opening of the works coincided with the visit of the International Conference with representatives of practically every government in attendance. Two hundred and fifty delegates were shown a demonstration of signals sent between Poldhu to the new works by means of a 15 kilowatt shore set connected to a 250 foot mast outside. There were already plans to erect two 450 feet masts with aerials between them. The visitors were also shown a replica of a wireless cabin used on board liners and battleships, and a wireless fitted on a motor car. (17) Marconi House, the new company headquarters was also opened in the Strand in the same year.

Marconi, New Street, 1912
(Courtesy of E.R.O.)

The Titanic disaster obviously did a great deal to make the name of the Marconi Company although the New Street factory was already being built when it occurred. All the 711 survivors owed their lives to the senior wireless operator who sent distress signals to ships in the vicinity. Actually many more might have been saved if the operator on one of those ships, the Californian, hadn't been off duty at the time. (18) Marconi radios had already saved lives after the collision of two ships in 1909 but this had garnered far less publicity. Marconi also gained a good deal of positive publicity through the sending of information across the Atlantic, which led to the capture of Dr Crippen. Even before the Titanic the company's financial position had improved through Isaacs methodically taking to court those who tried to break Marconi's patents, particularly the 4 Sevens patent. This involved the use of selective tuning where the transmitter and receiver were tuned to the same wavelength. The patent also gave Marconi a 50% share in wireless used at sea until its term ended in 1914.

Much of this progress was undone by the so called 'Marconi Scandal'. Marconi submitted a plan to the Government to link Britain and the countries of the Empire by a series of wireless stations. Initially Marconi asked for licences for the stations which it would erect and operate. It was decided however that Marconi should build the stations but that a Government owned system was desirable. (19) A contract was signed between the Post Office and Marconi for the first six stations without the project first being put out to tender. The stations were seen as an urgent priority because of the rise of German power internationally. Marconi's shares, including those of its U.S. subsidiary, rose sharply and then fell back. (20) Suspicion immediately fell on members of the government including Rufus Isaacs, the brother of Godfrey, who was the Postmaster General. It was alleged that members of the government had used their "privileged knowledge of the negotiations for the contract to speculate on Marconi shares". It was rumoured that Rufus Isaacs, the Postmaster General, had made £160,000 out of the sharp rise in the value of a new Marconi share issue in its U.S. subsidiary. Herbert Samuel, another member of the Cabinet, had made £250,000. It was also rumoured that Lloyd George had used this opportunity to add to his 'Treasure Chest'. Press hysteria forced the setting up of a Select Committee inquiry into the matter. It emerged that the company had been given a monopoly for five years and a virtual monopoly for 28 years. Critics said that the £60,000 cost per station was too high, as was the level of agreed royalties. In reply, Godfrey Isaacs argued Marconi was the only company that had maintained a continuous commercial service for distances comparable with those that would be needed. (21) Isaacs said that the charges were low compared with what European governments had paid the British Post Office for long distance radio installations. Although the company was formally absolved of any wrong doing, Marconi became embittered at being embroiled in the controversy. The company suffered a big loss because various activities had to be suspended while the hearings took place. Marconi's contract was finally cancelled in December 1914 because of the war. The company had spent £140,000 on the project and had turned down other work. (22)

Before the first war industrial relations at the works were not a problem in the normal sense. The original 'brotherhood of engineers' was now in control of the company. For them the constant source of irritation was not the workers but bureaucrats and red tape. The company had established a retirement age, a contributory pension fund and a sickness club.

Marconi had little time to recover from the scandal before the war put a stop to all commercial activities. After the British Admiralty had sent a message to its grand fleet the government took control of all messages. The commercial use of wireless telegraphy was stopped. Marconi's New Street works were taken over by the Admiralty. All the Company's trained wireless operatives were used for military work. The need for more wireless sets caused a big increase in their production at the factory. More operatives were trained at the Marconi College in Arbour Lane, Springfield. In all, 348 Marconi men died during the war, mostly at sea. (23) Marconi's other major contribution to the war was the use of Henry Round's direction finding equipment. Using it British warships could pick up German signals easily and pinpoint where they were coming from. Victory at the Battle of Jutland, which established British supremacy of the seas for the rest of the war, was only possible because of Round's painstaking research at the Chelmsford factories over the previous decade. By the end of the war his equipment was also being used on land and in the air. He was awarded the Military Cross for his contribution to the war effort. (24)

At the beginning of the war the British Expeditionary Force in France had only 10 transmitters. The New Street works were immediately tasked with producing hundreds more. By 1916 all three armed services were relying on the wireless for communication with aircraft, artillery and infantry. They had to withstand all conditions better than they had done during the Boer War. The Government gave the Company a cash payment of £596,000 after the war as compensation for use of its factory and research developments. This by no means covered what the company had lost in terms of its patents. (25) Marconi himself had been called up by the Italian forces when that country entered the war. In 1922 the company erected a roll of honour at the company's Strand headquarters to those Marconi men who had fallen during the war; many of them were from Chelmsford. (26) The plaque is now in the Chelmsford Museum Marconi exhibition.

With the return to peace, the Marconi engineers in New Street turned their attention back to the transmission of intelligible speech. This was known at the time as wireless telephony as opposed to wireless telegraphy. In 1919 a six kilowatt telephony transmitter was installed and testing began using an experimental transmission licence in order to investigate long distance speech transmission. A long 'T' shaped wire aerial that was suspended between the two 450 feet tall masts was connected to the transmitter. On the 15th of January 1920 Ditcham and Round started transmitting a programme of speech and gramophone music from the New Street research department's laboratory. 214 positive reports came from amateur enthusiasts and shipping operators amazed to hear words and music on the airwaves. The furthest report came from 1,450 miles away. Immediately a 15 kilowatt transmitter replaced its smaller predecessor. Although the company still saw radio in purely commercial terms rather than entertainment, for six weeks their continuing tests became a regular series of 30 minute broadcasts. These were mainly news with three or four short musical items. W.T. Ditcham organised the programmes and did the announcing with support from the Head of the Publicity department, Arthur Burrows. The first paid artiste was a Mrs Winifred Sayer. She sang with the well known local group the 'Funnions'. Sayer was an amateur soprano who happened to work for the Hoffmann Manufacturing Company in New Street. The instrumentalists who provided the first radio broadcasts were mainly drawn from the Marconi staff. (27) The 'Broadcast studio' was actually a packing shed next to the transmitting hut. Alfred Harmsworth (Lord Northcliffe) the owner of the Daily Mail, hired a top ranking professional singer to make a radio broadcast. (28) The artist who was chosen by Harmsworth, Dame Nellie Melba, was arguably the most popular singer in the world at the time. It took an enormous fee, £1,000 to attract the temperamental diva. Sayer had received ten shillings for her broadcasts. The heavy equipment and the aerials couldn't be moved, so Melba had to come to the New Street works. "Amazingly she agreed to leave the bright lights of the London stage for one night, and travel to a remote Essex factory." (29) Initially the elegant Executive Directors and Senior Dining rooms were chosen because of their "mahogany panelled walls, carpets and stylish decor". It was planned to connect the transmitter at the opposite end of the works to the 'studio' by means of a long cable. Effort was quickly put into improving the quality of the microphone, an adapted telephone mouthpiece, and the transmitter circuits. Almost at the last minute however, the cable burnt out because of the high frequency current. Cancelling would have hurt the company's image so it was decided to relocate the performance to a packing shed next to the transmitter hut. A thick pile carpet was put on the bare floor. Melba was picked up from the station by chauffeur driven car and driven around Chelmsford, cheered by a large flag-waving crowd. She was then given a tour of the works by Arthur Burrows, particularly the transmitter, and the huge masts. When Burrows remarked that her voice would be carried huge distances from the wires at the top she said "Young man, if you think I am going to climb up there at my time of life, you are very much mistaken". When a bulb from a camera went off, an engineer pulled all the plugs thinking the system was overloading. Ditcham however, quickly got everything ready again. The broadcast was progressing very well, but by the third song the transmitter began to cause problems. One of the valves began to fail and the broadcast went off the air. Repairs were quickly carried out but the third song had almost been entirely lost. When Melba was back on air, Round said "Madam Melba, the world is calling for more". "Are they?" she replied "Shall I go on singing?" She went on to sing four more songs. (30)

The broadcast was met with acclaim from everybody, except the Postmaster General, who sent a letter saying that a national service, such as wireless, should not be used for such frivolous purposes. Marconi's experimental broadcasts were suspended because, it was alleged, they were interfering with legitimate services. The Post Office was worried about their monopoly on communications in Britain. Later, Melchior's concert from Chelmsford certainly did cause jamming. The Company weren't concerned at the loss of their broadcasts because of the burden of their cost. As the British airwaves went silent the Americans started broadcasting, with hundreds of stations, to a rapidly expanding audience who demanded wireless sets. Demand from British amateur enthusiasts was such that eventually the Post office relented and Marconi was allowed to start broadcasting again. (31)

Arthur Burrows gave the responsibility for the new broadcasts to its Airborne Telephony Research Department based at Writtle. Immediately after the war Marconi had given a small group of ex-R.A.F. wireless experts the task of installing and testing wireless sets in planes. The Company thought that the development of commercial air transport was going to depend on significant progress in airborne radio communications. They had taken over an ex army hut in a small landing field next to the Writtle sewage works. The young Writtle team had already received a favourable reaction to their designing and installing a new transmitter for the Croydon Air Terminal. It was made at New Street. The task of managing the new broadcasting venture, which was to become 2MT Writtle, fell to Captain Peter Eckersley. (32)

Eckersley had fallen in love with the wireless whilst at Bedales School. Peter supported the Marconi system of radio transmission and this led in 1906 to a fight with a friend who supported the Lodge- Muirhead system that was in competition with Marconi. This had been encouraged by William Preece of the Post Office, to stem Marconi's alleged monopoly. (33) Eckersley was not very academic but had a sound practical sense. In addition he acted and wrote poetry, talents which were to become useful later on. Eckersley came from a Liberal dissenting background and was studying to be an electrical engineer when the first war broke out. He joined the Royal Flying Corps. His qualifications as an engineer, who knew about wireless, were very attractive to the fledgling organisation which was desperate for wireless operators. In 1915 he became a 2nd Lieutenant (Equipment Officer Class) at the age of 23. Eckersley was told not to fly but since he couldn't test wireless sets without being airborne, time and again he broke the rules. He was instructed by C.E. Prince, who had been a radio pioneer since 1907. Eckersley was present when the first telephony speech was successfully passed from Prince on the ground to a pilot overhead. Eckersley's plane was shot down at the Somme but Prince saw afterwards that he was attached to the Wireless Experimental Station at Biggin Hill. Prince wanted "observers in balloons and pilots in aircraft to be able to talk to each other and to the ground without having to switch over". After the war Eckersley initially wanted to become a regular R.A.F. officer but Prince persuaded him to join Marconi in 1919. (34)

In 1921 the newly formed Radio Society of Great Britain petitioned the Post Office for a special wireless transmission service. As a result a 15 minute programme of speech and music was authorised which Marconi successfully bid for. (35) Eckersley had been made head of the Airborne Research Department when Prince retired. He and the team were given the task of running the new radio broadcast project in addition to their normal research duties. Peter and his wife Stella had settled in a cottage in Writtle village.

The hut which was the centre of the team's operations was 16 foot wide and 66 foot long. There was no mains electricity. Power was provided by a 100 volt generator. The radio apparatus it used was all manufactured at New Street. Prior to being given the radio broadcast project, the team had been quite pleased that the Chelmsford radio station had been closed down because of the interference it caused with their work. By 1921 the team was the company's primary think tank for airborne wireless. Power was limited by the Post Office to 250 watts from two low power transmitters. Two portable Marconi masts that had been used in the Boer War were borrowed and set up in the field behind the hut. They decided to broadcast a single programme between 7.0. p.m. and 7.30. p.m on Thursdays. (36)

The first broadcast from 2MT Writtle went on the air on February the 14th 1922. It was followed by weekly broadcasts continuously for eleven months until the 7th of January 1923. The technical quality of the first broadcast was not a great success and there were complaints from amateur enthusiasts sitting patiently at home with their 'cat's whiskers'. The fault was soon found however, and the number of complaints soon fell. To start with Eckersley, having organised the programme, went home to listen to it himself. It was when he decided to become the "the power behind the microphone" that the broadcasts came alive. Immediately the programme was under the control of a part time comedian, actor and singer. His first programme included songs, rhymes and pub stories and went on until 9.0.p.m. Trains were interrupted by imaginary fog on the line: "if the porter even breathes on the line at Stratford, the London and North Eastern trains run late for the next fortnight". (37) The team was worried about the familiarity of the broadcast. It was possible to work at New Street for over a decade and still not know a colleague's first name. Despite 50 post cards being received congratulating Eckersley on the broadcast, the man who mattered, Arthur Burrows, was concerned at the likely reaction of the Post Office. Luckily Burrows soon left for the new B.B.C. and the Writtle team did their best to ignore Marconi headquarters. At the time the Writtle programmes were remarkable for their "gaiety and irresponsibility" and always contained a surprise; for example the broadcasts contained the first radio play 'Cyrano de Bergerac', with Eckersley playing Cyrano, and the first children's programme. (38) The Weekly News commented "The concerts which are now being sent out regularly from Writtle by wireless have become famous for the delights of listening to entertainments." (39)

Before the Writtle broadcasts finished, the Post Office issued another licence to Marconi. The 2LO station broadcast from Marconi House in London. This concentrated on much more formal broadcasting and featured only speech with no music. (40) While the Marconi broadcasting stations were still operating, Marconi was one of eight companies invited by the Post Office to form the British Broadcasting Company (to become the British Broadcasting Corporation in 1926). The wireless companies involved agreed to pay Marconi patent rights. They were to be the only makers of wireless sets on sale to the British public. It was hoped that foreign produced sets would be discouraged. It was agreed with 'Mr Reith' that the 2MT broadcasts would stop and the BBC took over the 2LO broadcasts. (41) The Marconi Company was tasked with designing the radio sets to receive the new BBC programmes. Eckersley applied for and got the job of Chief Engineer to the B.B.C.. Isaacs was annoyed at not being given one months notice but was anxious for commercial reasons for the new venture to be a success. (42) Ten thousand pounds was invested by the Marconi Company in the new venture. June 1923 saw simultaneous broadcasts in the eight regions. By this time there were over half a million radio licence holders. Marconi designed and built a huge transmitter for the BBC's new Daventry station which started being built in 1925. (43) Ironically for the 'Home of Radio', reception for the new B.B.C. broadcasts was not ideal in Chelmsford itself. (44)

Eckersley, himself, had a successful career at the B.B.C., but resigned in 1929. He then did very well paid consultancy work, including a contract back at Marconi, which was not renewed. (45) The famous hut, which was the focal point for 2MT Writtle, eventually saw service at Kings Road School. Now it is one of the exhibits that take pride of place at the Chelmsford Museum's industrial store and now education centre at Sandford Mill Museum.

F.G. Kellaway, previously a Liberal M.P., became the successor to Godfrey Isaacs as Managing Director of Marconi in 1924. The series of Imperial radio stations across the Empire were eventually built by Marconi despite initial opposition by the Post Office. A first beam station, using Marconi's newly developed shortwave beam system, opened in 1926 in Canada. Developing the beam system came at considerable financial cost but proved very successful. The Government were keen however, to prevent the Company getting into another monopoly situation. In 1928 a new company was formed that covered all the cable and wireless operations that carried messages across the Empire. This included all the Marconi beam stations and in 1934 became Cable and Wireless Limited.

After 1916 all British ships had to be fitted with radios. As the only British company in a position to carry out these installations, this greatly benefitted Marconi. Despite the fact that it was a great aid to safety, the increase in the use of direction-finding equipment on ships was slow, before it eventually became compulsory in 1952. It was later superseded by radar. (46) Marconi was also involved with the development of radio telephones. These were widely used in the inter war period for communication between lightships and the shore. The company was also involved with the use of automatic alarm systems on ships. Ships had to be always able to receive distress messages. (47) Marconi produced small radio sets for life boats. The first installation of a radio in a boat of the Royal National Lifeboat Institution was made in 1926. In 1923 the Weekly News reported proudly that wireless telephones manufactured at New Street were to be used by Scotland Yard for police purposes. Rapid transmission of messages with the descriptions of wanted men saved time. (See chapter 23) (48)

Marconi's entry into the manufacture of radio receiver sets was short lived. The Marconiphone sets, designed at Chelmsford, were made at Ilford by Plessey. Research for the sets continued at New Street however. The Marconiphone Company was sold to the Gramophone Company in 1929 and the company itself never again attempted to sell radio sets to the general public. The Gramophone Company became part of E.M.I. and they produced domestic sets until 1956 under the name of Marconiphone. (49)

Marconi himself led a somewhat chequered life. His marriage was dissolved after he started a relationship with a new Italian girlfriend. It was then discovered that he hadn't been properly married in the first place and he married again in 1927. The Italians had given him a knighthood as early as 1897. In 1915 he was made a Lieutenant in the Italian army but during 1916 he transferred to the sea and was given the rank of Commander. During 1923 he joined the fascist party and remained a fascist for the rest of his life, although he claimed not to be interested in politics. He was made the first President of the Mussolini Royal Academy. In 1935 Mussolini invited his "friend" to fight for Italy "not in the field in Africa, but over the airwaves" and Marconi was promoted to Rear Admiral. It is interesting to consider which side he would have chosen in the second war if his health hadn't broken down leading to his death from a heart attack in 1937. If he had lived beyond the outbreak of the war would he have been interned if he had set foot on British soil? After his death transmitters all over the world fell silent for two minutes. (50)

Despite his failing health the last ten years of his life saw Marconi continuing to work on all sorts of scientific developments. Much of this work was done on his yacht, Elettra. One of these areas of development was what was to become radar. As far back as 1916, Marconi and C.S. Franklin had found in their work on short waves that these were reflected back by objects in their path. Charles Samuel Franklin spent his entire career with the company. He had gone out to the Boer War to supervise transmissions and was credited a number of developments in radio including the Franklin Oscillator and the Franklin Beam Aerial. Little work was done on the phenomenon but the first mention of what was to become radar came at a lecture by Marconi in 1922. "In some of my tests I have noticed the effects of reflections of these waves by metallic objects miles away. It seems to me that it should be possible to design apparatus by means of which a ship could project a beam of these rays in any desired direction, which rays, if coming across an object, such as a steamer or ship, would be reflected back to a receiver on the sending ship and thereby immediately reveal the presence and bearing of another ship in fog or bad weather." (51) In the 1930s as German rearmament, especially in terms of its air force, came to be seen as a threat, much attention was given to using these reflected rays to detect aircraft. This came after the idea of developing a "death ray" was rejected as impractical. In 1935 a bomber was successfully detected after flying a through a beam from the Marconi built station at Daventry. Marconi then built 250 foot high towers to track aircraft flying at over 1,500 feet and 75 miles away. This work resulted in the Chain Home Stations being built right across East and South East England by the start of the war. Each C.H. station had four 360 feet masts for transmission. Antenna wires were strung between these masts 180 feet apart. The returned signal was received on four separate 240 foot masts. Only Marconi had the expertise in 1937 to fulfil the government's need for transmitter aerials for the C.H. beacons. After the first three stations were tested, a further 17 stations were commissioned. By 1938 Britain was covered by a system which could track aircraft up to 15,000 feet. Besides the development of antennae for radar the firm also worked on a new valve called the magnetron which was at the heart of the radar system. Although invented by John Randall and Harry Boot outside the company the 'resonant' cavity magnetron was produced in large numbers at Marconi, Chelmsford. This was capable of generating very powerful radio signals at very short wave lengths. The first magnetron 'blocks' were made under conditions of great secrecy at the firm's laboratories at Great Baddow. A 'block' was the intricate copper machining which formed the anode for the magnetron. Initially only 20 per week could be made. The company was one of three main suppliers of magnetrons during the conflict. After production was switched to a former van garage in Waterhouse Lane, a peak of 2,500 cavity magnetrons a month was reached by 1945. (52)

The Marconi Company was also closely connected with the development of television, although Marconi himself was not interested in its research and the company never attempted to make receiver sets. John Logie Baird approached the company with his invention in 1926 but Marconi decided to set up its own research group. Again Franklin was involved. During 1932 low definition television signals were sent from Chelmsford to Australia and the Marconi – E.M.I. Company was set up to carry out further research. In 1934 the Chronicle reported on a test transmission at Chelmsford where pictures were transmitted to an audience 100 feet away. It predicted a "tremendous future for television". (53) The B.B.C. chose the Marconi – E.M.I. system over that of Baird to launch its new service. (54) The first public service of high definition television programmes in the world started from the Alexandra Palace on the 2nd of November 1936. It used an aerial and transmitters designed and manufactured at New Street. The chosen system was much more flexible than Baird's and could transmit images simultaneously. Reception was only expected within a 25 mile radius, but pictures were actually seen as far as Manchester. Franklin designed both the sound and vision antennae, shortly before retiring in 1937. After trying both the Baird and Marconi – E.M.I. systems, the latter was found to be far superior and was used for all programmes until the outbreak of war. Although the new TV service covered a quarter of the population there were only 23,000 sets in use in 1939; they were very expensive to buy. Marconi – E.M. I. spent a great deal of money on new camera designs, better vacuums, new types of glassware, improving receiving cathode ray tubes and developing larger screens than the early seven inch ones. Much of this new technology was useful to radar and the Government requisitioned many of the scientists working for the joint company. (55)

    The company was certainly not immune to the depression but a big issue of three million new shares cleared off its debt. Kellaway ruthlessly pruned the staff. Marconi's problem was that all of its research normally took over 10 years before any commercial benefits were seen. Despite Kellway's economies, profits fell from £796,000 in 1929 to £260,000 in 1935. (56) The firm was now firmly a manufacturer of capital as opposed to consumer goods. Its skilled craftsmen had remained faithful to 'model shop' methods of manufacture. There was no use of 'conveyor belt' production, which was by then used in many industries, including the production of radio receivers. Considerable pieces of equipment were built however. In 1930 for example the company built the then most powerful transmitter in the world for the Polish Broadcasting Corporation. It was 150 times more powerful than that built for the first London broadcasting station. (57)

    In 1935 a Weekly News reporter was shown round the New Street works. Marconi's mammoth masts were in the process of being dismantled. The works then employed 1,250 people. Its basic layout was unchanged from when it was built but it had almost doubled in size. Raw materials still arrived by train on a siding from the Chelmsford goods station. A power test room was used for medium sized and small transmitters, while the station test room was large enough to accommodate the biggest transmitters produced by the works. Receivers and components were tested in the instrument area and large air-cooled, oil and water valves in the valve testing area. The portable test area was mainly used for testing aircraft wireless apparatus and military equipment. A beam test area was a replica of a wireless station for testing beam apparatus. The paper noted that all of the planes of Imperial Airways carried Marconi apparatus and that the London Airport at Croydon was fitted with apparatus for communication with aircraft that was made at Chelmsford. He was shown a device called the echometer which measured the depth of water beneath a ship. At the time the firm was still using Hall Street as a laboratory as well as other laboratories at Writtle and Broomfield. The Company's College at Arbour Lane was training British government and foreign users of Marconi apparatus, as well as Marconi engineers in the most up to date developments. (58)

Financial problems didn't prevent a big extension to the New Street works being carried out in 1937. Land was bought from Ridley and Son limited. A four story building, Marconi House, was built and office staff transferred from London. This coincided with the introduction of new working conditions. A new pension scheme was introduced, along with a five day working week of 45 hours, and a five and a half week of 47 hours. New facilities were introduced for morning and afternoon tea. All workers were given a week's holiday with pay. (59) By this time Marconi's social and sporting activities rivalled those of the Hoffmann Company. (See chapters 25 and 27)

As in the first war the Marconi Company made a big contribution to Britain's wartime success. The direct impact of bombing on the Chelmsford works is dealt with in chapter 24. Before the war, as well as the development of radar, crash programmes had already started to provide all three armed forces with radio equipment. By the end of 1938 the power station had been improved so that it could provide up to 80% of the works' electricity needs. Also the works' fire brigade strength had been doubled. After Munich the New Street works were camouflaged. (60) The Great Baddow Research Laboratory which had only just been opened was immediately taken over by the government.

On October the 6th 1939 the works manager received the instructions "This is a red hot job from the ministry". The firm had to install short wave transmitters into ten luxury motor coaches. These had to be converted into two heavy mobile field stations with a transmitter, power plant, central telegraph office, receivers and accommodation coach. The first station was completed six days later; the second five days after that. Marconi's team had worked 24 hour shifts. Before leaving the works they were christened the

'Blue trains'. Several months later the sole remaining transmitter limped back into the works. In all 380 such conversions were made at Chelmsford. (61)

Dramatically increased demand for receiver sets in all three armed forces meant that Marconi was forced to adopt standardisation for the first time. Just three types of receiver were designed and made. In total 10 thousand receiver sets were manufactured. Standardisation of production meant that a considerable amount of dilution of skills was inevitable. Like the other Chelmsford works, New Street lost many of its men to the call-up. (62) The girls and women brought in proved conscientious and often skilled workers. Very often they didn't know what they were making because production was piecemeal and they weren't told the nature of the final product. 1,200 were employed in June 1939 at New Street; by June 1940 this had gone up to 1,900; by August this had risen to 6,000. The works never shut down because shift work ensured 24 hour production (63)

One of the basic but vital components that Marconi made during the war were screening sets used to protect the wireless apparatus installed in planes from all the electrical noise created by the aircraft engines. The Company made over 72,000 of these sets. (64) Another was the stabilovolt, developed at Great Baddow, which controlled the voltage of radio receivers. Because of the vast numbers of these that were needed production was switched from Great Baddow to Waterhouse Lane. Marconi equipment was carried on all bombers and most Spitfires and Hurricanes. By the end of the war 350,000 stabilovolts had been produced.

Marconi had trained 2,000 radio officers before the war; by the end of 1940 this had risen to 6,000. (65) In all, 956 Marconi staff lost their lives carrying out their radio duties at sea. Marconi research staff developed a supersonic buoy for locating the enemy. It couldn't be picked up by the enemy but was also fitted with a 'hari kiri' device for blowing itself up. (66)

Wireless apparatus was also essential for the war in the desert. Each division had a Royal Signals Unit, 700 strong with 200 vehicles, many equipped with wireless apparatus. (67) The Commander could keep in touch with every unit. Wireless was important in reconnaissance and many spectacular raids. For the Chindits in South East Asia the valves in radio equipment were stored in jam jars containing silica gel to counteract the humidity. Fungi pests were finally countered with zinc varnishes. (68)

The increased demand for radio receivers led to an increased demand for crystals. In 1942 a separate department had to be set up for their production at New Street and by the end of the war this was employing 200, spread over two shifts. Another call to

Marconi during the war, this time from the B.B.C., was for more powerful transmitters. This was because of the increased demands put on this institution by the war. Twenty new two kilowatt transmitters were built. More than half the transmitters used by the B.B.C. were made by Marconi. (69)

In the first war direction finding equipment (D/F) had been used to a limited extent. During the second war D/F was used extensively, despite the development of radar, particularly the Marconi/Adcock HF D/F stations, which were used to identify the location of secret enemy transmitters in the U.K. and on the continent. After D-Day, mobile direction finders developed by Marconi with the National Physical Laboratories were used extensively in France. Direction finding equipment was also used in the Atlantic to protect British ships. At the end of the war many of the static stations in the U.K. continued to operate during the Cold war under the control of G.C.H.Q. (70)

By 1942 radar was being used not only to counter the threat from the air but also the threat at sea. The use of type 271 radar produced by Marconi saw a big increase in the number of U boats destroyed and a fall in the amount of British merchant shipping that was sunk by the Germans.

One of the most vital pieces of equipment used by the highly secret and highly trained Auxiliary Units was their special wireless sets weighing less than 40 pounds. The Units had been created with the aim of resisting the expected occupation by the Nazis. Marconi made many of these sets. (71)

The company and its now immensely skilled group of engineers made therefore, a great contribution to the war, but at a cost to the company. No records were kept of the Marconi technology used in the war. A large number of patents and production expertise was lost. By 1943 the company had supplied over 500 skilled men to the Government. Patents taken out by these seconded staff became owned by the particular Ministry. (72) The firm therefore, had lost much of the advantage it had over its competitors by the time the post war period began. Despite this much of the technology it had played such a vital part in developing during the war, such as the magnetron, was to be at the heart of the company's development over the next half century and indeed the development of its spin – off company, EEV.

1) Marconi and the discovery of radio L. Reade p.24
2) Reade p.33
3) Marconi Jubilee 1897 – 1947 p.15
4) Chelmsford Museums Sandford Mill records

5) Essex Weekly News 28 4 1899 p.5
6) Essex Chronicle 25 10 1901 p.4
7) A History of the Marconi Company W.J. Baker p.59
8) Reade p.38
9) Baker p.66
10) Reade p.62
11) Baker p.110
12) Baker p.113
13) Baker p.115
14) Baker p.121
15) Baker p.137
16) E.C. 21 6 1912 p.5
17) E.C. 28 6 1912 p.2
18) Baker p.137
19) The Marconi Scandal Frances Donaldson p.14
20) Donaldson p.19
21) Donaldson p.39
22) Baker p.156
23) Baker p.160
24) Baker p.164
25) Baker p.28
26) E.W.N. 9 6 1922 p.4
27) Marconi's New street Works Tim Wander p.78 - 81
28) Wander p.82
29) Wander p.83
30) Wander p.84 – 91
31) Wander 92 – 95
32) 2MT Writtle Wander p.111
33) 'Prospero's Wireless' 'P.P. Eckersley' by Myles Eckersley p.4
34) Myles Eckersley p.15 – 26
35) 2MT Writtle p.54
36) 2MT Writtle p.56 - 87
37) Myles Eckersley p.50
38) 2MT Writtle p.88 – 115
39) E.W.N. 9 6 1922 p.4

40) 2MT Writtle p.127 – 133
41) Myles Eckersley p. 58-69
42) 'The Power Behind the Microphone' Peter Eckersley p.46
43) Myles Eckersley p.113
44) E.C. 14 8 1925 p.7
45) Myles Eckersley p.94
46) The Economics of Radio S.G. Sturmey p.62
47) Sturmey p. 65
48) E.W.N. 3 8 1923
49) Wander p.100
50) Reader p.110-129
51) The ABC of Radar Colin Latham p.42
52) Wander p.115-119
53) E.C. 5 1 1934 p.10
54) Baker p.265
55) Wander p.120 – 129
56) Baker p.270 – 1
57) E.W.N. 26 11 1930
58) E.W.N. 23 8 1935 p.9
59) E.C. 6 8 1937 p.7
60) Tim Wander p.130 – 131
61) Marconi: A War Record George Godwin p.12
62) Godwin p.19
63) Godwin p.23
64) Godwin p.32
65) Godwin p.53
66) Godwin p.69
67) Godwin p.75
68) Godwin p.86
69) Wander p.137
70) Wander p.138 – 140
71) Wander p.175 – 177
72) Baker p.307

6

Marconi in Chelmsford after the Second War

'There was a high degree of skill at all levels with the top research people, who were leading the world, dealing with the skilled men on the shop floor'.

That Marconi no longer operates in the town at all is testimony to corporate mismanagement on a scale that can have rarely been seen before or since. The name disappeared from Chelmsford only a few years after Marconi Radar was producing half of the radar equipment in the country. Before its demise, Marconi in its various guises contributed a great deal towards technological development in Britain in the first 60 years after the second war. Marconi continued to be at the forefront of innovation in the transmission of sound and vision. The advent of the Cold War meant that new radar systems were needed for defence. Radar found numerous uses in civil aviation and maritime operations. The company appeared to have survived two take-overs but the attachment many workers felt towards the company, which had led to many examples of three generations of the same family working at the New street factory, gradually ebbed away. After the 1970s there was an increasing separation between managers and the workforce. The company frittered away its initial advantage in the field of computer technology and by the 1990s the top management was even resistant to the use of personal computers at the firm. Again the firm was at the forefront of mobile phone technology at the end of the twentieth century, only to throw this lead away. At the turn of the century the company's staple products, which were still earning the company significant income, were ditched in favour of investment in the new internet.com boom. Today only the BAE Systems Advanced Technology Centre, which was the old Marconi Research Laboratory at Great Baddow, the New Street site, which is now being redeveloped, and e2v on Waterhouse Lane (see chapter 8) remain.

The needs of war had led Marconi to have control of 36 factories in the Mid Essex area and in and around London. In the Chelmsford area the stands of Chelmsford City Football Club, a Methodist church, the old New London Road skating rink and two pubs had all been used. Many of these were used because of the dispersed sites plan and were soon sold off. Before the end of the war a certain amount of planning had been carried out for the time when the company became its own master again. Marconi looked at the likely competition it would face. Firstly there were a number of companies of similar size, experience and level of international sales. Secondly there had been a number of businesses which had concentrated on electrical engineering before the war, but which had been drawn into producing electronic equipment during the war, that were likely to continue after the war. Thirdly there were firms which before the war hadn't competed with Marconi because they concentrated on radio receivers for the domestic market, rather than transmitters, the capital equipment that Marconi concentrated on. These competitors had been drawn into the production of

Marconi Research Establishment, Great Baddow
(Courtesy of E.R.O.)

transmitters during the war and were likely to continue. Lastly Government research establishments, which had expanded rapidly during the war, were likely to continue to conduct this research. They had 'poached' a number of Marconi's best engineers and the company faced a severe shortage of skilled engineers. Another problem the company faced upon the cessation of hostilities was that the equipment at the New Street factory was antiquated and there was no chance given post war economic conditions of replacing it. This company had still retained however, a core of workers who were Marconi men to the bone. The Chairman, Admiral H.W. Grant, made it a principle to know each worker personally. He was quickly on the scene when the factory was bombed. (See chapter 24) (1)

Marconi's problems were added to by an unexpected development which was to have huge consequences for the company. Before the war, one of the company's strengths was its Imperial connections. The Imperial network of radio stations built by Marconi led it to dominate radio services in the Empire and Commonwealth. After the war, the government decided to nationalise these services that were run by Cable and Wireless Limited. C. and W. was also a holding company for Marconi. The Government had therefore, to dispose of the rest of the Marconi Company. A company of Marconi's standing with its vast amount of accumulated technological knowledge and acquired engineering expertise was bound to be an attractive proposition to major English and international companies. After much interest from the United States, where the electronics industry was making huge strides, the English Electric Company (E.E.) bought Marconi for £3,750,000. It also bought a 42% stake in Marconi International Marine Communications Company Limited and took complete control of Marconi Instruments Limited. English Electric had been formed in 1918 after a lateral merger between four companies involved in different areas of electrical engineering. After a good start the company, like Marconi, was affected by the depression of the late 1920s. Once G.H. Nelson was made managing director however, the company's fortunes revived and had considerably expanded by the time the Second World War started. During the war in addition to its normal products it built vast shadow factories and made huge amounts of armaments. (2) Nelson was a man of considerable foresight and saw that the fields of electric power and electronics were likely to converge. Marconi's leading position in radio and capital electronic equipment would, he felt, give E.E. a more balanced industrial base with which to compete at home and abroad.

The take-over caused shock and initial concern at Chelmsford. In addition the separation from Cable and Wireless meant a serious potential loss of revenue for

Marconi. Previously it had an almost complete monopoly in the supply of transmitting equipment to the imperial stations. Now it would have to compete with other firms for these orders. In addition the pre-war management structure dominated by engineers needed to be changed in favour of more managers with commercial acumen. Equipment built before the war was of "superlative craftsmanship built without regard to price". The specification delivered was often better than the customer required!

Grant resigned immediately after the take-over, which was not a surprise since he was 79 years of age: more unusual was that all the rest of the board of directors resigned 'en masse'. The thirteen members were replaced by a board of only five. Nelson chose F.N. Sutherland to be the new general manager of Marconi at New Street. He had started with E.E. as an apprentice in 1922. He was both a highly qualified engineer and a successful manager. Sutherland had no connection with Marconi's past way of doing things and was a good fighter. All the engineers thought he could have no knowledge of electronics; in fact he had a long standing interest in radio. After he took up his appointment initially he did little, preferring to assess his workforce and listen. In interview he said his aims were to increase production and improve the welfare of the workers. Although the workers were sceptical about the latter, there was a continuous improvement in working conditions and welfare facilities, in which Sutherland's wife played an important role. Sutherland showed the men a desire to run the company his way using methods that were often alien to them but he shared with them an urge to see the company make progress. Although he did not make the informal addresses which the workers had become used to, he quickly became recognised as a man who got things done. New equipment, which had been impossible to get immediately after the war, began arriving and was quickly installed. Methods of working were not changed drastically overnight. Model shop methods of assembly by skilled craftsmen were still retained for large pieces of equipment. A new accountancy system was quickly formed with a new form of developmental planning. In addition a technical sales department was established along with a new drawing office. When materials for production started arriving an increase in production finally came about after the fuel shortages abated. This was passed on in the form of increased wages and salaries resulting in a further improvement in the mood at the works. Another of Sutherland's successes was in the appointment of key staff. He made Robert Telford, a Marconi man, who he had met out in Brazil, his assistant. Twenty years later Sutherland was Chairman of the Company and Telford his managing director. Sutherland appointed R.J. Kemp as Chief of Research and a Dr E. Eastwood, who came from English Electric,

Deputy Chief. Eastwood had a high level background in radar research with the R.A.F. Nelson let Sutherland manage the company the way he wanted safe in the knowledge that he would approve of his methods. Sutherland applied the same approach to the six new company divisions which he established. Each division had its own sales force. He gave the chiefs of division considerable freedom in how they ran their particular area. The new divisions gave much greater incentives to individuals at various levels. (4)

The progress of radar during the war, and the company's role in it, had been staggering. Although it was almost certain that post war demand for military radar would continue to expand, the commercial possibilities for radar appeared more debateable. Eastwood however had no doubts. He bought with him a contract from English Electric for a reworking of one of the wartime types of radar. This was to play a vital role in the company's performance in markets for military and civil air traffic control. The sudden emergence of the Cold War made the building of new radars to wartime designs urgent. In a report requested by the R.A.F. Eastwood recommended the design of a completely new radar chain. After this was accepted by the government the New Street factory was put on a virtual war footing to produce the equipment for the new permanent and mobile stations which the company had designed. Despite extensive shift work, English Electric had to use a former shadow factory in Accrington and a hundred sub contractors. By the time the system was finished in 1955, the services equipment division had been renamed the radar division. At the same time civil aviation was beginning to recover and expand. This brought about a demand for improved methods of air traffic control. In 1950 the Ministry of Transport and Civil Aviation bought Marconi height finder and early warning radars for use at London Airport. Eastwood was heavily involved in the adaptation of new experimental defence radar for civil use. The first results of this research, the S232 50 cm radar was installed at London Airport in 1954. Its success was followed by many sales by the company in the following decade worth millions of pounds after the government allowed the sale of 'fixed coil' systems to N.A.T.O. countries. Marconi gradually increased the power of these systems in equipment produced for New Zealand and Sweden. The military and civil radar system developed for the latter in 1959 involved the use of a high speed digital computer to both overcome problems of interception and to bring into use various types of weapons such as fighters and guided missiles at the right instant. The system involved the use of closed circuit television. The company's high brightness display first used at Gatwick Airport in 1962 was extensively used by the mid 1960s. As early as 1950, a patent was taken out by Christopher Cockerell, later to be the inventor of the hovercraft. This was to find the height of aircraft electronically. Such equipment remained too expensive for a long time. By the 1960s Marconi's radar equipment was increasingly using transistor and microprocessor units. This involved the development of various forms of tabular display. The development of secondary radar allowing stations to identify 'friend or foe' aircraft was adapted for civil use.

The need for computers in the development of new complex radar systems brought about Marconi's involvement in new computer systems. This should have resulted in Marconi becoming a world leader in computer development. In the late 1950s a great deal of research went into microcircuit techniques, both semi-conductor and thin film. The production of previous computers, the MENTOR system was halted and a new machine called the MYRIAD using microcircuits went into production. By 1965 four out of five of British civil airways sites were equipped with Marconi radar. (5) In 1966 the company had produced a computerised air traffic control system for London Airport. (6)

Developments at Marconi Radar enabled it to get a foothold in the production of civil aircraft radar after the war. Post war aircraft such as the de Havilland Comet, the English Electric Canberra, the Armstrong Whitworth Apollo, the Bristol Freighter and the Handley Page Hermes iv were all installed with Marconi equipment. Marconi was just one of a large number of firms and government research departments which extensively researched the development of a device which would enable aircraft to navigate independently of all ground stations and the extremely limited conventional compass. By the early 1950's most of this research was concentrated on the use of the so called 'Doppler effect' in physics. After extensive research at the Great Baddow Laboratory a prototype was produced and tested at Writtle. After initial suspicion civil airlines embraced the 'Marconi doppler' with enthusiasm and in the 1960s whole fleets were fitted with the' black boxes'. This was followed by a new direction finder, the AD712 which sold well on the continent, but not in America because it wasn't adapted to meet U.S. standards. An adapted version of this was used in the Canberra which set three flight records. A Marconi engineer was present throughout. (7) By the late 1950s transistors were gradually replacing valves in transmitters and receivers. New transistor equipment was unveiled by the company at the 1960 Farnborough air show. "They set new standards in reduced size, weight and power consumption and in reliability and ease of maintenance." This was an example of years of Marconi research resulting in millions of pounds of orders. (8)

The reorganised company was in a good position to exploit its long standing connection with the B.B.C. In radio the B.B.C., like other stations, faced the problem after the war that had been building up before the conflict: the airwaves were becoming increasingly crowded. The company did some research into an FM station and in 1947 the B.B.C. gave an order to the company for an F.M. transmitter. A new B.B.C. transmitting station using this started in 1950. The station also used antennae and a feeder system designed and made by the company. Marconi also researched the development of high powered unattended stations using air cooled valves made by its sister company E.E.V. (9)

Before the war Marconi had produced television equipment for the B.B.C., in a joint venture with E.M.I. At the end of the war the two companies proposed abandoning the 405 lines system for the 525 which was standard in the U.S. The B.B.C. declined to adopt this and resumed their television service from Alexandra Palace using their old equipment in 1946. Before the war the company had concentrated on sound equipment for their part of the joint venture. Now as part of English Electric there was nothing to stop Marconi producing television tubes. This was a gamble because it meant the dissolution of the Marconi – E.M.I. partnership for television equipment and it was by no means certain that there would be a demand for televisions. Marconi experimented with camera design using image orthicon technology initially developed in the United States. One of the effects of this research was the remodelling of the Marconi valve laboratory into the English Electric Valve Company. Although it was part of the E.E. group and was very much a Marconi sister company, it has its own story and development through to the present where it still exists as the thriving firm e2v. It is therefore dealt with separately in the next chapter. For the second transmitting station erected near Birmingham the B.B.C. used the E.M.I's vision transmitter and Marconi's high powered sound transmitter. They had tendered competing contracts however and the partnership was dissolved in 1948. Sales of Marconi's first TV camera were slow however, but then the second version, the Mark 1B, was accepted by the B.B.C. who started using them for outside broadcasts. The company could start relying on EEV valves and didn't have to be dependent on American models. In 1951, after the development of the Mark 2 camera, the company broke into the foreign market supplying complete television systems in Canada, Spain and Bolivia. These included transmitters, antennas, cameras and studio equipment. The company then designed a new camera around a newly developed EEV four and a half inch image orthicon. By 1956 after considerable teething problems these Mark 3 cameras were being used by the B.B.C. Progress was such that Marconi and EEV won a joint engineering award at the American 'Emmy' s for their development of the new camera and tube. (10) It was the first time such an award had gone outside the United States. As early as 1953 Marconi had given its first demonstration of colour television, although it was another 13 years before a colour television service arrived in this country. As in the past with its tradition of training sound engineers, Marconi set up the world's first studio entirely for training purposes. (11) Considerable sales of colour television equipment were built up well before colour television was launched in this country in 1967. Marconi was awarded the contracts for the new Crystal Palace station that was needed to replace the old Alexandra Palace station. Some of the old equipment from the previous station found its way to Chelmsford, where it was added to the collection of company historical exhibits. The new station began transmitting in 1956. Marconi also benefitted from the establishment of the new Independent Television Authority in 1954. In that year the new Authority ordered three vision and three sound transmitters from the company. Other orders came in from the new programme companies. This influx of orders caused another temporary crisis at Chelmsford with the company full to capacity. Marconi completed the first station at Croydon in 7 months and within three years 7 other stations became operational. During the 1950's the company also carried out a great deal of research into closed circuit television, including underwater work. Its main use however was in heavy industry particularly in steel works and power generating stations. (12)

The company did a great deal of research into improving high frequency communications between countries and continents. Marconi of course had a tradition in this going back to 1900. In 1959 for example the company obtained a one and a half million pound order from the U.S. for a microwave telephone and telegraph system to link the U.S. Air Force with Great Britain. (13) The company received a major contract in 1964 for communication equipment to aid the search for North Sea Oil. It provided a G.P.O radio telegraph system for many mobile drilling rigs and two shore stations, one at the Humber and one near Aberdeen. (14) The 1960s saw the beginning of the introduction of a satellite link into high frequency transmissions. To begin with the company concentrated on providing ground stations for the satellites. The American end of the first Telstar broadcast used Marconi cameras. (15) Britain's first spaceship was 'guided towards the stars' by the Marconi direction finding equipment. Incidentally it was also equipped with Hoffmann bearings and Crompton Parkinson electrical circuits. (16)

As with sound broadcasting the company continued to develop its marine communication after the war. Marconi International Marine Communications Ltd. continued its practice, long established over more than 50 years, to provide ship owners with a rental and maintenance system. The company had over 250 depots all over the world, from which company technicians operated; to carry out maintenance and repairs on the equipment ship owners had hired from the company. Marconi applied developments in radar to mercantile shipping. The radio locator system proved very popular. Marconi was given the order to re-equip all lighthouses around Britain with new radio beacons. (17)

By 1964 the organisation of the company into semi autonomous divisions had worked so well that company turnover was ten times what it had been in 1947. Manufacture was carried on at numerous establishments but nearly all of them were within a few miles of the original New Street works. In 1954 however, a new factory was built at Basildon and in 1960 the company acquired an existing one at Wembley. The Baddow laboratories successful research into microcircuits led to a new factory being established at Witham. Marconi's expansion of its television interests led to a new plant in Waterhouse Lane being established in 1964. The production of components at Writtle was switched to a bigger factory at Billericay. (18) In 1968 the radar division moved from New Street to the then empty Crompton- Parkinson factory in Writtle Road. Part of that site also came to be used by the separate EEV Company. Marconi was able to give jobs to 150 of the remaining 900 Crompton Parkinson workers. (19) The Marine Company moved to Westway, Chelmsford in 1963. (20)

By 1962 at any one time there were 500 apprentices either at the local 'Tech' (Mid Essex Technical College) or Marconi College in Arbour Lane. (21) Most new Marconi apprentices stayed at the Brooklands hostel. They spent six months at the Apprentice Training Centre doing very basic tasks such as drilling, filing, welding and painting. This was followed by the first six months at the Mid Essex Technical College. By the end of the four year course only a few of the starting batch remained. (22)

Overall the 1960s were successful years for the company, with order books generally full and over half of all production being exported. Industrial relations were not always harmonious by this time however. In 1967 for example, nearly 1,500 workers at New Street walked out over a claim for longer holidays and a pay increase. This dispute covered all the hourly paid staff and was an illustration of the growing gap between them and salaried staff. (23)

In 1967/8 English Electric was initially the target of a takeover bid from the Plessey

Company but eventually accepted a rival bid from the General Electric Company (G.E.C.). The origins of G.E.C. went back to an electrical goods wholesaler started by a German living in London in the late nineteenth century, Gustav Binswanger, and the company acquired its first factory as early as 1888. The following year it was incorporated as the G.E.C. Limited and later became well known for its motto 'Everything electrical'. In 1900 it became a public limited company. It owned the Osram Lamp Company. G.E.C. expanded rapidly during the first war producing radios, signal lamps, and arc lamp carbons for searchlights. During the inter war period the company moved into heavy engineering and was heavily involved in the creation of the national grid. During the second war, G.E.C. was involved, like Marconi, with the development of the cavity magnetron for radar. Post war the company grew at a slower pace until Arnold Weinstock became managing director. After internal reorganisation and cut backs Weinstock embarked on a series of mergers aimed at rationalising the whole of the electrical industry. In 1967 G.E.C. acquired A.E.I., itself an industrial giant. 1968 saw the merger with English Electric., covering a number of companies, including EEV, apart from Marconi. As a result of these and later mergers, the conglomerate became well established on the F.T.S.E. top 100 shares index. By 1983 G.E.C. was the largest private employer in the U.K. with some quarter of a million workers.

Weinstock showed little interest in the developing fields of computers, microelectronics, mobile phones and consumer electronics, the very fields in which Marconi should have had a real technological advantage. He stood by the areas which had previously been successful for the group, defence, electricity generators and phone exchanges. At the end of the 1980s he deliberately entered into joint ventures with a number of foreign companies to make it difficult for the company to be taken over. (24)

An initial report on Marconi after the merger said that no work would be transferred from existing plant in the Chelmsford area to the Midlands or the North. (25) The following year saw Marconi develop and build a one million pound communication earth terminal. This was assembled at Rivenall and shipped out to the Ascension Islands. This resulted in the company being awarded the first of numerous Queens' Awards for Industry. (26) During the 1970s however the workforce at Marconi's factories in the Chelmsford area varied according to its order books. In 1971 for example the cancellation of a Libyan defence contract resulted in several hundred job losses. (27) After 600 redundancies were announced the following year Stevas, the local M.P., met with the Department of Trade and Industry to get assurances on employment at the firm. (28) Marconi Marine however, continued to flourish. In 1972 it received a big order from a Japanese firm. The same year it was the only one of G.E.C.'s hundreds of companies to receive a Queen's Award for Industry. This was for exports. (29) The following year Marconi Marine won a design award for its 'Seachart' echo finder. (30) An upturn in orders generally for the Marconi group of companies meant that its factories in the Chelmsford area were actually short of 350 workers in 1973 (31)

During the 1970s and the 1980s Marconi became increasingly dependent on defence orders from governments both at home and abroad in an era when the Cold War was still very much alive. In 1976 one such order caused a great deal of controversy. Marconi's contract with the South African Government led to a great deal of opposition from some of the trade unions at the Chelmsford works because of the apartheid issue. In the end the unions were forced to accept the order because jobs were at risk. (32) It put itself in a good position to win further defence contracts by developing the new Martello system of early warning radar. The RAF needed a new £100 million system to replace its out of date existing one. Marconi's Martello system could provide a picture of Russian bomber activity up to 300 miles from the coast. (33) These orders provided employment for Marconi Radar at their Writtle Road site. The firm was increasingly dependent however on the British government choosing Marconi tenders rather than their foreign competitors. In June 1980 the boss of Marconi Radar complained loudly after a major Civil Airports Authority order went to a Dutch company. Despite this, the company won a Queen's Award for Exports that year. (34) A delay to the government take up off the Martello system led Stevas to make representations again to the government, claiming that 30% of the jobs of the 3,700 workforce at Marconi Radar were under threat. One order went to the U.S. because of heavy subsidies. (35) The take – up of the Martello system by the British government, though belated, paved the way for many further orders for the system from abroad, particularly N.A.T.O. countries. As with many other Marconi technological achievements it had taken well over a decade to achieve positive results. Again it resulted in a Marconi company, Marconi Radar, receiving a Queen's Award for Industry.

Marconi Communication Systems Limited (M.C.S.) was also doing well, with over four and a half thousand people employed at New Street in 1980. Partly because of the local shortage of housing and transport problems, the factory was usually short of workers, particularly skilled engineers. (36) In 1981 M.C.S. won a Queen's Award for Technical Achievement for a fast tuning automatic radio transmitter which gained the company £50 million worth of business. This was the 25th Queen's Award for Industry to be awarded to the Marconi group of companies since the awards had started in 1965. (37) In 1982 M.C.S. became the first British company to build and install a satellite earth terminal. (38)

Not for the first time the outbreak of a conflict benefitted Marconi. As the British fleet sped to the Falklands there was an immediate call to the company for spares. Most of the warships were fitted with Marconi radar and missile guidance systems. (39) After the war M.C.S. received a massive military order for the defence of 'Fortress Falklands'.

After a difficult period in the early 1980s, marred by redundancies and poor industrial relations, the Marconi group became one of the most profitable sectors in the G.E.C. conglomerate. For a few years the order books for both Marconi Radar and M.C.S. were full. The shortage of skilled engineers became even more acute however. A company spokesman said "it (the business) is becoming higher and higher tech all the time". (40) In 1984 M.C.S. received a £11 million order for twenty thousand radio sets for British police and firemen to give them the best radio service in the world, in the face of stiff competition. M.C.S. also obtained a major order from the U.S. navy for radio equipment in 1984. (41)

During the 1980s the Great Baddow Laboratories were carrying out potentially vital research into automation and the robots of the future. By 1985 they were, it was thought, two and a half years away from having an assembly line prototype to demonstrate. This (Operation 'Gadfly') potentially gave the Marconi group one way of moving away from defence contracts. (42) Unfortunately for Marconi, this type of 'hi tech' computer dominated development was not compatible with Weinstock's view of how the company should be developing.

The 1990s saw two events, which in their different ways led to the demise of the Marconi name and group of companies. These were the end of the Cold War in 1991 and the retirement of Lord Weinstock in 1996. By the 1980s Marconi was the primary defence subsidiary of G.E.C. and was renamed Marconi – G.E.C. in 1987. The end of the Cold War drastically reduced the demand for ever more sophisticated defence systems which Marconi had played such a major part in producing. Initially the affect of this was masked by the outbreak of the first Gulf War. Marconi played a vital role in the war with its 'see in the dark' electronics. The low altitude infra-red night vision system used in the conflict had been developed at Great Baddow. Marconi Radar's main contribution to the war effort was target tracking and fine control radar for Sea

Wolf and Sea Dart missiles on board Royal Navy ships. They could take out incoming Exocet missiles. M.C.S. supplied high frequency radios for the Royal Navy and the Army. One hundred Marconi – G.E.C. workers were sent out to the Gulf to maintain equipment. (43)

The early 1990s saw a radical restructuring of the Marconi works in and around Chelmsford. New Street, the main base for M.C.S., saw a complete facelift and the Marconi Radar factory at Writtle Road was drastically scaled down. The concentration of Marconi Radar production in Fife and Leicester led to increased redundancies at that works. (44) This was followed by further redundancies at New Street and Great Baddow. M.C.S. and Marconi Radar continued however, to get big orders. M.C.S. received yet more Queen's Awards for industry for both Technology and exports for its new 'Scimitar' radio, which was sold to a large number of countries. (45)

By the time Arnold Weinstock retired he had made G.E.C. the 18th largest business in Britain, dominating the country's engineering, electronics and telecommunications business. George Simpson took over as Managing Director and began bringing in a new corporate style of management. (46) Initially of course there were assurances that the Chelmsford jobs were safe. (47) By 1997 however the workforce at New Street had been halved. In the same year the closure of the historic Marconi College in Arbour Lane was announced. Marconi Radar was still recruiting engineering graduates and in 1996 it announced plans to recruit half the 200 it needed from the new Anglia Ruskin University. (48) The Marconi laboratories at Great Baddow developed a miniature TV screen just over half an inch wide, for medical use and for the emergency services. (49)

In 1999 G.E.C. sold Marconi Electronic Systems, which included Marconi Radar, to British Aerospace for £7.2 billion. The latter became B.A.E. Systems, in which Marconi Electronic Systems was linked up to the Italian defence giant Alenia as Alenia Marconi Systems. They won a number of major contracts. In 2000 for example the company was awarded a £260 million order as part of a new Royal Navy anti aircraft system. (50)

Simpson and his aides decided to complete his reconfiguration of the G.E.C. empire, now renamed as Marconi P.L.C., by taking part in the infamous 'dot com' boom. He bought up overpriced United States telecommunications companies. Two big internet acquisitions in 1999 brought the company massively into debt. When the internet bubble burst, Marconi P.L.C.'s shares crashed. Within weeks the group of companies, which as G.E.C. had been worth as much as £35 billion, was reduced to a share value of £100 million. (51) This sealed the fate of the historic New Street works. Production was to be switched to their Waterhouse Lane site. (52) In the event, the groups mountain of debts necessitated further sell offs and the move never took place. In 2002 Marconi Strategic Communications (the old M.C.S.) was sold to the Italian giant Finmeccanica. (53) By the end of that year the Marconi name had all but left the town, with only 25 people working at New Street. Alenia Marconi Systems continued to make world beating radar but away from Chelmsford. (54) The A.E.U. shop steward Bill Pigram said "the new company is treating people as badly as the old one because of a complete miscalculation in the U.S". (55) In 2005 what remained of Marconi P.L.C. was sold off to the Swedish telecommunications company Eriksson who used the Marconi brand for a while then renamed it Telent. (56) Marconi Radar lives on as BAE Insyte (Integrated System Technologies) mainly working on advanced technology for the Royal Navy at Glebe Road. In 2010 jobs were being created at the old Great Baddow laboratories with BAE pioneering low carbon eco friendly technologies. (57)

Meanwhile a saga surrounding what would happen to the Marconi historical archive developed. During its long history the company had amassed a large collection of archives and artefacts. A sell off of the Marconi Historical collection was narrowly averted but negotiations with the then Borough Council failed. In 2004 it was announced the collection was not being transferred to Oxford University. (58) The University allowed the town to keep some exhibits on permanent display. During 2009 50 Marconi cameras were obtained from a private collection for the Museum, including one that was used to film and broadcast the Coronation. (59) In 2011 the late William Waters left his collection to the Industrial Heritage Centre at Sandford Mill, consisting of "every little bit of radio equipment you could want from 1890 to the 1960s". This made it possible to reconstruct the wireless room on the Titanic. (60) The collection remains divided with the archives and the products of the early firm at Oxford, while Sandford Mill holds the Marconi Hut and a range of later equipment including broadcast transmitters, TV cameras and the major national collection of Marconi marine radio equipment.

Even in the new millennium there were still some workers at New Street who had stuck with the company for decades, displaying dedication their corporate bosses would have hardly understood. Bill Lambert for example had helped with the Duke of Edinburgh's visit in 1962. He had explained to the Duke how his jig boring machine worked. His son said later that during an extensive stay in hospital "His boss went to the hospital to tell him that he'd had to put someone else in charge of the machine. He couldn't have Dad learn it from someone else." (61) Sir Robert Telford the last M.D.

of G.E.C. – Marconi Electronics Ltd, and later the company's life president had started as an apprentice in New Street in 1938. "Apprentices were expected to learn the job bottom up." He said that loyalty to Marconi had been built up by recruiting from all corners of the U.K. during the Depression years. "Working for Marconi was a good job. There was a high degree of skill at all levels with the top research people, who were leading the world, dealing with skilled men on the shop floor." (62) In 2008 Faheem Ahtar retired after 48 years with the company, starting immediately after he arrived from Pakistan as one of the first Asians in the town. (63)

The New Street site is now being developed with only the front facade having been given Grade 2 listed building status. A number of redevelopment plans had previously come to nothing, including one which would have retained key buildings, but also involved the demolition of most of the factory in order to provide new homes, a hotel, new business space and a new arrival space for Chelmsford station. The owners went into administration but in 2012 the site was bought by Bellway homes. (64) (65) Current plans involve the preservation of the front of the 1912 building along with the water tower and the power house. The rest of the site has now been demolished. A 'pocket' park will be the centrepiece of a pedestrian link between the Anglia Ruskin University and the railway station. (66)

It remains an absurdity that such a great amount of stored skill and technical ability, which was still proving itself in the 1990s, could be permanently wasted by corporate incompetence.

1) The History of the Marconi Company W.J. Baker p.324 – 6
2) Baker p.327
3) Baker 328 – 9
4) Baker 330 – 333
5) Baker p.338 – 345
6) E.W.N. 29 7 1966 p.20
7) E.C. 26 8 1955 p.1
8) Baker p.346 – 353
9) Baker p.354 – 360
10) E.C. 24 6 1955 p.7
11) E.C. 24 6 1955 p.7
12) Baker p.361 – 374
13) E.C. 26 3 1959

14) E.C. 8 1 1964 p.1
15) Baker p.375 – 386
16) Baker p.387 – 393
17) E.C. 3 6 1960 p.19
18) Baker 394 – 400
19) E.W.N. 24 5 1968 p.1
20) Marconi's New Street Works Tim Wander p.193
21) E.W.N. 23 3 1962
22) Wander p.249 – 251
23) E.W.N. 29 9 1967
24) Wander p.303 – 304
25) E.W.N. 2 5 1969 p.1
26) E.W.N. 15 7 1969 p.1
27) E.C. 19 2 1971 p.1
28) E.C. 28 1 1972 p.3
29) E.C. 21 4 1972 p.1
30) E.C. 27 4 1973 p.10
31) E.C. 12 5 1973 p.1
32) E.W.N. 12 2 1976
33) E.C. 4 2 1979
34) E.C. 20 6 1980 p.1
35) E.W.N. 12 8 1980 p.1
36) E.C. 13 2 1980 p.10
37) E.C. 24 4 1918 p.5
38) E.C. 9 7 1982 p.9
39) E.C. 9 4 1982 p.1
40) E.C. 13 8 1982 p.1
41) E.W.N. 18 8 1984 p.1
42) E.C. 18 3 1985 p.10
43) E.C. 25 1 1991 p.4
44) E.C. 5 6 1992 p.1
45) E.W.N. 25 4 1991 p.1
46) Wander p.304 – 305
47) E.W.N. 15 2 1996 p.4
48) E.W.N. 20 12 1996 p.3

49) E.W.N. 21 11 1997
50) E.W.N. 8 12 2000 p.1
51) Wander 305 – 306
52) E.W.N. 3 5 2001 p.21
53) E.W.N. 8 8 2002 p.1
54) E.C. 9 8 2002
55) E.C. 6 9 2002
56) Wander p.7
57) E.C. 15 4 2010
58) E.W.N. 9 12 2004
59) E.C. 19 11 2009 p.3
60) E.C. 14 4 2011 p.3
61) E.C. 1 2 2004 p.9
62) E.C. 2002 p.6
63) E.C. 17 1 2008 p.5
64) Wander p. 313
65) E.C. 2 8 2012 p.6
66) E.C. 20 12 2012 p.8

7

The Hoffmann Company in Chelmsford

"In 1930 the first five cars in the Le Mans 24 hour race were fitted with Hoffmann ball bearings."

In the early twentieth century the Hoffmann Company became one of the largest manufacturers of ball and roller bearings in the world. How it became located in Chelmsford was almost certainly not an accident. Although according to a later managing director T.W. Cooper, Ernst Hoffmann did little more than give his name to the company. M.H. Cobbold, in his history of the company, attached much more importance to Hoffmann's role in getting the company established. The company became a vital part of the town, employing at one time directly almost ten thousand workers and indirectly many more. Social and sporting activities were developed to such an extent that they matched and possibly even exceeded those of Marconi. (See chapters 25 – 28) Like the Crompton Company, the Hoffmann Company was not slow in developing sickness and pension schemes. Also mirroring that company Hoffmann was vehemently anti union in its early days; a stance which gradually had to soften. Both wars saw the company expand greatly with ball and roller bearings needed in all three armed forces. Employment almost halved in the immediate period after the second war but the firm remained a major manufacturer. Increasing competition in a declining world market in the 1960s led to the government's Industrial Reorganisation Corporation (I.R.C.) encouraging the firm to merge with two other major ball bearing producers to form Ransome, Hoffmann and Pollard (R.H.P.) Although this was competitive for well over a decade, by the 1980s the firm had a great deal of unused capacity at its Chelmsford works. The demise of the firm in Chelmsford was speeded by the Government's unfathomable encouragement of a Japanese competitor to set up a manufacturing base in the U.K. itself.

A ball bearing is an engineering term which refers to a type of roller bearing which uses balls to separate the moving parts of the bearing. In the later part of the nineteenth century two cousins Charles and Geoffrey Barrett were trying to make steel balls for use in the bicycles they were manufacturing at their foundry at the Barbican. R. Barrett and sons had been in business since 1720. (1) It is probable that the Christy Company in Broomfield had already played a role in a new company owned by the Barrett's (Westminster Engineering) coming to Chelmsford: Christy's certainly did in getting the company established at Springfield wharf in the early 1890s. The Barretts founded the Preston Davis Ball Bearing Company as the subsidiary to Westminster Engineering. The cousins found however that they couldn't make accurate balls in any reasonable quantity. Using their lathes, a little snag of metal was always left on the ball which had to be removed, leaving a ball which was not completely round.

Geoffrey Foster Barrett had left school at 15 and taken an electrical engineering course at Crystal Palace. He was apprenticed to a firm of electrical engineers travelling extensively for them home and abroad, in charge of erection and repair work mainly in coal mining plant, when his cousin Charles Arthur asked him to join him at his two Chelmsford companies.

The Barretts heard of a Swiss American engineer Ernst Hoffmann, who, working in the U.S., had developed a lathe which didn't leave the little piece of metal on the ball. The cousins persuaded him to come to London and bring his patent with him. With Hoffmann the Barretts formed the Hoffmann Manufacturing Company in 1898. It had the substantial capital of £100,000. They then submitted plans to Chelmsford Borough Council to develop four acres of land at the corner of Rectory Lane and New Street near Bishops Hall. (2) At this time it was opposite the Chelmsford Cricket ground. Fourteen years later of course it was to face the new Marconi factory. More importantly, from Hoffmann's point view, its initial site was surrounded by vast acres of empty land. The original main building, a single storey construction, was completed in 1899. This only carried back 256 feet which gave a floor space of 64,000 square feet. Additions started in 1906 and continued every year until 1914. (3) In time all the spare land was used, as the company eventually engulfed the mill on the River Chelmer in a little over two decades. Another crucial key to its successful location was its proximity to the railway line: a siding was quickly established. This was essential because huge amounts of metal and coal were needed.

The Barretts quarrelled with Hoffmann and he left the company when they bought him out in 1903. He was described by the board of the company as "a very impracticable inventor type". According to them he was only interested in further perfecting his patents rather than the urgent matter of making the machines to manufacture the ball bearings. Workers remembered him as a kindly man. He lived for a time in Baddow and also at Dovedale House in Moulsham. M.H. Cobbold, the firms publicity manager in the 1960s, gave Ernst Hoffmann credit however for undertaking the detailed responsibility for the layout of the factory. Cobbold published letters written by Hoffmann to a number of suppliers of steel tubes which reveal him to be not just an absent minded inventor. (4)

Of more use to the Barretts was Otto Schmidt, a practical and very able engineer. Schmidt happened to read an article which described an American Christian Hill's, method of grinding spheres and which said that the patent on this method were about to run out. G.F. Barrett was sent to America in 1901 to buy the patent which he successfully achieved. It was these patents, rather than those of Hoffmann, on which the success of the company was founded according to the Barretts. Cobbold however emphasised that the firm was still dependent for some time on the Hoffmann methods of turning the balls. Initially however production was confined to the Hoffmann Combined Free Wheel and Back Pedalling Cycle Hub. They manufactured a penny in the slot machine under the name of the Sweetmeat Automatic Company. This company also launched an automatic photographic machine, which consisted of a flashlight, sensitised plates and the necessary developing and fixing media; the whole process was completely automatic. Production of these machines was switched from the Barbican to Chelmsford in order to fill the gap before the machines for producing ball bearings were ready. The money to pay the workers had apparently run out when G.F. Barrett had to return to London to obtain the necessary cash! After the strain of the situation apparently took its toll on C.A. Barrett, he had a breakdown, retired from the Board and was absent for 15 months. The buying out of Hoffmann proved to be a turning point in the company's growth. Hoffmann's new board consisted of J. Ashby, Chairman, G.F. Barrett, P.C. Low and H.F. Knight.

The first works manager, F.W. Witte had arrived in May 1898 from the Hoffman Machine Company in New York. He brought with him Hugo Witte, a brother, who later became foreman of the Turret or Nearing Turning Department and E. Detert, who was the first foreman of the Ball Turning Department. According to the Barrett's, F.W. Witte did much to counteract the impracticable schemes of Hoffmann and was responsible for much of the progress in bearing production. He left in 1906 to start a ball bearing factory in Leipzig. Witte was succeeded by W.B. Mair, who had previously been the chief draughtsman. Mair was responsible for the development of the Hoffmann roller bearing. In 1913 C.A. Barrett suffered a second breakdown from which he failed to recover and he passed away in 1916. P.C. Low and G.F. Barrett as joint managing directors led the firm through the difficult war years. (5)

The Hoffman Company certainly benefitted from developing its improved product at the right time. Although the cycling craze had somewhat abated, motor cars were beginning to be bought in significant numbers and these of course used a variety of ball bearings. In addition the first experiments with flight were taking place. During 1901 the company designed its first bearing, a single thrust bearing designed for crane hooks. A thrust bearing is a type of rotary bearing which allows rotation between parts but they are designed to cope with a high axial load while they do this. By 1902 the company had started producing steel balls with a mirror finish. These were designed to be accurate to within 1/10,000 of an inch. In 1903 the firm patented a self adjusting ball journal bearing. The journal is the part of the shaft which slides over the bearing surface. During the same year a ball journal pedestal was patented. Roller bearings, which were later to become a large part of production, were beginning to be produced around 1903.

In 1902 the Company exhibited its products at a machinery exhibition at Wolverhampton. During 1907 it had a stand at the first International Motor Vehicles and Motor Boat Exhibition at Olympia and was already supplying Austin's and other motor vehicle manufacturers. Rolls Royce won the Tourist Trophy race of 1906 with a car fitted throughout with Hoffmann bearings. Both Rolls Royce and Napier Cars were to have long associations with the Hoffmann Company. The early de Havilland aircraft of 1910 used Hoffman bearings, for which the company received favourable comments. De Havilland was also to have a long association with the company.

The expansion of the company was inexorable. After starting in 1898 with 10 workers, in 1906 it employed 308; by 1914 this had risen to 1,800. Such was the wartime increase in demand for roller bearings that by 1921, 4,750 people were employed at the Chelmsford works. (6) Its capital rose from £100,000 in 1898 to £300,000 in 1911 and £700,000 in 1923.

Before the company was producing anything it kept an Employment Register: this starts on the 6th July 1898. The register had a very basic layout featuring the name and address of who was engaged, when they were engaged, when they left and why, their occupation and sometimes other remarks. It is very revealing about the company's early years before the war. In the first few months when the first works were being built, small numbers of carpenters, painters and general labourers were employed. When equipment was being installed fitters and pattern makers were taken on. All these were paid on daily rates. A fitter for example was paid 7d a day. 1900 saw the first 'wiremen' (electricians) employed. Christy's played a prominent role in lighting the factory.

The register shows that from the start the Barretts were hard taskmasters. A fitter, taken on in October 1898 for example, was let go two months later because he was too slow. A Mr Chapman of Friars Place, Chelmsford, taken on in December 1898 as a stoker for the furnace, was let go in June 1899 for "not being steady". He had been paid 20 shillings a week. In contrast a Mr Harvey of 23 Mildmay Road, a pattern maker, was transferred to permanent staff some months after being employed. Out of 5 workers taken on in January 1899, one was transferred to staff, one was let go for 'being no good' and another left because there wasn't enough work. Out of three taken on in February 1899, two didn't last more than a month because they were "not satisfactory". Some workers didn't last a week. The comment by the name of a fitter who left after a week was "he was not used to our class of work". It was rare for workers to leave of their own accord. Relations between employees and the acceptance of authority were seen as important. A worker was discharged in June 1899 for fighting with a foreman. The reason a fitter left in 1900 was put down as "trouble with the foreman". In the same month a turner was discharged for being intemperate. The firm were often blunt about the reasons for workers leaving. When production was getting going in the early 1900s there was a steady flow of workers departing because they were "lazy". A milling hand, who was a "union man", left supposedly because he objected to working on the machines. Indeed the term "union man" was used on a regular basis in reference to why a worker left and it was obviously an issue with the company. In February 1901 a grinder left and the comment was "not enough grinding work, a union man". The previous November saw the company's first apprentice taken on. In September 1900 an apprentice from Great Waltham, who had only joined in July, left because "he wanted to learn a trade and receive high wages at the same time". After a few years workers started leaving of their own accord. This was, almost certainly because their skills in the engineering industry became more transferable in the local area with the expansion of the other works.

In the early years nearly all the workmen lived in the local area i.e. Chelmsford, Moulsham and Springfield with only one or two living further afield in villages such as Writtle and Great Waltham. By 1909 the register shows a few more workers living in places like Sandon and Margaretting but the early starts and long hours meant that most lived within either walking or bike riding distance. In the years before the first war more workers on the permanent staff were beginning to live in the bigger houses in Mildmay Road.

It might be thought that the firm would have only started to employ a significant number of women workers during the first war. In actual fact the register reveals that the firm was taking on significant numbers of females, mainly for the packing department, from 1902 onwards. Just prior to the war a few women were being employed in the factory itself as photos in the Sandford Mill Museum Spalding collection show. Most of the females employed were teenagers, some as young as 15. Of the male employees, 14 and 15 year old boys were increasingly employed to be trained up. In 1909 the oldest worker was 52 but this was certainly exceptional. (7)

Despite the firm's initial anti union stance it was increasingly forced to negotiate with unions before the first war. After a small stoppage in 1910, over a new piece rate system, which led to a Works Committee being set up, there was a much more serious one in 1913 (see chapter 9). It revolved around the demand for a pay increase of 1/2d per hour because the men's leader, Tyrell Smith argued, of the increase in the cost of living in the town. After two weeks the strikers asked the local M.P. Pretyman to mediate and as a result 306 machine attendants and labourers had their minimum rate raised to 5d an hour based on a 55 hour week.

M.H. Cobbold, in his history of the company, said that in the early days of the company, local people tended to regard the firm as an inferior place to work compared with the other two big firms. Fathers tended to advise their sons to go to Crompton's or Marconi's rather than Hoffmann's. This prejudice tended to ebb away after the first decade.

A reporter from the Essex Chronicle was shown around the works in 1910 by B. Mair, the works manager. Close on 1,400 men were turning out one and half million ball bearings a day. "12 years ago the factory was driven by a steam engine. Today there is an immense power house containing two 300 h.p. dynamos in addition to others of lesser power. Another 300 h.p. dynamo is likely to be added. This electric machinery also supplies the lighting. Outside the power house there is a large collection of retorts for the manufacture of gas. Hoffmann is quite self contained and does everything for itself." The reporter crossed a line of rails directly connected to the G.E.R. "Raw material lies in tons including bars of mild (tool) steel about five feet long in various diameters. The next shop cuts the steel into various lengths." Oil was used to keep

New Building 1918
(Courtesy of E.R.O.)

knives and the bars cool and reduced friction which would have damaged the tools. One shop had a drilling machine which was invented by various members of the staff. It was supposed to be the fastest machine of its kind in the world at the time. Turning lathes produced rings of steel which would eventually become the ball bearings. Semi automatic and automatic machinery made the rings into the required shape. "Every department has a testing department. Up to date appliances ascertain the trueness of the articles." They were then put into an oven: carbonisation gave the balls greater wearing properties. A polish then followed. The balls then went to the assembling department where the various parts were put together. Lastly, blemishes were looked for in the "condemned cell". The biggest ball bearing was three and a half inches in diameter. The smallest was 1/32nd of an inch. Later the biggest was four inches and the smallest 1/64th of an inch. Every ball was guaranteed to 1/10,000 of an inch standard. (8)

Every year before the war had seen an incremental expansion in the physical size of the works but the war itself transformed the demands placed on the firm. The government took over the whole business for war purposes and Geoffrey Barrett was given a position of responsibility for the country's output of ball bearings. In 1916 the company submitted plans for a substantial expansion of the works to the council. (9) Later in the year the company drafted further plans for a new power station as well as extensions to the grinding and hardening shops and new sewers. (10) German prisoners of war were used towards the end of the war to build the extensions. The company had its own fire engine which it lent to the borough on occasion during the war. Hoffmann bearings were used in every facet of armed forces equipment from gun turrets on ships, to biplanes and tanks. The most important bearings were magneto bearings which supported moving parts without any physical contact.

In his war diaries Andrew Clark noted that one thousand men were taken from the firm during the first war. This, combined with the big increase in demand, meant that there was a further influx of women into the factory. A training school for these female workers as well as males was started at Rosling's Garage in Springfield Road. The firm promised to re-engage all the men after the war that had either volunteered or were later conscripted into the forces. As with the Crompton Company, this meant that most of the wartime women workers were replaced by the returning men at the end of the war, but women retained an important role at the factory. They had proved good at vetting the products by eye.

Immediately after the war the company was hit by the railway strike which caused a serious shortage of steel. (11) Although the economic problems of the 1920s did affect the firm, the growth in demand for cars, particularly in the 1930s meant that the company wasn't hit by the depression to the same extent as firms in Britain's older industries elsewhere in the country. The company gained a great deal of positive publicity through its bearings being used in numerous record attempts e.g. Donald Campbell's Thunderbolt. "In 1930 the first five cars in the Le Mans 24 hour race were fitted with Hoffmann ball bearings." By 1938 4,500 men worked at the factory. At that time two workers had been at the firm since the beginning, over 40 years. Five men had over 35 years and 41 over 30 year's service. (12)

After the first war the general level of wages at Hoffmann fluctuated with varying levels of economic prosperity. In the early post war boom a general labourer, who was over 21, was paid three pounds, three shillings and two pence increasing by seven pence after six months. During the recession that followed however, wages were cut by a third. (13)

During the inter war period the firm developed its own 'sick club'. Membership of the company's Hospital and Benevolent Fund had increased by 700 in the first five years after 1918. (14) The company was against the contributory scheme which the Chelmsford and Essex Hospital started in the 1930s. By this time the pension scheme had been extended to the hourly rate men and most workers had joined it. (15) Hoffmann's works had its own surgery with a trained nurse and an ambulance because some accidents were inevitable, although the company prided itself on its low accident record. The women had a welfare superintendent available to them. Its canteen could accommodate 776 people at a time. The social and sporting clubs were run by employees but the facilities provided by the firm were second to none (See chapters 25 and 27)

G.F. Barrett retired in 1921. He died in 1923 leaving a fortune of £413,932. Low continued as Managing Director until he retired in 1925, after which C. Pryke and T.W. Cooper were appointed joint managing directors.

In 1928 it was announced that the Chelmsford works was to be extended again because the existing site had become too cramped. (16) E.G. Brown, the Assistant Works Manager, said in a speech in 1933 that both the electric and the gas plant at the works were bigger than those that supplied the town. The firm had three power stations. Brown had been at the firm since 1908. It was a worldwide business. "In the month of April alone consignments were dispatched to 38 countries. The biggest shop was the grinding shop with 500 people working there; the cage had 280 workers and the turret shop 280." There were 580 'viewers' who viewed the production process. This inspection department measured balls, bearings and components with specialist gauges to maintain standards of precision. Brown emphasised that the firm used only British steel from Sheffield. He went on to say "The social club is a great thing to stop communism and dissatisfaction. When you are playing cricket it doesn't matter whether you are the manager or a labourer you are all playing the same game." (17) By 1935 the site covered 26 and a half acres having grown from an original 3.7 acres. (18)

Fuelled by the growth of the motor and aeroplane industries, the company made record sales and an improved dividend of seven and a half percent on preference shares and nine percent on ordinary shares in 1937. (19) Most cars incorporated between 20 and 30 rolling bearings. By this time bearings were used to a greater or lesser extent on almost every industrial machine. Such differing mechanisms as telescopes, elevating gear, artificial limbs, tuning condensers, artificial silk spinning machinery and naval gun mountings all needed ball bearings. Ball bearings were also used in locomotives and railway trucks both at home and abroad. In 1934 London Transport ordered Hoffman 'axle boxes' for its new Piccadilly line coaches. Similar orders came from the Indian government.

Not everybody had the rose tinted view of the company as the management. F.W. Warner, who joined the firm as a shop boy straight from school at the age of 13 just before the first war, remembered discipline being very strict. He worked from 7.30 a.m until 12.0 noon, then re-started at 1.0 p.m. and worked until 6.0. p.m.. Initially there were no unions but he later joined one when they became established. Warner was unemployed for two years in the recession that followed the post war boom. He restarted his job on £3 a week in 1922. A Mrs Claydon worked at the Chelmsford works before she married at the age of 24 and was not allowed to continue. Her husband also worked there and went on to complete 33 years. Her work was to check for any flaws in the bearings. Clarence Clamp, also a local left school at 15 in 1923 when his uncle got him a job in the machine shop at Hoffmann. He loathed it, and left as soon as he could when a friend of his father found him a junior office position at the Chelmsford Star Co-operative.

Like many workers in the town between the wars, Percy Rainbird switched between firms. He started working for Crompton after the first war and played for their football team. His father had been a hod carrier when building work was carried out there. A friend of his father got him a job at Hoffmann after he had been at Crompton for two or three years. It was "low grade work", working on the lathes. He worked a basic 48 hour week with eight and three quarter hour shifts, working at weekends and some nights. In the early years he could not afford to go on the works outings, which cost ten shillings and he never saw the seaside. By the 1930s seven of the extended family were working at the works. Several of the women in the family were employed grading and sorting different sizes of balls. By the time he married at the age of 30 in the 1930s Percy's wages were 48 shillings a week. Rainbird managed to obtain a new council house, the rent on which was 13 shillings a week. Nearly all Percy's life was tied to Hoffmann in some way. He and his wife danced at the ballroom in the Hoffmann clubhouse and went to the whist drives. Rainbird played football for the Hoffmann Strollers. His wife was moved around from job to job but was then made supervisor.

This was a big step up because she was in charge of 60 people. Her department had to produce a certain amount of bearings of different sizes and made large bearings for searchlights in the second war. They had to work all hours during the war. After each bomb that fell on Hoffmann during the war, the damage was usually cleared up after a day, although it obviously took longer for production to recover. (See chapter 24)

Philip Bartlett, having been made unemployed by Crompton, was sent by the Labour Exchange to Hoffmann in 1938. During the second war he was on day shifts, which was much safer than the night shift, as the factory was hit four times. He fell into the habit of picking up shrapnel pieces and selling them for the 'Build a Spitfire' campaign. Like the Rainbirds, he was given a council house, in his case on the Melbourne estate. (20)

The company was keen after the second war to show that Marconi was not the only Chelmsford based company to have made a considerable contribution to the war effort. They produced a small book somewhat ironically title "We Also Helped" The book detailed the four serious attacks on the firms Chelmsford works in July 1942, October 1942, April 1943 and December 1944. (See chapter 24) It emphasised the debt the firm owed to the A.R.P. In total there were no less than 1,343 alerts at the factory. When the war broke out the firm was building its Stonehouse factory at Gloucester for high precision bearings. During the war both factories made vast quantities of bullet cores of different types. A new factory in Northern Ireland was used to make aircraft propeller bearings. Towards the end of the war bullet core production was concentrated at a London factory so that the Chelmsford works could concentrate on bearings. Modifications were made to the factory in an attempt to minimise the disruptive effect of an enemy attack on production and to enable easier increased production. High precision bearings for gyros and other instruments were made at another new factory 8 miles outside Chelmsford, at Witham.

"We also Helped" emphasised the use of Hoffmann bearings in a number of different types of aircraft. "The Cheetah engine uses 74 bearings in 15 different sizes. The Merlin engine took over 60 bearings. The Griffin uses 40 bearings." Many bearings were used on the controls. The Lancaster bomber used as many as 950 bearings in total and the Mosquito 190. "Behind the actual aircraft there are the bomb loading trolleys, bomb winches, arresting gear, aerodrome floodlights, fog dispellers." All of those needed a multitude of bearings. In the actual aircraft there were mechanisms for bearings of the highest precision. These included gyroscopes, air position indicators, revolution indicators, automatic pilots and cameras. Hoffmann made contributions towards other equipment. The Sten gun could not operate without Hoffmann bearings. Steel balls helped retain the fire control mechanism. The most popular field gun in the war used five journal bearings. Primers for shells used 1/8th inch copper balls. The company supplied 72 million during the war. Motor generators usually had 8 bearings and hand driven generators for portable radios, which were used extensively on aircraft, used two bearings. In tanks two journal bearings were used for carrying the tracks. Compressors used on air fighters and bombers to get compressed air to various instruments used two ball journal bearings. The landing wheels of aircraft, both the main wheels and the tail wheels used two ball bearings. In the turret ring in tanks there were 72 steel balls in each tank. The planetary gear assembly for armoured cars used a thousand steel rollers and the same mechanism in tanks used 240 such rollers. During the war predictors were extensively used in AA guns to predict the course of enemy aircraft. Each predictor used 23 ball journal bearings and 34 ball thrust bearings. In bomb release gear, the trigger had to rub against the diameter of a ball bearing. The movement between these parts had to be absolutely free to cut out any time lag between when the button was pressed and the release of the bomb. In the control panel for the automatic bomb distributor there were two ball journal bearings and one single thrust bearing. This was used when a bomb armer wanted to drop a line of bombs across a target. The distant reading compass used 11 ball journal bearings and this controlled all the various compass dials used by the crew. (21)

All of this extraordinary range of ball and roller bearings contributed to Hoffmann's expansion. During 1939 – 1945 the company manufactured two and a half thousand million balls and rollers and many hundreds of thousands of complete ball and roller bearings. Towards the end of the war the Chelmsford works was employing a never to be exceeded ten thousand workers. This was only possible because of the use of extensive night shift work. Besides the millions of bearings the works also produced 1,500 million bullet cores. Hoffmann was serving 1,800 meals a day at their canteen. (22)

In 1943 the joint managing director T.W. Cooper retired in 1943 to be followed by his fellow managing director C. Pryke two years later. John W Garton, who had joined the board from Brown Bayley in 1941, became chairman in 1947 and then managing director in 1948.

The end of the war and the energy shortages that followed caused a good deal of problems for the company. There was the added difficulty that a number of workers did not want to move from 'non productive' work to production in the factory. When a number of such workers were given notices to transfer to the factory, 160 decided to leave instead. During the war there had been a great increase in the number of indirect personnel. (23) It was very difficult to get new workers into the area because of the housing shortage. (See chapter 18) In 1946 there was a plan to move part of the production from Chelmsford to the factory at Gloucester. This was abandoned but the problem remained. (24)

In 1947 the fuel crisis forced the firm to go on a four day week. (25) This was made worse by the loss of major contracts among them one for Czechoslovakia. J.W. Garton, Hoffmann's managing director was already warning that "overseas markets are closing in on us". "Other cancellations are happening almost every day" he said, speaking at the Mayor's banquet. (26) The company opened new branch offices in Leicester, Newcastle, Bristol, Cardiff, Liverpool and Dundee, as well as two foreign subsidiary companies, Hoffmann Belge in Brussels and Hoffmann Kogellagers (Nederland) in Amsterdam. Later a sales manager was appointed for the new European Economic Community.

By 1948 post war employment at the Chelmsford works had settled at around 5,400 workers; of these 34% were women. By this time the world wide deficiency in bearings, brought about by the diversion to wartime production, was bringing a big increase in demand which helped mask the increasingly severe competition. (27) Along with Marconi, the firm benefitted from a huge order in 1952 for bearings for American Centurion tanks. (28) In the 1950s continued expansion in the demand for motor cars helped the company cope with further foreign competition. Even the Suez crisis failed to make a serious dent in the company's profits. (29) The following year however, saw a business recession result in a falling order book and the company's workers back on a four day week. (30)

Hoffmann updated its facilities in the 1950s. "Now whenever work is in progress, by night as well by day, a doctor with a fully staffed surgery and trained nurses at his command is available to deal with any emergency. Workers stricken down with ill health remain on the company's books whenever possible, for as long as two years during which their financial position need not concern them. On returning to normal health they are able ….. to be given work suitable to their condition." Because foot conditions were a frequent problem at the factory, a chiropodist was available at the factory at minimal cost. Forty to fifty staff used this every week. Mass radiography was a feature of the company's health scheme. Recognition of long service included extra holidays and a special gift after forty years of service. In 1955 the firm had the 7th lowest accident record of the big firms in the country. Out of 7 million working hours only 5 thousand were lost through accidents.

Most of the firm's employees at Chelmsford in the 1950s still lived within a ten mile radius of the works. With the co-operation of Eastern National, 26 double decker buses served the works morning and night. Some of these buses went as far as Southend, Kelvedon, Braintree and Dunmow. Lunchtime services enabled some workers to go home for a midday meal.

By this time the firm ran a number of training schemes. One was for those who had received some extended education and wanted to aim for a technical staff post. Another allowed a pre graduate apprentice to gain an advanced level certificate which would exempt him from the Intermediate BsC exam, if he intended working for an engineering degree. Most of the training itself was conducted in the works own training school which was under the supervision of a supervisor and his staff. "The school has a large workshop fitted with modern machine tools and equipment, and a classroom with a film projector where lectures and discussions are part of the set up." Hoffmann also offered training for university graduates who wanted to make engineering their career. Another scheme took girls from school and gave them commercial training for office work. (31) In 1959 the firm carried out a works quiz, "What do you think of the boss?" This was a psychological study which was ahead of its time. (32)

Hoffmann was still getting exposure from high profile projects. In 1960 publicity was no longer obtained from racing cars but from satellites. All three major works played a role in Britain's first spaceship. Hoffmann of course supplied the bearings. (33)

By the mid 1960's Hoffmann was being affected by industrial disputes. (See chapter 9) Small groups of workers could cause a good deal of disruption when they reacted to government policies. In 1967 100 members of a white collar union were involved in a dispute which restricted production. (34) Such disputes didn't help the firm's ability to withstand foreign competition, particularly from the Japanese. Profits, which had risen from £164,819 in 1946, £1,636,743 in 1952, and to £2,197,594 in 1962, fell to only £922,650 in 1965. (35)

The Labour government set up the Industrial Reorganisation Corporation (I.R.C.) to encourage and actually carry out rationalisation in industries like the ball bearing industry. In other countries the bearing industry was highly concentrated but the British industry had too many manufacturing companies with small production units. This was the reason the industry in Europe had an output of £3,000 per employee whereas in Britain it was £2,000. After the takeover of the Brown Bayley Company by the I.R.C., it obviously had Hoffmann in its sights, because the firm were suppliers of steel to Hoffmann. Norman St John Stevas said that the danger with rationalisation was "that mass produced, long run bearing lines could be moved to Nottinghamshire and Yorkshire". "This could result in mass unemployment." "Some of the most modern processes in the industry are at Hoffmann." "I understand the I.R.C. officials paid only a cursory visit to Hoffmann to reach a decision which could affect thousands of my constituent's lives." By the end of the year Brown Bayley owned 60% of the Hoffmann Company and hence the company was not in charge of its own destiny. (36) Seven months later came the news that Hoffmann was to merge with the Newark firm Ransome and Marle, in a move planned by the I.R.C. The managing director at Chelmsford, A. Garton said "we have known for some time that some work done at Newark could sensibly be done here and vice versa". His father, J.W. Garton was now chairman of the Hoffmann board and had connections with Brown Bayley Company. Ransome and Marle had already bid for the company Pollard Ball Bearings Limited. (37) Stevas again led a delegation to see Wedgewood Benn the Minister for Technology about the threat of redundancies at the Chelmsford works. (38)The response was that the Government wanted to see a wholly British owned corporation operating efficiently in European and world markets. Initially there was a reshuffle of management but no redundancies within the new Ransome, Hoffmann, Pollard group (R.H.P.) (39)

The reorganisation didn't prevent another decline in industrial relations at the Chelmsford works. Again it only took 90 D.A.T.A members embarking on a 'go slow' to cause serious disruption. The company responded by "locking out" 30 draughtsmen. Despite this, 1970 saw the company doing well with a 27% increase in productivity. In the new R.H.P. group the Chelmsford factory was, in the general bearings group, the largest division. (40) This showed in a change of production later in the year which saw Chelmsford lose roller bearing production to Newark but the production of single row ball bearings extended at Chelmsford. (41)

The following years however, saw the R.H.P. group struggling to beat off foreign competition. Increased mechanisation saw 190 redundancies at Chelmsford with a resulting deterioration in industrial relations. (42) Unions felt there was a lack of communication between management and workers. They banned overtime, fearing further redundancies. The Chairman of the group pleaded with the Government to restrict Japanese imports of bearings. (43) He made the promise that the remaining 2, 800 jobs were "completely safe". Two million pounds was being spent on installing new plant and machinery at the works. (44) In 1973 5,000 people saw a fully automated bearing assembly line as part of an open day. Automation was now used in every point in the process from the steel tubes at the start, to the finished bearing. (45) The same year however, saw the company introduce a 3 day week as a result of the national power cuts which affected all the works in the area. (46)

R.H.P turned down a leading Japanese company's offer of a joint enterprise in Britain. The latter were then were granted permission to build a £6.5 million plant in a development area. (47) R.H.P. had only two years, while the factory was being built, to come up with a new manufacturing strategy. It did collaborate with a Japanese firm to build a huge telescope in Australia and also tried to diversify, taking over MTE Rayleigh, a firm making electric control gear in 1975. (48) Another rationalisation programme saw the number of office staff reduced. (49)

In 1974 the group had complained again about the level of foreign imports. This time Russian firms had been given the contract for supplying ball bearings for new British tanks. Deliberate overproduction in Eastern European countries was leading to a 'ball bearing mountain' being unloaded in Britain and other Western European countries. (50) The opening of the Japanese factory in Durham immediately caused a four day week at the Chelmsford works. Only three months earlier the factory had been working six days a week. Profits had suffered a big fall by 1981 and production fallen by a third. During that year the company shed 400 workers at the Chelmsford factory, leaving 1,500 remaining. (51) This still left the plant with overcapacity.

In 1989 the Chelmsford works was finally closed. Its bearing works were transferred to Newark, Notts. The R.H.P. group had been sold to a city consortium the previous year. "Chelmsford had been selected for closure because of the severe underutilisation of the large plant and continuing difficulties in retraining skilled staff." In the 1950s "the Chelmsford plant had been designed for larger production runs when it employed about four thousand people and the U.K. market was twice what it is today".(52) Plans to relocate the remaining workers from Chelmsford proved difficult because many workers didn't wish to move.

The R.H.P. site was first earmarked for office and high technology development but the developers went into receivership. Housing had already been built on the old Hoffmann sports ground. In 1992 it was announced that Anglia Polytechnic was to use the R.H.P. site. The first building of the soon to be Anglia Ruskin University was opened in 1993. It was ironic that, in the very year of the works closure a blue plaque to commemorate the Hoffmann Company was announced.

1) Essex Chronicle 14 8 1964 200 years memorial issue p.57
2) Chelmsford Borough Council minutes 25 5 1898
3) Essex Chronicle '40 years of progress' 4 3 1938 p.3
4) The Story of Hoffmann 1898 – 1969 M.E. Cobbold, Publicity Manager of the Hoffmann Company
5) Lecture given by T.W. Cooper, Managing Director of the Hoffmann Company, to the Chelmsford Lecture Society at the YMCA Hall on 27th February 1934
6) E.C. Memorial issue p.57
7) The Hoffmann employment register, Chelmsford Museums Sandford Mill records,
8) E.C. 17 11 1910 p.2
9) C.B.C. minutes 29 3 1916
10) C.B.C. 25 10 1916
11) E.C. 26 12 1919 p.3
12) E.C. 4 3 1938 p.3
13) Essex Weekly News 9 1 1920
14) E.W.N. 16 2 1923 p.5
15) E.C. 26 3 1937 p.2
16) E.W.N. 2 11 1928 p.7
17) E.W.N. 2 6 1933 p.10
18) E.W.N. 20 8 1935 p.9
19) E.C. 26 3 1937 p.2
20) Essex Record Office – Oral history records
21) 'We Also Helped' – Hoffmann
22) E.C. 4 1 1946 p.2
23) E.W.N. 5 7 1946 p.2
24) E.W.N. 23 8 1946 p.7
25) E.W.N. 7 2 1947 p.8
26) E.C. 3 6 1949 p.1
27) E.W.N. 16 4 1948 p.5
28) E.C. 19 12 1952
29) E.C. 10 5 1957 p.7
30) E.C. 6 6 1958 p.4
31) E.W.N. 4 5 1957 p.2
32) E.W.N. 10 9 1959

33) E.C. 3 6 1960 p.17
34) E.W.N. 3 3 1967 p.1
35) M.E. Cobbold p.65
36) E.W.N. 14 2 1969 p.1
37) E.W.N. 16 5 1969 p.1
38) E.W.N. 6 1 1969 p.1
39) E.W.N. 10 6 1969 p.1
40) E.C. 2 1970
41) E.C. 1 5 1970 p.1
42) E.W.N. 9 4 1971
43) E.C. 21 1 1972 p.13
44) E.C. 20 10 1972 p.1
45) E.W.N. 6 9 1973 p.7
46) E.W.N. 20 12 1973 p.1
47) E.W.N. 27 2 1974 p.3
48) E.W.N. 20 11 1975 p.3
49) E.C. 18 4 1975 p.1
50) E.C. 5 8 1977 p.1
51) E.C. 22 10 1982 p.1 and 6
52) E.C. 4 11 1988 p.1

8

Chelmsford Industry after the Second War – Britvic and EEV

'Conveyor belts jammed with bottles whizz behind Perspex screens at dizzying speeds'

The period since the second war has seen the demise of the four biggest industrial employers in Chelmsford. From the 1950s onwards there was a big increase in the number of adults not working in the town but in the main commuting into London. By the new millennium most people who worked in the town worked in the service sector: this was predominantly administration, insurance, banking, entertainment and retailing. The town has benefitted from rent levels that are lower than those in London and good schools make it easier to attract staff. As we shall see in the next chapter however, the decline of employment, particularly in the three big industrial firms caused severe structural employment problems in the town in the 1980s and 1990s. These difficulties would however been much greater without the survival and expansion of the two major remaining manufacturing firms, Britvic and EEV. Both had their origins in the town before 1945, Britvic as far back as the mid 19th century and EEV (now e2v) originally as part of Marconi, developing as it did the early prototypes of valves which were to become EEV's main lines of production. Both however, achieved their present form after the war. Britvic was essentially the creation of Ralph Chapman and has survived and prospered despite numerous takeovers, mergers and lateral aggregations. Although Britvic had other factories and its administrative base away from the town its main production base remained in Chelmsford, until the shock announcement of the closure of its Widford factory in 2014. EEV survived the end of the Cold War in the early 1990s, which initially decimated its order book because over 70% of its sales were connected with defence. Again it now has several factories away from Chelmsford, including one in France.

Britvic can definitely be traced back to a chemist shop run by a borough councillor James Tomlinson at 2 Tindal Square in the 1890s, although it is probable that its origins were even earlier in the middle of the century. The 1892 edition of Kelly's Directory lists Tomlinson as a chemist, druggist, mineral water manufacturer and interestingly an artificial manure merchant. Tomlinson moved the business way from upstairs at the shop to Cottage Place off Victoria Road. The 1902 entry in Kelly's has Tomlinson's premises being used solely as a chemist shop. Tom Turner remembered there being a small factory at Cottage Place during the Edwardian period. (1) In the Victorian period soft drinks became increasingly popular partly because of strong opposition to heavy drinking. 'Effervescent' concoctions were based on injecting carbon dioxide into drinks. New bottle stopping techniques meant that industrial production was possible. In most towns like Chelmsford however, production was on a very small scale often above pharmacists such as Tomlinson's. Tomlinson would have sold his tonics, lemonades and other soft drinks to his local customers along with his other products. He mixed fruit juices, sugar and other ingredients. By the early twentieth century the firm, now called British Vitamin Products, was based at the premises off Victoria Road.

Ralph Chapman was born in India but in the late 1930s after a spell as an electrical engineer he was looking for a business with potential to invest in. He recognised that the Depression had affected the health of many people in the country and therefore the firm he chose was British Vitamin Products. Chapman bought the existing business from J. Macpherson. His aim was to bottle fruit juices with concentrated vitamin C then sell them at affordable prices. In 1938 he started producing bottles at Victoria Road using a method which did not require using preservatives. A tomato cocktail produced that year did well enough to convince him he was on the right track. Chapman was making plans for a proper production line when the war broke out. He spent the conflict doing further research and making plans. (2) The product was re-launched in 1949 and tested first on the people of Chelmsford, Colchester and Brentwood. The firm grew very rapidly. In 1949 the firm employed 80 people at the Victoria Road works, but by 1954 this had increased to 800 and production was already getting too big for the existing works. Profits had increased from £2,352 to £304,533. (3) The quick expansion led to increasing complaints about conditions at the factory. For a while the nightshift had to be discontinued. (4) The firm made an application to acquire a larger site on the new Widford business park than they had originally been promised. (5)

In 1954 Chapman, perhaps surprisingly, decided to sell British Vitamin Products to Vine Products, the maker of V.P. Wines and Babycham. He received £1 million; not a bad return on his original small investment of a few thousand pounds. Chapman sold the business partly because the firm, even when its new factory at Widford was completed, would still have been too small to cope with the rapid increase in the demand for its products. He chose to sell rather than convert it into a public limited company. British Vitamins Products needed the expertise and capital of a larger firm behind it. Chapman remained managing director for a time but severed all connections with the fruit drinks industry in 1955. (6)

The first part of the new factory was built in the record time of 47 weeks, began production in May 1955, cost half a million pounds and immediately employed 500 people. It was reckoned to be the most modern fruit juice factory in the world. It could produce 250 thousand bottles of fruit juice a day. Huge storage tanks were built underground; meanwhile at Wembley the firm was already making automatic vending machines for its products. (7)

British Vitamin Products' continued expansion was of course helped by the boom in soft drinks in the 1950s. The advent of television played an important role in this. People needed something to drink when they were watching on the couch. During the start of commercial television and T.V. advertising opened the door to advertising by companies such as Britvic. Britvic regularly slashed its workforce in the winter months because it was the off season for many of its products. (8)

In 1961 Britvic became part of a larger group when V.P. merged with Showerings and Waterways. It was only a matter of time before this group was absorbed by a large alcoholic and non alcoholic drinks conglomerate and in 1968 Allied Breweries bought the firm for £100 million. Britvic then became Allied's operating company for its soft drinks division. In 1971 British Vitamins Products formally changed its name to Britvic. The link with a major brewer gave Britvic access to a nationally operating network of 'tied pubs'. This spurred the company to develop new products. In 1973 it launched a new brand of mixer drinks. Britvic also developed its own range of diet drinks starting with Slimsta in the early 1970s. In 1972, to take further advantage of the Allied Breweries pub network, it launched draught versions of its most popular soft drinks. Later the company launched Britvic 55 which was only available in pubs.

Britvic, like other U.K. soft drink producers was coming under pressure from U.S. competition. Coca Cola and Pepsi had been produced in the U.K. in the 1950s under licence. Britvic obtained the licence to sell Doctor Pepper in 1987, spending £600,000 to launch the new brand. The company was however suffering from intense competition. Half of the shares of Britvic were sold to Alan Bond's Australian conglomerate, Castlemain Tooley's. After a swift revival in the fortunes of the British company it was again sold, this time to the Bass group. It was then merged with Canada Dry Rawlings (C.D.R.) which produced the R. Whites brand. The new company was called Britvic Soft Drinks Limited. This was after the merger had been examined by the Office of Fair Trading. The new company was responsible for 9% of the British soft drinks market. Bass was in control of the company. C.D.R.'s offices at Kettering were closed and the newly merged company was run from Britvic's administrative offices in Broomfield Road. (9) The merger was quickly followed by another change of name to Britvic Corona. (10) In the same year, 1986, the company acquired the Tango brand. The advertising image was quickly changed for the latter to target the youth market. In 1995 Tango twice featured in the top 5 most complained about TV adverts. One advert showed Tango drinkers with their heads being blown off.

In 1987 Britvic made a major step forward by obtaining the U.K. production and bottling rights for Pepsi. The company also acquired the rights to produce and sell Seven Up, which Pepsi had only recently acquired. The deal worked for both companies because Pepsi, which had struggled to make headway in the U.K. market, soon established a strong market showing. In 1994 Bass appeared set to sell its 51% share in Britvic under pressure from the Monopolies Commission. The deal failed to go through however, after disagreement between the various parties, which also involved Allied-Lyons and Whitbread. (11) After this the company continued to look for new expansion possibilities obtaining the licence for launching Lipton Ice in Britain. In 1995 Britvic bought a major U.K. soft drinks rival, Robinsons. The latter had a history even longer than Britvic, going back to the early nineteenth century as Robinson and Bellville. With Britvic's marketing expertise Robinson began a major period of expansion. In 2000 Britvic bought Orchid Drinks which brought further brands to the company including Ame, Purdey's and Aqua Libra. The company entered the rapidly expanding bottled water market in 2001, when it acquired the marketing rights for Abbey Well in parts of the U.K. In 2002 it bought 'Red Devil' to get a share in the new market for 'stimulant' drinks.

In the mid 2000s Britvic's position again looked precarious when Bass announced its intention to sell its parent company Britannia Soft Drinks. Pepsi however, which owned 10% of Britvic shares and vitally owned the Pepsi brand in the U.K., was reluctant to let the company get into the hands of private equity groups. This it was felt might lead Coco Cola to obtain control of Britvic, Pepsi's U.K. bottler. Bass reversed their original decision. Britvic's intention to list on the Stock Exchange was also abandoned. Despite these various uncertainties an expansion was carried out at the Widford factory. A new high speed production line for Robinson Fruit Shoot led to a 17% increase in production in 2005. By this time Britvic had risen to be the second biggest producer of soft drinks in the U.K. (12)

By 2012 the Britvic site at Widford covered 15 acres, with its art deco clock tower still instantly recognisable to car passengers passing by. "Entering through the high green gates, conveyor belts jammed with bottles whizz behind Perspex screens at dizzying speeds while they are filled with colourful liquids, stamped with caps and smacked with labels." "Pipes and tubes churn out clouds of fruity aromas with members of staff kitted out in the trademark green coats, hard hats and blue hairnets, assessing each and every process that allow the 13 million cases of soft drink to be produced every year." In 2012 most of the staff lived in Chelmsford. By then it was producing with a Royal Warrant. There were production lines creating well known brands such as Pepsi, J2O and Fruit Shoot. "Each of lines produces thousands of litres an hour before automatically cleaning themselves before moving on to the next batch." Manufacturing manager Craig Sinclair said the process from start to finish took less than 10 minutes for mixing, pasteurisation and packaging. "On each of the lines, the drinks process starts at the beginning of the week with the diet, light in colour, fizzy drinks before moving on to the sugary, dark and more viscous products towards the end of the week." As with the previous big three firms in the town it was not uncommon for several generations of the same family to have worked for the firm by 2012.

Although the headquarters of the firm were moved to Hemel Hempstead, the firm remained a major employer at Widford despite having five factories elsewhere in the country. (13) Late in 2012 yet another merger was announced between Barr and Britvic. Barr are the Scottish manufacturer of Irn Bru. Britvic shareholders were to have 63% of the new company, Barr Britvic Limited, although its headquarters would now be in Cumbernauld. The company was strong enough to withstand this change as well as the enforced recall of Robinson Fruit Shoots in 2012 because of a safety issue with new packaging. This merger was on hold as it was being investigated by the Office of Fair Trading when early in 2013 the shock announcement that the Britvic factory at Chelmsford was to close was made. Two hundred and twenty seven people were employed at the factory. The decision was announced at a time when the company's

Fruit Shoots were increasingly being produced in France and a new factory was being established in Ireland.

The English Electric Valve Company (EEV) had its roots in Marconi research before the second war. Marconi had developed a vacuum laboratory for the production of valves. It used a corner of the New street factory and was run by Doctor George M. Brett. "The vacuum laboratory as I took it over was a single room, maybe 20ft by 25 ft which contained a diffusion pump outfit, glass bench, spot welder, hydrogen furnace, my desk and little else. The place was gloomy, claustrophobic and I thought a poor exchange for the HH Wills Physics Lab which I had just left in the summer." (14) Marconi's agreement with G.E.C. and E.M.I. prevented them from producing valves in the 1930s. For this reason the company established a factory in Czechoslovakia 1936. Jim Young went from the New Street Laboratory to take charge of production in that factory. The New Street laboratory was moved to Great Baddow but then taken over by the government when the war broke out. This produced the stabilovolt valve mentioned in chapter 5. Magnetron production, a key component in radar, started in 1940; however limited space caused Marconi to establish a manufacturing base at Waterhouse Lane, which was to become the centre of EEV after the war. After 1945 the demand for defence radar valves disappeared and the workforce at Waterhouse Lane declined from 450 to 150. (15)

A separate company had to be formed in 1947 away from Marconi to produce valves because the latter was still bound by the agreement not to produce valves, even after the takeover by English Electric. Initially the new company was known as the Phoenix Dynamo Company Ltd, but before one financial year was completed this was changed to English Electric Valves Limited. (E.E.V) (16) Most of the new company's orders were from Marconi in the first year but there was one from a French company. Soon the occasional order came from English Electric. Jim Young, back from Czechoslovakia, became a founding member of E.E.V. He and Maurice Esterson, an engineer who had joined Marconi in 1940 and spent the rest of his career at E.E.V., turned their attention to civil radar. (17) The company produced the first hydrogen thyratron which was used in radio receivers. EEV also started producing shutter tubes, which enabled pictures to be taken of x ray exposures. In the early 1950s the company started producing image orthicons which convert light into electronic signals in a television camera. The firm provided these for the cameras used in the TV broadcast of the Coronation. EEV also produced a new type of klystron used by Marconi in their transmitters at the new Crystal Palace station. (18) When the company became the biggest producer of orthicons in the country, the Waterhouse Lane factory had to be expanded. In 1952 for example, image orthicons were exported to Canada, Spain and Bolivia as well as being installed at the United Nations. They were also used in the first studio broadcasts by the BBC from the new Studio E at Lime Grove. (19) Two hundred and fifty thousand image orthicons had been produced by the company when production of these devices stopped in 1982.

Jim Young became general manager of E.E.V. in 1956. He replaced Simon Aseinstein, who had escaped from the Russian revolution and had risen within E.E.V. to become general manager. (20) In the 1950s, with enormous technological advances being made, most of the workers were women who had the manual dexterity required. Better cathode technology enabled the company to provide cathodes for televisions. The company produced magnetrons for civil radar which had a longer lifespan than their military predecessors. As with Marconi, the onset of the Cold War meant that military demand for the firm's products soon picked up. Image orthicons were adapted for use for underwater cameras. They were first used to identify a submarine. By the end of the 1950s EEV employed about 200 people. Its turnover was £2.5 million. (21)

The early 1960s saw a big expansion and increase in the variety of the firm's products fuelled by strong leadership by Jim Young. He achieved a balance of civil and military contracts, whilst also ensuring that exports remained healthy. The AEI Valve Company was acquired in London. A new factory was built in Maldon which opened in 1961. In a bid to further relieve pressure on the Waterhouse Lane factory, a factory was built at Benfleet but it soon closed in 1968. (22) In 1962 offices were opened in Toronto and New York. (23)

In 1968 after the G.E.C. takeover of English Electric, E.E.V. was merged with the G.E.C. Marconi Osram Valve Company. The company escaped the "Weinstock purge" mainly because Weinstock had faith in Young. By the end of the 1960s E.E.V. was producing over 200 different types of magnetron. (24) Five hundred of the company's klystrons were in use in TV transmitting stations around the world. (25) They were also used as oscillators in radar receivers and the Doppler radar used in navigation and speed measuring equipment. The 1960s saw the rapid expansion of the company's workforce to over 2,000. Two hundred of them were engineers and physicists, most of them graduates. Pressure of space saw the company bid for the old Crompton Parkinson site. Most of this site was taken over by Marconi but E.E.V. was given a small part of the rebuilt factory. (26) In 1968 the firm won a Queen's Award for Industry for the high degree of accuracy of its image orthicons. (27)

Despite this overall success the late 1960s saw the first signs of industrial unrest at the Chelmsford factory. A walk out by AEU workers in September 1968 was followed by a work to rule by the draughtsmen at Waterhouse Lane a few months later. (28) Just over a year later there was a full blown strike by 1,150 workers over pay. They came back for a day to qualify for holiday pay! (29) The workers were able to use their industrial muscle to get large pay increases several times in the 1970s.

By the early 1970s the Waterhouse Lane factory was ten times larger than it had been in 1947. Two further units were built on the site. By 1980 its space at the old Crompton works was open, as well as a previously empty factory which it took over at Witham. (30) Twenty years previously its main customers had been the U.K. government, Marconi and Decca but by the early 1970s it was selling a wide variety of power valves, microwave tubes and light conversion techniques to hundreds of customers from all over the world. The biggest export market was North America.

In the 1970s the company helped produce the thermal imaging camera and it was also involved with the development of the first full colour TV screens for outside events, which were known as Starvision. (31) These, using liquid crystal displays, were the earliest version of the large screen TV screens that are today such a part of outdoor events. The company also provided LCD s (liquid crystal displays) for TV game shows such as Family Fortunes, The Price Is Right, 15 to 1 and Bob's Full House. Later LEDs caught up with the Starvision technology and within a decade E.E.V. stopped producing its large screens. In October 1981 the company announced a takeover of the LCD division from a subsidiary of Westlands Aircraft Limited. Its manufacture of liquid crystal displays was transferred to the E.E.V. part of the Crompton site. During the 1970s big developments in the company's image intensifiers for night vision occurred. Initially they had weighed several pounds and were not easy to move. The second generation of this equipment was much more compact. (32) War in the Falklands resulted in a camera that could see through smoke and a camera for use specifically by fire fighters.

The 1980s saw strong progress in the company. There was a sense of community that perhaps hadn't been there in the 1970s. On one occasion there was a terrible August thunderstorm at the weekend. The company put out a message on the local radio asking for the employees to go in to work. Lydia Bridges recalled "going in just as we were, in shorts, with our wellies on". Everybody helped including management. "We worked non-stop to save all the electronic equipment." "We all felt that we were part of the E.E.V. family". (33)

The company won a £40 million order for its third generation intensifiers in 1986, securing work for 130 people. (34) Four hundred new jobs were created during the following year, 375 of them at Chelmsford. (35) In 1990 however, a recession resulted in 250 job losses overall. (36) The company's policy of long term development of new products did see returns in the long run but the end of the Cold War caused problems because 70% of its business was still defence related. This was something that Jim Young had worked hard to avoid.

New products allowed a slimmed down E.E.V. to gradually get back to acceptable levels of profitability. In 1990 it launched Nite-Watch, a pocket sized night vision viewer which was immediately popular with police forces in the U.K. and abroad. They also produced the first dental CCDs, which produced instant X rays of dental work. This removed the need to develop film and reduced X ray doses by 80%. The company supplied image sensors for several space missions and in 1984 it launched the light compact Stellar satellite communication amplifier, used to send live news across the globe. It was soon popular for use at outside events such as the Tour De France and was used for the BBC live broadcast of an ascent of Everest. This was followed by the next generation of the fire and rescue camera. The company's revival was helped by increasing demand for established products such as magnetrons and klystrons. (37)

This growth resulted in another expansion at the Waterhouse Lane complex. The company invested £1.2 million to double the floor space in 1993. (38) Further investment was also put into a new training centre. (39)

EEV briefly became Marconi Applied Technologies (M.A.T.) in 1999 when G.E.C. sold off its defence interests to BAE to focus on telecommunications. (See chapter 6) The collapse of the dot com boom had a dramatic effect on Marconi shares and an initially equally severe effect on the renamed company. M.A.T. did not really fit in the new Marconi telecom group because of its defence and fire fighting interests. (40) An attempt at selling the company came to nothing and attention turned to a possible management buyout. This started in 2001 and was completed by 2002. The buyout was backed by the venture company 3i. It was made easier by the fact that the business was profitable and had a high level of orders (41) The new company was immediately named e2v technologies after a deal was worth £42 million. (42) "The company is a worldwide leader in thermal imaging and components for space cameras" the Essex Chronicle commented. Only two years afterwards e2v was floated on the Stock Exchange and became a public limited company.

It was felt that the company needed to expand quickly and in 2005 the £5 million pound Gresham Scientific Instruments was taken over. This was renamed as e2v Scientific Instruments. The following year e2v bought Atmel Corporations facility in Grenoble for £76 million. Atmel's semi-conductor activities meshed well with e2v's and reflected the fact the company had a large market in France. e2v garnered prestige in 2001 by supplying CCDs for the Hubble space telescope upgrade. (43) In 2005 the company opened the e2v centre for electronic imaging at Brunel University. (44)

By 2006 the company had doubled its sales figures in three years, with orders from Germany now outstripping those from France. In 2007 e2v was helping to improve cancer treatment with its compact solid state modulator for radiotherapy equipment. "About 90% of the world's radiotherapy machines are reliant on components coming out of Chelmsford." (45) e2v CCD sensors were used on the Gaia satellite sent in 2011 to provide a 3D map of the galaxy. Defence technology represented a smaller percentage of total production by the new millennium but both the Chelmsford and Grenoble factories were involved in the Eurofighter programme. (46) The company received yet another Queen's Award for Industry in 2007 for its L3 Vision, low level imaging technology, the Argus 4 a thermal imaging camera for fire fighters and for its involvement in the Gaia project. (47) By 2011, e2v had contributed 106 CCDs for the enterprise which was involved in making a 3D map of our Milky Way galaxy. (48) In 2013 the firm made four image sensors costing one million pounds each for NASA's IRIS project. They were built to withstand extreme conditions and used to take pictures of the sun. In May 2012 Prime Minister David Cameron and Deputy Prime Minister Nick Clegg visited e2v after its 'Pro wave' project was given a £6 million grant from the Regional Growth Fund. (49)

Despite this progress, the firm was not unaffected by the economic downturn following the banking crisis. In 2009 employees agreed to work three days a week "in a drastic attempt to save jobs". This was after losses of £28 million. Workers blamed the company's poor position on the over expensive purchase of the French company Atmel in 2001 which had cost £70 million. The weakness of the pound had also contributed to the company's previous profits of £13 million being wiped out. (50) 2010 saw a revival in its order books however.

Apart from e2v and Britvic, the main industrial employers by the early 2,000s were BAE Systems. They are still based at the old Marconi research site in Great Baddow and were responsible for the new Ionosphere Forecast System that has been instrumental in improving weather forecasts. In 2013 the company was conducting research to help paralympics athletes by improving the wheels they use.

By the immediate post war period the expansion of the big engineering firms in the area had meant that there was a readily available supply of skilled labour in the town. This and the increased possibility of sub contract work resulted in the establishment of a number of new engineering and related manufacturing firms.

Horner and Wells was a firm of mechanical engineers founded in 1949 on Moulsham Street by D.J. Horner and E.C. Wells. They remained directors of the firm into the 1970s. The business owed its existence to the big engineering firms in the town. Early contracts were specialist items for Marconi, Crompton, Hoffmann and the Christy Group, making machines and gaskets for waveguides, which are hollow conductive metal pipes used to carry high frequency radio waves, particularly micro waves, metal fabrications for large valves and sheet metal radio equipment consoles. In the 1950s the firm developed a machine for measuring the strength of concrete on site, which was exported to 63 countries. In the 1960s this became the backbone of the business. In 1960 the firm moved to the Widford Industrial Estate. There it built a huge 400 ton down stroke hydraulic press. This was used for contract work straightening large steelwork. The firm diversified into making metal sculptures for artists. Its sculpture at the Royal Free Hospital in Hampstead was supposed to be the largest moving one in existence. It rotated on an RHP bearing. At the time Horner and Wells employed 50 people. Production was organised so that one worker saw a job through from start to finish. In the 1990s the company, in conjunction with a specialist at Brompton Hospital, designed a negative pressure unit for premature babies. (51) The firm still existed in 2013.

Another small light engineering firm was A.R. Cornell Limited, specialising in tool making and sub contracting work, which was established in 1964 on Navigation Road. One of its products was a injector food pump widely used in the food preserving industry. The firm supplied brackets for the fibreglass roofs of heavy goods vehicles and hydraulic spool valves to a tractor company. It also produced the tools for the manufacture of bottle openers.

Thanet Engineering Company Limited, established on Viaduct Road in 1966, was for a while one of the biggest trolley manufacturers in the country, making 1,000 trolleys a week and exporting to South Africa, Belgium, Eire , Hong Kong and France. Highfield Timber and Mouldings Ltd. were manufacturing precision mouldings in the late 1960s on a one and a half acre site at the Widford Industrial estate, after being an old established family business in central London. Timber was moulded for picture frames, radio television cabinets, display fitting, educational toys and furniture.

The results of the borough's and the county council's attempts to develop new businesses in the area have been mixed. Chelmsford Business Park, developed in the 1980's, promoted its links between London and the port of Felixstowe. One firm that did set up in the Business Park was Global Marine Systems, which had a history in underwater cables going back 150 years. The E.C.C.'s drive to promote the Springfield Lyon site as a 'silicon valley' was opposed by the borough council and never really took off. In 2012 plans were announced for a high tech business park, the Anglia Ruskin Medical Technology campus. This will be situated between the University and Broomfield hospital. It is hoped it will rival medical technology parks in Silicon Valley, California and other parts of the U.S. The partnership is a collaboration between Anglia Ruskin University and Chelmsford, Harlow and Southend councils. It is the first of its kind in Britain and building is scheduled to start in 2014.

As the manufacturing sector in the town has shrunk, the tertiary sector has continued to grow in the town with large investment and insurance companies like M and G attracted to the town. The building of two shopping centres (with a third in the pipeline) has increased the amount of retail employment in the town.

1) Chelmsford Museum Records – Oral history – Tom Turner
2) www.fundinguniverse.com/company-histories/Britannia-Soft-Drinks-Ltd-Britvic
3) Essex Weekly News 15 10 1954 p.1
4) Chelmsford Borough Council minutes 25 7 1951
5) C.B.C. minutes 25 4 1951
6) E.W.N. 21 10 1955
7) E.W.N. 2 1 1955 p.7
8) E.W.N. 10 10 1955 p.1
9) E.W.N. 20 2 1986 p.1
10) E.W.N. 20 11 1986 p.1
11) E.W.N. 13 1 1994 p.2
12) E.C. 9 2 2006
13) E.C. 14 6 2012 p.22 – 23
14) e2v Celebrating 60 years of bright ideas 1947 – 2007 Felicity Landon p.2
15) e2v p.6
16) e2v p.1
17) e2v p.11

18) e2v p.15
19) e2v p.13
20) E.C. 18 5 1956 p.11
21) e2v p.18
22) e2 p.29
23) e2v p.17
24) e2v p.30
25) e2v p.31
26) E.W.N. 7 3 1968 p.8
27) E.W.N. 20 4 1972 p.4
28) E.C. 20 9 1968 and 10 1 1969
29) E.C. 22 5 1970
30) e2v p.33
31) e2v p.43
32) e2v p.34
33) e2v p.44
34) E.W.N. 16 10 1986 p.1
35) E.W.N. 11 8 1987 p.1
36) E.W.N. 23 8 1980 p.1
37) e2v p.60
38) E.W.N. 31 7 1997 p.1
39) E.C. 18 10 1993 p.6
40) e2v p.71
41) E2V p.72-3
42) E.C. 19 7 2002 p.1
43) e2v p.79
44) e2v p.80
45) e2v p.93
46) e2v p.90
47) e2v p.92
48) E.C. 13 10 2011 p.10
49) E.C. 11 5 2012 p.4 - 5
50) E.C. 11 6 2009 p.1
51) Chelmsford firms Chelmsford Museums records Sandford Mill

9

Trade unions, the Chelmsford Star Co-operative and Employment

"Work is what we want; we demand justice; the right to an honest living"

This, the last of the chapters in this book directly related to industry in Chelmsford, looks at the history of the areas' trade unions, its Trades Council, the history of employment and unemployment in the area and the town's unique Chelmsford Star Co-operative. This co-operative has played a big role in the local community for almost 150 years. The trade union movement was slow to get established in the town until the years immediately before the first war. Chelmsford's rapid industrial growth then led to several unions becoming permanent. At least two of the town's big firms remained resolutely anti union and did everything they could to prevent unions from gaining a firm foothold. Similarly the area's Trades Council, first founded in 1899, retained a very precarious existence, ceasing to operate several times, before finally becoming well established in the 1930s.The rapid industrialisation in the 25 years before 1914, started to lay the town's workforce, many of whom had only recently come off the land, open to the vagaries of the trade cycle. After the war the depression was a severe example of this, affecting all the town's big firms. In the inter war period however, unemployment in general was not as severe as in other towns in the county and, particularly, in other parts of the country. Public works schemes did a good deal to minimise the worst effects of depression in the area. After a quiet period in the 1950s, the 1960s and 1970s saw all the main firms in the town affected by industrial relations problems. In part this was due to national economic problems. It was also however, the result of the paternalistic style of management of several of these firms disappearing. Large numbers of the town's workforce no longer felt the same connection with their employers that had been the case in previous generations. The decline of Chelmsford's industrial base in the 1980s and 1990s caused major problems in the town. Eventually however the restructuring of the area's employment resulted in most people of working age in the Chelmsford area, either commuting to London and other Essex towns, or being employed in the town's service sector.

The Chelmsford Star Co-operative (C.S.C.S.) was formed in 1867 but it had its roots in the Chelmsford Coal Club formed in 1847, only 3 years after the start of the co-operative venture of the Rochdale Pioneers. This club had been necessary because of the difficulty of heating working class homes during the winter when the price of coal rose dramatically. For twenty years the society prospered but increasingly members of the coal club could buy coal just as cheaply from other sources. By 1869 membership had fallen from 600 to 200 and the Club was dissolved with its small balance being donated to the local infirmary. At the time Chelmsford had about two thousand working men and the more affluent of them would have belonged to Friendly Societies. (1)

When the Chelmsford Star Co-operative was formed the town was extremely well provided for in terms of shops. There were 32 bakers and flour dealers, 11 coal and timber merchants, 21 grocers and tea dealers, 39 boot and shoe shops and 31 butchers. (2) The problem therefore was not one of getting goods; it was the difficulty of obtaining them at the right price and of decent quality. Adulteration of food was still rife in the town. Thomas Chapman, who worked at the Coleman and Morton Ironworks, suggested setting up a co-operative. Eighteen Coleman and Morton workers met in 1866 to discuss the issue. In March, 150 workers met at the Mechanics Institute to establish the venture. Shares were £1 each and no member was allowed to have more than 100 shares. A shop was soon leased in Tindal Street and townsfolk were immediately attracted by the quality of goods stocked. In September 1867 a customer dividend of 3 pence was approved. This rose to one shilling and two pence by 1871. For several decades prominent shopkeepers remained bemused how a shop which gave away a large part of its profits could be successful. Letters to the local paper showed how much the local traders felt threatened. (3) It was soon ready to start its own bakery. The opposition of the town's traders and the economic depression of the 1870s made life difficult for the new organisation, but the establishment of the Co-operative Wholesale Society (CWS) made it easier for the Chelmsford Society to get supplies. In 1880, with the depression receding, the society decided to build a new shop on the site of the present Quadrant store on Moulsham Street. On the ground floor was the grocery department, with the assembly rooms above and the stables and bakery at the back. At the end of the 1880s the Society started a butchery business but it had to close after two years because of continuous losses. In 1892 the Moulsham Street building was extended. The Society took the opportunity to install electric lighting which was carried out by Frank Christy who put in 50 electric lamps. In the same year the C.S.C.S. started its own coal delivery service. (4) A plot of land on the corner of Railway Street and Wells Street was bought for £380 for the coal yard and stables. Some of the land was used for the Cooperative's first branch store. This time T.H.P. Dennis supplied the electrical installations. Dennis also installed a phone connection between the two stores. The branch was extended immediately prior to the first war. In 1896 the Society opened a local agency for the Co-operative Permanent Building Society and in 1901 a similar agency for the Co-operative Insurance Society. By 1895 George Young had become the Society's full time secretary. He was one of those who had invested his own money in the Society.

The Society decided to help solve the housing problems affecting many of its members (See chapter 18). In 1895 it bought land on Goldlay Road, Old Moulsham, on which it had nine houses built at a cost of £270 each. These were rented out to members at seven shillings a week. Another plot in neighbouring Rochford Road was bought soon afterwards.

Trade prospered at the turn of the century and the Moulsham Street store was extended again. Rebuilding cost in excess of one and a half thousand pounds, with fittings supplied by the C.W.S., including mahogany and marble counters. Men's outfitting at the Moulsham Street store was transferred to a leased property on the Baddow Road. A new branch on corner of Arbour Lane and Springfield Road opened in 1912. The rapid industrialisation of the town before the first war and the establishment of an urban working class in Chelmsford did much to help the expansion of the Society.

The C.S.C.S. took on its first apprentices in 1872. Hours were long, despite its willingness to treat its employees well. Its branches closed at 1.0 p.m. on Wednesdays but the average working week was still 56 hours. The Chelmsford Traders' Association in contrast strongly resisted the one day a week early closing. (5) In 1900 the Society employed 48 workers in retailing and 8 in production. The Society's Educational Association established a wide variety of activities including football, athletics and cycling. A proposal by the newly formed Chelmsford Trades Council (see later) that the Society only employ only trade union members was resisted.

In the first year of the war 22 of the Society's 124 workers enlisted. The first war certainly saw rampant profiteering by the Society's competitors. A.R.P. Hickley (See chapter 13) thought the society wasn't doing enough to keep prices down. At the end of the war 28 Society workers who had enlisted were, as promised, reinstated. There was however some discontent because not all these workers were given back the positions they held before the war. A motion stating that all the returning workers should not be worse off was just passed. (6) The post war slump affected the C.S.C.S. like all other Chelmsford businesses. Its dividend went down from one shilling and four pence to three pence. Despite this, the Drapery Department, previously at Moulsham Street, was moved to the High Street. (7)

Although the Society was not immune to the depression of the late 1920s and 1930s, it did more than just survive. A fish shop opened in Wells Street in 1922 and the Society opened its first shop in the Boarded Barns estate on the Kings Road in 1927. It opened a branch in Writtle in October 1928. In 1921 the Society's milk operation celebrated 35 years even though milk supplying was very rare amongst co-operative societies nationally. The Society also finally established a successful meat operation. A fire in 1931 at the Moulsham Street branch caused £2,000 worth of damage but could not halt the general progress. All this expansion in activities resulted in the number of members increasing from 4,660 in 1919 to 13, 842 in 1939. (8) The Society of course did not ignore those affected by the severe economic conditions. There were regular donations to the towns Unemployment Relief Fund (See later this chapter). In 1923 a Sick Benefit club was started.

During the second war the Society experienced the same difficulty, as in the first, in obtaining supplies of sugar, butter and bacon as private shop keepers. The women's committee became actively involved with the Chelmsford Citizens Air Raid Committee (see chapter 24). (9) Only the Society's bakery in Railway Street and its grocery next door in Wells Street suffered any real damage. Despite the difficulties membership actually grew slightly during the war. At the end of the war the main building was destroyed by fire and no licence for rebuilding could be obtained until 1948. Prefabs were used for several years. During the early years after the war, the Society opened a number of stores in the rural area around Chelmsford; a bakery at Roxwell and a general store at Boreham. In 1949 it commenced selling fruit and vegetables from a mobile van. (10)

During the war the C.S.C.S. had decided to form its own political party, the Chelmsford Co-operative Party. Nationally in 1945 there were 23 Co-operative Party M.P.s who voted with the Labour government on nearly all issues. In Chelmsford the new local organisation was never going to be anything but a small pressure group. (11)

In the 1950s the Society quickly converted to self service stores after the first, the Kings Road store, was opened in 1955. By the late 1950s increased competition was causing financial difficulties for the society. Its funeral business was joined with several other co-operative funeral businesses. The Society stopped baking bread in 1957. Although the grocery store at Moulsham Street closed in 1967, the general store on these premises continued to expand. In 1973 a new extension was opened on the site of the old Congregational Church. (12)

The attraction of the dividend remained strong and dividend stamps weren't abolished until 1987. (13) This was replaced by a new membership card still based on the old dividend principle. In addition the society runs a Community Card which aims to raise money for local causes. The stores in outlying rural areas closed during the 1980s but the Moulsham Street store was re-launched as The Quadrant in 1988 and the Duke Street premises re-opened in 1992. Membership had risen to almost 60,000 by 1998. (14)

Trade unions had a difficult birth in the Chelmsford area. The first however, could be traced back to the eighteenth century: the United Cordwainers, who were shoemakers, formed an association in the town as early as 1785. Like many such associations at the time, it combined the functions of a trade union with that of a friendly society. During the early nineteenth century all such groups were likely to be treated as illegal groups. In 1814 the Chelmsford Society of Carpenters was refused recognition despite its attempt to disguise itself as a Friendly Society. Despite the Repeal of the Combination Acts in 1824 - 1825, unions still found it difficult to get established in the town. In 1861 the Friendly Society of Skinners was the only union recorded in the town. (15)

A big influence on the formation of trade union branches in the town was the rapid industrialisation of Chelmsford at the end of the nineteenth century. The establishment of Christy and Norris and the Crompton Company did a great deal to help form an urban working class in the area. This of course was further enhanced by the establishment of the Marconi and Hoffmann companies at the turn of the century. The growth of engineering firms in the town led the Amalgamated Society of Engineers (A.S.E.) to try to establish a foothold. This was made difficult by the outright opposition of Colonel Crompton to having union members in the workforce. A branch had been formed in Chelmsford in 1855, but this had closed down in 1888. Before this, a strike had occurred at the Arc works involving fitters and turners. The Essex Chronicle reported

"The firm had changed the men from hourly work to piece work and also reduced the rate for overtime. Such alterations are contrary to the rules of the A.S.E. Mr Kyle one of the partners said the firm was not overburdened with work and they could easily get more men before any pressure came." Mr Pear the secretary of the local branch of the A.S.E. said "The strikers include some of the oldest hands in the works and as the majority of them are married men with families the struggle is no light one for them to take up. The firm yesterday advertised for turners; and after their experience it is not surprising that they ask for not society men." (16) The local members of the A.S.E. came out again in 1897 – 8 as part of a national stoppage. One alleged 'blackleg' was pelted with eggs and flour at the Crompton Company. Despite the strikers getting some financial support from the well funded union and the C.S.C.S., the strike ended in a major national defeat for the union. (17) Membership at the Chelmsford branch was reduced to 40 but the A.S.E. did not disappear in the town.

Attempts by the Workers Union (later to be the T.G.W.U.) to get members at the Hoffmann Company led to a similar response from the Barretts, the cousins who ran the firm, as had happened at Crompton. Before the first war the Barretts did everything they could to remove union members from their workforce. (See chapter 7) Eventually they had to recognise the union in 1912.

A branch of the Operatives Bricklayers Society was formed in 1892. The Amalgamated Society of House Decorators and Painters (A.S.H.D.P.) was very small nationally but very active in the Chelmsford area. It was the latter which played a major role in getting a local trades council started.

The Chelmsford and District Trades Union Council was formed in October 1899 after a meeting at the Black Boy Inn, Springfield Road. A trades council brings together local unions and workers to campaign on issues affecting local working people. The A.S.H.D.P. had sent invitations to the Society of Operative Bricklayers, the General Union of Operative Carpenters and Joiners, the United Builders Labourers Union and the A.S.E. These five original members represented only 155 members locally. (18) In its early years, the Council was concerned that there were few if any councillors to raise the issues that it thought were important to local people. The only councillor to regularly put forward working class issues was Arthur Lunney. (See chapter 13) Although he belonged to the Conservative Party he consistently raised the need for a public baths, public conveniences and most of all the need for improved working class housing. He and the Trades Council had no success trying to persuade the borough council to adopt the 1890 Housing of the Working Classes Act. The Council ignored a letter from the painters union saying that they were paying council employees at lower than the accepted pay rates.

A downturn in local trade union membership in 1902 – 1904 led the Trades Council to temporarily cease to exist. The big increase in trade union membership nationally towards the end of the decade saw it revived however. Several new union branches were started in the town in the Edwardian decade, including the N.U.T. and the Chelmsford Railway Clerks Association. A branch of the National Association of Operative Plasterers was also re-established. There were two strikes at Hoffmann, one before and one during the first war, during a period of intense confrontation nationally. The first strike, in 1913, was settled after, according to the Essex Chronicle, "Mr Pretyman (the Chelmsford M.P.)'s successful mediation". A minimum wage was settled at 5d for all workers over the age of 21 who had worked for the firm more than 24 weeks. It should be born in mind however that half the workforce were under 21 at the time. One thousand employees had joined the strike. (19) Prominent in the strike was Fred Tyrell Smith leader of the local Workers Union, who later set up his own business, joined the Conservative party and became a councillor in the borough. (20) The second strike at the factory occurred in 1918 when electricians successfully stopped work to obtain London overtime rates. (21)

Immediately before the war the Chelmsford Trades Council was reformed and tried to see that the "Fair wage clause" was carried out locally. In practice it was widely evaded by local traders and manufacturers. The Trades Council also tried to encourage women workers, who were employed in large numbers in the Chelmsford factories, to join local union branches. (22) It protested that food prices were rising rapidly during the war and that the Food Control Committee was doing little to prevent this. Wages of the workforce in Chelmsford's factories were lagging well behind prices. During the first war the membership of those union branches attached to the Chelmsford Trades Council rose to five thousand. By the end of the war the Workers Union alone had one thousand members in the town. The extent of the increase in working class organisation is reflected by the fact that the Labour candidate for Mid Essex in the 1918 general election polled over 5,000 votes, although the party had only recently been established locally. (See chapter 13) Union support allowed three candidates to run in the municipal elections for the first time. Two of these were elected, including A.R.P. Hickley. (23)

After the war the painters in the town struck for several weeks in 1919. This happened after the workers refused to sign a set of rules which the masters had drawn up. Another cause of the conflict was the employment of unskilled men at below the union rate of one shilling and three pence per day, which had become common practice during the war. (24) In 1920 a strike of moulders severely affected the Crompton works but once settled the factory quickly went back to full time working. (25)

The post war years were to reveal how exposed the Chelmsford workforce was to the vagaries of the trade cycle. A short lived boom quickly gave way to a deep recession. Although Marconi and Crompton were not hit immediately, Hoffmann went onto a three day week in 1921 and then let five hundred workers go. (26) The firm had undergone a great expansion during the war (See chapter 7) but the demand from the armed forces ceased at the end of 1918 and was not immediately made up by peacetime uses for ball bearings. By February 1921 there were over 1,400 unemployed in the town, with a further 2,454 on short-time working. (27) As elsewhere in the country, the recession left the local community unable to cope. National insurance was not yet developed enough to act as an adequate safety net and the Chelmsford Poor Law Union was hampered by regulations dating back almost a hundred years, which severely prescribed the extent to which it could help those cast adrift. (See chapter 19) The community reacted as best it could: a voluntary Unemployment Relief Fund was set up and the borough council immediately began looking at the possibility of local public works schemes if the Ministry of Transport would give 60% grants. (28) Mayor Thompson and the Council drew up a list of road widening schemes. (See chapter 10) An Unemployment Relief Fund committee was established in March 1921 to oversee the collection and distribution of funds. The poor law guardians voted to contribute £500. Some councillors thought that a significant number of those laid off at Hoffmann's could go back to their rural jobs. These workers had however moved to be close to their work and even if farm jobs had been available there would have been considerable resistance to moving back. Later in the year the slump began to affect Marconi as well, with its workers put on short time working. As was the case nationally, employers were putting downward pressure on wages. The borough council reduced the wages of its gas workers. By September 1920 the Unemployment Relief Fund was drying up and 1,000 unemployed workers in the town were not receiving help from any source. The Board of Guardians stepped in offering outdoor relief of 19 shillings for a married man, 19 shillings for his wife and three shillings and sixpence for each child. Money for rent was given in cash. A single man was given 10 shillings in kind each week and 5 shillings for lodgings. (29)

The Trades Council continued to press for schemes that created work, under the banner "Work better than dole" but it took time for the borough engineer to draw up road widening and flood protection schemes and then get approval for them from the central government. In October 1921 approval was gained for a new road from Springfield Road to Victoria Road. By the end of the year a number of schemes had been approved for both the borough and the rural area, with the Ministry of Transport paying 50%. (See chapter 10) (30)

In 1922, a dispute between the National Federation of Engineers and the A.E.U., led to 240 workers at Crompton and Marconi being 'locked out' while work carried on as normal inside. The Weekly News reported "A few men have resigned from the union but generally speaking the workers have remained loyal to their organisation." In May 1922 a deputation of 50 of those locked out went to see the Board of Guardians. The Board granted a low level of relief on the understanding that the money the men were receiving from their union was taken into account. (31) Their leader Cotton said the men would not return to work until a Board of Enquiry had reported. It was a dispute between the national union and the federation rather than the men and their immediate employers, but they had already been on half time working for twelve months before the dispute. During the same week 25 of those locked out returned to work on the employer's terms.

By July 1922 the Geddes Axe, with its effect on national spending, had begun to limit public works schemes of the type that were being carried out in the Chelmsford area. This time a deputation of the local unemployed invaded the Board Room at the Wood Street workhouse. "Work is what we want; we demand justice; the right to an honest living." The Chairman of the Board defended the recent reduction in relief, saying it was commensurate with the fall in local wages. A member of the deputation, R. Harrington said there were 700 registered for work but many public works were waiting to be done. Fred Marriage , the Chairman, said "dole is a matter for the Government." Younger members of the deputation talked about having "fought the Germans and now we have to fight the British."(32)

The government turned down the council's request for a further grant, this time towards a public works sewerage scheme. By 1923 the worst of the unemployment crisis in the town was over, with registered unemployment down to 387. (33) Until the general strike employment began to increase once more in the town particularly at Hoffmann. (See chapter 7)

Employment in the town in 1925 was as follows –

Hoffmann Ball Bearing Works	3,115
Crompton's Engineering	1,400
Marconi	700
Brown's timber works	150
Christy and Norris engineering	128
Chelmsford Borough Gasworks	76
National Omnibus Company	58
Britain Pash Engineering	55
Christy Brothers Electrical Engineering	36
Pinkhams Glove factory	25

At the time a total of 6,958 men and 2,608 women were employed in the borough. 4000 workers were employed in agriculture in the Chelmsford area. Whilst most of these lived in the Rural District 300 lived in the borough itself. Over 2,000 women still worked in domestic service in both the district and the borough.

The General Strike of 1926 came two years after the Chelmsford Trades Council had again ceased to function. It reconvened to co-ordinate the action of local unions in the strike. (34) These included the local railwaymen, the A.E.U. and the Workers Union. The involvement of the latter two meant that Crompton, Hoffmann and Marconi were all affected. Local opinion was polarised by the strike, much as the Chartist movement had done 80 years previously. A volunteer force was set up, based at the Shire Hall, to work against the strike. (35) The local papers regarded the strike as an almost military conflict and had no doubt that nationally it had a political purpose; an assertion that has been proved to be incorrect. (36) Chelmsford Trades Council and the Star Co-operative raised money for the miners. Before a meeting designed to highlight the plight of the miners 'Abandoned' stickers were placed over adverts to prevent it going ahead. At the actual meeting speakers were pelted with flour and eggs. After the protracted failure of the dispute the employers took revenge both nationally and locally. When the Chelmsford railway workers went back to work they were forced to sign a harsh new contract. The government of course also exacted retribution in the form of the Trades Disputes and Trades Unions Act of 1927, which was an attempt to take the right of collective bargaining from the unions. (37) Chelmsford Trades Council saw it as a 'blackleg's charter'. Fortunately unemployment in the late 1920s was low in the Chelmsford area. In September 1928 just 123 men and 11 women were registered as unemployed. (38)

Like all towns in Essex, Chelmsford wasn't as badly affected by the Great Depression, which started in 1929, as the so called 'Distressed Areas' elsewhere in the country; however unemployment was soon rising sufficiently for the Chelmsford Trades Council to press for a return to public works schemes. Roads, sewer and water schemes were soon being prepared for the council by the Borough Engineer. This time however, the government insisted on a certain proportion of those employed on the schemes being from the Distressed Areas rather than from the local area. When the first scheme came to fruition in the Chelmsford area in 1930, of the 100 men employed 60 were local but 40 were from other parts of the country. (39) By August 1930 unemployment in Chelmsford had tripled in a year to 500. (40) This was less than most Essex towns and a drop in the ocean compared with the levels being experienced in other parts of the country. By 1932 however, this figure had risen to 1,700. (41) The government's policy of financial retrenchment meant that relief was continually being cut. The Public Assistance Committee (the successor to the Chelmsford Poor Law Union) gave 8 shillings a week to the unemployed single man but he had to work for 16 hours to receive it. In October 1931 a deputation representing the local unemployed went to the town council. It made a number of demands that were mostly beyond the council's power to meet. The deputation asked for all cuts to the 'dole' to be put back plus an extra 5 shillings per head, 2 cwt coal per household, 2 shillings a week off council rents and schemes of work for local men at trade union rates. At the council meeting the Mayor said four of the requests were outside the council's control but the request for rent reductions would be passed on to the housing committee. The latter was turned down even though the request was backed up by a petition signed by 700 tenants and submitted by Councillor Brown. (42) As elsewhere the imposition of the means test to assess whether the unemployed had private means caused considerable antagonism in the town. In October 1932 a group of unemployed workers invaded a council meeting at the Shire Hall. Again the Mayor said they were only implementing government policy. A letter to the Weekly News reflected the views of many when it said 'Why should the thrifty be penalised?' (43) The Unemployment Relief Committee was revived with all the major works making a contribution. (44) 1,500 vouchers were distributed for groceries and coal etc; 450 boots were supplied with clothing and bed linen from the distribution centre in Broomfield Road. A year later the Committee was distributing fish as well as other food and coal. Chelmsford's Mayor thought the goods shouldn't be sold because this would be unfair competition for the town's traders. (45) The

Trades Council argued the unemployed could not afford to pay the prices in the shops and therefore this was not hurting the traders.

During 1933 unemployment began to ease in the county town. By the end of the year it was only half the level of the previous year. In April the unemployed marched on the town from all parts of the county. Ten thousand people were expected but only 500 arrived. (46) By 1935 only 300 people were registered as unemployed in Chelmsford. This was because all the local firms were very busy. They were part of the newer industries in the economy that were doing much better than the old 'staple' industries concentrated in other parts of country.

In the 1930s the Chelmsford Trades Council was finally established on a permanent footing. It made sure all three hunger marches received a warm reception in the town. (47) Members did their best to disrupt Fascist meetings in the town. (See chapter 13) With the local Labour Party it established the Searchlight magazine. (48) This put forward views that it felt were not getting expressed in the local papers.

The only major dispute in Chelmsford in the 1930s involved the busmen, part of a national dispute for a nine hour day and a 2d increase per hour. One hundred and sixty of the town's one hundred and seventy four busmen came out on an unsuccessful strike. This reflected the loss of effective influence of unions after the General Strike. (49)

The second war saw the opening of branches of several unions new to the town, including two white collar unions N.U.P.E. and the A.S.W (50) This reflected the type of work being carried out at the main works and some of the laboratories around Chelmsford. The Trades Council had been forced during the 1930s to bar communists from holding office but during the war communist trade unionists, such as Sybil Olive, were very active particularly in the campaign to get more air raid shelters and contributing towards the pressure for nurseries. Before the end of the war the Trades Council held public meetings on the need for a National Health Service.

The immediate post war period was one of low unemployment in the town with all the major works re-establishing themselves. In 1951 there were over 1,500 unfilled vacancies in Chelmsford. (51) During the 1950s industrial relations at the big works were generally more peaceful than they were to become in succeeding decades. In 1953 there was an engineering strike but the Weekly News described this as a "tame docile affair". (52) 1957 and 1958 saw increased militancy amongst local bus drivers however, with the emergence of the lightning strike phenomenon. By 1959 the Weekly News could say "This is one of the nation's boom towns." Whereas unemployment was increasing in the rest of the country "so attractive is the position that at the local Employment Exchange enquiries are being received from many parts of the country." Unemployment was about 320, whereas there were 380 job vacancies. In Colchester unemployment was 774 but there were only 243 job vacancies. (53)

Discontent grew at Crompton Parkinson in the early 1960s. Its workers felt they were the lowest paid of the big Chelmsford works. (54) The early part of the decade saw the rise of the instant walkout at the big works. In 1964 for example several hundred workers walked out at Marconi's factories in the town over the dismissal of one trainee. (55) Two years previously the management's refusal to enforce a 'closed shop' had resulted in a token walk out. In 1965 there were a number of disputes in the town. Six hundred workers voted to walk out by a show of hands at EEV. Subsequent negotiations resulted in an improvement of conditions at EEV and Marconi. (56) Another possible strike of bus workers was averted after negotiations. (57) Two years later the governments pay freeze saw EEV workers again in conflict with the management. Workers felt the pay structure needed to be overhauled after productivity had been increased by 30%. Eventually Barbara Castle, the Secretary of State for Employment allowed a big pay rise at EEV. (58) With women making up a large part of the workforce at all the major works, the passing of the Equal Pay Act led all the major unions to press for better pay and conditions for their female workforce but progress in the early years was slow. The early 1970s saw further attempts by the white collar unions to attract the middle managers of the big works. Clive Jenkins, Joint Secretary of the A.S.T.M.S. addressed middle managers of Marconi, Hoffmann and EEV at the Saracens Head Hotel. (59)

In the main the decade after 1968 was marked by unprecedented levels of industrial unrest in the town. Very few trade unions in Chelmsford were not involved in this unrest at some stage and engineers, teachers, firemen, draughtsmen, bank employees, agricultural and bus workers and others in public and welfare services were all drawn to protest activities. There were three main reasons for this industrial unrest; high rates of inflation, government industrial relations policy and the loss of jobs in all the major works. The closure of the Crompton Parkinson factory at Writtle Road resulted in the loss of 1,500 jobs. (60) During the early 1970s there were job losses at the Hoffmann factory after the merger which saw the formation of R.H.P. Industrial relations remained poor at EEV with several disputes over pay and conditions. In 1972 came the first major strike at Marconi. 900 workers were on strike at Marconi and EEV by April. The dispute lasted over 4 weeks. (61) A year later the Marconi workers threatened another strike, maintaining their pay was less than the prevailing rates in other G.E.C. factories. There was a further protracted dispute at EEV in 1976. (62) The same year saw a walk out by 1,000 employees at the factory.

During the middle of the decade Chelmsford's public sector workers began to take action. In 1975 the town's firemen joined a national protest. Three years later they came out on a strike which lasted 8 weeks before they were forced back to work. (63) At the end of the 1970s the dustmen's strike saw piles of rubbish lying all around the town. (64) Industrial action which limited laundry supplies, reduced admissions to Chelmsford's hospitals to emergencies only. (65) Caretakers at local schools also came out in a dispute.

National economic problems led to all the major works shedding further labour towards the end of the decade. In 1977, unemployment in the town rose to two and a half thousand. (66) After an economic upswing caused the level to dip to a thousand three years later, a severe recession in 1981 saw registered unemployment reach almost three thousand with both Marconi and R.H.P. shedding further jobs. (67) The rate of unemployment was still marginally lower than the average in the South East of England. By 1985 the level had increased to over four and a half thousand. Over 1,750 of these were women.

In 1979 the Chelmsford Trades Council had 41 branches representing 23 unions. By 2,000 this had declined to 17 branches representing 11 unions. (68) This was largely due to the decline in manufacturing in the town and the privatisation of public utilities which weakened the strength of unions in the area. Despite this contraction, the organisation did a great deal to help the miners during the 1984 strike. One miner, staying with Malcolm Wallace, a prominent local trade unionist, was later sentenced to 5 years at Chelmsford Crown Court for attacking a policeman. A further 5 received three years each for their involvement in the incident. (69) The increased unemployment in the town in the early 1980s led the council to press for an unemployment centre in the town. When one was opened, heavily subsidized, it only lasted a matter of months. (70)

The town's structural economic problems remained severe at the end of the 1980s and well into the 1990s. The effect of the closure of R.H.P. in Chelmsford was worsened by the various Marconi companies regularly shedding workers. (See chapter 6) By 1991 unemployment was up to five thousand having doubled in a year. (71) In 1992 the once prosperous new town of South Woodham Ferrers featured in a TV programme highlighting economic gloom in the South East of England. (72)

The biggest and certainly most acrimonious strike in the Chelmsford area towards the end of the century was the busmen's dispute of 1994 – 1995. Serious job losses and cuts particularly to rural services had followed the privatisation of Eastern National in 1985 and deregulation the following year. The job losses continued into the 1990s when conductors disappeared and traffic density was many times heavier than it had been previously. A new agreement in 1992 involved an increase in hours for bus drivers to eight and a half hours. Ninety six men refused to sign and the company then sacked these men claiming they had broken the agreement. . They brought in managers and retired bus drivers to man the buses, paying for them to stay in hotels at considerable expense. In retaliation the strikers started a regular free bus service which the police tried to ban. One hundred thousand people travelled on the free service. (73) A picket by the strikers at the town's bus station led to five arrests. In June 1995 after 7 months the dispute was finally settled. Three quarters of the striking drivers voted to accept the company's revised offer of £400 per year of service. Forty four of these drivers were still without a job and re-applied for their jobs under the new conditions. (74) Predictably both sides claimed victory.

Despite further job losses at the Marconi factories, unemployment was drastically reduced at the end of the century, reaching a twenty year low of just over 1,000 in 2001. (75) The unemployment rate was only 1.4%, half the national rate. In 2009 the financial crisis led to this increasing to 4.0%. By 2011 this had fallen again to 2.5% against a national average of 3.7%. The local economy had made the necessary structural adjustment by de-industrialising. In 2011 over 85% of jobs in the district were in the service sector. Between 1998 and 2003 alone, 16,000 jobs were created in the town. (76) In 2011 there were almost 80,000 jobs in the Chelmsford district. Many people were commuting into Chelmsford to work from the rest of the county. In addition to Chelmsford people commuting into London, which had been increasing ever since the 1950s, many more people were commuting to other Essex towns particularly to Basildon.

1) The Chelmsford Star Co-operative Society Malcolm Wallace p.8
2) The Chelmsford Star p.11
3) The Chelmsford Star p.12-15
4) The Chelmsford Star p.22 – 23
5) The Chelmsford Star p. 29 – 31
6) The Chelmsford Star p.39 – 41
7) The Chelmsford Star p.42 -43

8) The Chelmsford Star p. 48
9) The Chelmsford Star p.59
10) The Chelmsford Star p.71
11) The Chelmsford Star p.63
12) The Chelmsford Star p.80
13) The Chelmsford Star p.87
14) The Chelmsford Star p.106
15) Nothing to Lose A World To Win Malcolm Wallace p.12 - 15
16) Essex Chronicle 9 3 1888
17) Nothing to losep.20 – 22
18) Nothing to losep.11
19) Essex Weekly News 27 12 1918 p.3
20) Nothing to p.30 – 34
21) E.W.N. 27 12 1918 p.3
22) Nothing to lose p.37
23) Nothing to lose p.44 – 49
24) E.W.N. 22 8 1919 p.5
25) E.W.N. 2 1 1920 p.5
26) E.C. 14 1 1921 p.5
27) E.C. 4 2 1921 p.5
28) E.C. 11 3 1921 p.3
29) E.C. 16 9 1921 p.3
30) E.C. 2 12 1921 p.5
31) E.W.N. 5 5 1922 p.5
32) E.W.N. 23 7 1922 p.2
33) E.W.N. 11 5 1923 p.5
34) Nothing to lose p.63 – 64
35) Nothing to lose p.67
36) E.W.N. 14 5 1926 p.6 (Editorial)
37) E.W.N. 29 7 1927 p.7
38) E.W.N. 7 9 1928 p.7
39) E.W.N. 22 8 1930 p.2
40) E.C. 22 8 1930 p.7
41) E.C. 29 1 1932 p.6
42) E.W.N. 30 10 1931 p.7

43) E.W.N. 4 11 1932 p.6
44) E.W.N. 20 1 1933 p.7
45) E.W.N. 3 3 1933 p.7
46) E.W.N. 7 4 1933
47) Nothing to lose p.79
48) Nothing to lose p.89
49) Nothing to lose p.81 - 84
50) Nothing to lose p.90
51) E.W.N. 20 4 1951 p.1
52) E.W.N. 4 12 1953 p.1
53) E.W.N. 6 5 1960 p.1
54) E.W.N. 6 5 1960 p.1
55) E.W.N. 10 4 1964 p.1
56) E.W.N. 13 8 1965 p.1
57) E.W.N. 12 11 1965 p.1
58) E.W.N. 15 1 1968 p.1
59) E.W.N. 13 3 1970
60) Nothing to lose p.119 - 120
61) E.C. 25 4 1972 p.9
62) E.W.N. 8 7 1976 p.1
63) E.W.N. 12 7 1978 p.1
64) E.W.N. 15 2 1979 p.1
65) E.W.N. 15 3 1979 p.1
66) E.W.N. 28 7 1977 p.1
67) E.W.N. 26 2 1981 p.1
68) The Struggle Continues Malcolm Wallace p.5
69) The Struggle Continues p.16 – 19
70) The Struggle Continues p.23
71) E.C. 8 2 1991 p.1
72) E.W.N. 29 10 1992 p.2
73) The Struggle Continues p.35 - 41
74) E.W.N. 22 6 1995 p.1
75) E.C. 27 7 2001 p.1
76) E.C. 23 2006 p.1

10

Transport in and around Chelmsford

"This smelly, scruffy embarrassment to our county town"

The above verdict of Chelmsford's bus station was delivered by a local newspaper in 2002. It could equally have been applied to Chelmsford's transport system in the late twentieth century, which had evolved over the previous century but was manifestly not 'fit for purpose'. As a market town, roads were always likely to be crucial to Chelmsford's development. Much of the town had been wedged in between two rivers since the Middle Ages, which with a network of narrow streets, threatened in the early part of our period at least, to limit the expansion of the town. Chelmsford's rivers were susceptible to serious flooding until they were reconfigured in the centre of the town during the 1960s. The Chelmer and Blackwater Navigation had played an important part in the previous expansion of the town but by the 1880s it was declining in importance. Chelmsford had been reached by the railways 40 years before municipalisation and these were to play a vital role in its industrialisation. As was the case with many towns of its size, the advent of the motor car put pressures on the traditional structure of the town which it hadn't been designed to handle. It is strange that all the controversy and enquiries into Chelmsford's bypass made it the last major town on the A12 to receive one. Its County town status obviously didn't bear any weight when it came to a major decision such as this.

Prior to the creation of the borough, and also of the Essex County Council, the maintenance and building of roads in the Chelmsford area had been the responsibility of the local Highways Board which covered the rural district as well as the town. As early as 1880 there was discussion in the local papers about the possible dissolution of this board. (1) The Essex Chronicle was critical of the state of the local roads. It thought gravel, the local stone, shouldn't be used, but didn't want any more money being spent, in this case on bringing in granite by railway, because the Board of Health was already spending large amounts on its new sewerage scheme. (2) Its dissolution would have meant the responsibility for the roads falling on the parishes. This ensured the immediate survival of the Highways Board. Footpaths remained often in an appalling state especially in rural area, with little or no scavenging carried out. One cause of the roads being broken up was the increasing use of heavy traction engines by farmers. They also caused problems in Chelmsford itself. In 1885 the Weekly News complained that "traction engines are constantly being driven through the town at a speed far in excess of the two miles an hour allowed by parliament." "On many occasions within the last few months these ponderous engines have passed through the High Street at a speed of at least four or five miles hour, causing houses on either side to oscillate to an extent which must be dangerous both to buildings and occupants." (3) In 1883 the Highways Board bought a new road roller which was drawn by two horses to try to roll the granite in better. (4)

Another, more easily seen cause of destruction of the roads, was the susceptibility of low-lying Chelmsford to regular spells of flooding. In 1882 both the Chelmer and the Can overflowed their banks and submerged large areas either side. (5) Severe storms in 1885, with two and a half inches of rain in two hours, made the roads and streets impassable. In 1888 a rapid thaw of snow and ice caused the overflowing water to cover Victoria Road and much of Broomfield, Springfield and Baddow. Several cottages at Springfield wharf were covered. (6) Because of widespread damage to the houses of poor residents in the town a relief fund was set up with a committee to administer it. The committee prided itself that of over £333, raised 16 shillings were spent on expenses. (7) Another natural phenomenon, the earthquake of 1884, did a lot more damage in Colchester, but it was certainly felt in Chelmsford. "Even the prison at Chelmsford was said to have looked like a ship rolling on the sea." (8)

With the establishment of a roads committee on the new Borough Council, the local papers kept up the pressure concerning the state of the roads. The Essex Chronicle thought that the town's roads were in a better state than other Essex towns but "still compare badly with those of equal size to Chelmsford outside the county." It urged members of the committee to visit other towns to see what could be done. (9) In 1890 the committee bought the town's first steam roller. (10) The same year the Council trialled a new road sweeper made by the local firm Coleman and Morton. It was judged to be better than the one already used, being adaptable to any variation in the road and sweeping to a width of ten feet. (11)

The floods of 1888 indirectly brought about one of a number of disputes between the Borough Council and the new County Council. An iron bridge in New London Road had been swept away. Initially the town council were willing to a pay a quarter of the cost of the new bridge, but the E.C.C. were willing to pay only half. Part of the problem was that the responsibilities of the new county council had yet to be clearly defined. (12) The County Council took the borough to court, but inevitably a compromise was reached with the borough paying 1/3 and the County 2/3 of the £2,100 for the new bridge. The new bridge consisted of six iron composite arched ribs laid on brick built piers. (13) Several hundred people went to its opening. The Chelmsford Rural Sanitary Authority (the forerunner of the Rural District Council) also had to replace a bridge at Writtle, which had been destroyed in the floods. (14)

As at Norwich, the main streets in Chelmsford were wood paved, even though flooding often raised and warped the blocks. In 1901 for example £450 was raised for the cost of new wood paving in Duke Street. (15) The council made persistent efforts to get shops and public houses in the town to pay for the paving outside their premises. There was a long standing dispute for example with the owners of the White Hart Hotel. (16)

Before the first war the borough council, along with the new rural district council, made persistent attempts to widen key roads. In the absence of compulsory purchase orders however, the councils had to wait for properties to be offered for sale and then widen small sections in roads, such as New Street and Duke Street. This explains the 'hotch potch' of road widths we have today. In 1906 for example, the Council applied to the Local Government Board to widen parts of Duke Street because of the increased traffic to the railway station. (17) Previously the Council had widened the entrance to New Street from the High Street which had been particularly narrow. (18) A strip of land from the corner of the Shire Hall to the churchyard was bought for £1,400. Half the cost was born by the E.C.C. (19) In the years immediately before the war, the council carried out a good deal of widening on the approaches to Chelmsford, including Wood Street, Baddow Road and Rainsford Road. (20) This usually involved using pieces of garden and parts of buildings. (21) The Rural District Council widened part of Gaol Lane (Sandford Road) in 1899 and part of Navigation Road in 1901. (22) Improving the often poor state of its roads and footpaths was expensive for the new R.D.C.. It ordered all new and repaired roads to be steam rollered in 1906. (23) By 1914 the district council was spending over two and a half thousand pounds a year on road maintenance. (24)

At the turn of the century the first motor car related accidents were occurring in the town. Most of them were due to the comparative rarity of cars, with people and animals not being used to them, rather than sheer speed. Cyril Frost remembered the very early 'Red Flag cars', so called because a man had to march 60 yards in front with a red flag, driving through the town. (25) In one incident a horse spooked by a car engine bolted into a shop window. (26) A boy was caught on a car's lamp bracket in 1903 and carried some yards, fracturing his thigh. (27) In 1907 the council applied to the Local Government Board for regulations to limit the speed of motorised vehicles in the borough to 10 miles an hour but the Chief Constable said the limit was not necessary. (28) The editor of the Weekly News was evidently in two minds about the new vehicles. "The new motor car is not in favour with many, indeed it is much disliked but they have come to stay, if they are driven with due care and attention." (29) World War One saw a lot more cases of cars colliding, with the increase of military vehicles in the town. (30) The advent of the motor car also made the work of the petroleum inspectors, checking that petrol was kept safely and securely, more important. In 1911 for example the Anglo American company sought permission to store 2,000 gallons at their garage near the railway station. (31) Of course, before the war cars were greatly outnumbered by bikes and horse drawn vehicles as means of transport. Penny-farthings were particularly popular in the rural areas around Chelmsford. Prior to the war an increasing number of employees of Chelmsford's new factories used bikes to get to and from work.

Despite some criticism from farmers, the Great Eastern Railway (G.E.R.) became increasingly popular with passengers. In October 1889 The Times described the company's trains as the most punctual in the country. The same year a new line was opened from Chelmsford to Wickford. (32) Some local politicians, particularly Frederic Chancellor, tried to promote the idea of a line joining Ongar and the Epping line to Chelmsford. This would not only provide another route for Londoners to the coast, but it would also improve links with the country town and make it easier for those on county and judicial business to travel to Chelmsford. (33) Chancellor thought such a line would greatly weaken the argument for moving the county administration to London, which was being widely touted at the time. A meeting was held at the Corn Exchange in May 1891 to get support for the idea. (34) The Directors of the Company decided however that they couldn't consider the scheme because of expensive work being carried out at Liverpool Street Station. To mollify the town's politicians and newspapers the directors stated "the lines will be connected before many years". (35)

The following year, the Essex Chronicle revived the idea, emboldened by the fact that the company had just opened a new line from Upminster to Grays. (36) They found it difficult to get widespread public support. Another campaign by the paper, which had more success, was the pressure for a new railway station. The original station had been opened in 1856 and in the opinion of the newspaper was in a worse condition than Colchester's railway station which was already being rebuilt. (37) In April 1892 the Borough Council's seal was attached to a petition asking for a new railway station. A second petition was signed by the town's inhabitants. (38) When completed the new Edwardian building was an impressive brick design.

In 1893 the steamship 'Chelmsford' was launched. It was built for the G.E.R. for the new route from Harwich to the Hook of Holland. The ship was 300 feet long and had a breadth of 34 feet, with a depth of 16 feet. It could accommodate 200 first class passengers, 602 second class and a limited number of third class passengers. A number of townspeople went on early trips to Berlin and elsewhere. (39) The G.E.R., itself, was to disappear in 1929 with its absorption along with a number of other lines into the London and North Eastern Railway Line (L.N.E.R.)

In 1891 there was a public meeting in Chelmsford on the need for a telephone link with London. Discussions took place with the National Telephone Company. 20 firms and traders had to sign contracts at an annual rental of £10 each. The company opened a local exchange within months. (40)

In 1905 the G.E.R. decided, like other railway companies, to operate buses. These operated between the station and the rural areas around Chelmsford. The three services were to Great Waltham via Broomfield, to Danbury via Great Baddow and to Writtle. G.E.R. was the first railway company to build their own buses. They were designed by James Holden, a carriage and wagon superintendent at the company. The buses had seating for 36 passengers inside and 18 outside. (41) Thomas Clarkson (See chapter 2) took over these bus services in 1913. During the war Clarkson's steamers went to Billericay, Broomfield and "even up and over the hills to Maldon". (42) His National Omnibus Company's first garage was under one of the arches in the railway viaduct. Women were brought in during the war because of the shortage of male drivers.

Immediately after the first war the number of accidents in the town increased rapidly, particularly in Duke Street. Collisions between cars and motorbikes, which had increased rapidly in popularity, were common. (43) The situation was not improved by the path of the water conduit down the middle of the High Street. The editor of the Essex Chronicle thought it was a traffic hazard. (44)

A proposed road from Duke Street to the Springfield Road, which it was thought would relieve some of the traffic congestion, was opposed by some local traders and a public inquiry was held. The £36,000 project was approved and the road was opened in 1924 by the Mayor, Fred Spalding. (45) In the same year the first mention was made of a possible bypass for the town, in this case by the County Surveyor. (46) In the end Chelmsford's first bypass, taking in the Widford Bridge and Van Dieman's Road, wasn't built for another ten years. (47) It cost £200,000 to build. A quarter of the labour used to build the road had to consist of previously unemployed workers from the distressed areas. Two miles of the road were within the borough. The bypass was officially opened by George V in May 1932. Chelmsford Borough Council and the R.D.C. continued with various road widening schemes between the wars, taking advantage of public works

Opening of Chelmsford Bus Station 1937
(Courtesy of E.R.O.)

grants which were given to help with the unemployment problem (see chapter 9). Further widening took place in Duke Street, as well as Rainsford Road, Rainsford Lane, Coval Lane and Waterhouse Lane, in the early 1920s. (48) In 1922, 55 men worked on a Galleywood road widening scheme. (49) A similar scheme was started in New Writtle Street, Moulsham.

After the first war the National Omnibus and Transport Company went over to petrol driven buses as soon as Clarkson left the company (see chapter 2). In 1919 it started a service from Chelmsford to Woodham Ferrers, via Howe Green, East Hanningfield and Bicnacre. (50) Hawksley, who took over as chairman of the company from Clarkson, was an able businessman who turned the company's fortunes around after it made a loss in 1919, due to Clarkson's steam obsession. (51) In June 1918 the company had bought a yard and premises from Messrs Wells and Perry. This was adjacent to the railway viaduct and fronting on to Duke Street. Its first buildings were demolished in 1930. The company and two railway companies joined forces to form the Eastern National Company in 1929. In 1935 it submitted plans for a new bus station in Duke Street and this was opened in 1937. (52)

As early as 1928 there was discussion of a possible airport in Essex. It was to be located between Shoeburyness and Brightlingsea. (53) Meanwhile the intrepid members of the Chelmsford and District Flying Club operated out of an aerodrome at Broomfield. The aerodrome was opened by the Lord Lieutenant of Essex in 1932. (54) Another site for an aerodrome, just outside the then borough boundary at Bowers farm, Springfield, was being considered before the second war. (55)

The growth in motorised traffic between the wars meant that the council had to provide car parks. From 1922 parking was allowed at the rear of the market. (56) In 1938 part of Kings Head Meadow was leased to the council for parking. (57) From 1925 the council started issuing parking tickets to the owners of cars parked in the market itself. (58) The county council started erecting traffic islands in the High Street just before the outbreak of the war to streamline the hectic traffic. (59) Despite this progress a number of the town's main streets were still wood paved between the wars.

Even before the first war the only businesses using the Chelmer and Blackwater Navigation were the Chelmsford Gasworks and the timber firm Brown and Co. (60) The Navigation was the focus of a public works scheme in 1922 to make it easier to use both for commercial and pleasure purposes. At one point in 1922 five gangs employing a total of 308 men were cleaning and widening the river. (61) In the 1920s the gasworks stopped getting its coal by the canal. This left only Brown and Son Limited using it to bring timber from Heybridge to its wharf at Chelmsford. The timber was bought by ship as far as Osea Island on the Blackwater estuary and it was then loaded into barges which were towed into the estuary at Heybridge Basin. After this the timber was then transferred into horse drawn barges. (62)

After the first war telephone extension lines were set up in the rural area around Chelmsford bringing this method of communication to better off households. (63) The rural council also continued widening the often narrow and dangerous country lanes and making a number of corners less dangerous. (64)

Traffic in the town was very congested immediately after the second war. Possible improvements were included in both the Minoprio Plan and the town's first official plan (see chapter 12). In 1947 the editor of the Weekly News berated the often chaotic traffic conditions in the town. "Public safety is the main issue not the timekeeping of the buses." "Parking on both sides of certain roads at the same time should no longer be permitted." "There are municipal car parks not so far away." (65) He also commented that continued petrol rationing didn't seem to be having much effect on the number of cars in the town. In 1950 the town council prohibited vehicles waiting in certain roads between 8 a.m. and 6 p.m.. A ban was also placed on loading and unloading of goods between 12 p.m. and 2 p.m. in New Street and the High Street. (66) A one way traffic system was experimented with on Moulsham Street from the Baddow Road corner to Queen Street and St John's Road. (67) In 1952 the editor did not think much progress had been made. "We have a pre war bypass that takes the London coastal traffic past the town instead of through it. Is this all we can do? The main bottleneck remains under the railway." Double decker buses had to go under the archway. (68) The one way scheme in parts of the High Street and Moulsham Street was stopped then resumed after pressure from the local papers. This caused a big improvement in the traffic through the busy centre of town. (69) Eastern National rerouted buses away from Moulsham Street but the council withstood pressure to make the whole of the street one-way. (70) The 1950s also saw the introduction of parking charges at what had previously been free council car parks. Although there was a shortage of parking spaces Chelmsford was better provided for than most towns. In 1963 a survey of 107 councils showed an average of 11 car spaces for every 1,000 people. In Chelmsford it was 44 per 1,000 people. (71)

The late 1950s saw the introduction of offences for speeding in Essex. Radar was used for the first time to measure car speeds. One of the first 'magic eyes' in the country was used at Ingatestone. (72) The early 60s saw the introduction of the breathalyser. (73) In the middle of the decade traffic wardens were introduced in the town. (74)

An inner ring road had long been seen, by some at least, as a solution to the town's traffic problems. Initial plans in the 1950s, which included a flyover at the Army and Navy, had to be downscaled because of a reduced government grant. The revised plan of 1961 allowed for a dual carriageway between Coval Lane and the London Road. (75) An original decision of the Ministry of Transport to put a roundabout at the Army and Navy crossroads received a good deal of criticism. (76) By 1962 the first stage of the ring road, running through Central Park, was nearing completion. After an original estimate of £90,000 the final cost was £382,000. The opening of this first stage in 1965 led to premature claims that the town's traffic problems had been ended. (77) Plans for the second stage, a dual carriageway from Friars Place to the Army and Navy, had already been submitted two years previously. This would have to cut through the line of shops in Moulsham Street and across a residential area. It was planned to link up with Baddow Road near the Odeon cinema. (78) By 1968 the council was still pressing for a flyover at the Army and Navy, but the Borough Engineer stressed that it would only be temporary if a new bypass was built for Chelmsford. By this time bypasses had already been built for most towns along the A12. Chelmsford's original bypass had long since been absorbed into the fabric of the town.

In the 1950s and 1960s a number of the villages in the rural area around Chelmsford had bypasses built to ease their traffic problems. Ingatestone's opened in 1959. (79) The Great Baddow bypass opened in 1966. (80)

Regular flooding continued in the Chelmsford area. In 1947 a Flood Relief Committee once again had to be established and over £1,000 collected. Individual cases of damage had to be looked at by an independent assessor. (81) These floods brought about a limited flood prevention scheme. It was the extreme floods of 1958 that forced the authorities to finally take action to protect the centre of the county town. The flooding was the worst in the area for seventy years. 3.15 inches of rainfall fell at West Hanningfield and 2.73 in Chelmsford itself. Parked cars were swept away in Kings Head Meadow. The bridge in New London Road was destroyed. Moulsham Street, the High Street and the Springfield road were all covered by several feet of water. The Mayor toured the affected areas of the town and immediately launched an appeal for £10,000 to aid "those whose homes and premises have been affected by this tragedy." (82) By 1960 the Borough Council were in talks with the Essex River

Board about a flood prevention scheme in the centre of town which was likely to cost a quarter of a million pounds. (83) The initial scheme to replace the meandering stretch of the Can between Rainsford Lane and the railway viaduct by a straight cut with steel pilings was described as vandalism in some quarters. (84) When the scheme was finally agreed it took two and a half years to complete. This affected the building of the first stage of the ring road because the road would have to cross the Can. (85) Upstream of the town both the Chelmer and the Can were widened and deepened. In the centre of the town completely new channels were built as far as the junction of the two rivers. Beyond this junction an automatic sluice gate was built to control the flow of water. In the town deep concrete walls gave what many felt was a dull appearance. A number of people, including the local historian John Marriage, bemoaned the removal of the gullet and other channels that made up the area known as Mesopotamia (see chapters 11 and 12). (86)

The railway line through Chelmsford was not electrified until the mid 1950s. Like the rest of the country the replacement of steam by electric trains was slow compared with the continent, whereas countries like Switzerland had largely electric trains before the second war. When plans were announced for electrification in 1953 it was believed that "Population will follow the trains". It was assumed that electrification would speed up the development of Chelmsford as a dormitory for London. (87) The extension of overhead cables the nine and a half miles from Shenfield to Chelmsford was to cost two and a half million pounds. Twenty two electric trains each day were to run, in tandem with the steam service. There wasn't the money available to immediately extend the service to Colchester. (88) The Mayor welcomed electric trains to Chelmsford in June 1956. (89) By 1968 Chelmsford railway station was struggling to cope with 7,000 passengers a day. (90)

The late 1960s saw the first serious proposals for a new Chelmsford bypass. In 1966 a "Mile a minute motorway plan" involved a giant loop around the town linking the A12 at Widford and Springfield and skirting Broomfield. (91) A new plan in 1968 raised fears that a motorway might be an elevated road alongside the existing A12 bypass between Springfield and Widford. (92) In 1971 opposition to a central bypass became more organised with Stevas, the Chelmsford M.P., being prominent. (93) By the end of 1972 a proposed southern route was on the table which would take the new route near Sandon. (94) Naturally opposition groups to both routes were formed. A public exhibition showed three possible routes including a new northern one. Those in favour of the southern route pointed out that it would only result in 5 houses having to be demolished whereas the central route, going as it would through the centre of town, would result in the demolition of 176 houses. (95) The opponents of the southern route emphasised the likely environmental damage to the area. In August 1972 the Ministry of Transport appeared to come down in favour of the southern route. (96) Sandon Parish Council prepared for a fight claiming their village would be cut in half. (97) The E.C.C. came out in favour of the northern route. (98) A distraction from this controversy was the possible placing of a motorway only one mile from Chelmsford if the projected airport at Maplin went ahead. (99) Continued protests against the new A12 route inevitably led to a public inquiry which was delayed until 1975. (100)

Meanwhile the traffic congestion in the town was getting worse. The existing Army and Navy roundabout which had been designed for 3,800 vehicles an hour was being used by 9,000 vehicles an hour at peak times. (101) A report commissioned by the R.D.C. said that the A12 bypass would be a 'white elephant' which would not ease the town's traffic problems. The six roads around Chelmsford would need to be widened, for example the A130 from Broomfield into Chelmsford. (102) Chelmsford Borough Council considered a switch to the northern route in 1974. (103) The first inquiry after being postponed three times, showed that the southern route would use 300 acres of land and that the upgrade of the central route would drastically increase pollution. (104) In early 1976 a bizarre plan emerged to scrap the railway in the town centre and replace it with a fleet of buses! The bypass could then go through the centre of town. (105)

In 1976 the bypass question was thrown into chaos again, with the southern route thrown out by the Department of the Environment and the central route being favoured. The loss of agricultural land was adjudged to outweigh the loss of houses on the central route. It was thought that a new central route could be designed with less environmental damage. (106) In 1977 the central route looked certain when it emerged that the Ministry had already bought 19 houses along that route, with another 12 under consideration. (107) The following year however, the recently unified council rejected the central route by 17 votes to 6. "It would run mostly alongside the existing A12, avoiding the congested Army and Navy roundabout and requiring the building of new cuttings, embankments and bridges." (108) In June 1978 the council voted for the southern route after a heated debate, as did the County Council. (109) The following year the Ministry of Transport finally backed a rural bypass a u turn on their decision of three years before. Further delays occurred however and it wasn't until 1981 that the Department decided to press ahead. The Great Baddow parish council then forced another public inquiry. (110) At the inquiry the Department of the Environment maintained that the new flyover at the Army and Navy (see later) had improved traffic considerably at peak hours, but was already working at full capacity and congestion would inevitably get worse again. (111) Perhaps the most telling evidence came from the town's firms, particularly the boss of EEV. He said that his and the other Chelmsford companies needed an effective bypass. The lack of one made the town unsuitable for big firms. "No less than 26,000 people were dependent on the continued presence of G.E.C. in the town. The firms needed the best brains but prospective recruits were put off by the traffic holdups. We have had first class engineers resign because the journey across town to work is found to be slow and expensive. We are aware of customers who prefer not to visit us in Chelmsford." A recent accident which had caused a five hour traffic standstill had cost his company £200,000. The total cost for Chelmsford as a whole would have been far greater. (112) In August 1984 work on the 9.2 mile detour finally started. It eventually opened in November 1986 and immediately relieved pressure on the Army and Navy roundabout. (113) By 1987 the new road was taking traffic far in excess of predicted levels and experts were forecasting that a third lane would be necessary. In 2008 the A12 was named the worst road in England and Wales by the R.A.C. as it was "plagued by closures and long queues as a result of accidents". (114) The road was given a highway patrol and the police were allowed to treat it like a motorway but cutbacks reduced its effectiveness. (115)

While the interminable bypass saga lumbered on another contentious issue, the inner ring road also caused sporadic disagreements in the 1970s. The second stage from the London Road to the Army and Navy was opened in October 1971, seven months ahead of schedule. Once opened however, it attracted a good deal of criticism for separating Moulsham from the town. (116) Stage 3 Parkway also caused much debate. Public pressure led to some properties being saved but the scheme would have still resulted in 45 properties being demolished. In 1975 the £3 million scheme from Coval Lane to Rectory Lane was called off because of lack of money. (117) A revived scheme in 1970 involved bulldozing 70 homes and was designed to link the new Parkway with the Chelmer Valley Route. This involved a big roundabout at the junction of Rainsford Road and Rainsford Lane. (118) A further scheme two years later would have involved the partial demolition of the County Hotel. (117) In 1981 construction was again put back to 1985 or 6. Three years later however, the green light was finally given for the 70 shops and houses to come down and building to start the following year. (120) Parkway stage 3 finally opened in September 1987. (121) Traffic travelling to and from the North and West of Chelmsford was now able to avoid the town centre completely. Critics pointed out however that the new dual carriageway had turned Chelmsford's West End into a dead zone. The two hundred yards of Broomfield Road between its junction with Duke Street and Parkway became a dead end as soon as the new circulatory system opened. (122)

In 1988 a new scheme was announced which would link Springfield Road with the ring road. The scheme was designed to keep traffic out of the lower end of the High Street and enable the long awaited shopping development to go ahead on Kings Head Meadow and at the rear of Debenhams. (123) It would have to include a viaduct over both the Can and the Chelmer.

A third drawn out transport saga involving the town was the projected flyover at the Army and Navy roundabout. As early as 1972 Stevas had a meeting with the transport minister to try to get one built. He was of the opinion that if one was built it might make the building of a bypass unnecessary. There was strong opposition to the flyover from local residents. (124) The plans were heavily criticised for allowing only for inexpensive foundations, which would only be strong enough for cars. This was a purely financial decision. A public inquiry delayed the decision further. (125) When the contract was finally awarded in 1978 costs had to soared to well over half a million pounds. Half the finance came from the county council and half from the government. It was designed to be open only during peak hours. In the morning cars were to use it heading from Southend to Parkway and in the reverse direction in the evening. (126) The flyover opened in December 1978 and the council were delighted with the results. On average 950 vehicles used it in the morning and 1,150 in the evening. (127) Two years later however, it was already carrying far more traffic than it was designed to take. This was because people who had been avoiding the Army and Navy had now gone back to using it.(128) In 1990 an E.C.C. survey said that the flyover could go but nothing happened despite regular accidents which have carried on to the present. (129) A 2013 scheme to create third lane on a short stretch of Parkway west wards from the Army and Navy roundabout was criticised for being far too little. Critics argue a new two-way flyover is needed to replace the temporary one built 35 years ago but it is highly unlikely the finance will be forthcoming from the government in the foreseeable future.

The closing decades of the twentieth century saw a number of further bypasses for villages around Chelmsford, including the Boreham bypass which opened in 1971.

(130) The new Chelmer Valley route was proposed in 1972 to link Chelmsford and Little Waltham but opposition and delays meant that government approval was not given until 1982. (131) Yet another public inquiry was held before the Chelmer Valley Road was finally opened in October 1989. (132) A new bypass around Writtle, between Little Oxney Green and the A12 at Widford was opened in August 1987 after another public inquiry. "In addition to relieving the traffic through the village, the new road will enable traffic from the south and east of Chelmsford to avoid the town centre. It helps make the link between the A12 and the M11." (133) Proposals for a bypass around Danbury were abandoned but one was built around Great Leighs in the early years of the new millennium. It was to link Chelmsford with Braintree and "return the village to its rural idyll". (134)

In 1989 an M12 link to join the M25 with Chelmsford was announced to run north of the existing A12. Part of the £13 million pound package included widening the existing A12 bypass to three lanes. The plans were initially welcomed by the Council and Simon Burns , the local M.P. It was projected as a toll road. (135) Opinion moved against the road with concerns about the environmental effect on Highwood. (136) The plan was eventually abandoned by the government in 1994. (137)

The problem of traffic in the High Street was only going to be solved by pedestrianisation. In 1974 a new plan for the town's road system involved the pedestrianisation of both Duke Street and the High Street. (138) A limited scheme was introduced in 1981 applying previous Saturday restrictions to weekdays. It didn't apply to buses and bikes however. (139) By 1988 the complete pedestrianisation of a large part of the centre of the town was being introduced, boosted by the Meadows development. It was not finished for another four years. (140) Park and ride schemes were obviously necessary but the first scheme from Sandon, close to the A12, didn't open until 2004. (141) A second was opened in 2011 on Essex Regiment Way. (142)

In 1979 had come the bombshell that several large areas to the north and west of Chelmsford were being considered for London's third airport. Initially it was thought the disused wartime airfield at Boreham might be a contender, but when the shortlist was announced it featured Willingale, nine miles from the town. (143) From the start it was unlikely to be chosen but local campaigners and farmers wasted a great deal of time and effort before Stansted was chosen. Of course the choice of Stansted was not without implications for Chelmsford, especially when a second runway was later first mooted. (144)

When Brown's stopped using the Navigation in 1972 commercial trade on the

Chelmer and Blackwater ceased. Timber companies were introducing new methods of packaging timber. This made the unloading of timber from large ships much quicker, but these packages wasted too much space on Brown's barges and the company didn't have cranes. (145) In 1973 the Chelmer and Blackwater Navigation Company produced a plan for reviving the fortunes of the navigation. This involved boat trips down the canal, using licences to the owners of private boats and building landing stages along the canal. (146) In 1998 the Navigation reached its 200th birthday, as the second oldest navigation in the country. The National River Authority dredged the channel and new lock gates were built by the canal employees at Springfield. They used timber given by the Essex Wildlife Trust. (147) Increased revenue was generated by these means but the company fell into financial problems. Debts had reached half a million pounds by 2002 and it went into administration in 2003. (148) The Inland Waterways Association agreed to take over the maintenance of the Navigation in 2005 as a subsidiary called Essex Waterways Limited.

Much of the work maintaining the Navigation is undertaken by a group of local volunteers. By 2003 'Susan' was the last wooden barge on the waterway. It was built in 1953 to the design of the old horse drawn barges. It was flat bottomed because of the limited depth of water in the Chelmer. 'Susan' was 55 feet long and 13 feet wide and built for Brown and Son. The use of an inboard engine was not a success because of the weeds on the river. It was used as a maintenance vessel after being acquired by the Inland Waterways association. The 'Susan' was then owned by the Passmore Edwards Museum at Stratford before being acquired by the Chelmsford and Essex Museum. (149) It is now owned by a charitable trust and is undergoing renovation.

In the 1980s the county town's railway station was beginning to look increasingly worn and the narrow staircases were unsuitable for the large number of commuters. In 1983 a £1 million facelift was announced. (150) The station was almost completely rebuilt. At the same time there were persistent calls for a second station in the Chelmsford area, or at least a halt to relieve some of the pressure on Chelmsford station. In 1984 there was a new bid for a relatively inexpensive railway halt at Springfield after a previous proposal had been rejected as too expensive. When Stevas met with British Rail, the company said costs would have to be shared with the county council and that providing just a halt, was not feasible. (151) Support for the scheme appeared to be gaining momentum when a number of Springfield residents objected. (152) Planners were saying that a second station was essential because of the new houses to be built in Springfield. In the event the scheme was vetoed by British rail in 1988, citing the likely cost of at least £8 million. (153) The following year the idea of a halt, this time at Pump Lane, was again on the table. This would have served passengers arriving on foot, so that no parking would have to be provided. Despite the need being greater than ever, no progress was made in the 1990s. A new plan for a station at Beaulieu Park was proposed in 2000 to tie in with the new housing development there. This proposal has surfaced several times since (154) In 2002 a new plan surfaced for a half a billion pound railway which would link North London and Stansted via Ongar and Chelmsford thus reviving the idea for such a railway more than a century earlier. This failed, as did the idea to get Crossrail extended to Chelmsford, in addition to a proposal for a super-link through Essex to include Chelmsford, Colchester and Stansted. (155)

In 2008 Essex trains were named the worst in the country and as a result of this NXEA lost the franchise. A recent survey has shown some improvement in consumer satisfaction under the new Dutch owners but there remains a good deal of customer discontent. Over 20,000 journeys are made each day from Chelmsford station. (156) (157) In July 2013 plans to increase line speeds along routes running through Chelmsford and the introduction of "4 tracking " to improve capacity along a section north of the city remained on hold. This means the envisaged station at Beaulieu Park remains a pipe dream.

The 1970s saw Eastern National cut a number of rural bus services. (158) By 1980 it was making giant losses of £400,000. (159) In 1984 it was announced that the company was to be privatised by being offered to the highest bidder. The county council were heavily subsidizing the borough's remaining rural routes. (160) By 1986 de-regulation had meant that Eastern National had lost the tender for the subsidized weekend services in Chelmsford and the surrounding villages. Minibuses were already operating on some routes. (161) In 1991 the Badger Line replaced Eastern National. (162)

As early as 1994 a new bus station was planned for the town. (163) The existing one was commonly seen as an eyesore. A £30 million pound development was envisaged next to the Civic Centre. This originally was to include an office block, a depot under cover and basement parking for 300 cars. (164) A new plan in 2002 was to include offices, shops and homes as part of the scheme to re-develop the West End area of the town. The new bus station would replace "this smelly, scruffy embarrassment to our town." (165) By 2003 the plans had changed again with the depot set to move to the Westway. The Chelmsford Society was in favour of a proper bus to train interchange.

(166) Chelmsford's old bus station was finally demolished in 2005 and the new one opened in the beginning of 2007. (167)

The new millennium saw new concerns about possible flooding in the centre of Chelmsford. A scheme to construct a flood barrier across the River Wid, so that water could then be released gradually, has been delayed because of the cost and the opposition of local villagers. (168) It would be capable of holding 500 million gallons of water but it is envisaged that the barrier would only be needed on one or two days every ten years.

The early years of the new millennium brought forth the usual quota of schemes to head off the still likely possibility of gridlock in the town, despite all the supposed improvements. A number of people are worried that the building of a third shopping centre in the town will make the problems a good deal worse. In 2004 there was a proposal for environmentally friendly trams. (169) The same year an electronic management system was introduced for the town's traffic. (170) Members of the Chelmsford Civic Society and others feel that the town's transport 'improvements' including the ring road and the town's 'spaghetti junction', have removed a lot the town's individuality.

1) Essex Weekly News 7 5 1880 p.1
2) Essex Chronicle 5 3 1880 p.5
3) E.W.N. 19 5 1885 p.5
4) E.C. 14 12 1883 p.5
5) E.W.N. 3 11 1882 p.5
6) E.W.N. 21 1 1888 p.5
7) E.W.N. 31 8 1888 p.2
8) Essex Countryside Vol.1 1953 J.R. Milsome
9) E.C. 13 12 1889 p.5
10) E.C. 2 5 1890 p.5
11) E.W.N. 7 11 1890 p.2
12) E.W.N. 28 6 1889 p.5
13) E.W.N. 31 10 1890 p.4
14) E.W.N. 25 4 1890 p.5
15) E.W.N. 6 3 1901 p.3
16) Chelmsford Borough Council minutes 26 2 1896
17) E.W.N. 31 8 1906 p.5

18) E.C. 19 6 1903 p.4
19) C.B.C. minutes 12 5 1902
20) C.B.C. minutes 29 11 1911
21) C.B.C. 25 2 1914
22) Chelmsford Rural District Council minutes 20 8 1901
23) C.R.D.C. minutes 18 12 1906
24) C.R.D.C. minutes 31 3 1914
25) Essex Record Office SA/702
26) E.W.N. 27 9 1900 p.5
27) E.W.N. 2 1 1903 p.5
28) E.W.N. 31 7 1908 p.8
29) E.W.N. 13 5 1904 p.8
30) E.W.N. 21 4 1915 p.5
31) C.B.C. minutes 27 12 1911
32) E.C. 4 1 1889 p.6
33) E.C. 28 3 1890 p.5
34) E.C. 8 5 1891 p.5
35) E.C. 24 7 1891 p.5
36) E.C. 8 7 1892 p.5
37) E.C. 25 3 1892
38) E.C. 29 4 1892 p.5
39) E.C. 24 2 1893 p.5
40) E.C. 4 12 1891 p.5
41) Chelmsford Museums Records – 'Just the ticket' David Thornton
42) C. Museums records 'On the buses' Derek Wilks
43) E.W.N. 14 3 1919 p.3
44) E.W.N. 28 12 1919 p.4
45) E.W.N. 7 10 1924 p.7
46) E.W.N. 26 9 1924 p.7
47) E.C. 4 3 1982 p.2
48) C.B.C. minutes 19 6 1918 and 26 1 1921
49) C.B.C. minutes 31 5 1932
50) C.R.D.C. minutes 18 11 1950 p.50
51) 'The National 1909 to 1929' RJ Crawley etc
52) E.C. 30 8 1935 p.7

53) E.W.N. 28 12 1928 p.6
54) E.W.N. 20 5 1932 p.7
55) C.B.C. minutes 29 7 1936
56) C.B.C. minutes 29 3 1922
57) C.B.C. minutes 29 6 1938
58) C.B.C. minutes 23 1 1925
59) E.C.C. minutes 15 1 1939
60) Essex Review 1955 'Navigation on the Chelmer' John Marriage
61) C.B.C. 31 5 1932
62) E.R. 1955 John Marriage
63) C.R.D.C. minutes 19 9 1922 p.169
64) C.R.D.C. minutes 2 12 1926 p.593
65) E.W.N. 10 10 1947
66) E.W.N. 31 1 1950 p.1
67) E.W.N. 9 9 1949 p.1
68) E.W.N. 15 2 1952 p.1
69) E.W.N. 25 3 1952 p.1
70) E.W.N. 27 3 1953 p.1
71) E.W.N. 27 9 1963 p.1
72) E.W.N. 11 7 1958 p.1
73) E.W.N. 29 1 1960 p.7
74) E.W.N. 30 8 1963 p.1
75) E.W.N. 28 7 1961 p.1
76) E.W.N. 14 9 1962 p.1
77) E.C. 9 7 1965 p.3
78) E.W.N. 1 1 1965 p.1
79) E.W.N. 20 11 1959 p.1
80) E.C. 1 4 1966 p.1
81) C.B.C. minutes 26 11 1947
82) E.W.N. 12 9 1958 p.1
83) E.W.N. 29 1 1960 p.7
84) E.W.N. 29 1 1960 p.16
85) C.B.C. minutes 27 6 1962
86) Essex Countryside Vol. 29 June 1981 John Marriage
87) E.W.N. 2 10 1953 p.1

88) E.W.N. 16 9 1955 p.1
89) E.W.N. 15 6 1956 p.3
90) E.C. 23 8 1968 p.1
91) E.C. 12 2 1966 p.1
92) E.C. 5 4 1968
93) E.C. 19 2 1971 p.64
94) E.C. 25 8 1972 p.22
95) E.C. 27 4 1973 p.1
96) E.W.N. 24 8 1972 p.2
97) E.W.N. 14 9 1972 p.1
98) E.W.N. 25 6 1973 p.7
99) E.C. 27 7 1973 p.1
100) E.C. 20 5 1975 p.1
101) E.W.N. 18 10 1973 p.1
102) E.W.N. 31 1 1974 p.1
103) E.W.N. 25 7 1974 p.1
104) E.W.N. 22 5 1975 p.5
105) E.W.N. 5 2 1976 p.1
106) E.C. 16 7 1976 p.1
107) E.C. 30 9 1977 p.1
108) E.C. 9 6 1978 p.1
109) E.C. 23 6 1978 p.1
110) E.W.N. 20 8 1981 p.1
111) E.C. 10 9 1982 p.2
112) E.C. 24 9 1982 p.3
113) E.C. 21 11 1986 p.1
114) E.C. 14 2 2008 p.1
115) E.C. 2 9 2010 p.1
116) E.W.N. 14 10 1971 p.1
117) E.C. 11 6 1976 p.1
118) E.W.N. 17 8 1978 p.1
119) E.W.N. 24 7 1980
120) E.W.N. 24 7 1981 p.1
121) E.W.N. 24 9 1987 p.1
122) E.W.N. 15 10 1987 p.1

123) E.W.N. 26 5 1988 p.1
124) E.W.N. 5 12 1974 p.3
125) E.W.N. 11 8 1977 p.1
126) E.C. 20 1 1978 p.1
127) E.C. 29 12 1978 p.1
128) E.C. 11 7 1980 p.1
129) E.C. 26 10 1990 p.1
130) E.C. 19 2 1971 p.3
131) E.W.N. 1 7 1982 p.1
132) E.W.N. 12 10 1989 p.1
133) E.W.N. 6 8 1987 p.1
134) E.C. 20 9 2002 p.1
135) E.C. 26 5 1989 p.1
136) E.C. 6 9 1991 p.6
137) E.C. 1 4 1994 p.1
138) E.W.N. 31 1 1974 p.11
139) E.W.N. 26 3 1981 p.3
140) E.C. 14 9 1988 p.3
141) E.C. 4 11 2004 p.1
142) E.C. 24 2 2011
143) E.C. 25 5 1979 p.5
144) E.C. 1 2 2002
145) E.C. 11 21979 p.9
146) E.C. 1 6 1973 p.3
147) Essex Countryside Vol. 41 1993 Jan. John Marriage
148) E.W.N. 25 8 2003 p.3
149) E.C. 10 1 2002
150) E.C. 25 2 1983 p.1
151) E.W.N. 7 3 1985 p.1
152) E.C. 15 1 1985 p.1
153) E.C. 16 9 1988 p.1
154) E.C. 14 4 2000 p.6
155) E.C. 12 2002 p.3
156) E.C. 7 7 2011 p.18 – 19
157) E.C. 27 10 2011 p.7

158) E.W.N. 17 3 1977 p.5
159) E.W.N. 28 8 1980 p.1
160) E.C. 20 7 1984 p.9
161) E.C. 17 10 1986 p.1
162) E.C. 26 4 1991 p.1
163) E.C. 25 2 1994 p.1
164) E.W.N. 5 8 1993 p.3
165) E.C. 23 8 2002 p. 1
166) E.W.N. 8 3 2003 p.1
167) E.C. 19 1 2006 p.1
168) E.C. 8 2 2007 p.
169) E.C. 27 5 2004 p.1
170) E.C. 15 1 2004 p.1

11

The development of the town before 1945

*"Cattle and sheep were still driven down the High Street
until well into the twentieth century"*

The sixty years before 1945 saw a transformation in the town of Chelmsford. At the time of the 1881 census Chelmsford was a small county and market town boosted to a small extent by being a centre of judicial administration. The rural area around the town was actually declining in population and the town itself was growing very slowly. The foundation of an engineering industry from the late nineteenth century in the town caused an expansion both physically and in the population of the town. Between the two wars the growth of the town began to absorb rural parishes such as Springfield and Great Baddow. In 1880, as this chapter shows, the town was a largely piecemeal jumble of Medieval, Tudor and eighteenth and nineteenth century developments. Early Roman settlements in Moulsham were unseen and largely unknown, not to be excavated until the later twentieth century (see chapter 12). Successive ordinance survey maps from 1876 show the gradual spread of the town up through Moulsham and also along the Springfield, Rainsford and Broomfield Roads. Although New London Road had been developed during the mid 19th century, housing was not built along its upper reaches until the end of the century. In the late nineteenth century the beginnings of the influx of people into the town from rural areas started. The centre of the town remained laid out in a grid system that had originated in the 15th century, compressed as it was between the two rivers. Lying back from the main roads was a mass of often impenetrable yards and courts which remained more unless unchanged until well after the second war. Spalding's photos reveal the large number and variety of shops that existed in both Chelmsford and Moulsham. The inter war period saw a great expansion in working class council housing (see chapter 18). A big increase in middle class housing also occurred in the town between the wars. Private development was largely unplanned with the borough council showing little interest in taking advantage of planning acts. The Rural District Council showed a much more positive attitude towards planning interventions before the second war. Despite the industrialisation of the town, commentators, such as Fred Spalding junior, emphasised the rural orientation of Chelmsford between the wars with its important market and the wide variety of shops, serving those who came into the town from the surrounding areas as much as those who lived in the town. Even with these changes a citizen of Chelmsford brought forward from 1880 to 1939 would have recognised the town on the cusp of the second war. Those who were adults in 1945 would not recognise the Chelmsford of today.

The 1871 and 1881 Censuses reveal the parish of Chelmsford, within the Chelmsford Union, to be a small town with its population barely only increasing by 567 to 9,885. For the Censuses the Union was divided into 62 districts with two special enumerators for Chelmsford prison and the workhouse. Both Censuses were organised by W.W. Duffield (see chapter 13) as Superintendent registrar of the union; he used 70 enumerators. The work cost a penny per head of the population.

Union district	1881	Increase	Decrease
Great Baddow	2055		2
Little Baddow	549		61
Boreham	902	41	
Broomfield	855	65	
Buttsbury	452		35
Chelmsford (incl. Moulsham)	9885	567	
Chignal St James	224		66
Chignal Smealy	134	1	
Danbury	974		69
Fryening	704		13
Good Easter	520		61
East Hanningfield	404		86
South Hanningfield	234		13
West Hanningfield	430		130
Ingatestone	926	28	

Great Leighs	753		110
Little Leighs	125		24
Margaretting	526		4
Mashbury	143		0
Pleshey	302		73
Rettendon	720		88
Roxwell	814		145
Runwell	393	20	
Sandon	466		38
Springfield	2528		119
Stock	565		67
Great Waltham	2349		113
Little Waltham	580		117
Widford	300	7	
Woodham Ferrers	613		164
Writtle	2412		13

The total population of the Chelmsford Union in 1881 was 32,923. This was a decrease of 849 on the 1871 Census. Almost three quarters of the population lived in rural areas. It is noticeable that a considerable number of parishes such as East and West Hanningfield, Great Leighs, Roxwell, Great Waltham, Little Waltham and Woodham Ferrers experienced a major decrease in their population. The principal cause of decline was the agricultural depression (see chapter 1) It was not until the two decades before the first war that the expansion of industry in the county town was able to take up the surplus population from the surrounding rural areas. (1) Some villages continued to decline. Great Leighs had lost another 140 people by 1900. (2) Even the opening of the railway line through Woodham Ferrers for example failed to halt that villages decline. (3) This stagnation of the population of the Chelmsford Union overall was followed by two decades of slow but steady growth. Chelmsford should be compared with the county as a whole, where the rapid expansion of metropolitan boroughs such as West Ham, caused the population of the county to more than double between 1851 and 1891 (369 thousand to 785 thousand). (4)

By 1901 the beginnings of important industry had began to result in the more rapid expansion of the borough's population. In that census it was 12,627 but by 1921 this had increased to 20,769. Some of this was accounted for by the boundary changes of 1907. In this census the population of the rural district was still slightly greater than the borough's with 24,545. (5) This growth was dwarfed by the rapid expansion of the county's population, again particularly in the metropolitan boroughs. By 1911 the county's population had almost doubled to more than 1,350,000. (6) By the time of the first war many of the population of the outer Chelmsford parishes particularly Springfield, Great Baddow, Boreham, Broomfield and Writtle worked in the borough. Boreham for example, which had a stable population of just over 800 in the last two decades of the 19th century, almost doubled its population in the first half of the twentieth century. (7) Danbury was another village which benefitted from proximity to the town and its available work. (8) Despite the depression the borough's population continued to increase during the inter war period. It was estimated at 35,500 in 1944. This increased population came from the rural areas and to a lesser extent from the distressed areas elsewhere in the country. In addition the borough's birth rate, although lower than it had been, was still higher than the national average. (9)

The 1876 large scale ordinance survey map reveals a great deal about the limited development of Chelmsford and Moulsham at the time. On the edge of Moulsham, Oaklands House, at the top of Moulsham Street, had been built by Frederick Wells the brewer, in 1867. His 'FW' appears on three places on the outside of the building. The gatehouse to Oaklands Park is now Oaklands Lodge on the corner of Rothesay Avenue. Further down towards the town at no. 103 Moulsham Street today is the former bailiff's house which also has the 'FW' motif. Henry Guy, who gave money for St John's church and is buried in the churchyard, had built Hamlet House, now named Dovedale House. After later being the residence of Ernst Hoffmann, it is today in the grounds of Chelmsford College. Further down on the left were the six Tudor almshouses, which had been rebuilt by William Mildmay of Moulsham Hall in 1758. (10) In Anchor Street off Moulsham Street on the left, was the ironworks of T.H.P. Dennis later to be taken over by R.E.B. Crompton (see chapters 2 and 4).

On the other side of Moulsham Street on the way out of town on the map, St John's school was smaller than it was to become. It later bore the inscription "This school was erected and the adjoining schools enlarged in loving memory of Thomas Tidboald, Churchwarden of St John's, by his widow, A.D. 1885". The tomb of Thomas Clarkson Neale, the secretary of the Chelmsford Philosophical Society and who played a major role in the establishment of the museum, (see chapter 27) was and is still to the rear of the church (see chapter 22). Behind St John's Church was a brickfield. Next to the school there were a number of terraced houses one of which was called 'Hemp Cottage'. They are still present. Further down back towards town on the right was H. and T. Godfrey who had been rope makers and producing marquees, netting, yarn and sacks since 1828 (see chapter 2).Today this is the site of Godfrey Mews. Beyond this was Rope Walk (roughly in the position of today's Grove Road). On the other side also going down towards the town was the 'Bay Horse Inn', which is still there. It was originally a 17th century building with weather boards and a peg tiled roof. Like Chelmsford itself, the Moulsham of the 1880s was well served with pubs between Hall Street and Rope Walk (see later) including the Mason Arms and the Kings Arms. The British School was between Blackfriars Place and Friars Place and fronted onto Friars Road. This of course has all been replaced by a section of Parkway. Lady Lane was just a track with no houses at all on either side. Lying back from Lady Lane was the 'Town sewerage depot'. Heading up from Baddow Road, Mildmay Road was not built up beyond Woodford villas, i.e. beyond Lady Lane. On the lower end of Mildmay Road was a stone and timber yard as well as another maltings. On the corner of Mildmay Road and Hall Street was the silk mill built by John Hall of Coggleshall, later to be used as Marconi's first factory. A tannery was close to the Can by the Baddow Road.

Towards Baddow Road on Moulsham Street in the 1880s was the 'Windmill Arms'. Also towards the town on the corner of Baddow Road and Moulsham Street was the 'Old White Hart Inn'. Just before the stone bridge was the Cross Keys Inn on the site of what is now the Regent. It was a medieval gabled building, the last of the town's medieval inns. The stone bridge had been built by John Johnson in 1787, probably on the site of the Roman bridge. At the start of Moulsham Street before the stone bridge the militia barracks covered a large area including a parade ground that was also the Armoury and Depot of the West Essex Militia. It had been built on the site of the old prison. The Militia's headquarters were transferred to Brentwood and the buildings were sold around 1890. Most of the site is now occupied by the Chelmsford Star Co-operative (see chapter 9).

Out of the village, Moulsham Hall had been demolished as early as 1814. It stood near the entrance to the present day Moulsham Infants and Junior Schools. The 1876 map shows the site of Moulsham Lodge as completely detached from town, approachable by a lane off the Baddow Road. Oaklands itself was surrounded by a large area of gardens and woodlands. It fronted onto Moulsham Street up to beyond the Lodge house going back towards the town. Beyond it was Saltmarsh's nursery with an organised layout of fruit trees and glass houses. On the other side of Moulsham

Street there was another nursery between Moulsham Street and the New London Road. John Saltmarsh lived in the building on Moulsham Street which is now the Conservative Club. Nursery Road built at the end of the century refers to the nurseries. Further out of town beyond Oaklands there were gravel pits. St John's Vicarage is shown on what was then called Longstomps Road (now Vicarage Road).

In the middle of the 19th century James Fenton, the architect, had been involved with the Copland family in developing a large area, previously part of the Mildmay estate, which became the tree lined New London Road. (11) Arguably his work for the 'Chelmsford Company' left a much more pleasing legacy than the work of the planners who succeeded him more than a century later. It included a mixture of high quality terraced, semi detached and detached properties.

Either side of New London Road was by no means completely built up in 1876. Bellefield, later to be the home of Frederic Chancellor, Thornwoods and Chestnutt Villas are clearly shown but land which was later to be used for the building of the Chelmsford and Essex Hospital was empty. After the hospital was opened in 1883, Spalding took many photos of the building both outside and inside. In 1880 next to the field that became the Chelmsford and Essex Hospital was the Ebenezer Chapel, designed by James Fenton in 1847 – 1848. On the corner of New London Road and New Writtle Street was the Laurel Grove house, now occupied by the Chelmsford Club, where Fenton himself had lived. Coleman and Morton's Iron foundry (see chapter 2) fronted on to New Writtle Street and New London Road on the left hand side going out of town. The site was later used by the Crown Windley company (see chapter 2) On the 1876 map was the Church of the Immaculate Conception, a Roman Catholic Church which had been built in 1846 – 1847 (see chapter 22). Next to the church, Albert Place had been built in the 1840s. On the opposite side of the road was the Red Lion pub which had originally been built in 1842. In 1876 there were a number of small private schools on both sides of the road, many of which didn't last very long. (see chapter 20) There were several clay pits on the either side of the road up from Queen Street and the Nonconformist cemetery. On the right the land fell away due to brickwork where Brierly Place, the home of John Ockelford Thompson, was later to be built. It is now the United Reform Church. There were no houses between Mason's Villa and Melford Villas which had been built in the middle of the century.

In 1883 William Augustus Lucking, the son of William Lucking, who was already an undertaker, bought a property next to the Nonconformist Cemetery in New London Road. George William, his son, carried on the business. He died aged 41 and his wife continued the business with Gus, their second son, eventually taking it over. Lucking and Son is still there today after Darren Lucking, a great nephew of Gus took control in 1996. (12) The Nonconformist cemetery had been designed by James Fenton himself and had opened in 1846. Later eminent Chelmsford people to be buried there included Brittain Pash, Frederick Wells and A.G.E. Morton.

In 1887 the Chelmsford Cemetery opened in Writtle Road (see chapter 13). The cemetery later contained the graves from the fallen of both world wars. It has since received over 21,000 burials. Forty one burials and commemorations were carried out after the first war. There were 38 burials during the second war; 32 of them on a western part of the cemetery. The cemetery contains the Hoffmann memorial (see chapter 24). A crematorium was a much later addition to the cemetery in 1961. This original chapel was added to by a second. The original was renovated in 2011. Chelmsford cemetery now has cremated remains plots and a Muslim section. There are now a number of closed cemeteries around the city including St Mary's churchyard, Widford, St John's Churchyard, Moulsham Street, the New London Road cemetery (the former Nonconformist cemetery), St Mary's churchyard, Great Baddow, Rectory Lane Churchyard, the Cathedral Church of St Mary, St Peter and St Cedd, Holy Trinity, Springfield and All Saints, Springfield.

Opposite the Nonconformist cemetery was the Claremont Villas originally built in 1851 and later to be occupied by the St Philip's Priory. On the corner of Elm Road, Cherry Garden villas had also been completed by 1851. On the other side was Orchard Lodge, which had been built in 1841 – 2 and which is now the South Lodge Hotel. Numerous Spalding photos show the new Chelmsford and Essex buildings after they had been completed in 1883, both of the outside and the inside.

In 1876 on the New London Road was the original bridge across the Can, later to be swept away in the floods of August 1888. It was replaced by an iron bridge in 1890. Next to the Moulsham side of the bridge was the Congregational Church, again designed by James Fenton in 1840 (see chapter 22). On the other side of the bridge was the Mechanics Institute built in 1841, which flourished in the middle of the century but was well in decline by 1880, and later to close in 1899. It has since been used by the Museum and today is used by the Coroner's service. James Dace, the music specialist, was established next to the Institute as early as 1859. The firm soon established shops in Stratford, Romford and Colchester and by the end of the century had moved in Chelmsford to opposite Bolingbroke's and Wenley's in the High Street.

In the town itself in 1876, Mesopotamia Island was either side of the Springfield

Bridge over the River Chelmer and on either side of the Springfield Road. It was caused by the gulleys of the river. The island included the Dukes Head Inn, Oriel House and a stone yard. Earlier in the century mock elections had been held on Mesopotamia when real elections campaigns were being held in the town. Speeches lampooned local Whigs and Tories with little difference between them. 'Candidates' were paraded around the town on horseback. The losing candidate was thrown into the horse pond. Later the winner met the same fate. (13) A brewery and malt house surrounded the 'Black Boy Inn'. There was a temperance hotel on the High Street. The 'Kings Head', backed on to a meadow, and was one premise down from the Springfield Road corner. The 'Queen's Head Inn', was on the other side of the High Street not quite opposite, on the site of the present day Marks and Spencer; between the two was the conduit. The 'Kings Head' had been a medieval inn and was later demolished in the 1930s, to be replaced by Woolworths. Two premises up from the 'Queens Head' was the Post Office. On the corner of the High Street and New Bridge Street was the 'Old Oak Inn'. Further up the High Street was another public house the 'Half Moon Inn'. According to Fred Spalding junior, in his reminiscences on his childhood, the 'Saracen's Head Hotel' had a backroom which served as a club room. Meetings of the Old Town Jury Club and the Beefsteak Club were held there (see chapter 27). (14) According to Spalding, just down from the Saracens Head was a wine and spirits shop run by a Mr Champ a teetotaller. Next door was occupied in the 1870s by a Doctor Gibson who had a large private practice. He was the medical officer for the West Essex Militia. Two premises further down was Courts, a baby linen shop. This was followed by the London and Westminster Bank. Next came Medlicott's, the tallow chandler, known to all the farmers for his candles or 'dips'. (15) During Spalding's childhood in the 1870's there were more private houses in the High Street than shops. The map of 1876 does show however that a promontory of permanent shops had encroached on what was previously the main area for the market. On the site of the later Barclays Bank was a house where Frederic Chancellor lived. It had previously been the site of the original Chelmsford Bank at the end of the eighteenth century and in the middle of the nineteenth century, Sparrow, Tufnell and Co, later to merge with Barclays in 1896 (see chapter 2). Most of the shops had similar windows; mostly semi circular in shape, supported by an iron post in the centre and had panes of glass. Down the High Street on both sides there were iron posts. Midway down each post there were holes about three inches in diameter, through which ropes were pulled. The aim was to stop the animals that were driven down the High Street getting on to the pavement and causing mayhem. 'Dilly' Miller was employed to do this job. Although the market was moved out of the High Street in 1881 this did not completely remove the problem, because cattle and sheep were still being driven down the High Street until well into the twentieth century. Spalding junior remembered the annual army training with the men going from the Moulsham barracks to Durrant's field which later became the goods yard of Hoffmann's. Next door to Spalding's father's original shop on the other side of the Saracens Head was the Freestons shop selling caps, bonnets, leather leggings and gloves. Close by was Pool, the sadler, and Pertwee, the chemist.

In Tindal Street in 1880, moving towards Tindal Square was the 'Spotted Dog' with its courtyard and the Dolphin Inn on the left. (16) Further beyond the 'Spotted Dog' was the 'White Hart Hotel'. Behind the hotel was a 'Tonic ale brewery', the forerunner of Britvic. (see chapter 8.) Next to it was the 'Bell Hotel', just before the Corn Exchange, fronting out on to the Square, which was much larger than it is today. The Corn Exchange had opened in 1857, one year before Spalding's birth. According to him auctioneers and other agents did their business in the vestibule of the building and in front of the Shire Hall. The market inspector in Spalding's youth was Richard Francis. He had a difficult if not impossible job, because the area where the market was held had so many entrances and exits, making it difficult for him to find his clients and get them to pay the charges they owed. At the rear of the Corn Exchange was a large warehouse owned by Brittain Pash (see chapter 1). (17) The cattle dealers wore top hats. Horse buyers tried out the horses in Duke Street, Tindal Street and other side streets. (18)

Behind the Bell Hotel was a malt house. Also by the Corn Exchange was the Golden Lion on the corner of Tindal Square. Just past the Shire Passage on the right hand side was yet another public house, the Market House. This was a very dilapidated building in Spalding junior's youth. Frank Whitmore, the county architect, later to be the provisional mayor when the town was incorporated, rebuilt it. In front of the Shire Hall was the so called 'Russian gun'. The 'Sebastapol cannon' had been presented to the town in 1858. St Mary's parish church was surrounded on three sides by graves (See chapter 22). As late as 1870 there was still a stream of water down the High Street from Tindal Square even though the statue of Judge Tindal had replaced the old conduit head in 1852. Chelmsford's conduit padoga was removed to the corner of the High Street and the Springfield Road. (19) It had itself replaced the Naiad, Chelmsford's water nymph', which later was moved into the Shire Hall. (20) The clock on the Shire Hall was not added until 1887.Spalding also remembered the town fairs, which were held twice a year. During the fairs Tindal Square was full of booths and caravans. There were usually three roundabouts in the square and one in front of the cannon. It was usually well conducted, but later in the century shopkeepers had the fair first moved, then banned (see chapter 27). (21)

By the 1870s the Wenleys had already had a store in the town for over a quarter of a century. In 1845 William Wenley and his son of the same name had gone into partnership with each other and opened their first store on the Baddow Road. They were already accomplished cabinet workers and specialised in high quality furniture. In 1869 the firm had opened a store at 55 the High Street, near the stone bridge. This also stocked carpets, wallpapers and timber and in addition began to run a removal business. (22) About the same time as Wenley's started, George Bolingbroke arrived in Chelmsford. He had worked for Marshall and Snellgrove, later to become Debenhams. Bolingbroke opened a drapery shop with his brother in law John Ling, at number 74, next to Wenley's store. (23) He retired in 1882 and left the business to his son. Ten years later the son took over the shop next door. Because he thought J.G. Bond, the shop owner on the other side of the High Street, would make a bid, he had a butcher friend bid for the premises on his behalf. (24) Despite this and one or two other takeovers, the town still had 287 shops in 1887.

At the time of the incorporation there were still a mass of yards and courts in central Chelmsford seemingly cut off from the town's main thoroughfares because they were only reached by passing under archways. Union Court for example started from halfway up Tindal Street and went a long way down to almost behind Museum Terrace on New Bridge Street. Spalding's photos of Angel yard, once an entrance to a Tudor inn, later the site of the Spotted Dog, showed how decrepit many of the yards were. The entrance was eventually demolished in 1927. Crane Court, an important place for political and educational meetings, was reached by a passageway one premises up from the London and County Bank and two premises before the Saracen's Head. Off Legg Street, a turning off New Street, was Legg Yard. Almost opposite Legg Street in New Street was Marriage Square.

The entrance to Waterloo Lane was very narrow in the 1870s, as was the entrance to New Street next to the Shire Hall. Beyond Marriage Square was Eddington's foundry. Houses had already been built up on both sides of Victoria Road. On the corner of New Street and Victoria Road was the Victoria National School. Beyond the railway line there were fields both sides of New Street. In Duke Street going towards the railway station there was first the 'Golden Fleece', which is still there, then the 'George'. The

Grammar school fronted on to Duke Street and went a fair way back. Opposite the station the Friends Meeting house was a dominant building seating 800. Behind it was the large Vineyards house. On the other side of the railway was the 'Plough', also still there, with a timber yard opposite. Behind the yard was Fairfield House. In the 1880s it was occupied by the public vaccinator, Henry Newton. A new road, Market road was built to provide access for cattle to the new market.

In Springfield the original County Police station was shown in the 1876 map almost opposite the gaol. (see chapter 23) Springfield Place was shown situated completely in the countryside. A series of Spalding photos show the new County Police headquarters which were built in 1902. There were five blocks of buildings in crescent form, each two or three stories high. It had residences for the Chief Constable and his deputy and quarters for clerks and other members of staff. The premises were fitted with electric light. Another photo shows a fleet of Austin Seven cars supplied for the police by Pollards garages.

Although Chelmsford's industrial expansion was still in its infancy, the ordnance survey map of 1897 shows clearly the start of the urban spread of Chelmsford. In Springfield there were new houses around Springfield Green. On the Springfield road going out of town there was much more housing on both sides. The Broomfield Ironworks (Christy's) on the Broomfield Road now had houses on both sides. Also on the Broomfield Road, the new grammar school site was prominent. There was also new housing along the Rainsford Road. The top of New Street was still empty except for the field used for cricket and other sports. Admirals Park was already laid out and the Recreation Ground was clearly developed, tree lined with a bandstand. (25) At the back of the park was the water tower and main reservoir run by the 'Chelmsford Corporation'. The Industrial School was set well back from the Rainsford Road in large grounds. Rainsford Lane, off Writtle Road was still completely in the countryside in 1897.

What is now Old Moulsham was showing distinct signs of further development by the turn of the century. There were houses along one side of Grove Road, with a nursery still on the other. Houses had been built on both sides of Nursery Street. Oaklands was however still well out of the town. The Lodge now marked the beginning of the estate which went back to Longstomps Road. Crompton's Arc Works now extended back from Anchor Street to Queen Street. St John's vicarage was still isolated on the Longstomps (Vicarage) Road. Housing had started being built on Upper Bridge Road, Seymour Street and Wolseley Road off New Writtle Street by the railway line. There were also some signs of development on the Baddow Road end of Van Diemans Road. In Lady Lane there were just 12 houses past Mildmay Road but as yet there was no Manor Road. A local man John Janker (1902 – 1993) recalled it being a country lane with just a few houses on it. There were now a few houses on the first part of Rochford Road and Goldlay Road. Janker also remembered two lodging houses in Moulsham Street, the Model and the Kettle. These mainly served wayfarers and were usually busy. (26)

Tom Turner remembered the electric lighting in the town early in the twentieth century (see chapter 4). "Arc lamps were fitted to high standards in the main streets while the side streets were lit by carbon filament lamps about 30 watts connected to wooden poles fitted in familiar cast iron pipes with overhead wiring and a curious type of lantern for the lamp to protect it." The arc lamps had to be serviced almost every day. "This was carried out by two fitters who had to push around the town a ladder on a very heavy wooden truck, complete with tool box and spares." The truck

Looking up Tindal Street, Towards Tindal Square during the early 1900s
(Courtesy of E.R.O.)

could weigh up to half a cwt. Its ladder had to extend to 25 feet to reach the arc lamps which were high to spread the light. Turner also recalled the time the council decided to substitute gas lighting for electric but after a few years they reverted back to electric (see chapter 13). Blondel electric lights were installed. Like the originals these were made at the Crompton Arc Works. (27) Spalding's photos of Moulsham Street and elsewhere in the town in the early years of the twentieth century show the rapid proliferation of phone wires and telegraph poles because of a big increase in the use of telephones.

In the early 1900s the first County Hall, red brick buildings in Duke Street, removed both the old Grammar School and the 'Coach and Horses' Inn early in the new century. Tindal Square was still much larger than it is today. It was still dominated by the Sebastapol cannon, the Judge Tindal Statue, and the Corn Exchange but it also had numerous shops. In 1915 these included Orams, the watchmakers and jewellers, and Collins, the china and glass shop, where the Midland bank, now H.S.B.C., stood. By 1930 Spalding Junior's shop with its distinctive greenhouse (his studio) on the roof, had been replaced by Harrison's the ironmongers. In 1937 this in turn had been replaced by the Employer's Liability Assurance Corporation. Next to it was Bellamy's the chemists. The gun was removed to Oaklands Park in 1936. Spaldings photos of Tindal Street 1916 – 1918, show the street had retained much of its character with the Spotted Dog and White Hart Hotel featuring prominently. His photos of Angel Yard behind the Spotted Dog, reveal however how much the area known as the 'Yards' was in need of repair.

The effect of Chelmsford's dramatic industrial progress on the development of the town is well illustrated by the ordnance survey map of 1921. In 1907 boundary changes also had a big effect on the original size of the town (see chapter 13). Hoffmann's factory was three big buildings on the corner of Rectory Road and New Street but it now went right back to the corn mill. It also included extensive railway sidings. One of Spalding's many photos of the Hoffmann's works shows its own, very necessary, fire brigade in 1921. Another set of pictures shows its very large gas plant for power. On the opposite side of New Street was the new Marconi works. Houses had been built for workers on Marconi Road and Bishops Road. The area of Primrose Hill was now much more built up including Cramphorn Road and Nelson Road. Extensive building had taken place during the previous twenty years towards the railway line along roads such as Lower Anchor Street and Bradford Street. Along the railway both sides of Upper Bridge Road were now built up.

Angel Yard behind the Spotted Dog during the early 1900s
(Courtesy of E.R.O.)

After the first war the Wells and Perry factory was still operating in Duke Street. The fire station remained on Market Road. There was now a bowling green behind the Corn Exchange. The Recreation Ground also had two well cared for greens. Barrack Square was now built up with the Star Co-operative covering most of it. The Congregational Chapel still fronted on to New London Road. By the stone bridge was the Wesleyan Methodist chapel (see chapter 22) The chapel had been built in 1898 replacing the Cock Inn. It was demolished in 1971 to be replaced by Caters supermarket, later Presto's. Also by the stone bridge in 1929 was the Pearl Assurance building. Off Waterloo Lane was the swimming baths. The Empire theatre had been built on Mesopotamia Island. On the High Street, the Regent Theatre was a prominent building going back a fair distance (see chapter 27). There was a football pitch on Kings Head Meadow. Spalding's photographs between the wars show the wealth of public houses that remained in the town. The greatest concentration was still in Tindal

Street, including the 'Spotted Dog'. An inter war Spalding photograph of Victoria Road South shows the Public Library, Museum and School of Art built in 1904 – 1906 and a a needle shaped monument to those who fell in the Boer War which now resides in Central Park (28).

After the first war both Wenley's and Bolingbrokes secured steady expansion until the 1930s. Bolingbroke's had Father Christmas flown in to the town one year. Wenleys was the first shop in the town to have lifts installed in 1927. (29) Both firms were badly hit by the depression of the 1930s however, as well as the rise of the chain stores with their greater buying power. Bond's like Bolingbrokes started as a drapery business. Its founder in the mid 19th century had been John George Bond, who died in 1924, when he was one of the few remaining original members of the town council. (30) In 1890 a business review of the eastern counties said "Few houses in the country can boast of so widespread and influential a patronage". During the 1920s Bonds began acquiring neighbouring stores on the High Street. A Spalding photo of the 1930s shows the firm covering three shop fronts. (31)

In the 1930s there was still a library above Boots in the High Street. There was a Liptons store next to Woolworths (which has recently become a branch of Barclays). (32) Next to Bolingbrokes was Luckin Smith, a grocer's. Spalding's photos show all the shops had window displays even the Electricity shop. Before the second war there remained four butchers in the High Street. In the early 1930s crowds gathered on the corner of Springfield Road and the High Street to watch P.C. Henry Baker direct the traffic in a super efficient manner. Spalding's photos show the inside of the Shire Hall after improvements had been made in the 1930's. "Inside the ground floor has been refurbished to find room for the Crown Court and jury retiring rooms, but the great ballroom (or county room) upstairs remains virtually in its original state."

Moulsham had become much more built up by 1921. Houses had been built on one side of what is now Vicarage Road. There were more houses on the Hamlet Road end of Lady Lane but still allotments going down towards Van Dieman's Road. Off Lady Lane both sides of Roseberry Road had houses and one side of Bouverie Road was built on. Manor Road had been built up on both sides down to the Corporation depot. Houses had also been built on Braemar Avenue going towards Oaklands. (33) Several of Spalding's 1928 photos show the large three story 'Pendeen' house in Moulsham Street with very big ornate gardens at the back. Friars Place, a gabled house, remained a prominent building but it was demolished in 1930 to make way for a new road. At the time of the first war a number of gabled shops were still in the Old Friary including

Wright the butcher and Bellamy the chemist. (34) By 1933 Wright and Joseph Ellis, the bookseller were still there, as was the Windmill Inn. After the first war the Anchor Inn on Moulsham Street was a Wells and Perry pub. The Rising Sun at the top of New London Road was owned by the Poor Law guardian Alfred Conybeare.

Spalding's photos reveal how far Brown and Son had developed their main premises at Coates wharf, at the town end of the Navigation, between the wars (see chapter 2). (35) They also show the imposing nature of the front of Marconi's New Street works and how the masts dominated the town before they were taken down in the 1930s. (36) The Marconi College in Arbour Lane, Springfield was well established by the 1930s. (37) There was further expansion at Hoffmann's in the 1920s and 1930s, with huge new sheds with glass roofs being built and the railway sidings being covered over, when they were no longer used. By the 1930s the medieval cottages of New Street were showing their age, having been patched up and repainted for centuries. Bishops Hall stood off Rectory Lane, near the Bishops Hall mill by the river. It was demolished in 1928.

The 1930s saw major changes in Duke Street. By 1936 the brewery had been demolished. A large building next to it, Dorset House, previously known as Brewery House continued, first as a dentist, then a youth club, before becoming a ruin until it was finally demolished in 1981. The foundation stone for the new County Council block was laid in 1933. When finished the building (see chapter 13) was certainly not universally liked. In 1954, Nikolaus Pevsner, in his 'Buildings of England' series, regarded the building as a "sad anti climax". "The height of the building ruins the skyline of the town from many points by depriving the Cathedral tower of its pre-eminence." (38)

The 1939 ordnance survey map confirmed the building of the Boarded Barns council housing estate. This included Corporation Road, Kings Road, and North Avenue. Christy's on the Broomfield Road was completely surrounded by houses, as was the Essex Industrial School. By the start of the second war Springfield had become much more densely populated particularly Stump Lane and around the prison. The 'ribbon development' that had started earlier in the century had spread further along the Springfield Road. Springfield Lyon however was still completely in the countryside.

By 1939 there had been further development along the New London Road, with Brierly Place, later to be destroyed during the war, built next to Claremont villas. The football ground was now at New Writtle Street having moved from Kings Head Meadow. There was new housing development beyond the Arc Works on Writtle Road including Crompton Street and Waterhouse Street.

In Moulsham middle class housing had been built in Rothesay and Finchley Avenues by 1939. Oaklands was consequently much reduced in size. Moulsham Drive now had housing on both sides. Lady Lane was now fully built up on both sides down to Van Dieman's Road apart from one small allotment where council houses were later built. There was a small amount of housing on the other side of Van Dieman's Road. The new Moulsham Schools were shown off Princes Road on the ordnance survey map but there was no housing around them or around Moulsham Lodge. Longstomps Avenue was now built up all the way down to the junction of Galleywood Road and Wood Street. Galleywood was now built up on both sides down to Tile Kiln Road, in another example of ribbon development. (39)

A first national planning act was passed in 1909. It allowed a council to prepare schemes for any land "which is in the course of development or appears likely to be used for building purposes". The number of buildings on a site could be regulated and the space around them, as well as their appearance and the way they might be used. This Act proved slow and cumbersome. A 1919 Act allowed interim development of a scheme before final approval was considered. Chelmsford Borough council showed little inclination to take advantage of either Act. The Chelmsford Rural District Council was much more proactive. Its first attempt at planning came with the parish of Runwell in 1926. Chelmsford R.D.C. was concerned that the motor car was already affecting such places. The Weekly News commented "there can be no doubt that local authorities ought to bestir themselves to ensure their areas are not disfigured by gimcrack bungalows". "The Chelmsford R.D.C. deserves the thanks of the public for the adoption of a town policy." To some extent however, the R.D.C. were pushed into the decision, because the Rochford authority, which bordered on to Runwell, already had a planning policy and the council was concerned that private builders might move their schemes to Runwell to escape controls. (40) Two years later the R.D.C. was again making proposals for the Central Essex Town Planning Scheme. It wanted 19 miles of new road to enable the further development of rural parishes. The borough council showed little interest in doing the same although its transport problems were already emerging (see chapter 10) with six main road intersecting in the town. (41) In 1930 the R.D.C. put forward a new plan for Ingatestone and Fryerning. It was increasingly obvious that any planning had to be conducted with both authorities co-operating with each other. Any further growth in the borough would increasingly overflow into the surrounding rural areas. (42)

The 1932 Act enabled local authorities to prepare schemes for any land not just suburban land. It was supplemented by the 1935 Ribbon Development Act. This made development of all land within 220 feet of roads subject to controls. After the 1932 Act the Borough began to show a more positive attitude to planning, attending the Statutory Regional Committee. In 1935 agreement was reached on new business and industrial areas. After much discussion between the two authorities a Springfield site was agreed for a new aerodrome by the joint committee. The war intervened before this plan could reach fruition. (43)

One significant event in the development of the town during the second war was the removal of the 'Conduit' padoga from the corner of the High Street and Springfield Road in 1940, because it was causing such an obstruction to the flow of traffic. It was rebuilt in Tower Gardens where it is now a grade two listed building. It consists of a dome of stone on six tapered Doric columns. On one side there is the inscription 'This conduit was erected A.D. 1814 by the parish, aided by a subscription of one hundred pounds by Robert Greenwood, merchant.' On the other side it says 'Rebuilt by the parish A.D. 1852'. Spalding Junior's photos show the outside and inside of the Saracens Head when it was taken over by American soldiers. One of his many photos of his shop windows shows an advert for fund raising in 1942.

1) Essex Weekly News 13 5 1881 p.8
2) Great Leighs and Little Leighs Pat Watkinson
3) History of South Woodham Ferrers Floyd Watersworth p.9
4) Essex Review 1894 Vol.3 p.220
5) Chelmsford Through the Ages Torry p.63
6) E.R. 1915 13 5 1881 p.8
7) Boreham E. Burgess p.15 and 42
8) Danbury Kelly's Directory 1924
9) Chelmsford Borough Council minutes 31 5 1922
10) Chelmsford and Moulsham: An historical walking guide David Jones and Janette Scarborough. Friends of Chelmsford Museum
11) Essex Chronicle 29 8 2003 p.41 article by John Marriage
12) Chelmsford Museums records –Lucking and Son
13) Chelmsford in My Younger Days Alderman Fred Spalding p.3
14) Fred Spalding p.4
15) Essex Countryside 1958/9 Vol. 8 p.10 – 11
16) Fred Spalding p.7

17) Fred Spalding p.8
18) Essex Countryside 1962/3 Vol. 11 p.62 – 63
19) Essex Countryside 1979 Col. 27 Dec.
20) Fred Spalding p.11
21) Essex Chronicle 21 2 2003 p.34
22) Bolingbroke and Wenley's Furnishings (2005)
23) Essex Life and Countryside Mar. 2005
24) E.R.O. Ordnance survey map 1876
25) E.R.O. Ordnance survey map 1897
26) Chelmsford Museums Oral records John Janker
27) C. Museums Oral records Tom Turner.
28) E.R.O. Spalding photo collection
29) Essex Life and Countryside Mar. 2005
30) C. and E. Museum Chelmsford people records
31) E.R.O. Spalding collection photo 1745
32) E.R.O. Spalding collection Photo number 1503
33) E.R.O. Ordnance survey map 1921
34) E.R.O. Spalding collection Photo number 616
35) E.R.O. Spalding collection Photo number 748
36) E.R.O. Spalding collection Photo number 754
37) Chelmsford in Old Picture Postcards
38) E.R.O. Spalding collection Photo number 778
39) E.R.O Ordnance survey map 1939
40) E.W.N. 3 9 1926 p.7
41) E.W.N. 11 4 1930 p.6
42) E.W.N. 5 10 1928 p.11
43) E.C. 28 6 1935 p.3

12

The development of the town and rural area and planning after 1945

"Its pretty Shire Hall, the water meadows and parks along the rivers, the tiny flint studded cathedral"

"Irredeemably mediocre Chelmsford" was the title of an article in the satirical magazine Private Eye which appeared in 1990. This was one of a number of pieces that have appeared both nationally and locally in the last 40 years criticising the town's architectural blandness. Although some of the remarks of a recent story in the Guardian (see later) were certainly unfair, it has to be admitted that the planning decisions made on the development of the town in the 1960s and 1970s did a good deal to remove the individual character of the town. Although Anthony Minoprio's post war plan for the town was not officially adopted in the early post war years, a number of its proposals did eventually come about including the town's first shopping centre and the inner ring road. Critics of recent development can blame Minoprio for getting the idea accepted that there was little of architectural worth in the town to be saved for posterity. This idea certainly played its part in the sweeping away of all the town's courts and yards in the name of progress. Colchester took the view however that it was in the end no more expensive to renovate and improve at least some of its yards and cottages. Minoprio's views were also a factor which led to the desecration of Tindal Street, certainly one of the streets which had given Chelmsford its individual character, when Chelmsford's first shopping centre was finally built. Late in the day National Heritage money saved some of the old buildings of Moulsham Street, but still more could have been done to keep its centuries' old character. The removal of Mesopotamia and the river gulleys that caused it was also, in the opinion of John Marriage, another unnecessary contribution to the increasing sameness of Chelmsford towards the end of the century. Despite these criticisms of the town people still generally rate it a pleasant place to live and this is the reason why the population of the city is rising rapidly in the new Millennium. The borough increasingly had to do battle with the County Council to limit new housing in the area in the late 20th century. Despite this the green belt around Chelmsford generally held and a number of villages within the area have retained their character. Lack of available land plus the determined opposition of conservationists has meant that the population of the new city falls well short of the 200,000 predicted 30 years ago.

Chelmsford's first census for 20 years in 1951 revealed that the increase in the town's industry had caused a big increase in both the population of the borough from 27,457 in 1931 to 37,858 and the Chelmsford Rural District which had risen from 27,836 to 39,258. (1) The faster growth of the Rural District reflected the continued urban spread of the town of Chelmsford into parishes such as Great Baddow and Springfield. In the next two decades the population of the area as a whole doubled to just over 120,000 by the 1971 census. This was despite the predicted overspill population from Greater London in the main not fully materialising. In the 1960s the area's population increased by 30,000. (2) A limited exodus from metropolitan Essex was fuelled by cheaper house prices in the town but Chelmsford's rate of growth of population slowed considerably after the two districts merged in the early 1970s. The population of the area grew by roughly 15,000 in both the 1970s and the 1980s but only by 3,000 on the 1990s. Limited land available for new housing restricted the opportunities for people to move into the area and reinforced the slow rate of local growth in population which was a feature nationally. By 2001 there were 157,000 people in the Chelmsford metropolitan district. Recent estimates from the Office for National Statistics show Chelmsford's population as 168,500, an increase of over 11,000. This compares with 173,600 for Colchester, 174,300 for Southend and 175,000 for Basildon. In contrast in the same set of figures Norwich has only 132,200 and Ipswich 133,700 people. (3) All the indications are that the population of the new city is rising rapidly. By 2007 the BMI (Black and ethnic minority) had grown to 17,500; 1 in 10 of the population. (4)

Immediately after the war it seemed likely that Chelmsford would be affected by the implementation of the Greater London Plan. In 1944 this had allowed for the decentralisation of a million people from the Inner Urban ring to the Outer Country Ring which included Chelmsford. The 1945 Minoprio Plan for Chelmsford was one of 250 such plans submitted at the end of the war for the U.K. Anthony Minoprio had been appointed to prepare a survey and plan for the Borough and Rural District of Chelmsford in 1944, not by the local authorities but by an unofficial group, 'the Chelmsford Area Planning Group'. They were made up of leading citizens and industrialists. The aim of the report was to "encourage the adoption of good design and wise long term planning". In his preface to the Minoprio plan, Sir Patrick Abercrombe, the author of the preface to the Greater London Plan, raised the danger of the town falling under the influence of London and losing its individual character. Minoprio had trained as an architect in Liverpool and supported large scale neoclassical designs with wide avenues, rather than the small scale garden city forms of Raymond Unwin. "Good architecture can do more than any other factor to foster civic pride and the self respect of a town." Minoprio held the view that the architect should be in control with no need to consult the local community. In this his approach was similar to that of the Chelmsford Company in developing the New London area a century earlier. Both schemes were initiated by unelected 'city fathers'. The latter arguably however, left a much better legacy for the town. Minoprio contrasted the slow piecemeal growth of the town up to the end of the nineteenth century with the rapid growth of the town in the twentieth century, which had resulted in sprawling ribbon development along the main roads out of the town. (5) He identified 7 main problems. Firstly, there was an insufficient provision of car parks. Secondly, the market was badly sited and too small. Thirdly, there was a lack of well designed amenities. Fourthly, the town was disfigured by advertisements and rubbish dumps. Fifth, there was a need to develop residential areas as neighbourhood units, not just collections of houses. This was connected with a sixth problem, a lack of clinics, shops, public halls, playgrounds and allotments. Seventh, insufficient use had been made of the two rivers. He noted that since the turn of the century a new problem had arisen in the town with the rapid development of motor transport. Any new road plan would be hampered by the presence of the two rivers and a railway viaduct. By the second war the town was hopelessly congested by traffic (see chapter 10). The area between the High Street and the existing market was being wasted by a layout which had existed in 1591 but had great potential. Minoprio berated the general low level of design and amenities in the town. There were however, several buildings designed to a high standard of architecture, notably the Shire Hall and the Cathedral. These two buildings were not shown to their best effect because of the shapeless muddle of the other buildings around Tindal Square. (6)

Minoprio tried to show how the defects of the road system could be rectified, the central land re-planned, the rivers used to benefit the town and new buildings and residential areas used to benefit the "dignity and character of the town". (7) Vehicles coming from London towards Colchester and the coast were compelled to go through the High Street and Duke Street. A bypass had been included in both the Mid Essex Plan and the Greater London Plan. This led Minoprio to propose an inner ring road. (8) He put forward two new roundabouts, one at what is now the Army and Navy and one at the southern end of the Springfield Road.

Minoprio saw no redeeming features in the area between the High Street and the Can known as the 'Yards'. The layout and design of the buildings had, he felt, serious defects which could not be put right. What was needed was a total re-planning of Tindal Street and the area between the High Street and the Recreation Ground. Tindal Square should be reduced in size and the Corn Exchange, a building which he had little affection for, demolished. This was Minoprio following the general reaction against Victorian buildings. The view of Chelmsford's timber framed buildings as being of little value became ingrained in the local authorities perception for just long enough for all these buildings to be swept away a quarter of a century later. If they had been retained for another ten years new conservation forces would have ensured the preservation of at least some of them. Minoprio envisaged the resulting area being filled with a large shopping space, public buildings and large car parks. These would be designed as rectangular blocks with internal courtyards giving car parks and delivery access. His civic centre would have been placed on the banks of the Can with public spaces, cafes and boating. (9) Minoprio proposed 10 new residential areas (Typical Neighbourhood Units). Each was to have between 5 and 10,000 inhabitants, with its own shops and amenities. Each unit was to be reached by a walk from the centre not exceeding ten minutes. (10) He gave complete specifications for the amenities in each T.N.U. such as 130 shops, 4 nursery schools, 1 community hall, an ante natal clinic and a welfare clinic. (11) Minoprio predicted the further development of the Melbourne estate and the spread of Springfield north of the railway. (12) He maintained that without encroaching on the green belt Chelmsford's existing residential areas could be re-planned to comfortably house a further 15,000 people. (13) Minoprio identified a shortage of housing in nearly all the surrounding rural parishes and a lack of amenities, particularly piped water in many of them. (14)

The plan failed to make an immediate impression on either local businessmen or the local authorities. Those councillors who were on the town Planning Committee failed to make time to officially discuss it. The Weekly News did however report on the drastic changes envisaged in the scheme in 1950. (15) Most of his proposals were however, incorporated into Chelmsford's first town map which formed part of the 1952 Development Plan for Essex. It included a possible increase in the population of 21,000 to be located in 9 residential areas on the Minoprio model. The redevelopment of the town centre was delayed until it could be financed by private enterprise in the 1960s and 1970s, but by and large followed his scheme. (16)

Chelmsford became an early target for London's overspill population because there was plenty of employment. It was therefore felt that people would be able to settle and work locally without time consuming travel. (17) The 1952 plan was taken on a tour of Essex including Chelmsford by Essex County Council. It provided for 9 thousand new homes to be built by 1971 in the area to cater for the arrival of the allotted 'overspill' population. An inner relief road was to be built within the first five years of the plan. It was felt its route would be comparatively inexpensive with few houses having to be demolished. The proposed shopping centre followed Minoprio's plan as did the inclusion of clearance around the cathedral, to make the latter a more prominent feature in the town. (18) As was to be the case with succeeding plans, the proposals caused a good deal of opposition and resulted in a lengthy inquiry which was initially held in the county town. Protests were particularly strong in the rural parishes such as Galleywood, which didn't want large scale house building. In a prophetic article in the Joseph Billio column in the Weekly News in 1957, the lack of a Civic Society, similar to that formed in Maldon before the war, was highlighted. It was already felt that the planners were taking over and much of the value in the town would be lost. (19) A year later the same column was complaining that Colchester was leading the county town in cottage preservation. There, 42 crumbling cottages had been brought up to date in one year. This had involved all but rebuilding the cottages. (20) A number of Spalding's photographs reveal that a similar amount of work would certainly have been needed in the case of Chelmsford's cottages. In contrast, a planner commented on the revised plan for the county town in 1958 "Chelmsford's shortcomings are of course the planners opportunities. Having virtually no problem of preservation on historical, architectural or aesthetic grounds and with a great deal of open, derelict or underdeveloped space at their disposal they have almost as free a hand as the creator of new towns." (21) The plan drawn up by the borough engineer involved two large quadrangles of shops and a paved market place and differed in a number of respects from that drawn up by the County Planning Officer, Leslie Leaver. There would have been two squares for pedestrian use. The borough engineer emphasised that the county town was being left behind as a shopping centre by the new towns of Harlow and Basildon and an early start was needed. This however, was delayed by the need to first move the cattle market (see chapter 1) and the planning restrictions which affected one third of Chelmsford. Compulsory purchase orders would be needed for much of the 'Yards'. (22)

In addition to the scheme for the centre of Chelmsford, the borough authorities wanted to build its quota of new houses but were restricted by the lack of unused space, despite the assertion of the planner mentioned earlier. For this reason they decided to fight for proposals to restrict the green belt. The Rural District Council however, concerned at proposals for further housing in Great Baddow and Writtle, pushed for a further extension of the green belt. (23) Although the expected influx of overspill population hadn't materialised in the early 1950s, it was greater than predicted during the later part of the decade. This put pressure on the remaining underdeveloped land in the town in the south and south east of the town. (24) In the review of the Chelmsford district plan in 1962 a new planner J.E. Grant, who had come from the new town at Basildon, envisaged a town centre serving 100,000 people, plus another 100,000 in the Mid Essex area. In his plan cars and shoppers would be separated in the new Chelmsford. He put forward a pedestrian deck bounded by Market Road, Tindal Street, Moulsham Street, Friars Road, London Road and the River Can as well as a new inner relief road. Warehouses, garages and service roads would be under the deck level. All the shops would be reached by stairs, ramps and possibly escalators. (25) Councillor Bellamy baulked at the cost but Councillor Roberts felt it would be eventually the cheapest way of easing the chronic congestion in the town. (26) The town's civic trust was finally brought in for consultation. It criticised the new scheme along with the two previous schemes. The borough engineer himself felt the new scheme was inflexible and too costly. Another problem was that many of the property owners were objecting. Nineteen sixty three saw a new plan for the town centre with one central square. A development was to be built mainly on land already owned by the council. (27) The new one level scheme would yield 170,000 square feet of shopping space with 133 shops. A start was made in July 1964 with the council carrying out compulsory purchase orders on 20 shops, 3 pubs and 3 cafes. (28) The plan for the central area didn't however get the green light from the government until 1968. This was despite determined opposition from local architects and the Civic Trust (later the Chelmsford Society and then the Civic Society). They put forward alternative proposals that would have 'saved' both Tindal Street and Tindal Square. A pub and a restaurant proposed in the new official scheme would jut out into Tindal Square and ruin it. The adopted plan sacrificed residential accommodation and it was predicted that the new area would become dead and deserted after the shops had closed. A previous scheme had at least enlarged Tindal Square to form a new heart for Chelmsford and had included residential accommodation. Instead every possible foot of lettable space had been crammed into the central area. The result was no provision for wide pedestrian walkways and initially no central space. (29)

The first High Chelmer shopping centre opened in 1973 with a fountain in the centre. (30) John Marriage bemoaned the reduction of Tindal Square to little more than a traffic junction and in particular the demolition of the Corn Exchange. "It was a great loss to the character of the town when this building of character was destroyed in 1969 as its rather run down condition made it ideal for activities unable to afford high hire charges." (31) Marriage was concerned at how little had been done to conserve the best of the past. "A whole side of Tindal Street, one of the town's most interesting streets containing a wealth of old buildings, was demolished to make way for the present blank uninteresting wall of a large underused service yard. This destruction was an act of pure vandalism, needlessly perpetrated and is now still mourned by older Chelmsfordians." he wrote in 1982. (32) Marriage felt that the merger of the two Chelmsford districts, bringing in as it did councillors who took a wider view on what was important in the development of the area, came just a few years too late to save a lot of what was individual about Chelmsford. He felt that Mesopotamia Island, swept away as part of the remodelling of the two rivers in the town, could and should have been saved. The channels which created the island were filled in by the River Authority in the early 1970s.

Marriage also thought that Moulsham Street, another street like Tindal Street with a large number of buildings worth preserving, was also under threat. In 1973 a private company put forward a big scheme to redevelop a large part of the street. Fortunately this company folded before the scheme could get underway. (33) Despite it being a conservation area a number of buildings of historical interest in the street disappeared in the later 1970s. National Heritage money at the end of the 1980s saved some of the oldest cottages, including several with Tudor overhangs, but many were still lost. (34) In the new millennium the street retained some of its individuality but more could have been done.

The town's conservation movement did manage to preserve most of the features of Gray's brewery on the Springfield Road, near the High Street, after it had appeared that they would disappear. Initially Debenhams wanted to knock down the old listed brewery and build an extension to their then present complex. Eventually part of the old brewery was kept and converted into 9 small shops. (35)

After the completion of Parkway in the 1970s, the West End part of the town was in serious decline. The newly formed Civic Trust vowed to improve the area in 1985. (36) In 1997 a scheme was introduced to part pedestrianise the area. (37) It wasn't until the new millennium that some improvement was introduced to this part of town. The first plans for the new bus station (see chapter 10) drew severe criticism from the Chelmsford Society but what was actually built was a significant improvement on the initial plans. A new public square, now renamed Marconi Square, should be a focal point for leisure use but this has yet to be consistently the case. The Marconi Statue was moved to the Square from the Record Office in 2007. (38)

A number of the rural parishes were more successful in preserving their identities. In Great and Little Leighs after the 1920s, when farmers had been quite happy to sell land to builders, without any controls and with no planning permission then needed, the villagers formed the Great and Little Leighs Protection Society to preserve the village way of life. After the second war Writtle was in danger of becoming another suburb of Chelmsford, like Springfield and Great Baddow, but was saved by the operation of the green belt that has kept it separate from the town. Keeping the village shop was often seen as a key issue as was the development of a community hall and other amenities.

1971 saw the first Essex County Council plans to turn Woodham Ferrers from a small rural parish into a new town with a predicted population of nine thousand. (39) Two years later the E.C.C. made a compulsory purchase order for 1,000 acres at what was to become South Woodham Ferrers. (40) Opposition to the scheme on environmental and cost grounds led to a public inquiry, but the government approved the scheme the following year, partly because it lay between two major centres of employment in Basildon and Chelmsford. The borough agreed to the development because if they hadn't the equivalent number of houses would have to be built elsewhere in the district. By this time the projected number of expected residents had risen to 20,000. (41) Work started on the project in 1975 and by 1983 there were seven and a half thousand residents. Much was made of the 1,300 acre development on the banks of the River Crouch. The town bordered on a 300 acre country park and 200 acres of further open spaces and playing fields. Its shops were arranged carefully in courtyards. Despite this attractive layout many of the residents in the original village refused to use the new amenities. (42) When the town was completed it won many plaudits until rising unemployment towards the end of the century limited its success story.

By the early 1980s the prediction that the redevelopment of the centre of Chelmsford would lead it to being a quiet and deserted zone in the evening had come true. "The town that dies in the evening" was the comment of Councillor Lander. (43) The new centre was becoming a "precinct of fear" with older townsfolk wary of entering the area at night. (44) By 1983 the shopping centre was already proving too small for the needs of super stores, with supermarkets such as Sainsbury's moving out of town. The centre was already being described as 'tatty' with its openness leading to much vandalism at night. A two million pound facelift eventually included sealing the renovated shopping centre in the evening and removing the fountain from the centre. (45) The second shopping centre for the town was planned in 1985 on land in Kings Head Meadow. This also involved a new road over the two rivers and a new car park (see chapter 10). Work started in 1989. The Meadows finally opened in 1992. (46) As early as 1985 a third shopping centre was planned for the large empty space down to the river. Several planned developments came to nothing before the new millennium. Another scheme, this time involving the John Lewis Partnership, received planning permission in 2012. The revised plans mean that the new development could rival Westfield at Stratford. (47) In June 2013 the demolition of the old Barclays Bank and National Westminster Bank in the High Street were taking place as the first part of the development. The year 2012 also saw progress on two other proposed developments. Firstly planning permission has been given for Waitrose to return to the town by developing the Royal Mail site on Victoria Road. This development will also include a new mosque (see chapter 22). (48) Even well before these developments, the town was voted one of the best shopping centres in the south east. Progress was also finally made on the old Anglia Ruskin site. In the new plans there will be pedestrian routes either side of the Ann Knight building. (49) Work on this was underway in 2013.The refurbished Quaker building will be the centrepiece of a new square. So far all plans for the gasworks site have come to nothing. The latest scheme for this area, by the retail owners of Bluewater, collapsed in 2010. (50)

The new millennium saw the disappearance of two of Chelmsford's best known names, Bolingbroke and Wenley. Both adjacent shops were completely gutted by fire in 1947. Quick work by those on the scene enabled much of the stock to be saved. The customers of both shops were honest enough to pay back their debts even though the shop's ledgers had been destroyed in the fire. Post war restrictions meant it was several years before the shops could re-open. When they did they were both modernised. Wenley's now had a top floor restaurant that could seat 100 people. New fire regulations meant that passages had to be created through the walls between the two buildings. This gave Richard Wenley an idea and he went to Wray Bolingbroke to see if he would be interested in a merger. Both families admitted later that their businesses would not have survived separately. It was a further two years before work began on joining the two shops together with the creation of a single trading floor. In the late 1990s the shop closed its High Street site and moved to a site in Springfield. The business moved again to premises on the Parkway near the Army and Navy in 2001. (51) This was finally closed in 2006.

One man who did his best to keep at least some individuality in the buildings in and around Chelmsford was Fred Willett, who was an expert in the ancient craft of pargetting. This involves ornamental designs on plaster reliefs. He was also an accomplished painter but taught himself the craft of pargetting in the 1930s. Operating out of a side street in Chelmsford he continued his work for over 40 years and his handiwork can still be seen on houses throughout East Anglia as well as in the Chelmsford area. Examples of his work included the design of a cricketer on the wall of a house fronting on to the main street in Writtle. He completed works for a number of brewers, e.g. the 6 Bells at Great Waltham. (52)

With regard to the development of Chelmsford as a whole, the last three decades of the century saw an increasing conflict between the local authority and both the county council and the government. Rural parishes in particular had to fight to keep their individual identity. As early as 1971 a government plan earmarked Chelmsford for medium growth expanding to a projected 220 thousand people, just short of the accepted city size of 250,000. (53) The plan for South Woodham Ferrers could only account for 20,000. Some of the necessary house building was achieved in the North Springfield area surrounding Pump Lane. By 1976 the county was insisting that further development go ahead in Melbourne and North Springfield, as well as South Woodham Ferrers but the Chelmsford authority thought that existing public services were already overstretched. Continual rearguard actions by Chelmsford Borough Council managed to limit the number of houses actually built. In 1991 there was all party opposition to a Chelmsford Borough Plan which was based on the premise that the town needed 10,700 more homes in the new century. The Plan maintained that more residential development in the North West and North East of the borough was possible." The town has reached its logical capacity. It just cannot take any more lumps on the edge of town. We do not have the highway infrastructure for anymore." (54) The borough tried to limit this by proposing the extension of the green belt around the entire town. Despite this a new scheme for Beaulieu Park was proposed in 1999. (55) In 2012 it finally looked as though this scheme would achieve fruition, with the first of 3,200 houses due for completion in 2013. Land has been allocated for a new secondary school. (56)

Another plan for a mini new town, at Margaretting was eventually turned down by the County Council in 2,000 because it was in the green belt. (57) This was the second time the village had featured in such a scheme, having originally been considered for one of the post war new towns in 1944. This decision led to pressure to find room for a further 7,000 houses. A new proposal for a mini town at Boreham in 2,001 immediately raised the opposition of the newly formed Boreham Conservation Society. (58) Resistance to the Boreham development continued well into the new millennium.

Despite the green belt being 'under siege' at villages such as Writtle, many local villages have more than held their own. (59) In 2009 Binacre for example, was runner up in the best village in Essex competition. Some of the remaining land for development there had been given to the council to be used for open spaces in 2009. The village was raising £3 million for a local church and community centre. (60) In 2010 Great Waltham won an annual award from the Rural Community Council. "Although close to Chelmsford it retains a real village atmosphere." (61)

The rural area around Chelmsford has also managed to keep a number of substantial houses. Apart from Hylands (see chapters 27 and 28) these include Langley's at Great Waltham, New Hall and Boreham House.

Boreham is of course home to New Hall, a palace of Henry the Eighth which he had rebuilt. It declined during the following two centuries but was converted to a Catholic School by the end of the century (see chapters 20 and 21). The architectural critic Pevsner stated that New Hall is one of the foremost remaining brick built sixteenth century buildings, which accounts for its grade one listed status. It has retained this status despite its setting being affected first by the coming of the railway, then more recently the Boreham bypass and now in the twenty first century the Beaulieu Park Development.

In the grounds of New Hall, the Hoare banking family, had Boreham House, now a grade one listed building, built in the early eighteenth century after which New Hall was sold. The two buildings have been separate ever since. In 1877 it was inherited by Lieutenant Colonel Tyrell Tufnell. It stayed in the Tufnell family until Henry Ford bought it in 1931. He established Fordson Estate Limited with the house as its base, to show that British agriculture could raise itself out of the depression. After 1937 it became a college. Since 1997 it has again been privately owned and is currently hired out, like Hylands, for private weddings and functions.

Part of Leez Priory lies in Great Leighs and is within the Chelmsford City area. This was the medieval house of the Rich family and is a Grade One listed building. Great Leighs also encompasses Lyons Hall the long time residence of the Tritton family, with their close connections with Barclays Bank (see chapters 1 and 2). It is a Grade 2 listed timber framed building with fifteenth century origins.

Langley's at Great Waltham was rebuilt in its present form to designs by William Tufnell, after the original Tudor house had been partly demolished. The park had been extended by 1875 and an elaborate formal 'parterre' garden laid out.

Great changes have taken place in Chelmsford's High Street apart from the two shopping centres. Superstores moved to the outskirts of the town. There was a decline in the number of shops from 87 in the 1900s to 67 in the new millennium. Even by 1955 the number of shops that were locally owned had fallen from 78 to 51. In the 1900s households had shopped two or three times a week for fresh food. By the new millennium only Marks and Spencer sold fresh food on the High Street. Smaller shops had been replaced by banks and building societies "Today only three stores sell household items but five sell mobile phones." Chelmsford's centre still ranked fifth nationwide in 2003 for the number of shops. Bolinbroke and Wenley was not the only store to close because of internet competition. (62)

One positive effect of the relentless drive to redevelop Chelmsford was the archaeological finds that have been discovered as a result, particularly those which have given further proof of an extensive Roman development (Caesaromagus). Roman finds in the town started with excavations in 1849 by Frederic Chancellor which had revealed the first signs of the bath house of the Mansio. In the late nineteenth century building in Moulsham had seen regular finds of Roman pottery, coins and burials. Immediately after the second war Major Jack Brinson carried out further excavations which unearthed more of the baths. The beginning of the construction of Parkway from the late 1960s made further excavation urgent. Chelmsford Excavation Committee excavated 40 sites in Chelmsford up to 1978. Its work was then taken over by the Archaeology Section of the Essex County Council. (63) Further excavation on the site of the present Godfreys Mews revealed the south gatehouse bank and ditches built in the second century A.D. In 1987 a stone coffin was found, which can now be seen at the museum. On the left hand corner of Rochford Road off Mildmay Road is the site of a Romano – Celtic temple. It was an eight sided stone building erected in the fourth century used for the individual worship of gods and goddesses. (64)

One example of an old industrial brownfield site eventually being used against the odds to improve the local environment has been the establishment of the Marconi Ponds Nature Reserve during the new millennium. This is the area known by former Marconi workers as the Filter Beds or the Crompton ponds. Before Crompton established his second Arc Works there, it had been used as clay pits for local brickworks. After Crompton began building on the site in 1896, an artesian well was sunk nearby. "The waste or surplus flowed into tanks and ponds that supplied water for industrial plant and flushing water for lavatories". All this water was piped to the filter beds that became the two pieces of water known as the Marconi Ponds. The ponds had ceased to be used as filter beds by 1959. After Marconi Radar left the old Crompton site in 1994, the planning agreement for the development known as 'The Village', involved the Chelmsford Borough Council being given the strip of land that now makes up the wildlife site plus £80,000 for community participation. After several plans came to nothing, progress was started by the clearance of bottles by the Essex Bottle Diggers Association in 2005. After the Chelmsford Environment Partnership took over the management of the project, the Friends of Marconi Nature Reserve was set up in 2007. The new group was allowed to use e2v's sports pavilion for meetings which was next to the site. Kingfishers and herons were already present and foxes and deer are being encouraged to return. The Friends of Marconi Ponds have received National Green Flag awards in each of the last three years and they now justify the title 'A Rural Retreat in Central Chelmsford'. (65)

On balance it is hard to disagree with some of the criticisms of the town in the controversial article which appeared in the Guardian in August 2010. "In the 1960s it forgot it was a pleasant historic county town and threw in its lot with Los Angeles, covering the place with ring roads and pumping it full of commuters." The author Tom Dyckoff did list the reminders of Chelmsford's halcyon age; namely "its pretty Shire Hall, the water meadows and parks along the rivers, the tiny flint studded cathedral" but rightly bemoaned the fact that these features were cut off from each other. (66) Dyckoff praised the area's schools as well as the local villages that had retained their character such as Sandon and Writtle. He was unfair with regard to the area's transport never having experienced the dire congestion up to the 1970s, but the new developments in various parts of the city may see a return to those days if sufficient regard isn't paid to the transport infrastructure (see chapter 10).

1) Essex Weekly News 13 7 1951 p.1
2) E.W.N. 12 5 1976 p.7
3) Population estimates for England and Wales Mid 2011 Census from The Office For National Statistics.
4) Essex Chronicle 15 2 2010 p.5
5) On the planning history of Chelmsford Ana Lescenko Fuller and Robert Home p.14
6) Chelmsford Planning Survey Minoprio p.13
7) Minoprio p.14
8) Minoprio p.15 – 17
9) Fuller Home p.16
10) Fuller and Home p.17
11) Minoprio p.34
12) Minoprio p.36
13) Minoprio p.37
14) Minoprio p.39 - 47
15) E.W.N. 20 10 1950 p.1
16) Fuller and Home p.19
17) E.W.N. 6 6 1952 p.1
18) E.W.N. 24 10 1952 p.1
19) E.W.N. 20 9 !957 p.9
20) E.W.N. 26 9 1958 p.9
21) E.W.N. 4 7 1958 p.9
22) E.W.N. 2 1 1959 Editorial
23) Chelmsford Rural District Council minutes 16 12 1960
24) C.R.D.C. minutes 27 8 1962
25) E.W.N. 5 1 1962 p.7
26) E.W.N. 2 2 1962 p.1
27) E.W.N. 7 8 1963
28) E.W.N. 31 7 1964 p.1
29) E.W.N. 4 7 1969 p.1
30) E.C. 26 10 1973 p.6

31) Essex Countryside 1979 Vol. 27 May
32) Essex Countryside 1982 Vol. 30 May
33) E.C. 19 10 1973 p.1
34) E.W.N. 8 5 1988 p.1
35) E.C. 25 4 1980 p.5
36) E.C. 26 7 1985 p.2
37) E.C. 19 9 1997 p.1
38) E.W.N. 25 9 2006
39) E.W.N. 12 2 1971
40) E.W.N. 26 7 1973 p.1
41) E.W.N. 13 6 1974 p.1
42) Essex Countryside 1983 Vo. 31 Mar.
43) E.W.N. 18 6 1981 p.1
44) E.C. 13 1 p.1 1984
45) E.C. 11 11 1983 p.1
46) E.W.N. 29 10 1992 p.6
47) E.C. 22 9 2011 p.1
48) E.C. 18 10 2012 p.1
49) E.C. 18 8 2012 p.3
50) E.C. 18 2 2010 p.1
51) Essex Life and Countryside Mar. 2005
52) Essex Countryside 1978 Vol. 26 Aug.
53) E.C. 8 1 1971 p.36
54) E.C. 6 9 1991 p.1
55) E.C. 30 4 1999 p.1
56) E.C. 21 7 2011 p.7
57) E.C. 7 7 2000 p.5
58) E.C. 9 2 2001 p.5
59) E.C. 29 3 2007 p.2
60) E.C. 16 7 2009 p.5
61) E.C. 15 7 2010 p.23
62) Survey of Chelmsford's Retailing Anne Lloyd 2003
63) Caesaromagus: Roman Chelmsford p.3 – 5
64) Chelmsford Museum and Moulsham: An historical walking guide David Jones and Janette Scarborough p.5

65) www.marconiponds.btck.co.uk/
66) http://www.guardian.co.uk/money/2010/aug/28/lets-move-to-chelmsford-essex

13

Politics in the Chelmsford area before 1945

"They should not have invented, the sewing machine, the wringing machine and all the things which lessened labour and gave women time to think"

The early years of the period this book deals with were obviously dominated by the incorporation of the town so that it became a borough with the greater access to funding which this offered. Anybody expecting a rush to municipal excess, with a number of public buildings being built at lavish expense, would have been disappointed. We will see elsewhere that the late Victorian and Edwardian period were characterised by a very cautious approach to public spending in the town. It was a source of much municipal pride that in the two decades that followed incorporation, average rates were below their pre 1888 level. On a parliamentary level the Mid Essex constituency was frequently not contested because of the failure of the local Liberals to get themselves sufficiently organised. Another feature of Chelmsford politics before the first war was the inability of any political labour organisation to get established. Rapid industrialisation in the town in the years before the first war should have provided fertile ground for the establishment of the Independent Labour Party (I.L.P.) or another similar organisation, as it did in Ipswich and Norwich. A major political conflict in the area during the years before the first war concerned the borough's boundary extension. The rural council's sense of independence and refusal to be browbeaten resulted in the issue being taken all the way to the House of Lords. One of the great national political issues which had a big effect on local politics in Chelmsford was the movement for women's suffrage. A feature of the movement in the town was the support it received from a number of prominent men as well as women. In the 1930s when one might have expected another major political movement, fascism, to gain considerable local support, it failed to get a real foothold. In 1914 the borough's politicians thought it was inevitable that the awarding of cathedral status would lead to the county town becoming a city. In the past such towns just had to apply to the Letters Patent Office but when Chelmsford did so it was passed over in favour of towns with much greater population. The town was unlucky in the sense that in 1907 the Home Office had introduced minimum population of 300,000 for towns wishing to become cities. Even Ipswich with a population of almost 74,000, compared with Chelmsford's 18,000, was thought of as a minor town by government officials. It was to be almost a hundred years before the town finally became a city.

Chelmsford was a borough from 1888 to 1974. The town had ignored the possibility of incorporation for more than five decades after the Municipal Corporations Act of 1835. This had been amended by an Act of 1882. The question of incorporation was first mentioned in the town as part of very early discussions about what the town could do to commemorate the Queen's Jubilee. (1) By August 1887 the Croydon Review noted "The inhabitants of Chelmsford are considering whether the time has at last arrived when they should have a......corporation." (2) It was the involvement of A.J. Furbank, a solicitor new to the area, in the incorporation movement which was a key factor in its eventual success. He believed a corporation was the best form of municipal government and intrinsically superior to anything a local board could offer. In August 1887 a memorial in favour of incorporation, signed by 50 taxpayers "undaunted by the indifference which has been exhibited in the matter by the local Board of Health" was submitted to the local board. (3) The Board of Health appointed a committee to look into the matter. Furbank said he had received 30 letters from town clerks on the subject saying that it was frequently possible to run boroughs cheaper than their predecessors, Boards of Health. He thought that this should definitely be the case in Chelmsford, because expensive sewerage work had already been carried on in the town, resulting in a rise in the rates. He maintained that the Board was unpopular with a large section of the public. Only 1,500 people usually voted and "many of the papers were filled by outsiders." (i.e. people from outside the town) He also said that there were 8 county towns that had been incorporated, with a smaller population than Chelmsford. This answered W.W. Duffield's argument that Chelmsford was too small to be a borough. At the same Board meeting Edmund Durrant made the point that the local government bill might result in Chelmsford being merged into a district of the county and the Board of Health abolished. G.W. Gepp, one of the opponents of incorporation within the Board, steadfastly maintained that it would result in an increase in the rates. (4) The tide began to turn in favour of the incorporation movement with the holding of a public meeting at the Corn Exchange. (5) This drew 500 people with only a dozen voting against the motion in favour of incorporation. Fourteen Board of Health members refused to join the committee that was set up to look into the issue. Two petitions were submitted, the one in favour with 1,063 signatures, the one against with 346. What those in favour found interesting, was that the two petitions represented an almost equal value of property. (6) Those signing the smaller petition in general had much greater wealth, at least when judged by the amount of property they owned. They argued that this showed how vested interests were operating. It was said that they didn't want to lose their cumulative voting rights under the existing board system, which favoured those with valuable property interests. By November 1887, 1,400 names were attached to the petition in favour. (7) The election of members of the Board of Health in April 1888 saw the 'Incorporation 6' returned. (8) These included Frederic Chancellor, who being the astute politician he was, saw the change in broad opinion that was taking place and became a late convert to the cause. In January 1888 the editor of the Essex Chronicle had estimated that four fifths of the town's population were in favour of incorporation. (9) At the inquiry into the issue, witnesses spoke of the difficulty of getting working men on to the existing Board. Representatives of both the Bolingbroke and Wenley shops thought that the move would benefit business in the town. It was Chancellor's voice however that resonated most powerfully at the inquiry. Whilst he thought that the works of the board had been undervalued he was now satisfied that the majority of ratepayers were in favour of incorporation. (10)

The Local Government Board Commissioner appointed by the Privy Council reassured the committee that the charter would be granted. Initially he seemed strongly inclined to draw the boundary across the parish of Springfield, a move that would have been very controversial. In order to get the charter granted as quickly as possible no part of Springfield was included. Two wards, North and South were agreed. It was also decided not to include a part of Widford. In August the Charter for Chelmsford was approved by the Queen and on Wednesday the 19th of September the Charter was brought by train to Chelmsford. The train arrived at 3.25 p.m. and the Charter was carried by the acting mayor, Frank Whitmore and the acting town clerk. (11) Evidently the town did the occasion proud, although the Weekly News thought that the decoration was not as complete as for the previous Essex show to be held in the town. (12) A large red banner emblazoned with 'God Save the Queen and Success to our Borough' was unfurled at the Railway Tavern in Duke Street. All the traders made an effort. The parapet at Mr Chancellor's house in the High Street was covered with crimson baize looped with white cords and tassels and on it were the local historic dates 1100, 1337, 1850 and 1888. The first being the date of the first bridge over the Can, the second was when the town sent four members to parliament, the third when the Board of Health first met and the fourth was the year of the charter. All the pubs and hotels were covered with flags."Undoubtedly one of the great attractions which brought many people into the town was that through the generosity of Crompton and Co., there would be a general illumination of the town by electric light." This installation covered the town from the Arc Works to the railway station and the cable used was over three miles in length.

A large number of people crowded around the station and a few got onto the platform to greet the arrival of the train bearing the Charter and the party which had gone to fetch it. When the train arrived the Chelmsford Town Band played 'See the Conquering Hero Comes'. The procession through the town included the Grammar School boys, 360 boys and girls of the Victoria National School, 410 boys and girls of the British schools, 60 boys and girls of the Catholic school and 120 boys of the Essex Industrial School. (13) There were also the 2nd battalion of the Essex Regiment and members of the Suffolk Hussars as well as police constables and members of the local fire brigade. They took the route down the High Street, up through Moulsham Street, across Queen Street past the Arc Works, and down the New London Road. The procession arrived back in a packed Tindal Street at 4.45 p.m. Whitmore asked for three rousing cheers for the Queen and the acting town clerk read the charter. (14)

For the borough's arms a sketch was elicited from the Herald's College which illustrated interesting periods from Chelmsford's history. Furbank himself suggested the 'Many minds one heart' motto. "Across the centre of the shield itself, there is a bridge of three arches at the base of which there are bars, wavy, signifying water. The bridge is surmounted by crosiers crossed or 'in saltire' flanked either side by a lion rampant. The crest is charged with a pair of crossed swords and portcullis and a circlet of oak leaves." (15)

Furbank organised the first elections in the borough but he had left the town by 1899. Ten of the eighteen councillors elected were former Board of Health members. When the six aldermen were elected at the first council meeting in November 1888 all 6 were former Board members. Duffield and Durrant had topped the original poll in the North ward, with Taylor Ridley and Chancellor further down the poll. In the South ward, long time eminent citizens such as Gray, Bodkin, Wells, Copland and Darby featured prominently. (16) The spaces left by the election of the aldermen were filled by supplementary elections, which resulted in more well known townsfolk such as Gepp and Whitmore being voted in. (17)

After the elections Chancellor was voted in by the councillors as the town's first mayor. This was celebrated by a "huge torchlight procession followed by a bonfire and a display of fireworks". (18) The Mayor's robe was made by the local shop Bolingbrokes. "The robe is composed of superfine broadcloth lined throughout with white silk, trimmed with velvet and sable edging, with a costly Russian sable round the neck and down the fronts reaching to the bottom." The papers pointed out that the aldermen had to buy their own robes. (19)

The following year C.E. Ridley, the brewer, presented the Mace to the borough. It "is of solid silver, weighing 140 ounces and is about four feet in length." "It is a handsome piece of work and the ornamentation is symbolical of agricultural and kindred pursuits." "On the boss or head of the mace, there are two beautiful enamelled shields laid on 18 carat gold. One of these contains the Royal Arms of England and the other the Borough Arms with the motto 'Many minds one heart'." "On the intermediate parts of the boss there are representations of oak leaves and acorns, barley, oats and wheat engraves in low relief upon the silver." "The boss is surmounted by a model of the Royal Crown, with a ball and cross across the apex." "Round the middle is the inscription 'Presented by Charles Ernest Ridley of the Elms, Chelmsford, A.D. 1889'." The Mace was in two pieces, screwed together in the middle. (20) Henry Collings Wells, of the local brewing family and the town's first member of Essex County Council, presented the mayoral chain and insignia to the town. (21) This was designed by Arthur Raven, who worked for Lovedays.

In 1889 the editor of the Weekly News said that the cost of becoming a borough was a thousand pounds but still thought it was well worth it; the cost would have been less if the opposition hadn't forced an inquiry. He pointed out that incorporation had already yielded a financial dividend enabling a consolidated loan which saved £300 a year. (22)

Prior to the major boundary changes in the Redistribution of Seats Act 1885, Chelmsford had fallen within the constituency of West Essex. Between 1868 and 1885 this returned two members of parliament. Throughout this time these were the Conservative M.P.s Sir H.J. Selwyn Ibbetson and Lord Eustace Cecil. In the 1880 election Ibbetson recorded 2,664 votes and Cecil 2,397, comfortably beating the Liberal candidate Buxton. (23) Ibbetson was a regular speaker at Conservative meetings at the County town, sharing a platform for example with the owner of Hylands, Arthur Prior at a meeting in the Shire Hall in 1883. (24) Later that year he spoke again, blaming the Liberal government for the depression in agriculture, specifically their failure to limit the imports of livestock. (25)

1885 saw the inaugural meeting of the Chelmsford branch of the Conservative Women's Primrose League. (26) Although nationally the League didn't officially support women's suffrage, its active role in the party did much to raise the political consciousness of women locally. The following year a Conservative Working Men's Club was founded in the town. Meanwhile the local Conservative Regional Association met for the first time at the White Hart Hotel in 1882. (27) In 1884 the two local Liberal organisations, the Chelmsford and District Liberal Association and the Chelmsford and West Essex Liberal Association sensibly decided to combine. (28) A Chelmsford Working Men's Liberal Five Hundred was also started in the early 1880s. The Liberals were often poorly organised but didn't have any difficulty in getting people to attend meetings. One was held at the Corn Exchange in 1884, on the then current reform bill. "A few members of the opposition mustered at the back and created a disturbance during part of the proceedings: some of them were forcibly ejected." (29)

Under the government scheme for the redistribution of seats, the Boundary Commissioners held an inquiry in the Grand Jury Room of the Shire Hall in 1885. As a result the Dengie Hundred was added to the new Chelmsford constituency, and consequently removed from the Southend Constituency. (30) For the resulting election the Conservatives selected William Beadel as their candidate. (31) His first election was a lively affair with Beadel polling 4,221 votes and the Liberal candidate Martin, 3,071. The Weekly News reported "the election is being carried on with considerable vigour and both parties are confident of success. One of the features of the struggle is the defacing of election bills by each side." (32) Previously, rowdyism had broken up a Primrose League meeting. Before the election the following year the Liberals nominated John Kempster, who had the advantage to the constituency party that he offered to pay his own expenses. In the event he withdrew and the 1886 election was uncontested. (33) This was not before a soiree organised by the Primrose League had drawn 1,100 people. (34) In 1887 the eminent local politician and administrator W.W. Duffield was asked to stand by the Liberals. He was well known and the Essex Chronicle felt "he is a fluent speaker, had a good grasp of the political questions of the day and is personally popular on the Board of Health." Duffield declined after evidently much thought. (35) Beadel died in 1892 and his funeral was at Hutton. The Irishman Thomas Usborne was adopted as the Conservative candidate. (36) Usborne was born in Limerick and went to Harrow and then to Trinity College, Cambridge. Once again the Liberals were insufficiently well organised to fight the by election and he was returned unopposed. He considered Home Rule in Ireland, which of course he opposed, to be the only major question at issue in the general election which followed a few months later. The town had already seen several large meetings on the question. In 1889 a group of Liberals met at the Corn Exchange to protest against the treatment of political prisoners in Ireland by the government. "There was a crowded attendance, which included several Conservatives and Unionists and a large number of ladies." (37) It emerged that Usborne would be opposed by a Liberal, Dr Grigsby. In one week the latter spoke at Chelmsford, Sandon, Billericay and Little Baddow. (38) After some rowdy meetings Usborne polled 4,168 votes and Dr Grigsby, 2,799, a comfortable majority of 1,369. (39) Usborne was one of seven Conservatives elected in the county: 4 Liberals were returned. (40) The editor of the Weekly News hoped, rather forlornly, that the local Liberals "are not going to sleep again for six years". (41) Two years later Usborne was receiving criticism from some quarters for treating his Chelmsford constituency as a sinecure seat. Major Carne Rasch, who held the neighbouring constituency of South East Essex, came to his defence. "He did not attempt to ignore the fact that he has taken part in fewer divisions than any other Essex county member." Rasch said "there is a great deal of humbug talked about being continually in the voting lobby and that voting on every trivial question which comes before the House would neither benefit him, nor his constituency, nor his party". He obtained a pair when absent. The editor of the Weekly News supported Usborne saying that he only spoke in the House on subjects which he had expert knowledge. (42) Despite the criticism he was returned unopposed in the general election of 1895. (43)

In 1899 the Mid Essex Conservative Association, meeting at the Crane Court rooms, received a letter from Usborne stating that he had decided to retire. He had recently helped greatly to raise funds for the Farming Relief Fund, for those who had suffered in the great storm. Carne Rasch was immediately asked to move from his existing seat. (44) Rasch showed his popularity, defeating a lacklustre Liberal candidate, C.S. Henry, 4,975 votes to 1,849. Almost 7,000 people voted out of a total electorate of just over 10,000. Rasch had polled more votes than any previous candidate. (45) The result was the signal for a euphoric torchlight procession. Rasch had been a popular M.P. in South East Essex, but if anything this popularity increased. A month later

Major Rasch "proceeding on the Broomfield Road came upon some men who were at work with a steam roller belonging to the Essex County Council." "As he was passing the men asked him whether he did not think they ought to come under the Working Men's Compensation Act, so as to be entitled to compensation in case of accident." The Weekly News was impressed. "Major Rasch immediately contacted the Home Secretary. A reply is imminent. In the meantime he will keep pegging away." (46) Rasch was by no means a typical landowning, hunting, Conservative of the period, although he was a member of the Beefsteak Club along with' the great and good of Chelmsford'. Rasch was a long time supporter of an eight hour day for workers saying that this was necessary "to give the masses that condition of life which is the aim of all true social reformers". (47) He was however against the raising of the school leaving age from 11 to 12 because he thought it would put too much pressure on parents who depended on their children's wages. Rasch also campaigned for shorter speeches in parliament. It was for his trenchant views on military inefficiency, especially in the Boer War, that he is perhaps best known (see chapter 15). He desperately didn't want his beloved military make the same mistakes in another, perhaps greater conflict. Perhaps it was as well that he died before the main tragedy of the Great War occurred. Rasch was made a coronet in 1903. In 1906 he scored another victory in the general election but this time it was a very close run thing. Rasch polled 4,915 votes but his Liberal opponent Dence received 4,461. His majority of 454 was reduced from 3,129 in 1900. (48) This was the first election where locally the women's suffrage issue played a part (see later). Afterwards Rasch held a huge victory dinner with a record 730 diners. (49) In May 1908 Rasch returned to the Commons after a long absence due to illness, but in August of that year he resigned from representing the constituency after 22 years in the House of Commons overall. (50)(51) Major Rasch died in October 1914 at his beautiful home of Woodhill. (52) It was fitting that some of the funds made available after his death were used to finance a memorial in the town towards those who had lost their lives in the Boer War.

In the early municipal elections Liberals were in the ascendancy. (53) Several attempts to establish the Independent Labour League in the town by leaders from Ipswich and Colchester floundered. The Labour League achieved some support locally, but in order to get elected a left wing politician, Dixon had to change the name of the League locally to the Ratepayers Association, for voting. When the League criticised the Poor Law guardians for their inflexibility (see chapter 19) they drew considerable criticism from the Essex Chronicle. In 1891 the Labour League put up a candidate, G.

Chalcroft up against the chemist J. Tomlinson in a by-election. Tomlinson had traps conveying the voters to the polls. He won comfortably by 422 votes to 177. Chalcroft said "we working men can do very well without the shopkeeper". (54) It was the shopkeepers and professionals however, who had a stranglehold on the political life of the town. A working class politician Arthur Lunney was eventually elected. Despite being a Conservative Party member, his demagoguery and battles at the meetings of the Poor Law guardians provoked the ire of the Chronicle. He again topped the council poll in 1902. (55)

Rates were kept low; in 1890 two shillings and eleven pence in the pound against three shillings and four pence the previous year. The dispute with the County Council, mentioned in chapter 10, was fuelled by an obsession with limiting council spending. In 1892 the borough council decided against buying the old grammar school premises to use as municipal buildings. The editor of the Weekly News said this would have put an extra 2d or 3d on the rates for 30 years. (56) In the event the County Council bought the premises. Part of the building was to be used by their accountants and surveyors etc, the rest was to be used for technical instruction (see chapter 20). (57)

The question of how to celebrate the Queens Jubilee in 1897 sorely tested the resolve of the town's politicians to limit spending, but the suggestions of a free library and a town hall came to nought. The proposal for a free public library was defeated because it was felt that the Beech Report on sanitation meant that the latter had to come first in terms of municipal spending. (58) There was considerable criticism of the Jubilee celebrations that did go ahead. Chelmsford had been the only council in England that had held its discussions 'in camera'. (59) Many felt that a Punch and Judy show was not a suitable entertainment for a County town! The Chronicle regretted that the Chelmsford celebrations were outdone by those of Galleywood. (60)

When Chelmsford eventually did get a public library, it had to be combined with a museum and school of art and science for the borough to get full value (see chapter 27). The total estimated cost of £6,500 was deemed 'exceedingly moderate'. (61) A scheme for a public swimming baths was repeatedly shelved for reasons of economy until finally reaching fruition in 1906. This steadfastly parsimonious approach meant that in 1903 rates were still 1d less in the pound than they had been when incorporation occurred. This of course meant that the type of town hall that was opened in Colchester in 1898 was inconceivable in the borough.

The council bought a steam fire engine but was very reluctant for it to be used outside the borough. (62) Some of the surrounding parishes refused the offer of 'certain terms' for the use of the engine. (63) There was also considerable criticism of the fire service provided by the council. In the opinion of the newspapers they needed to get away more smartly. "There might sooner or later be a serious conflagration". (64) This was despite the local firm of T.H.P. Dennis recently fixing alarm connections to the homes of all fire officers, thus ensuring they could be contacted immediately in an emergency.

1908 saw the retirement from Chelmsford public life of William Ward Duffield. Duffield was born in Great Baddow in 1820 and died aged 92 in 1912. He became a solicitor in 1846, founding the family firm, which he left to his son A.S. Duffield. Interestingly he had a season ticket with the Great Eastern Railway for over half a century. Duffield became clerk to the Board of Guardians, then taking up a similar responsibility with a number of other bodies, including the Highways Board, the Rural Sanitary Authority and from 1873 the clerk to the Justices, a post which he held for 35 years. He became Registrar of the County Court and the Bankruptcy Court in Chelmsford in 1883. Duffield had been the secretary of the town's Literary Institute. He was a Director of the Reliance Life Assurance Company which later became the Norwich Union and was a long time zealous supporter of the Chelmsford Gas Company. In addition he was a member of the Board of Health and a Borough councillor for a combined total of 40 years. Duffield was elected as one of the first aldermen of the new borough. (65) (66) He was succeeded to a number of his administrative posts by his son.

1908 also saw a number of Chelmsford politicians, but particularly Frederic Chancellor, heavily involved in making a strong case as possible for the town's parish church to be made a cathedral (see chapter 22). The success of this campaign made the local papers assume that Chelmsford would become a city over a century before it actually happened. (67) The first steps to become a city had been started by the council when the war broke out. (68)

Carne Rasch was succeeded in the Chelmsford constituency by Ernest George Pretyman, who had previously been M.P. for Woodbridge in Suffolk from 1895 to 1906. He was from a religious family, his father and great grandfather being clerics, but he was educated at Eton and the Royal Military Academy, Greenwich. Like a number of Chelmsford's late 19th and early 20th century M.Ps, he had strong military connections. This was by no means unusual as the majority of Conservatives in the Commons had a military background. He had spent the 1880s in the Royal Artillery. In December 1908 Pretyman recorded a large victory over the Liberals in Chelmsford. He polled

6,132 votes and Dence, standing again for the Liberals, gained 3,387 votes. (69) The suffragists claimed success in lowering the Liberal vote, but the truth was that locally the Liberals were still insufficiently organised. Pretyman had already been Civil Lord of the Admiralty from 1900 to 1903 and he was again from 1916 to 1919. (70)

A huge battle over the proposed extension of the boundaries of the borough was always likely because the two local councils did not have a high opinion of each other. This, added to the fierce sense of independence of the rural parishes and many of their citizens, meant that conflict was ensured. In essence the borough's case was that the town had expanded much more rapidly than could have been predicted and was already absorbing large parts of the previously rural areas around it (see chapter 11). This process was likely to continue, and if anything given the rate of industrial growth, become more rapid, and it therefore made sense for the unitary body to provide the services for the whole area. The initial proposals were published in September 1906 and would have affected five parishes, namely Great Baddow, Springfield, Widford, Writtle and Broomfield. (71) Within a month all the parish councils to be affected had expressed their opposition, but so had parishes such as Great Waltham, that wouldn't be directly affected. (72) Two months later the Local Government Board asked for the R.D.C.'s reactions to the proposals. It was referred to that council's solicitors. In 1907 the L.G.B. held a public inquiry into the issue at the Shire Hall. The Borough Surveyor played a central role; he knew every "twist and turn in the eccentric current boundary". (73) Chelmsford's Rural District Council claimed the superiority of their water supply, but the borough said they hadn't received a complaint in three and a half years. One witness said "whenever I have been in the public library I have seen someone from Springfield there". A Dr Reid saw some unsatisfactory conditions in the borough's dairies and said there was a lack of inspections. In contrast the rural dairies were in a good condition. "I was never in a rural district which is better managed from a sanitary and administrative point a view." (74) The R.D.C. produced an accountant who said that the extension would lead to an increase in the rate of 3d in the £ over the greater part of the area, and in some parts more. Special expenses to provide services would place a heavy burden on the excluded portions. At the inquiry it was maintained that all 29 parishes, with the exception of Little Leighs, had passed a resolution urging the District Council to oppose the extension. It was claimed that 93% of the population signed the resolution in Springfield; in Great Baddow it was 97%, in Broomfield 87.5%, in Widford 99%, in Ingatestone 88.7% and in Writtle 67%. The chairman of Springfield parish council claimed that only 102 Springfield residents worked in Chelmsford. He also maintained that only 1/3 of all land in Chelmsford was currently built on. The Essex Chronicle felt that the L.G.B. might feel that the parishes have "protesteth too much". Whatever happened, the paper felt that harmonious relations needed to be restored!

After the inquiry the Board proposed to give the town council 2/3 of what it asked for, including a large slice of Springfield and part of the Rainsford Road. The council took the view that it could afford to wait for the rest. Springfield would however lose practically all its population and rateable value. (75) At the special R.D.C. meeting it was stated that taking the matter to the Lords would cost up to £3,200 and would have to be borrowed on a short term loan. It was still approved with 14 in favour and 2 against. The total costs to the R.D.C. of the campaign were over £7,000.

The peers decided against them without the Corporation having to reply to the R.D.C.'s case. They did however succeed in getting the House of Commons to hand back to them a considerable amount of rural territory, which however did not yield much in terms of rates. (76) In addition the final act included a small part of Admirals Park and the part of Writtle known as the Waterhouse estate. (77) Chelmsford Borough Council was expanded to 3 wards, with 18 councillors and 6 aldermen. Springfield was to have 6 councillors and 2 aldermen.

A major feature of politics in the Chelmsford area in the Edwardian period was the women's suffrage movement; it certainly didn't start then however. This should be no surprise because Anne Knight, the Chelmsford anti slavery campaigner and member of the Chartist movement, had published one of the first leaflets to call for votes for women in 1847. (78) In the Victorian period, petitions were commonly used by the movement to gain attention to their cause. The first petition from the town was presented on the 26th of April 1872. Chelmsford's first suffrage meeting was held on the 12th of March 1874 by a Miss Beedy and Helena Downing. A Jessie Craigen held a similar meeting at the Literary and Mechanics Institute. In 1886 the same venue hosted a meeting where the main visiting speakers were Florence Fenwick Miller and Florence Balgarnie, who was the secretary of the Women's Suffrage Society. (79) Interestingly there was considerable support from local clerics, with the Reverend Stanley Gibson, the Rector of Sandon, the Reverend J.W. Crompton from the Free Church at Danbury and the Reverend G.C. Postans, the Congregationalist minister in Chelmsford all present. (80) The meeting was well attended and chaired by W.W. Duffield. Carne Rasch was quoted at the meeting "I wish the women's suffrage every success". (81) A Reverend Gibson was concerned that it might cause discontent amongst married women if, as the Women's Suffrage Society proposed, they didn't get the vote. Mrs Fenwick Miller opposed this clause. James Pertwee said that "when it was considered that ladies could take degrees in universities and that the franchise was now lowered to the illiterate farm labourer, he thought it was a disgrace to men and a degradation to women to keep her out of the franchise". Miss Balgarnie then said if those men who held their hands up against the resolution, wished to keep women out of the franchise, "they should not have invented the sewing machine, the wringing machine and all the things which lessened labour and gave women time to think".

As in much of the country the women's suffrage issue was fairly quiet in the Chelmsford area during the 1890s. The work of the Women's Liberal Association and the Primrose League showed the increased involvement of women in politics however. In 1894 there was a meeting on the issue at the Chelmsford Y.M.C.A. The Reverend F.W. Atkin moved a resolution in favour of extending the parliamentary franchise "to all duly qualified women being ratepayers". It was only just passed by 2 votes. (82) In 1899 a Mr Hoare spoke at a Women's Liberal Association meeting held at Crane Court. "I believe in women's suffrage but the majority of the Liberal party may not be in favour of it". (83)

In the early 1900s the women's suffrage movement was once again in the public eye, with the founding of the Women's Social and Political Union (W.S.P.U.) which favoured more militant tactics than the more moderate National Union of Women's Suffrage Societies (N.U.W.S.S.). A 1904 meeting on extending the franchise to women at the Corn Exchange was attended by locals prominent in the cause such as Aylmer Maude, Richenda Christy, Mrs Catherine Munnion and Mrs Sarah Hickley. In 1905 Mrs Dence, the wife of the prospective Liberal candidate, presided at a meeting of the Chelmsford Liberal Club when a local woman Miss Copland lectured on women's suffrage. "Parliament ought to be a reflection of the people but it would not be while women were without the vote". Mr Dence also spoke in favour of the vote being given to women. (84)

Cristabel Pankhurst of the W.S.P.U. and George Bernard Shaw, spoke at a meeting of the Chelmsford Discussion Society in 1907. Later in the year after an unruly Liberal meeting Lord Tweedmouth commented "The way the suffragettes were ejected from the meeting at the Corn Exchange cannot be justified and people of all shades of opinion are unanimous in condemning the methods used. A political meeting is not a religious service and it is open for anyone to ask questions. The instant each suffragette rose to ask a question, they were grabbed by a number of political "understrappers" and thrown onto the street." Apparently "despite great care being taken with the distribution of tickets, five members of the W.S.P.U. got into the building". Heckling followed "Women are taxpayers aren't they?" When one man shouted back "Then give them the vote then" he was put out. Lord Tweedmouth said women should have patience. Mrs Drummond, who was also on the platform, replied "We have had patience for 40 years". Whilst this was occurring, another suffragette, Miss Maloney, addressed a crowd from the cannon in front of the Shire Hall. She complained about the way she had been ejected from the meeting. Drummond and the other suffragettes were taken by the police to the railway station accompanied by a cheering crowd of 1,000. A letter from a resident of Hamlet Road, Moulsham, appeared in the Weekly News, blaming the stewards for problems at the meeting. (85)

As elsewhere, 1908 saw perhaps the peak of suffragette activity in the town. August saw Mrs Billington Craig, secretary to the Women's Freedom League speak 'on the gun'. She had previously been one of those who had chained herself to the 'grille' at the Commons. Despite this militancy she and her supporters did not see eye to eye with the W.S.P.U.. On the same day a Miss Higgins, of the W.S.P.U., led a meeting at the conduit with addresses from a Mrs Meyer from Australia and Mrs Drummond. Mrs Cooper and Miss Joseph, of the N.U.W.S.S., spoke near the Marconi works in Hall Street during the workers' lunch hour. (86)

It was the November 1908 election that brought all three wings of the national women's movement to the County town. The W.S.P.U. under 'General' Drummond was highly organised and very efficient. It was the failure of the Liberal party to translate their supposed support for women's suffrage that led the W.S.P.U. to oppose their most fervent supporters. In the 1908 election the N.U.W.S.S. put three questions to each local candidate. If they answered 'yes' to each question they would get the organisation's support. Both Dence and Pretyman failed the test in Chelmsford. By this time many Liberal politicians looked upon the matter in purely pragmatic terms. It was considered that most enfranchised women would vote Conservative, so they would not give effective backing to such a measure. The Women's Freedom League, with strong Labour affiliations, led by Mrs Despard, was also in the town for the two weeks before the election. On November the 19th the W.S.P.U. led by Sylvia Pankhurst, Mrs Pankhurst's second daughter and Helen Ogston arrived in the town. Pankhurst apparently looked like an artist, slim and slight with a shrill voice. Ogston on the other hand was a brawny Scottish graduate. Later, after being on the receiving end of a sexual molestation, she took to carrying a whip around with her. The crowd were orderly to begin with but when Sylvia Pankhurst began to speak, some youths began to drag the cart she was standing on towards the market. She asked for the help of someone who she believed was a policeman, but whom it transpired was a postman. Despite further drunken interruptions "the suffragettes determined good humour and above all their logical presentation of a case which had not been put before the people of Essex, finally won sympathy". The crowd however, made a rush at them and they had to be protected by the police. "The police escorted them from the market to the Shire Hall." On the Saturday evening before the election there were four open air meetings in the town. The Tariff Reform League held a meeting near the Shire Hall, the National Trade Defence League spoke near the market, the N.U.W.S.S. spoke in Tindal Square and Mrs Drummond spoke to the crowd from the balcony of the Bell Hotel. (87) Drummond had hired one of Thomas Clarkson's buses and a full 12 piece brass band for a procession through the town. In the photos taken by Frederick Spalding the bus was bedecked with 'Votes for Women' signs and W.S.P.U. banners. A poster urged the voters to 'Keep the Liberals out'. (88) The bus was then used to take the suffragettes who were recently released from prison and who were also featured in

Mrs Drummond and Suffragettes in prison dress 1908 (Courtesy of Chelmsford Museums)

the photos on the posters, around the villages of Essex. They returned to Chelmsford at 9.30 p.m. to a huge crowd. There wasn't any excitement on the actual polling day but there were suffragettes outside every polling station. The suffragettes said that the increased majority for the Conservatives was due to their work. Dence certainly blamed his defeat on them.

The following month the Young Liberals, despite the opposition to women's suffrage of their seniors, invited Miss E.M. Gardiner of the N.U.W.S.S. to speak. Most at the meeting agreed with her views. (89) This and the furore over the election were probably instrumental in the establishment of a local branch of the N.U.W.S.S. in December 1908. Lady Rayleigh was President. The Reverend Canon Lake and the Reverend T. Macdougal Mundle became Vice Presidents and another prominent citizen Aylmer Maude of Great Baddow joined the committee. (90) Miss Ridley and Miss Chancellor were also vice presidents. Herbert Pash was one of a number of prominent Chelmsford men, along with John Ockelford Thompson, A.R.P. Hickley and C. Conybeare, who gave active support to the women's suffrage movement. Pash gave a talk on women's suffrage at K.E.G.S. in March 1909 (91). Apart from meeting regularly at the Institute in 1910, the local N.U.W.S.S. met at the Shire Hall with the Reverend Canon Lake presiding, when it seemed likely that a bill might be introduced into Parliament. (92) In November 1910 Mrs Richenda Christy the honorary secretary of the local branch of the N.U.W.S.S. explained the Conciliation Bill in the Essex Chronicle. "It proposed to give the vote to those women only who are on the municipal register and that it excludes ownership qualification, except where the owner actually occupies her property". (93)

Amongst 119 suffragettes arrested for a raid on the House of Commons, were Misses Dorothea and Madeleine Rook of Ingatestone and Miss Grace Chapelow. Chapelow was a well known figure in the Chelmsford area. She had been born in London in 1884 but later lived in Hatfield Peverel with her mother and brother. Her mother, Emily was prominent in Victorian social reform movement and she carried the flag at the funeral of Emily Davidson. During her 20s Grace became a militant suffragette and was a friend of the Pankhursts. In 1912 she was part of a W.S.P.U. campaign in Chelmsford along with Pethwick Lawrence to explain the militant tactics used by the suffragettes. (94) This was the start of the attacks on property. After Chapelow had spoken at the Shire Hall, a Colonel Wood cancelled further lettings by the suffragists. He was worried after damage to properties in London. When she and Grace were arrested for breaking windows with hammers and stones at the Mansion House Dorothea Rook said "This is not done as wanton destruction, we have done it as a protest against being deprived of the vote". (95) They were sentenced to two months imprisonment. According to her close friend Florrie Kantner, Chapelow suffered physical pain, being forcibly fed in prison. She smuggled a prison cup and a knife out of Holloway in the hem of her skirt and these are now on display in Chelmsford Museum. The knife has 'Down with Asquith' scratched on it. Her treatment in prison may have contributed to her becoming somewhat reclusive later in life. In 1912 she was sent to prison for refusing to pay 14 shillings costs in a case involving dogs. Chapelow, along with other W.S.P.U. members, gave up the suffrage movement during the war. In the first war she did well out of selling goats' milk. She was a strict vegetarian and kept thirteen cats. Chapelow died in Stock in 1971.

The movement continued to be active in Chelmsford before the first war. At the A.G.M. of the Chelmsford and District N.U.W.S.S. in January 1911 Miss Tabor of Brentwood regretted that the ordinary quiet work of the Suffrage Societies was completely neglected in the papers. (96) Another member, R.D. Courtney said in the same year that resistance to the Census, a new tactic, would be futile. (97) Miss Rook however defended this action. "Women shouldn't be treated as chattels." By 1912 a branch of the Church League for Women's Suffrage was well established, meeting at Crane Court. It had been established in 1909 by Georgina Brackenbury and the Reverend Claud Hinchcliffe. In 1914 some members formed the Suffragists Church Women Protest Committee. This objected to "the servile attitude of the heads of the church to an unjust and irresponsible government". (97) These certainly included the new Bishop of Chelmsford. After receiving a letter from them he replied "I have never been able to advise the extension of the franchise to women because I honestly feel that.... it would be detrimental to the cause of women." (98) In the years before the first war the local meetings of the N.U.W.S.S. always emphasised their moderation. Most of their meetings were chaired by Lady Rayleigh who regarded the widespread law breaking as foolish. (99) Miss E.M. Bancroft the headmistress of the Chelmsford County High School for Girls, said in 1911 that she "doubted whether any good cause had been so maligned and misinterpreted as that of women's suffrage". "Not only women but men were now working for its so many leagues established to support it from different points of view." (100) Despite Chelmsford being a hotbed of suffragism it was frequently observed that female participation in local politics could have been greater. The town didn't have a female councillor until Frances Chancellor, Frederic's daughter was elected in 1920. In 1913 there were only two female poor law guardians in the Chelmsford Union. The Church League for Women's Suffrage said there should have been ten. (101)

In January 1918 Frederic Chancellor died just after being made a freeman of the town. Most of the town was temporarily closed as a mark of respect. (102) Part of his legacy was the large number of churches and schools he designed, both in the town and the county, as well as the Corn Exchange and what became the cathedral. He also played a major role in keeping the museum in the town and finally getting a public library for the town built. Most of all however, he stood over politics in the late Victorian and Edwardian town like a giant. He was the town's first mayor and mayor seven times in all. Chancellor was described by one person as "an autocrat of a person not easily approached". "He was a familiar figure around Chelmsford in horse and trap with driver and his expeditions into the country were as carefully planned manoeuvres." "His arrival on the job was in the nature of a parade ground inspection with everyone literally standing to attention." "No one would dare to approach him unless requested and he spoke only with the foreman or master builder, who was usually there to receive him." This makes it difficult to explain his use of the modest 'Fred' instead of Frederic at the bottom of his drawings. (103) His blue plaque, unveiled in 1991, was placed at Bellefield, his house in New London Road. (103)

After the war Pretyman won the 1919 general election by a big majority of five and a half thousand. (104) Labour were now finally organised enough in the constituency to put forward a candidate and did gain over 5,000 votes in the absence of a Liberal candidate. In 1922 the Labour candidate W.F. Toynbee criticised the Wage Committee for Essex that had agreed to every Farmers Union demand for a decrease in wages. During the previous six months wages had fallen by £1 a week. (105) In the November 1922 election the Chelmsford constituency electorate had grown to just over 35,000. Of these just over 15,000 were women, after the 1918 Representation of the People Act had enfranchised propertied women over 30. Pretyman polled 11,267 votes and the Liberal candidate, Sidney Walter Robinson 6,380, a majority of 4,887. (106) The Labour candidate was Mrs C.D. Rackman, an accountant from Cambridge, who polled 3, 767 votes. During the post war depression Pretyman saw no answer but a reduction in the general level of wages, the classical economic approach. "The workers must see that unless we get somewhere near an economic wage we could not restore trade and industry." (107) By November however, Pretyman was calling for protection as a cure for unemployment. His opponent at the next election in 1923 was again the Liberal Robinson. He was a building contractor and also a farmer with land near Chelmsford.

Robinson was well known for his breeding of pedigree short horn cows. He was a J.P. in the County and a Freeman of the City of London. Robinson was also a member of E.C.C. before first contesting Essex South East in 1918. After losing to Pretyman in 1922 he was lucky in 1923 in the sense that there was no Labour candidate to split the Liberal vote. He recorded 12,877 votes against Pretyman's 10,185. (108) The first and so far only Liberal M.P. in Chelmsford thanked his labour friends in the constituency. Pretyman decided not to stand again after representing the constituency for 15 years. (109)

During the short period Robinson was an M.P. he was best known for his introduction of a bill to include farm workers in the National Insurance scheme. Asquith, the former Liberal Prime Minister, visited the town and spoke at the Corn Exchange. The building was full but because there was amplification outside there were more people outside than inside. Portable apparatus had been developed by Captain H.J. Round of Marconi

Election 29th of October 1924 Candidates standing in front of the Gun addressing the crowd (Courtesy of E.R.O.)

and this was the first time it had been used. (110) During the next election campaign Robinson again spoke in favour of Free Trade. At a meeting of the Liberals at the Gun he said "Repeal would cost a great deal of unemployment in Chelmsford." (111) Labour's candidate was a General Moller. Herbert Morrison was a visiting speaker at a Labour meeting at the Corn Exchange. It was "perfectly clear that the Labour Party was not Bolshevic or Communist, did believe in using the constitutional power of parliament and the municipalities for the good of the public". (112) In the 1924 election the participation of the Labour candidate did not make a decisive difference because nationally and locally the tide had turned in favour of the Conservatives. The Tory candidate was Henry Curtis-Bennett who was a prominent solicitor. He polled 15,815 against the 10,244 of Robinson. Moller only polled 2,904 votes and lost his deposit. (113) In 1926 Curtis-Bennett retired citing the strain of his divorce as the reason for his withdrawal.

The new Conservative candidate was Colonel Charles Kenneth Howard-Bury, D.C.O., D.L., J. P. He was born in Ireland in 1881 and went to India with the King's Royal Rifle Corps. In 1921 he led a Mount Everest reconnaissance expedition. This expedition was instrumental in creating the myth of the abominable snowman. He was elected M.P. for Bilston in 1922 but lost the seat in 1924. At the next election both Robinson and Moller stood again. Although Howard-Bury's majority was nearly five thousand, this time the participation of Labour perhaps did make a difference because the combined Liberal and Labour vote was a thousand more than the Conservative vote. The main issues had been coal (this was just after the general strike) and once again agriculture. (114) During the following year Neville Chamberlain spoke at Chelmsford. He described the town as being at the centre of a great agricultural county but he did not promise the farmers protection. The editor of the Weekly News saw no alternative to protection to help agriculture. (115) In 1929 Howard-Bury was attacked by a Labour M.P. for being anti miner at a meeting in Chelmsford in accusing them of not being willing to work. He said many miners had fought alongside Major Moller during the war. (116)

In 1930 Howard-Bury decided not to stand again, citing the pressure of 'private affairs'. The new Conservative candidate was Lieutenant-Colonel Sir Vivian Leonard Henderson. Like Howard-Bury he had been educated at Sandhurst and was commissioned as an officer in the Loyal North Lancashire Regiment, with whom he served during the first war being awarded the Military Cross. In 1918 he was elected to Glasgow Tradeston but then lost the seat to a Labour Co-operative candidate in 1922.

During 1923 he stood for the Bootle constituency near where he had been born. He lost a very close election but then took the seat comfortably in 1924. Henderson lost the seat in 1929 when the Labour majority included the gain of his Bootle constituency. He had previously been Secretary of State to the Home Department. (117) During the 1931 election campaign Henderson said that cuts in unemployment benefit were a necessary sacrifice. He was in favour of preferential treatment regarding trade with the Empire. Henderson was a supporter of the National Government. (118) J.A. Sparks, the Labour candidate, spoke at the Corn Exchange. He said the country should refuse to be dictated to by the financiers and that tariffs wouldn't help as they hadn't done anything for the United States, which had the highest unemployment in the world. (119) Not surprisingly the editor of the Weekly News was in favour of the National Government being given a free hand on tariffs. In the election Henderson achieved a landslide, polling 31,961 votes to Sparks' 7,755, a majority of 24,206. (120) Unfortunately Henderson's health deteriorated markedly from 1934 onwards and he stepped down at the 1935 election.

Henderson's successor to what was now a very safe Conservative seat was Colonel John Robert Macnamara. In the election he polled 28,314 votes to the 11,590 of the Labour candidate Hughes: a majority of over 16,000. (121) Macnamara attended over 70 meetings in the area. He was deeply affected by the Spanish Civil War and was joint secretary of the Basque Children's Committee. In 1924 he had joined the Territorial Army as a second lieutenant in the 3rd London Regiment. Macnamara was certainly on the far right of the Conservative party. His secretary was Guy Burgess, later to find notoriety as a spy, with whom he frequently visited Germany before the second war. In World War Two he went to Italy as a colonel of the Royal Ulster Rifles. He was killed in December 1944 during the fighting in northern Italy. Macnamara was watching his troops take part in the allied offensive. He was buried in the Forli War cemetery in Italy. (122)

After the first war the local Labour Party made attempts to fight every council seat in the borough. In November 1919 they put up 7 candidates in 8 vacant seats. Four were successful. (123) Unfortunately they lost all four seats in 1920. The successful candidates that beat them were all supported by the new local branch of the Middle Class Union. A Chelmsford League of Young Liberals was re-established in 1927, but in general the movement was in decline in the borough, as elsewhere. (124)

In 1927 A.R.P. Hickley was the only Labour candidate to be returned, in his case for the second time. (125) Augustus Richards Potterton Hickley was born in 1861 and emigrated to Australia, where he made his fortune. On the return he bought the Chelmsford skating rink and opened the Picture House (later the Select) cinema in New Writtle Street. The latter was the first in the town and one of the first in England. He was secretary of the local Trades Council when it reformed (see chapter 9). Hickley belonged to the Workers Union and was first elected to the South Ward in 1913. He was an early supporter of planning and was Chairman of the Town Planning Committee in 1916. Hickley retired from business in 1920 but remained a Labour councillor until 1930. He later joined the Chelmsford Communist party and was Treasurer until his death after the Second World War. In addition he was a spiritualist and a poet. (126)

Overall the Labour Party struggled to make progress in the municipal elections. In 1926 Minnie Pallister, a Labour candidate for Bournemouth, remarked at a meeting in a meeting in the vestry Hall, New Street "Chelmsford is a difficult town for the Labour movement". Each time a branch of the I.L.P. had been formed the branch had fizzled out. (127) There was a strong anti Labour feeling across Essex in the 1930s.In 1934 none of the four Labour candidates in the borough were elected. In 1937 Labour did finally gain a seat, with C. Langton becoming a councillor. (128) During the same year a woman candidate, a Miss B.S. White succeeded in being elected at the first attempt. (129)

One of the unanswered questions about politics between the wars in the Chelmsford area is why fascism didn't gain a greater hold. Around Ipswich, where there were a large number of farmers who were disaffected with the National Government, the movement gained rapid momentum. Perhaps Chelmsford lacked well known landowners around whom the movement could coalesce. In 1934 there was a small fascist meeting in the town, but Sir Oswald Mosley was unable to attend and the meeting was led by one of his lieutenants. (130) During 1936 a much more lively meeting was held at the Corn Exchange by the British Union of Fascists. The efforts of opponents to hold a meeting outside in Tindal Square were banned by the police, but they distributed leaflets requesting people not to attend a Fascist meeting. The appearance of a 'blackshirt' was the signal for an outburst of cat calls and boos outside. One speaker at the meeting was a Mr Raven Thompson from the B.U.F. headquarters. The audience of 100 inside reduced considerably during the evening. A crowd surged forward outside but were unable to break the cordon of police on the edge of the movement. "At 20 to 10 a number of young men detached themselves from the crowd and entered the building". "They worked their way into Market Road and as fascists left the Corn Exchange they shouted their disapproval". The Weekly

News praised the "Tactful handling of the crowd by the police". It observed that the "fascists were not popular in Essex". (131) In 1937 Mosley finally arrived in Chelmsford. The meeting was held at the Recreation Ground. Whilst he explained the aims of the movement, there were occasional interruptions, but the meeting was generally a quiet one. Mosley had two microphones and spoke from the top of a motor car. Before the meeting members of the Chelmsford Branch of the Communist Party were giving out leaflets entitled 'Fascism Means War'. There was some heckling when Robert East, the district Fascist leader for the Maldon division, spoke. Mosley himself was greeted by the fascist salute. In his speech he attacked the 'Reds.' There would be voting as at present. All foreign produce would be excluded. He introduced a Mr C.H. Blacker, whom he said would represent the Chelmsford division in the next election. (132)

As early as 1923 the borough council was talking about extending the borough boundaries again. Attention initially focused on including Great Baddow and Galleywood (133). In 1926 an ambitious scheme involving the whole five parishes of Great Baddow (including Galleywood), Broomfield, Springfield, Widford and Writtle was dropped because of the expense. The council thought that the parishes "with the exception of Springfield were favourably disposed to the move". (134) In 1932 a new scheme proposed extending the borough boundary to include Great Baddow and a further part of Springfield and Sandford Mill. (135) At a meeting in the Great Baddow Parish Hall, a resolution favouring inclusion in the borough was heavily defeated (57 for, 230 against). The borough swiftly dropped plans to include Great Baddow. (136) In 1933 a new proposal included parts of Broomfield, Springfield, Widford and Writtle. (137) Following their acceptance an inquiry was held into increasing the number of wards from three to four. A west ward was added to the North, South and Springfield wards to gain a more equal distribution of rateable value. Previously the North ward had almost twice the rateable value of the South ward. (138)

Immediately after the first war there was considerable pressure for the borough to finally have a town hall. The pressing need to push on with the housing programme (see chapter 18) prevented a scheme from coming to fruition. A committee considered various sites, including one at the rear of the Bell Hotel with a frontage onto Threadneedle Street. Another site on the London Road did not have sufficient vacant land for future possible extensions. The Council bought Rainsford House as its municipal offices. Rents from previous offices in Duke Street meant there was no additional burden to the taxpayer. (139)

Proposals for new county offices in Chelmsford had originally been made as early as 1912. E.C.C. wanted larger conference rooms to allow council meetings to be held there. (140) The plans were not proceeded with because of the first war, but they were revived in 1925. They involved a site bought by the E.C.C. which bordered on Duke Street, Threadneedle Street and King Edwards Avenue. Office staff were at the time housed in nine different buildings, some of them quite unsuitable for use as offices. (141) The first section of the new County Hall was started in 1931, fronting onto Threadneedle Street and Kings Edwards Avenue. This was to cost £87,000, but the next section including a portion of Duke Street as far as the then county offices was estimated at £135,000. (142) The magnificence of the interior of the County Hall that finally was completed was almost entirely due to a generous donation from W.J. Courtauld, of the well known business empire. He contributed £21,000 to the fittings and furnishings of the Council Chamber. (143) "The Council had really provided the shell of a council chamber and the lobby adjoining, while he had been responsible for the interior including the decoration and furniture." "The decorations are works of art, illustrating in pictures, writing and glass the story of the Essex people." "Eminent Royal Academy artists have produced beautiful wall paintings and there are numerous illustrations of coats of arms in coloured glass of the abbeys, priories, schools, and colleges in Essex, two great maps and many portraits, coats of arms of the Essex boroughs and flags of the Essex Regiment." (144)

The Rural District Council was operating from cramped offices in Waterloo Lane and was looking to expand them by 1923. (145) Expansion occurred in 1925 on the original site but this soon proved insufficient. (146) Plans to reconstruct the existing offices were dropped in 1935 and land was found for new offices in New London Road. (147) (148) After the new building was opened the old offices were sold to the Post Office. (149)

One of the town council's more strange decisions after the first war was to end the electricity lighting contract in 1920. The town's gas company had been bought by the town council in 1916 (see chapter 2). (150) Fred Spalding said there was "nothing else to do". "It only showed what a great mistake they made years ago in allowing the Electric Light Company a monopoly." George Taylor predicted a large saving on the rates of 2d or 3d in the £. (151) As a result when most towns were moving or had moved to lighting by electricity, the town that had complete electric lighting first, went back to lighting by gas. One possible explanation is that some of the town's politicians, had shares in the gas company and had done well out of the sale and felt they needed to justify the municipalisation of the company. By 1924 the editor of the Weekly News said he would welcome a return to electric lighting. (152) In 1925 the council decided not to buy the local electric works, but in 1929 there was a proposal to return local lighting to electricity put before the Lighting committee. Gas had doubled in cost since 1920. The local electricity company however, was not in a position to provide lighting because the original equipment had deteriorated. (153) In 1936 the town still wasn't lit by electricity, although all the other local towns were, including Romford, Brentwood and Witham. (154) Fred Spalding had certainly changed his mind. "If it were not for the tradesman's lights in the High Street the place would be in almost total darkness." In 1937 Mayor Bellamy finally announced the return to electric lighting for the whole borough. (155)

The borough council made some attempt, during the recession after the first war and the depression after the Great Crash, to alleviate local unemployment (see chapter 9). This was mainly limited to schemes that were eligible for Government grants. The large amount of municipal house building that was essential, meant that other measures that would have created further employment, for example a new public library, had to be delayed or abandoned. A draft scheme for the latter had been drawn up in 1926 but in 1932 the government refused to sanction a loan for the building. Eventually the town got its separate library when one opened in Duke Street in 1935. (156)

The second war saw the death of one of Chelmsford's most distinguished politicians, John Ockelford Thompson (see chapter 24). In 1885 Thompson's father had bought a share in the Essex Chronicle. A young Thompson worked at the paper was to inherit part ownership of the paper. "It is essentially a paper of county news, but devoted above all things to the agricultural interests of Essex." (157) After his father's death he became editor of the paper. He was elected to the council in 1907. For some years he was a member of E.C.C. (158) Thompson was mayor of the town 7 times before his death. Whilst this, along with other small group of politicians who were multiple holders of the post, says something about the cosy nature of Chelmsford politics, it also reveals the extent to which he was respected in the town. He was a member of the Essex Territorial Association and a leading supporter of the League of Nations. Thompson, as we have seen was also active in the Women's Suffrage movement, and he supported numerous philanthropic and religious organisations in the town. He also played a prominent role in establishing the sport of bowls in the town, even later having a green at his house at Brierly Place (see chapter 25).

In 1937 the 'gun' was removed from in front of the Shire Hall to Oaklands Park.

This move was carried out ostensibly to remove an obstacle to traffic, but at the same time Chelmsford lost the focal point for many impromptu and unofficial meetings. The death of Chelmsford's M.P. Colonel Macnamara was to bring about the start of perhaps the most unusual period in Chelmsford's political history.

1) 'The Sleeper and the Shadows' Vol.2 Hilda Grieve p.386
2) Essex Chronicle 12 8 1887 p.5
3) E.C. 19 8 1887 p.5
4) Essex Weekly News 30 9 1987 p.5
5) Hilda Grieve p.388
6) Hilda Grieve p.389
7) E.W.N. 18 11 1887 p.8
8) E.W.N. 13 4 1888 p.7
9) E.C. 27 1 1888
10) Hilda Grieve p.393
11) Hilda Grieve p.396
12) E.W.N. 19 9 1888 p.3
13) E.W.N. 19 9 1888 p.3
14) Hilda Grieve p.396
15) E.W.N. 16 11 1888 p.2
16) E.W.N. 2 11 1888 p.8
17) E.W.N. 23 11 1888 p.8
18) E.W.N. 16 11 1888 p.2
19) E.W.N. 30 11 1888 p.5
20) E.W.N. 29 3 1889 p.5
21) Essex Review 1909 Vol. 18 p.53
22) E.W.N. 29 3 1889 p.5
23) E.C. 16 4 1880 p.5
24) E.C. 6 4 1883
25) E.W.N. 28 9 1883 p.7
26) E.C. 24 9 1885 p.5
27) E.W.N. 7 7 1882 p.5
28) E.W.N. 29 8 1884 p.5
29) E.W.N. 10 10 1884
30) E.W.N. 16 1 1885 p.6

31) E.W.N. 13 11 1885 p.7
32) E.C. 16 4 1896 p.5
33) E.C. 9 7 1886 p.8
34) E.C. 21 5 1886 p.7
35) E.C. 9 9 1887 p.8
36) E.W.N. 22 4 1892
37) E.W.N. 8 3 1889 p.6
38) E.W.N. 20 5 1892 p.5
39) E.W.N. 13 7 1892 p.2
40) E.W.N. 22 7 1892 p.4
41) E.W.N. 22 7 1892 p.4
42) E.W.N. 2 2 1894 p.4
43) E.W.N. 7 1895 p.4
44) E.W.N. 25 8 1899 p.7
45) E.C. 19 10 1900 p.2
46) E.W.N. 16 11 1900 p.2
47) E.W.N. 25 7 1890 p.4
48) E.W.N. 26 1 1906 p.6
49) E.W.N. 16 3 1906 p.4
50) E.W.N. 1 5 1908 p.4
51) E.W.N. 20 8 1908 p.6
52) E.W.N. 2 10 1914 p.2
53) E.C. 8 11 1895 p.5
54) E.W.N. 27 12 1891 p.2
55) E.W.N. 7 11 1902 p.6
56) E.W.N. 10 6 1892 p.5
57) E.W.N. 16 2 1894 p.5
58) E.C. 28 5 1897
59) E.C. 17 5 1897 p.4
60) E.C. 25 6 1897 p.5
61) E.W.N. 27 2 1903
62) E.W.N. 21 7 1893 p.7
63) E.W.N. 27 3 1903 p.4
64) E.W.N. 2 10 1908 p.6
65) Essex Review Vol.21 1912

66) E.W.N. 28 2 1908
67) E.C. 14 2 1908
68) E.W.N. 24 3 1914 p.5
69) E.W.N. 4 12 1908 p.6
70) E.W.N. 18 1 1918 p.3
71) E.W.N. 27 9 1906 p.2
72) Chelmsford Rural District Council minutes 23 10 1908
73) E.W.N. 18 1 1907 p.4
74) E.C. 25 1 1907 p.2
75) C.R.D.C minutes 12 7 1907 p.96
76) E.W.N. 2 8 1907 p.4
77) Chelmsford Borough Council minutes 25 9 1907
78) The Women's Suffrage Movement in Britain and Ireland: A Regional Survey Elizabeth Crawford p.92
79) E.C. 9 4 1886 p.6
80) Elizabeth Crawford p.92
81) E.C. 16 4 1889 p.6
82) E.W.N. 19 1 1894 p.5
83) E.W.N. 6 1 1899
84) E.W.N. 1 12 1905 p.5
85) E.W.N. 6 12 1907 p.4
86) E.W.N. 27 8 1908
87) Essex Countryside Dec. 1977 'The day the suffragettes came to Chelmsford ' Jennifer Durtacher
88) Elizabeth Crawford p.96
89) E.W.N. 18 12 1908 p.8
90) E.W.N. 25 12 1908 p.8
91) E.W.N. 12 3 1909
92) E.W.N. 24 6 1910 p.8
93) E.C. 11 11 1910
94) Chelmsford Museums Records
95) E.W.N. 14 11 1911
96) E.W.N. 31 3 1911
97) E.W.N. 26 4 1912
98) E.W.N. 5 12 1913

99) E.W.N. 15 3 1912
100) E.W.N. 13 10 1911
101) E.W.N. 21 11 1913 p.8
102) E.W.N. 11 1 9 1918
103) Chelmsford Museums records – Chelmsford people
104) E.W.N. 3 1 1919 p.3
105) E.W.N. 3 2 1922 p.6
106) E.W.N. 17 11 1922 p.2
107) E.W.N. 26 1 1923 p.2
108) E.W.N. 14 12 1923 p.3
109) E.W.N. 18 1 1924 p.5
110) E.W.N. 2 5 1924 p.8
111) E.W.N. 15 8 1924 p.5
112) E.W.N. 17 9 1924 p.3
113) E.W.N. 31 10 1924 p.5
114) E.W.N. 10 12 1926
115) E.W.N. 29 7 1927 p.6
116) E.W.N. 1 3 1929 p.3
117) http://en.wikipedia.org/wiki/Vivian Henderson
118) E.W.N. 23 10 1931 p.4
119) E.W.N. 23 10 1931 p.4
120) E.W.N. 30 10 1931 p.9
121) E.W.N. 22 11 1935
122) http://en.wikipedia.org/wiki/John Macnamara
123) E.W.N. 7 11 1919 p.5
124) E.W.N. 28 1 1927
125) E.W.N. 4 11 1927 p.11
126) Chelmsford Museums records – Chelmsford people
127) E.W.N. 8 1 1926 p.7
128) E.W.N. 2 11 1934 p.12
129) E.W.N. 5 12 1937 p.8
130) E.W.N. 16 11 1934
131) E.W.N. 6 11 1936
132) E.W.N. 15 6 1937 p.7
133) E.W.N.16 3 1923 p.8

134) E.W.N. 17 8 1928 p.6
135) E.C. 1 4 1932 p.2
136) E.C. 15 4 1932 p.4
137) E.W.N. 12 5 1933 p.11
138) E.W.N. 29 3 1933 p.11
139) E.W.N. E.W.N. 14 7 1922
140) Essex County Council minutes 6 1 1914
141) E.C.C. minutes 17 2 1925 p.361
142) E.W.N. 13 3 1931
143) E.C.C. minutes 17 11 1936 p.2193
144) E.W.N. 30 9 1938 p.6
145) Chelmsford Rural District council minutes 16 10 1914
146) C.R.D.C. minutes 14 7 1925 p.147
147) C.R.D.C. minutes 30 1 1935 p.508
148) C.R.D.C. minutes 12 6 1935 p.112
149) C.R.D.C. minutes 22 8 1939 P.217
150) E.W.N. 3 11 1916 p.6
151) E.W.N. 7 2 1920 p.2
152) E.W.N. 25 1 1924
153) E.W.N. 1 2 1929 p.7
154) E.W.N. 29 3 1935
155) E.W.N. 17 12 1937 p.6
156) E.W.N. 12 4 1935 p.6
157) Essex Review Vol.6 1897 p.155
158) Essex Review Vol. 50 1941 p.54

14

Politics in the Chelmsford area after 1945

*"An unforeseen and virtually unexpressed deep
and almost universal desire for change"*

Chelmsford's politics immediately after the second war was dominated by the election of a candidate from a little known, extreme left wing party to the parliamentary constituency. This in a constituency that had returned a Conservative member of parliament for all of the previous 75 years with the exception of a few months in the 1920s. Five years later a Conservative candidate was returned and normal service was resumed until the present day. In 2012 there had still only been four Chelmsford M.P.'s since the war, if the brief period when there were two at the same time is discounted. In these days of politicians with uniform early careers as political advisors it is interesting that the first three especially had diverse backgrounds. The biggest change in local municipal politics has been the merger of the two local councils into one district council. Like the Millington phenomenon, the existence of a Labour led municipal council proved very short lived. The closing decades of the last century and the early years of the new millennium saw the Liberals in control of the council for all but four years. The later years of the twentieth century also saw several bids for city status, which was finally unexpectedly granted in 2012.

The parliamentary vacancy in Chelmsford in 1945 came about because of the death of the sitting M.P. Colonel Macnamara (see the previous chapter). Ernest Millington's chance came because of the agreement of the Conservative and Labour parties not to fight by elections during the war and to leave the incumbent party to win comfortably. The Commonwealth Party showed no such compunction in fighting the by election that was held in February 1945.

Millington grew up in Ilford. He won a county scholarship to go to Chigwell School. (1) This was a "small but highly successful minor, public school". (2) His father, a High Tory, seems to have rather resented his son's acquisition of a wide range of knowledge. He had been "a successful soldier and leader of men" but "now he was a poorly paid unskilled labourer and all his ideas and beliefs were regularly being challenged by a half grown lad". (3) Ernest joined the Labour Party League of Youth at the age of 14. Political and educational differences led to him being ordered out of the house in 1932. He was "homeless, jobless, penniless" and technically still at school. Millington had to phone the school and tell the headmaster he would not be returning after the holidays. (4) Whilst doing a variety of jobs, he completed his unofficial education at the Ilford Workers' Association. There he met his first wife and they married in 1937. (5) He joined the Territorial Army and was with a searchlight unit when the war broke out. (6) Millington was sent to the Officer Cadet Training Unit in Wiltshire and emerged as a 2nd Lieutenant in the Royal Artillery. (7) He was briefly in charge of six searchlight sites. At the end of 1939 he volunteered for the rapidly expanding R.A.F. Six weeks training in a Tiger Moth followed. When he qualified as a pilot, Officer Millington was selected for training as a flying officer. Millington was posted to R.A.F. Spitalgate, just outside Grantham. (8) He had a year in Flying Training Command learning the basics of flying but repeatedly requested operational flying and was eventually sent to be trained on Wellington bombers. (9) Millington later recalled that commanding a squadron of Lancaster bombers had given him the greatest pleasure. After speaking out at a conference of senior officers, where he was the most junior person present, about the need to fly in groups, he was promoted to the rank of Wing Commander. (10) Interestingly Millington in his autobiography spoke up for Air Chief Marshall Harris, the Commander in Chief of Bomber Command, castigating the establishment for disowning him after the war. Millington thought that all possible methods were legitimate to extinguish the Nazi threat. (11) In 1945 having almost completed his tour of operations and been awarded the D.F.C. he offered himself as an election candidate for the left wing Commonwealth Party. This was on the understanding that he would stand in a constituency that he couldn't possibly win! (12)

The Commonwealth Party had amongst its founders the writer J.B. Priestley and the former Liberal M.P. Sir Richard Ackland. It took a 'libertarian socialist view' rejecting the State owned form of socialism. The party wasn't bound by the wartime agreement on by elections and it was able to take advantage of a wartime electorate looking forward to the introduction of Beveridge's welfare state and win three constituencies before the end of the war. These were at Edisbury, Skipton and Chelmsford. As Macnamara had previously had a majority of sixteen thousand, Millington looked to have chosen a safely unwinnable seat. The audiences at meetings were enormous and asked him endless questions about bombing operations. "They seemed to hold me personally responsible for the destruction of German cities." "The Daily Mirror which, to my embarrassment, adopted my candidature made much of the fact that 'while Wing Commander Millington was flying though thick flack to bomb Berlin, his Tory opponent, Flight Lieutenant Cooke was signing important documents in the Air Ministry'." His military background and the temporary socialist fervour of the Chelmsford electorate led him to a majority of 6,431, overturning the sixth largest Conservative majority in the country. (13) Part of the reason for this gigantic turnaround was that Chelmsford's electoral register had been updated to include the masses of industrial workers who had come to Chelmsford during the war. In addition Millington thought one reason for his success was an "unforeseen and virtually unexpressed deep and almost universal desire for change". (14) "Traditional trade union and Labour Party members and supporters reacted adversely to their leadership, which gave them explicit instructions to vote for the Tory candidate. (15) Sybil Olive remembered when interviewed that she hadn't been surprised that Millington had won. His campaign was well organised and, although there was an element of a protest vote, people in the constituency genuinely wanted change. (16) He became the youngest sitting M.P.

Millington bought a small house in Boreham. After being presented with the D.F.C., he went into the House of Commons where a Tory M.P., who had been a military officer in the R.A.F., with the rank of quadroon leader, came up to him saying "You are improperly dressed." "Your D.F.C. ribbon is too wide." He was not expecting Millington's reply. "If you are talking to me as an R.A.F. officer: stand to attention, take your hand out of your trouser pocket and address a senior officer as 'Sir'." "If you are talking as a fellow member of parliament, mind your business and '.......off'." Evidently the Tory M.P. was in parliamentary mode as he '........ off'! (17) At the general election which immediately followed the end of the war Millington initially offered to step aside, so as not to split the vote with the prospective Labour candidate, Baker Smith. In the event it was the latter who stepped down, because he felt Millington was now better known. Millington won beating the Conservative candidate Hubert Ashton but by a reduced majority of 2,220 votes. (18)

The shock of winning the seat at Chelmsford did not prevent Millington from attempting to fulfil his parliamentary duties diligently. He went to the Commons four nights a week not arriving home until after midnight and spent most weekends on constituency and party duties. At a time when most M.P.'s were still the sons of wealthy families, he had no other income other than his parliamentary salary of £1,000 and he had a wife and four children to support. This was to put a strain on his marriage that was to lead eventually to divorce. "To me and my family it was a period of status accompanied by grinding poverty." (19) He did however, become close friends with several parliamentary colleagues, particularly John Strachey, who despite representing Dundee lived in the Chelmsford constituency. (20) In January 1950 Strachey spoke in Chelmsford as the Minister of Food. (21) Several of his military friends dropped Millington immediately his election made his politics clear.

Chelmsford's local papers certainly gave Millington a chance before turning resolutely against him. The Essex Chronicle criticised the fact that he wasn't invited to the hospital carnival in 1947 saying it was a matter of courtesy rather than politics. (22) As was now the tradition he was given a column in the Essex Chronicle. He viewed the need for three thousand houses as the most pressing need in the constituency. After an initial positive start to council house building (see chapter 18), this slowed alarmingly and he blamed the local authority, probably sensing that the links with local builders were too close. After the fire at Bolingbrokes and Wenleys he campaigned for an immediate public inquiry to determine whether there was any deficiency in the fire fighting fire service and whether there were any dangers posed by out of date wiring in the town as a whole. In 1946 Millington crossed over the floor of the House to the Labour Party. This had become increasingly likely because the Commonwealth Party was already a declining force. In the 1945 general election Chelmsford was the only one of the original seats it retained. Millington's move annoyed the Essex Chronicle who demanded that he resign and allow a by election to be called. Millington refused to vote with the Labour government on a number of occasions. He was, for example one of fifteen M.P.s who didn't support conscription in peace time. In general he allied himself with the Bevanite wing of the party. Aneurin Bevan was the politician he most admired until his major volte face as Foreign Secretary over the atomic bomb. (23) In 1949 Millington chaired a world government week in Chelmsford. This sought to reorganise the United Nations into an effective world government! (24)

It was evidently a relief to Millington that he was beaten in the election of March 1950. The second time Conservative candidate Hubert Ashton polled 28,541 votes and Millington 23,682. (25) "I did not enjoy being a member of parliament. The hours away from home, wife and children were interminable. Income was nugatory, expenditure high. Everyone came with a problem for a M.P. to solve. Some were even satisfied. One wonders whether a young man with little to offer in the way of expertise and experience other than in killing and devastation could achieve anything of value to justify such a neglect of family." (26) Four months after defeat he stood down as the Labour candidate. It was he said "a reluctant decision forced on me by the needs of my family". (27)

After an assortment of odd jobs Millington applied to rejoin the R.A.F. as a non-flying Lieutenant. (28) After his views on Suez became known he was sent to Malta. (29) When he got there he was accused of stealing 28 shillings and sixpence, the proceeds of an airman's dance, which had been given to him when he left. With his wife, he was also accused of stealing £50 from the Wives club. The first amount "was a clear oversight and would be repaid immediately". He was told the police would not pursue the case against his wife if he confessed. The Essex Chronicle made much of his parlous financial state. (30) Millington was convinced that the Commander in Chief was under instructions to "get him discharged from the R.A.F. by hook or by crook". He was found guilty and "cashiered from the R.A.F". (31) After a successful teaching career in London he remarried and moved to the Dordogne. His political views didn't change however, and he was very critical of New Labour. He died in May 2006. (32)

The temporary radicalisation of the Chelmsford electorate at the end of the war also had a big effect on municipal politics in the borough. In the November elections in 1945 Labour did far better than it had ever done before in the borough. They won 10 out of 17 seats; nine of these being Labour gains. Once aldermanic vacancies had been filled, it had a working majority for the first time. Labour councillor A.E.Hodge was mayor, replacing Sidney Taylor, who was one of five sitting councillors to fail to retain their seat. Hodge's main interest was housing and there was no doubt this was the main issue as far as the local electorate were concerned. (33)

Concern with the lack of progress on the housing issue was the main reason the Labour majority lasted only a year. Although the curtailment of Marshall Aid and the resulting national programme of austerity was the reason all municipal councils couldn't keep their election pledges, the Chelmsford electorate were not in a forgiving mood. In the elections of November 1946 Independents regained a majority on the council with 18 members to 14. A row ensued when the Independents took control of all of the committees. Labour had pointed out that they had allowed Independents to chair several committees when they held control. (34)

January 1947 saw the death of Fred Spalding, aged 88. Spalding had been a member of the town council for a record 54 years, a mayor three times and a freeman of the borough. He only retired from the council two years before his death. (35) He had taken over his father's shop when Spalding Senior retired to farm Meadgate farm. His photos left a record of all aspects of life in Chelmsford covering half a century. In all there were over 8,000 photographic prints stored in County Hall before being taken over by the Essex Record Office. His original shop, in Tindal Square, had an 'attractive greenhouse structure' on the top floor and is now an estate agency. Spalding was also involved in promoting concerts and pantomimes at the Corn Exchange and elsewhere. He had been a fast bike rider and was President of the Essex County Cycle Association. Spalding was instrumental in bringing County cricket to Chelmsford and was President of Chelmsford Cricket Week. He was a local J.P. and Chair of the Chelmsford and Essex Hospital committee as well as being involved in the founding of the St John's Ambulance in the town. Spalding was a freemason and also governor of K.E.G.S. (36)

In February 1947 the Mayor, Arthur Andrews was sent for trial over a mayoral banquet. The Ministry of Food, anxious that the austerity drive should apply to everybody, had sent out an order that mayoral dinners should be limited to three courses. Andrew's banquet had included five courses. (37) The judge fined him £25 and said "you unwittingly broke the law". (38) It could be argued that the Mayor should have realised that such lavishness was inappropriate given the general food shortages that were prevalent and that rationing was still being imposed. The incident however, did little to harm Andrew's popularity and he was later made a freeman of the borough. This may have been one of the issues leading to the use of the derogatory epithet 'the 40 thieves' with regard to Chelmsford's councillors. The term originated in Robert Tressell's book the 'Ragged Trousered Philanthropists' although there is little evidence that Chelmsford has been worse in this respect than most towns of its size.

The 1947 local elections saw a drive by both the Conservatives and Liberals to put forward more candidates but Independents remained in the majority on the council. (39) By 1951 however the Independents had been absorbed into the Conservative party. (40) The Weekly News complained that the post of Chelmsford mayor should be shared around more evenly but Councillor Andrews was still elected again by councillors. The same year the row over the chairmanship of borough council committees flared up again with a Labour walk out at a council meeting. (41)

In these days of identikit politicians, who join the House of Commons after short careers as political advisers, the Chelmsford M.P. Hubert Ashton would be considered highly unusual. Ashton was born in Calcutta, India, in 1896. After an education at

Winchester College and Trinity College, Cambridge, he was commissioned in the Royal Field Artillery in the first war and was awarded the Military Cross. Incredibly he managed to play cricket for Essex in vacations during the war. Immediately after the war he was a batsman in a strong Cambridge university side. In 1921 and 1922 he scored more than 1,000 runs in a season. After three years in first class cricket Ashton was averaging 46. In 1921 he was a member of a scratch team assembled to take on the 'invincible' Australians at Eastbourne. Ashton rescued 'England' by hitting 75 in 72 minutes which helped his side win by 28 runs. This exploit contributed to him being named as one of Wisden's five cricketers of the year. That august tome also felt he should have been picked for the test side. In an extraordinary incident in a match against Lancashire he was bowled, but both bails returned to the top of the stumps, resulting in him being given not out. He was also evidently a good footballer playing for a number of clubs including West Bromwich Albion, the amateur team the Corinthians, Bristol Rovers and Clapton Orient. In 1941 Ashton became President of Essex County Cricket Club. (42)

Ashton started his political career by being a member of the E.C.C. After losing to Millington in 1945, he benefited from the local Conservatives being much more organised in 1950 when he won by almost 5,000. In October 1952 he beat the new Labour party candidate Norman Hadden by 29,069 votes to 23,775, a majority of 5,294. (43) Hadden had originally withdrawn his candidature after the Labour Party Centre Office nominated Sir Lesley Plummer who had run a ground nut enterprise for the government and managed several socialist magazines. The local party resented somebody they didn't know being parachuted in and selected Hadden anyway. (44) Four years later Ashton beat a new Labour candidate F.C. Floud by 25,450 votes to 20,301. Floud certainly livened up constituency politics. A year after the election he attacked the Tories as "miserable scum" at a meeting on the Suez crisis. When he started the meeting with 'Friends and comrades' he was shouted down by some 'loud mouthed' Young Tories' at the front. (45)

For the 1959 election Labour chose their fourth different candidate in successive elections. He was Brian Clapham, a barrister. A brawl was feared on the eve of the election when the Labour Party held a meeting on the Bell car park right next door to a Conservative party meeting at the Corn Exchange. ITV cameras showed up in Chelmsford because R.A. Butler was speaking. (46) By this time Labour were without a full time agent, and this in addition to the fact that the Conservatives were still benefitting from the 'You've never had it so good' period, saw Ashton increase his majority to almost 10,000. (47) In 1962 Ashton decided he wouldn't seek re-election, which didn't actually happen until 1964. (48) He was still heavily involved in cricket, being President of the M.C.C. in 1961. He died in South Weald in 1979. Throughout his period as M.P. for Chelmsford Ashton was a fervent supporter of the Agricultural College at Writtle.

During the early 1950s Labour had more success in the rural district elections. In 1952 it made a clean sweep of the seats on Springfield parish council. By 1964 however, the Conservatives were in control of three of the four wards in the borough, with Labour only doing well in the North Ward, partly because of the Boarded Barns council estate. (49) In 1956 the new council comprised 18 Conservatives, 10 Labour and 4 Independents. (50) Two Labour gains in 1957 was the start of a revival in the fortunes of the party. The party again protested that it should have been Labour's turn to provide the Mayor. In 1958 F.C. Langton, the leader of the Labour group and freeman of the borough, was indeed made Mayor. Further Labour gains meant that the Mayor had the casting vote with the parties tied. (51) The Conservatives however, regained control the following year. (52) By 1960 they had 20 seats to Labour's 11. At the end of 1961 the situation was similar to four years previously with Labour only controlling North Ward. (53) Labour was reduced to holding 10 seats but in the same year the Labour councillor Mrs Jean Roberts became Chelmsford's first female mayor. (54) She was quickly followed by a second, the Conservatives' Mrs M.M. Davies. (55)

1962 saw the beginnings of a Liberal revival in the borough. Nationally the party were riding high after the victory at Orpington. In the East ward the Liberals won two seats from the Conservatives but one of these had been lost by the end of the year, when Conservatives had 17 members, Labour 14 and Liberals 1. (56) (57) In 1964 the national swing towards Labour in the general election saw the Conservatives lose overall control in Chelmsford. Conservatives were left with 16 seats, Labour 15 and Liberals 1. (58)

The general election in 1964 saw Norman St John Stevas stand for the first time after the retirement of Hubert Ashton. He was given the Christian names Norman Panayea St John by his parents. His mother hyphenated St John to the Stevas surname after she divorced his father. He went to St Joseph's Salesians School, Sussex and then the Catholic Radcliffe College, Leicester. In these early years he was active on both Catholic and Young Conservative platforms. He once reported Gordon Reece, later the journalist, TV producer and strategist for Margaret Thatcher, for atheism. Stevas started to train for the former Roman Catholic priesthood at the English College,

Rome but found he had no vocation. He then went to Fitzwilliam College, Cambridge, graduating with a first class honours degree in Law. Whilst there he won the Whitlock prize and served as President of the Union in 1950. He then went to Oxford where he gained a Bachelor in Civil Law degree. Later he obtained a PhD at London University on the early work of Walter Bagehot and a Doctor of Judicial Science degree from Yale University. In 1952 he was called to the bar at Middle Temple. For most of the 1950's he followed an academic career, lecturing at Southhampton University and Kings College London, as well as receiving fellowship at Yale. His book 'Obscenity and the Law' was later referred to regularly as legislation gradually removed 'the pulpit from the law' and this was followed by several other books on difficult questions of law. (59) Between 1966 and 1986 Stevas produced 15 volumes on Walter Bagehot. Bagehot is principally known for his book the English constitution which explored the nature of the parliamentary constitution but he also wrote on the nature of financial crises. In 1959 Stevas joined the Economist as its Legal and Political correspondent. (60)

It was perhaps inevitable that such a high achiever and egotist would enter politics. If it hadn't been for his private life, which prevented him from standing against Margaret Thatcher for the leadership of the Conservative party, it is entirely conceivable that he could have gone on to become Prime Minister. Stevas had first contested a parliamentary seat as early as 1951 in the Labour stronghold of East Dagenham. The 1964 election was seen as a possible marginal in Chelmsford, despite the previous 10,000 majority, and was fiercely contested. In September George Brown spoke at an open air meeting in the Tindal Square and the Foreign Secretary R.A. Butler gave a speech at the Corn Exchange. Brown's meeting only attracted 150 people. (61) During October 1964 Sir Alec Douglas Home made a helicopter visit to Chelmsford, Maldon and Colchester. (62) In the event Stevas won comfortably with a majority of over 7,000. The Essex Chronicle noted that the Chelmsford result was in contrast with the prevailing swing in East Anglia in general. (63)

Stevas was certainly busy in his first year in the constituency, writing 1,500 letters for his constituents. (64) In 1966 he introduced a bill of rights for illegitimate children. (65) He was always on the liberal wing of the Conservative party, had long been an opponent of capital punishment and the limiting of immigrations on race grounds and was in favour of a relaxation of the obscenity laws. Stevas however, opposed both Leo Abse's Divorce Bill and David Steel's Abortion Bill because of his catholic beliefs. He was however, co-sponsor of Abse's Private Members Bill to permit homosexual acts between consenting adults which became the Sexual Offences Act of 1967.

The 1966 election saw Stevas' majority cut to just under 5,000. Ninety sixty six also saw him clash with a constituent when he would not discuss the Vietnam issue at his surgery because he said it was not a personal problem. (66) In the 1970 general election, which saw the Conservatives returned to power under Ted Heath, Stevas increased his majority to just over 13,000. This time George Brown was consistently heckled when he spoke at the Civic Centre. (67)

By the time of the next election the Liberals were a much more powerful force in the constituency: this was almost entirely due to the fact that their candidate Stuart Mole was a councillor and very well known locally. In the election of February 1974 Mole managed to poll 21,929 votes, but with 28,560 votes Stevas still had a majority of over seven thousand. (68) Mole did however defeat the Labour candidate by well over five thousand votes. The second election of 1974 saw a good deal of tactical voting with probably several thousand Labour voters switching to the Liberals. This time Stevas' majority was reduced to just over four thousand votes. A late straw poll in the constituency had actually put Mole ahead. (69)

Towards the end of Edward Heath's government Stevas was Under Secretary of State at the D.E.S. when Margaret Thatcher was Minister of Education. Between 1973 and 1974 he was Minister for the Arts for the first time. Stevas supported Heath in the first ballot of the 1975 Conservative Party leadership election but switched his vote to Thatcher in the second round after he had originally considered standing himself but was advised against doing so. He then served as a member of the shadow cabinet from 1974 to 1978 when he was the shadow spokesman for education. Stevas later became the Shadow Leader of the House of Commons.

The 1979 general election, which saw the Conservatives return to power, was predicted to be close in Chelmsford and the campaign saw Stuart Mole prematurely predicting victory. In the end Stevas slightly increased his majority to almost five and a half thousand. It was this sixth time he had been returned in 15 years. (70) Boundary changes the following year saw the whole of Boreham and Springfield return to the constituency but South Woodham Ferrers, Ramsden Heath and Rettendon go to the Rochford constituency. (71)

In 1979 Stevas was appointed by Margaret Thatcher as Minister for the Arts for the second time and in addition he was given the roles of Leader of the House of Commons and Chancellor of the Duchy of Lancaster. It was during the next two years that he was the driving force behind the creation of the current system of Select Committees. Select Committees today play a vital role in making ministers more accountable to backbench M.P.'s than they would otherwise be. Stevas was the first of the Tory 'wets' to be fired in 1981 as Margaret Thatcher gradually exerted her authority. "Cabinet ministers recalled St John Stevas, as he sat at the end of the cabinet table, drawing laughter from other dissenters, often invoking his nicknames for her, including the 'leaderene' and, most irritating for Mrs Thatcher, Tina, coined from her battle cry at the time 'There is no alternative'." (72) On one occasion he asked to be excused from a meeting at 10 Downing Street because he had a meeting to attend. "But I'm going to the same meeting" Mrs Thatcher replied. "Yes" he said "but it takes me so much longer to change." Stevas refused the role of Arts Minister as a non cabinet role.

The 1983 election saw Mole stand for the fourth time, this time for the new Social Democrats. (73) This time the seat was a genuine marginal. A number of high powered visitors were drafted into the constituency including Norman Lamont and Shirley Williams. In the end Stevas survived but his majority of 378 was the smallest in the new House of Commons. (74) Three years later Stevas announced that he was retiring at the next election realising that he was unlikely to win. He had already tried without success to get selected for the safe neighbouring seat of Rochford.

Stevas went on to become Chairman of the Royal Art Commission from 1985 to 1999, causing a good deal of controversy. Some thought that he put his own views and choices above those of other people. Paintings from national collections were hung in his office, documents were presented in red boxes and he had a chauffeur and ex civil servants doing his bidding. One commentator said "if he cannot have power, he must have the trappings". A governmental review was very critical of the way the Arts Commission was run. The Commission strongly criticised the plans for the Millenium Wheel although three of his fellow commissioners had been in favour of it. Despite this he was re-appointed for a third time.

Stevas was also no stranger to controversy in his period as the Master of Emmanuel College, Cambridge from 1991 to 1996. He had a new conference centre built at a cost of £8 million, partly due to his insistence that the limestone had to be obtained from the same source from which the college's Wren chapel had been built. Stevas successfully promoted the college through 'House and Garden' and 'Hello' magazines but relations between the Master and some of those at the college were strained. He was an eminent royalist and had a close relationship with the royal family. All his personal notes were written in purple ink and he only used official House of Lords stationery after he became a Lord. He died in March 2012, aged 82. (75)

During the municipal elections the trend against Labour continued and they were reduced to just 6 seats in 1968. (76) In advance of a likely reorganisation of local government under the Heath government the borough suggested a 'marriage' with the district council. Not surprisingly the rural parishes' response was frosty to say the least. Nevertheless the R.D.C. was prepared to hand over the urbanised areas close to the town, namely Great Baddow but not Springfield and Galleywood. (77) In the event the rural area had no opportunity to repeat their fight of 1907 because national legislation was introduced under the 1972 Local Government Act. The new council was to have 60 seats, with 28 members from the borough and 32 from the rural district. (78)

In the old council there were gains for both Labour and the Liberals in 1972, which mirrored the swing to the left in the county as a whole. In September 1973 the Prime Minister Ted Heath went on a walkabout around the town during extremely tight security because of the danger of an I.R.A. bomb.

The early 1970s saw another brief flurry of activity in the county town from the far right of British politics. In the 1950's Oswald Mosley had again spoken in Chelmsford as leader of his new Union movement. He spoke at the Shire Hall in 1957 but generally had difficulty in getting halls for meetings. (79) In February 1973 left wing activists clashed with members of the National Front and the Essex Monday Club outside a meeting at the Shire Hall addressed by the National Front chairman, John Tindall. 100 police were drafted in from all over the county but there was no violence. This was after a petition went to the county council against the decision to let the Hall to the Front. (80) In May 1973 a Monday Club meeting at the Shire Hall featured an anti immigration film. (81) Generally however, as before the war, the extreme right gained little support in the town. A National Front march in 1977 starting at the Golden Fleece pub in Duke Street gained little support. The party had at most 40 members in the town. (82) Another march in 1982 only attracted 100 supporters when 500 had been expected. The march was against the jailing of the editor of the Front's Bulldog paper in Chelmsford prison. (83) Recently the English Defence League (E.D.L.) has tried to get established in the town on the back of the supposed issue of a new mosque. Again it has gained little support.

The first election for the new district council saw the Conservatives winning comfortably with 30 seats, Labour 16, the Liberals 8 and 6 Independents. (84) Conservatives claimed that the Independents would normally vote with them. The Labour chairman R. Hadley said that if that was the case then they should stand for re-election as Tories.

A committee of the new council recommended that the office of mayor should be abolished arguing that it was ceremonial and expensive. (85) A petition for a royal charter would have to be applied for the new council to have a mayor. The Weekly News conducted a poll on the issue, which voted to keep the office, but a low turnout of the readership suggests there wasn't much interest either way. Eventually in October 1973 the new council voted 30 votes to 20 to end the mayoral office. (86) The following month a campaign was launched to keep the post. (87) Eventually there was a free vote, with 38 in favour and 15 against replacing the current council chairman by a mayor. (88)

The early years of the new council saw the Liberals become the second force with the Labour Party fading rapidly. By 1980 the Liberals had 20 seats to the Conservatives 34. (89) The influx of a new affluent electorate and the decline in the number of industrial workers was certainly a factor in this turnaround. In the 1983 election the new Liberal – S.D.P. alliance fought 59 of the 60 seats. The alliance squeezed home to get overall control by a single seat. "For the first time in living memory not one Labour councillor was returned." (90) Within the Alliance, 3 S.D.P. councillors were returned for the first time. In 1985 the Boundaries Commission looked at the imbalance between some wards in Chelmsford but the Alliance stayed in control in the municipal elections later that year. (91)

Nineteen eighty four saw the first calls for a modern bid for city status. This was led by the Mayor Mrs C. Johnson and the Provost of the Cathedral John Moses. Only 11 bids for city status had been granted during the century. (92) The bid failed to materialise but a new bid was launched in 1991. This time there was evidently a greater chance of success because the Home Office invited Chelmsford to apply. It was the favourite in the early betting; according to the papers it was a town of over 150,000 people, Essex didn't have a City and Chelmsford's Polytechnic looked set to be a University. (93) The following year came the news that the town had lost out to Sunderland. In 1996 the Council prepared a new bid, hoping to get city status to coincide with the 800th anniversary of the town's charter. (94) The Home Office invited Chelmsford to bid again in 2,000 but this failed as well. (95) During following year a new bid was submitted for the Queen's Jubilee. (96) The collapse of a number of regeneration plans were thought to probably limit the chances of success as they had done the previous bid. It looked like Chelmsford was to remain a town, despite the name of its football team! Sixty percent of the town's population were in favour of becoming a city. K. Attwood, the boss of e2v said "Obtaining city status would be good for businesses of all sizes, raising Chelmsford's profile and attracting investment". (97)

The granting of city status in 2012 was a surprise to many in the town, although those involved had certainly put a great deal of effort and organisation into the bid; Reading was a strong favourite and Chelmsford outsiders at 18 to one with the bookmakers. City status is certainly one race which defies logical prediction. The cost of the bid was estimated at under £20,000 which is likely to be seen as real value for money in years to come. (98) Simon Heffer, the eminent journalist, himself an old Chelmsfordian, was somewhat equivocal on Chelmsford's new status. He is not the only one however to bemoan the continued lack of a symphony hall, which you would expect to find in most cities. (99)

It was announced in 1974 that a new multi million pound County Hall complex was to be built on the out of town on the edge of Springfield. This was to replace the existing buildings and the latter were to be sold or rented out. (100) There was strong opposition to this from various quarters however, and the Queen finally opened the £12,500,000 extension to the existing County Hall in 1988. (101)

Nineteen eighty six saw the selection of a new Conservative parliamentary candidate, Simon Burns from a field of more than 100 candidates. Burns was educated at the Christ the King School, Accra, Ghana, Stamford School and Worcester College, Oxford. He is a second cousin of David Bowie. Burns was a founder member of the Rutland and Stamford Young Conservatives. In 1972 he worked for the Democrat Senator George McGovern in his presidential bid against Richard Nixon. From 1973 – 1975 he was a committee member and Secretary of Oxford University Conservative Association. (102) Between 1977 and 1981 he was a member of the Putney Conservative Association. In 1983 he stood in the Alyn and Deeside (North Wales) constituency where he reduced the Labour majority from 6,800 to 1,368.

In the build up to the 1987 election a poll for Anglia TV had the Alliance and the Conservatives neck and neck with 41% each. (103) Eventually he gained a majority of over 7,700 over Stuart Mole. (104) The alliance met resistance in the new housing estates on the outskirts of Chelmsford, which had boosted the electorate by 5,000 since 1983. The following year Mole stood down saying he would not fight the constituency again. (105) He was credited by the Chronicle for being responsible for the increase in Liberal support in the town in the previous twenty years and having played a large role in the creation of the administration that then ran the town. (106) From the outset Burns has lived in the Chelmsford area, thus answering one of the perceived weaknesses of Stevas as a constituency M.P.

The election defeat was followed by a split in the local Alliance party in council politics. Four out of six holders of top posts in Chelmsford's S.D.P., announced they would not be supporting efforts to merge their party with the Liberals. Mole supported the merger but there was a strong anti merger feeling amongst S.D.P. supporters in the town. (107) The Chelmsford S.D.L.P. was launched in May 1988. (108)

Simon Burns' early years as M.P. for Chelmsford were characterised by a series disagreements with the local Alliance government. Initially these were arguments over the Poll Tax. Burns insisted that the council was using the Poll tax as a cover for a big increase in spending on the rates before the new tax was introduced. (109) At first the Poll Tax was expected to be around £300 per person in Chelmsford but when it was finally announced it was £392. This was largely because of a 'safety net' which would have to go to other higher spending areas in the country. Burns maintained that the high charge was also due to the council's continued high spending. (110) He said "I have a strong suspicion that the borough council's spending has been done to try to take advantage of the change over in the system of financing local government in order that they can hide their profligacy by blaming the increase on the Government". (111) March 1990 saw the protests against the Poll Tax outside the council offices organised by a 'Chelmsford Against the Poll Tax' organisation. (112) By June there were more than 20 thousand unpaid tax bills and the council was owed £5 million. (113) The C.A.T.P. argued that many people couldn't afford to pay. 300 summonses for non payment were sent out in October. Forty seven staff were struggling to deal with the 115,000 residents in the borough that were liable to the charge. (114) By then the shortfall had been cut to seven and a half percent. In 1991 the new community charge was reduced by £30. Burns argued that this was due to the County Council cutting its share of the charge, rather than anything the local council had done. (115) In 1992 Poll Tax bills rose by 15% after the new Tory council had cut spending to avoid being rate capped. (116) By 1993 when the new Council tax started Chelmsford council still had three and half million pounds owing on the Poll Tax. (117)

In 1991 the Conservatives had regained control of the Chelmsford council, winning 29 out of 56 seats. Labour did gain 2 seats in All Saints ward, the first time it had held seats since 1979. Simon Burns commented 'I am delighted that Chelmsford has got rid of the Liberal Democrats. I look forward to working with the new council." (118) Despite his predictions that the Liberal Democrats were a fading force in the town they won a majority again in 1995 winning 32 seats. (119)

Until 1994 Burns was P.P.S. at the Ministry of Agriculture, Fisheries and Food. He was then assistant government whip, Lord Commissioner of Her Majesty's Treasury and then Parliamentary Under-Secretary for Health. In 1992 he won a majority of 18 thousand in the general election. (120) At this time he was working a 72 hour week, not including travelling, which was extensive because he lived in the constituency. (121)

Proposed boundary changes announced in 1993, would have transferred St Andrews ward, Writtle and Chignal to Brentwood and Ongar. The Hanningfields, Margaretting and Stock would go to Billericay. A Liberal Democrat commented "This seems to be a case of people playing games with pencils on maps without any knowledge or understanding of local circumstances." (122) Simon Burns was against the changes which would have made the constituency geographically smaller. The resulting boundary changes created two constituencies involving the borough. These were West Chelmsford, which Burns stood for, and Maldon and East Chelmsford which included the villages of Danbury and Great Baddow. (123)

In the 1997 election Simon Burns saw his majority reduced from 18,000 to 6,000. After the Conservative defeat Burns was Opposition Front Bench spokesman for Social Security until 1998, when he became the spokesman for the Environment, Housing and Planning. From 2001 to 2005 he was the Shadow Health Minister, after which he became an opposition whip. Meanwhile he had been elected to the executive of the influential 1922 committee and became its Treasurer in 1999. One of his principal achievements was to get his private members bill, the Football (Offences and disorder) Act through parliament, which tightened up the law on football hooligans. In 2000 he pressured the government to strengthen the law further by giving the courts the power to withdraw hooligan's passports in order to prevent them causing trouble abroad. His election majority was again just over 6,000 in 2001. (124)

John Wittingale was elected to the constituency of Maldon and East Chelmsford in 1997 after previously being M.P. for Maldon since 1992. He was educated at Winchester and the University of London, graduating in economics. Wittingale was Special adviser to several Secretaries of State for Industry in the 1980's before becoming political adviser to Margaret Thatcher when she was Prime Minister. He was awarded an O.B.E. for his work in that role.

Despite their decline in parliamentary elections the Liberal Democrats remained a strong force in municipal elections. In 1999 however they lost control, when Labour councillors could exercise the balance of power. (125) They regained power in 2003 but depended on support of the Independents. (126) In 2003 the Conservatives finally regained control of the council, which they held again in 2007. (127) Despite persistent criticism of the council in the later years of the twentieth century the council was able to announce in 2001 that it was debt free having paid off its previous £27 million loan. (128)

After proposals in 2003 a new streamlined single constituency for Chelmsford finally came into being in 2010. (129) In the 2010 election Simon Burns was again victorious beating the Liberal Democrat candidate Stephen Robinson by just over 5,000 votes. (130) Before this Burns had worked for Hillary Clinton in her campaign to be nominated as the Democrat candidate in the 2008 election. Burns has an extensive library of books on the Kennedy family. He quit his London flat in the wake of the expenses scandal after "inadvertently" overcharging on the flat. (131) Burns was Minster of State for Health in the new Conservative government until 2012 when he became Minister for Transport. In May of that year he celebrated 25 years representing Chelmsford. (132) Recent years have been marked by an argument with John Bercow, the Speaker in the House of Commons. Burns had to apologise after calling the latter a "stupid sanctimonious dwarf". In 2011 he compared the campaigning group '38 degrees' to 'zombies' resulting in thousands of complaints. The same year there was a controversy over the M.P.'s £41 thousand 'chauffeur bill', necessary he maintained because he needed to work on confidential papers. (133) This led him to start using the train again to get to the House of Commons. In October 2013 he somewhat surprisingly resigned from his government post in order too, unsuccessfully as it turned out, stand for the vacant post of deputy speaker of the House of Commons. If he had won Burns would have been deputy to Bercow.

In the most recent municipal elections there was a further swing to the Conservatives, with the party achieving 40 seats and the Liberals only 15, a loss of 11. (134)

In May 2012 Christopher Kingsley became the first Mayor of the new city. In June the letters patent regarding city status arrived from the House of Lords. (135) A visit from Princess Anne during December 2012 gave the new city the Royal seal of approval. (136)

1) 'Was that really me?' Ernest Millington p.20
2) Millington p.27
3) Millington p.32
4) Millington p.39
5) Millington p.45-47

6) Millington p.48
7) Millington p.50
8) Millington p.57-58
9) Millington p.68
10) Millington p.84
11) Millington p.91
12) Millington p.104
13) Essex Weekly News 4 5 1945
14) Millington p.109
15) Millington p.111
16) Essex Record Office Oral records Mrs Sybil Olive
17) Millington p.116
18) E.W.N. 27 7 1945
19) Millington p.106
20) Millington p.117
21) E.W.N. 27 1 1950 p.7
22) Essex Chronicle 4 7 1947
23) Millington p.118
24) E.W.N. 1 4 1949 p.5
25) E.W.N. 3 3 1950 p.8
26) Millington p.134 – 5
27) E.W.N. 19 1 1950 p.1
28) Millington p.139
29) Millington p.141
30) E.C. 3 1 1958 p.1
31) Millington p.144
32) The Independent – Obituaries 15 5 2009
33) E.W.N. 9 11 1945 p.3
34) E.W.N. 8 11 1946 p.2
35) E.W.N. 31 1 1947
36) Essex Countryside Vol.33 – Article by Rosemary Devon.
37) E.W.N. 7 2 1947 p.8
38) E.W.N. 21 2 1947 p.8
39) E.W.N. 24 10 1947 p.8
40) E.W.N. 24 10 1947 p.8

41) E.W.N. 1 6 1951 p.1
42) Wikipedia http://en.wikipedia.org/wiki/Hubert Ashton
43) E.W.N. 12 10 1951 p.1
44) E.W.N. 19 1 1951 p.1
45) E.W.N. 9 11 1956 p.1
46) E.W.N. 2 10 1959 p.9
47) E.W.N. 10 10 1959 p.3
48) E.W.N. 23 3 1962 p.1
49) E.W.N. 8 5 1953 p.1
50) E.W.N. 11 5 1956 p.1
51) E.W.N. 9 5 1958 p.1
52) E.W.N. 8 5 1959 p.1
53) E.W.N. 21 4 1961 p.8
54) E.W.N. 16 6 1961 p.9
55) E.W.N. 23 3 1962
56) E.W.N. 19 4 1963 p.1
57) E.W.N. 10 5 1963
58) E.W.N. 8 5 1964 p.1
59) Guardian obituary 5 3 2012
60) Wikipedia Norman St John Stevas, Baron St John Fawsley
61) E.W.N. 18 9 1964 p.1
62) E.W.N. 9 10 1964 p.1
63) E.C. 23 10 1964 p.19
64) E.W.N. 1 10 1965 p.11
65) E.W.N. 4 2 1966 p.9
66) E.W.N. 15 7 1966 p.1
67) E.W.N. 19 6 1971
68) E.C. 1 3 1974
69) E.W.N. 10 10 1974 p.1
70) E.C. 11 5 1979 p.2
71) E.C. 22 8 1980.1
72) The New York Times obituary 9 3 2012
73) E.C. 15 1 1982 p.14
74) E.C. 30 9 1983 p.8
75) Wikipedia obituary

76) E.W.N. 10 5 1968 p.5
77) E.C. 27 8 1971 p.1
78) E.W.N. 13 7 1972 p.1
79) E.C. 22 2 1957 p.1
80) E.W.N. 15 2 1973 p.1
81) E.W.N. 31 5 1973 p.5
82) E.C. 1 8 1977 p.3
83) E.C. 29 11982 p.4
84) E.C. 15 6 1973 p.1
85) E.W.N. 23 8 1973 p.12
86) E.W.N. 4 10 1973 p.12
87) E.W.N. 29 11 1973 p.1
88) E.C. 24 6 1977 p.1
89) E.W.N. 19 10 1980
90) E.W.N. 12 5 1983 p.1
91) E.W.N. 14 2 1985 p.3, E.W.N. 9 5 1985 p.1
92) E.C. 25 5 1984 p.3
93) E.W.N. 24 10 1991 p.3
94) E.C. 23 1 1998 p.1
95) E.C. 16 7 1999 p.1,
96) E.W.N. 11 10 2001 p.1
97) E.C. 14 1 2010 p.5
98) E.C. 15 3 2012 p.1
99) E.C. 22 3 2012 p.8
100) E.W.N. 24 10 1974
101) E.C. 8 7 1988
102) The National Archives: Department of Health Simon Burns.
103) E.W.N. 2 4 1987 p.1
104) E.W.N. 18 6 1987 p.7
105) E.W.N. 14 2 1988 p.14
106) E.C. 5 2 1988 p.9
107) E.W.N. 20 8 1987 p.1
108) E.C. 20 5 1988 p.9
109) E.C. 8 7 1988 p.6
110) E.C. 9 2 1990 p.1

111) E.C. 25 2 1990 p.1
112) E.C. 2 3 1990 p.3
113) E.C. 22 6 1990 p.1
114) E.W.N. 11 10 1990 p.3
115) E.W.N. 21 3 1991 p.1
116) E.W.N. 13 2 1992 p.1
117) E.W.N. 13 5 1993 p.1
118) E.W.N. 9 5 1991 p.8
119) E.W.N. 11 5 1995 p.1
120) E.C. 16 4 1992 p.1
121) E.C. 24 5 1991 p.1
122) E.C. 17 6 1993 p.1
123) E.C. 28 4 1997
124) E.C. 15 6 2001 p.9
125) E.W.N. 13 5 1999 p.7
126) E.C. 10 5 2002 p.12
127) E.C. 9 5 2003 p.1
128) E.C. 11 10 2001
129) E.C. 2 5 2003 p.1
130) E.C. 13 5 2010 p.3 – 4
131) E.C. 14 1 2010 p.1
132) E.C. 3 5 2012 p.8
133) E.C. 14 4 2011 p.1
134) E.C. 12 5 2011 p.12
135) E.C. 7 6 2012 p.1
136) E.C. 6 12 2012 p.2

15

Chelmsford during the Great War

"Age shall not weary them nor the years condemn"

The above quote is of course from the almost universally well known poem 'To the fallen' by Lawrence Binyon (1869 – 1945). The sombre lines of the fourth verse are spoken at every Remembrance Day service. It was originally published on the 21st of September 1914 at the start of the war. He lived in Chelmsford as a boy and attended K.E.G.S. when it was at Duke Street. Binyon went on to St Pauls School, London then Trinity College Oxford. He was the son of Frederick Binyon, curate at St Mary's Chelmsford. As well as being a poet Binyon was a museum curator at the British Museum and an art critic. He worked with Elgar on a play about the Arthurian legends. (1)

Although less than half a dozen bombs were dropped on Chelmsford during the first war, the town and its surrounding area were affected by the war in a wide variety of ways. Besides like every town in the country losing large numbers of its young men to the extent that virtually every extended family suffered at least one bereavement or a member with a serious injury. The Essex Chronicle started the war publishing a full roll call of casualties, but the lists quickly grew to such a length that the paper had to limit this to a monthly record. There was a shortage of newsprint which exacerbated this problem. The Chronicle was soon limited to four pages per issue. As we shall see the area was flooded with military personnel. Although many did not stay longer than a night or two, the thousands of soldiers put a great strain on the areas' resources; billets had to be found for the men and horses. Also the men had to be kept occupied. This and the possible likelihood, however remote, of invasion meant that the town's authorities, and those of the rural district, had to be well organised. Towards the end of the war they had to exert a large amount of control on food distribution. All the big firms were involved in producing munitions and Hoffmann especially underwent a huge expansion. This meant drafting in a large number of women to factory work for the first time. Chelmsford, with one or two exceptions, like Norwich, had escaped direct targeting, but the area was directly in the flight path of, firstly the cumbersome Zeppelins and later the German Gotha aircraft on the way to and from London.

More than a decade before the start of the first war, Chelmsford had been affected to a lesser extent by the Boer War (1899 – 1902). Unlike most countries on the continent which had conscription, Britain had no large standing army. The Essex Regiment had been formed in 1881 following the union of two foot regiments, after the Cardwell reforms had led to the establishment of territorial grouping of soldiers. Both the first and second battalions, the third militia battalion and elements of the volunteer battalions, served in that war. The first battalion were honoured for their involvement with the relief of Kimberley and Paardeberg.

The Boer war was the first in which, despite problems, wireless was used (See chapter 5). In addition, as we have seen, Colonel Crompton and his Company were instrumental in the establishment of a company of Electrical Engineers. He went out with them on their first tour of duty, establishing amongst other things the use of searchlights which he had designed. Crompton also had efficient trains built for use at the front. (2) Chelmsford contributed to the City Imperial Volunteers and the Chelmsford detachment of the Essex Regiment was asked to provide 110 volunteers and four officers and to hold a similar number in reserve. "They will have to be good shots; they will take the place of men in the 1st battalion of the Essex Regiment who have trained to act as mounted infantry." (3) Unlike the first war the Boer War was extensively reported on by the local papers; letters from serving solders filled the pages, and from the outset revealed some of the limitations in the way the war was being fought. A Chelmsford reservist, who was the son of the landlord of the Orange Tree, Anchor Street, wrote to his father in 1900 "We have only the clothes we stand up in, with an extra shirt and a pair of socks. All of our other things were left at Capetown. This will be a longer job than many people have bargained for. Things are very dear. Butter is two shillings and sixpence, beer eight pence a quart and six pence for a small loaf." (4) A couple of months later a Private W. Rawlinson of the Border Regiment wrote to his parents in Upper Bridge Road Chelmsford, "I am glad to say that I have come through another long battle, which lasted seven days; it was a most trying time. The losses in our regiment were 130 killed and wounded. I had a very narrow escape, for there were ten of us lying in a trench when a shell dropped between us, and killed a poor chap right out, but never touched any other." At night "we were lying out in the open in just what we stood up in, for we did not even get our greatcoats, and we could not sleep as it has been bitter cold at night lately." "We have had to live on biscuits, bully beef and a drop of coffee." He was only allowed two washes a fortnight. (5)

From the start of the war in South Africa Major Carne Rasch, the M.P. for Chelmsford, was critical of the War Office and the army system. "As to the generals" he remarked "the less said about them the better." He described the War Office as "that epitome of red tapism of the one man in Pall Mall." Rasch declared that the system provided at a "maximum cost and minimum efficiency." Never one to hold back he said "our guns in South Africa are outclassed and out ranged; the cavalry are without enough horses." The National Defence Committee "whose combined ages equalled that of Methuselah" did not meet for six months after their appointment. (6) Rasch's speech was a mistake and ill timed according to the editor of the Weekly News. Certainly it was brave, appearing to go against the prevailing jingoistic tide. Four months later Rasch said he didn't want what the Essex Regiment had done in the Transvaal to be thrown away and count for nothing. (7) Before the end of 1900 he made another speech in which he pronounced that the whole system of army administration was "rotten to the core". In a prophetic pronouncement he stated that red tape needed to be removed to "prevent in future wars the repetition of the blunders that have been committed in South Africa." (8)

During January 1901 another detachment of Electrical Engineer Volunteers was selected for service after the previous one under Colonel Crompton's command had returned home the previous month. (9) The City Imperial Volunteers also returned home to Chelmsford and "the heartiness of the welcome could not be matched anywhere". (10) The need for more volunteers led to a recruiting office being opened in Chelmsford and the Weekly News reported that recruiting "has since been proceeding briskly".

In April 1900 the Weekly News published a Chelmsford man's story about the siege of Ladysmith. He was the son of a Tindal Street furniture dealer. "Of course there have been many escapes and I have been twice hit by spent bullets from shrapnel but without piercing the skin thank God." "Our beef has run out and we are now living on horse flesh served up as follows – 1st pure joints of horse meat, undisguised; 2nd minced meat, much disguised; 3rd soup, disgusting; 4th sausages, revolting. But we don't live to eat but eat to live consequently we hold our noses, shut our eyes and get it downstairs as quickly as possible. God send the relief quick or the Boers won't have much to shoot at." Three weeks later he wrote "Today has been a joyful one. About 5 p.m. two heads came over a hill to our south and then two more, till at last about 400 men mounted could be seen right along the hill and then we could see they were colonial troops. Needless to say the cheers were deafening and continuous." (11)

Fund raising was common in the war, again a precedent for the later world conflict. In February 1901 a concert was given at the Shire Hall in aid of the Chelmsford division of the Soldiers and Sailors Families association. (12) The war established the need for a drill hall in a town like Chelmsford; a place where volunteers could train and relax. This was to be built on a site on Market Road and was to cost £3,000. (13) In three months £2,000 was raised by events at the Shire Hall and elsewhere. (14) Lord Roberts, the Commander in Chief of Essex Regiment opened the hall in Chelmsford 1904. The immediate commencement of a gym class twice a week at the hall reflected the widespread concern at the fitness levels of the soldiers who went to South Africa. (15) A large recreation room was set aside for corporals and privates. In an era when memorials were still unusual, some of the money left by Rasch was used to erect a memorial to those who died in the Boer war in 1910.

From 1902 to 1914 the first battalion of the Essex Regiment served in India, Burma and Mauritius while the second battalion stayed at home. Large scale reforms in 1908 saw the volunteers absorbed into the territorial force and the militia into the special reserve. At the outbreak of war in 1914 the 3rd Special Reserve Battalion was based at Warley and the 5th Territorial Force was based at Chelmsford. (16) During the war the regiment as a whole provided thirty infantry battalions, receiving battle honours at Le Cateau, Ypres, Loos, Somme, Cambrai, Gallipoli and Gaza.

"The great Nations of Europe are now involved in one of the largest wars the world has ever seen"; so the Essex Chronicle announced the start of the war. (17) As elsewhere there was a rush to voluntarily enlist. Would be volunteers were given all possible encouragement. Two weeks after the commencement of hostilities the Chronicle recorded "Colonel Travers drove into Chelmsford bedecked with the Union Jack and from the gun platform in front of the Shire Hall appealed to the farmers to assist in recruiting for Lord Kitchener's army." (18) Chelmsford was one of the three main recruitment centres in the county. By the middle of September 1,000 men had enlisted in the County town. (19) The big employers in the town were encouraging their workers to enlist with the promise that their jobs would be safe at the end of the war. In the rural areas the larger landowners often put heavy pressure on young tenants to enlist. In his wartime diaries Reverend Andrew Clark mentioned the ill feeling stirred up in Great Leighs village by the high handed stance of the Tritton family, who thought all young men in the area should join up and those who were older should join the reserve to protect the roads, bridges and telegraph posts. The squire's daughters put up recruiting posters. Despite this "there was a great village feeling against lads who are of age and physique to enlist and who have not done so." J.H. Tritton and Clark himself were the names at the top of the list for the volunteer reserve in the village. (20) Tritton chaired a recruitment meeting at his residence Lyons Hall. After his initial speech came several by recruiting officers. (21) A villager, H. Sergeant, an employee at Marconi, was turned down at the recruiting office because his chest size was just below the minimum required. He bought himself a pair of dumbbells and a fortnight later successfully offered himself for service again. (22) Not everybody was caught up in the tide of jingoistic fever however. A well attended peace meeting was held at the Shire Hall in August and the Chelmsford Adult School based at the Friends Meeting House sent a resolution to Asquith in favour of peace. (23)

As elsewhere, after six months there was a fall in recruiting. (24) The National Registration Act of 1915 revealed there were a large number of men who should have been available. Under Lord Derby's scheme, door to door visits in the town forced men to 'attest' that they would be available if needed. Reports in the local papers of anti German riots elsewhere in the country were also used to encourage men to enlist. (25) Already the previous October 'evidence' of German atrocities had been used at a recruitment meeting at the Shire Hall. (26) By June 1915 recruitment was again rising but a considerable number of those enlisting were either unfit or classified to class 3, the reserves. (27) In October 1915 there was a final march of Yeomanry through the county for recruitment. (28)

Nationally there was no avoiding conscription. In January 1916 a Military Service Bill was introduced for single men and this was extended to married men in May. A tribunal had already been set up in Chelmsford to hear appeal cases. George Taylor, the Mayor, chaired the tribunal which heard 40 cases in the first month of the year. (29) The editor of the Weekly News probably spoke for the majority when he said that a few conscientious objectors had a genuine conscience but most were frauds. "There was a particularly fine specimen of the class at Chelmsford..... who refused to enrol as a fighting man or take service as a non combatant." (30) By March most of those who appealed were being passed for non combatant service and were being put to work as farmers. (31) Those appeals that claimed likely hardship to the family were often refused. (32) Farmers were often appealing on behalf of their men. (33) In January 1917 it was announced that no further Essex men were to be called up if they were involved in the production of milk. (34) The growing shortage of soldiers meant that medical exemption was sometimes revoked, as happened to a Chelmsford man with a serious heart condition. (35) Those with key council jobs, like the borough engineer and the surveyor, were automatically given a conditional exemption. (36) The tribunals exhibited a class bias. When Edward Craggs, a former officer in the Sportsmen's Battalion, was in Chelmsford court applying for a discharge of his bankruptcy, the possibility of sending him to the forces did not arise. (37) After resigning his commission he was allowed to stay at home.

By September 1914 thousands of troops were in the Chelmsford area and the King inspected a large number in the grounds of Hylands House in October. (38) Many of the troops just passed through the area. In August 1914, for example, the East Anglian Division of Territorials marched through the town. (39) During September the Berkshire Territorials were billeted in the town for several weeks before moving on to Broomfield. They were praised for their conduct and behaviour. (40) The number of troops that had to be found billets varied during the war but may have been up to seven thousand. In December 1914 the council were finding it difficult to find billets due to the fact that many houses were affected by measles, whooping cough and chicken pox. (41) During 1915 the military authorities requisitioned the casual wards of the workhouse. (42) Eventually a large number of huts had to be built on the Recreation ground. Although the soldiers were a boost to the local economy, the military authorities frequently had to give compensation to house owners for damage to their property. In August 1916 Andrew Clark reported that "Plenty of empty houses are to be obtained in Chelmsford, but all are so badly damaged by soldiers as to be almost uninhabitable." He described a house in Hamlet Road, Moulsham. "In it the soldiers have torn up the boards just to make firewood and in compensation the military authorities have given the landlord the wholly inadequate sum of £12." (43) Besides the soldiers themselves, accommodation also had to be found for a large number of horses. In the town the military authorities used the market premises at a charge of 6d, per horse, per night. (44)

In a town where even before the war the water supply and drainage system was, only just coping, the arrival of such a large number of people was bound to put that part of the town's infrastructure under intolerable strain. The military authorities tried to reduce the need for the soldiers to wash at their billets by negotiating with the council for use of the slipper baths at the town's baths every afternoon. Many of the facilities where the soldiers billeted were anyway still very primitive. By September the need for water was reaching a record 440,000 thousand gallons per day. The deficiency in the daily supply resulted in the level at the Longstomps reservoir falling to only four feet deep. A new borehole at Admirals Park (See chapter 17) only just saved the town from imminent disaster. (45) The Inspector of Nuisances was often called in to investigate cases of overcrowding where soldiers were billeted. Dr Thresh blamed the military authorities for the first outbreak of pneumonia in the town in 1915. They had failed to disinfect houses and huts where soldiers had succumbed to the disease. An outbreak of cerebro-meningitis in the area in the winter of 1914-1915 was also attributed to soldiers. (46) These medical cases were dealt with at Oaklands hospital, where huts were built in the grounds. In addition to having to pay for the construction of several short roads for their soldiers to use, the military authorities also had to pay for damage inflicted on existing public roads. In 1915 after a road in Great Baddow had been badly damaged, the Chelmsford R.D.C. applied to have it repaired under the Military Traffic Scheme. (47) Just like the town, villages such as Stock found it difficult to cope with the number of soldiers billeted there. In its case this was because of its position on a possible invasion route and the fact that it was surrounded by gun placements and large searchlights. (48) Within a week of the war breaking out, an infantry regiment was stationed in the village, a complement a thousand strong. A Scottish Regiment of the Royal Artillery was also stationed in the village. Most of these soldiers were placed in private houses. Incredibly, in addition to all these soldiers, Belgian refugees were also placed in the village.

 By 1917 the Chelmsford area also had to find room for the large numbers of munitions workers flooding in. Conscription had meant that large numbers of existing workers were called up and had to be replaced. Hoffmann alone lost 1,000 workers. This led to the establishment of a central billeting board. The increasing employment of women in the big factories and the municipal gasworks still did not solve the shortage. (49)

 One of the most immediate pressing problems regarding the stationing of soldiers in the area was the question of what they were going to do in their spare time. From the outset, excessive drinking was a likely problem. Heavy fines were often imposed on out of hours drinking; for example on the landlord of the White Hart in 1916. (50) Licensing hours were not altered in Chelmsford until September 1915. Public house closing times were put back from 11 p.m. to 10 p.m. on Mondays to Thursdays and from 10 p.m. to 9 p.m. on Sundays. Alternatives to heavy drinking needed to be provided however. (51) The Corn Exchange was immediately established as the centre of entertainment activities for the soldiers but all the town's cinemas, the Regent Theatre, when it opened in 1916, a skating rink and a number of churches were also used. (52) Soldiers clubs were quickly established, one in the hall at St John's, Moulsham and another at St Peter's School in Rainsford End. (53) Concerts were put on weekly at the Corn Exchange, often by the soldiers themselves. In December 1914 there was a military tattoo at the Recreation Ground with officers at the garrison meeting the expense. (54) By January 1915 weekly entertainments were taking place at least three places other than the Corn Exchange. (55) The Woolpack Inn for example held a concert in 1916 to raise money for cigarettes and tobacco for the wounded soldiers at the Hylands hospital and the Chelmsford Red Cross hospital. A New Years social for soldiers was held in the Wesleyan school room. (56) The Society of Friends opened their premises for the troops' recreation. (57) Chelmsford's best known entertainment group was the 'Funnions', led by Fred Munnion, 'the Funnion'. They played all the Y.M.C.A. huts, Hylands hospital, Oaklands hospital and most of the military camps. The 'Funnions' always played for charity. They gave a concert for example in the Primitive Methodist church in Hall Street to a large audience of 130 in order to raise money for the nearby Red Cross Hospital. Entertainments were also put on by and on behalf of soldiers stationed in the outlying villages. The soldiers of the Oxford and Buckinghamshire Light Infantry put on entertainments in Writtle for the Writtle and Widford Nursing Association and the Belgian refugees. (58)

Patriotic fervour led to a great deal of fund raising activity in Chelmsford. Nationally a relief fund was established for the distribution of funds to the dependants of soldiers and sailors killed or wounded in action. Several Flag days, when flags with Russian emblems on them were sold in town, were held for the huge amount of soldiers wounded in the war. (59) Before Lenin took Russia out of the war, glowing tributes were made to the Russians at a fete held in the town in September 1916. (60) A local War Savings Committee was established with the Mayor J.O. Thompson as president. (61) By November 1917 it had raised almost £17,000 in nine months. (62) In January 1918 the Essex Chronicle maintained that there were two ways readers could help Britain win. One was by buying War Bonds the other was by drinking coffee rather than tea, because there was an acute shortage of tea. (63) By February 1918 Chelmsford had raised £100,000, the third highest amount in the county. (64) In May 1918 Chelmsford held an 'Aeroplane week', with an aim of raising £50,000 which would be sufficient for 20 planes at £2,500 each. (65) The Bishop, Watts Ditchfield, strongly supported this move, which was aided by the display of an aircraft in front of the Shire Hall. Local papers pointed out roller bearings for the biplanes were made at the Hoffmann factory. (66) A tank week was also held when a tank stood in front of the Sebastapol cannon at the Shire Hall. Apart from monetary fund raising blankets were regularly collected for the troops. (67) A boot and shoe fund was also started and orders given to the Industrial School. (68) Mrs Aylmer Maude organised the provision of clothing for soldiers. The Y.M.C.A. collected magazines for the troops. (69)

As happened in the rest of the country, large mansions in the area were converted into much needed hospitals and convalescent homes. Sir Daniel Gooch was on his way to the Antarctic with Shackleton when the war broke out. He immediately sent a message that Hylands should be used as a hospital, but it was Lady Gooch who did much of the organising. It helped that the estate was close to the railway line, with its own siding. (70) By October Belgian wounded were arriving at the hospital and by May 1915 the wounded at Hylands included Canadians. (71) At the end of 1914 a temporary hospital was erected at the back of the Chelmsford and Essex Hospital on London Road. This was a Red Cross hospital for the treatment of sick and wounded officers. (72) In September 1915 this accepted a party of 18 wounded officers from the Dardanelles. (73) During August 1917 this hospital admitted its 1000th patient. (74) In June 1918 Bellefield, the former home of Frederic Chancellor, was taken over to get more space. (75) During July 1917 it was arranged that the voluntary aid detachment of the Red Cross Society was to assign a member to visit each school upon public warning being given of a hostile air raid. (76) Oaklands was also used, with military cases of influenza being taken there. A number of houses in the rural areas around Chelmsford were made into convalescent homes for the wounded, including Skreens Park, at Roxwell, which was demolished after the war in 1920. (77)

By the end of the war the home economy was under much more State control than had been known before. Imported food supplies were being increasingly disrupted leading to big increases in food prices and necessitating food controls. As early as 1914 the local Trades Council wrote to the Chelmsford Star Co-operative about the need to keep prices down. (78) Wheat prices increased by over a quarter in the last four months of 1914 alone, with a consequent effect on bread prices. There was an immediate demand to increase home food production, with a consequent effect on the farming areas around Chelmsford (See chapter 1). By 1915 sugar beet production had started in the local area. (79) The Cultivation of Land Act of 1917 resulted in much unused land being dug up including part of the Recreation Ground, which was used to grow potatoes. (80) In January 1917 the Council said all possible measures had to be taken to use all unused land in the borough. (81) Essex, like Kent, became one of the leading counties for the Women's Land Army. (82) In 1918 there had to be a recruitment drive to save the harvest. (83) Despite the increase in mechanisation of local agriculture shortages of equipment was an increasing problem, as was the lack of personnel after conscription to train the women workers. Clark reported in September 1915 "Most of the women in the parish, and in the district are potato lifting today and have been for some days." (84) Ploughmen were exempted from conscription and in 1917 the two councils were instructed to release any council workers, who had knowledge of ploughing, for two months work on the farms. (85)

Towards the end of the war many townspeople increasingly felt that the town's traders were taking advantage of the food situation to make excessive profits. The introduction of rationing probably came just in time to prevent serious outbreaks of civil disobedience in the town. In January 1918 a Local Food Control Committee was set up. (86) All households had to register for supplies of butter or margarine. Volunteers had to fill out and distribute the eventual 20,000 cards produced for the Chelmsford area. (87) The committee attempted to buy up and keep a store of frozen meat (88). Towards the end of the war it was pressed to set up communal kitchens, partly because so many women were working and had little time to cook. (89) A major conflict occurred in the town over the price of milk that the Food Control Committee had set, which retailers thought was too low and caused them to go 'on strike'. This proved unsuccessful partly because the Star Co-operative refused to participate. June 1918 saw a public meeting at the Drill Hall discussing food prices and rationing. (90) The issuing of ration cards did not proceed easily because not everybody had put their addresses on the cards. There was also no co-operation from the Education Committee. In Colchester, schools were closed for a week to enable teachers to help the process to proceed more smoothly. (91) Instead, in Chelmsford twelve temporary clerks had to be employed to assist regular staff in this work. The composition of the F.C.C. had to be extended to meet mounting criticism; the extra members included a nominee from the trades council, a further women's representative and a member of the co-operative society. It had previously been felt that the original committee was dominated by the town's traders. Towards the end of the war there were a number of reports of discontent at the military camps. At the Lyons Hall barracks, Great Leighs, for example this was caused by poor food.

All the town's big firms benefitted from the war, especially the Hoffmann Company, whose bearings were used in all three armed force (see chapters 4, 5 and 7). German prisoners of war were used for the big expansion of the Hoffmann site that occurred towards the end of the conflict. Crompton's fully exploited the production of munitions and as a result in 1916 was subjected to the excess profits tax. (92)

One aspect of increased State control was on communications at home, especially with regard to the newspapers. Unlike the Boer War there was little reporting allowed on the war in the Weekly News and the Chronicle and no letters from the front were published. Clark's diaries reveal that almost all the official news in Great Leighs was local. This didn't prevent news of military successes and setbacks reaching the village quickly. In October 1914 Clark reported that the 12th weekly news bulletin pinned up in the village "contained no reference to the sinking of a cruiser in the Straits of Dover, but that adverse item of news was widely known in the village on Sunday morning." This was not officially confirmed by the Government until November 1917. (93)

The lack of official news caused rumours to flourish, especially in the early stages of the war when Germans were thought to be everywhere, although the true number of German born aliens in the area was actually very small. In a meeting at Great Leighs, villagers were told to watch for spies. The chairman, Tritton said there were 50,000 Germans, Austrians and Hungarians in the country. "Of these a large number come week by week to the market at Chelmsford and elsewhere." (94) It was this type of fuelling of hysteria which led to five 'foreigners' being seized supposedly attempting to poison the reservoir at Chingford. In 1914 another report which gained a good deal of currency in the Chelmsford area was that the Germans had actually landed. (95)

Compared with the second war, crime was low in Chelmsford during the conflict. Special constables were however enlisted to protect the roads, bridges, telegraph posts, lakes and reservoirs. They were supposed to arrest anybody "speaking to the dishonour of the country". There was usually a shortage of such constables, especially in the rural areas. The police themselves were "required to keep a register of every alien to make sure that no alien goes more than 5 miles from his address." (96)

By 1915 the borough council were taking the threat of air raids very seriously and took steps to deal with such an emergency. Chelmsford's Chief Fire Officer was adamant that the fire brigade could cope with two fires at once. The fear remained however that the Germans might use incendiaries which "would stretch the brigades' capabilities beyond breaking point". (97) As a result the fire brigade was enlarged by using military personnel and special constables. Members of other local brigades were used and former brigade members were asked to rejoin. Fifteen volunteered their services without pay within a day and in return were insured by the council. In October 1915 the fire brigade was called out five times but no damage was inflicted on the town. For air raids the specials were divided into five 'piquets' in different parts of the town. Watching posts included the police station, St John's church and one on the cathedral tower. (98) Likely routes for evacuation of people in the Chelmsford area proved difficult to determine because moving people northward would have interfered with troop movements. (99)

The G.E.R., whose line passed through Chelmsford, was, like other railway companies, taken over by the government at the beginning of the war. (100) Two months later the Essex Chronicle could report "Not only have naval and military needs been met but the usual passenger service has been maintained with few exceptions." (101) In an interview in the Chronicle with H.W. Thornton, the general manager of the G.E.R. in 1915 stated "There are more trains in and out of Liverpool Street station than any other station in the world." Between 6 a.m. and 9. 30 a.m. there were 278 trains arriving and 75,000 passengers alighting. On a typical day 700 trains arrived over 24 hours. He described one particular ambulance train which was constructed for use at the battle front. Almost thirteen thousand people went to see it when it had been built. (102)

Both councils in the area urged the government to compensate victims of air raids for damage to their property. In the event this proved barely necessary. Some threat came from the Zeppelins and later from German biplanes. The Germans made extensive use of Zeppelins for bombing and scouting after the outbreak of the war. People in the Chelmsford area got regular first hand sightings of the cumbersome giant airships because it was directly on their route to London. In the end these bombing raids only had a psychological value and were not a military success. After blackouts were imposed most bombs were dropped at random in East Anglia, including the Chelmsford area, and nearly all missed any target. One of the first of the super airships, the L33, reached Chelmsford by following the G.E.R. railway line on the way back from London. After coming under fire at Kelvedon Hatch it came down at Little Wigborough. The crew apparently warned villagers that the Zeppelin was about to be fired. A special constable came across the crew walking along the road. They identified themselves and were arrested. "The back of the airship had been broken in the fall and the covering of the immense gas bag had been burnt off but otherwise she was little damaged." A large crowd gathered but the military were able to protect the remains which were studied by experts and later some of the details were incorporated into

British airship design. (103) The L33 was one of 14 or 15 airships which wandered over Eastern England on the night of 23-24 September 1916.

Miller Christy lived in the Chignalls and was in the perfect position to see all the activity, as he lived not far from a landing strip from which planes took off to deal with the 'foe'. A Zeppelin had tried to bomb this but had missed by more than half a mile. On the night of the 23rd of September he saw the L32 pass over his house on its way back from London: it was 'wheezy' and 'slow of gait'. He then heard another, the previously mentioned L33, which was even more grievously injured than the first. Two anti aircraft guns were firing at it, then a plane attacked the wounded Zeppelin. "Scarcely had I caught sight of these tiny tinkling flashes, before both sky and earth were suddenly lit up by an unearthly lurid red glare. In a second or two I saw that the glow came from behind the large cloud, a little below the spot I had been watching and was due to a Zeppelin slowly falling. At once there broke out a mighty cheer. Every cottage, every man and women within miles, seemed to be cheering." (104) "Its flames lit up the whole neighbourhood. The airship fell very deliberately in stages. At certain points the airship remained almost stationary blazing furiously. Material would drop out of the middle." He guessed that the L33 had gone to ground just beyond Stock, 8 miles away, at 1 20 a.m. Looking out East he saw another red glare from a Zeppelin blazing on the ground. Police found articles in the fields at the back of his house. "To lighten the vessel the crew had to throw belts of cartridges, a large aluminium petrol tank, a tool box and the like." Christy went to Billericay to inspect the wreck of the L32. There had been no survivors and the 22 German bodies had been put in a barn. All the crew had been clad in very thick clothing. He couldn't get close because of the military cordon and all the people there. Such was the hysteria that when the wreckage of one Zeppelin was being carried down Chelmsford High Street it was stopped by a crowd who took parts as souvenirs. The same lorry was looted again when it stopped for petrol and had to be defended by soldiers. (105) During the month before, the L10 airship had managed to drop two bombs on Chelmsford but there was no damage. (106) An attempt may have been made to destroy the masts at Marconi's factory without success.

Christy was also well placed to report on the dawn of aircraft raids on London. Most of the Zeppelins, although they were capable of causing significant damage, were destroyed. He then observed a string of audacious raids by aircraft. "No longer one or two machines which just dropped a bomb or two", the raids "were now made in squadrons of ten, fifteen, twenty or even more." (107) In the early part of the war planes had been used mainly for reconnaissance, but with technical improvements they were able to hold bigger bomb loads. Eventually the problem of synchronisation was overcome which ensured that machine gun bullets wouldn't hit the planes' propellers. The Gotha aircraft were the first bombers to be used from 1917 onwards. On the July the 7th Christy noted that 22 Gothas passed near his house. They were met by British planes, but the Germans went through because they were faster and more manoeuvrable. Percy Rainbird, a local man, remembered 40 German planes flying very low across Chelmsford on their way to London. (108)

On the November the 11th 1918, news of the armistice and the end of the war spread like wildfire in the town. "The hooters of all the works were sounded and thousands of employees rushed into the streets shouting and cheering." Nearly all the shops closed immediately. Flags were displayed everywhere from the houses. "The streets were thronged with children for the rest of the day." The Mayor announced a general holiday. At the Regent Theatre, before the commencement of the variety show, the orchestra played 'Rule Britannia' which was taken over by the audience and this was followed by the singing of the national anthem. As soon as the news became known bell ringers rushed to the Cathedral to ring the bells. In the evening there were crowded services at the Cathedral and the London Road Congregational church. (109) No doubt the fact that the final outcome of the war was uncertain until well into the middle of 1918 added to the general feeling of jubilation. In Clarks' Great Leighs news of the armistice reached the Post Office, passed on from Chelmsford, the same day. (110) A return to normality was by no means immediate. The severe outbreak of influenza, which affected the entire country, closed the town's schools for a month. Chelmsford's Food Control Committee had to remain in operation because rationing and control of prices were still needed. The bishop and local dignitaries were alarmed at the apparent outbreak of lawlessness and disregard for authority at the war's close.

Early plans to include a war memorial in the town's new municipal buildings caused an outcry from those who wanted something separate. It was also criticised by others as being too expensive and less necessary than working class housing. (111) When the town's memorial was finally unveiled five years to the day after the end of the war in front of Fairfield House, nearly all the surrounding villages had already erected their own memorials. This didn't stop the ceremony being suitably grand with the whole council present and the Archbishop of Canterbury attending the memorial service at the Cathedral. (112) Most of the memorials in the rural areas were simple affairs, such as Writtle's white cross. (113)

Inspecting of troops at unveiling of war memorial during 1923
(Courtesy of E.R.O.)

The town's big factories gradually returned to business as usual, letting their women workers go, in favour of previous employees, who had been promised their jobs back at the end of the war. The people were reminded daily of the awful conflict by the wounded who sat on seats that had been especially erected for them around the town. (114) Chelmsford's branch of the Old Contemptibles Association was formed in 1928 and at one time had 300 members. Stan Brown was the last to pass away in 1987. (115)

1) Essex Chronicle 8 11 2002
2) Essex Weekly News 12 1 1900 p.2
3) E.W.N. 22 12 1899
4) E.W.N. 5 1 1900

5) E.W.N. 9 3 1900 p.4
6) E.W.N. 19 1 1900 p.4
7) E.W.N. 4 5 1900 p.2
8) E.W.N. 24 8 1900 p.5
9) E.W.N. 11 1 1901
10) E.W.N. 2 11 1900 p.4
11) E.W.N. 6 4 1900 p.2
12) E.W.N. 1 2 1901 p.5
13) E.W.N. 17 1 1902
14) E.W.N. 4 2 1902 p.5
15) E.W.N. 8 1 1904 p.5
16) History of the Essex Regiment 1741 – 1958 http://www.1914-1918.net/essex.htm
17) E.C. 7 8 1914 p.8
18) E.C. 21 8 1914 p.3
19) E.C. 11 9 1914
20) Echoes of the Great War The Diary of the Reverend Andrew Clark 1914 – 1919 (Ed. James Munson)
21) Clark p.13
22) Clark p. 17
23) E.C. 7 8 1914 p.8
24) E.C. 5 3 1915 p.5
25) E.C. 14 5 1915
26) E.W.N. 9 10 1914
27) E.C. 11 6 1915
28) E.W.N. 27 10 1915 p.3
29) E.W.N. 23 1 1916 p.5
30) E.W.N. 10 3 1916 p.4
31) E.W.N. 24 3 1916
32) E.W.N. 14 4 1916 p.5
33) E.W.N. 9 6 1916
34) E.W.N. 26 1 1917 p.3
35) E.W.N. 6 7 1917 p.6
36) E.W.N. 16 11 1917 p.6
37) Essex In World War One Foley

38) E.C. 16 10 1914 p.5
39) E.W.N. 21 8 1914 p.5
40) E.C. 25 9 1914
41) Chelmsford Borough Council minutes 30 12 1914
42) E.W.N. 8 1 1915 p.3
43) Clark 3 8 1916 p.145
44) C.B.C. minutes 27 1 1915
45) 'The Impact of Catastrophe: The People of Essex and the First World War (1914 – 1920) Paul Rusecki p.112
46) Rusecki p.113
47) Chelmsford Rural District Council minutes 7 12 1915 p.35
48) Stock Charles Phillips p.43
49) C.B.C. minutes 12 12 1917
50) E.W.N. 15 12 1916 p.3
51) Rusecki p.124
52) The Chelmsford Museums records
53) E.W.N. 21 8 1914 p.5
54) E.W.N. 23 12 1914 p.5
55) E.W.N. 8 1 1915 p.5
56) E.C. 7 1 1916
57) C. Museums records
58) 'Local heroes' The villagers of Writtle who gave their lives in the great war John W Trusler
59) E.C. 19 11 1915 p.8
60) E.C. 8 9 1916 p.1
61) E.W.N. 22 2 12 1916
62) E.C. 2 11 1917
63) E.C. 4 1 1918
64) E.W.N. 15 2 1918 p.3
65) E.W.N. 12 4 1918
66) E.W.N. 10 5 1918 p.5
67) E.W.N. 25 9 1914 p.5
68) E.C. 9 10 1914
69) C. Museums records
70) E.C. 21 8 1914 p.8

71) E.C. 7 5 1915
72) E.W.N. 27 11 1914 p.5
73) E.W.N. 10 9 1915 p.5
74) E.W.N. 29 3 1917 p.5
75) E.W.N. 14 6 1918 p.3
76) C.B.C. minutes 25 7 1917
77) E.C. 23 10 1914
78) E.C. 14 8 1914 p.3
79) E.C. 12 2 1915 p.6
80) C.B.C. minutes 29 11 1916
81) C.B.C. minutes 31 11 1916
82) E.W.N. 23 8 1918 p.3
83) E.W.N. 28 6 1918 p.3
84) Clark 21 9 1915 p.83
85) C.B.C. minutes 28 3 1917
86) E.C. 25 1 1918 p.5
87) C.B.C. – Report of the Food Control Committee 26 6 1918
88) E.C. 17 5 1918 p.3
89) C.B.C. minutes 27 2 1918
90) C.B.C. minutes 26 6 1918
91) C.B.C. minutes 26 6 1918
92) E.C. 30 6 1916 p.3
93) Clark 30 10 1914 p.27
94) Clark 31 8 1914
95) Clark 27 4 1916 p.121
96) Clark 31 8 1914 p.11
97) Ruzecki p.144
98) Ruzecki p.145
99) Ruzecki p.160
100) E.C. 14 8 1914 p.8
101) E.C. 9 10 1914 p.4
102) E.C. 13 8 1915 p.5
103) History House Essex www.historyhouse.co.uk
104) C. and E. Museum records
105) Foley

106) Rusecki p.147
107) C. Museums – oral history records
108) Essex Record Office Oral tapes Percy Rainbird
109) E.W.N. 15 11 1918 p.6
110) Clark p.258
111) Rusecki p.314
112) Rusecki p.316
113) Trusler p.231
114) C.B.C. minutes 16 6 1918
115) www.worldwar1veterans.blogspot/2009/06/chelmsfords-old-contemptibles.html

16

Health

"The dead hand of the State will be between the doctor and the patient"

The next three chapters, dealing with the health, sanitation and housing of the area, may seem arcane at times but are essential to the story of the evolution of the modern city. In the late Victorian period people in the country as a whole were at the mercy of epidemics. Increasing effort was made to prevent outbreaks as their causes became increasingly clear and to isolate them if they occurred. Chelmsford adhered resolutely to voluntary hospitals before the advent of the N.H.S., although raising funds, despite a new system of contributions, became increasingly difficult. The period since the second war has seen incredible advances in modern medicine but the last third of the twentieth century was characterised by a very tortuous path for the hospitals of Mid Essex.

In Chelmsford the work of the local Board of Health had done much to lay the foundation of the town's public health system, but the unexpected growth of the town's population due to its industrialisation, was to put that in jeopardy. The town's growth also began to put pressure on the town's woefully inadequate infirmary, even though the current one in Moulsham Street, next to a public house, had only been used since 1871. In 1880 the chairman of the Infirmary and Dispensary committee said "the present Infirmary and Dispensary is totally inadequate to the wants and needs of the local neighbourhood." In 1869 only 390 people had been seen at the dispensary but by 1879 this had risen to 3,164. Every day 100 patients were waiting in the cramped quarters. The Medical Officer, E.H. Carter, emphasised the grave nature of the cases received at the Infirmary stating that if a death occurred there was nowhere to place the body. He suggested that a committee be set up to buy a new site. As in nearly all towns of Chelmsford's size the new infirmary depended on voluntary contributions. (1) Immediately, a donation of £500 was received from St Mary's Church; a Subscription Ball was held at the Shire Hall and a concert given for the building fund. A sum of £2,500 needed to be raised but the existing infirmary's endowment fund could not be touched for the new building. (2) Concerts continued throughout the year. Early possible building sites included Mildmay Road, the Barrack ground, and land opposite the Museum in Bridge Street. Workmen of the Anchor Works gave a donation as did the Star Co-operative. The site chosen was a piece of land next to the Ebenezer Chapel in New London Road, which was opposite the Coleman and Morton factory. (3) Pertwee and Chancellor designed the building. A bid of £3,485 from the local firm of Choat and Saltmarsh was accepted. (4) Prominent in the fundraising had been H.T. Veley, a partner in the towns' leading solicitors, Gepp and Sons. The new buildings were formally opened in November 1883 by Lady Brooke and were viewed as a great achievement by the townsfolk. Inside, the dispensary on the ground floor was separated from the infirmary by a door and there were two large waiting rooms, one for women and one for men. There was a mortuary at the back. The fund raising committee had appealed to the towns' civic pride for enough money but local doctors had also provided funds, as well as their often free services. (5) In the event costs were higher than anticipated and a debt of £252 had to be paid off by the local brewing magnate Henry Collings Wells. (6) By 1887 1,300 patients were using the dispensary each year and 112 the infirmary. The endowment fund had now reached a more satisfactory five thousand pounds. (7) Funds were still needed however, as the collecting box for the infirmary in the wall outside the railway station illustrated.

Although Chelmsford was regarded as healthy area, concern was regularly voiced about damp conditions in the town. In 1892 a discussion took place in that august journal 'The Lancet', as to whether Chelmsford was waterlogged. (8) One of the diseases most widely associated with damp conditions was diphtheria, although impure milk was also identified as a likely cause. Numerous school log books attest to the prevalence of the disease and the severity of the attacks. In 1900, for example, there was a severe outbreak in the Chignals, made worse by many parents refusing to hospitalise their children. Lessons were learnt in those villages and during further outbreaks in 1907 and 1914 the disease failed to take hold. (9) The old grammar school buildings in Duke Street were damp and insanitary. K.E.G.S. headmaster was criticised by the editor of the Weekly News in 1888 when he failed to give details of the preventive steps he was taking after several deaths from the disease. (10) In the same year an outbreak was traced to impure milk. (11) An 8 year old boy from Mildmay Road died from the disease in 1900. (12) In 1895 Dr John Thresh, the medical officer for the rural district and by this time also the medical officer for the county, first used an anti toxin against the disease, but it was to be several decades before this became really effective. (13) As late as the 1920s it was still a major disease, with 11 cases in the infectious diseases hospital in 1922. (14) Four years later there were 10 cases in Woodham Ferris. (15)

Dr. Thresh was an extremely important figure in the development of the county and the Chelmsford rural area in particular. Thresh was born in Wakefield in 1859 and apprenticed to a chemist, but his handwriting was too poor to be a clerk. He studied science at the Owen College in Manchester and graduated from London University in 1882. His first experience of public health administration had been when he was consulted about water and sewage disposal problems at Buxton, while he was a pharmaceutical chemist there. After he came to Chelmsford as the Rural District Health Officer in 1892 his good work came to the attention of the E.C.C. and he was appointed as the first Essex County Medical Officer of Health. There was some opposition to his appointment on the grounds it would lead to unjustified expense. Thresh had proved his worth many times over when he finally retired from the county position in 1919. He was an impressive teacher in laboratories and nine of his thirteen assistants became Medical Officers of Health in other towns. The house he lived in on New London Road was later used by the Farleigh Hospice. Thresh died in 1932 and was buried in the Widford church yard. (16)

An infectious disease which still caused panic out of all proportion, to its incidence in the town and elsewhere, was smallpox. An outbreak in 1885 led E.H. Carter, the town's medical officer, to call for re-vaccination and a tent to be erected outside the town. (17) The Weekly News reported "The disease was introduced into the place by a travelling tailor and the three cases which we reported were all traced directly to him." Smallpox was the one vaccination that was effective but this was an emotive issue. The anti-compulsory vaccination league met regularly in the town in the 1880s and the Reverend John Morgan Whiteman, the Primitive Methodist minister at Hall Street Moulsham, was president of the local league. (18) It felt that vaccination could often do more harm than good. Dr Thresh stated that an unvaccinated child under 10 was 440 times more likely to die of smallpox than a vaccinated child but the opposition to vaccination did not cease. (19) In 1893 two vicars were fined for refusing to have their children vaccinated and it was not uncommon for people to be imprisoned and have their property seized. (20) A poll on vaccination however, revealed little overall enthusiasm for the anti vaccination cause, as did the votes of anti vaccination candidates at council elections. (21) The town was congratulated by a government inspector in 1885 on an exceptionally well attended vaccination. (22)

Other diseases which are easily controllable today, such as measles and scarlet fever, caused widespread problems in the late Victorian and the Edwardian periods. In 1883 a measles epidemic claimed five deaths and various schools in the area were closed for weeks. (23) Serious outbreaks were still causing school closures well into the twentieth century, despite doubts that such closures didn't prevent the spread of the disease. Scarlet fever was known to spread particularly quickly but schools were not always closed. (24) In 1893 a serious outbreak occurred at New Hall School in Boreham; three pupils died and the school was closed for three months, before a new drainage scheme meant that the next outbreak at the school was much milder. (25) After 1902, outbreaks in the councils' schools were usually followed by rooms being disinfected. (26) As late as 1928 scarlet fever was still the most prominent type of case in the joint isolation hospital. (27) This was despite medical officers becoming more adept at pinpointing the causes of outbreaks. An outbreak in 1913 for example was traced to contaminated water in the well at Admirals Park. (28)

Another disease to cause periodic panic in the area was typhoid. After an outbreak in 1897, an inspector of the Local Government Board emphasised the defects of the local water supply. (29) The towns' surveyor instructed the borough's drains to be flushed after the outbreak. Chelmsford's Borough Council maintained there was nothing wrong with the towns' water supply or its milk supply. (30) The R.D.C., urged on by Dr Thresh, was more vigilant in regularly checking the water supplies for the bacteria. In his report on the housing of the working classes in the Chelmsford and Maldon area, Thresh cited a group of four houses with "an abominable nuisance" as the cause of seven typhoid cases. (31) In a case in 1907 the cause was traced to a defective drain. (32)

Cancer cases became increasingly common in the early twentieth century, possibly due to improved diagnosis, although there was almost completed ignorance as to its causes. In 1907 there was a serious discussion in the Weekly News as to whether cancer patients should be isolated, treating as an infectious disease! (33) On one occasion Dr Newton, the M.O.H., even gave a gift of tobacco to the inmates of the workhouse.

In both the town and the surrounding rural area there was a pressing need to isolate cases of these infectious diseases. The desire to have a permanent isolation hospital led to a disagreement that was to provide a foretaste of the battle over the borough boundary extension that was to follow (See chapter 13). After the borough had used tents to isolate various outbreaks of smallpox and scarlet fever etc, houses were used in Coval Lane and then in Beehive Lane as isolation hospitals. In 1897 Dr Newton, recently appointed as the borough's M.O.H., complained about the damp conditions at the hospital. (34) The rural district sanitary authority had bought a site in Baddow in 1893 and built an isolation hospital on it which was set well back from the road. (35) Chelmsford Borough Council bought a site in Baddow Road in 1899 for a possible isolation hospital. (36) The L.G.B. was in favour of one joint isolation hospital for the two authorities but from the outset the newly formed R.D.C. was not. (37) Chelmsford borough council was willing to accede to the Board's request, probably because it would involve less expense. A year later the R.D.C. was still set against the proposal and the Board sanctioned a loan for the borough's new isolation hospital. (38) Plans were submitted with four wards of four beds each. The Board reasserted the need for a joint hospital the following year however. (39) Chelmsford borough was now using a temporary hospital in Coval Lane but a smallpox hospital in Galleywood was closed. In 1902 the L.G.B. finally sent out an order for a joint hospital to be built. (40) A joint hospital board was set up and a new site found in Great Baddow. (41) Eventually however, to save expense, the two councils agreed on extending the rural district's existing hospital at a cost of £2,500. (42) Interestingly Dr Thresh was not in favour of this expense arguing that a smaller hospital would suffice. By 1914, however, he was urging the board to enlarge the hospital. (43) The hospital was regularly used for isolating infectious cases up to the second war and remained in use until 1969. (44)

    At the end of the nineteenth and the beginning of the twentieth century, the Chelmsford and West Essex Infirmary, as it was then called, flourished in terms of donations including one of £1,000. (45) Money was also received from subscriptions. The subscribers received tickets and, later in the early twentieth century, letters to be used by patients. A collection box was erected on the platform at Chelmsford railway station in 1909.This expanding income and the growing needs of Chelmsford's expanding population led the infirmary to be expanded with four extra wards, two nurses' rooms, a bathroom and a lavatory built over the ground floor dispensary, connected by a corridor to the central building. When the new buildings were opened by Lady Rayleigh in 1909, the women's ward had been made into a children's ward and a new outpatients department established with consulting and waiting rooms. Walls were hard plastered and enamel painted so that they could be washed with ease. (46)

A deficiency of £2,000 was made up by Mr C.E. Ridley, the brewer. Right up to the formation of the N.H.S., the Chelmsford and Essex was to suffer periodically from a lack of funds. The lack of a sufficient number of local large landowners willing to make big donations became an increasing hindrance after the first war. Despite this, there was never any concerted demand for the type of municipal hospital common in larger towns and cities. The new firms, like Hoffmann, were making smallish donations but organising their own scheme in order that their workers were covered if they went into the infirmary. (47)

The hospital was managed by a General Committee and a House Committee, as well as various sub-committees. It was the House Committee who did most of the work, scrutinizing the tenders for groceries, hiring and firing and dealing with the not so infrequent complaints about treatment. In 1915 a group of nurses raised the behaviour of the Matron and a Ward Sister late at night. They had 'entertained' a few military medical officers, who had disturbed the whole hospital. The eight nurses then resigned when they thought the matter was not being taken seriously. Evidently the House Committee brought pressure to bear and the Matron and Ward Sister resigned allowing the nurses to withdraw their resignations. Interestingly the matter was not discussed at the General Committee and therefore did not reach the local papers. During the Edwardian period the House Committee found it more financially prudent to obtain its groceries from a number of different specialist suppliers of meat, vegetables etc., than one general grocer. The Committee also set different levels of fees for private patients. It also oversaw the contracts and work of the three medical officers working at the hospital in the early 1900s. The House committee spent a good deal of time discussing the acquisition of new apparatus; firstly anaesthetic equipment and in 1906 there was the first consideration of 'Rontgen Ray' treatment. X-rays had only been discovered in 1895. By the outbreak of the first war X-ray equipment was being intensively used at the hospital. In 1907 the hospital received 376 patients, with a daily average of 27.80 and 201 operations were carried out. (48) An article in the Hospital magazine in 1915 gave the hospital an almost completely clean 'bill of health', although it did conclude that the local community needed to increase its contribution to the hospital by £500 per annum and the administration of the institution could be improved. The name of the infirmary was officially changed to the Chelmsford and Essex Hospital in 1908. (49)

A major health issue in late Victorian Chelmsford was cemetery provision. As early as 1881 the Sanitary Committee of the old Board of Health was considering a new cemetery because the old cemetery at St John's was seriously overcrowded and needed closing. (50) Initially the Board of Health were reluctant to provide a new cemetery for Moulsham. (51) The following year it agreed to allow the Sanitary Committee see what sites might be available. (52) Further delays led the L.G.B. to hold an inquiry at the Corn Exchange to see whether it should instruct the Board of Health to provide a new cemetery for the Moulsham district. (53) After trial bores at Wood Street found the ground too hard, a 14 acre site was found in Writtle Road, for which compulsory purchase orders had to be used. Chancellor, in typically forthright fashion, stated that "The desire of the Board is to complete the cemetery with as little expense to the ratepayer as possible." (54) This financial penny pinching was unfortunately necessary because of the imminent considerable expense of improving the town's water supply. The first body was interred in the cemetery in 1887. (55)

Doctor Thresh and his borough counterpart frequently commented on the comparative health of people in the area. In 1880 for example the death rate in the Chelmsford area was under 17 per 1,000, which was over seven points below the national average. (56) Even though the rate varied considerably from year to year, depending on the effect of epidemics, the area's death rate was normally at least four points below the national average. Epidemics such as diphtheria always caused a spike in the death rate; the one in 1900 caused the highest death rates in the area for ten years. (57) When epidemics were absent, the effect on the death rate could be dramatic. In 1909 the borough death rate was below 5 per 1,000. (58)

Despite the apparent healthiness of the local populace Dr Thresh spent much of his time, in both his jobs, exposing overcrowding in working-class housing and the effect of insanitary conditions, working closely with the sanitary and nuisance inspectors. The identification of the cause of typhoid led to a big increase in the installation of flushing toilets. (See chapter 17) Insanitary living conditions were increasingly realised to be a cause of the severe outbreaks of diarrhoea which were a frequent killer in the summer months. (59) Despite living to a longer age, many people were condemned to decades of suffering from acute arthritis and bronchial complaints.

Damp living conditions were also associated with another major killer, consumption or tuberculosis (TB.). Here again Dr Thresh was in the vanguard of change, pushing for the introduction of sanatoria. In 1910 the Alfred Boyd sanatorium was opened in Little Baddow. (60) During 1912 it was decided that a new County sanatorium should be situated in the Chelmsford area. (61) A sanatorium was established at Sandon in 1912 and in the same year a conference on the treatment of the disease was held at Chelmsford. (62)

The impact of the war on the town's health and hospitals has been dealt with in the previous chapter, but during it Dr Thresh led the fight against the spread of venereal disease producing a county scheme for its treatment in 1917. (63) At the end of the war there was a conference on the disease held in the County town. (64)

After 1918 doctors and hospitals increasingly had the means not only to prevent the spread of infectious diseases but also cure and treat invasive illnesses. Equipment like x ray units for example was expensive however, and made big demands on voluntary hospitals such as the Chelmsford and Essex. Another problem after the war was that it was obvious that the number of beds at the hospital needed doubling because of the growth of population in the area. The hospital was forced to increase its charges and all the town's big employers now subscribed. After the war the recession led the hospital to reduce or abandon altogether the charges on a significant number of 'hardship cases'. A start was made on the extension in 1921, although only £18,000 of the £20,000 had been raised. (65) In 1924 two new wards were opened at the hospital. (66) A nurses' home was added and a kitchen block built. Marconi made a gift of a wireless to the hospital as early as 1925. That year also saw the start of the town's carnival to raise funds for the hospital. (67) In 1927 for example £1,000 was donated to the Hospital by the Carnival Committee (See chapter 27) Continued growth in the number of patients and the necessary further expansion of the hospital made the start of a contributory scheme inevitable. (68) The new scheme cost married men 3d a week and benefitted themselves, their wives and their children up to the age of 16. (69) Chelmsford's large works did not join, preferring to have their own hospital funds as in the past and pay the ordinary weekly sum for their members who required hospital treatment. The hospital scheme achieved members in 90 Essex towns and villages and by 1939 total membership was over 15,000. Administrative costs were also cut. The new scheme was a success and the hospital did better in the 1930s than that in Colchester, although debts were beginning to accumulate by the outbreak of the second war. (70) A new block was opened in 1931 at a cost of £30,000, which included a new children's ward. (71) The newly expanded hospital could now accommodate 114 patients in 4 men's wards, 3 women's, a children's ward and a private ward. There were now two operating theatres, a large outpatients department and an x ray unit. (72) The hospital was still very dependent on voluntary contributions and in a typical year needed to get £10,000 of the £20,000 running costs from such contributions. In April 1932 schoolchildren collected over three thousand eggs as a contribution to the patients' food at the hospital as a contribution to the food of patients. (73) The expansion of the hospital necessitated an extension of the nursing home, which was opened in July 1932. (74) By 1935 the hospital was again full and being stretched beyond its capacity. It was then offered the lifeline of a gift of Mrs J.H. Keane of Carlton House, Galleywood for the specific purpose of building an extension. (75) This enabled the building of the John Henry Keane block with three new wards. Extra voluntary contributions were still needed, however for a further extension to the nursing block. 'Bellefields', formerly Chancellor's home, was taken over to be used for the convalescence of patients. Hospital debts grew despite the Keane gift. The chairman of the hospital's committee in 1938 said "the town's lack of support was one of the hospital's greatest weaknesses." He described the £500 received that year from the carnival as "pitiful". (76) The amount of new equipment which needed to be bought was one of the reasons for the greatly increased cost of running the hospital. In 1934 the hospital received a valve diathermy apparatus at a reduced price, which

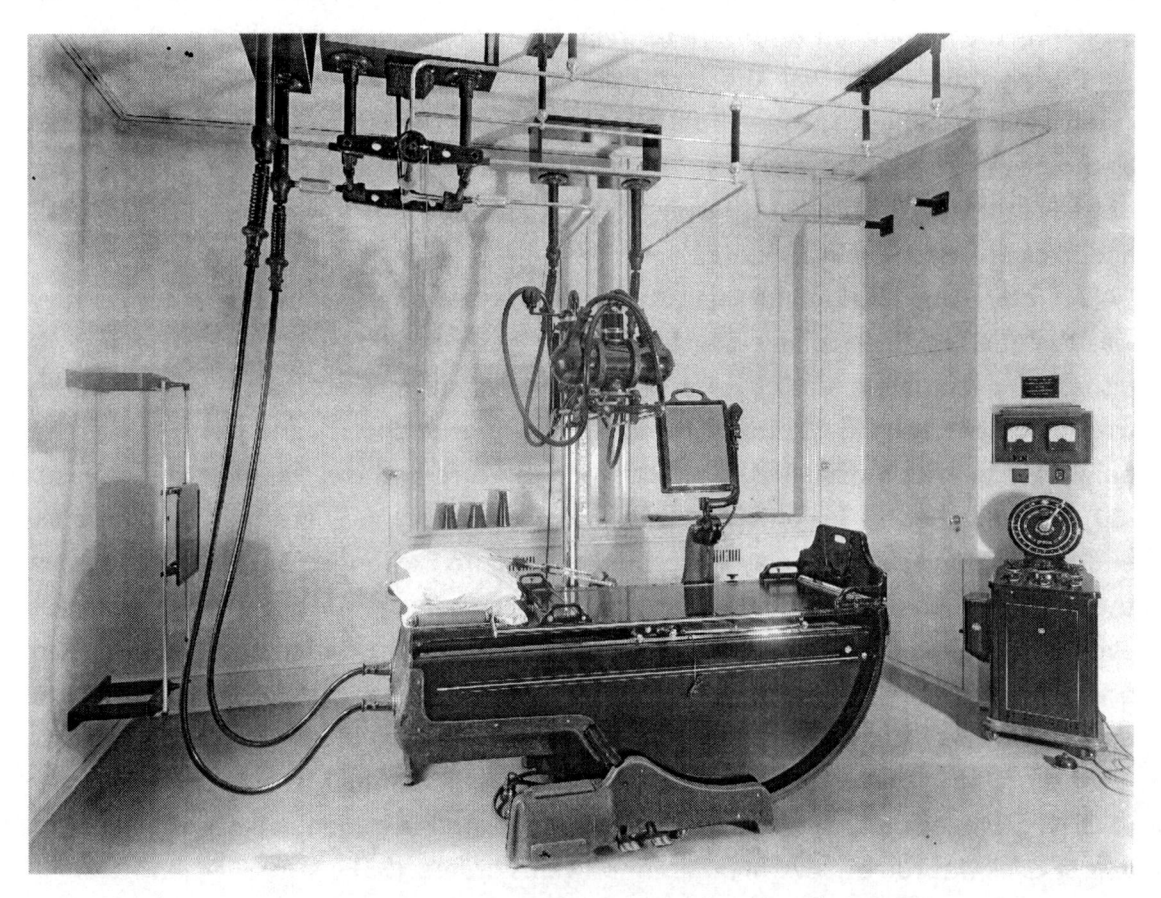

X ray equipment at Chelmsford and Essex Hospital 1939
(Courtesy of E.R.O.)

was instrumental in one of the major advances in bloodless surgery. It was produced by A.E. Dean and Marconi Wireless and Telegraph Co. Ltd! (77) National insurance was perceived as another threat to the voluntary hospital, although national financial stringencies meant that the scheme was not extended in the 1930s. Before the second war the County Council were looking at establishing the Chelmsford and Essex as a base hospital for the county, which would have provided it with a financial lifeline.

In 1926 a new infirmary was built at the workhouse and this was to become St John's hospital. It had four wards with 24 beds each. (78) It had a maternity ward on the second floor with 9 beds and one labour ward bed. There was also a children's ward with 6 cots. The new building reflected the fact that the workhouse was by this time dominated by the aged and infirm, but from the outset it could be used by ordinary patients in the town. By 1936 300 operations a year were being carried out. Staff and equipment were transferred from the Chelmsford and Essex to carry out tonsil operations etc. Plans to extend St John's by adding a further 100 beds, an operating theatre and an extension to the nursing home were curtailed by the war.

During the second war the institution's residents were evacuated so it could receive war casualties. Thirteen huts were built under the emergency medical services to provide extra wards; these later became part of the general hospital. The number of beds at the hospital went up from 109 in 1934, to a wartime peak of 705 in 1942 and back down to 354 in 1950. (79)

An interesting local health institution which lasted most of the twentieth century was the St Giles leper colony, which was later given the title of a hospital. Hansen's disease had long been eradicated in Britain, but British sufferers caught it while in the tropics. When set up in 1914 at Bicknacre by a group of doctors and clergy, it was the only place in Britain designed specifically for the care and treatment of the disease. (80) All funds had to be provided privately. Various events were held to create an endowment fund such as a play performed at the Corn Exchange. (81) In the early years the institution was subjected to a serious N.I.M.B.Y. campaign. Local traders wouldn't even deliver groceries and essential supplies and the first patients had to arrive in blacked out cabs. (82) Relations with the people of Bicknacre gradually improved, with bread and meat being delivered to the door rather than thrown over the fence. Patients went shooting in the woods for rabbit and pigeon. In 1923 the Marconi Company gave St Giles a wireless, which was particularly useful for blind patients. Before the second war St Giles was run by several different religious orders. (83)

From the early twentieth century onwards the Medical Officers of Health were helped by the School Medical Officers of Health (see chapter 16). As early as 1908 the S.M.O. for the rural district was pressing for the appointment of a school nurse and an inspection room in each school. In his 1910 report 32% of the girls inspected were found to have head lice. Initial pressure for a school nurse and a health visitor was ignored by the borough council but eventually a joint one was appointed in 1917. (84) After the first war the M.O.H. pressed for a full time health visitor to spread good domestic health practice and the establishment of a Maternity and Child Welfare Centre in the town. (85) A health visitor was appointed in 1920 and the Friends Meeting House began to be used as an infant centre; a second centre was soon opened in Orchard Street, Moulsham, taking advantage of recent national legislation. (86) By 1928 a third clinic had been opened, this time at the Chelmsford and Essex hospital. (87) Similarly in the rural district, three infant welfare clinics were quickly opened at Great Waltham, East Hanningfield and Danbury. (88) There was evidently some resistance to using them and attendance was low. (89) Initially an ante natal clinic in the borough was not considered cost effective. However by 1925 the M.O.H. was carrying out ante natal work at the hospital. Also by the same year there were 3 midwives, one in each political ward. (90) The disappearance of the so called 'handy women', who had been totally unqualified and delivered babies, was a major factor in reducing the infant mortality rate in the town.

The depression immediately after the first war (see chapter 9) led to much discussion in the town as to whether malnutrition was increasing, especially amongst schoolchildren. (91) In 1921 the S.M.O. said there was no evidence of this and refused to support the distribution of free school milk. (92) A year later however, cocoa was being given to 50 school children. (93) The fact that Chelmsford wasn't acutely depressed by the standards of the 1930s meant that the borough council was able to hold back from distributing free school milk until the second war.

During the war the Chelmsford and Essex dealt with 15,903 service cases and 595 air raid casualties. Blood was taken from 9,092 individuals. The new buildings at the Chelmsford and Essex were opened in 1943. (94) Its General Committee hoped forlornly that the hospital might be able to continue with voluntary donations after 1948, with the commencement of the State run National Health Service. In 1946 there was a meeting held at the Shire Hall to explain Nye Bevan's new scheme. The hospital's endowment of £125,000 was to be passed to a new board. Immediately a £35,000 individual donation was withdrawn. The Essex Chronicle commented "The dead hand of the State will be between the doctor and the patient." Millington the

Chelmsford M.P. said however, "Do not be fooled by the sectional interests in the papers." (95)The immediate pre N.H.S. years were a time of acute shortages of nurses in the Chelmsford hospitals. Waiting lists at the Chelmsford and Essex rose sharply, particularly for surgery. In 1947 St John's had 60 nurses when it needed 140 and it was feared the hospital might have to close. (96) Three hundred beds had to be kept empty. An appeal was put out for untrained nurses. Long hours and little pay were cited as reasons for the shortage. (97) Problems at the Chelmsford and Essex were exacerbated by severe flooding in 1947.

The voluntary Chelmsford and Essex Hospital closed after, ironically, the hospital's highest ever donations. (98) A Chelmsford hospital group was to be formed under the northeast metropolitan group. (99) As elsewhere, the government's austerity drive meant that the local N.H.S. faced immediate cutbacks. These were made worse by the dwindling voluntary contributions. No new equipment such as x ray machines could be bought. (100)

As the N.H.S. service began the already hard pressed Essex health services were hit by a serious outbreak of polio. In October 1947 there were 33 cases in the county but only 2 in Chelmsford. (101) During a later outbreak in 1953 however, there were 7 cases in the county town. In an effort to curb its spread, the M.O.H. led a campaign to increase ventilation in schools and swimming galas were abandoned. (102) The outbreak of 1955 was less virulent but still resulted in the death of one mother. (103) During the following year the new anti polio drug reached Essex and was immediately used on 7,500 children in the county. (104) In 1957 however, an outbreak caused cuts to the carnival programme in Chelmsford. (105) By 1961 vaccination was considered essential and jabs were stepped up to avoid people being crippled for life. (106) Polio was the last infectious disease to cause major problems.

Broomfield Hospital had its origins before the second war. Ironically, given its recent 21st century transformation into an ultra modern general hospital, it was originally chosen as a TB sanatorium for the out of the way location. Essex County Council bought a seventy acre site from the owners of Broomfield Court. The first patients didn't arrive until 1940 and it continued to specialise in chest illness until the mid 1950s.Treatment normally lasted from one to three years but in some cases five years. The vogue for fresh air was often taken to extreme lengths. There was no glass on the veranda making the wards open to all weathers. A nurse recalled "I have seen snow on the patient's beds." (107) With the decline in the number of TB sufferers it became a general hospital dealing with acute illnesses.

As early as 1959 the Chelmsford group of hospitals were being regarded as out of date. St John's Hospital had been expanded by means of a succession of ad hoc huts and the ante natal clinic and operating theatre were not up to modern standards. A nurse there in the 1950s remembered the operating theatre being a shock to her because she had been used to working in a modern hospital. She also recalled one of the Grace Bartlett nurseries being converted into an operating theatre for caesarean sections. There had however, been a good deal of piecemeal improvement since the war. These included a new obstetrics theatre, an X ray unit and waiting room, a new teaching unit, a staff canteen, a new dispensary and an occupational therapy department. In 1959 the hospital had 77 maternity beds and a premature baby unit of 10 beds. It had 12 resident house officers and registrars but over 18 visiting specialists. (108) At the Chelmsford and Essex the two operating theatres were regarded as unsatisfactory. The x ray department was in inadequate accommodation, the outpatients centre was cramped and the casualty block also lacked space. At Broomfield there was a shortage of accommodation for nursing and other staff. (109)

The first mention of centralising health provision for mid Essex came as early as 1961. Already the Chelmsford Group Hospital Managing Committee was recommending the closure of the Chelmsford and Essex, St John's and Baddow Road hospitals. Staff at the hospitals objected immediately. The Chronicle thought that the idea of replacing four inadequate and scattered hospitals by providing a single centre offering a single service was a good one, but doubted whether Broomfield was the right location. (110)) In 1962 Broomfield was selected as one of five sites for new hospitals in Essex. (111) A potential one thousand acre site was found but, as was to happen many times in the future, financial constraints caused a delay. During 1964 the hospital board was informed that Broomfield was unlikely to be included in the building programme for another ten years. (112) In 1968 the Regional Board drew up plans for the first stage to be completed by 1976/7. (113) The cost was estimated at £3 million in 1970 but four years later anger was mounting at the delay in even starting the district hospital scheme. (114) In 1976 doctors were still maintaining it was wrong to build the hospital three and a half miles away from the town centre. (115) One year later the Health Minister David Ennals was promising a start within two years but a postponed sewerage scheme at Broomfield led to another postponement in 1978. (116) (117) Part of a £39 million cash boost was earmarked for the new hospital in 1980 but then cash shortages forced further delay. (118)

The local papers frequently asked the question; why was it that Chelmsford always seemed to be last in getting money for its health services? In 1974 conditions at the Chelmsford and Essex were deemed atrocious by the town's Community Health Council. (119) The following year part of a new surgery complex collapsed at the hospital. (120) By the mid 1970s hospital spending in Mid Essex was the lowest in the county. (121) Cutbacks caused theatre and ward closures in all three hospitals. In 1979 there was an announcement that there would be no extra hospital beds in the next ten years despite the projected increase of population in the area to 170,000 by 1991. (122) A TV series on St John's maternity ward had given a positive impression but the hospital was increasingly restricted by nursing shortages. (123)

St Giles was given the status of a hospital in 1969, after leprosy had been declared a notifiable disease in 1951. Most of the hospital's costs were born by the N.H.S. but voluntary contributions were still important. The heavy expense of running the hospital led to St Giles being sold to the housing association Springboard, in 1984. The original residents did not welcome the newcomers, who were mentally or physically handicapped. A Channel 4 documentary on the institution did not give a rosy picture. By 2005 St Giles was no longer a hospital, having been re-classified as a hostel. Hansen's disease patients still got the specialised care they needed, although there had been no new patients for ten years. (124) Most sufferers had jobs in the local community.

The drive for a local hospice started in 1981. In 1983 the Essex County Council agreed to sell the site of a former boys' home in New London Road to the hospice appeal. (125) In 1985 the fund stood at a quarter of a million with an estimated one million needed. Four years later the Farleigh Hospice was ready to open with likely running costs of one thousand pounds a day. (126) It was always likely that the hospice would be better suited to a purpose built centre and a move was announced in 1996. The original 10 bed hostel was caring for about 500 patients a year and costs had risen to two and a half thousand pounds a day. (127) A site for the new £3 million hospital was found next to Broomfield hospital. (128) In 2004 J's hospice, a new care at home service for the 16 to 40 age group, was founded by Denise Wiffen. (129)

The 1980s also saw the establishment of several private hospitals in the Chelmsford area. One at Springfield Place was vetoed by the Council for being incompatible with the surroundings but allowed later. (130) Another such hospital at Lawn Lane went ahead. Several were built later including the Springfield Medical Centre, which was built in 18 months. In 2006 the Chelmsford Medical Centre opened at Fenton House, New London Road.

In contrast with the money available to private hospitals, the N.H.S. in Mid Essex continued to be starved of cash, at the time the population of an area was growing by two and a half percent per year. A newspaper article in 1980 claimed that Chelmsford's hospitals were the worst in Europe, citing overcrowded wards and inadequate heating. The report condemned the use of Victorian buildings at the Chelmsford and Essex and part of St John's, as well as the continued use of wartime huts at the latter. (131)

In 1989 the possibility of Mid Essex opting out of the existing State system was first raised and in 1991 this was carried out along with the local ambulance service. (132) During the mid 1990s the Mid Essex hospitals group was merged with N.W and N.E. Essex health authorities to create a larger, and it was hoped, more efficient health service. (133) The saga of the creation of a modern Broomfield hospital lumbered on against this background of change. Further cutbacks in the early 1980s caused major parts of the Broomfield plan, including a new accident and emergency unit, an x ray department, an intensive care department and a fracture clinic, to be postponed. (134) The local M.P.s Norman St John Stevas and Newton said "we will fight these cuts" but proved powerless to do anything. (135) A new ward block was finally opened at Broomfield in 1987, which represented the first new wards in the district for 40 years! (136) A new £3 million cancer centre was proposed but eventually Broomfield wasn't awarded it. (137) The next stage of building at Broomfield was axed in 1990 when it was announced that the district was £32 million in debt on building spending. (138)

In 1991 the idea of a 'super hospital' at Broomfield was again revived. (139) This led to moves to close St John's and move the remaining services at the Chelmsford and Essex to Broomfield. Despite the background of further cuts to the N.H.S. further expansion of Broomfield hospital did take place with the start of building on the new £3.2 million 'Linden' mental health centre, and a new £10 million pound orthopaedic centre was planned. (140) In 1994 a burns unit was moved from Billericay to Broomfield. (141) A familiar pattern of financial restrictions prevented a 1997 multi million pound plan from achieving fruition. (142) Finally in 2000 a £70 million pound plan was given the green light in the following year to transform the hospital. (143) A private finance initiative was to provide most of the capital. (144)

Plans for the Chelmsford and Essex to close were announced in 1985. (145) Acute services were to transfer to Broomfield and St John's. (146) A consultant came up with a plan whereby various clinics could be concentrated at the London Road site, to supplement the services at Broomfield. (147) This plan, rather than the one that would have seen the hospital converted into a nursing home, was largely followed. (148) Large amounts of surplus land were sold off for commercial development. (149)

St John's hospital somehow survived in the 1980s and 1990s despite the perennial threat of the axe. In the early 1990s a new children's ward, the Sunshine ward, was even opened after fund raising by the public. (150) The former infirmary had been the birthplace of most of the town's babies. The hospital finally closed its doors in 2010. In 2011 the hospital site came back on the market after the initial owners went into administration. (151)

Despite the almost continual financial crises and often high waiting lists, the Mid Essex hospitals often performed well in the new ratings brought in during the early twenty first century. (152) In November 2010 the £148 million pound super hospital was finally opened at Broomfield. It included an ultra modern Accident and Emergency facility, a new Maternity Unit and 336 new beds. The Essex Air Ambulance opened a helipad at the top of the building. In November 2012 however there were already predictions that the Trust faced a dire financial crisis with a predicted £27 million loss on the year. Research indicated that the true cost of the P.F.I. initiative at Broomfield hospital was likely to be £766 million over 32 years rather than the supposed £148 million. (153) Simon Burns said "They never should have started these P.F.Is in the first place". (154) Severe teething problems at the super hospital led to its boss Graham Ramsey quitting in January 2011. The recruitment of Malcolm Stamp as Chief Executive resulted in a quick turnaround in Broomfield's performance. "Now our cancer waiting times are the best in Essex and 95% of patients go through A and E within four hours: we weren't meeting any of those targets two years ago." "The staff have been absolutely magnificent, from the clinicians to the porters and the cleaners." By 2013 the trust was consistently in the top ten performers of 46 trusts in the East of England and Midlands. Stamp did not believe that the budget deficit and the P.F.I. would result in service cuts. (155)

1) Essex Chronicle 30 7 1880
2) Essex Weekly News 23 12 1881
3) E.W.N. 27 1 1882
4) E.C. 29 9 1882
5) Chelmsford Museums records
6) E.W.N. 30 1 1985
7) E.C. 27 5 1887
8) E.W.N. 29 1 1892
9) Around the Chignalls Stan Jarvis

10) E.W.N. 2 3 1888
11) E.W.N. 20 7 1888
12) E.W.N. 12 10 1900
13) E.W.N. 1 4 1895
14) E.W.N. 17 2 1922
15) Chelmsford Rural District Council minutes 1926
16) Essex Countryside Vol. 8 p.175
17) E.C. 16 1 1885
18) E.W.N. 9 5 1884
19) E.C. 20 5 1892
20) E.C. 8 9 1893
21) E.W.N. 12 2 1892
22) E.W.N. 27 2 1885
23) E.C. 20 4 1883
24) E.C. 6 5 1892
25) New Hall and Its School Tony Tuckwell.
26) Trinity Road School log book
27) E.W.N. 6 7 1928
28) Chelmsford Borough Council minutes 26 3 1913
29) E.W.N. 26 8 1897
30) E.W.N. 26 8 1897
31) John Thresh: The Housing of the Working Classes in the Chelmsford and Rural Districts
32) E.C. 2 8 1907
33) E.W.N. 13 9 1907
34) C.B.C. minutes 30 6 1897
35) Chelmsford Rural Sanitary District Authority 1893
36) C.B.C. minutes 26 7 1899
37) C.B.C. minutes 25 10 1899
38) C.B.C. minutes 28 8 1901
39) C.B.C. minutes 25 9 1901
40) C.B.C. minutes 30 4 1902
41) C.B.C. minutes 31 12 1902
42) C.B.C. minutes 28 8 1907
43) Essex County Council minutes 1914

44) E.C. 9 5 1969
45) E.C. 16 10 1896
46) E.C. 11 6 1909
47) E.W.N. 24 2 1911
48) E.C. 15 2 1907
49) Chelmsford and Essex Infirmary minutes 1890- 1905 and 1905-1917 E.R.O.
50) E.W.N. 16 9 1881
51) E.W.N. 29 9 1882
52) E.W.N. 31 8 1883
53) E.W.N. 19 9 1884
54) E.W.N. 24 4 1885
55) E.W.N. 14 4 1887
56) E.W.N. 31 1 1880
57) E.C. 11 1 1901
58) C.B.C. minutes 24 11 1909
59) C.B.C. minutes22 9 1903
60) E.C. 12 8 1910
61) E.C. 9 6 1912
62) C.R.D.C. minutes 25 6 1912
63) C.R.D.C. minutes 13 2 1917
64) C.R.D.C. minutes 4 6 1918
65) E.C. 1 4 19121
66) E.C. 20 6 1924
67) E.C. 19 6 1926
68) E.C. 21 3 1930
69) E.C. 24 10 1930
70) E.C. 26 2 1932
71) E.C. 28 8 1931
72) E.C. 10 2 1932
73) E.C. 22 4 1932
74) E.C. 15 7 1932
75) E.W.N. 26 4 1935
76) E.W.N. 6 51938
77) E.C. 19 10 1934
78) C.B.C. 29 9 1926

79) Chelmsford Museums records
80) Caring for Hansen's Disease Nicholas Rose p.1
81) E.W.N. 22 2 1924
82) Rose p.2
83) Rose p.7
84) Legacy of the Rural Guardians G. Cuttle p.208 - 210
85) C.B.C. minutes 30 12 1919
86) C.B.C. minutes 25 2 1920
87) C.B.C. minutes 28 12 1928
88) C.R.D.C. minutes 8 9 1925
89) C.R.D.C minutes 2 10 1928
90) C.B.C. minutes 24 7 1925
91) C.B.C. minutes 19 7 1920
92) C.B.C. minutes 26 9 1921
93) C.B.C. minutes 29 3 1922
94) E.W.N. 19 2 1943
95) E.C. 29 3 1946
96) E.C. 24 1 1947
97) E.C. 31 1 1947
98) E.C. 14 3 1947
99) E.W.N. 11 5 1948
100) E.C. 8 4 1949
101) E.W.N. 27 10 1949
102) E.W.N. 10 7 1953
103) E.W.N. 12 8 1955
104) E.W.N. 4 5 1956
105) E.C. 2 8 1957
106) E.C. 16 6 1961
107) Broomfield 100 years of the Parish Council p.49
108) C. Museums records
109) E.W.N. 27 11 1959
110) E.W.N. 26 5 1961
111) E.W.N. 26 1 1962
112) E.W.N. 8 5 1964
113) E.W.N. 23 2 1968

114) E.C. 6 10 1974
115) E.C. 14 5 1976
116) E.C. 8 7 1977
117) E.C. 26 5 1978
118) E.C. 12 9 1980
119) E.C. 8 11 1974
120) E.C. 17 10 1975
121) E.C. 7 10 1977
122) E.C. 30 11 1979
123) C. Museums records
124) Rose p.8-11
125) E.C. 2 12 1983
126) E.C. 22 9 1989
127) E.C. 197 1996
128) E.C. 13 12 1996
129) E.C. 16 9 2010
130) E.C. 17 10 1980
131) E.C. 17 10 1980
132) E.C. 18 10 1991
133) E.W.N. 6 2 1997
134) E.C. 16 9 1983
135) E.C. 14 10 1983
136) E.C. 14 8 1987
137) E.C. 27 9 1985
138) E.C. 26 10 1985
139) E.C. 31 5 1991
140) E.W.N. 29 10 1992
141) E.W.N. 18 8 1984
142) E.W.N. 3 4 1997
143) E.W.N. 30 11 2000
144) E.C. 17 5 2002
145) E.C. 4 10 1985
146) E.C. 10 10 1986
147) E.C. 13 2 1987
148) E.W.N. 21 5 1987

149) E.W.N. 22 8 1991
150) C. Museums records
151) E.C. 27 4 2011 p.1
152) E.W.N. 27 9 2001
153) James Drummond jamesdrummond@essexchronicle.co.uk
154) E.C. 8 11 2012 p.14
155) E.C. 14 3 2013 p.22 - 23

17

Sanitation in the Chelmsford area

"The privy midden is now a thing of the past"

The above quote, from the county medical officer of health in 1920, reflected the change that had come over domestic sanitary arrangements in the previous 50 years. (1) In the late nineteenth and early twentieth century much emphasis was placed on the need to improve the water supply and sewage systems in both the borough and the rural district. People in the Chelmsford area increasingly wouldn't put up with three hours water a day for their baths and new water closet. This was an age after all when "cleanliness was next to godliness". Great improvements in the area's sanitation during the first 50 years of the borough owed a great deal to the indefatigable work of the sanitary and nuisance inspectors, with the help of Dr John Thresh (see chapter 16), for a considerable part of that period. The rapid expansion in the area's population made their work even more essential. Chelmsford's sanitation was always made more difficult by the lack of steep gradients and the presence of two rivers; around or under which pipes had to be built.

As Hilda Grieve stated, the early nineteenth century town had drained naturally into its two rivers. The only public drain was the sewer running from the conduit in the market place down the middle of the High Street. The "confused anarchy of individual or shared, open or covered drains, privies and cesspools with holes and pits in the ground for filth and dung" show how much work there was for the later inspectors to accomplish. (2) A sewer had been built in Rainsford Lane in 1857. (3) Fenton's temporary treatment tanks in Kings Head Meadow were replaced by permanent filtration tanks off the then isolated Lady Lane. In the 1880s a great deal of housing occurred in Moulsham, (see chapter 18) ahead of sewers and water drains, despite the best efforts of the Board of Health. (4) Chancellor was warning of the town's insufficient water supply before he resigned as the Board's engineer. Summer droughts would cut off the water from Burgess Well and leave the town dependent on the small reservoir at Hall Street. (5) A bore had been drilled at Hall Street/ Mildmay Road in 1868. (6)

The pressing need to deal with the problems of sewage disposal led the town and the rural area to agree on a joint scheme in a rare display of unanimity. A £13,000 loan was negotiated for the Brook End sewage farm scheme in 1881. (7) Another loan of almost £8,000 was negotiated for a new main sewer. (8) Sewage was carried by gravitation rather than being pumped, which was much more expensive. (9) The Board of Health also arranged for the streets to be swept once a week and a scavenger was sent round twice a week "to collect all the refuse not collected in the brick pits". (10) It made at least some attempt to stop the major firms of the town causing a nuisance through their smoke. (11) The water shortage of 1884 caused the matter of the town's water supply to be referred to the Sanitary Committee of the Board. A scheme was put forward by Pertwee, the Board's engineer. This led to a spring being exploited at Admirals Park and a reservoir and tank was built to accommodate the resulting supply. (12) The reservoir was 7 feet deep, 170 feet long and 36 feet wide. It held 150 thousand gallons and was covered by an iron roof. The reservoir took 2 days to fill. Nearby was the water tower; at 37 ft square and 65 ft high, it hardly matched Colchester's monstrosity. Colchester's 'Jumbo' tower, nicknamed after an elephant, was completed in 1883 and was claimed to be the second biggest in England at the time. The iron tank put on top of Chelmsford's tower contained 8,000 gallons. T.H.P. Dennis laid a new eight inch main to convey this water to the town.

One of the problems of the expanding town was that so many of the existing pipes were defective and prone to leakages. In addition, the new borough council committed itself in 1891 to connecting all houses to the new mains. (13) In May 1896 there was a general shortage of water in the town with most houses reduced to 3 hours supply a day. (14) The crisis put a lot of pressure on the fledgling borough council. They hired Joseph Francis, an engineer from the New River Water Supply Company, to advise the Sewer and Water Supply sub-committee and he considered the town's water supply to be imperfect as well as insufficient. A typical days' water supply was 150,000 gallons when 500,000 was normal for a town of Chelmsford's size. Existing sources of water supply were far too shallow and there was a need for a well to be bored down to the chalk at 7 to 8 hundred feet. (15) The first site considered was in the Recreation

Ground because Francis considered deepening the Mildmay Road well to be too expensive an option. By 1899, the Beech Report, commissioned by the borough into the town's sanitation, highlighted the need for a greatly enlarged water supply as well as attention to numerous sanitary defects. (16) In 1900 the Essex Chronicle thought the council was still not taking the town's water supply issue seriously enough and endangering the town's public health as a result. (17) Finally the council ordered the sub-committee to prepare a scheme.

The problems of the town's water supply were probably exceeded by those of the rural area. In the 1880s there was virtually no public water supply, very few public wells and almost no pipes. The wide geographical area was a considerable hindrance to establishing a public water supply before the first war. The rural area's acute water shortage, highlighted by Dr Thresh in 1891, was by no means unusual. (18) A large number of private wells were usually shallow and unreliable and they also normally lacked pumps because of the expense. The rural authority made the first move to conserve water by building a reservoir on Danbury common in 1893. (19) In 1894 the Rural Sanitary Authority negotiated a deal to extend the water supply from Wickford to Rettendon, Runwell and Woodham Ferris. (20) Dr Thresh stated that only six villages in the rural area had a public water supply in 1895. Thresh was often concerned with the all too common instances of impure and contaminated water from private wells. In many parishes water was only available from ponds, or by collecting rainwater from roofs. When a public water supply was established the rural district often had the problem of getting the owners of cottages to use it, for example at Broomfield in 1900. (21) Both councils increasingly used water certificates, which owners of new houses had to have before these could be let. The new Rural District Council did try to establish as many public wells as possible, obtaining loans from the Public Loans Board, for example for trial bores at Writtle and Rettendon. (22) Regarding sewage, Thresh bemoaned the fact that most cottage residents in the rural area had large enough gardens to dispose of their slop, if only they took the trouble. "The effluvia from rotting vegetable and animal matters pollute the air." (23) Old fashioned conveniences were generally in use, which were generally made out of wood. During the summer they caused "a most abominable nuisance."

The need to tackle the various nuisances was the reason much importance was attached to appointing Nuisance Inspectors, who then worked in tandem with the local Sanitary Authority. Overcrowding in houses was identified as a major potential nuisance which often led to insanitary conditions. In 1895 Thresh identified the

Chelmsford area as the worst in the Home Counties for overcrowding. (24) In 1899 for example the owners of three Moulsham houses were threatened with closing orders because of overcrowding. (25) Conditions in Moulsham's two lodging houses were notorious for overcrowding and were attracting the attention of the Council's Sanitary Committee as early as 1888. (26) The problem persisted and 13 years later the Travellers' Rest lodging house had only 1 water closet for 13 people. (27) Well into the new century the inspectors were carrying out several hundred inspections a year and sending out multiple closing orders. For example the rural inspector of nuisances sent closing orders to the owners of 69 houses in Baddow Road in 1912. (28) By the Edwardian period, demands were increasing for the councils to reduce overcrowding by building houses themselves (see chapter 18).

Thresh also criticised the fact that cottagers often could not be persuaded to burn their refuse. Ditches full of refuse remained a health hazard as parishes were often unwilling to pay for scavengers and increasingly expected the R.D.C. to take the responsibility. Even when contacts were given to private scavenging firms their efficiency left much to be desired. The R.D.C. frequently advertised for scavenging firms to collect house rubbish, in the vain hope of getting a better service. (29) Both the borough and the rural district used refuse destructors. Ironically the latter were sometimes the cause of a nuisance themselves, because of the smoke they let into the atmosphere. (30) Parishes were not the only ones to complain about the lack of efficient scavenging services. During 1904 the Springfield prison complained to the R.D.C. that it paid taxes and therefore was entitled to have its premises scavenged. (31) In 1929 some private scavenging firms were still employed although by now they were mainly dispensing their rubbish at the council dumps. (32) A tip at Longstomps was used for 40 years. The street sweeping system first established under the old Board of Health did not work satisfactorily. In 1902 the sanitary inspector was forced to print cards telling residents to sweep their footways and pavements outside their houses. (33)

In an era before effective damp courses were developed, let alone generally introduced, damp presented another common nuisance. During 1913 the R.D.C. was increasingly mentioning damp courses as a possible solution. (34) By 1920 it was being found that damp courses could extend the life of otherwise unfit houses but it was still a struggle to get owners to install them. (35) As late as 1932 a statutory notice was placed on a house in Fryerning because of excessive damp. (36) By 1913 inspectors in both districts were regularly meeting with owners and their agents to encourage them to abate nuisances, rather than immediately issuing notices. Most of them increasingly realised that they would have to comply. In 1909 the Borough's Inspector of Nuisances alone inspected 905 houses. (37) Another branch of the local inspectorate was the petroleum inspectors, first appointed under the old Board of Health, who became increasingly important with the increase in the number of motor cars in the Edwardian era. Safety concerning the storage of petrol became a major issue. In 1911 for example, the Anglo American Company sought permission to store two thousand gallons near the railway station. (38)

The extension to the town's water supply caused much debate after the turn of the century amongst both politicians and in the newspapers. Eventually the council opted for a relatively cheap scheme, drilling a trial bore at Mildmay Road. (39) An accident at the trial bore only added to the criticism. (40) The subsidence that occurred was fairly typical of the problems encountered in sinking new deep wells. Chancellor correctly predicted that the new scheme would only be a temporary solution. By 1903 the Mildmay Well was not yielding what had been expected. Councillors Chancellor and Lunney criticised the efficiency of the Mildmay pumping station. Thresh was convinced that a new well was needed at Admirals Park. (41) Part of the problem was the great deal of wastage from the old main, which was still being used. The extension of the water supply necessitated an alteration to the reservoir at Longstomps, which by 1908 was storing 610 thousand gallons out of a total of 760 thousand gallons, with only small amounts stored at Mildmay Road and the Admirals Park water tower. (42) (43) The town's water supply situation had certainly improved by 1910 as there was a constant supply, with no cut off at 11 a.m. as previously. (44) Chelmsford's 657 flushing cisterns, which had been installed between 1904 and 1908, stood a much better chance of having water.

Of course the first war brought a great increase in the demand for water in the area as well as vastly increased pressure on the sanitation system in general (see chapter 15). After the war and the departure of the soldiers, demand for water did drop, but not by much, because of the growth in the population. In 1921 average daily consumption was still 470 thousand gallons, compared with a peak of just over 500 thousand gallons during the war. (45) A new source of supply at Brockley Road, Springfield couldn't offset the declining yields of the borough's established wells. (46) By 1925 the pressure of consumption meant that supply had again to be limited in the town to between 6 a.m. and 10 p.m. (47)

In the early twentieth century a number of deep wells were sunk in the rural area, including Great Baddow, Ingatestone and Writtle. (48) The bores often took months to drill and were beset by difficulties, e.g. in 1902 a trial bore at Writtle came to an end because of an influx of sand. (49) Water towers were built at Great Baddow and Springfield. (50) By 1905 the Rural District engineer could state that the areas water supply was good except for Ingatestone. (51) By 1909 however all the surface springs in the rural area were showing decreasing yields. Demand for water in villages such as Broomfield, which was becoming a suburb of Chelmsford, was increasing rapidly.

By 1914 the joint sewage farm had grown into a fully commercial operation with crops such as celery and rye grass grown and sold. (52) The farm was seriously in danger of being overworked and it was extended in 1914. A main trunk had to be built from the Kings Head to the sewage farm in 1922 to relieve the pressure of sewage. (53) Many of the rural parishes had problems with gravitational schemes because they feared the cost of expensive pumping systems. As late as 1925, plans to send Writtle sewage to Chelmsford had to be altered to include a pumping system because the gravitational system wouldn't work. (54)

One sanitation problem which vexed the borough council for nearly three decades was the pollution of the Chelmer. The Public Health Act of 1876 had prohibited the passage of sewage into streams and made it an offence to continue the pollution. In 1898 the borough accused Writtle parish of polluting the river by discharging raw untreated sewage into it. (55) As County Medical Officer of Health, Dr Thresh, took water samples. In 1901 the Weekly News was telling the R.D.C. it needed to be more prompt in its action. (56) Further water tests showed the water was still impregnated with sewage. (57) Eventually the R.D.C. came to legal terms with the borough, agreeing a small amount of compensation. (58) By October of the same year however, the river was being seriously polluted again. (59) Writtle's new sewage scheme eventually solved the problem. Over a decade later the Chelmer was again being polluted but this time the source was further up the river at Great Waltham. (60) Essex County Council put pressure on the R.D.C. to solve the problem but almost a decade later however, it had to start proceedings against the district council for polluting the river at Broomfield and the Walthams. (61)(62) The problem was eventually traced to two slaughterhouses at Little Waltham. (63) Sometimes the source of the pollution was outside the Chelmsford area itself. In 1904 and 1911 pollution was traced by Thresh to Dunmow. (64) Waste from a sugar beet factory at Felsted caused serious pollution of the river in 1926. (65)

By 1925 it was obvious that another new borehole in the borough would only bring temporary relief to the pressure on its water supply. The borough decided to take advantage of the new methods of purification that were being applied to river water. A scheme was drawn up to take up to a million gallons a day at Sandford Mill. The cost was likely to be £50,000 but, like the new sewage mains from Kings Head Meadow, the project was conceived to provide work for those unemployed locally (see chapter 9). (66) Chelmsford Borough Council was told that they could take the water from the river without affecting the paper mill further downstream. Sandford Mill itself had been vacant for some years and the property sold. The need for a big increase to the water supply was shown by an acute water shortage on the new Boarded Barns estate. (67) A new borehole on the estate had to be abandoned. A Chelmsford water bill had first to go through parliament. Sandford Mill Waterworks was opened in 1929 and was a testament to the skill of the borough's engineer Ernest J Miles. The intake was made on the mill stream and the river flowed by gravity over a weir 66 feet long into an open channel leading to a storage reservoir. This was built of reinforced concrete and could contain over 3 million gallons of water. From the storage reservoir the water flowed over another weir into the channel leading to the treatment tanks with one million gallons capacity. In the tanks, sulphur of alumina and lime were added. After 24 hours all impurities were removed. CO_2 was then added to improve the water's drinking qualities. Water was then delivered by mains to the reservoir at Longstomps two and a half miles away. (68) The Weekly News said "It was a fine achievement on the part of Mr Miles, the borough engineer, that the great river supply works were planned by him and carried out with great success." (69) Chelmsford Corporation had a new reservoir built at Galleywood in 1930, with the permission of the R.D.C.. In 1948 the borough was allowed to increase the rate of abstraction from the river by half a million gallons a day, to meet the ever increasing demand. (70) This was despite the opposition of Brown's, the timber merchants, who feared it would interfere with their use of the Chelmer. In addition, the council sank a new borehole by the Sandford Mill works. All this didn't prevent the Weekly News from describing the quality of Chelmsford water as "nauseating". (71)

In the inter war period the R.D.C. strived to bring proper sewerage schemes to many of its parishes. Often however, the government refused to sanction significant spending. In 1931, for example, the Ministry of Health blocked the council borrowing for a scheme for Stock, Ingatestone and Fryerning. (72) A further extension to the sewage farm was agreed to by the R.D.C. but delayed by the financial crisis. (73)

Opening of Sandford Mill 1929
(Courtesy of Chelmsford Museums)

After the second war the borough and the surrounding area were having considerable difficulty in storing enough water. The projected consumption of water was expected to increase from one million gallons to three and a half million gallons a day in the next thirty years. A first suggested site for a new reservoir at Ingatestone was eventually dropped in favour of one at Hanningfield. (74) Work started in 1952 to create a massive new reservoir by flooding the Sandon valley, covering part of South Hanningfield. (75) Despite opposition from the local parish the scheme received government approval after an inquiry. (76) Besides the Mid Essex area, the Hanningfield reservoir was to serve Basildon, Harold Hill and other rapidly growing urban areas in Essex. (77) A sixty foot dam was built. (78) When the six million gallon reservoir was opened in 1957 it quickly became established as a nature reserve. In the 1980s it was supplying a quarter of the counties water and was also one of the country's largest still water fisheries, producing especially high quality rainbow trout. The estate around the lake is now leased by the Essex Wildlife Trust and is especially popular with bird watchers.

By the 1920s the declining yields of wells in the rural parishes was causing real concern. The Danbury waterworks in particular was finding it difficult to meet the demands of its own district, including Rettendon and Woodham Ferrers, because several wells in the district had run dry. (79) (80) This problem was solved by getting water supplied from outside the Mid Essex area. In 1932 a connection was made to the South Essex Waterworks Company mains near Danbury, after the latter had negotiated for the company to supply water to Stock. (81) The company obtained its water from the River Stour. (82) In 1933, 800th gallons every four weeks were being obtained by the rural district from the South Essex Water Company and 250th gallons were coming from the Southend Water Company. (83) Two years later the waterworks at Danbury and Ingatestone were made redundant and water for Writtle was being obtained from the borough. (84) By 1935 the rural district was only producing one third of the total amount of water it was consuming and by 1937 this proportion was down to 1/8th. (85) It was never a viable financial proposition for the rural district to have its own river water purification works.

By the inter war period nearly all inspections of houses were re-inspections, but they were still frequent. In 1926, 206 inspections were carried out in the rural district by the sanitary inspectors, leading to 14 informal notices, but only one of these was made statutory. (86) By this time most notices were to install water cisterns, but the Nuisance Inspectors were still dealing with cases of overcrowding. In 1925 the Borough still enacted 51 closing notices for overcrowding. (87) The R.D.C. was collecting all rubbish by 1930 but this was still not always effective. (88) In 1935 the local Womens Institute complained that rubbish wasn't always being collected at Woodham Ferrers. (89) Water mains had to be completed for all the new housing estates that were springing up in both areas by the 1930s. Mains water arrived in Stock by 1930 but there was no mains sewer until after the second war. (90) Although Chelmsford's sanitary problems were now largely a thing of the past it was still at the centre of the driest part of the country. In 1958 the area was close to general water rationing. (91) By 1965 Chelmsford, whose water consumption had doubled in the previous ten years, was again threatened by drought. Its independent supplies were no longer sufficient and it took the balance it needed from the South Essex Water Company. It was getting one and a half million gallons a day from the river, 300,000 gallons from deep boreholes, 200 thousand gallons from springs and 900th gallons had to be obtained from the Company. (92) The Sandford Mill site was acquired by the Essex Water company but it was decided to concentrate water treatment at the Langford works and therefore Sandford Mill was no longer needed. In 1984 the pumping machinery was taken out and the works was returned to the borough.

In 2003 Essex and Suffolk Water completed works to enable treatment of effluent from Chelmsford to be treated at the Langford treatment works, before being put back into the river for subsequent re-use. A report commissioned by the Borough Council and amended in 2010, emphasised the likely pressure on both water supply and sewage treatment caused by the planned for increase in population in the city of up to 16,000 people by 2021, especially in the N.E. of the area. The Chelmsford North development will require a dedicated sewer direct to the Chelmsford Wastewater Treatment Works, to avoid the risk of serious sewer flooding within the centre of Chelmsford. The treatment works at Chelmer Village (formerly Brook End) needs upgrading at a cost of £12million. (93) Although closer to the Hanningfield Reservoir, the city now receives it water from the Abberton reservoir. Both now hold the equivalent of 312 million bathfuls of water. (94) In 2011 twelve decommissioned water tanks at East Hanningfield were used for the making of a zombie film. (95)

1) Essex County Council minutes 5 10 1920
2) Hilda Grieve the Sleeper and the Shadows p.312
3) Grieve p.347
4) Grieve p.353
5) Grieve p.357
6) The Chelmsford Borough Water Undertaking p.2
7) Essex Chronicle 28 1 1881
8) Essex Weekly News 18 3 1881 p.6
9) Grieve p.365
10) Grieve p.341
11) Grieve p.358-359
12) E.W.N. 27 12 1888 p.5
13) E.C. 27 2 1891 p.5
14) E.C. 24 5 1895
15) E.C. 11 2 1898 p.4
16) E.C. 20 10 1899
17) E.C. 29 6 1900 p.5
18) E.W.N. 22 5 1891 p.2

19) Chelmsford Rural Sanitary Authority minutes 20 6 1893
20) C.R.S.A. minutes 31 12 1895 p.20
21) Chelmsford Rural District Council minutes 9 2 1900 p.245
22) C.R.D.C. minutes 11 6 1901 p.189
23) Essex Review Vol.1 p.31
24) C.R.D.C. minutes 24 5 1895
25) C.B.C. minutes 28 8 1899
26) C.B.C. minutes 28 12 1888
27) C.B.C. minutes 10 1897
28) C.R.D.C. minutes 24 12 1912
29) C.R.D.C. minutes 6 3 1900 p.283
30) C.B.C. minutes 26 7 1911
31) C.R.D.C. minutes24 11 1904
32) C.R.D.C. minutes 29 10 1929
33) C.B.C. minutes 31 12 1902
34) C.R.D.C. minutes 13 5 1913
35) C.B.C. 26 5 1920
36) C.R.D.C. minutes 30 5 1932
37) C.B.C. minutes 24 11 1909
38) C.B.C. minutes 27 12 1911
39) E.W.N. 27 10 1899
40) E.W.N. 11 5 1900
41) E.W.N. 31 7 1903
42) E.W.N. 31 7 1903
43) C.B.C. minutes 20 12 1908
44) C.B.C. minutes 29 6 1910
45) C.B.C. minutes 27 4 1921
46) C.B.C. minutes 20 3 1919
47) C.B.C. minutes 24 7 1925
48) C.R.D.C. minutes 27 7 1902 p.40
49) C.R.D.C. minutes 19 8 1902
50) C.R.D.C. minutes 7 6 1904 p.83
51) C.R.D.C. minutes 11 4 1905
52) C.B.C. minutes 22 12 1908
53) C.R.D.C. minutes 19 91922

54) C.R.D.C. minutes 3 11 1925
55) E.C. 30 12 1898
56) E.W.N. 25 10 1901
57) E.W.N. 29 11 1901
58) C.R.D.C. minutes 9 1 1900
59) C.R.D.C. minutes 29 10 1901
60) C.R.D.C. minutes 17 2 1914
61) C.R.D.C. minutes 21 7 1914
62) C.R.D.C. minutes 1 5 1923
63) C.R.D.C. minutes 26 6 1923
64) E.C.C. minutes 3 1911
65) C.R.D.C. minutes 30 11 1926
66) E.W.N. 15 9 1922 p.2
67) E.W.N. 31 8 1923
68) E.W.N. 18 7 1930 p.7
69) E.W.N. 19 7 1929
70) The Chelmsford Borough Water Undertaking p.3
71) E.W.N. 10 10 1947
72) E.W.N. 24 5 1931 p.9
73) E.W.N. 6 11 1931
74) E.W.N. 1 7 1949
75) E.W.N. 21 3 1952 p.1
76) E.W.N. 10 3 1950
77) E.W.N. 19 11 1954 p.1
78) Essex Countryside Vol.35 1987
79) C.R.D.C. minutes 20 9 1921 p.214
80) C.R.D.C. minutes 28 9 1921 p.182
81) C.R.D.C. minutes 5 7 1932 p.142
82) C.R.D.C. minutes 3 1 1934 p.188
83) C.R.D.C. minutes 6 6 1933 p.160
84) C.R.D.C. minutes 3 1 1934 p.237
85) C.R.D.C. minutes 20 7 1937 p.157
86) C.R.D.C. minutes 15 6 1926 p.371
87) C.B.C. minutes 24 7 1925
88) C.R.D.C. minutes 8 7 1930 p.167

89) C.R.D.C. minutes 17 9 1935
90) Stock Charles Phillips
91) E.W.N. 11 7 1958 p.12
92) E.W.N. 19 3 1965 p.1
93) Updated report for C.B.C. on Chelmsford Water Cycle Study Technical Report by Halcrow Group Limited 2010
94) E.C. 7 7 2011 p.13
95) E.C. 27 6 2013 p.15

18

Housing in the Chelmsford area

"On a clear day you could see Bradwell"

As we have seen in chapter 11, the geographical area of built up Chelmsford was much more restricted in 1880 than it was to be come during the next four decades because of the industrialisation of the town. Nearly all of the housing that occurred before the first war was private, but after 1918 the building of council houses took off both in the borough and the rural area, dominated initially by the building of the Boarded Barns estate. The immediate post Second World War period saw the council unable to build permanent new houses and being forced to use a large number of military huts at Boreham and elsewhere, as well as large numbers of 'prefabs'. Although Marconi was involved in house building on a small scale the idea of any of the big three building their own Silver End was never a realistic possibility. Half a century after it was built, the Boarded Barns estate had become an eyesore, constituting a deprived area. During later part of the twentieth century the newly expanded district council gradually ceased house building, which was replaced by increased private house building on the edges of the district. The new millennium saw the council's housing stock being sold off to a housing association.

In the 1880s, house building began to accelerate, particularly in the Moulsham area. The Board of Health and then the Borough struggled to use the powers of 1876 Health Act to prevent overcrowding and insanitary conditions (see chapter 17). Chelmsford Borough Council managed to get the builders of the first houses in Lady Lane to extend their back rooms. (1) Builders in Mildmay Road and Manor Road, off Lady Lane, were not allowed to have houses occupied until they were connected up to the drains. In 1902 the council found that the builders of houses in Manor Road had not drained, levelled and paved the kerb properly. The Borough also struggled for decades to improve conditions in existing housing particularly in the warren of alleyways and yards between Tindal Street and the market. It tried without success to use the Housing of the Working Classes Act of 1890 to improve the appalling conditions in the housing around the Union Yard.

As early as 1892, in an article in the Essex Review, Doctor Thresh outlined the problems of working class housing in the rural area around Chelmsford. The character of the houses varied greatly in different villages. "In some there are very few dilapidated houses, with very few with the old lath and plaster cottages roofed with thatch: few without ample gardens. In others the cottages are crowded together and a large proportion of them are so old or so structurally defective that they are really unfit for human habitation." Many of the cottages were built on narrow strips of land besides roads. They had "a timber framework, studied outside with laths and daubed over with plaster, or with a mixture of clay and chopped straw, and are roofed with thatch". These cottages were fearfully cold in the winter. "Walls were sometimes not an inch thick." The floors downstairs are usually of brick, laid on the ground, and are almost invariably damp." When bricks were broken, bare earth would be exposed. Bits of board were laid down and several thicknesses of matting over them; but damp caused them to rot. The bedrooms were frequently in the roof without a fireplace. "The doors and windows are often of the most rickety description causing the room to be exceedingly draughty and cold." In some villages "the more modern cottages are built of wood or brick and covered with tiles or slates". Even so many of these were in a deplorable state. "The weather boards, from age and want of paint have become so rotten, that it is almost impossible to repair them." Although loftier than lath and plaster ones, they generally had less space. The second bedroom was often a lean-to, without a fireplace and utterly unsuitable as a bedroom. Thresh blamed the agents who set the tenants' rents and the landlords who had not seen the properties for years. There were often no better cottages in the village to move to, so the tenants stayed put. (2)

In Chelmsford the houses which sprang up towards the end of the century, both in Moulsham and near the railway line, were brick built and generally of a much better standard than in the rural areas. The garden city movement had some influence on local builders, like Saltmarsh. Nevertheless terraces of four to six houses were the norm. There was a variation in the types of houses built to reflect the differing circumstances of the tenants. Many of those on the salaried staff at Hoffmann's, during its early years before the first war, lived in the bigger third and four bedroom houses in Mildmay Road. Some of the smaller terraced houses for example, in the lower part of Roman Road, had no front gardens. The rapid growth in Chelmsford's population in the decades before the first war led to the first demands for council housing in the borough. (3) Overcrowding, despite the tireless work of the inspectors, was an increasing problem in the town (see also chapter 17). Although by the end of the century the average number of people per dwelling was 4.5, many houses had a much larger number living in them. In 1899 Arthur Lunney, soon to be a councillor, was pressing for the overcrowding problem to be tackled. (4) He cited the case of one house with four families living in it, but refused to say where the house was. Chancellor doubted the veracity of the story.

In the rural area the problem of overcrowding was as bad, if not worse. At Highwood near Writtle, Dr Thresh identified a house where "in one small one storied house, live the father, mother, married son and wife, two adult sons, one adult daughter and three girls of school age; besides these there were often as many as three men lodgers ". Thresh went on to say "if we take legal proceedings the people turned out will be compelled to move into some other house already fully occupied, and the final condition may be worse". (5) At Little Baddow many cottages remained overcrowded in the early years of the twentieth century, despite the fall in the village's population. (6) All the villages had very few people who owned their own house. In Howe Green, part of the parish of Great Waltham, for example, there was only one house owner, the local landowner Colonel Tufnell (7) The so-called 'Champagne' sales of the Champions estate brought owners of houses to Woodham Ferris, but this was comparatively rare. (8) Thresh initially had doubts whether the Act of 1890 could be used to produce the necessary housing, but by the turn of the century he saw that it might offer at least a partial solution.

Meanwhile in the borough, the council set up a sub-committee in 1900 to look into providing dwellings for the working-classes. (9) A scheme was produced for 10 to 12 dwellings each containing front and back rooms, a scullery and three bedrooms. The full council however, decided not to take up the committee's recommendations. (10) Having given up issuing notices on the houses in Union Yard, the council tried to use the 1890 Act in order to carry out improvements, but the Local Government Board refused permission. (11) Three years later the borough considered using the 1899 Small Dwellings Act, which allowed councils to loan money to enable people to buy houses but this was rejected as being unfeasible. (12) In 1910 the shortage of houses forced the council to consider a new scheme in which 20 dwellings were to be built on land off Moulsham Street. The houses were not to include baths as it was felt that they would only be used for storing coal! Rents should be set no higher than six shillings and sixpence, so that the poorer classes could afford them. (13) Lunney hailed the scheme as "the best thing that had ever happened in Chelmsford" but the L.G.B. declined to approve it. The editor of the Weekly News pointed out that the rent level would be well beyond families receiving eighteen to twenty shillings a week in income. (14) This was at a time when rents generally took about one ninth of the average family's earnings. Another site was briefly considered off Goldlay Road but eventually a proposal was accepted to build thirty eight cottages in Rainsford End and the Council applied to the L.G.B. to borrow £7,000. (15) After an inspector from the Board visited the town and looked at the plans, the scheme was accepted and the following year 14 firms put forward tenders. (16) Plans for 8 more houses in Lady Lane were submitted. (17) Meanwhile Hoffmann asked for some of the Rainsford Lane houses to be reserved specifically for their workers, but the council refused, saying that applications would be invited at a later date. (18) All the applicants for the first Rainsford Lane houses, let at four shillings and sixpence a week, were on a weekly wage of between fifteen and twenty seven shillings. (19) A new scheme for further houses in Rainsford Lane resulted in a total of 106 cottages being built before the war. All were let by the time the war broke out. (20) As early as April 1913 rent arrears were being built up by some tenants because of the strike at the Hoffmann Company. (21)

In the rural area, as early as 1893 the then Rural Sanitary Authority identified certain parishes, particularly Good Easter, as needing working class dwellings. (22) Thresh said the District Council should consider using the 1890 Act to improve those cottages that were in a considerable state of disrepair. (23) Six years later after an investigation into the cottages of Little Waltham he noted that elsewhere, where authorities had erected working class dwellings, they cost more than those built by private firms and the rents were more than the agricultural labourers could afford. (24) By 1917 however, the housing committee was reporting that cottages were needed in "a great many parishes". It identified two types of cottages that were needed; those with 3 bedrooms and two good living rooms for families, and one storied cottages with three rooms, which would be suitable for young married couples and old age pensioners. (25) A scheme was drawn up a year later for a total of 16 cottages spread between the three parishes of Little Baddow, Danbury and Sandon. Whilst these were being built further land for council house building was acquired in Runwell and Roxwell. (26)

These early cottages were built in pairs even though the L.G.B. had suggested blocks of four or six. Rent levels were set at four shillings and nine pence for the larger houses and three and nine pence for the smaller ones. The Rural District Council agreed to pay all the rates on each house. (27) Before the outbreak of the war the Council was looking at further sites in East Hanningfield and Stock. (28)

During the Great War, billets were found for six thousand men in the town (see chapter 15), but as early as 1917 the borough council decided that working class housing was going to be a pressing issue after the war. (29) Many of the new influx of workers into the town had families, unlike the soldiers who were on their own. The council were already coming under pressure from the local Trades Council. In view of the national 'Homes Fit For Heroes' campaign, a big post war local scheme was always likely. (30) An initial scheme submitted to the L.G.B. in 1918 for 1,000 houses, was criticised for being too rushed. After liaising with the big firms in the town, the council was concerned that married men with families, particularly skilled mechanics, wouldn't move to the town unless they had a house ready to be occupied. The council's intended purchase of land in Springfield was opposed by local residents who didn't want council houses close to them. (31) After the Council had originally voted to purchase the Springfield site, it eventually opted for a site at Boarded Barns. Purchase of the farm and existing buildings cost just over £12,000. The layout of the scheme was heavily influenced by the 'Garden City' movement of Ebenezer Howard and Raymond Unwin, for example the tree lined North Avenue. In the council the vote was very close, the motion only being passed on the casting vote of the mayor, because many of the town's traders, who made up the majority of the town's councillors, were still worried about the expense on the rates and increased council debt. (32) In July 1919 the Ministry of Health approved the layout of the houses in the Boarded Barns scheme. Two bedrooms and the living room in each house were to have a sunny aspect. Access to the coal shed and the water closet was to be under cover. Further land had to be acquired from Wells and Perry for the whole scheme to be completed. The council houses were very popular with their new occupants, which contrasted with the general poor view of the condition of the same houses half a century later. In the meantime, the pressing need for temporary housing led to very serious consideration being given to using the prison, which had been used as a hostel since the start of the war. Surprisingly the letter columns of the local papers show that a number of people were desperate enough to use the cells voluntarily! (33) The council eventually declined to go ahead with using it and also refused the offer of wartime hutments. It received a letter from the Chelmsford branch of the National Federation of Discharged and Demobilised Prisoners asking for preferential treatment in applications for council houses. The council, unwilling to set a precedent, avoided giving a positive reply. (34)

The Ministry of Health allowed the borough to obtain a loan for a further 72 houses on the estate and the council approached the big three firms for a loan. Marconi and Crompton agreed immediately; Hoffmann delayed a response but eventually agreed. (35) Although Marconi announced the formation of a public utility company to build houses for their workers, this was not followed up until after the second war. Chelmsford Borough Council said they wouldn't consider selling any part of the Boarded Barns estate to the firms. (36)

The Borough Council, concerned at the slow rate of progress on the Boarded Barns estate, used the 1919 Addison Housing Act to make sure that other building work, in particular the cinema at Rainsford Road and a bank at Tindal Square, didn't interfere any further with the rate of building. (37) At the end of 1920 the three building firms involved said they were having problems obtaining bricks. (38) By May 1921 only 37 houses had been built in the previous year. (39) Much more progress was made the following year and by May 1922 146 houses had been completed and 118 nearly completed, out of a total of 260. (40) Then, as elsewhere, the effect of the national Geddes Axe on public spending stopped all building of council houses in Chelmsford. At the end of 1923 the council received Ministry of Health approval to use the new subsidy scheme to sell Boarded Barns land to builders. This scheme covered a further 150 houses and was followed by a further scheme for 250 houses in 1924. (41) In the same year the council made the first of a number of requests to the Ministry of Health to reduce rent levels because of the recession that was hitting the town's industry. (42) The housing shortage was still such that the council gave serious consideration to erecting Athol steel houses. (43) By 1929 there were 629 council houses being built, with another 226 under contract. (44)

After the first war the borough had 150 houses that could not be made fit to live in and 300 that could be improved and made habitable. The development of more effective damp courses made it possible to insert them into the latter type of house. (45) Four houses in Griggs Yard were demolished in 1927. (46) In 1929 a further 31 houses were demolished in New Writtle Street and Griggs Yard but there remained 50 still only fit for demolition. (47) The council were taking advantage of increased powers to demolish unfit houses. Already improved facilities were being demanded and in 1920 baths were fitted in the Rainsford End council houses. (48)

The R.D.C. received permission from the Ministry of Health to acquire 9 sites for building. It was looking to build 500 houses compared with the borough's 1,000. (49) There was often a big difference in the tenders for the new council houses. In Boreham for example, there was a gap of £3,000 on two tenders but usually the lowest tender was accepted. (50) Often only one tender was put forward however, which put the R.D.C. in a difficult position. Increasingly the council sought and obtained a reduction in tenders. Another problem was rent levels. In 1920 the Ministry of Health wouldn't accept the level of rents the District Council wanted to charge for houses at Sandon. (51) Eventually the Ministry accepted the low rent of seven shillings and sixpence, on the understanding that the houses were allocated to agricultural labourers. (52) As with the Borough Council, the Ministry repeatedly refused the District Council's requests for a reduction in rents. The rent levels did vary from village to village. Those where many workers worked in Chelmsford tended to have higher levels of rent. In Good Easter the smaller council houses were six shillings a week, compared with eight and six pence in Margaretting and eleven shillings in Writtle. (53) Those without a parlour were cheaper than those with one. As with the borough, the district council was under increasing pressure to provide better facilities in its council houses. In 1922 gas mains were laid to council houses in Great Baddow and Writtle. (54) Also, as in the borough, the new scheme enabled the district council to get rid of the worst of its houses. Nineteen were demolished in 1922. (55) The 1924 Wheatley Act, passed under the short lived Labour government, enabled the R.D.C., like the borough, to take advantage of higher subsidies and increase house building. There was however, a similar shortage of workers and materials. In 1920 the Housing Commissioner refused to allow the authority to use artificial tiles. (56) By 1927, 354 council houses had been built or started in the rural area. (57) Subsidy payments were only made to the building firms after water and pavement certificates had been granted. (58) In 1926 the District Valuer was involved in fixing the value of the land that the rural authority purchased. (59)

By 1931 the corporation had built three thousand council houses in twenty years. (60) If the total did not compare with places like Norwich and Ipswich, where the Labour Council built four thousand houses between 1918 and 1939, this was still an impressive total. The depression resulted in the period of subsidies to council housing coming to an end. In Chelmsford the 1930s saw a revival in private house building for owner occupiers, with low house prices and mortgage rates making the acquisition of a house a realistic aspiration for middle class families. Privately built working class housing in Moulsham in the early part of the century, (see chapter 11), was supplanted by middle class housing in roads like Rothesay Avenue and Finchley Avenue. (61) In these roads were a mixture of semi detached houses, detached houses and bungalows with no overriding layout; in all of these gas and electricity were considered essential.

In 1936 all 236 houses built in the borough were private houses. (62) Before the second war the Corporation was considering substantial further council housing with land being bought, in what became the Melbourne estate. (63) It was originally envisaged that part of the estate would be private houses. A council housing scheme was started and completed in Widford before the outbreak of war. (64)

In the rural area, like the town, comparatively few council houses were built in the 1930s. The R.D.C. did however establish a slum clearance committee, and demolitions enabled them to build a few more council houses, because they satisfied government criteria. Most of the new houses were specifically for re-housing. By 1936 the district council was considering five areas for slum clearance and made use of compulsory purchase orders e.g. in East Hanningfield. (65) Rent reductions were finally allowed for agricultural labourers just before the start of the war. (66) When war broke out a few council houses were being built in Springfield and Writtle, house building was about to start in Chignal and demolitions were proceeding apace. (67) (68)

As during the Great War, plans for post war housing were well advanced before the end of the second war. In the town, although the degree of destruction didn't match that in the major cities, it was still sufficient to require considerable rebuilding. This, along with the continued growth of the population, because of the rapid expansion of the town's firms during the war, ensured that the provision of housing was a key issue in the minds of the town's voters in the parliamentary and municipal elections at the end of the war. An early version of the Corporation's scheme in 1943 estimated that 500 houses would be needed. Over half of these came directly from estimates the big three firms gave for the number of houses their workers would need. (69) Before the end of the war the borough council submitted a scheme to the Ministry of Health, which included houses on Upper Bridge Road, Rainsford Lane and on the Melbourne estate. (70) At the end of 1944 the Corporation made a decision to erect 150 factory made houses at Barnes Mill, rather than on the Springfield estate. (71) During the second war 283 houses were demolished and 476 badly damaged.

By 1945 the borough owned land sufficient to build 1,300 houses, but the acute shortage of materials and labour forced it to look at various types of prefabs, including those made by the British Iron and Steel Federation (B.I.S.F.). (72) These were to be temporary, but the council did decide to build 70 permanent Duplex houses for pairs of families. (73) The new Labour council resolved to use direct labour to try to speed up building and also put a veto on private house building. (74) (75) Chelmsford Corporation declined to give special assistance to the Hoffmann Housing Association because of the pressure to build houses from all sides. (76) A hundred B.I.S.F. houses were put up, with the workers staying in the Y.M.C.A. By September 1946, 58 Duplex flats had been occupied but the contractors on the Melbourne Park estate were finding it impossible to find billets for their workers. (77) In August 1946 the Borough's waiting list was already up above 2,300. (78) Many of those who would have been homeless were living with their in-laws. Chelmsford Borough Council had declined the offer by the military authorities of using the wartime huts on the Recreation Ground, but by then they were occupied by increasingly desperate squatters. The Marconi Company told the council it was finding it increasingly difficult to meet the Government's required output targets, because of the housing shortage. They had 500 workers requiring accommodation, 250 of which were urgent cases. (79) Marconi, through its Kingsway Housing Association, wanted to build a number of traditional houses, supplemented by some prefabricated ones. The council regretted that this would not be possible because of the lack of available labour. A few months later the big 3 put forward a new scheme, which would entail 100 prefabs. of the Arcon type on the Patching Hall estate and this time the council agreed. (80) By 1947 402 houses were under construction in the borough, only 79 of which were being privately built. (81) During these early post war years the borough's house building record compared with any town of its size in the country. This didn't prevent consistent accusations of profiteering by local building firms, especially when it came to war damage repairs. On one notable occasion the borough engineer refused to pass on one builder's cheque to the council because he considered it so extortionate. (82) The borough increasingly complained about the restricted quota of houses allowed for the town by the government. By 1949 the rate of house building had slowed markedly to the consternation of an increasingly angry local public. Less than half the number of houses was built compared with the previous year. (83) The borough turned to another type of prefab., Easiform houses, which were being recommended by the government. Twenty were erected in Chignall. (84) Aluminium houses, made in Braintree, had already been put up on the Melbourne estate. (85) The continued housing difficulties were a principal reason for defeats in Chelmsford for the Labour Party in the parliamentary and municipal elections, but national circumstances meant it was virtually impossible for any local party administration to have achieved much better results.

The housing problems, although severe, would have been virtually impossible if the rural area hadn't come to the rescue. At their peak occupation, the previously, military huts at Boreham, Roxwell and Gibcracks at Danbury provided homes for over two thousand people, most of them from the town. Boreham airfield had been empty since the American planes had left in 1944, leaving 212 Nissen huts (see chapter 24). Initially the government didn't think they would be suitable as social housing but the sheer scale of the housing problem soon changed their minds. Squatters soon took matters into their own hands, but at first they had to do without basic facilities such as running water and electricity. (86) Some worked for Hoffmann and one person who was interviewed was employed by the Gas Board. He and his family moved in with camp beds but no furniture. (87) Their first meal was cooked outside. All water had to be collected at the local farm. The father contacted the district council saying he wanted to pay rent to make his family's occupation official and they agreed. In October 1946 the district council took control of 150 of the hutments at Boreham and converted them. First of all they partitioned the long huts to make them suitable for families; then they installed electricity and cooking stoves. After the very cold winter of 1947, the snow thawed very quickly and the gas worker's family woke up to find their bed and possessions floating. Another occupant, Jean Hunwick and her husband, used Utility furniture to make some sort of home and paid ten shillings a week in rent. (88) She said that other occupants there included surveyors, policemen and artisans. A. Piska, who had come to England to escape the Czech Communist Party and had flown with the R.A.F. in the war, was offered a hut at Boreham. It was cold and unfurnished but he managed to buy a few pieces of furniture with money given by a R.A.F. association. John Trusler moved to the airfield in 1949 when he was four years old. Trusler had to get a coach to travel to Boreham School, which was put under pressure to accommodate an increased number of pupils. He and his family were still there for the Coronation, when several families crowded into one of the rooms in the community centre to watch the ceremony on a television. Another boy took the eleven plus exam and went to K.E.G.S. Olivia Hale and her husband were married in 1950 when they both worked at Marconi, New Street. Whilst at the airfield they bought their first car for £65. When she became pregnant in 1953 they moved out to a house on the Melbourne Park estate, after being on the waiting list for three years. (89) A Mrs Manning arrived at the airfield after being evicted by a Rettendon farmer, who needed accommodation for his workers. She came with her father, who worked for Eastern National and after living in one big room they moved into a smaller hut divided into two bedrooms and a living area. Initially there was no water, with a tin bath once a week. Boreham's NAFFI and mess rooms were also used for housing, but part of the hospital block was used for a community centre. (90) The R.D.C. managed to get Eastern National to provide a bus service into town. (91) Other facilities that were added included permanent shops, mobile shops, a telephone box and a welfare clinic.

Roxwell Labour Camp was also wanted for temporary housing but it was initially to be turned over to a manufacturing firm. Again the housing crisis forced the Ministry of Health to change its mind. (92) Roxwell's huts were partitioned and occupied by the end of 1946. (93) Chelmsford Borough Council then took over huts at the military camp at Roxwell and at Gibcracks in Danbury in 1947. (94)

Despite occasional complaints that the camps were unsafe for children, no attempt was made to reduce the use of the huts until 1950. In 1953, 291 of the huts on the four sites were still occupied. (95) All the huts were not demolished at Boreham airfield until 1958. (96) The final hut at Gibcracks was not removed until 1961. (97)

The rural area faced the same post-war housing shortage as the borough, even though it managed to build a few cottages during the war for agricultural labourers. Chelmsford R.D.C. built large numbers of permanent, prefabricated Airey houses, which were to cause serious problems thirty years later. At the time however, they were favoured because they could be erected quickly. The authority turned down the government's offer of Swedish timber houses. (98) By 1949 218 Airey houses had been built since the war in the rural district, compared with only 82 traditional houses and 90 temporary prefabricated bungalows. (99)

In the borough, prefabs. were the first houses to be built in Queensland Crescent on the Melbourne Park estate, after prisoners of war had helped to build the roads. They were followed on the estate by steel houses and only later by brick houses. The only shops were in Kings Road and a parade of shops wasn't built for the Melbourne estate until the early 1950s. The idea of providing neighbourhood shops was slow to catch on in the borough.

In 1948 houses had been fully built along Mousham Drive in the southern part of the borough, but there were still no houses built around the Moulsham schools the other side of Princes Road, which became the Mousham Lodge estate. This estate had been built by 1960, as had the Tile Kiln estate. The Melbourne estate, in the northern part of the borough, mentioned in the previous paragraph, had been started but not finished in 1948. It had been completed by 1960.

The Chelmsford Borough Council passed the total of two thousand houses built since the war in 1953. (100) At the same time over one thousand council houses were under contract. During the year 370 council houses were built. (101) Better economic conditions nationally made it easier for houses to be constructed. New council houses were built on the Westlands and Woodhall estates and more prefabs on the Barnes Mill estate, but land was becoming increasingly in short supply, forcing up the prices the borough had to pay. Land at Moulsham Lodge was subject to a compulsory purchase order. (102) There was already very little land available for residential development in Springfield. The continuing housing shortage was the reason 380 of the 685 council houses that were built in the borough in 1954, were of non traditional types. (103) Again local industry expressed concern that the housing shortage was a threat to the town's prosperity. (104) Council houses were offered for sale in the 1950s but there were few actual sales.

The shortage of space led to the building of Chelmsford's only multi-storey block of flats. It was designed to be part of a mixed development usually associated with Corbusier. Initially the borough had a choice between a ten storey block and a fifteen storey one. The lower one would be more economical, but the taller one would receive a higher rate of subsidy. (105) In the event the latter was chosen in 1959. Four years earlier the Weekly News had expressed concern that the need to take some of London's overspill population would lead to Chelmsford becoming a town of skyscrapers. (106) After the building of Melbourne Court all attempts to build multi-storey blocks floundered because of opposition. A concerted campaign in the local parish prevented a tall block of flats being built in Great Baddow in 1962. (107) As happened elsewhere, the disaster at Ronan Court, Newham, removed any remaining pressure to build tall tower blocks of flats. Melbourne Court was opened in July 1962 at a cost of £250,000. It was 150 foot tall and provided 58 flats. "From the fifteenth floor on a clear day you could see Bradwell." (108)

Council house building had slowed to a trickle by the mid 1950s, which followed a national trend. In 1956, although 3,500 houses had been built since the war, only 62 were currently being built. (109) There was much criticism of the Conservative council, for not being willing to build further council houses. Similar concerns were being expressed a decade later when Alderman Richardson said plans to cut down council building would drive industry away from the town. (110) The Marconi

Company did its best to lessen the accommodation difficulties through its Kingsway Housing Association. This built 150 houses in the early 1950s in Baddow. (111) It went on to build further houses in Dorset Avenue, Great Baddow in the late 1950s and early 1960s and two blocks of flats in Noakes End. (112) The firm made this consistent effort, because although there were an increasing number of privately built houses for sale, the majority of Marconi workers could not afford to buy them.

Chelmsford's continued housing shortage and the attachment to them of many residents, ensured that a considerable number of prefabs. remained, both in the town and the rural area. Indeed once the sale of council houses gained momentum in the 1970s some residents obtained mortgages on permanent prefabs.. Sixty eight prefabs. remained in the town in 1969. (113) In 1974 the borough recommended them for use by the homeless. (114) By 1985 the B.I.S.F. houses in North Melbourne were being modernised to further extend their use. (115) In 2001 owners were selling their 'unique' bungalows made from aircraft fuselages! Owners of prefabs. in Beeches Road did not want preservation orders put on them because they feared this might depress prices, when they were looking forward to getting £70,000 for them! (116)

In 1968 the borough decided to sell council houses, but again there were initially few takers. (117) A new scheme was put into action in 1971 with a maximum of 10% reduction in prices, but this was doubled to 20% in 1977. (118) (119) During 1979 some council houses were being sold for half price in a fulfilment of the Conservatives election pledge. (120) By 1986 approaching two and a half thousand council houses had been sold in the borough.

In the early 1970s the first council houses, in both the borough and the rural area, were beginning to show signs of age. During 1971 a borough councillor said that the early estates could be slums within ten years. (121) Many of these houses were still lacking basic facilities. In 1973 one in seven council tenants were without exclusive use of hot water, a fixed bath or shower, or inside flush toilets. (122) The first stage of a £9 million modernisation programme for the Boarded Barns estate was approved in 1973, but this was subject to numerous delays, resulting in parts of the estate, particularly Tennyson Road, being described as Chelmsford's most deprived area. (123) It was then decided that some of the houses had to be pulled down. At the same time another estate, the 'Cornish' Woodhall, was described as being "mildew ridden" by the local politician Stuart Mole. (124) Tenants at Boarded Barns had to be re-housed and the government initially deemed the scheme too expensive. (125) The following year residents and trade unionists were complaining of '"the shoddy work" being carried out on those homes being improved. (126) Ten years after the first phase of the Boarded Barns improvements had started, Phase 11 had still to commence. (127) The 1970s saw a further reduction in the number of council houses built, largely due to changing council attitudes towards them. In contrast there was a boom in private house building in the early 1970s, with upwards of 300 built each year, but then private developers began to suffer from the same shortage of land as the council had earlier. A housing shortage led to rises in the housing waiting lists in both the borough and rural areas. The new private housing boom in North Melbourne and East and North Springfield eased the situation. (129) By 1989 a great deal of private house building had occurred in Springfield in the area between Pump Lane and White Hart Lane. The Chelmer Village area which had been completely rural in 1960 was now fully built up.

In 1985 however there were still 2,000 on the council waiting list. The expanded borough had ten thousand council houses. (130) Housing associations such as Springboard, which developed a site in Chelmer village, began to play an increasing role, especially in sheltered housing and housing for the handicapped. The setting up of co-operatives on the part of tenants, which were successful elsewhere in the mid 1970s, was not supported by the council.

After the tireless efforts of Joan Bliss, a four bedroomed women's refuge was set up by the Chelmsford Women's Aid Group in 1990. (131) The refuge celebrated its twentieth anniversary in the new millennium. (132) High rents and a lack of council houses led to an increase in the number of homeless in the town. The number without homes was exceeding the 150 council houses being built. A proposed hostel for the homeless was opposed by some residents in Moulsham in 1996, but one was eventually established in George Street. (133) The recent recession had led to a revival in the number of homeless in the new city and made them an increasingly visible problem, especially in Moulsham Street.

Many of the remaining council houses had serious defects by the 1980s. The concrete pillars of the Airey houses were found to have deteriorated. (134) At the same time un-modernised Boarded Barns homes were offered to would be owners at £10,000. The estate was certainly run down and 450 out of 659 people who responded to a survey of residents were unemployed in 1994. (135) In a new £23 million plan, 288 of the original houses were to be scrapped and replaced by 227 two and three bedroomed houses and two bedroomed bungalows. These would be built by a housing association for rent or part purchase. In the next few years those people that remained had to endure squalid conditions and were at the mercy of vandals, thieves and dumpers. The first bulldozers moved into Browning Avenue in 1996. (136) Plans to demolish a large number of houses in the second phase of the scheme were changed to improving and refurbishing the majority of the existing houses. (137)

Increasingly the council was an enabler rather than a provider of homes; making land available to housing associations at no cost and with a local authority grant. (138) The council eventually decided in 2000 to offload the running of its existing council houses. It proposed to transfer the entire council housing stock of 7,300 homes to a social landlord in a deal worth £89 million. The council said it could not afford the £40 million needed to bring the houses up to twenty first century standards, while keeping rents at a fair level. Tenants were to have a greater role in managing the estates. (139) At the time the tenants voted on the transfer, the modernisation of Boarded Barns was at a standstill, with no money available and the waiting list up to 4,000. (140) The transfer of the council houses went through in 2002. After the completion of the Boarded Barns modernisation, the Melbourne estate including Melbourne Court was upgraded by the non-for-profit housing association. (141)

As we have seen in chapter 12, by the year 2000 private house building, encouraged by several Essex plans, was stretching the areas land and essential services to breaking point. This led to the plan for an extra 2,000 houses at Boreham being abandoned. The need for new houses continually came up against the desire to protect the green belt. Plans published since 2005 included a new neighbourhood to the N.E. of Springfield, but also an alternative which would allow new houses in villages like Broomfield, Boreham and Little Baddow. (142) At the time of writing the need to provide adequate services is the major obstacle to a major new development at Beaulieu Park (see chapter 12).

Interestingly a few of the post-war prefabs. still remain in the new millennium. Some of these are the aluminium BL8 homes built by Hawker Siddeley in Gloucester and erected in Beeches Road. Gladys and Neville Harding are still in one having moved in during 1954. "I thought it was a wonderful house when I arrived because it came with a fridge and cooker, which was extremely rare at the time." They bought the house in the 1980s. "It still gets very warm in the summer and cold in the winter." During 2009 one of these bungalows was on the market for £149,950 to cash buyers with no mortgages available. (143) In terms of housing as a whole in the city, homes in Goat Hall, Galleywood, can fetch £1 million whereas the cheaper houses tend to be found on ex-council estates such as at Melbourne and Westlands. (144)

1) Chelmsford Borough Council minutes 27 9 1893
2) Essex Review Vol. 1 p.31
3) Chelmsford Council Housing Between the Wars S. Duggan 1918 – 1939 p.1
4) Essex Weekly News 28 4 1899
5) E.W.N. 27 3 1891 p.6
6) Sheila Rowley Little Baddow
7) An Edwardian Hamlet Howe Street in Great Waltham 1901 – 1910 Alan Maddock p.97
8) A History of South Woodham Ferrers
9) C.B.C. minutes 28 3 1900
10) C.B.C. minutes 26 3 1902
11) C.B.C. minutes 26 9 1906
12) C.B.C. minutes 31 3 1909
13) E.W.N. 29 7 1910 p.5
14) E.W.N. 2 12 1910 p.4
15) E.W.N. 29 9 1911 p.6
16) C.B.C. minutes 27 3 1912 p.377
17) C.B.C. minutes 29 5 1912
18) C.B.C. minutes 26 6 1912
19) C.B.C. minutes 29 1 1913
20) C.B.C. minutes 9 11 1914
21) C.B.C. minutes 30 4 1913
22) Chelmsford Rural Sanitary Authority minutes 25 4 1893
23) Chelmsford Rural District Council minutes 1 9 1903
24) C.R.D.C. minutes 18 5 1909 p.131-2
25) C.R.D.C. Housing committee minutes 1911 p.21
26) C.R.D.C. minutes 6 8 1912
27) C.R.D.C. minutes 20 1 1914 p.152
28) C.R.D.C. minutes 3 2 1914
29) C.R.D.C. minutes 29 8 1917
30) E.W.N. 31 8 1917
31) C.B.C. minutes 29 1 1919
32) C.B.C. minutes 30 4 1919
33) C.B.C. minutes 30 7 1919
34) C.B.C. minutes 26 11 1919

35) C.B.C. minutes 26 5 1920
36) C.B.C. minutes 30 4 1920
37) C.B.C. minutes 30 6 1920
38) C.B.C. minutes 21 3 1921
39) C.B.C. minutes 25 5 1921
40) C.B.C. minutes 31 5 1922
41) C.B.C. minutes 30 4 1924
42) C.B.C. minutes 30 1 1924
43) C.B.C. minutes 20 3 1925
44) C.B.C. minutes 25 9 1929
45) C.B.C. minutes 26 5 1920
46) C.B.C. minutes 30 11 1927
47) C.B.C. minutes 30 10 1929
48) C.B.C. minutes 26 1 1921
49) C.R.D.C. minutes 16 12 1919 p.69
50) C.R.D.C. minutes 1 7 1920 p.196
51) C.R.D. C. minutes 1 10 1920
52) C.R.D.C. minutes 22 10 1922
53) C.R.D.C. minutes 29 4 1921
54) C.R.D.C. minutes 27 6 1922
55) C.R.D.C. minutes 25 7 1922
56) C.R.D.C. minutes 30 11 1920
57) C.R.D.C. minutes 25 1 1927 p.732
58) C.R.D.C. minutes 19 4 1927 p.33
59) C.R.D.C. minutes 18 5 1926
60) C.B.C. minutes 27 5 1931
61) Ordnance survey map 1939
62) C.B.C. minutes 28 8 1936
63) C.B.C. minutes 30 12 1936
64) C.B.C. minutes 30 3 1938
65) C.R.D.C. minutes 27 10 1936
66) C.R.D.C. minutes 25 4 1939
67) C.R.D.C. minutes 16 5 1939
68) C.R.D.C. minutes 15 8 1939
69) C.B.C. minutes 27 1 1943

70) C.B.C. minutes 26 5 1943
71) C.B.C. minutes 15 12 1944
72) C.B.C. minutes 16 5 1946
73) C.B.C. minutes 28 11 1945
74) C.B.C. minutes 26 6 1946
75) Essex Chronicle 26 4 1946
76) C.B.C. minutes 26 6 1946
77) C.B.C. minutes 25 9 1946
78) C.B.C. minutes 28 8 1946
79) C.B.C. minutes 30 12 1946
80) C.B.C. minutes 26 2 1947
81) C.B.C. minutes 30 4 1947
82) E.C. 3 1 1947
83) C.B.C. minutes 25 1 1950
84) C.B.C. minutes 28 11 1951
85) E.C. 4 7 1947
86) Ericprobert.pwp.blueyonder.co.uk
87) C. Museums records
88) C. Museums records
89) C. Museums records
90) C.R.D.C. minutes 26 11 1946
91) C.R.D.C. minutes 17 12 1946
92) C.R.D.C. minutes 27 8 1948 p.198
93) C.R.D.C. minutes 17 12 1946 p.511
94) C.R.D.C. minutes 25 2 1947 p.625
95) C.R.D.C. minutes 17 3 1953
96) C.R.D.C. minutes 11 1958
97) C.R.D.C. minutes 9 5 1961
98) C.R.D.C. minutes 17 7 1945
99) C.R.D.C. minutes 11 4 1949 p. 12
100) C.B.C. minutes 25 3 1953
101) C.B.C. minutes 27 1 1954
102) C.B.C. minutes 31 3 1954
103) C.B.C. minutes 27 12 1954
104) E.W.N. 27 1 1956

105) C.B.C. minutes 30 9 1959
106) E.W.N. 30 12 1955 p.4
107) C.B.C. minutes 27 3 1962
108) E.W.N. 20 7 1962 p.4
109) E.W.N. 27 4 1956
110) E.W.N. 11 10 1968 p.1
111) C.R.D.C. minutes 16 5 1950
112) C.R.D.C. minutes 10 11 1959
113) E.W.N. 5 7 1979
114) C.B.C. minutes 6 2 1974
115) C.B.C. minutes 10 9 1985
116) E.C. 16 3 2001 p.21
117) E.C. 3 10 1969
118) E.C. 26 3 1971
119) E.C. 23 12 1977 p.1
120) E.C. 5 12 1986
121) E.C. 10 1 1971 p.1
122) E.C. 26 1 1973 p.3
123) E.C. 16 7 1976 p.1
124) E.C. 27 1 1978 p.1
125) E.W.N. 9 1 1975 p.1
126) E.W.N. 12 2 1976 p.5
127) C.B.C. minutes 6 12 1983
128) E.W.N. 14 3 1974 p.1
129) E.W.N. 17 11 1977 p.3
130) E.W.N. 30 5 1985 p.1
131) C.B.C. minutes 17 1 1990
132) E.C. 4 1 2002
133) C.B.C. minutes 1996
134) E.C. 12 3 1982 p.1
135) E.C. 25 11 1994 p.1
136) E.W.N. 26 9 1996
137) E.C. 31 7 1998
138) E.C. 7 5 1993 p.3
139) E.C. 17 4 200 p.1

140) E.C. 20 10 2000 p.9
141) E.C. 4 2 2010 p.7
142) E.W.N. 13 10 2005 p.3
143) E.C. 13 10 2009 p.13
144) E.C. 22 4 2010 p.18

19

The Chelmsford Union Poor Law

"Chained to a workhouse wall"

At the beginning of the 1880s attitudes to the Poor Law in Chelmsford, as elsewhere, were imbued with the idea that there was no real reason that adults should be unemployed. Forty years later the industrialisation of the town had led to a change in attitudes, both of the elected Poor Law guardians and the general townsfolk. It was realised that the large numbers of workers in the town's big factories were prey at regular intervals to the vagaries of the business cycle.

The Chelmsford Poor Law Union in the 1880s dated back to the 1834 Poor Law Amendment Act. The Act was originally intended to abolish the giving of outdoor relief i.e. outside the workhouse, to paupers. Under the principle of 'less eligibility' the relief given inside the new workhouses was intended to be slightly worse than the lowest independent worker could obtain. The workhouse was supposed to be a forbidding place with its high walls, rigid separation of the sexes and different types of poor people, and dull monotonous work for the able bodied pauper. Nationally the landscape had changed considerably by the 1880s. The scandal at Andover in 1847, where inmates were forced by their starvation rations to gnaw at the bones they were supposed to be crushing for fertiliser, caused an outcry when exposed in the Times. Afterwards relief was increasingly allowed outside the workhouse and under the Labour Test the able paupers were supposed to be put to work in the local community by the relieving officers. Those being given relief outside the workhouse were to be given at least half in food and kind if they were able bodied and one third if they were women, sick or aged. The relaxation of the rules led to a reaction in the 1860s because of the increased cost of the system and it was still felt by most people that pauperism was the result of idleness and lack of character. This view was underpinned by classical economics that maintained there was no inherent reason for unemployment. In the mid Victorian period there was an increasing distinction made between the deserving poor, who included the aged and infirm, and the undeserving poor. A great number of charitable societies grew up to help the former, dominated eventually by the Charity Organisation Society. The C.O.S. failed to get a hold in the Chelmsford area.

The Chelmsford Poor Law Union was a small one by Victorian city standards. By 1900 the Union covered both the area of the Borough and the R.D.C.; it consisted of 31 parishes represented by 38 elected and voluntary guardians as shown below.

Great Baddow, Little Baddow, Boreham, Broomfield, Buttsbury, Chelmsford, Chignal, Danbury, Good Easter, High Easter, Fryerning, East Hanningfield, South Hanningfield, West Hanningfield, Ingatestone, Great Leighs, Little Leighs, Margaretting, Mashbury, Pleshey, Rettendon, Roxwell, Runwell, Sandon, Springfield, Stock, Great Waltham, Little Waltham, Widford, Woodham Ferris, Writtle (1)

Chelmsford borough had six elected guardians and consistently felt it was underrepresented, especially when the vexed question of rateable values came up. By the 1880s elections for guardians were frequently not contested in certain parishes and voting in those that were, was normally very low. The guardians were dominated by well off tradesmen and landowners, with normally one or two vicars. Despite the lack of interest in the elections, there is plenty of evidence to suggest that most of the guardians in the Chelmsford area were diligent in what was voluntary work. There is nothing to show that the sort of corruption that occurred in cities was a common practice in Chelmsford. In the former, owners of large tenements, whose tenants were receiving relief, were often guardians. The meetings often lasted for three hours and most of the guardians knew that they also had to attend a meeting of the R.D.C., which usually followed at the workhouse boardroom. Guardians regularly went to conferences and visited the county lunatic asylum and other workhouses. This was in addition to the normal work of inspecting the workhouse, vetting applicants for outdoor relief, interviewing would-be staff and checking the tenders for bread, meat, and coal etc. Many guardians served for a large part of their adult lives. When Fred Marriage became chairman of the local assistance committee in 1930, after the break-up of the poor law union, he had already been a guardian for 40 years. Algar and Corder, who were both chairmen of the board in the late nineteenth century, achieved a similar length of service. The overwhelming view of the local guardians in the late 19th and early 20th century was that work was character forming and that as little encouragement as possible should be given to the undeserving poor. Although most charity work seems to have been for foreign missions in Chelmsford, the guardians didn't forget those in the workhouse at Christmas. In 1894 for example, the wives of councillors and guardians helped with the carving of the Christmas dinner, with tobacco and beer being provided by the guardians. At New Year a free hot dinner was given to the aged poor. (2) In 1901, 300 pounds of beef, pork and mutton were provided for the Christmas dinner plus an equal weight of plum pudding. (3) Increasingly there were occasional trips out: in 1914 A.R.P. Hickley, the town's first Labour councillor, put on a Christmas trip to his Picture Palace (later the Select) cinema in New Writtle Street. (4) In contrast, a workhouse celebration for a royal wedding in 1893 was cancelled, because according to the local newspapers, it was considered too extravagant. (5)

The biggest event of the union in the late nineteenth century, which affected the work of the guardians, the lives of the inmates, and the poor rates of the property owning class, was the fire which gutted most of the existing workhouse in Wood Street at the beginning of December 1886. A local newspaper reported that "The principal buildings of the workhouse were laid out in the form of a cross, the chapel and master's room being the centre, from which ran out the infirm, aged, women and young women's wards on the north, terminating in the board room; another old men's ward in the east, and the able bodied women's wards on the south." (6) The chapel was on the second floor and was heated by a stove which was in full blaze. At two o'clock painters saw flames leaping through the roof. It was thought that a spark might have ignited the wooden fittings that lined the whole roof underneath the slates. Passersby threw buckets of water on the fire, while they waited for the fire engine to turn up, but they had to withdraw from the chapel. A hose and hydrant could have brought the fire to an immediate halt. All the inmates were put out in a field and a few old women in the aged ward were removed to safety. Meanwhile the crowd grew as the fire spread and some of the local unemployed were keen to earn something by helping. When the roof started to collapse, men and women went running from room to room, throwing bedding and furniture out of the windows: the objects being picked up and then taken to a safe distance. The fire brigade didn't turn up until ten past four. Apparently there was a difficulty in getting enough hoses and nobody gave the order for the brigade to leave for the workhouse. When they did arrive, the hoses were trained on those parts of the building not already alight. Water was obtained from the mains at Wood Street and the pond at the back of the workhouse. By 5 o'clock the fire had entirely gutted the centre of the building. Only one of the women's wards and the infirmary were saved.

The building was insured for six and a half thousand pounds, which was always likely to be less than the cost of the necessary re-building. In the event the insurance company only gave three and a half thousand pounds, which the guardians surprisingly accepted as being fair. (7) A repairs committee was set up immediately and visited the workhouse committee a week after the fire. Inmates were dispersed amongst the surrounding unions, particularly Maldon. The guardians invited the local architects Chancellor, Pertwee and Whitmore to send in plans for the new building which would incorporate the old infirmary. (8) Chancellor's design was eventually chosen and the tenders for the construction varied from £13,000 to £18,000, with that chosen being just under £14,000. (9) The Weekly News was not impressed with the guardians' assertion that it would only mean an extra penny rate. A memorial was handed in by 400 ratepayers, requesting that the matter be referred back to the board for reconsideration. They wanted new plans drawn up, but in the event only one guardian supported this proposal. (10) The first brick was laid the following month and sixty men were employed. Given the controversy the paper did note "the contract is only considered a small one by the firm, their last one being £32,000." (11) The criticism in the press was probably a factor in the guardian's decision to ban the press from their meetings. This unwise decision was rescinded later after the Weekly News had commented "the guardians overlook the general principle that people who pay the money ought to know how it is spent." (12) Eventually £16,855 was spent on the new workhouse and the Weekly News refused to drop the subject. "There seems to be more difficulty in getting the diet of poor workhouse inmates improved by the addition of a morsel of food, or the substitution of a warm nourishing meal for a cold one, than there is in spending thousands of pounds over palatial buildings and offices and a boardroom fitted up with the lavishness that the large ratepayers even cannot afford to indulge in their own premises." (13) The guardians had the temerity to ask Chancellor how his architect's fees of £23 and 17 shillings were made up, but they were quickly satisfied when he had explained them. (14) Chancellor evidently outstayed his welcome, frequently turning up at meetings after the buildings had opened, to the irritation of the guardians. (15)

The number of staff at the new workhouse was much more limited than the big city workhouses, consisting of a master and matron, a part time chaplain, a gate porter and a medical officer. A decision had been made not to teach pauper children in the new workhouse. The quality of education at the previous workhouse had not been high and there had been a rapid turnover of schoolmasters. The passing of the 1870

Forster Education Act had meant that education of a reasonably high quality was now available in the town, but in reality the overriding factor was that of expense.

The role of the master was wide ranging, including overseeing the able bodied poor, their work and discipline, as well as supervising the wards and the distribution of food in the workhouse. His wife, the matron, was responsible for the women and children. Before the fire a new couple, a Captain and Mrs Pollard, previously a master and matron at the Witham workhouse, had been appointed to the same posts at Chelmsford. They were selected from 52 couples, at a salary of £65 for the master and £35 for the matron, together with meals and furnished apartments. (16)The Captain evidently tried to make changes establishing a library at the workhouse, but less than two years later, in 1882, he and his wife were replaced by a Mr and Mrs Martin from Petersfield. (17) (18) Later that year a new head nurse was appointed from 52 applications, but the Union found it very difficult to keep nurses towards the end of the century because of the long hours and poor conditions. In contrast, two clerks, W.W. Duffield and his son A.S. Duffield, gave over 60 year's service between them. Perhaps this was not surprising because they were the best rewarded of the Union staff, augmented as they were by other sources of income including the post of clerk to the R.D.C. Outside the workhouse the guardians employed four relieving officers to administer outdoor relief.

Two of the main tasks of the guardians were to monitor the tenders for food and other provisions and keep a check on the diet of the inmates. Guardians spent a great deal of time discussing the former. A major disagreement occurred in 1892 between fellow guardians over the coal tender, after the they voted to put their tender with a London firm, rather than the local supplier, even though the latter gave a lower quote. (19) In 1889 the master said the wastage of food was unavoidable because the L.G.B. instructions insisted on a certain amount of food being served each day. (20) The same year the dietary committee looked at the official workhouse diet. They considered adding an onion to the Sunday dinner; previously it was just bread and cheese. Breakfast every day was eight ounces of bread and a pint and a half of porridge for the men and six ounces of bread and a pint of porridge for the women. Dinner was of equal quantities for men and women. On Monday and Thursday it consisted of 14 ounces of suet or rice pudding and "not a smell of anything else". The meal on Tuesday and Friday consisted of five ounces of meat with twelve ounces of vegetables or four ounces of bread. On Wednesday and Saturday four ounces of bread and a pint and a half of soup sufficed. Supper each day consisted of eight ounces of bread and one ounce of cheese for the men and six ounces of bread and one ounce of cheese for the women. "What a relish that onion will give the cheese on a Sunday" the Weekly News tartly commented. (21) The following year, when they conducted a forensic examination of the accounts of the workhouse, the guardians found the reality very different. They discovered a number of items of expense that were certainly not in the L.G.B's strict dietary tables. These made no mention of beer, yet 7,404 pints of beer and 407 pints of porter had been paid for. The guardians were shocked to find that the amount spent on beer was four times that spent on potatoes. Inmates had smoked 53 and a quarter pounds of 'weed' in the previous six months. Even worse the guardians found that they were paying one shilling and six pence over the odds for each pound of tobacco. In addition there was spending on 1,170 pounds of bacon and 1,023 eggs which of course were not mentioned in the tables. A considerable tightening in the spending on food followed! (22)

One type of poor on which the Poor Law was consistently strictly imposed in late Victorian England, was the vagrants or casuals. In depressed times there were hundreds of these passing through Essex. The guardians were against the latter sleeping rough and supported the police when they brought them before magistrates. A labourer from Galleywood in 1884 for example, was apprehended and charged with begging on New London Road. (23) Leaflets were frequently distributed to the townspeople asking them not to give alms. The L.G.B. had been keen to get the union to impose a two day rule on casuals who turned up at the workhouse. This was to make it easier to make them do some monotonous work, e.g. oakum picking, in the hope it would keep the numbers down to a minimum. A vagrant, who refused to break stones in the workhouse in 1881, was sentenced by the magistrates, to 21 days hard labour. A temporary abolition of the labour task brought a surge in the number of tramps before the new workhouse was ready. (24) Considerable discussion occurred in 1890 about how the casuals should be admitted to the workhouse. They had to go first to the police at Shire Hall to get a ticket for entry at Wood Street. The journey was doubtless deliberately imposed to reduce the number of tramps deciding to gain entry for the night. An informal restriction of ten o'clock was imposed by the master and night porter. In 1894 the master was finally instructed to detain them for two nights, because the number of tramps was threatening to become more than the workhouse could manage. (25) This had little effect in stemming the flow of tramps through the town and on one occasion later in the year 45 vagrants had to be put up at lodging houses at a cost of 4d a night each. The guardians were particularly worried that the tramps had no task to perform in the morning. (26) A year later an ambulance shed had to be converted into an extra tramp ward. (27) Later, a tramp was locked up for having 8d on him when he tried to enter the workhouse. (28) Arthur Lunney, who later became a councillor, often seemed to be a lone humanitarian voice on the guardians in the 1890s. His perseverance and obstinacy, which sometimes led to fellow guardians walking out at the end of meetings while he was still talking, also raised the ire of the Essex Chronicle. The paper accused him of hypocrisy when he campaigned against guardians taking excessive expenses, when he himself had once done so. He tried for several years to change the ticket system for tramps. "It had been a great cruelty to make poor half starved creatures tramp over two miles when there was no necessity for it." He also objected to women and children having to stand outside, while their husbands went for a ticket at the Shire Hall. (29) Finally in 1898 Lunney managed to get a Poor Law Inspector to agree with him and the system was changed two years later, even though the chairman and several guardians still disagreed with him. (30) (31) The following year one of the guardians Mrs Conybeare, visited the workhouse at Billericay and found it operated a cell system for tramps, with each cell attached to the stone breaking yard. Within 10 months of the cells being introduced the number of tramps had reduced from 8,600 to 1,000 because it robbed the tramps of half of the workhouse's charms, unable as they were to pass on the experiences and incidents of the day. Mrs Conybeare also thought that the re-introduction of a bread and water diet might be necessary because to make "an idle life attractive was a mistaken kindness". (32) There was a big decrease in the number of casuals at Chelmsford in the early years of the century from 4,668 in 1897 to 2,500 in 1903. (33) By 1905 however, the swarms of tramps were such that tents had to be put in the grounds of the workhouse. (34) Doubtless economic conditions played a part but so did the relative attractiveness of various workhouses. In 1909 7,743 tramps were relieved at the workhouse, the most at any workhouse in the Eastern Counties. (35) Vagrants disappeared from the workhouse during the first war, replaced by prisoners of war, but made an immediate re-appearance after it had finished. In 1928 there were up to 800 casuals a week using the workhouse. (36) An extra ward for them was built in 1929, despite continued misgivings that the ward, completed at the Ministry of Health's request, would simply attract casuals from other workhouses (37)

By the time of the late Victorian period, the Chelmsford guardians don't appear to have attempted to send back any able bodied poor, who they thought they were not responsible for under the old (i.e. pre 1834) Settlement Laws. Every attempt was made however to make the new workhouse as unattractive as possible to the able-bodied pauper. The new workhouse had a wall built around it to prevent escape. (38) It was a regular occurrence for the master to be instructed to clear out the able bodied currently in the workhouse, with the aim of getting them to look for work and so that they would not get accustomed to workhouse life. The Essex Chronicle often castigated inmates for refusing to look for work. In one case the paper said "if he persists he will be packed off to prison. That is the place to shake off these fits of laziness contracted in our luxurious workhouses." (39) In 1894 for example, a number of able bodied men were sent out of the workhouse and instructed to look for work at the waterworks then being constructed at Danbury. The Chronicle said that "Some of them shrank from the prospect of renewing the struggle for existence outside." (40) Both Chairmen of the Chelmsford guardians in the late 19th century failed to accept the connection between the agricultural depression and the level of poverty. Most guardians felt that there was work available if the paupers would look for it. Herbert Marriage frequently offered work to the able bodied men that appeared before them. (41) The guardians always made sure that the master gave regular work to the able bodied in the workhouse. In 1902 a trial was given to stone pounding but oakum picking was the mainstay. (42) The following year a magistrate sent a man to prison for refusing to pick oakum in the workhouse. He was given a further seven days for having one shilling and five pence on him when he applied for relief. (43) In 1905 the master was instructed to make life more uncomfortable for the able bodied in the workhouse after a man was allowed out to see his children. (44) In 1908 there were only 15 able bodied men in the workhouse but 12 of those were over 40. (45) Several guardians thought it was difficult for men of their age to find employment, but the Chairman typically disagreed. By 1911 some of the able bodied were in the workhouse because of the shortage of housing in the area. (46)

The often harsh attitude of the guardians to those able bodied paupers who went into the workhouse was mirrored in their view of those obtaining outdoor relief. Those who, driven onto the Poor Law by circumstances, for example widows and their children and families deserted by their male breadwinner, could be usually supported considerably cheaper by means of relief outside the workhouse rather than inside. Guardians recognised that paupers often became institutionalised very quickly in the workhouse. They supported the police and magistrates who sought and punished those who deserted their families and made them dependant on the Poor Law and the culprits were frequently given a month's hard labour. (47) Later the guardians followed the practice, commonly used in the north, of rewarding the police for catching such deserters. (48)

In the 1880s there was no uniform system of distributing outdoor relief. The guardians themselves were given tickets which a pauper could exchange at one of the relieving stations for either provisions or money. (49) In 1896 it was agreed after heated discussion that no new names could be added to the outdoor relief list without the person concerned coming before the Board. (50) No outdoor relief was to be given to the able bodied and widows without children or having only one child to support. The rules were also applied to those married women, with or without children, whose husbands were in prison or had deserted them, or whose husbands were training with the militia. This was a reaction to the increased cost of relief because it had become common practice to give relief to the casually unemployed. The Weekly News thought the new rules were very harsh and was astonished that it had been a Reverend Barnyard who had proposed them. (51) There was further heated discussion at a meeting of guardians after they had received a letter from the local Labour League criticising the new rules. Unusually the clerk, Duffield, intervened saying "the inspectors have said you are too liberal in outside relief." Reverend E.P. Gibson retorted "They are horrible fellows who know nothing about poor people." (52) The chairman replied "You gentlemen (Gibson and the other opponents of the new rules) will do away with the idea of thrift altogether." (53) Arthur Lunney repeatedly put proposals to increase outdoor relief during poor weather but this was always turned down. By 1906 he was claiming that Chelmsford was the only Essex Union not giving such relief. (54) He sent a letter to the L.G.B. on the matter, but some of the guardians objected to him acting independently and sent their own, disowning his views. In 1904 the outdoor relief stations were abolished and the relieving officers were paid an increased salary to visit those receiving payments in their own homes. (55) This certainly helped those who were elderly or infirm. The relieving officers were quickly dissatisfied with the new system but the guardians refused to go back to the old one. (56) During the war some townsfolk had their outdoor relief withdrawn if soldiers were billeted with them. (57)

The guardians were very slow to recognise that the numbers claiming poor relief were increasingly tied, because of the industrialisation of the town, to the trade cycle. A majority of guardians still thought there was no genuine unemployment. During February 1909, soup kitchens were set up independently of the poor law to help the unemployed. (58) In 1916 despite the drastic increase in the cost of living, the guardians still felt unable to increase outdoor relief. The depression after the Great

War did apparently bring about a change in the guardian's attitude towards the unemployed. Although National Insurance had been introduced, it still only covered a minority of trades and many of those supposedly covered did not possess a National Insurance card. Chelmsford was still not so large that the guardians couldn't see the comparatively large number of unemployed on their doorstep. The guardians agreed that receipt of unemployment relief would not automatically prevent someone getting poor relief. For several years the guardians had an unemployment relief post, which was closed in 1923, when the worst of the recession had passed. (59) The guardians were not immune to pressure, such as the Hoffmann strikers marching on the workhouse (see chapter 9). For a while the Poor law was just one part of a local bureaucratic muddle which included outdoor relief, unemployment benefit and the mayor's charitable relief fund.

With regard to the workhouse children, after making the decision to send them to the borough's schools, the guardians expressly wished that they wouldn't stand out, but curiously decided to have them dressed in a distinctive uniform, which would surely have had the opposite effect! The guardians regularly inspected the children in the Boardroom. This didn't prevent occasional accusations of ill treatment of children in the workhouse, including one of excessive whipping in 1894. The children said they had not been ill treated but what they really thought can only be guessed. (60) Most guardians were in favour of severe treatment in the workhouse where necessary. When a boy was ordered to be birched for stealing in the workhouse, even the Reverend Gibson supported the decision. (61) In 1898 the surprisingly benevolent decision was made to give the children half a penny a week pocket money, although this was not passed unanimously. (62) The money was only to be withheld in cases of misconduct. Early in the twentieth century many Poor Law Unions were putting their pauper children in cottage homes. It was hoped that taking them out of the workhouse would make them less institutionalised, but the Chelmsford Union was slow to take up the idea after such homes were first suggested by Mrs Conybeare in 1901. The cost was to be about 4 shillings and sixpence per child per week. (63) Chelmsford guardians shuddered when the cost of the first houses was announced at three thousand pounds. (64) The following month a proposal to build two cottages, costing £1,000 each was passed but only by thirteen votes to eleven. (65) By 1904 the home for girls at Baddow was almost complete and the following year a foster mother was appointed. (66)(67) In 1906 the guardians congratulated themselves that only 2 of 40 similar homes around the country had been completed as cheaply. (68) A proposal to board out the boys was blocked by the L.G.B. initially but allowed later. (69) Eventually pressure of numbers led to the establishment of a boy's home in Writtle in 1908. (70) Those children already boarded out were left where they were rather than uprooted again. (71) Some of the boys at Writtle were persistently unruly. They were given bread and water as punishment. (72) Continual problems were reported however, immediately before the outbreak of the first war. (73)

One of the problems of a late Victorian and Edwardian workhouse, like that at Wood Street, was the increasing average age of the paupers, leading to more of them being infirm. In 1892 the oldest inmate of the workhouse died aged 94. (74) The following year 6 inmates were over 90, 18 between 80 and 90, 78 between 70 and 80, giving a total of 108 that had exceeded the allotted span of three score and ten. (75) During the 1880s mental patients were being placed at the county lunatic asylum and were visited regularly by the guardians, but increasingly however the medical officer may have been under pressure to keep such patients at the workhouse. In 1896 the Reverend Gibson reported that one of the female patients "who is well over 90 years of age" was "chained to a wall". The master said there was no chain and "what was done was done solely to prevent her from doing harm to herself". A reporter was taken to see for himself. Conditions were of "scrupulous cleanliness and an air of comfort". An old lady was wearing a restraint, which was a belt, four or five inches wide, stoutly made and padded. One end of the strap is locked on to an iron loop on the wall. She seemed quiet and harmless and was taken off the restraint for several hours. The woman had fallen down several weeks ago which had led to the restraint. (76) The medical officer said he had not declared her insane because he thought her "restlessness" would disappear. A L.G.B. inspector was not convinced but the chairman E. Corder expressed himself "satisfied that proper care was being taken of the woman." To the surprise of the rest of the Board it was then announced that the woman had been transferred to the asylum. The editor of the Weekly News noted that the matter showed that there was a need for an institution between the workhouse and the asylum, in which "people whose mental weakness arises simply from senile decay can be tenderly and effectively guarded." (77) The introduction of Old Age Pensions in 1908 does not appear to have had any marked effect on the numbers of old people staying in the Chelmsford workhouse.

Increasing numbers of sick put great pressure on the nurses and the existing infirmary, which had survived the fire. In January 1899 of 227 adults in the workhouse, 127 were in the infirmary. (78) During 1900 it was announced that a new infirmary was to be built because of overcrowding, but concern over the poor rate was the reason nothing was done until after the Great War. (79) During the war the infirmary was used for wounded soldiers but it also housed injured prisoners of war. (80) Lunney continually raised the matter of the poor conditions of nurses. In 1902 he said the night nurse was looking after 120 patients, but received no support for his suggestion for an extra night nurse. (81) Five months later he said that three nurses had resigned because of their miserable conditions. (82) A few months later three additional nurses were employed, doubling the nursing staff at the workhouse. (83) Some attempt was made to improve conditions for the patients. After 1902 a screen was erected around the dying whenever possible. (84) Post 1907 an effort was made to isolate cancer patients and in 1911 an observation ward was set up for mental cases. (85)(86) After

Chelmsford Union Infirmary (St John's Hospital) which was built in 1926
(Courtesy of E.R.O.)

the guardians initially refused one, a padded cell was included in this ward. (87) The elderly were still allowed few comforts. In 1895 six new seats were purchased to replace the broken ones in the old men's yard. It was not until 1905 that they had seats in the grounds, although they had been allowed to walk there since 1901. (88)

After the guardians had ignored the suggestion of the L.G.B., to build a new infirmary in 1914, they had finally accepted by 1923 that the old one had to be pulled down. (89) Room for 120 beds was to be available at once, with possibly two hundred and forty in the future. (90) The nursing block was a separate building. Once opened, non-pauper cases were admitted into the maternity wing of the new building at a charge of thirty shillings a week (see chapter 16) (91). This paved the way for the emergence of St John's as a hospital separate from the rest of the institution.

The guardians had discussed the Majority and Minority Reports of the Royal Commission into the Poor Laws before the war, but in 1919 there was a conference at the Shire Hall on the possible abolition of the Poor Law and its replacement by a scheme of national assistance. (92) From the outset they maintained that a system of local representatives was best, knowing as they did the needs of the local poor. In 1925 the guardians discussed a letter from the President of the Association of Poor Law Unions. This said that the government's proposals were unnecessary and would lead to increased bureaucracy and centralisation as well as a loss of liberty. Mr Conybeare noted that the Commission before the war had refused to hear any evidence from Boards of Guardians. (93) A year later the guardians accepted the inevitable but did agree that the new authority which replaced them should have control over all forms of national assistance. (94) The local guardians were still taking part in the propaganda against their abolition when the bill was going through parliament. (95)

An Essex County Public Assistance Committee was set up, with all the Poor law powers transferred to it. Eight area guardian or assistance committees were established for the county, including one for the Chelmsford area. These had the powers of carrying out the new public assistance system delegated to them. (96) When the new system started in 1930 three county council members were appointed to the Chelmsford guardians committee. In some ways little changed. Fred Marriage was elected to chair the new local committee, just as he had chaired the old board. (97) Proposals to merge the two children's homes, which were housing reduced numbers, were abandoned. (98) The biggest change was probably that the local committee were responsible for imposing the hated means test in the local area. It did initially have some control over who was paid relief and how much they were paid but soon however the county committee was setting the relief scales for single men, families and widows. (99) Rates did vary from urban to rural areas. (100) "In no case should the relief granted, including the rent allowance, exceed the normal wages of the applicant when at work or the unemployment benefit." (101) In 1930 the Chelmsford committee obtained five rooms above Liptons at 42, the High Street.

During the second war the workhouse's residents were evacuated and the casual wards closed. The public assistance system remained in operation until replaced by the new Welfare State after the war. A Mrs I.J. Gilbey, who worked at St John's as a nurse after the war, remembered that the workhouse still had some residents, who worked if able in the laundry or as domestics in the nursing home. (102) The Writtle boys home continued to be used until the 1970s.

1) www.institution.org.uk/workhouse/England.Essex/Chelmsford
2) Essex Weekly News 7 12 1894
3) E.W.N. 27 12 1901 p.8
4) E.W.N. 2 1 1914
5) E.C. 23 6 1893
6) E.C. 2 12 1886 p.5
7) E.C. 11 2 1887 p.7
8) E.W.N. 3 6 1887
9) E.W.N. 18 5 1888
10) E.W.N. 25 5 1888 p.7
11) E.W.N. 18 6 1888
12) E.W.N. 3 5 1889 p.5
13) E.W.N. 11 7 1890 p.4
14) E.W.N. 8 8 1890 p.2
15) E.W.N. 8 11 1889 p.5
16) E.C. 20 8 1880 p.5
17) E.C. 3 9 1880 p.5
18) E.W.N. 1 7 1982 p.5
19) E.C. 13 5 1892 p.5
20) E.C. 29 5 1891 p.5
21) E.W.N. 23 5 1889 p.5
22) E.W.N. 5 9 1890 p.5
23) E.W.N. 5 5 1884 p.5

24) E.W.N. 17 5 1889 p.6
25) E.W.N. 8 6 1894 p.6
26) E.W.N. 7 12 1894 p.6
27) E.W.N. 2 8 1895 p.2
28) E.W.N. 18 10 1895 p.5
29) E.W.N. 6 5 1898 p.6
30) E.W.N. 6 5 1898 p.6
31) E.W.N. 16 11 1900 p.6
32) E.W.N. 26 7 1901 p.2
33) E.W.N. 4 3 1904 p.4
34) E.W.N. 9 6 1905 p.3
35) E.W.N. 11 6 1910 p.2
36) E.W.N. 22 6 1928 p.2
37) E.W.N. 6 12 1929 p.2
38) The Legacy of the Rural Guardians G. Cuttle p.40-41
39) E.C. 17 2 1893 p.5
40) E.C. 24 11 1893 p.4
41) E.W.N. 4 8 1893 p.4
42) E.W.N. 5 9 1902 p.6
43) E.W.N. 17 4 1903
44) E.W.N. 13 10 1905 p.3
45) E.W.N. 27 3 1908 p.3
46) E.W.N. 2 6 1911
47) E.W.N. 11 2 1881 p.3
48) E.C. 3 7 1894 p.3
49) E.C. 23 1 1891
50) E.C. 3 7 1894 p.3
51) E.W.N. 3 7 1896 p.6
52) E.W.N. 31 7 1896 p.6
53) E.W.N. 28 9 1896 p.6
54) E.W.N. 19 3 1900 p.5
55) E.W.N. 15 4 1904 p.2
56) E.W.N. 9 12 1904 p.2
57) E.W.N. 16 10 1914 p.3
58) E.C. 12 5 1909 p.5

59) E.W.N. 1 6 1923 p.2
60) E.W.N. 17 8 1894 p.6
61) E.W.N. 31 8 1894 p.6
62) E.W.N. 1 7 1898 p.6
63) E.W.N. 1 1 1901
64) E.W.N. 19 9 1902 p.6
65) E.W.N. 3 10 1902 p.6
66) E.W.N. 19 2 1904 p.6
67) E.W.N. 12 5 1905 p.2
68) E.W.N. 21 12 1906 p.2
69) E.W.N. 21 6 1907 p.2
70) E.W.N. 27 3 1908 p.3
71) E.W.N. 11 3 1913 p.2
72) E.W.N. 10 2 1911 p.2
73) E.W. N. 11 7 1913 p.2
74) E.W.N. 5 2 1893=2 p.5
75) E.W.N. 8 12 1893 p.4
76) E.W.N. 5 6 1896 p.5
77) E.W.N. 20 6 1896 p.4
78) E.W.N. 12 1 1899
79) E.W.N. 10 8 1900 p.2
80) Press release on St John's Hospital – Chelmsford Museums records
81) E.W.N. 27 2 1902 p.6
82) E.W.N. 25 7 1902 p.2
83) E.W.N. 31 10 1902 p.2
84) E.W.N. 5 9 1902 p.6
85) E.W.N. 10 9 1907 p.2
86) E.W.N. 24 2 1911 p.2
87) E.W.N. 7 4 1911 p.2
88) Cuttle p.40-1
89) E.W.N. 5 5 1914 p.3
90) E.W.N. 10 3 1922 p.3
91) E.W.N. 4 2 1927 p.2
92) E.W.N. 22 11 1919
93) E.W.N. 21 8 1925 p.3

94) E.W.N. 2 5 6 1926 p.3
95) E.W.N. 7 12 1928 p.2
96) E.W.N. 8 7 1929
97) E.W.N. 28 2 1930 p.2
98) E.W.N. 7 12 1928 p.2
99) Essex County Council minutes 1929 p.1178
100) E.C.C. minutes 1 4 1930 p.735
101) E.C.C. minutes 1 4 1930 p.737
102) Chelmsford Museums records – St John's Hospital

20

Education in the Chelmsford area before 1945

"Cinemas, dancing, motor jaunts, all were enemies of the weekly work routine"

In the mid 19th century Chelmsford had a thriving voluntary schools' system. The 1870 Forster Education Act meant that these schools had to obtain enough income from subscriptions and fees. An act of 1891 cut off this source of income. By the 1890s Chelmsford was increasingly surrounded by board schools that had been set up in areas where considerable numbers of children were without schooling. The boards were elected and given the power to charge a rate to pay for the cost of the schools. In Writtle, for example, a school board was set up because the lack of subscriptions. (1) In Chelmsford both the National and British Schools made every effort to keep out a school board before school board and voluntary schools were integrated into the new local education authorities under the Balfour Education Act of 1902. The National Schools were supported by the established church and the British schools by the nonconformists. Elsewhere, nonconformists often pushed for the establishment of a board, because of their difficulty in raising enough money to run their British Schools. In Chelmsford both Anglicans and Nonconformists took the view that a school board would result in an unnecessary layer of bureaucracy and therefore considerable expense. One effect the lack of a school board had on Chelmsford was that a generation of adults that might have entered politics through this route didn't do so. Another effect, which was to have lasting consequences for Chelmsford education well into the twentieth century, was that the higher grade elementary schools, which became common elsewhere, didn't develop in the town. This was a principal reason for the borough still only having two secondary schools in 1923. The lack of a school board may also be the reason Chelmsford still had 'a ragged school' for poor children in

1896, ten to fifteen years after they had died out in most other areas. A new ragged school had been opened in 1886 in George Street off Moulsham Street. The absence of a school board also meant that, under the Mundella Act of 1880, Chelmsford had to have an attendance committee. As the Revised Code (see later) and payment by results became less important, schools had to show a good record of attendance to obtain the essential grant from the government.

Even before Chelmsford became a borough, both National Schools were experiencing financial problems. In 1881 the congregation of St Mary's Anglican Church were told that a proportion of their offertory collection was going to the National school and if they subscribed to the latter they would keep it going at 30% less cost than the equivalent board school. (2) The Victoria National School's board of management, elected by subscribers, included a number of the local Board of Health politicians including Chancellor, Gepp, Veley and Durrant. Later the same year the committee were told that £150 had been spent on repairs the previous year and "it was not to be wondered that the committee were in debt. The government were expecting more from the schools, more books and desks were required." (3) In 1882 the British Schools for nonconformists in Chelmsford, had to consider raising a fund to cover the cost of building the necessary extension at the Friars. They briefly considered the idea of a school board before agreeing to set up the fund and increasing the fees from 3d to 4d per week. (4) After the 1870 Elementary Schools Act, the Charity School, which was situated on the north east corner of the present cathedral churchyard, was too small to justify its continued existence. The winding up of the Charity School gave the National schools in Chelmsford and Moulsham the chance to fund their essential new buildings. Chancellor and other governors were careful however, not to use all the Amy Johnson funds from the Charity school for the new venture. They were aware that the funds belonged to all the townspeople, although the former Charity School pupils were being currently educated at the National Schools. (5) The rest was to be used for exhibitions and scholarships for pupils from all the town's elementary schools to enter the grammar school. (6) These disbursements continued for well over half a century. The administrators of the Charity School funds, who included W.W. Duffield, Chancellor and Durrant, also paid for the annual examinations in the town which were used to assess who might be of sufficient standard to qualify for the scholarships.

Initially the Charity school managers had petitioned the Charity Commissioners to divert the school funds in order to establish a "middle class" girls' school. (7) This was dropped through lack of support and through opposition from the government. Girls' education was perceived as being of secondary importance and being well catered for by the multiplicity of small private girls' schools in the New London Road and the surrounding area. In 1880 for example a Mrs Baker advertised the Sutherland Lodge. This offered "a sound practical education on moderate terms." (8) Many such schools didn't last long. A ladies' school on Museum terrace was run by the three Wilshere sisters between 1890 and 1895. Another was run by Miss Ann Rope at St John's Terrace between 1878 and 1895. Dr Bodkin, father of four very intelligent daughters, did not consider that Chelmsford was large enough for a girls' high school given that the boys' grammar only contained 75 boys. (9) The managers of St John's National schools in Moulsham were also pushing for a share of the charity school funds. They were fortunate however, when Mrs Tidboald, whose husband had been a church warden at St John's church for many years, gave a large donation of £1,600 enabling the necessary extension to that school to take place. (10) The Charity School fund money was used by the Chelmsford Victoria National Schools for a new two storey building, on the corner of New Street and Victora Road, designed by Chancellor, which was opened in 1885. He had designed many board schools in London. The early 1880s also saw the opening of a small new National school, St Peters, on the Rainsford Road. It was maintained by four voluntary collectors in the town.

Chelmsford's attendance committee had been in existence since 1877. In 1879 there were 1,497 pupils in the town, of which 461 were at the British schools, 490 at the Victoria National schools, 450 at the St John's schools and 73 at the Catholic School in London Road. (11) The work of the attendance committee and the attendance officer cost £96 in that year. Warnings about attendance issued to parents went down in number from 127 in 1878 to 60 in 1890. (12) In 1880, 46 summonses were issued resulting in 29 orders and 13 fines. The committee felt no compunction in taking this action swiftly and decisively. Special exams were arranged in the town to enable children obtain a level of proficiency at standard four, sufficient to enable them to leave school. (13) The Victoria National Schools also regularly hosted the pupil teacher exams because all the local schools were dependent on a steady supply of the latter.

By the time Chelmsford became a borough, managers of schools and the local press were panicking that a school board was inevitable. It was noted that the Writtle school board was working well. (14) The fees at the British Schools had to be raised but attendances didn't fall. For several years they received excellent inspection reports and the maximum grant available. The 1891 Education Act however meant that the Victoria National and Moulsham Schools had to be free, although they were able to claim for government grants. This and a big rise in pupil numbers led to further anxiety in the papers. According to the Essex Chronicle, infant schools were besieged by mothers of children, some of them not more than three years old. (15) The pressure of numbers was exacerbated by an increasing tendency of Chelmsford parents to keep their children on at school until the fifth rather than the fourth standard. (16) In 1898 the newspapers used polite blackmail to get those in Moulsham to raise money for an essential expansion. Perhaps surprisingly nonconformists were well represented amongst the list of subscribers. The Essex Chronicle said a school board was inevitable if the necessary money wasn't raised, adding probably incorrectly that the nonconformists were already in favour of such a board. (17) This publicity had the right effect and the new buildings were opened at St John's in 1899, although a bazaar had to be held at the Shire Hall to raise the final amount of £500. (18) By 1901 the British Schools were also considerably in debt and had to raise money to avoid a school board. An inspector again spoke highly of the quality of work, but mentioned overcrowding in the girls department. The British Schools were educating 633 children, 205 boys, 223 girls and 205 infants. (19) In the 1890s the Springfield schools were also suffering from a lack of subscriptions but the Reverend Pearson managed to stave off a school board by allowing the nonconformists some representation on the board of managers. (20) During the 1890s the Amy Johnson charity fund money was used to pay for scholarships in Chelmsford. In 1890 60 sat a competitive examination, but the prizes were extremely limited; a payment of £5 each to four boys and £3 each to four girls, tenable for one year. These were for elementary school pupils. In addition there were two exhibitions of £10 each to one boy and one girl, for two years at any place of education higher than elementary school. Apart from the grammar school this could also be used for apprenticeships. (21) Despite the financial problems of the town's schools, the attendance rates were high in the years immediately before the 1902 Act and compared well with the surrounding rural areas board schools. (22) In 1897 a council resolution to pass the formal raising of the school leaving age to the fifth standard was implemented, despite the opposition of a number of prominent local people including Major Carne Rasch, who thought it would bring hardship to some working parents, who depended on their children going out to work or working with them. (23) The six standards had been established under the Revised Code of 1862 and roughly conformed to the ages 7 to 12. They were responsible for restricting most learning to the three R's.

    The rural areas around Chelmsford faced greater problems enforcing attendance than the borough. Prosecutions were carried out by the school attendance officers, but often the schools tried to fit in with the harvesting times. In Great Waltham for example, "the managers closed the schools on the 27th of June for pea-picking until re-opening on 23rd of July". (24) This did not change after attendance had been made compulsory. The attendance officers tried to tackle the problem of agricultural employment at source by interviewing farmers who were employing children contrary to the Act of 1873. (25) A flourishing school board operated in the Chignalls from the 1870s but the school still faced acute attendance problems. The schoolmaster Edward Joliffe, who was paid by attendance, complained in the school log book "of children being kept away to work in the fields and gardens often owned by members of the board themselves". (26) His stridency on attendance led to him being asked to leave. Joliffe's successor had a simpler solution; he fiddled the figures!

The 1902 Education Act established local education authorities. In Chelmsford this meant that the inevitable school board didn't come about. By this time Chelmsford was well behind other large towns in the Eastern counties in the provision of post elementary education. By the 1890s the Norwich school board had built a purpose built college for pupils from its elementary schools who had received scholarships. (27) The school board there had a strong socialist element and from the start women were elected. In Ipswich the school board used ratepayers' money to provide higher grade elementary schools, which didn't emerge in Chelmsford. (28) Colchester had also gone over to a school board, but not until the 1890s. (29)

After the 1902 Act the E.C.C. Education Committee contained 45 members, 30 of whom had to come from the council and the rest from the outside, with various denominations represented. (30) As a county borough, Chelmsford gained control of most aspects of its education and a rate of 3d in the pound was set. (31) The buildings of the voluntary schools in Chelmsford were taken over on 21 year leases and the Chelmsford Education Committee appointed additional managers to the schools and a survey of all the buildings was carried out. (32) Fred Chancellor and his daughter Frances were on the managing body of both the Victoria and the St Peters' schools. Frances was heavily involved in establishing the teaching of needlework in the borough. Councillor Wells and Miss R. Pertwee became managers of the Friars. Aldermen Bond and Whitmore became managers of the Catholic school. The Friars School, formerly the British School, was found to be in a deplorable state. (33) After the extension of the borough boundary the local education committee immediately recommended a new elementary school for Springfield and two years later the Trinity

Road School was built along with the rebuilding of the Friars School. (34) (35) The 1900s also saw the first inspections by the schools medical officer and as elsewhere there was the immediate exposure of 'dirty children'. In 1910, 107 children in the borough were classified as unclean. (36) Demands for a school nurse in Chelmsford fell on deaf ears until the first war. Successive inspectors found that improvements were desirable in water for drinking and washing purposes in Chelmsford schools as elsewhere and the cleanliness of the borough's schools was not of a high standard. The Council tried without success to get teachers to take on cleaning of their class rooms. (37) Arrangements for drying children's clothes and boots usually left a lot to be desired.

After 1902 nationally the pupil teacher system went into decline but in 1904 the County said it could continue in the short term. (38) A pupil teacher centre was established by the County in the town. In 1907 a County report said Chelmsford needed 7 pupil teachers. Girls were to receive £16 in their first year and £18 in their second and boys £20 in their first and £24 in their second. (39) After 1909 they were renamed student teachers. (40) They were supplemented by uncertificated teachers, who had passed their London, Oxford or Cambridge matriculations.

In 1904 the first specialist teaching centre, in this case for cookery, was established at the Friars School by a full time teacher, after classes had previously been held at Great Baddow. (41) Swimming lessons were established for older pupils after the Waterloo Lane pool was opened in 1906. (42) As in other areas Chelmsford had to deal with children who are today described as having 'learning difficulties' and in 1909, 5 "dull and defective children" were identified. (43) In 1923 such children were being held back in the same class year after year. By 1921 Victoria girls' school had established a special class of 30 for below average pupils. (44) The education committee decided that the number did not warrant the starting of a special school.

By 1910 most school leavers in Chelmsford were 13 and over. They were only allowed to leave if they had beneficial employment to go to and they had to be furnished with a leaving card, which could be used at the new Labour Exchanges. (45) (46) An increasing number of leavers were going to the three big firms.

In 1910 came the first serious criticisms of St John's school, which were to lead to its closure less than thirty years later. A HMI inspection said the grounds were too small and partitions were needed within the classrooms. (47) Increasing importance was attached to H.M.I. reports and the Friars School received an excellent one in 1912. "The teaching is kind and earnest, and very good progress is being made by the children, whose general intelligence and proficiency in reading is selected for particular praise." (48) In contrast in the same year the Victoria schools were given a very unsatisfactory report. At the school "the appearance of discipline is achieved by methods which cannot be conducive to good work". (49) The governors told the teachers they were expecting a big improvement.

In the borough those with a good attendance were still given the curious incentive of half a day off. The school with the best attendance in the borough was given the attendance shield. (50) A need for an extra school in both the North and South Wards was identified, with sites at Rainsford Lane and Bradford Street originally earmarked. The 2,500 existing places became insufficient with the rapidly increasing population. (51) After the 1902 Act 250 pupils were being educated from outside the borough and the council insisted on being reimbursed by the E.C.C. (52)

The war caused immediate problems with staffing in the borough's schools with teachers volunteering for the military. At the Victoria school the managers took the view that a particular teacher was of more use to the country at the moment by staying and teaching, but they couldn't prevent him leaving. He enlisted and his teaching salary was paid in full, less his army pay with his job held for him at the end of the war. (53) The new Trinity Road School used the Friends Meeting House when the school was taken over by the military. (54)

Chelmsford had an industrial school for wayward and destitute boys since 1872 and it was certified in 1873. Joseph Brittain Pash had opened the school in several houses in Baddow Road. It was initially financed by subscriptions. Subscribers could nominate boys who would benefit from being sent there. In 1876 a £5,000 grant was given by the Essex Quarter Sessions and £2,000 by the West Ham school board in return for 20 reserved places. A new purpose building was opened off the Rainsford Road in 1879, at a cost of £10,000. The police and magistrates could use the 1866 Industrial Schools Act when boys were caught stealing, begging, or were simply homeless. By the end of 1879 111 boys had been admitted from all over Essex. There were subscribers from all parts the county, but a large number of them were from Chelmsford. The Essex Chronicle was pleased that the "average cost per boy was only 17 – 18 shillings per weeks". (55) Pupils were given a basic education and were also taught practical skills in "tailoring, shoemaking, carpentry, gardening, laundry and kitchen work". (56) Despite this the Chronicle reported in 1880 that "there was considerable difficulty at the present time in obtaining a suitable situation for the lads". Successful attempts were made to get some of the boys to settle abroad. In 1882 13 boys were placed in Canada and 3 boys went to Queensland. (57) An inspector gave a good report on the school saying "The boys are in good health and look cheerful and bright and well cared for."(58) A good proportion of the boys were on the 4th and 5th standards. A later inspector did however mention that the level of punishments could be reduced by a "more carefully drawn out system of rewards, marks and encouragements". (59) Perhaps therefore it was not surprising that there were regular newspaper reports about boys escaping from the home. In 1883 there was evidently a serious lapse of discipline by boys "who had produced much mischief and incited others to defiance and disorder and had to be sent away to prison". Five years earlier cells had been added for unruly boys. (60) The timetable was devised so that there were few moments for relaxation; an early start was followed by half a day's schoolwork and half a day's industrial training plus housework. There were no servants apart from the housekeeper. Firm religious education was considered essential but was non denominational, although some of the local Church of England clergy expressed concern that the school was founded and run by nonconformists. Despite the tough elements of the regime at the school there is little doubt that Pash and his extended family cared a great deal about the welfare of the boys. His daughter Ellen was secretary of the boy's Band of Hope and for many years she took a class on Sunday evenings when her mother, Mrs Pash, was in charge of the Sunday evening class arrangements. As an honorary lecturer under the Essex Technical Instruction Committee she used to lecture the boys on a wide variety of useful subjects. She also used to speak to the boys at meal times and on wet days. Ellen started a wild flower garden for the boys after collecting the necessary plants and seeds on trips into the countryside with the boys. In 1902, the year before she died, she gave each boy a cedar wooden pencil with his name upon it in gilt letters. She had recently been involved in the establishment of a magazine at the school.

By the 1890s most of the funding for the Industrial School was coming from the county council. As with the workhouse however, the great and good of the town liked to support the institution. During 1890 the Weekly News noted that the boys at the school, who had behaved well during the year, were taken on a day excursion to Southend and that this was funded by local dignitaries. (61) In the same year "The Christmas Day dinner consisted mainly of roast beef and plum pudding; and several old boys shared in the repast, having come home for the holidays". (62) The Mayoress, Mrs F.A. Wells, was present for the 1901 prize giving at the school. (63)

By the 1880s the Chelmsford grammar school had existed for well over 300 years and was based in Duke Street. At this time the King Edward the Sixth school was not particularly distinguished. Unlike other such schools, which had broadened their curriculum after the report of the Taunton Commission in the 1860s and the Endowed Schools Act of 1869, K.E.G.S. remained un- reformed with a narrow classical curriculum. (64) In 1884 the decision was made to make the school a centre for the Cambridge examinations but this didn't occur immediately; the editor of the Essex Chronicle thought that this should have happened before to improve standards. (65) This was the last major act of the Reverend J.A. Kershaw who resigned later that year, moving to a school and parish at Kelvedon. The new head Frank Rogers, who was appointed the following year, left an indelible mark on the school. (66) An early decision was taken to apply to the Science and Art Department to take classes in Higher Maths, Photography, Magnetism and Electricity, and Agricultural Science. (67) Rogers increased the fees from £6 to £8 per year. (68) Rogers told the governors, just before Chelmsford became a borough, that the school couldn't be properly remodelled for modern needs without having new buildings. (69)

After the inauguration of the town as a borough, the pressing need of its grammar school was for new premises. The existing buildings in Duke Street were cramped and insanitary, as outbreaks of diphtheria resulting in several deaths testified. A site was identified in Moulsham but Sir Henry Mildmay declined to sell. Then a four acre site in Broomfield Road belonging to Ernest Ridley was acquired. The only doubt was whether it was large enough to include a full sized cricket field. There was the possibility of obtaining extra land next to the site, and Rogers and his staff were in favour. (70) Delays followed due the governors initially choosing a site on Market Road. (71) Lack of parental support for this decision led to the foundation stone being laid at the Broomfield Road site. (72) This was only after the Charity School Commissioners removed their objections to the school using its endowed funds for the new buildings. (73) Its new buildings were formally opened in 1892 by Lord Rayleigh, the Lord Lieutenant of Essex, with a number of Essex M.P.s and the Mayor and other councillors present. (74) "The structure stands on the high ground of one of the pleasantest and healthiest parts of the borough" the Weekly News commented. Its architecture was a mix of Gothic and Elizabethan and the paper also mentioned, importantly given the difficulties in the previous buildings, "the sanitary arrangements and drainage comprising all the latest improvements". (75) The new buildings could take a roll of 160 including 20 boarders. Rogers had already almost doubled the roll to 120. In 1893 the school asked the Charity Commissioners for permission to raise the maximum age of students from 17 to 19 to enable some of them to go on to university. (76) The endowed fund stood at only £700, when £2,000 was needed for scholarships, both for new entrants and prospective University entrants, and an effort was made to increase the size of the fund. (77) In 1894 a new gymnasium was opened after a gift from Gray, the brewer. Another significant event of the Rogers headmastership was the founding of the Chelmsfordian magazine in 1895, which was praised by both the Daily Mail and the Spectator. (78) The 1890s saw the foundation of the old boys' association and the football, hockey and cycling clubs. A debating society was also formed before the turn of the century: in time to debate the start of the Boer War. (79) Eighteen ninety six saw the first female teacher, Elsie Slader, who taught the younger boys of the Preparatory School. After leaving in 1898 she came back in 1910, teaching there until 1918. After 1918 she was secretary to the later Headmaster Thomas Hay.

The grammar school had received several very positive inspection reports in the 1890s as the changes instituted by Rogers took root and by 1905 it was full with 105 pupils. (80) In 1907 however, the first time it had been inspected by independent State inspectors, it had a critical report; ironically the only well taught subject was science. (81) K.E.G.S. had acquired a significant debt in the move to Broomfield Road and this had meant Rogers hadn't been able to afford quality staff. The governors took immediate action with P.E. being made compulsory and Rogers had to resume teaching. K.E.G.S. was on course to lose £250 a year and the council, now responsible for a quarter of the school's intake, had to pay more for their scholarships. Rogers reacted angrily to his pay being cut by 27%, maintaining that he had given £2,000 over the course of 16 years towards the cost of new buildings and another £1,400 towards the pay of assistant teachers. (82) He didn't accept the findings of the H.M.I. report and resigned to live in Bournemouth. (83) Two years later he was involved in a scandal when a wealthy woman poisoned herself after '"loaning" Rogers £3,000. The jury at her inquest wanted him censured for his attitude. (84)

K.E.G.S. new head, Thomas Hay, had been senior science master at the school and now had to manage the school under stringent financial conditions. The number of free places was cut back from 25% to 12.5%. (85) Tuition fees were between £6 and £12 for fee paying day boys. (86) The County Council paid for £1,400 of the £2,000 cost of essential new buildings and a new inspection report gave the school a qualified bill of health, but the first war drastically reduced the staff, with qualified teachers hard to find. During the war 376 old boys and masters fought for their country during which they won 21 medals, 17 of them military crosses, but 60 of them died. (87)

By the 1880s Chelmsford's Mechanics Institute had declined as a means of educating the working classes in the town and it eventually closed in 1898. (88) As early as 1881 there was a night school at St John's for men and youths. The vicar then established similar classes for women. (89) In town, by 1882, a teacher at the Victoria National School was teaching evening classes in science, particularly electricity. Not surprisingly 14 of those enrolled on the classes were from the Arc Works. (90)

Like other authorities, the E.C.C. decided to fund technical instruction, using the so called 'whisky money' available by Act of Parliament from 1890. Proper further education in Chelmsford dated from 1895 with classes at Crane Court (where the National Westminster Bank was later to be situated). (91) In the early 1900s, 300 students were registered and larger premises become essential. (92) By this time evening classes were also being held in Chemistry at the Grammar School. (93) In 1892 the County Council's Technical Instruction committee had taken over the empty old Grammar School buildings for a day class "in practical instruction in structural physiological botany as applied to agriculture and horticulture". (94) This started the School of Agriculture (see chapter 1). In 1894 new chemistry and biological laboratories were opened in the same buildings by the County Committee. (95)

New Hall, the oldest Catholic school in England to take girls, suffered a decline in numbers towards the end of the century. The school had opened on its present site in 1799. By 1913 there was only an average of 13 pupils on the roll. This was due to the lack of new educational thinking and the insanitary conditions at the school which led to several cases of diphtheria. (96) The school's Eaton theatre was opened in 1925.

In the depression after the war the S.M.O., initially said there was no need for school meals, although some towns were providing food at breakfast and lunchtime. (97) Later he did produce a scheme but asked for voluntary help, after admitting that a considerable number of children were suffering some impairment of health due to lack of food. Cocoa was provided to the 50 worst cases. This was not enough when as many as a third of the parents of schoolchildren in the borough were either unemployed or underemployed (see chapter 9). In Springfield a generous doctor enabled anaemic children to be supplied with cod liver oil and malt extract. (98) A.R.P. Hickley campaigned unsuccessfully to have two teachers placed on Chelmsford's education committee. (99)

The 1918 Fisher Education Act included the raising of the school leaving age to 14. Luckily given the problems Chelmsford had in accommodating all its pupils, the depression and the resulting Geddes Axe meant that the borough was under no pressure to carry this out in the 1920s. The County Council and the Borough education committee were both initially against the establishment of the national Burnham pay scales and the E.C.C. even contemplated moving away from the national arbitration award. After their introduction the local teachers were still against Burnham, especially when pay rates were reduced in the 1920s. (100) In 1925 the situation was reversed when the education committee didn't accept the Burnham pay scales but the teachers did. (101)

By 1925 house building on the Boarded Barns estate had made a new elementary school essential. The Kings Road School was built for 840 pupils: 320 boys, 320 girls and 200 infants. After the Catholic School in Chelmsford received a poor inspection report and was seriously overcrowded, a new school preparatory school was established on the St Philip's Priory site on London Road. (102) The Board of Education was increasingly concerned with St John's school; besides the lack of playground space, there was no staffroom, no proper hall and a number of small rooms in the Girls department. (103) In the southern part of the borough the Bradford Street site could not be bought. A site in Lady Lane was then identified but the Board of Education didn't think it was large enough to accommodate the infants, junior and senior schools which were necessary. (104)

The early twentieth century continued to see small private schools set up, such as Mrs Bird's school which was opposite the Congregational Church in London Road. Apparently she was a strict, evangelical spinster, who always dressed in black. With two assistant teachers she taught about three dozen pupils and most of these lived close enough to go home at lunchtime. There was a narrow curriculum of Scripture, Grammar, Geography, Arithmetic, Spelling, Reading and Drill. St Anne's was a preparatory school set up in 1925 by two sisters Misses C. and E. Martin who used their own home at 27 New London Road. After starting with only 10 girls it expanded in the 1930s and became a limited company. During the second war the school had to be moved to Danbury. (105)

In 1926 the principal recommendation of the Hadow Report was the separation of primary education and secondary education at the age of 11. Both Chelmsford Borough and the Rural District had Higher Education Committees, but no senior schools had resulted, apart from the Girls High School (see later). By the 1930s the borough's extension proposals included new senior schools at Sandon and Baddow. (106) In 1937 the decision was made to build a new church school to replace the Victoria schools. (107) The county council had opposed the Church's proposal for a Church of England senior school because the state of the Victoria schools made a new elementary school essential. By the outbreak of the second war there was a need for a new infants and junior school on the planned Melbourne estate. In 1935 the proposed Moulsham Schools were switched from Lady Lane to their eventual site off the Princes Road. (108) The opening of the Moulsham Schools enabled the closure of St John's and the small Widford school. (109)

    The school log books, which had to be kept by head teachers, reveal a great deal about life in schools during the early part of the twentieth century. After its opening in 1911, the Trinity Road School logbook shows the frequent visits by Temperance societies, including the Band of Hope. (110) At the Widford Church of England school the Reverend Thurlow gave weekly lessons. (111) One inspection mentioned the "friendly discipline". But "it is a pity that more children cannot work by themselves". (112) Both the Widford and Trinity Road schools, like all the Chelmsford schools, celebrated Empire day, on which the flag was saluted and national songs sung. (113) In 1919 a school nurse was finally appointed to the district and visited the Widford school. During 1923 the school competed in the first Chelmsford Schools sports day, which was held at the Crompton sports ground. (114) After the first war the school always held a memorial service on Armistice Day at the Widford War Memorial, by the churchyard gate. (115) Diphtheria remained a dangerous disease and in 1928 a case at the school was removed to the isolation hospital. The drains and lavatories were inspected and swabs taken from the children. (116) Widford's log book finishes in 1934 when boundary changes meant that the school became the responsibility of the borough. At the new Trinity School the inspectors from the beginning identified a major failing, common to all the Chelmsford schools; namely the lack of facilities for practical manual occupations. (117) During the first war Trinity, like the other schools, contributed to war savings. (118) In 1917 each child was given instruction in what to do in the event of an air raid. (119) By 1918 the absence of two teachers who had been called up was causing the school great difficulties. (120) A student teacher was given a class of 21 "backward" pupils in 1921. In the same year the S.M.O. examined those pupils whose parents were unemployed. (121) By 1924 the school nurse was coming in to weigh, measure and test the eyesight of the boys. (122) The absence of woodwork was still being mentioned in 1929. (123) A 1931 report on Trinity again mentioned the "kindly discipline" which conflicts with many other recollections of life in Chelmsford schools in the early part of the century. Vic Hales remembered the regular use of the cane at the Friars school before the first war, as did Fred Warner who went to the Church of England School, Springfield. (124).

Economic depression after the war meant that the aim of raising the amount of free places to 40% at the boys' grammar school had to be abandoned. (125) The school introduced the School Certificate and Higher School Certificate to try to get pupils to say on to the sixth form and a written contract with parents ensured that parents did stay on until 16, but only a few stayed beyond that. Further scholarships were needed for higher education after the first scholarships had been named after Frederick Chancellor. Despite the cuts imposed by the Geddes Axe, a well qualified teaching staff was built up and by 1922 only one teacher remained from before the war. (126) By 1927 money from the Board of Education had ceased going straight to the school and was going first to the education authority. (127) The school continued to improve under a new head H. Bailey, and by 1930 County scholarships were taking 19% of entrance places. (128) A new head Norman Squier took over in 1934, after being a pupil from 1902 to 1906. (129) Bailey left when questions were raised about his wife's relationship with several of the boarders! (130) In 1935 the County Council said they would only finance necessary new buildings in return for the school taking fully maintained status. This would have meant giving all the foundation property to the County Council. Instead the governors mortgaged the Broomfield Road site with the right of repossession should the governors default. The depression meant that fewer pupils stayed on past 16 and prior to the outbreak of the second war there were only six boys in the 6th form and none went on to University. (131) Even so, the grammar school was well established as a state school with two thirds of its entrants coming from the elementary schools. (132)

By the 1900s Chelmsford still didn't have a girls' secondary school but the success of female adults in the Cambridge University extension classes, held at the Museum (see chapter 27) had showed the need was present. (133) The new county education authority recognised that there were very few girls' secondary schools in Essex and one was earmarked for Chelmsford. It was to give a general education for those who could afford payment or those who could secure free places. (134) The school opened in May 1907 and by July had 77 scholars. (135) By 1909 it had 110 pupils, almost equal to K.E.G.S., of which 35 were fee payers and 20 boarders who stayed in an approved lodging hostel. (136)(137) In 1910 Miss Harcourt, the first headmistress announced her wedding and, as was the custom, had to leave. The new headmistress was Edith Bancroft from Radford School, Bristol, who was to leave an indelible mark on the school. (138) The school soon reached 150 pupils and in 1914 the county gave a grant for enlargement. (139) Gymnasiums were started but not finished until after the first war. A domestic science room was completed in 1916. (140) During the war the school provided an education for students who had fled from Belgium. (141) By 1922 the school had reached a peak of 350 but was seriously overcrowded. The County had bought army huts as a temporary measure but they were still there 25 years later. (142) The school received a large donation of £500 in 1924 but that had to be used for school leaving scholarships. (143) Inspectors of the school had a very high opinion of Miss Bancroft. At the speech day of 1922 her warning was "cinemas, dancing, motor jaunts all were enemies of the weekly work routine". (144) In 1929 she said that women aged 21 would soon have the vote and "it was very important that a girl should be well educated so that she can think, weigh and choose". (145) She retired in 1935 but never missed a speech day afterwards until her death in 1971. The year before, she had attended a dinner to mark her 100th birthday and when a Bancroft wing was opened in 1950s she had performed the opening ceremony.

Chelmsford High School For Girls built 1907, extended 1914 and 1932
(Courtesy of E.R.O.)

As with the boys, numbers declined during the 1930s because of the depression. (146) Fees were raised to £4. 6 s. 6d. for parents in the Chelmsford area, and £4. 11 s. for parents elsewhere in the county. In 1935 the County said that one of each year's three forms had to be "scholars", with no automatic entry from the Preparatory School. (147) The County had sanctioned £2,500 for essential building work when the second war started. (148)

By the early twentieth century, towns such as Ipswich had their own technical colleges. The borough, with doubtless one eye as usual on expense, built its school of science and art as part of buildings which also housed the museum and the library (see chapter 27). It was soon renamed the School of Art and Technology. (149) At the same time the County opened its new laboratories in Chelmsford, designed by Frank Whitmore the County architect. (150) As the demand for evening classes grew rapidly after the first war, with the further the expansion of the big three firms, a new technology block was built in 1929, allowing for classes in cookery, woodwork and metalwork. These facilities were used by local schoolchildren during the day, making up, to some extent, for the lack of facilities in their own schools. (151) The big three firms were sending their women and boys to special classes. In 1935 the College again changed its name to the Mid Essex Technical College. (152) Fees were charged to most of the boys and girls going to the day college but in 1937 there were 35 free places for boys and 33 for girls. (153) By 1938 the Marconi Company was releasing 52 students each day to go to the college. Prior to the second war, new buildings were finished with extra workshops. (154)

The Industrial School had 150 boys in January 1915. Forty four left during that year and 42 were admitted. Of the 44, 16 were placed on farms, 10 returned to home, 3 went to Canada, 5 joined the army, 2 went into the hotel service, 7 went into other occupations and 1 was boarded out. (155) In 1920 a new uniform for going out was introduced, designed to look less institutionalised. (156) Three years later, there were rumours the school was to be closed because numbers had fallen from 150 to 90. It was now sustained by government grants, subscriptions and contributions from parents. (157) The rumours proved to be unfounded and the school was renamed the Essex Home School in 1925. (158) Nineteen twenty six saw the death of the school's founder Joseph Brittain Pash aged 87. (159) He had also run the agricultural machinery business opposite the market (see chapter 1). By the time of its jubilee in 1922 more than 1,800 boys had passed through the school. (160) In 1929 a new hall for recreation and gymnastics was opened by the Lord Lieutenant of Essex. (161) The school went on to have considerable success at boxing. (162) By the 1930s the school had its own theatre and swimming pool, as well as the band which had been originally formed back in the previous century. In 1933 the school was certified as an Approved School for boys between 6 and 16.

In May 1939 Chelmsford was told to expect 9,500 evacuees, of which up to half were likely to be children. (163) The Education Committee was told it couldn't expect to evacuate any children elsewhere. Teachers were given a course in anti gas protection and first aid. (164) After requests to be taken off the receiving list for evacuees, the number was at least reduced to 7,000 in June. Schools were to operate a double shift system. In the event 2,543 evacuees had arrived in Chelmsford by the 12th of September, although some who arrived at the station were simply ferried to the rural areas; of these 1,437 were children. (165) A request for 200,000 sandbags to defend the schools was turned down. (166) A proposed "scattering scheme", which involved letting pupils go to local houses in the event of a raid, was abandoned in favour of providing shelters for schools. (167) The unclean state of many of the evacuee children caused much comment and the S.M.O. was asked to inspect them. During the "phoney war" most of the children returned to London and in May 1940 the Government decided the town would not be used in the phase 4 evacuation plans. (168) Meanwhile the education committee was complaining about the slow completion of the shelters. By May 1940, 15 were in various stages of completion. If children were in school when the bombing started they were instructed to take up positions away from the windows. By December netting had been provided for windows in all the schools except Rainsford Senior, which had internal shelters. (169) The committee opposed the use of shelters by adults after school had finished but was overruled. They were supposed to be handed over in a clean condition. The camouflage of schools was considered undesirable because the Germans might think it concealed military targets. (170) From the outset the war had an adverse effect on attendance. Warning letters were regularly sent out but the absence of males in most households and the necessity for women to work had a marked effect on attitudes to school and behaviour. This led to the opening of a youth centre in 1942 at Friars School. (171) (172) By the end of the war the education committee were finally forced to start prosecuting the parents of absentees and to provide school dinners, 6d a day was charged for all but a small number of pupils. The meals had to be ferried in from Billericay. Once built, the shelters worked well, although several had to be strengthened.

As during the first war, the boys' grammar school was profoundly affected by the second war. Initially the school had to receive boys from Tottenham Grammar School but most quickly went back to London and by the end of August 1940 there were only 40 such pupils left. (173) Air raid trenches were quickly available at the school. Soon 200 boys were having school dinners because their mothers were working. (174) Half of the leavers opted to join the Air Force. (175) In 1942 the school was directly in the 'firing range' when the nearby Hoffmann factory was attacked and at the end of that year the school was used for two air balloons. Remains of the concrete bases used for securing the balloons, could still be seen fifty years later. (176)

As at the boys, school trenches had been dug at the girls' school when the second war broke out. The fact that it still admitted boarders led to record numbers at the school, with 381 pupils in 1943. School buildings were damaged and the worst raid was in December 1944 "when windows were broken in nearly every room, the roof and brickwork was damaged, all doors burst open". The girls spent long hours in the shelters and Miss Cadbury, who had taken over from Miss Bancroft in 1935, remembered "the courage of the girls, many of them who spent their nights and much of their days in shelters but regarded it as a point of honour to be at the school on time". (177)

The 1944 Butler Education Act not only laid out the tripartite system of secondary education, which was to be introduced after the war, but it also provided for the transfer of the borough's powers with regard to education to the county council.

1) Essex Weekly News 13 9 1889
2) Essex Chronicle 1 7 1881 p.5
3) E.C. 8 7 1881 p.9
4) E.C. 15 9 1882 p.5
5) E.W.N. 24 3 1880
6) E.C. 24 3 1883 p.6
7) E.W.N. 26 6 1882 p.5
8) E.W.N. 7 5 1880 p.4
9) E.W.N. 30 10 1885 p.5
10) E.C. 5 6 1885 p.5
11) Hilda Grieve The Sleepers and the Shadows Vol.2 p.368
12) E.W.N. 1 4 1881
13) E.W.N. 1 8 1884 p.5

14) E.C. 21 3 1890 p.5
15) E.C. 28 8 1891
16) E.C. 30 7 1897 p.4
17) E.C. 14 4 1898 p.4
18) E.C. 28 4 1898 p.4
19) E.C. 25 3 1901
20) E.W.N. 13 9 1889 p.5
21) E.W.N. 10 5 1899 p.5
22) Chelmsford Borough Council minutes 25 7 1894
23) C.B.C. minutes 2 5 1897
24) An Edwardian Hamlet: Howe Street in Great Waltham 1901 – 1910 Alan Maddock p.74
25) Little Baddow Sheila Rowley p.32
26) The Chignalls Wilkins p.73
27) A History of Norwich F. Mears p.172
28) History of Ipswich P. Bishop p.134
29) A Portrait of Victorian Colchester Peter Cherry p.85
30) E.W.N. 20 2 1903 p.3
31) Essex County Council minutes July 1906 p.296
32) Chelmsford Borough Council minutes 27 5 1902
33) E.W.N. 20 9 1907 p.2
34) E.W.N. 27 3 1908 p.4
35) E.W.N. 27 8 1908 p.4
36) E.W.N. 15 2 1910 p.2
37) E.C.C. minutes p.267
38) E.C.C. minutes 1904 p.218
39) E.C.C. minutes 1907 p.51
40) E.C.C. minutes January 1909
41) C.B.C. minutes 29 4 1904
42) Chelmsford Education Committee minutes 19 3 1907
43) C.E.C. minutes 19 10 1909
44) C.E.C. minutes 13 12 1921
45) C.B.C. minutes 20 3 1910
46) C.B.C. minutes 25 10 1910
47) C.B.C. minutes 31 8 1910

48) C.B.C. minutes 27 3 1912
49) C.B.C. minutes 24 4 1912
50) C.B.C. minutes 29 10 1919
51) C.E.C. minutes 30 8 1908
52) C.E.C. minutes 14 7 1903
53) C.B.C. minutes 24 2 1915
54) C.E.C. minutes 20 6 1917
55) E.C. 14 5 1889 p.6
56) Grieve p.370
57) E.C. 12 3 1882 p.5
58) E.C. 29 9 1882 p.5
59) E.W.N. 23 9 1887 p.8
60) Grieve p.370
61) E.W.N. 25 7 1890 p.5
62) E.W.N. 2 1 1891 p.5
63) E.W.N. 18 10 1901
64) E.C. 1 8 1884 p.5
65) E.W.N. 21 8 1885
66) E.C. 17 7 1885 p.5
67) E.W.N. 2 10 1885 p.5
68) E.W.N. 25 1 1887 p.5*
69) E.C. 27 1 1888 p.5
70) E.C. 16 8 1889 p.5
71) E.W.N. 7 11 1889 p.5
72) E.C. 14 8 1891 p.5
73) E.W.N. 1 8 1890 p.5
74) E.W.N. 13 5 1892 p.2
75) E.W.N. 1 7 1892 p.2
76) E.C. 1 12 1893 p.4
77) E.C. 9 9 1892 p.5
78) Tuckwell p.82
79) Tuckwell p.89
80) E.W.N. 3 11 1905 p.5
81) Tuckwell p.101
82) Tuckwell p.101*

83) Tuckwell p.104
84) E.W.N. 25 3 1910
85) Tuckwell p.110
86) Tuckwell p.111
87) Tuckwell p.117
88) The Chelmsford Museums records
89) E.W.N. 24 10 1881 p.5
90) E.W.N. 18 5 1883 p.2
91) "I went to the Tech" Edited by John Marriage
92) Marriage p.17
93) Tuckwell p.72
94) E.W.N. 11 11 1892 p.5
95) E.C. 23 2 1894 p.4
96) New Hall Tuckwell p. 141
97) C.E.C. minutes 8 11 1921
98) C.E.C. minutes 13 12 1921
99) C.E.C. minutes 14 9 1920
100) E.C. 25 10 1920
101) C.E.C. minutes 8 9 1925
102) C.E.C. minutes 8 9 1931
103) C.E.C. minutes !4 9 1926
104) C.E.C. minutes 8 3 1927
105) C. Museums records
106) C.E.C. minutes 21 9 1932
107) C.E.C. minutes 10 11 1937
108) C.E.C. minutes 10 1 1939
109) C.E.C. minutes 2 9 1940
110) Trinity Road Boys School Log Book p.2
111) Widford C.of E. School Log Book p.9
112) Widford School p.16
113) Widford School Log Book p.24
114) Widford School Log Book p.165
115) Widford School Log Book p.196
116) Widford School Log Book p.215
117) Trinity Log Book P15

118) Trinity Log Book 15 1 1917
119) Trinity Log Book 22 1 1917
120) Trinity Log Book 8 7 1918
121) Trinity Log Book 5 9 1921
122) Trinity Log book 23 1 1924
123) Trinity Log Book 13 12 1929
124) E.R.O. Oral library
125) Tuckwell p.121
126) Tuckwell p.124
127) Tuckwell p.127
128) Tuckwell p.129
129) E.W.N. 15 6 1934 p.6
130) Tuckwell p.131
131) Tuckwell p.136
132) Tuckwell p.138
133) C. Museums records
134) History of Chelmsford County High School for Girls Mary Kenyon p.3
135) E.C.C. minutes 1907 p.348
136) E.C.C. minutes 1909 p.61
137) Kenyon p.14
138) Kenyon p.17
139) E.C.C. minutes 6 1 1914
140) Kenyon p.21
141) C. Museums records
142) Kenyon p.22
143) E.C. C. minutes 1 1 1924 p.159
144) Kenyon p.26
145) C. Museums records Chelmsford people
146) Kenyon p.28
147) Kenyon p.28
148) Kenyon p.35
149) "I went to the Tech." Edited by John Marriage p.17
150) E.W.N. 4 9 1903 p.6
151) Marriage p.21
152) Marriage p.22

153) C.E.C. 8 6 1937 p.16
154) E.W.N. 21 10 1938 p.7
155) E.W.N. 26 3 1915
156) E.W.N. 20 8 1920 p.5
157) E.W.N. 18 5 1923 p.2
158) E.W.N. 10 7 1925 p.3
159) E.W.N. 12 2 1926 p.6
160) C. Museums records – Chelmsford people
161) E.W.N. 4 2 1929 p.3
162) E.W.N. 4 4 1930 p.11
163) C.E.C. minutes 9 5 1939 p.256
164) C.E.C. minutes 9 5 1939 p.256
165) C.E.C. minutes 12 9 1939
166) C.E.C. minutes 8 9 1938 p.207
167) C.E.C. minutes 1 12 1939 p.302
168) C.E.C. minutes 14 5 1940 p.13
169) C.E.C. minutes 3 12 1940 p.55
170) C.E.C. minutes 14 4 1941 p.56
171) C.E.C. minutes 3 6 1941 p.88
172) C.E.C. minutes 27 11 1941 p.114
173) Tuckwell p.144
174) Tuckwell p. 140
175) Tuckwell p.141
176) Tuckwell p.147
177) Kenyon p.35

21

Education in Chelmsford after 1945

"Only if selective schools go will we have genuine comprehensive education"

In the almost seventy years since the end of the second war, the Chelmsford area has gone from having a limited secondary education system and a significant number of village schools under threat, to having one of the best sets of schools at both primary and secondary level in the country. The process of improvement was not smooth however with overcrowding being a significant problem in the 1950s. Chelmsford's two selective schools have survived and the King Edward Grammar School remains in the State system after looking at various times almost certain to go independent. The area's general high standard of both primary and secondary education has made a significant contribution to the attractiveness of the area to newcomers. Although Chelmsford failed in its attempt to get Essex's first university, by the new millennium it had a thriving university of its own on a brand new campus.

The 1944 Education Act, as with every area of the country, had enormous effects on Chelmsford. First it established uniform change from primary school to secondary school at eleven. This meant the remaining elementary schools becoming primary schools and teaching pupils up to the age of 11 instead of 14. The Act introduced compulsory secondary education for all children up to the age of 15. Secondary schools were to be divided by the tripartite system, namely grammar schools, technical schools and secondary modern schools. Even then it did allow for comprehensive schools which would take mixed ability intakes. Pupils took the 11 plus because it was thought abilities and aptitudes were more or less fixed. The Act also resulted in Chelmsford losing control over education and a Mid Essex Education Executive Committee was set up, one of six in the County. This central division included Chelmsford, Maldon and

Saffron Walden, and the Ongar and Dunmow rural districts. Both, Chelmsford Borough and the R.D.C., had two representatives each, with the other authorities having one each. The Butler Education Act also mentioned that the L.E.A. should give support to nursery education but this was certainly not a priority. The Ministry of Education decided that nurseries should be provided by schools but the borough council allowed the Waterloo Lane, Corporation Road and London Road nurseries should continue until the schools could provide them. (2)(3) A month later the county education committee decided to take over the three nurseries.

These nurseries had finally been started during the war, after pressure from mothers working in the Chelmsford factories. (4) The chair of the Women at Work Committee Jean Roberts had played a prominent role and the Trades Council also played a part. (5)

By 1942 the nursery at Corporation Road was almost finished but the two others had barely been started because of the lack of materials. (6) Ministry of Health officials set high standards preferring that the nurseries be overstaffed rather than understaffed. The Corporation Road nursery opened in August and the one at Waterloo Lane a few weeks later and were judged a great success, even though they were viewed as a social experiment. Their positive inspection was due in no small part to the help given by the Women's Volunteer Service. (7) Attendance did however drop and by the beginning of 1943 the three nurseries were only operating at less than one third of capacity. (8) The Council was however pleased that the National Society of Child Nurseries reported that they were running smoothly and that they appeared to be a happy atmosphere in all three. (9) Working mothers also pressed for play centres to look after their children after school. This demand was resisted because it was felt that it would set a dangerous precedent and allow mothers to shirk their responsibilities. Even though the demand for nursery places hadn't quite matched what had been expected, the likely growth of industry in post war Chelmsford and with it the continued employment of many women in the factories meant that continued nursery provision was essential. Indeed the council quickly identified the need for additional nursery facilities in the Melbourne Park and Springfield Park estates. (10) Severe financial stringencies meant that the government's initial desire for nursery facilities in the schools was never a serious prospect in the Chelmsford area, in the immediate post war era.

The Butler Act also included the compulsory provision of school meals by L.E.A.s. Chelmsford and also the E.C.C. had a long standing resistance to providing such meals. In 1908 the Essex County Council had declined to do anything about meals. (11) As seen in chapter 19 Chelmsford's S.M.O. was forced to provide cocoa to the most malnourished children in the depression of the early 1920s but refused to provide proper meals. During the second war the provision of school meals became essential because so many mothers were working. The borough considered two schemes; firstly providing its own meals from three Chelmsford schools and secondly using a Ministry of Food cooking depot. (12) Chelmsford borough council came under strong pressure to provide midday meals for the 400 pupils now receiving free milk. (13) It was not until August 1942 that a scheme involving a depot was approved. Parents were to be charged 6d a meal. (14) The meals were delivered from Witham and there were frequent complaints about their quality and the fact that they were often not hot. (15) Inevitably there were problems getting the food from the depot to the schools. In the first three weeks of the scheme an average of 900 meals was sent, but by the beginning of 1943 this had fallen to below 800. (16)(17) The Government were pursuing an objective of 95% of pupils receiving school meals and the council were forced to consider at least some of its schools providing meals. By the end of the war the Moulsham and Rainsford Schools were each providing 1,000 meals a day, with the latter cooking meals for Kings Road pupils. (18) In 1945 the proportion of Chelmsford children receiving school meals was not far short of the national average (22% compared with 30%) (19). The Witham depot was still providing 5,000 meals a week, by far the majority. (20) After the war all schools had to have dining rooms, although for a long while they were not purpose built.

In the immediate post war period the conversion of elementary schools to primary schools threatened 60 schools in the county, of which 2 were in the borough and thirteen in the rural area. These were Friars Infants and St Peter's in the borough and included East, West and South Hanningfield Voluntary Schools, Good Easter County School and Writtle Junior Boys and Girls in the rural area. The Weekly News said "Many of the smaller schools were in scattered villages and hamlets and often were dark, insanitary and inconvenient." Great Leighs School had toilets that consisted of buckets, cleaned three times a week by contractors. These were so awful that some children refused to use them. (21) In the event no schools closed immediately because the remaining pupils would have to be educated somewhere. There would be the logistic problem and the expense of bussing them to surrounding villages. The very small school of St Peter's in the borough wasn't even scheduled for closure until 1959. (22)

The immediate education problems in the Chelmsford area were not going to be improved by closing schools. They were caused by the rapid growth of population in the area, which would necessitate new schools, coupled with the severe financial constraints of the post war era. The latter meant that no new schools were built immediately. In 1952 the Ministry of Education and the County Council were blocking a new primary school on the Chignal estate and a new secondary school at Broomfield. The Rainsford and Moulsham secondary schools already had almost 2,000 pupils between them. (23) "Overcrowded conditions in Mid Essex" ran the headline in a 1954 edition of the Weekly News. School space was only 65% of the standards set by the Ministry that year. (24) In the Chelmsford area 3,510 pupils were taught in classes of more than 40, 2,166 in classes of more than 45 and 850 in classes of more than 50 or more. A report to the Mid Essex Executive committee had already outlined the slum conditions in which thousands of children were being educated. It had cited the gross overcrowding, primitive sanitary conditions, lack of modern drainage and leaking roofs in a number of schools. (25) Although the financial conditions in the country as a whole had greatly eased by the mid 1950s, it was several years before this resulted in the necessary new schools in the Chelmsford area. Councillors repeatedly claimed that new towns such as Basildon and Harlow were receiving preferential treatment. Seven new schools were put forward for the Chelmsford area in 1954, including secondary schools at Sandon and Broomfield and junior schools at Great Baddow and Melbourne Park but two years later several building projects put forward by Mid Essex were still being blocked by the County. By this time the post war baby boom was beginning to affect the school intake and there would be a serious shortage of places even if the building programme was carried out. The reserve building programme needed to be put into operation as well. (26) In October 1956, Rab Butler opened the Broomfield Secondary School. Broomfield was designed to take 450 boys and girls and was described as "light and airy". (27) By this time the county's capital spending on education was second only to London. In the early 1960s some of the closures of village schools anticipated 15 years earlier did finally come about but in most cases they were replaced by new schools, for example at Great Baddow and Boreham. (28)

As early as 1963 the Mid Essex education executive discussed the idea of transforming the area's secondary education system into a comprehensive one with a mixed ability intake. In the post-war period the Chelmsford area had followed the tripartite system with a number of secondary modern schools, a technical school and two selective schools. At this time the comprehensive issue was not the controversial one that it was to become, with even some Conservatives giving support to the idea.

In Mid Essex, the grammar, technical and second modern schools would have been substituted by 8 much bigger comprehensive schools. K.E.G.S. and the Girls' High School were to be combined into a junior college for 'A' level students. Broomfield, Westlands, Sandon and Moulsham Schools were to become 8 form entry and Rainsford and Boswells Schools were to become 10 form entry. (29) The proposals came from a sub-committee, but were actually passed by the whole executive, provoking a furious response in the readers' letters columns of the local papers. (30) Not surprisingly, nothing came of these proposals but at the end of 1964 an early 11 to 18 comprehensive was opened at Great Baddow, with a proposed sixth form of 120. (31) The John Payne School, which had opened in 1959 as a Roman Catholic school, took its first steps towards becoming fully comprehensive in 1965 and its extension was to lead to a doubling in of its size. (32) From the mid 1960s the Labour government began encouraging the introduction of comprehensive schools and the phasing out of grammar schools and in 1966 the Mid Essex Executive voted 16 votes to 5 in favour of a scheme which would have set up 12 comprehensives in the Chelmsford area, 10 of which would have been co-educational, including a new school at Barnes Farm. The committee voted by 13 to 10 to retain K.E.G.S. and the Girls' High School as single sex schools but to phase out selection by 1973. (33) This led to an immediate public meeting at the Shire Hall. Public pressure led to a further scheme the following year where the two selective schools would only combine at the sixth form stage. (34) A previous proposal to combine K.E.G.S. and Rainsford School was abandoned. Parental opposition meant that by July 1967 Mid Essex was the only area in the county not to have submitted a comprehensive scheme to the E.C.C. (35) In June 1970 Mr W. Primmer, the Mid Essex Divisional Educational Officer stated "all Chelmsford's schools must go comprehensive". "Only if selective schools go will we have genuine comprehensive education". (36)

The election of a Conservative government in 1970 changed everything. Edward Heath's new government did not attempt to roll back those changes in education that had occurred, but supported the retention of existing selective schools. This enabled the controlling Conservative group on the County Council to keep the remaining selective schools, including K.E.G.S. (37)

Norman St John Stevas supported the 90% of parents who wanted the Moulsham schools to be co-educational, after the county council had originally decided to keep the sexes separate. (38) It went co-educational, with the option of reversing back if the parents wished by the end of the decade. A decision to close Ingatestone

Secondary School, which had only been opened in 1959, was also postponed after public pressure. (39) Continued increased population led the area to follow the vogue for large schools. An extension was carried out to the Sandon School to enable it to accommodate 1,320 pupils. (40) Extension plans for Moulsham School were scrapped however, and it stayed at 10 form entry. (41) The new Boswells School increased from 2 to 8 and eventually 12 forms of entry. Hylands comprehensive school was formed out of an expanded Westlands School, eventually rising to 1,320 pupils. New primary schools were approved at Beehive Lane, at Great Baddow and at Danbury Park and Binacre. (42)(43)

In 1973 the Essex Education Committee voted in favour of the two Chelmsford selective schools remaining single sex selective schools; each would remain at 3 forms of entry and accommodate only 5% of pupils in the area. (44) Essex County Council was to stick resolutely to its policy of keeping the two selective schools in the area, whilst turning the rest of the areas secondary schools comprehensive. (44) The fact that the areas' two selective schools only took a small proportion of the total number of pupils helped them to maintain this strategy, legitimately arguing that the comprehensives did take a wide range of abilities.

After a prolonged battle, which went to the Minister of Education, Margaret Thatcher, the Mid Essex Technical School merged with Broomfield School (see later). (45) The performance of the new comprehensives was hotly debated and a local newspaper had to apologise for an inaccurate article when it alleged pupil violence at the giant Great Baddow comprehensive. (46) The mid 1970s was a difficult period for education in the Chelmsford area generally, with teachers finding it difficult to get accommodation, which led to a shortage. Essex as a whole was low in its average spending on pupils and its pupil teacher ratio at primary school level was 1:28, the highest in the South East: in the secondary list Chelmsford had the second highest ratio. (47)

After 1974 the new Labour government wanted to complete the move to comprehensive education. The Education Minister wanted a pledge from the County Council that it would remove all its grammar schools after 1978. (48) Stevas spearheaded the opposition to plans to scrap the local selective schools. Local Liberal councillor Bob Battey criticised Stevas, saying Essex was creating a "super selective process" for the very small minority going to grammar schools. (49) The Tameside decision by the Law Lords allowed local grammar schools to continue there and gave the two Chelmsford schools hope, but a new Education Bill would force E.C.C. to come up with plans for full comprehensives. (50)

Before the end of the second war the governors of K.E.G.S. had to consider the Butler Act. They had the choice of taking voluntary aided status, which would have given maximum independence or voluntary controlled status, which would lay the school open to maximum interference. One problem was that the endowments now brought in only a little income. The separation of pupils at the age of 11 meant that the preparatory school would have to disappear. (51) The change to voluntary controlled status proved too much for the head Norman Squier, who found the regulation under the new regime irritating and he retired in 1949. (52) Under the new head, Nigel Fanshawe, the school would flourish but initially it had to recover from the war. The buildings were filthy and there had been no maintenance. E.C.C. wanted a three form entry school with 500 pupils and a 'fast stream' was established to enable the A level students to take the Oxbridge entrance exams. (53) In the early 1950s the foundation governors were restored as a governing body separate from the managing governors. It was found that the local authority had kept no proper spending records and a new scheme of management was not agreed by the local authority and the Charity Commissioners until 1966. (54) The 'baby bulge' began to have a affect on pupil numbers in the late 1950s and in 1957 the school became 4 form entry, with numbers topping 640 the following year. (55) (56). An inspection in 1955 was generally good but noted that the hall was too small and pressure of numbers meant that for four years K.E.G.S. used the Rectory Lane Youth Centre. (57) For a short period the school also used the disused Friars School before the construction of Parkway started.

Fanshawe thought the numbers entering the two sixth forms would plunge if K.E.G.S. and the Girls High School were merged at sixth form level as mentioned earlier. (58) To an extent K.E.G.S. was always in control of its own destiny because, unlike the girls' school, the Broomfield Road site belonged to the foundation trust and not the county council. (59) In 1976 the Church of England made the suggestion that K.E.G.s. and the High School might become voluntary aided C. of E. schools but the fact that parents would have to give £600 per annum meant that this was never a serious proposition. (60)

The Butler Act changed the Girls' High School radically because it had not become a grant aided foundation and could no longer charge fees. Its preparatory school had to close in 1947. Because the war had prevented scheduled extension to the buildings, the accommodation problem became increasingly severe in the 1950s and the huts and prefabs became a permanent feature. By 1958 the pupil roll had risen to 584 and space was at a premium with 30 girls packed into rooms designed for 18. In 1959 plans were submitted for a three storey block consisting of a hall, kitchen, library as well as music, art and science complexes, which finally allowed the huts and prefabs to go. (61) The new accommodation was actually built in 1961 and also included extra sporting facilities. (62) It had celebrated its jubilee with a service at the cathedral in 1957. (63)

By 1977, K.E.G.S. had announced its intention to go independent; this would have turned the clock back 33 years when it was an independent grant aided school. (64) This route was not open to the girls' school because it had no endowment funds of its own and did not own the site. If the go-ahead to abolish the two schools had been given by Shirley Williams, the move would have cost the K.E.G.S. 2 million pounds. This would have been the cost of compensation to the E.C.C. for equipment and buildings supplied to the school. The foundation governors couldn't have raised that amount of money and it would have had to revert to a fee paying school. (65) Plans for the Girls' High school to become a mixed ability comprehensive were found to be impractical by the D.E.S. Then the D.E.S. vetoed the plans by K.E.G.S. to go independent and also a plan to convert the girls' school to a Church of England comprehensive. (66) In October 1977 the government threatened to take the County Council to court for failing to meet the latest deadline for phasing out selective schools in breach of the 1976 Education Act. (67) A further deadline was set for October 1978, but K.E.G.S. had decided to go independent irrespective of whether the Conservatives won the coming election. The County Council managed to successfully argue that yet another deadline for September 1980 was impractical. (68) At the beginning of 1979 a further deadline was set for September 1981 but the election of the Conservatives settled the issue for the foreseeable future.

The Home School (previously the Industrial School) was now under the full control of the County Council. In 1976 the school's pupils were entered for the first time in 'O' level and C.S.E. exams. (69) This and other changes were introduced by the new principal Alan Stephens but he was hindered by a long term fall in numbers. Three years later the County Council took the decision to close the school. This caused an outcry locally, but the school then only housed 22 boys when it had the accommodation and facilities to keep 82 'wayward' children. (70) There had been a withdrawal of referrals by London boroughs, with a resulting loss of income. (71) A heated debate followed as to whether the school had gradually obtained a bad reputation but it was certainly very expensive, costing £301 per child per week, 4 times the cost of a boy at Eton! (72) Existing staff tried to get support for a move to accept girls in a newly created school.

This would not however, have produced the required numbers and the school closed in 1980. The buildings were demolished in 1987. (73)

By the second war, Chelmsford had a secondary technical school and a technical college on the same site, which had been the old museum, library and school of art. Unlike the South East Technical College it was not taken over by army trainees and both the Junior and Senior School managed to keep going. (74) Special courses were put on for the forces, including fitters, electricians, carpenters and joiners. Under the Butler Act the technical school was due to increase to 540 pupils, giving parents in the borough the choice of a practical education for their children. (75) The school had the advantage that the local engineering firms were always ready to accept boys from the school. From the outset a larger technical college for adults was being planned. Dovedale House in Moulsham was already being used and negotiation took place to use the old Victoria boys' school, but new buildings were needed. (76) In 1947 there were 2,500 students taking evening classes coming from a very wide area. By 1967 the college was the most popular in East Anglia. (77)

The technical school changed its name to the Technical High School in 1962 after it had moved to Patching Hall Lane in 1958. Against the prevailing trend towards comprehensives, there were plans on the part of the Mid Essex Executive and the governors to make it selective. Frank Cooper had been appointed head in 1961 and under him the sixth form flourished with an increasing number going on to University. The important strand of technical education was retained, with metalwork, woodwork, technical drawing and applied science and technology all being studied. There was an increasing "use of engineering and technology to solve problems regarding design, construction and the use of working models". (78) In 1975 the move away from the original site was achieved by a merger with Broomfield Secondary Modern School. The resulting Chelmer Valley High School had to overcome significant problems including initially being split site and also having to combine two separate staffs. Cooper took most of his staff with him and the L.E.A. made them heads of department because the technical school had won the reputation for being of grammar school standard.

In 1960 the government proposed the establishment of a new university in Essex. At the start the local papers considered Chelmsford the favourite, with Hylands the preferred site. (79) Colchester was chosen however, allegedly because it was further away from London and there would be less likelihood of students travelling backwards and forwards to and from London. This it was hoped would create a better community spirit. (80)

The election of the Thatcher government in 1979 was to bring about a profound change in the education of the country over the next two decades. Apart from the cessation of the move towards the abolition of the remaining grammar schools little happened until the passing of the 1988 Education Act. Previously however supporters of the introduction of market forces into State education had raised the idea of an educational voucher giving concrete choices to parents, but this idea was abandoned as being impractical. The 1988 act introduced a quasi voucher system because parents could exercise their choice with regard to the schools for their children and school budgets were determined by the number of parents who chose their school. This introduced a measure of market forces into the State sector for the first time. The act also introduced Local Management of Schools, whereby all schools were taken out of the direct financial control of local authorities, with financial control being handed to the head teacher and governors of a school. Grant maintained schools were introduced, whereby primary and secondary schools could remove themselves from their respective local authorities and would be completely funded by central government. The Act also allowed for the establishment of City Technology Colleges and the establishment of the National Curriculum, but it was the first three measures that had a significant effect on the Chelmsford area.

Given the long standing interest in education in the area and an equally well documented aversion to bureaucracy, it is perhaps not surprising that schools in the area reacted positively to the new opportunities that were now available. Putting a positive face on their school, especially with introduction of league tables, enabled schools to increase their rolls and their budgets when the quasi market worked in their favour. Whereas in most of the rest of the country the move towards G.M.S. was slow, in the Chelmsford area it was grasped quickly and not just by the two selective schools. The perceived advantages in terms of independence and access to greater capital were seen as being significant. Both K.E.G.S. and the Girls High School decided to opt out in 1991. (81) Hylands and Boswells schools both opted out soon afterwards, followed by Chelmer Valley High School and Rainsford School. (82)

The 10 Essex Grammar Schools decided to scrap the 11 plus and operate their own selective exam in 1993. (83) Tony Tuckwell, the head teacher at K.E.G.S. hinted in 1991 that his school would become independent if Labour won the next election and tried to abolish grammar schools. "K.E.G.S. independence will be preserved by any means necessary." (84)

In 1993 the Girls' High School came top for all State schools in England for G.C.S.E.

results in the new league tables and K.E.G.S. came 25th. (85) In 1994 K.E.G.S. and the County High were first and second amongst the State Schools as measured by 'A' level results. (86) By the new millennium nearly all the secondary schools in the area were performing well in the league tables. In 1998 the St John Payne School, Moulsham School and Boswells School were 21st, 22nd and 29th in the national tables for G.C.S.E. results. Great Baddow High School was highlighted as one of the most improved schools. (87)

When a Labour government was elected in 1997 it did nothing to reverse the role of market forces in education, although it did not allow any new grammar schools. (88) The 1998 School Standards and Framework Act encouraged diversity by allowing secondary schools to take specialist college status and also replaced G.M.S. with Foundation Schools. After the 1998 Act those schools with specialist college status were eligible to receive additional capital and current grants from central government to complement business sponsorship. (89) Again Chelmsford's schools were amongst the first to obtain specialist college status. Rainsford School obtained specialist status for the performing arts in 2002 and other local schools followed with Hylands getting specialist science status in 2003. (90) This included a sponsorship from GlaxoSmithKline. (91) Chelmer Valley High School obtained specialist engineering status in 2003. Moulsham School was given humanities status in 2005. (92) The new millennium saw most of Chelmsford's secondary schools continue to show very high standards.

K.E.G.S. obtained specialist science status in 2003. Towards the end of the 1990s the school's facilities had been in great need of improvement and in 2000 funds raised by an appeal topped £1 million, which was used for new science laboratories, a music block and new classrooms. In 2001 the school was named school of the year by the Sunday Times. (93) By 2008 it was in the top 5 state schools in the country, when judged by 'A' level results. (94) The Girls' County High School obtained the status of a specialist Technology college in 2000 and in 2004 it was given a second specialism, Music (with English). It had opened the new Cadbury Science block in 1995. (95) Apart from the two selective schools New Hall, Boswells School and John Payne still continued to rate very highly in the league tables well into the new millennium. New Hall is now mixed having 1,150 pupils, both boarding and day, in 2011.

The Chelmsford Technical College, in Victoria Road, merged with Brentwood College in 1975 under the name of the Chelmer Institute of Further Education. (96) By the 1980s the separate Chelmsford College was well established at Moulsham Street and in 1985 the decision was taken to build an extension on Princes Road next to the Moulsham schools. By the new millennium the Moulsham Street campus was concentrating on sixth form courses and the Princes Street site housed the Adult Education Learning Centre.

In the early 1970s East Anglia had the lowest rate of participation in Higher education in the country and the local engineering employers in the town could not recruit staff with the necessary skills. The Chelmer Institute, based at the old Victoria Road South site became the Essex Institute of Higher Education in 1984 but a plan for a federal centre of higher education spanning four counties came to nothing when the centres couldn't agree on the proposals. (97) By 1986 the Chelmsford based Institute had 14,000 students but only 1,000 of these were full time. (98) There was no polytechnic in the whole of East Anglia. Plans were drawn up for a merger between the Essex Institute and the Cambridgeshire College. A major site outside Chelmsford with residential accommodation for 2,500 students was proposed. (99) The college was to have the largest business school in Europe and a big law department as well as facilities for the training of teachers and nurses. Few possible sites remained because of green belt restrictions, with the exception of one on the Boreham interchange. (100) Meanwhile the merged colleges became the Anglia Higher Education College and this then became the Anglia Polytechnic in 1991. The existing buildings were obviously unsuitable and the following year plans were announced to take over the disused Ransome, Hoffmann, Pollard site, at the junction of Rectory Road and New Street. (101) In 1995 the Queen opened the Anglia Ruskin University. (102) The decision to move the whole campus to Rivermead was helped by a gift of £5 million by Michael Ashcroft to build a new business school. In 2005 the name was changed to Anglia Ruskin University, the name Ruskin referring to the John Ruskin School of Art in Cambridge originally opened in 1858. (103) The Rivermead campus was the newest in the U.K. and at the end of the 2000s was offering degree and post graduate courses in Business Studies, Law, Computing and Electronics, Construction, Architecture, Science, Language and arts and Nursing and Health Studies.

Recent years have seen the area consolidate its attractiveness because of the quality of its schools. As before, K.E.G.S., the Girls High School and New Hall have all regularly achieved close to 100% of their pupils gaining 5 A – C Grades at G.C.S.E., but other schools such as Sandon, Hylands and Moulsham consistently achieve about 80% figures. In 2013, St John Payne Roman Catholic School was named in the top ten schools in the country in terms of the number of entrants into Oxbridge. It was the only non selective school in Essex on the list. Unsurprisingly, many of these schools as well as a number of primary schools were keen to take advantage of the greater opportunities to acquire Academy status after 2010. (104) In contrast it was announced in 2009 that St Peter's College (formerly Rainsford School) was to close. Its pupil roll was only 452, when its capacity was 1,030 pupils. It had only come out of special measures in 2007, after previously being deemed a failing school. "The council has a duty of care to take action if there are more than 25% spare places in a school." Opposition to the closure was limited. (105) At the time of writing Meadgate primary school has just been identified as a failing school and put into special measures.

2011 saw the announcement of the £17 million redevelopment of the Columbus Special School which was the result of two major mergers. (106) In 2012 it gained academy status and in March 2013 received commendations in the Civic Trust awards.

November 2012 saw planning permission passed by the city council for the Beaulieu Park development which includes several new primary schools and a secondary school. In contrast, the same year also featured the centenary of the Trinity Road Primary school. (107) Two years earlier, a school with a much greater historical pedigree, New Hall, welcomed television's Time Team. Digging on two sites in the school's grounds they uncovered proof of Henry the Eighths's palace, including the chapel, the gatehouse and the living quarters. (108)

1) Essex Weekly News 23 6 1944 p.9
2) Chelmsford Borough Council minutes 30 1 1946
3) C.B.C. minutes 27 3 1946
4) Essex Chronicle 27 3 1942
5) Malcolm Wallace 'Nothing to Lose and a War to Win'
6) E.C. 10 7 1942
7) E.W.N. 26 11 1943 p.2
8) C.B.C. minutes 24 3 1943
9) C.B.C. minutes 24 11 1943
10) C.B.C. minutes 25 2 1948
11) Essex County Council minutes 4 1908
12) Chelmsford Education Committee 27 11 1941
13) C.B.C. minutes 25 2 1948
14) E.C. 28 8 1942
15) E.W.N. 30 7 1943

16) C.B.C. minutes 11 1942
17) C.B.C. minutes 24 2 1943
18) C.B.C. minutes 28 7 1943
19) C.B.C. minutes 28 6 1944
20) C.B.C. minutes 28 3 1945
21) E.W.N. 17 1 1947 p.10
22) E.C.C. 19 5 1959 p.934
23) E.W.N. 29 2 1952 p.1
24) E.W.N. 25 11 1954
25) E.C. 24 7 1953
26) E.C. 6 4 1956
27) E.W.N. 19 10 1956 p.11
28) E.W.N. 14 7 1961 p.5
29) E.W,N. 6 4 1963 p.9
30) E.W.N. 29 3 1963 p.41
31) E.W.N. 18 12 1964 p.3
32) E.W.N. 17 12 1965
33) E.W.N. 23 11 1966 p.20
34) E.W.N. 19 5 1967 p.11
35) E.W.N. 15 10 1967 p.11
36) E.C. 5 6 1970 p.7
37) E.C. 22 1 1971
38) E.W.N. 26 3 1971
39) E.W.N. 19 3 1971
40) E.W.N. 1 7 1971
41) E.W.N. 10 2 1972 p.1
42) E.W.N. 10 2 1972 p.3
43) E.W.N. 1 2 1973 p.1
44) E.W.N 18 1 1973 p.1
45) E.W.N. 7 11 1974 p.5
46) E.W.N. 17 7 1975 p.1
47) E.W.N. 25 7 1974 p.1
48) E.C. 30 5 1975 p.48
49) E.C. 31 1 1975 p.48
50) E.C. 6 8 1976 p.1

51) Tuckwell p.148
52) Tuckwell p.154
53) Tuckwell p.155
54) Tuckwell p.158
55) Tuckwell p.159
56) Tuckwell p.162
57) Tuckwell p.163
58) Tuckwell p.166
59) Tuckwell p.169
60) www.cchs.co.uk/prospective-students/history-cchs.php
61) History of Chelmsford County High School for Girls Mary Kenyon p.35
62) www.cchs.co.uk/prospective-students/history-cchs.php
63) E.W.N. 10 5 1957 p.5
64) E.C. 13 5 1977 p.1
65) E.C. 14 10 1977 p.1
66) E.W.N. 29 9 1977 p.1
67) E.W.N. 20 10 1977 p.1
68) E.C. 15 9 1978 p.1
69) E.C. 3 9 1976 p.1
70) E.C. 23 11 1979
71) E.C. 1 2 1980 p.1
72) E.C. 1 2 1980 p.88
73) www.freeewebs.com/essexhomesschools/
74) 'I went to the tech.' John Marriage
75) E.W.N. 9 8 1946 p.6
76) E.C. 23 1 1967
77) Marriage p.39
78) E.R.O. SA 24/267/1
79) E.C. 8 7 1960 p.11
80) E.C. 26 1 1962
81) E.C. 13 9 1991 p.3
82) E.C. 2 4 1993 p.3
83) E.C. 17 9 1993 p.1
84) E.W.N. 19 12 1991 p.4
85) E.C. 4 9 1992 p.3

86) E.C. 10 11 1994 p.1
87) E.C. 4 12 1998 p.7
88) How new is New Labour? The quasi market and English schools 1997 to 2001 Anne West and Hazel Pennell p.2
89) West and Pennell p.7
90) E.C. 19 7 2002
91) E.C. 5 2 2003 p.4
92) E.W.N. 30 6 2005 p.5
93) E.W.N. 6 4 2001
94) E.C. 10 1 2008
95) www.cchs.co.uk/prospective-students/history-cchs.php
96) E.C. 18 7 1975
97) E.C. 22 2 1985 p.6
98) E.W.N. 13 11 1986 p.1
99) E.C. 7 10 1983 p.3
100) E.C. 12 1 1990 p.1
101) E.W.N. 23 4 1992 p.1
102) E.W.N. 15 6 1995 p.1
103) Marriage p.56
104) E.C. 23 7 2010 p.27
105) E.C. 5 3 2009 p.6
106) E.C. 20 1 2011
107) E.C. 9 6 2011 p.26
108) E.C. 2 2 2009 p. 4

22

Faith in the Chelmsford area

"We have a parish church Cathedral and we want to make it less like a parish church and more like a Cathedral"

The last 130 years have seen a huge change in the role of religion in peoples' lives. In a small town such as Chelmsford, most people attended church regularly in 1880. Even if they didn't they would ensure that their children attended Sunday school. In the rural area around Chelmsford, church attendance was probably even higher; the established order being reinforced by the reserved pews for landowners and their families and the fact that they often paid for the building and alterations to their local church. We shall see that the various strands of nonconformity were well established in both the town and the rural area by the late Victorian period. The early years of the twentieth century saw the establishment of the Essex Diocese of the Church of England with Chelmsford as its cathedral town. Despite a wide number of alterations and improvements the cathedral remains recognisably the same as the late nineteenth century parish church. The pronouncements of successive bishops were an interesting barometer, both of the changes that occurred in the attitudes of the church and the degree of influence the church has on people. A survey in the 1990s, which revealed that Chelmsford had the fourth lowest church attendance rates in the country, reflected the increasing secularisation of society. (1)

By the 1880s the temperance movement had a strong hold over the middle class trades people and administrators of the town and the promise of the occasional tea and excursion also attracted a large number of working people, whose diet was restricted and access to entertainment almost non-existent. By the 1890s there were up to a dozen temperance societies operating in the Chelmsford and Moulsham parishes. The plethora of public houses and drinking booths gave these societies a good target as did the drinking habits of the expanding number of working people in the town. Some of these societies, like the Band of Hope which had been originally established in 1846, lasted a long time. In 1881 it had 500 members in the town and also had a branch in Great Baddow. (2) The Church of England also had its own well supported Temperance Society in the town, which was even older and met at the Shire Hall and for which services were held at the St Mary's parish church (now the Cathedral). (3) A sermon in 1882 said "drunkenness was essentially the national sin". (4) One feature of these societies was a move towards total abstention. For example, the John Copland Temperance Association, which met regularly in the early 1880s, had turned into the John Copland Abstemers Army by the end of the decade. (5) The Moulsham Teetotal Army met in the Roman Road Mission room. In 1887 it held a "successful entertainment there" with "many not able to get admission" and "twenty pledges were taken during the evening". (6) By 1895 a Women's Total Abstinence Union had been formed, with 200 regularly attending meetings at the Shire Hall out of a total membership of 450. (7) The local papers regarded this development with suspicion, supporting the need to reduce the number of drinking places in the town but regarded the cause of total abstention as being rather extreme. In 1884 the first conference of temperance societies in the Chelmsford area was held at the Co-operative stores. (8) Nine hundred sat down to tea at the Corn Exchange in 1888 after every society sent a contingent. (9)

In the late nineteenth century there were four temperance hotels in Chelmsford. The best known of these was the Roseberry Hotel on Mesopotamia Island (see chapter 11). James Frost was born at the hotel and his parents ran it. He remembered it having 26 bedrooms and his parents employing kitchen and cleaning maids. Two permanent blacksmiths also worked for them. Of course no hard drinks were allowed on the premises, in marked contrast with the other hotels in the town. His father had to sell the business after he developed asthma during the war. (10) S.T. Shipman remembered the hotel and its yard being the hub of activity on the island. (11) Thomas Thorne recalled political parties congregating outside the hotel during election campaigns. (12) Fred Spalding senior remembered a temperance hotel on the site of the old Black Boy public house on the corner of the High Street and Springfield road. Another was the Red Cow at the junction of Rainsford Rd and Broomfield Road.

After the war there was a big fall in the popularity of the temperance societies due in part no doubt to the increase in both the amount of leisure time and the types of leisure activity available. The big organised teas and short trips out no longer seemed so attractive. By 1930 the True Temperance Association was one of the few still operating locally. Nevertheless the evils of drink remained a core theme of all the local church sermons, particularly those of Chelmsford's first Anglican bishop.

The need to refuse the temptation of drink was a common theme of another religious based organisation in the Chelmsford area, namely the Salvation Army. The Chelmsford branch of the S.A. was officially formed in 1886, 21 years after the organisation's foundation in East London by William Booth and his wife Catherine. What is interesting is the amount of outcry the fledgling organisation caused in Chelmsford, as happened in a number of other places. This wasn't due to its theology, which was mainstream Protestant, but its 'quasi' military structure. It was the military type of uniform and the preponderance of marching which supposedly caused much of the fuss, in a country which had a long tradition of avoiding a standing army. In reality it was probably the brewery companies and publicans, alarmed by the organisation's denouncement of drinking, which financially supported the establishment of a 'skeletal army' whose members were dedicated to opposing the 'Army' by fair means or foul.

The 'Army' started holding meetings at the 'Red Cow' public house in Coval Lane in 1885. In July 1885 the Essex Chronicle reported "A contingent of Salvation Army consisting of about a dozen 'soldiers' dressed in scarlet tunics passed through the town and along the Springfield Road yesterday afternoon. A large and imposing caravan with flags flying, drawn by three splendid horses, accompanied them." (13) The following year the paper wrote "on Saturday evening some vendors of the 'War Cry' received somewhat severe treatment from the Chelmsford populace, small crowds hooting and jostling and following them up and down the principal streets." (14) Evidently it was the arrival of a Captain Brewster in the town and the opening of a 'barracks' on the Springfield Road that caused the increased conflict. They were soon attracting big audiences by a combination of marches through the town and music that at the beginning was of dubious quality. (15) At the beginning of 1887 the 'Army' proceeding up Moulsham Street were met by a herd of bullocks turning the Baddow Road corner. "Some of the crowd accompanying the army saw this was an opportunity for a spree and drove the animals forward scattering the soldiers right and left." (16) The following month "'Colonel' Hayward, his wife and daughter were marching from the barracks to the primitive Methodist chapel in Hall Street where they intended holding a service." "On reaching the High Street however they were met by a large crowd of roughs, who formed in front and preceded them to Moulsham Street." "Here they turned and charged the red jerseyed soldiers and completely routed them." Hayward and his wife and daughter had to shelter for two and a half hours in a butcher's shop before the mob left. (17) There was mounting criticism in the local papers who blamed their 'countenance' for the trouble. After one concert in front of the 'Gun' the 'soldiers' left their brass instruments at various shops for safety. (18) The opposition seems to have been able to parade its 'skeletal army', with its flag unhindered. One aim was often to capture the Army's flag or to duck the leader in the pond or the river. The Essex Chronicle admitted that the S.A. did "great good amongst the dwellers in the slums and amongst the poorer classes generally" but that "these ends.... it could attain without all this parade and noise". (19) This opposition was probably the reason why it wasn't until 17 years after the arrival of the 'Army' in the town that it opened its citadel in Moulsham Street. This had a main hall, built to accommodate 350 people, but also had a young people's hall for a further 200. One hundred and fifty sat down for the opening celebratory meal in 1902. (20) The Chelmsford branch established a lodging house and a mission. In the early 1890s it invited the inmates of the Model and Kettle lodging houses in Moulsham as well as a number of those who lived in the town's yards to an annual 'knife and fork' tea. (21). By the early twentieth century the opposition to the 'Army' in the town had largely dissipated and when General Booth came to the town in 1905 he was met by the Mayor, Councillor Gepp, and treated to a dinner at the Corn Exchange presided over by Carne Rasch. (22) In 1936 the Salvation Army celebrated its silver jubilee in the town with around 300 members. (23) Eight years previously it had built a hall on the Boarded Barns estate in the northern part of the town. (24) A number of its followers were conscientious objectors during the second war. Most went into non military occupations but one Salvation Army Insurance agent refused to be conscripted and was given three months imprisonment. (25) In 2009 the organisation became slightly controversial again when it opened its new buildings in Baddow Road, which although its modern design received plaudits in the architectural world divided the townsfolk of Chelmsford to say the least! The church was constructed entirely from laminated pinewood and made in Austria before being transported by a convoy of low loaders and slotted together by a giant crane. In 2011 the organisation celebrated its 125th anniversary in the borough. Nick Simmons Smith, a composer, who is a resident in the U.S., but who was born in Chelmsford, wrote a piece "Chelmsford 125" to commemorate the event.

In the late 19th century the Chelmsford and Moulsham parishes were part of the Diocese of St Albans but prior to 1874 they had been part of the Diocese of Rochester.

(26) St Mary's was basically the church of a prosperous medieval town. Today the church, now of course the cathedral, mainly dates from the 15th and 16th centuries. It was a gothic design with flint work predominating. During the alterations carried out in the 1980s remnants of a 13th century church was found. The nave of the church had been reconstructed after parts of it had collapsed due to gravediggers undermining one of the piers in 1800. (27) In 1880 a new Chancel screen was erected "to the memory of the late Archdeacon Mildmay". (28) The 1876 ordnance survey map shows the church surrounded on three sides by graveyards and noted that there were pews and seating for 1,000. (29) Various galleries had been removed in 1867 and 1873. Also in 1873 an outer north aisle was added with the organ chamber and vestries. (30) In 1882 Chancellor designed and donated as a gift a new south porch. He aimed to restore it as it was in 1424. (31) Work started in 1884 on a number of alterations proposed by the Bishop of St Albans that included the raising of the chancel floor and the erection of choir seats. (32) During 1887 there was public subscription to restore the tomb in the churchyard which was in memory of three women who had perished in a fire in 1808. (33) In 1899 a new timber roof replaced the old one. (34)

After St Mary's became a cathedral in 1914 (see later) there were immediate demands to alter and extend it but this was delayed because of other priorities in establishing the new diocese. After the death of Bishop Watts Ditchfield the demand for alterations coalesced around the need for a suitable memorial to him. Although serious consideration was given to building a permanent house of retreat, eventually it was decided to make major alterations to the chancel. The architect Charles Nicholson had originally produced plans which would have led to the cathedral doubling in size and altering its whole character as the second smallest cathedral in the country after the one in Derby. Companion towers would have been built to add to the original single one. (35) A strong argument against Nicholson's plans was the huge cost of the proposals for what was still a young diocese. The actual alterations carried out added all of fifteen feet in an easterly direction to the chancel and two bays. (36) A statue to Watts Ditchfield was also erected. Nineteen twenty nine also saw new building in the form of new vestries and a chapter house. The organ was moved away from the north aisle. (37) A £20,000 donation in 1932 was partly used for renovation of the organ. (38) In 1934 a report by Wykham Chancellor, Fred's son, outlined that extensive repairs were needed to the nave. Johnson's work had stood the test of time but there were "loose and defective patches all over" and repairs were started immediately. (39) The sculptor Harley Jones completed 16 stone carvings on the outside of the cathedral, including the one of St. Peter on the south east corner of the transept which faces Bradwell. After the war in 1953 the South porch was altered to include a memorial to the friendships forged between U.S. forces and the people of Essex between 1942 and 1945. (40)

In 1954 came the first proposal to develop the Cathedral precincts, arising out of the Minoprio Plan (see chapter 11), which wanted to clear the area around the cathedral so that it could play a more prominent role in the skyline. (41) Plans were prepared that involved again a larger Cathedral and the Council paying part of the cost as well as the compulsory purchase of 27 cottages on the north side of the cathedral. Strong public opposition to the scheme and the abject failure of a £50,000 fund raising scheme for the borough meant that the original plan was stillborn. (42) Initially the money raised only allowed work on restoring the tower to continue, but by 1961 enough had been raised to allow other internal work to start. (43) The condition of the south porch was one factor resulting in the appeal being extended yet again. (44) Financial plans for a new headquarters of the diocese in New Street next to Guy Harlings, the cramped mansion previously used as the headquarters, had to be abandoned in 1977. (45) However the period did see, Beryl Dean embroider the cathedral banner and the colourful hanging beneath the east window comprising a patchwork of 1,250 individual pieces.

In 1982 a £400,000 appeal was set up for improvements to the cathedral. Bishop John Trillo managed to achieve agreement amongst the diocese authorities that what was needed was not a big extension, but internal improvements that would give the building more flexibility and make it less dark and forbidding. The borough gave £20,000 towards the cost and restoration work on the tower and windows was carried out first. (46) By 1983 the initial amount had been raised but costs had risen to over half a million pounds. The money was used to install a new under floor heating system, a new stone floor and the replacement of the old pews with movable chairs. John Moses, the provost, said "We have a parish church Cathedral and we want to make it less like a parish church and more like a Cathedral". (47) A Sanctuary was moved from the East End wall to the central position in the area previously occupied by the choir, who transferred to the east end wall. The high altar, which had been dedicated in 1931, was shortened and placed in the new Sanctuary area. Two side chapels, to St. Peters and St. Cedd were transferred from the East to the West side. (48) In 1991 another Cathedral appeal was launched, this time for a new organ and bursaries; after a century of use the former had broken down and was beyond repair threatening the future of the internationally known choir. (49) During 1994 a new nave organ was installed, the first in an Anglican cathedral for more than thirty years: it has 2,600 pipes; the smallest are ¾ inches long and the longest 16 inches. (50) The choir remained in the chancel but this necessitated the building of another organ. The diocese acquired the pipe work of an 1844 organ and this became the basis of the new organ in the chancel. (51) In 1995 Princess Margaret visited the cathedral for the unveiling of the two organs and the establishment of an organ foundation. The north transept where the previous organ stood now houses the 'Tree of Life'. This is a 20 foot painting by Mark Cazalet unveiled in 2004 depicting an Essex oak in high summer bloom, though it is dying on the left side.

In 2000 yet another appeal was announced for the restoration of the cathedral. £800,000 was needed for renovation work and this had risen to £1.25 million by 2003. (52) This was needed for repairs to the roof, masonry and stain glass. £75,000 of this was to come from the congregation, who had to find another £1.30 a week on top of their existing weekly payments. £200,000 was promised by pledges and grants and £50,000 was raised on a single gift day. (53) Bishop John Perry opposed a £100,000 donation by the masons but was overruled by the diocese authorities. In 2004 the Duke of Kent paid a return visit to the town, to see the cathedral's latest improvements; these included a new vestry, a new learning centre at Guy Harlings, the diocese office, a new lighting and sound system in the cathedral itself as well as the restoration of the east window and the reroofing of the north transept. (54)

In Mousham, the parish church St John's had not been built until 1841 to a design by Thomas Webb, with a transept and chapel added in 1851- 2. (55) The tower, including the clock, was built in 1883 when the nave was enlarged because congregations at the church were beginning to grow rapidly. (56) A fund raising entertainment was held at the Shire Hall and permission for the work had to be obtained from the Charity Commissioners. (57) There were occasional demands towards the end of the century for a second church to be built in the parish.

In the late 19th century, Chancellor designed and carrying out improvements to St Mary's church and many other Essex churches in the Chelmsford area. He oversaw for example the complete restoration of St Mary's at Fryerning in 1869. The modern glass in the nave of this church includes the memorial to Airy Neave M.P., who spent his early life in the parish and was killed by an I.N.L.A. bomb on 1979. (58) Chancellor also helped to restore All Saints Church in Springfield in 1881. He was also involved in restoring St Martin's at Little Waltham between 1882 and 1884, when the north aisle was added. (59)(60)

In 1862 Arthur Prior, the then owner of Hylands House (see chapters 27 and 28), employed the well known church architect, Sir Piers Aubyn to build a replacement for the existing church of St. Mary's at Widford. (61) Eleven years later he instructed Aubyn to build the church of St. Michael and All Angels at Galleywood. (62) Widford had been gothic in style but St. Michael's, the larger of the two, was in the decorated style with yellow brick with bands of red. The latter was unique amongst English churches having been built in the middle of Galleywood racecourse. It stood over 200 feet above sea level and could be seen from miles around. (63)

Other notable churches include St. Mary's at Broomfield because of the work there by the artist Rosemary Rutherwood who designed four windows and painted the fresco on the ground floor. (64) St. Mary the Virgin at High Easter has a window made in 1931 commemorating the two Edward Gepps, father and son vicars at the church between 1848 and 1916. (65) The Chancel of All Saints Church at Writtle was restored after two fires in 1974 and 1991. (66) A church at Essex's last new town, Holy Trinity at South Woodham Ferrers, was built as an ecumenical church which is shared by Anglicans, Methodists and Roman Catholics. (67) St. John's church at Danbury was rebuilt in 1951-2 after being damaged during the war. (68) All Saints Church in Chelmsford was built originally as a temporary mission church for the new Boarded Barns estate in 1930. (69)

The first discussion of a proposed Essex diocese came at a diocesan conference at Barnet in 1905. (70) The Bishop of St Albans asked for the separation of Essex from Hertfordshire. (71) In 1906 a Bishopric fund was set up to help with the cost of a new diocese and thirty five pounds had been raised by the end of the year. (72) The town's two newspapers thought the decision regarding the choice of cathedral town for the new diocese was almost a foregone conclusion. (73) Others saw the issue differently, with the Guardian thinking that Chelmsford came second to Colchester. It was the capital of the county but "had little else to commend it". Colchester was the seat of the oldest recorded bishop and was the largest town in extra metropolitan Essex. It also claimed to have a donation of £2,000 to go towards the upgrading of one of the churches. (74) West Ham pointed towards the large number of new parishes in East London, whereas there hadn't been one in Chelmsford. Woodford claimed to have two churches suitable for the cathedral and two houses suitable for a bishop to reside in. (75)

Chelmsford, like Colchester formed a cathedral committee which was headed by Frederic Chancellor. His son, Wykeham, was also involved and in 1907 "father and son communicated with a large number of gentlemen in the county". Further publicity included a 12 page brochure extolling the virtues of the county town. Chancellor in a letter to the Church Times recognised "the needs of London over the border", but he felt that "unless the Bishop's residence as well as the Cathedral was at Chelmsford, the county districts will hardly recognise that it is an Essex Diocese". (76) Each of the seven applicants sent a deputation of three to a small committee of the executive committee of the Bishopric fund, which heard the case of each. Four hundred and sixty one parishes in the county were sent voting papers to express an opinion on the issue; of these 383 were returned. The voting was as follows

	1st preference	2nd preference	3rd preference
Chelmsford	191	66	34
Colchester	101	77	38
West Ham	63	91	47
Woodford	13	28	31
Barking	8	25	53
Waltham	6	7	21
Thaxted	1	4	39

After the voting, the executive committee decided, not unsurprisingly, to recommend Chelmsford to be the cathedral town of the new diocese. (77) Chelmsford had to wait a further 7 years to actually become the cathedral town with the final establishment of the new diocese. A bishoprics' bill which was necessary for a new bishopric, cathedral and change of diocesan boundaries was held up by the momentous issue of the time, the Parliament Bill. The stress of the delay almost killed the then Bishop of St Albans, Edgar Jacob. Eventually the bishoprics' bill was abandoned but Chelmsford was included in similar legislation for Suffolk and Sheffield. (78)

The first Bishop of Chelmsford, John Edwin Watts Ditchfield was ordained late in life. He was brought up as a Methodist and began work as a local Methodist preacher in Manchester and Cumbria. After training for the full Methodist ministry he found there was no place as a circuit minister. Unable to find a vacancy in the Transvaal he turned to the Church of England. (79) Three years after being confirmed in 1888 he was working as a curate in Upper Holloway. Showing a lifelong tendency to overwork he was sent on a sea cruise to Egypt and the Holy Land to recuperate. He became the vicar of Bethnal Green in 1897. Watts Ditchfield saw fifteen hundred people confirmed, was a successful fund raiser and was the chair of the local board of guardians. (80) He was convinced that drink was the root of all evil. Apart from his sermons he became a very effective speaker for various missionary societies.

Watts Ditchfield was enthroned on 23. 4. 1914, St Georges Day. The town had all its bunting out and schoolchildren, all given the day off, waved their flags. His sermon was mainly directed towards the 450 clergymen present in the cathedral but afterwards he mounted the gun in front of the Shire Hall and repeated the same message for the large waiting crowd. This occurrence was also followed by the next two bishops. (81) 'Redgates' on the Colchester Road had been bought by the Ecclesiastical Commissioners as the bishop's residence. Like his first two successors he was on the evangelical wing of the established church. He was against aspects of the 'High' church such as the burning of incense and the wearing of vestments, but said there must be a degree of give and take. In the early part of his time he appeared to be rather inflexible and overestimated the power of a bishop to enforce changes on the diocese clergy. (82) His early monthly letters to the clergy showed a rather menacing note to those who showed any doctrinal disloyalty for example in denying the virgin birth. He disliked memorials to the fallen in the first war being placed inside churches, but they were still placed there in many churches in the county. In Chelmsford Cathedral itself, a memorial, was dedicated in 1921. Like most church leaders he was totally in support of the war, although he was opposed to clergy signing up for war service. In 1917 he said "We as lovers of peace must resolutely oppose those who argue in favour of a premature peace, which would probably lead to another and probably even more disastrous war in future". (83) Watts Ditchfield was disgusted however when certain newspapers started arguing in favour of revenge attacks on German towns after aircraft started killing women and children in English towns. He considered it "a monstrous suggestion" that Sunday evening classes should be suspended to save gas and coal. By the time he died in 1923, after he had delayed an operation to his appendix, his views had broadened. (84) He still tried to ban whist drives in the diocese as a means of fund raising in the year before his death however. (85)

In his years as bishop most emphasis was placed on raising money to finish incomplete churches and build new ones, particularly in those metropolitan areas rapidly growing in population. He also established the long term aim of raising vicars' stipends, which were often as low as £250 per annum. (86) Watts Ditchfield put a great deal of emphasis on the importance of retreats, using a house at Pleshey which is still used for this purpose. This frequently put him into conflict with vicars like the diarist Andrew Clark, who was more concerned with his work in his parish (See chapter 15). Clark opposed attempts to modernise the prayer book and refused to attend clerical meetings and 'quiet days'. (87) The Bishop's evangelical fervour was matched by the principal landowners in Clark's parish, the Tritton family, but Clark tried hard to establish a working relationship with the village's important benefactors. (88)

Chelmsford's second bishop, Dr Frederick Sumpter Guy Warman, had been the Bishop of Truro and was a friend of Watts Ditchfield. His career path had followed a more typical route than his predecessor. He went to public school, then Pembroke College, Oxford. Although he was only bishop for six years, before becoming Bishop of Manchester, he further developed the diocese in its administration and pastoral care and achieved the first significant increases in stipends. (89)

Warman was succeeded in 1929 by Henry Wilson, who was bishop for over twenty years. (90) Wilson came from southern Scotland and had been to Cambridge before taking an M.A. in Dublin. By 1934 Wilson was finding it difficult to fill some country livings, with an income of £350 and a large country house to maintain. By the time of Wilson's resignation the Diocesan Sustentation Fund, which was used for church building and raising stipends, had risen to £50,000. (91) Wilson tried to deal with the problem of how to respond to the Hadow Report on Schools, which meant that new church secondary schools would have to be established; also many existing church schools already needed a large amount of repairs. In 1929 it was estimated that the diocese needed £125,000 for new churches, £25,000 for new vicarages and £15-20,000 for reconditioning schools. (92) The economic depression did not help but by 1935, 15 permanent churches, 15 temporary or mission churches and 15 parsonages had been built, along with numerous grants to enlarge church schools. (93)

Wilson took a more realistic attitude to church attendances than his predecessors. The church had to "look at things as they exist". "Instead of going to church on a Sunday morning the family get into the car and drive off for the day into the country or to the seaside." He concluded however that the main reason why people do not observe Sunday by churchgoing is "because they do not want to go to church". (94) In 1937 however he came out strongly against the new Divorce Act, arguing that religion should have an important role in the issue and that marriage should be lifelong. He felt the inclusion of prevalent cruelty as a possible cause of divorce "opened a very wide door". (95) In the post war period the issue of re-marriages in church remained a big issue amongst the Essex clergy.

Wilson was very active during the second war. He strongly made the case for a Home Guard before one was established and then joined it immediately. When a German plane came down at Bishopscourt, Springfield, a strange tale went round that the Bishop had shot it down with his pistol! He had no doubt that Britain would not fall like France. "The fall of France came from within." "No doubt the crooked scheming elements now called the fifth column are represented amongst us, but they are few in number, many of their representatives are shut up and none of their qualities are typical of our national spirit." (96) He was strongly critical of the role of the Pope in both wars. "The Papacy is now as was the case in the last war and indeed always in the past four hundred years, anti British and anti democratic." (97) At the end of 1940 he said "Had it not been for the miracle of Dunkirk and the victory of our airmen over the German air force it might well be that many of us would have to face a German firing squad or disappeared into concentration camps." (98) Like other local leaders he was alarmed at the "Grave moral collapse of our young people". Wilson suggested an 8 o'clock curfew for girls. (99) Like most religious leaders he regarded the use of the atomic bomb at the end of the war as morally indefensible. "The use of this missile wiped out scores of thousands of young people and women, who were no more a target than are the people who read these words." (100) He had no compunction in involving himself in politics, expressing disquiet at the general election result after the war which removed "an indispensible leader". (101) Wilson's last big speech was on the dangers of Communism where he sought to guard against panic. (102)

The fourth bishop in October 1950 was the Reverend Falkner Allison who became the youngest diocesan bishop at the time. (103) Two key problems in the diocese remained essentially the same, namely the building of enough new churches to meet potential new congregations in the Essex new towns and London overspill and doing something about the general miserable level of stipends. Help for building now came from the Church Commissioners rather than the Sustentation Fund. (104) Some £35,000 of the money raised in the county went on new churches in housing estates in Chelmsford, including St Andrew's on the Chignal estate, a new church on the Woodhall estate in Broomfield, a new church on the Moulsham Lodge estate and one on the Westlands estate in Widford. (105)

The new bishop in 1962 was John Tiarks who had been a parish priest for 36 years after attending the Westminster School, then Cambridge University. In his early years at Chelmsford, possible moves to merge the Church with the Methodist Church, met with strong opposition from the Essex clergy. (106) Tiarks thought it was "inevitable that the Diocese of Chelmsford, the third largest in the country would be reduced in size". (107) Perhaps surprisingly there was no enthusiasm from the churches in metropolitan Essex to move away from the Essex diocese. The cathedral successfully restarted holding flower festivals, which proved very popular. "For perhaps the first time ever thousands queued to get into the cathedral." (108)

The next Bishop, John Trillo, was initially shocked by the size of his official residence, Bishopscourt, and made plans to move to a £65,000 Georgian house with a swimming pool at the front. Perhaps unsurprisingly one observer on a Boreham council estate said "he should live more like us". (109) He stayed at Bishopscourt for a further 10 years. Trillo described himself as a "moderate radical". In 1976 he spoke against gay marriage but called for greater understanding of homosexuality. (110) During 1979, a pivotal year in politics, he said unemployment was destroying the lives of millions and also dealt with racism and unconscious racist attitudes. (111) In 1980 he spoke out against the so called Moonie cult (the Unification church), which was very active in Essex, bemoaning their effect on young people, who were attracted by the communal lifestyle. At the same time the local Elim Evangelical Church made a film focusing on those cults, after parents had often been prevented from seeing their children. (112) Several village church halls in the county banned the cult, including one at Boreham. (113) The early 1980s saw the Church Evangelical Council fighting a battle over council approval for an Adult shop in Moulsham Street. (114)

After John Trillo resigned due to ill health, he was replaced by John Waine in 1986. (115) Four years later Waine was surprisingly seen as a front runner to replace Archbishop Robert Runcie as Archbishop of Canterbury. (115) His problem was unifying the diocese as the Essex clergy struggled to come to terms with the issue of the ordination of women priests, a problem which still exists. (116) Waine was against the current church legislation but said that women deacons would be in charge of many churches in the diocese. (117) The ordination of 53 women priests in 1994 caused 8 male priests to resign in Essex. (118) Waine's successor John Perry played a leading role in the cathedral forging new links with the Brentwood Catholic Cathedral, in what was the first such link in the U.K. (119) Perry received national prominence criticising Channel 4 for showing 'Queer as Folk', depicting what he regarded as 'paedophile activity' (120) When Perry retired as bishop in 2003, Essex was the second largest diocese in the country with a population of 2.6 million people but only 50,000 of these attended Anglican churches in the county each week. At the start of the new millennium however, the cathedral was one of only a handful which had increasing attendances. The new bishop John Gladwin came from Guildford. In 2008 he attacked 'the moral affront' of the banking crisis. "It is surely time for all of us to challenge this nightmare culture where people are encouraged to think they can have what they want, be it binge drinking or binge banking" (121) Gladwin was succeeded in 2009 by Stephen Cottrell. He is the 10th bishop and took over the second largest diocese in the country. On his enthronement he saw the need to combat racism as a major requirement. Although Cottrell was in favour of the ordination of women priests a number of male priests in the diocese threatened to switch to the Catholic Church over the issue. (122)

One of the most successful activities in the diocese in the late 20th century was the revived Chelmsford Festival (see chapters 27 and 28). Originally started as a choir competition in the 19th century it was first revived in the 1950s but revived again in 1983. By 1994 it was attracting 11,000 performers taking part in events in the cathedral and elsewhere in the town, most with a religious theme. The festival was even large enough to have its own fringe for a while. Famous musicians such as Yehudi Menuhin were attracted. In 2005 the Southbank Sinfonia held a concert at the Cathedral as part of the festival. (123)

Unlike the established church locally, the Catholic Church has not had a problem attracting a congregation in recent years. Our Lady Immaculate Church on New London Road started as a temporary mission in the Catholic school in the mid 19th century. (124) The actual church was built in just over year but early attendances were small, averaging just over 100 with a further 36 attending Mass at New Hall, Boreham. (125) In the 1880s the Catholic school had 66 children but money to run it had to come from the mission. Until the 1870s the Diocesan Inspector of Schools had direct control over such schools. After the Forster and Mundella Acts (see chapter 20) the school had its first inspection by a government H.M.I. in 1879. (126) The creation of a new Catholic diocese in Essex almost led the church in New London Road becoming the catholic cathedral. Cardinal Bourne, who played a major role in the decision, favoured Chelmsford but the new administrator favoured Ilford as the cathedral site. In the end Brentwood was chosen as a geographical compromise in 1917. (127) In the inter war period St Philip's Priory was established at Claremont Villas on the New London Road, which included a small preparatory school and a chapel. (128) The main school was rebuilt in 1934. By the 1930s pressure of numbers led to Brooklands house in Broomfield being used to hold Mass, as was a temporary mission at Danbury. (129) By 1946 the Catholic parish had a population of 1,728 but the average at Mass at New

London Road on a Sunday was 1,110 and there were 277 pupils at the school. (130) This led to St. Pius being built and in 1959 the new secondary school, the Blessed John Payne opened (see chapter 21). (131) The growth of further potential followers in the southern part of the borough led to the Church of Holy Name being built in 1965 in Moulsham Lodge. (132) A similar growth of potential congregation led to a further church, Saint Augustine of Canterbury being built in North Springfield. (133)

By the time our period starts, nonconformism had been well established in the Chelmsford area for over two centuries after the 'Great Ejection' of ministers from the established church in 1662. Nonconformists played a major role in the expansion of the town in the mid 19th century; in particular they were responsible for the development of the New London Road estate. By the late 19th century virtually every type of dissenting group was well established in the town.

By the early 18th century the local Baptists had already split into two groups. The original Baptist group were based in Baddow Lane but a strict Ebenezer group of Baptists had built a chapel on the south side of Duke Street. (134) The distinctive New London Road building of the current Ebenezer Chapel was a design by the well known local architect James Fenton, who is buried in the nonconformist cemetery in New London Road. He and his family worshipped at the Baddow Lane meeting house. Land had to be bought on either side of the chapel so that no noise could disturb the worshippers. Fred Spalding senior remembered it being built. By the late 19th century a Sunday school had been established at the chapel and this was used by the Red Cross during the war. During the second war the building was used as a rest centre after aerial bombardment, with stores of blankets and non perishable food provided for emergency use. In the 1930s and 1940s the chapel developed an open air mission which preached around the Chelmsford area. The portable building used was lost in the 1958 flood. (135) This was the third time the buildings had been flooded. (136)

In 1903 a group of Baptists were meeting in Crane Court, off the High Street, but increasing numbers led them to use the Corn Exchange. Originally they bought a site on the New London Road but this was sold and the site on the current church on Market Road acquired. Building was started in 1908 and the church opened in 1909 with a Sunday school quickly being established. (137) As with the Church of England, concern for the children on the new Boarded Barns estate led to the formation of a Sunday school there, initially in the homes of followers. This was handed over to the Congregational Church who then built a church on North Avenue. (138)

Apart from its two main established churches, the town's landscape at the end of the 19th century was dominated by its Congregational and Wesleyan chapels. The Congregational Chapel, situated opposite the Mechanics Institute in New London Road, was capable of holding 1,400 and had been designed by David Rackham for Pertwee's firm. (139) It was opened in 1882 and was always well filled. (140) "The floor of the church was reached from a platform and steps, some fifteen feet over the platform and thus above the New London Road level." "It had a fine facade with a central opening of considerable height, two columns of stone carrying a very simple and straight entablature." At road level there was a set of majestic wrought iron gates and railings, in all a very imposing building worthy of its place and really the beginning of the New London Road." "It was a grand sight to see all the Sunday churchgoers, all dressed up in their Sunday clothes, standing chatting after the services and a place where the congregation very much enjoyed attending." (141) The interior was very large and wide with a large organ in the balcony. (142) The church was restored in

Interior of Congregational Chapel, New London Road during the early 1920s
(Courtesy of E.R.O.)

1926 including an enlargement of the organ. (143) After the building was demolished, the Chelmsford Star Co-operative Society developed the site in the 1970s. During this period the Congregational Church in the U.K. merged with the Presbyterian Church to form the United Reform Church. The local U.R.C. now occupies Christchurch on New London Road on the site of the old home of John Ockelford Thompson, which was destroyed during the second war.

Chelmsford's Wesleyan chapel was also an imposing building with seating for 650 on the ground floor and a further 100 in the gallery. The chapel and the Sunday school were situated on the north bank of the Cam by the stone bridge on the site of the current Cater House. (144) It opened in 1898 replacing the old chapel in Springfield Road. A writer in the Essex Review commented "It occupies a prominent position in the High Street..... and it is a very handsome structure". The fact that the building was so near the river was the cause of considerable difficulty when it came to the

Wesleyan Chapel by the stone bridge during early 1900s
(Courtesy of E.R.O.)

foundations. It was built on broad belts of concrete continuing to the river bed. The building was designed in the perpendicular gothic, predominantly in red brick. "The maintenance is in the High Street and is formed by a four centred arch over which is a large mullioned window." (145) The building was demolished in 1962 when the foundations were causing considerable difficulties.

Like a number of dissenting groups, the Quakers had their origins in Chelmsford as early as the seventeenth century. As well as from Anne Knight (see chapter 13), the movement made a considerable impact on the area through the work of the Christy and Marriage families. The first permanent meeting house was built as early as 1699. This was replaced by the building opposite the railway station which remained in use for 130 years. It was sold in 1957 to fund the present Meeting House in Rainsford Road. (146)

The wide variety of churches in the borough was matched in the surrounding rural area. Great Leighs had a Baptist chapel which later became non denominational. (147) Woodham Ferris had a Congregational Chapel built in 1882 to seat 150 people. (148) Kelly's Directory mentions a Congregational chapel on Writtle Green as well as one at Howe Green and a Methodist chapel at Oxney Green. (149) In 1906 the Kelly's Directory mentions a non denominational chapel in Danbury. (150) The rise of non denominational churches in the rural parishes put pressure on the local Church of England churches. A church at Chignal St James for example slowly declined and was deconsecrated in 1982. The lack of sufficient funds for a Church school in the Chignalls led to a thriving school board by the 1880s (see chapter 20), fully supported by the surrounding chapels. (151) In general the rancour between the chapels and the established church, principally over tithes, did die down. During 1904 for example, All Saints Church at Springfield was ransacked. Altar ornaments and vases were stolen and pews vandalised. Afterwards however donations came in from all sections of the religious community and the items were soon replaced. This came less than a generation after there had been serious disagreements between the different religious groups within the same community. (152)

Chelmsford Young Men's Christians Association (Y.M.C.A.) celebrated its centenary in the town in 1977. It had been founded barely thirty years after the original Y.M.C.A. started in St Paul's churchyard, London, in 1844. The first building in Chelmsford was above Bonds (now Debenhams). In 1927 the organisation moved to its current headquarters in Victoria Road. During the war the Y.M.C.A. provided canteen services until a new wing which had been built in 1935 received bomb damage. Today the organisation provides child care and youth work services in the city. In November 2013 a new Y.M.C.A. Youth Club started in Moulsham School.

In the new millennium, evangelical groups such as the Elim in Hall Street continue to thrive as do the two Muslim organisations. One mosque is by the Parkway, off Moulsham Street. The other was at a small house in Regina Way. This has been demolished and planning permission had been granted to build a four storey mosque and community centre. At the time of writing there had been two small protests at the proposed new mosque by the right wing English Defence League. All the protestors were from outside Chelmsford. (153)(154)

1) Essex Weekly News 8 1996
2) E.W.N. 10 10 1881
3) E.W.N. 30 9 1881 p.2
4) E.W.N. 15 8 1882 p.5
5) E.W.N. 13 1 1888
6) E.W.N. 28 1 1887 p.5
7) E.W.N. 17 2 1896 p.5
8) E.W.N. 17 2 1899 p.5
9) E.W.N. 10 2 1888 p.7
10) E.R.O. SA 15/702/1
11) Chelmsford Museums records Oral histories folder
12) C. Museums Oral histories
13) Essex Chronicle 3 7 1885 p.15
14) E.C. 7 5 1886 p.5
15) C. Museums records
16) E.C. 27 1 1887
17) E.C. 25 2 1887 p.5
18) E.C. 22 4 1887 p.5
19) E.C. 24 12 1886
20) E.W.N. 30 10 1902 p.5
21) E.W.N. 27 1 1893 p.5
22) E.W.N. 8 9 1905 p.3
23) E.C. 17 6 1936 p.4
24) Chelmsford Borough Council minutes 25 6 1928
25) E.C. 30 1 1942

26) Chelmsford Cathedral pamphlet p.4
27) Essex Churches and Chapels-the Friends of Essex Churches p.61
28) E.C. 26 3 1880 p.3
29) E.R.O. 1876 Ordnance survey map
30) Chelmsford through the Ages Torry p.55
31) E.W.N. 27 4 1882 p.5
32) E.C. 7 12 1883 p.5
33) E.W.N. 27 5 1887
34) Torry p.55
35) E.C. 3 2 1922 p.2
36) Chelmsford Cathedral Geoffrey Wrayford p.5
37) E.W.N. 27 11 1929 p.5
38) E.W.N. 18 3 1932
39) E.W.N. 12 2 1934 p.7
40) Chelmsford Cathedral pamphlet p.20
41) E.W.N. 30 7 1954 p.1
42) E.W.N. 29 8 1958 p.1
43) E.W.N. 14 8 1959 p.1
44) E.W.N. 7 4 1961 p.1
45) E.C. 25 2 1977 p.1
46) E.W.N. 4 3 1882 p.1
47) E.W.N. 3 2 1983
48) E.C. 17 6 1983 p.5
49) E.W.N. 7 3 1991
50) Chelmsford Cathedral pamphlet
51) E.C. 6 10 1995 p.5
52) E.W.N. 4 5 2000 p.1
53) E.W.N. 29 6 2000 p.1
54) E.C. 28 3 2004 p.4
55) E.R.O. –The Spalding collection
56) E.C. 28 3 1883 p.5
57) E.W.N.27 5 1889 p.5
58) Essex Churches and Chapels p.92-3
59) E. C. and C. p.163
60) E.C. and C. p.193

61) E.C. and C. p.188-200
62) E.C. and C. p.93-4
63) Essex Countryside Vol.21 1973
64) E.C. and C. p.54
65) E.C. and C. p.82=3
66) E.C. and C. p.205
67) E.C. and C. p.203
68) E.C. and C. p.74
69) Essex Review Vol. 39 1930
70) E.W.N. 24 11 1905 p.6
71) History of the Diocese of Chelmsford Gordon Hewitt p.40
72) Hewitt p.41
73) E.C. 27 7 1907
74) Hewitt p.43
75) Hewitt p.44
76) Hewitt p.43
77) Hewitt p.46
78) Hewitt p. 47-49
79) Hewitt p.52
80) Hewitt p.57
81) Hewitt p.60
82) Hewitt p.61
83) E.W.N. 7 1917 p.3
84) E.W.N. 20 7 1923 p.3
85) E.W.N. 8 12 1922
86) Hewitt p.75
87) 'Echoes of the Great War' The Diaries of the Reverend Andrew Clark p.vii (Introduction)
88) Clark p.viii
89) Hewitt p.75
90) Hewitt p.100
91) Hewitt p.108
92) Hewitt p.112
93) Hewitt p.117
94) E.W.N. 7 9 1934 p.6

95) E.W.N. 27 8 1937 p.5
96) E.W.N. 26 7 1940 p.4
97) E.W.N. 11 10 1940 p.4
98) E.W.N. 12 11 1940 p.4
99) E.W.N. 22 10 1943 p.12
100) E.W.N. 24 8 1945 p.2
101) E.W.N. 24 8 1945 p.2
102) E.W.N. 8 10 1948
103) E.W.N. 29 9 1950 p.5
104) Hewitt p.150
105) E.W.N. p.1
106) Hewitt p.180
107) Hewitt p.152
108) E.C. 1 10 1971 p.14
109) E.C. 27 6 1975 p.1
110) E.C. 5 11 1978 p.11
111) E.W.N. 4 1 1979 p.1
112) E.C. 6 6 1980 p.3
113) E.C. 8 8 1980 p.1
114) E.W.N. 13 1983
115) E.W.N. 12 12 1985 p.1
116) E.W.N. 12 5 1994
117) E.W.N. 19 11 1992 p.4
118) E.W.N. 12 5 1994 p.7
119) E.C. 25 9 1998 p.2
120) E.W.N. 18 3 1999
121) E.C. 6 11 2008 p.6
122) E.C. 3 2 2011 p.13
123) E.W.N. 12 5 2005
124) The Parish of Our Lady Immaculate Father Stewart Foster p.46
125) Foster p.61
126) Foster p.60
127) Foster p.90
128) Foster p.91
129) Foster p.112

130) Foster p.113
131) Foster p.115
132) Foster p.117
133) Foster p.127
134) The Ebenezer Chapel 182 – 2002 p.5
135) Ebenezer P.10
136) Ebenezer p.14
137) The Baptist Church, Market Road p.3
138) Baptist Church p.4
139) Essex Almanac 1906
140) E.W.N. 13 1 1882 p.5
141) C. Museums oral history records Stanley Bragg
142) E.R.O. Spalding photo collection 518
143) E.W.N. 23 9 1927 p.11
144) Essex Almanac 1906
145) Essex Review 1898 Vol. 7
146) www.quakersmidessex.plu.com/our.History.3htm
147) Great and Little Leighs Pat Watkinson
148) Kelly's Directory 1937
149) Kelly's Directory 1908
150) Kelly's Directory 1906
151) The Chignalls 1888 – 1988
152) A History of Springfield Ian Clark
153) E.C. 26 7 2012
154) E.C. 23 8 201

23

Crime, the police, the courts and the prison in the Chelmsford area

"Evil beyond belief"

Chelmsford, as the County town, has been at the centre of the County's judicial system since the Middle Ages. It has also been the headquarters of the County's police force for more than a century. Chelmsford is also the site of one of the country's major prisons which has a colourful history to say the least. The late 19th and 20th centuries saw a number of major murder trials at the Assize Court at the Shire Hall, some of which made national headlines. Until 1914 executions were regularly held at the prison.

There has been a gaol in Chelmsford since the seventeenth century. It stood in Moulsham St, along with the House of Correction, which had been in the High Street, and was eventually demolished in 1859. (1) The new prison at Springfield was started in 1822. It was built with an outer wall 20 feet high and an inner wall 30 feet high which was 60 foot from the boundary wall. The centre of the prison was the governor's house. From it, spreading outwards there were seven radii, which contained the wards that held the prisoners. There were 204 cells, each 8 feet by 6 and a half feet and 9 feet high. In addition there were 14 large cells that were 14 by 8 foot. Originally it was supposed to house 225 prisoners but by 1837 it was already sleeping 628! (2)

Until the end of the 19th century the principal means of occupying the prisoner's time was the treadmill. It was not attached to any form of machinery and was therefore totally unproductive. In 1880 there were 8 treadmills and the prisoner spent 6 to 10 hours on one of them each day. (3) Discipline was very strict with the prisoners being unlocked at 6 in the morning and locked up at 8 in the evening. After making their beds and washing they worked on the treadmill until half past 7. They then went to chapel and at 8 a.m. took one and a half pounds of bread baked in the prison plus a quart of beer to their cells. The prisoners then worked on the treadmill until 1.0 p.m. Lunch consisted of a pint of gruel plus an onion in their cells. At half past one they were allowed out of their cells to attend school. They then started work again on the treadmill until 7 p.m. The prisoners were given a supper of four ounces of bread and two ounces of cheese in their cells. A breach of discipline resulted in solitary confinement night and day.

The treadmill was still the main type of hard labour in the prison in the 1890s with up to 89 men on the treadmills at any one time. In August 1888 a man died after a fortnight on the treadmill. He was only 23 and his body was very emaciated. The coroner recorded his death as caused by jaundice and acute of atrophy of the liver. He did however say to the prison representative "if you could modify your punishments I think it would be advisable". (4) The treadmill was finally abolished in the prison in 1896. (5) It was replaced largely by oakum picking but no attempt was made to make a record of how much the convicts collected.

The middle of the 19th century had brought some recognition that prisoners needed some help after they had been released, to try to ensure that they did not re-offend. A Society for the Essex Female Discharged Prisoners was formed first, for the small number of women prisoners in the gaol and this was followed by a Male Society. By 1880 the latter was trying to find places in homes, situations with respectable tradesmen or berths on long sea voyages, for boys who had come out of the prison. For adult men they tried to obtain suitable lodgings, temporary employment or tools for a trade. The Male Society also gave assistance for emigration in a few cases. (6) A register of the local society shows this was expensive, usually costing eight pounds, whereas the cost of railway fares, tools and the most common type of support, clothes was usually measured in shillings. By 1885 the Female Society was helping half the 53 women prisoners who passed through the prison that year. Of the 26 helped, 4 were found new homes, 2 sent to hospital, 11 were given clothing and 5 others were counselled. Eight took the temperance pledge, probably as a way of avoiding the principal reason why they were in prison in the first place!

In 1880 the prison held 201 male and 19 female prisoners. At the end of that year the prison staff consisted of a governor, chaplain, surgeon, clerk, a schoolmaster, four male and two female wardens and two other subordinate male officers. Punishments were frequent: during 1880 202 males and 12 females were punished. It cost just over £20 per annum to keep each prisoner. The register of the Discharged Prisoners Society shows that well over a half of all prisoners were classed as labourers. It was common for the prison to receive over a 100 military prisoners a year, who had transgressed while in service, and this was a bone of contention with the prison authorities. (7) They were imprisoned for desertion or other offences.

Most of the prisoners were between the ages of 20 and 40, although a few were teenagers and a small number over 60. A very few were still at school with several in the 1880s as young as 12. The registers kept by the Society show the variations in the lengths of sentences from a few days for begging to two years for serious felonies. Easily the most common form of offence, which resulted in imprisonment, was theft and burglary. (8)

In 1880 the Essex County Police Force had been in existence for 40 years. Incredibly the first Chief Constable John McHardy was still in office. Like most early Chief Constables he came from a career in the armed forces. He was only 38 when he was appointed but had already had a long career in the Royal Navy. McHardy was appointed from 31 candidates and didn't retire until 1881. He had kept his position in the navy and attained the rank of Rear Admiral in 1870. It was quite common for men to rise in rank long after they had left the navy. (9)

Early constables wore a dress coat, but this had been replaced by a frock coat by the 1880s. Constables were given a rattle, truncheon and a pair of handcuffs. They had to provide themselves with two pairs of white drill trousers. The familiar helmet had been first used in the 1870s. McHardy had introduced the Merit Star in 1871 which was given to officers doing "highly distinguished and discreet conduct in the discharge of their duty particularly when accompanied by the risk of life, personal courage and coolness, aided by marked intelligence".

McHardy was succeeded as Chief Constable by William Poyntz, who had been in the Royal Marine Light infantry, before being appointed Chief Constable of Nottingham in 1871. Like McHardy, Poyntz was a strict disciplinarian, particularly with policemen who drank while on duty. (10) In an

The first Chief Constable of Essex Captain John McHardy (Courtesy of the Essex Police Museum)

area like Chelmsford, where nearly all the offences were probably alcohol related, the constable had to be sober if he was to get the respect of his local community. Drinking amongst constables, especially in the rural area around Chelmsford, remained a problem however. Poyntz issued a general set of orders. "Hair was to be of a reasonable length, boots were to be issued instead of shoes and decorated truncheons were to be scraped clean and varnished. (11) He also published a new booklet setting out how the constabulary was to be managed, which replaced one originally issued by McHardy in 1849. Poyntz also issued the Force Orders, which included all disciplinary offences by policemen, who had committed them and what they covered. All officers were supposed to read them, to dissuade other officers from making similar mistakes, but the new system was much disliked and Poyntz's successor Captain Showers removed it. In Poyntz's rule of conduct was "The principal purposes for which a police force is established is the prevention and detention of crime, the suppression of vagrancy, and the maintenance of peace and good order". (12) Instilling a sense of discipline and respect for superiors such as higher ranking officers and Justices of the Peace was not always easy, as constables were almost exclusively from working class backgrounds and were usually paid little more than an agricultural labourer. The constable was expected to adhere strictly to his patrol times in the same way as the Victorian factory worker would clock on and off. Following the shooting of Inspector Simmons in 1885 (see later) after the officer had interrupted a burglary, Poyntz allowed revolvers to be issued to officers on night patrol but only to those who wanted them. The armed criminal knew he might be shot if the drew a weapon and it was another 40 years before the next Essex policeman was killed. (13)

In 1880 there were 28 policemen in the Chelmsford division, consisting of a Deputy Chief Constable, a Superintendent, an Inspector, four sergeants and twenty one constables. (14) Many local policemen achieved long service. An Inspector Peagram for example, was promoted to inspector after 16 years service in 1881. When he was promoted three years later £100 was raised for him as a testimonial, which showed the respect in which he was held by the local community. (15)

The local police were usually involved in cases which ended up in the Petty Sessions at the Shire Hall. A typical petty session in 1885 for example involved a Springfield man drunk in charge of horses and a Chelmsford woman who refused to send her son to school; the boy was sent to the Industrial School. (16) There was also a case of a shopkeeper infringing the Petroleum Act, a man charged with setting fire to grass in Woodham Ferris and an indecent assault charge against a labourer. It was alleged that he bought a child a bag of sweets and then assaulted her but the case was dropped through lack of evidence. A poacher from Little Waltham was fined 10 shillings with 12 shillings costs. In another case a labourer was found guilty of breach of contract for failing to hoe 6 acres of peas. He was fined 7 shillings and 6 pence with 5 shillings costs. In the same session a publican from Great Baddow was charged with keeping his house open during prohibited hours. These sessions also regularly saw cases on the adulteration of milk by shopkeepers, brought by the County Medical Officer of Health.

Housebreaking was considered a sufficient problem in the Chelmsford area to merit a regular weekly column in the Essex Chronicle. Break-ins were especially common during Sunday services because a large proportion of property owners went to church. (17) Partly to apprehend burglars the Essex Joint Standing Committee, which controlled the constabulary's finances, approved the establishment of a telephone link between the headquarters of the county police at Chelmsford and Brentwood, Romford and Chadwell Heath and thereby to London. The cost was justified on the grounds that burglars often carried out a series of burglaries and then disappeared into 'the smoke'. (18)

Cases of ill treatment to children were beginning to be taken seriously and the Society for the Prevention of Cruelty to Children, which had established a branch in the town, put forward a case at the Chelmsford Quarter Sessions in 1893. A woman was committed for trial for ill treating a servant who was under 16. After arriving in Chelmsford well fed, within five weeks "she was a bundle of rags and in an emaciated condition". "The prisoner began to knock off her breakfasts, then her dinners......., and at times kept her three days without food". She "knocked her about with various instruments". The defendant was bound over to the Central Criminal Court and there found guilty and given the maximum possible sentence of two years hard labour. (19) Late Victorian society was also less inclined to accept abuse within marriage where it was exposed. In 1898 the local papers gave a lot of prominence to the "Brutality of a Broomfield husband". The man, a fitter, was charged with assaulting his wife, who applied for a separation order. "After knocking her down and hitting her in the face twice...... she was so frightened that she was unable to go to bed with him and consequently sat up all night." In the last year he had only given her £4 or £5 for the maintenance of her and her children, even though he had a steady job at the Crompton Arc Works. The Chelmsford bench convicted him of aggravated assault and he was ordered to pay 5 shillings a week for maintenance to his wife and children, a sum hardly sufficient for the family to survive. (20)

In 1905 a woman being attacked in her own house was headline news in the Essex Chronicle, when £24 was stolen from a house in Roman Road, Moulsham. (21) Towards the end of the century a new type of offence was beginning to occur. In 1899 Colonel Crompton of the Arc Works was called as an expert witness at Chelmsford in a speeding case involving one of the new motor cars. It was shown that the maximum possible speed of the car was nine and a half miles an hour in 65 yards, after which it declined. The summons was dismissed. (22) We tend to think of vandalism as a modern occurrence but it did occasionally occur in late Victorian Chelmsford. In 1899 there was an attempt at train wrecking. "On Sunday evening somebody placed a number of stones and a large iron bolt on the down line near the bridge in Stump Lane, Springfield." It nearly caused serious damage to a train bound for Chelmsford but luckily the bolt was crushed flat. (23)

One 'crime' which attracted considerable attention in the town was the so called "Chelmsford mystery" of 1905. A female tramp on her way to Wood Street workhouse for the night had fallen asleep on the Jubilee seat at the junction of Wood Street and New London Road. A few hours' later neighbours were disturbed by the sound of loud female shrieks. Fred Taylor, a prominent Widford citizen went to see what the fuss was. He first saw a local policeman, Sergeant Peters walking quickly away from the seat, appearing to want to get away from the screaming woman as quickly possible. Another person heard the old woman cry out "You brute you kicked me." Peters said he had merely prodded her to see if she was alive. According to her he had woken her and demanded to know why she was there. She said she had been too late to get into the workhouse. When examined by the nurse at the workhouse, she had bloodstained undergarments and bruised and cut buttocks. The Chief Constable Captain Showers refused to take disciplinary action against Peters and as a result Taylor decided to take up the case privately and raised £50 for the case. The Essex Chronicle, aware of the interest the case had caused, raised £380 from readers for Peters' defence. In court it came to light that Peters and Taylor had a disagreement before, with Peters allegedly telling Taylor a deliberate lie. The defence said the woman had on her five pence and a farthing which was sufficient for a night's lodgings and didn't need to go to the workhouse and she couldn't produce the workhouse ticket. Before the bench arrived at its decision it was revealed that the woman had several convictions including a seven years prison sentence in Cardiff for theft. The bench had to decide whether to send Peters for trial but the case was dismissed quickly leaving numerous witnesses uncalled. Taylor paid for a cab to take the woman to the railway station at Shenfield and she wasn't heard from again. The case raised a number of prejudices regarding the attitudes of different groups of people to both vagrants and the police. (24) (25)

The County's headquarters at Arbour Lane, Springfield were used for the training of new Essex constables. In 1892 for example 27 were given training which included a course in ambulance work. (26) The Chelmsford division itself lacked a proper police station and was based inside the Shire Hall. Police numbers grew only slowly with an 1896 annual inspection of the division at the County Headquarters revealing 34 officers, a deputy chief constable, two inspectors, 5 sergeants and 26 constables. (27)

By 1896 the County Headquarters were inadequate because of defective drainage and restricted accommodation. The £9,000 it would have cost to repair the defects was considered prohibitive. (28) After considering a site on land owned jointly by the Marriage and the Chancellor families but deciding it was too expensive, the Standing Joint Committee bought a three acre site in Gaol Lane which is now Sandford Road. A prize of £100 for the best design for the new headquarters was won by a Chelmsford man, Mr George E Clare. The new complex cost £18,000 and included a lodge, the Chief Constable's house and its stables, a main block and further stables. (29)

By 1902 the Chelmsford police could no longer operate effectively out of the Shire Hall. The Judges of the Assize complained that this had an effect on their accommodation at the Shire Hall and the working of the various courts. (30) A property was bought from Gepp and Sons on the east side of New Street, opposite one side of Shire Hall. New police cells and police quarters were erected. They were connected by a subway to the Shire Hall as a means of quietly and efficiently getting prisoners to court. (31) The old cells in the Shire Hall were removed, enabling an increase in the size of the Crown Court. The new police building was 3 storeys high and remained operational until 1969, after which it was used for a while by the Essex Record Office.

In the late Victorian period the Chelmsford Assize Court held many famous trials, a number of which resulted in executions at Chelmsford prison. One of those which made national headlines was the murder of Sergeant John Eves whose mutilated body was found at Purleigh. He had been battered around the head and his throat cut from ear to ear. Four local poachers were arrested on suspicion. They had carried out a bungled theft of corn which they had previously been hired to thresh. Eves had already been assaulted by one of the poachers, a John Davis, who had been given two months imprisonment with hard labour for the offence. The police found three sacks of corn at Davis' brother's home and blood was found on John Davis' cart and on Richard Davis' coat and shoe. Charles Sales and John Bateman, who were friends of the Davis brothers, made up the four. James Ramsey and his son had been heard making threats against Eve and were also arrested. The Davis brothers, Sales and James Ramsey were committed for trial at Chelmsford. All four pleaded not guilty at the trial which started in August 1893. The case against John Bateman had been dropped for insufficient evidence but he told the magistrates that Sales had admitted his guilt and also implicated the Davis brothers. According to the prosecution Eves had come across the men stealing the corn and had challenged them. The case against Sales was dismissed despite Bateman's evidence and the jury then took one hour and twenty minutes to find the Davis brothers guilty and James Ramsey not guilty. John Davis confessed to the murder but Richard Davis appealed. He said he was struggling with Eve when Ramsey came up and struck a number of blows to Eve's head with a cudgel and then cut his throat. John Davis was hanged at Chelmsford prison on 16. 8. 1893.. When Ramsey later came to court in a different case, Richard Davis gave evidence against him on the matter of Eve's murder and the jury gave him 14 years without leaving the box. (32)

Another famous trial at Chelmsford concerned a murder which actually took place in the Chelmsford area at the Admiral Rous Inn, Galleywood. Sam Crozier had been a regular at The Fleece, Duke Street, Chelmsford when he met and married one of the barmaids there in January 1898. Three months later they took over the Admiral Rous, near Galleywood racecourse, despite both having a reputation for liking more than the odd drink. Customers soon commented on his wife's cuts and bruises. One day when Crozier met the previous landlord on the common he said his wife was lying dead at home. When the police arrived she had two black eyes and cuts to her chin. Crozier said the wounds were old and caused when she had fallen down in a drunken state. The doctor was satisfied it was an accident and gave permission for the funeral to go ahead. A policeman, Sergeant Scott thought there were grounds for suspicion however, and made further

Sergeant Eves (Courtesy of the Essex Police Museum)

enquiries. It emerged that Crozier had consistently ill treated his wife and abused her. Scott applied for a warrant on a charge of manslaughter and he was actually led away from her graveside at her funeral, four days after the body had been found. (33) At the inquest Crozier said she had nothing to eat and had drunk heavily but one witness saw him throw his wife and another heard the sound of blows. As a result of the exhumation it was found that the victim hadn't been persistently indulging in alcohol and could have lived to an old age. A verdict of manslaughter was recorded at the inquest but he was then convicted of murder at the Chelmsford Assize and hanged at Chelmsford Prison on the 5th of December 1898. (34)

Another trial at Chelmsford which achieved national prominence was the so called Moat Farm Murder. In 1903 Samuel Dougal was tried for the murder of Camille Holland. After a successful career in the Royal Engineers he had spent 9 years in Canada when he had lost two wives in quick succession in mysterious circumstances. Working in Dublin he was given 12 months hard labour for forgery. During the sentence he tried to kill himself. In 1898 he met Camille possibly through a 'lonely hearts' advert. She was a person of independent means having inherited £6,000 from her aunt. In 1899 they moved to Coldham Farm, Clavering, which he renamed Moat Farm. They lived as man and wife but Camille refused to put the property in their joint names. A maid was subjected to inappropriate advances which she reported to her mistress. The maid was waiting for her mother to collect her so that she could leave, when Camille disappeared after going out for a ride with Samuel. In the coming months he was joined by another Mrs Dougal, who was in fact his third wife. During the next four years he was seen with a number of different women from the village. By this time Dougal had gained access to all Camille's money, forging her signature and even having the farm, made over to him, which fell rapidly into disuse. In the spring of 1903 his trial for forging a cheque prompted a police investigation into Camille's disappearance. When the police took over the farm attracting the attention of the national press, a body was found which was identified by her body garments. In the trial at the Shire Hall it came out that Dougal had taken her out for a ride in their pony and trap and shot her once in the head. The shoes she was wearing are displayed at the Police Museum at County Headquarters. He was executed at Chelmsford Prison on 26. 6. 1903.. (35) (36)

By 1880 executions at Chelmsford prison had already been held in private for over ten years. It was felt that public executions, which were supposed to deter working class criminals, stirred up too many base emotions. Even though the public and reporters were excluded from this spectacle, this did not prevent large crowds from gathering outside the prison when an execution was expected, waiting for the time when "the black flag floated dismally in the air". Accompanying the executioner was a representative of the Sherriff's Office and Charles Gepp, the Under Sherriff (see later). "The scaffold itself is a very simple structure, consisting of a cross bar resting on some cobbles in the wall at the other end of the room". "The room itself is very small". (37) In all, 17 executions were carried out at the Chelmsford Prison between 1880 and the last which took take place just before the start of the war in 1914.

James Lee was executed on 18. 5. 1885. for the Inspector Simmons shooting. Simmons was shot after stopping three men. Lee claimed his identification was worthless because he had been publicly dragged through the streets of Romford. In 1887 a 17 year old, James Morley was executed for the murder at Chigwell Row of a young married woman, whom he had lodged with. At his trial at the Chelmsford Assize he denied entering her bedroom intending to kill her. George Sargent a poacher from Copford was hanged in August 1888 for cutting the throat of his wife who had left him and refused to return home. Sargent, like Morley, was executed by the executioner James Berry, who also executed Thomas Sadler five years later. (38) Sadler, a labourer had killed his lover's husband in a dispute over custody of the children at Colchester. In the report on the trial at Chelmsford in The Times it was reported that Sadler had been drinking and had killed on impulse. He pleaded manslaughter but a murder verdict was recorded. (39) The following year an outwardly respectable, middle aged, married bookkeeper was hung for the murder of one of his several mistresses at Prittlewell. (40) In 1898 William Wilkes was hanged for kicking his wife to death. (41) A 35 year old unemployed hawker William Burnett was hanged in 1900 for murdering his prostitute wife. She had told him she would not give him her earnings. The trial was at the Old Bailey but he was executed at Chelmsford. After Sam Dougal had been hanged, Bernard White was hung in December 1903. He had beaten to death his 20 year old girlfriend at Warley because she was seeing somebody else. This execution was notable because it was the first at Chelmsford to be carried out by the famous executioner Henry Pierrepoint. Pierrepoint had originally been an apprentice butcher at Bradford. He was appointed to the list of executioners after repeatedly writing to the Home Office to offer his services. Pierrepoint became the principal executioner in Britain in 1905 and in 1906 he carried out all 8 hangings that were carried out in the country. In total he carried out 105 executions. His brother Thomas and his son Albert joined "the family business". (42) Pierrepoint was in charge for the next execution at Chelmsford, that of Richard Buickham who was found guilty of shooting an elderly couple at Basildon. His last execution at Chelmsford was of Fred Foreham. Foreham was a 45 year old labourer who had battered to death the woman that he lived with. Pierrepoint did arrive for another execution at Chelmsford but his assistant Ellis thought he was drunk and a fight ensued. Ellis reported the incident and he was struck off from the list of approved executioners and didn't officiate at an execution again. After Pierrepoint left, George Newton a 19 year old gas worker was executed for cutting his fiancee's throat. Two years later in a remarkably similar case William Beal was hanged for slitting his fiancee's throat as they kissed. The oldest person to be executed at Chelmsford was also the last. Charles Fremd, ironically a German born grocer, was hanged for murdering his wife in Leytonstone. Shortly afterwards the prison was taken over by the military and there were no more executions at the prison although they carried on in Britain for another half century. (43)

1889 saw a civil engineer, who spent 18 months in the prison write an account of life inside the gaol. He described how prisoners were punished severely for offences such as turning their heads in chapel. The Governor was evidently worried about what he might say and he and the chaplain appealed for him to go straight out of town. He alleged that the chief warden had knifed him! The engineer was given the task of picking oakum but no checks were made on how much he did. Long timers were placed in cells for substantial periods so that they couldn't escape. The engineer said that the governor was fined £50 per escapee. In his time there several wardens were discharged for their behaviour including violence against prisoners and the trafficking of contraband. (44) A few months later a letter to the Essex Chronicle, from one of the wardens who had been dismissed, said that the trafficking was because of the heavy fines on wardens for frivolous offences. Grave offences went unnoticed. He said that old convicts shuddered if they had to go to Chelmsford prison and that wardens 'were afraid for their very lives'. (45) Conditions were not helped by it becoming an exclusively convict prison in the mid 1890s with a good deal more long term prisoners. (46)

The poor quality of the warden workforce led to a school for wardens being set up in 1897. Fifteen wardens were trained at a time and the course included being in charge of convicts inside and out of the prison, being in charge of work shifts, the systematic issue and collection of stores, being in charge of the infirmary and the kitchen and the writing of reports about prisoners. The Essex Chronicle expressed surprise that something like this hadn't been tried before. After passing the course, the wardens didn't stay at Chelmsford being sent on to other prisons around the country. (47) The school quickly gained a very good reputation. Its first warden, a Mr Box, came from Holloway prison.

The regular reports of the Police Commissioners reveal other interesting aspects of life at the prison. In 1889 1,658 males and 98 females passed through the prison. Of the men 323 could neither read nor write at all. One thousand and two hundred and twenty five men and seventy one women could do one or both imperfectly. Only 26 men and one woman could do both well. (48) The Discharged Prisoners Society in 1902 reported a resistance to associating with ex prisoners in the Chelmsford workplaces, which apparently didn't occur in large cities. (49)

The 1907 Probation of Offenders Act enabled courts to release offenders into the care of probation officers and led to the establishment of a local service in Chelmsford, as illustrated by the officers' early case books, particularly of J. Hirst who had previously been the schoolmaster at the prison. Magistrates increasingly tried to avoid sending offenders to prison in cases such as petty theft. It is interesting to note that the case books show that incidents of indecent assault and exposure were usually not considered serious enough to warrant a prison sentence. Hirst was also a Discharged Prisoners Aid Officer and was known as the 'Prisoners' Man' because of his kindness and thoughtfulness. (50)

1900 saw the start of the building of a new hospital at the prison, on the site of the old debtors' prison in the north east of the complex, costing £5,000. It was three floors high and could be seen from outside the prison wall. There were five cells for convalescents, a padded cell and various rooms for the medical officer. (51) By June 1915 the number of prisoners was declining and afterwards the gaol was taken over by the military authorities. The prison was then used for the confinement of military prisoners and German prisoners of war. (52)

The firm of Gepp and Sons, solicitors, has been connected with the judicial, religious and political administration of Essex in Chelmsford for nearly 250 years. From 1832 a member of the firm was almost continuously Under Sheriff to the County. In addition, in the mid 19th century T.M. Gepp was steward to 39 manors, the Essex County Treasurer, Registrar of the Chelmsford County Court, Registrar of the Archdeacon of St Albans, Clerk to the Commissioners of Income Tax, Governor of Chelmsford Grammar School, Trustee of the Chelmsford Charity School and a Trustee of the Chelmsford and Dengie Savings Bank. (53) The Under Sherriff was employed by the High Sherriff of the County to assist at the court. He employed an assistant and often a bailiff to carry out the instructions of the court, which usually involved collecting fines. (54) The

Under Sherriff also had to arrange the execution of prisoners, employ a hangman and even test the strengths of the ropes. (55) G.P. Gepp and W.P. Gepp had been closely involved with setting up the Discharged Prisoners Society (see earlier). (56)

At the outbreak of the first war there were only 450 officers in the county and a volunteer force had to be recruited to help the regular officers. Five hundred special constables were recruited with further numbers held in reserve. They were not issued with uniforms, but were given armbands to show their authority (see chapter 23). The 'specials' kept their day jobs but were expected to carry out four hours patrol near their homes. They were eventually given a peaked cap and a whistle. (57) A Special Chief Constable position was established with a proper ranking structure under him. Women were employed during the war as Auxiliaries, mainly to deal with women and children. There was considerable opposition within the County's force to women in the police, particularly from the later Chief Constable, Francis Peel and Essex was the last county in the country to employ women in 1946. (58)

Captain Showers retired in 1915 after 31 years as Chief Constable. The new Chief Constable John Unett had started with the City of London force and had been appointed Chief Constable of Preston in 1912. He introduced new measures to deal with speeding motorists, where police had to use stop watches. They checked the time taken for a motorist to travel along a quarter of a mile length of road. He died whilst still Chief Constable in 1932. (59) During the first war the regular force had become increasingly disenchanted with the job, both locally and nationally, because inflation meant that police wages in real terms fell drastically. A local branch of the National Union of Police was formed and there was a threat of strike action. (60) With the rise of Bolshevikism, this was the last thing the national government wanted and it set up the Police Federation. Essex Police didn't support the 1919 national police strike. (61)

The first motor car for the force was bought by Captain Unett in 1915 but they still used 16 horses. In 1918 four new Ford Cars were bought and in 1931 10 Triumph motor cycles were acquired, but the new chief constable did not use these as police transport; he felt the officer should concentrate on controlling the vehicle not chasing villains. In 1936 the first cars were installed with radio receivers. (62)

Unett's successor Francis Peel was a direct descendant of Robert Peel. He went to Cambridge University after the army, but then was a beat constable in Liverpool in a tough area where he had to be armed on his patrols. Peel was the youngest Chief Constable when appointed at Bath, becoming also the first to rise through all the ranks from beat constable. (63)

The inter war period saw an increase in thefts involving cars. In 1930 for example, several public houses between Ongar and Chelmsford were broken into and one of the publicans chased the men in his car. (64) By 1931 over 1/3 non indictable offences in the county were involving motor cars, as the number of accidents inevitably increased. From 1927 phones were installed in all police houses in the county. (65) By 1935 the motor patrol department based at police headquarters in Chelmsford consisted of one sergeant with 20 constables and 10 cars. This was obviously insufficient and was increased to 40 constables and 20 cars before the second war. (66) Even before the second war the chief constable was concerned at the growth of juvenile crime, with amongst other things the first recorded cases of' joy riding'. (67) The County's Detective and Inquiry Department was set up after the first war: detectives were needed to deal in particular with the increasing number of robberies from safes that were occurring in towns like Chelmsford. Training continued to be carried out at the County headquarters. Until 1923 it was carried out by Sergeant John Brooks. In 1926 he was promoted to Inspector in the Special Constabulary for training purposes. The specials were kept on as a reserve in the county after the war. (68)

Chelmsford prison was not re-opened until 1931. Initially 150 convicts were brought from Parkhurst and Dartmoor. According to the new governor "They were some of the worst boys in the country". (69) There was to be a special regime with regular employment, physical training and open air exercise. Voluntary workers and teachers were to be involved. Each prisoner was to have a regular visitor. These good intentions, unfortunately counted for little and within a year a prisoner was attacked with a bar and an attempted escape by four prisoners had to be foiled. (70) Two weeks later there was a danger of a serious disorder and a service in a chapel had to be cancelled because of shouting prisoners and an undercurrent of discontent in the prison generally. Conditions certainly improved later in the decade. In 1938 a vicar from Stratford, East London, who had been holding a mission at the prison, reported that it was a great deal better than previously. An attempt was made to reform the character of the prisoners and there was good, sufficient food. The men worked at carpentry and engineering workshops. He said the religious services were well attended. (71) During 1937, prisoners were entertained for the first time by sound pictures. (72) In 1943 the prison was damaged by incendiaries. There was no loss of life and the damage would have been worse but for prisoners and wardens working together to extinguish fires. (73)

By the 1930s the great processions associated with the arrival of a judge in the town to open the assize were a thing of the past. Fred Spalding remembered "It was a great thing in my younger days – the High Sherriff with his carriage and four horses, trumpeters, marshals, footmen with powdered wigs." "A procession of tradesmen, farmers and others from the town and surrounding villages of nearly a mile long went out to Broomfield to meet him and to accompany him to church with the Judge."

The County's police force was greatly reduced in the second war. By December 1939, 101 officers had gone to the army. By 1941 a further 73 had volunteered and conscription resulted in another 117 being called up. In all, 291 officers served in the war, of which 24 were killed in action. (74) In November 1940 the Police Headquarters at Springfield were hit in a bomb attack. Two policemen on guard duty were killed. They were the only policemen to die in Essex whilst on active police service. (75) Again, special constables played a noteworthy part in relieving the pressure on the regular police. Many of the local police were involved in training workers in ARP. An Inspector Hodges, for example, trained workers at the Hoffmann factory, which proved vital when the works was hit several times. (76) Three hundred and fifty auxiliaries were employed in the County's force, including the Women's Peace Corp. Peel however, remained implacably opposed to women joining the force.

The immediate post war years were marked by an increase in robberies in the Chelmsford area and the County as a whole. This caused alarm, partly because there was severe shortage of police. "The police complain that they are severely handicapped through lack of men particularly on patrol duties." (77) A year later the Weekly News said one officer was responsible for investigating 60 robberies. (78) Police were still resigning for better paid jobs in the 1950s. Robberies continued, particularly in the rural areas. Most raids on houses were small scale but a burglary on the outskirts of Chelmsford in 1948 resulted in £1,000 worth of jewels being stolen. (79) In 1950 the Essex force launched a big recruiting campaign with a window display in Bonds on the High Street. There were 140 vacancies in the county. (80) Concern was heightened by the increase in armed robberies in the area. At a robbery at East Hanningfield where £350 in cash and jewellery was stolen, a woman had a revolver stuck in her ribs. (81) The robbers were caught and were jailed for 6 years.

One new phenomenon in the area after the war was teenage gangs. One was reported to be terrorising the area around the Boreham airfield. (82) Initially this was frequently attributed to the increased amount of freedom children had during the war years. Another concern was the high road accident rate particularly amongst children. The Kerb Drill was taught in schools, which was particularly important on crowded streets such as those in Chelmsford. (83) In 1953, 1,000 motorcyclists were killed or injured on the roads of Essex. Police motorcyclists, who had been re-introduced to the county, had to wear crash helmets on patrol duty.

Increasing crime during the 1950s caused a big increase in the number of cases dealt with at the Shire Hall. The number of judges at the Essex Assize was increased to two to deal with the large number of serious crimes. (84) 1951 was the busiest year on record for the six courts in Chelmsford. (85) A common crime for judges to hear in the early post war years was bigamy due to couples being separated during the war years. (86) By 1952 the Quarter Sessions were meeting monthly. On Thursdays there were two Courts of Assize, two of Quarter Sessions, and two of Petty Sessions. Despite improvements carried out in the 1930s there were only two properly equipped courts. One court was criticised by an Essex Quarter Session judge as "the black hole of Calcutta". Four of the courts were held in small rooms of varying degrees of unsuitability. The confusion and overcrowding was even worse when the when the Coroner sought accommodation for an inquest. (87)

The 1950s saw further complaints about the behaviour of teenagers on the streets of Chelmsford after dark. A new hostel for difficult boys at Farleigh on the New London Road was quickly closed. "The boys do not take kindly to discipline." (88) A year later several Chelmsford boys were sent to approved schools for a raid on a church at Maldon. They "threw prayer books stole wine and rosary beads" and caused considerable damage. (89) Nineteen fifty five saw the appearance of 'teddy boys' in the town. The Essex Police's first police dogs Senta and Remoh were used to control them. (90) A purpose built dog section was later built at Sandon in 1970. When a park keeper was threatened by gangs it was front page news in the local papers. "Hooligans drove him to resign." Councillors called for police protection for park keepers in 1955, when a 62 year old gave up his job after he was threatened at Central Park by youths. (91) One estate which was particularly bad was Melbourne Park, where popular Saturday night dances were actually stopped. In 1959 gangs roamed Oaklands Park, armed with knives, chains, and sticks. Here, as well, attacks on the park keeper occurred and the public stopped coming to the park. (92) Vandalism at the Museum itself meant that children under 14 had to be accompanied by an adult. In 1959 the Essex Police tried a different approach to the gang problem, with an amnesty on knives and knuckledusters. (93)

The late 1950s and early 1960s were the age of 'smash and grab' raids in the Mid Essex area. It was an era when businesses still kept cash on the premises. In 1960 for example three shops, a cafe and a private house were raided on the same night by a thief who used a jemmy. (94) During 1962 a thief with a gun was chased through the streets of Chelmsford after he broke into an electrical shop and stole a portable radio. (95) In 1963 raiders blew a safe in the Eastern Gas Board's showroom and got away with £800.

The mid 1960s saw the first signs of a drug problem in the town. In 1965 an 18 year old youth who worked for Marconi was charged with buying amphetamines at a dance in the town. (96) During 1968 a youth died by drowning in the Can after taking L.S.D.. (97) In the same year it came to light that '5 bob' deals of cannabis were common in the prison after being brought in by outside working parties. (98)

1970 saw major flare ups in the town involving 'mods' and 'rockers'. Gangs came from West Ham, Basildon, Southend etc. In May there was a night of skinhead violence in the town. The police cleared the bus station but a mob moved through the town breaking windows and picking fights with those who they called 'greasers'. (99) The following weekend the police were evidently more organised, meeting some 200 youths at the railway station and persuading some to go back. Eighty escaped but were broken up into small groups and were put back on a London bound train. The youths then stopped the train by the viaduct and went down the embankment and into Central Park. They were rounded up again but stopped a second train. This time they were escorted by police on a long walk home! (100)

In 1968 plans were announced for a new police station in Chelmsford. The original one in New Street was far too small and outdated. Land, further down New Street, was bought under a compulsory purchase order. It was four years before the new station was opened. (101) The new station at the junction of New Street and Victoria Road had an underground car park for 23 cars and 10 cells, 8 for men and 2 for women. It had room for a staff of 275, a modern communication room, offices, an assembly room, a games room, a lounge and a restaurant. (102)

Prisoner – warden relations started the post second war period in a poor state at Chelmsford prison. There was a sit down strike in the gaol with boys from borstals refusing to work and there were several attempted escapes. In 1949 two prisoners "played hare and hounds" with wardens and the police after an escape in daylight and they were not re-captured. (103) By this time the local press were asking what was wrong with the prison.

In 1952 a Weekly News reporter was allowed inside. He found 229 young men serving sentences from two to four years corrective training. Co-operative and trustworthy young prisoners went to open prisons but the least amenable went to Chelmsford. The reporter said that the average occupant at Chelmsford prison was

"27 years old, has seven previous convictions and is doing three years, probably for housebreaking". "He is more likely to have been a barrow boy than a skilled tradesman". Only 2% had served an apprenticeship of any kind. Corrective training was supposed to use educational and industrial experiences and the personal influence of the prison staff to produce a good and useful citizen. Chelmsford was the first local prison to be turned over completely to corrective training. The reporter was given an obviously stage managed tour. There were three workshops involving sheet metal work, brush making and tailoring. All prisoners started in the mail bag shop. Thirty men were also being trained in building work. The governor's house, destroyed in the war by a German bomb, had been completely rebuilt by prisoners. Forty prisoners also worked outside in the town, working on housing sites, laying sewers as well as gas, electricity and water mains. A smaller group grew vegetables and looked after the flower beds inside the prison. (104) In all, young offenders worked for 40 hours a week and there were evening classes on making soft toys and musical appreciation. The reporter maintained that the prison had a high success rate with only 30% of those discharged re-offending. Voluntary prison visitors played an important role but there were only 11 for the 229 prisoners. (105) Predictably this enlightened policy did not last and by 1956 the prison housed hardened criminals of all ages. (106)

The twentieth century saw a downgrading of the role played by the High Sherriff and the Under Sherriff, to playing a part in royal visits to the county town and the protection and well being of the judiciary and magistrates. As a result, the stranglehold of Gepp and Sons on civic life in the town waned. H.H. Gepp could always be seen at elections however, looking 'dapper'. (107)

In 1975 a new County Police headquarters was announced, to be built at Springfield on roughly the same site as the old one. This was to house communication and C.I.D. units, a rifle range, a dining room and a recreation area. It opened in 1979 and included a computer run technology centre, one of the functions of which was to monitor traffic conditions in the county, including the smooth running of the Army and Navy roundabout through the use of close circuit T.V. All Essex police operations would be run from a control room by a twenty man team. At the time this represented one of the most advanced systems in the world. (108) The Essex Police Training School, which had only opened in 1969 at Springfield, was closed. All recruitment in future was to be from those over eighteen and a half. (109)

In 1973 Chelmsford's historic Assize Court was replaced by the Crown Court system. May 1973 saw the Barn Murder trial open at the Shire Hall to national interest.

Henry George Ince was accused of the murder of Muriel Patience and the attempted murder of George Patience during a robbery at Mountnessing. The jury failed to reach a sufficient majority after six and a half hours. (110) In January 1974 there was a retrial with a further two men on trial for the crimes. These two men were convicted. George Ince was acquitted of the murder but given 15 years for the robbery. At his retrial there was a good deal of criticism of the police's actions. (111) There had been a 'Free George Ince campaign' which was on a smaller scale than the 'Free George Davis' saga, which had involved the digging up of a Test Match pitch and the involvement of several rock stars! (112) After several police officers had already been disciplined, Ince was forced to reveal in court that on the night of the murder he was in bed with the gangster Charlie Kray's wife! (113)

The early 1970s also saw a good deal of criticism of the police in the Chelmsford division itself. In 1972 there was an inquiry into alleged local police brutality, with the Chelmsford M.P., Stevas, receiving a number of complaints about police behaviour. (114) Until 1975 there was a separate Women's Police Department in the county. After 1975, women had equal pay and could start to do the same jobs as male officers. (115) Nineteen seventy three saw the first use of speed cameras in the area with those caught appearing in the Chelmsford courts. (116)

By 1972 the prison was again causing concern. A detective questioning an inmate said the jail was "loaded up with drugs" and that there was widespread drug trafficking. (117) One month later, there was a riot with prisoners staging a sit in demonstration on the prison roof. A special disciplinary board of visiting magistrates was brought in to hear the 56 cases, of which only 3 were dismissed. (118) Seventy prisoners had caused £5,000 of damage. The riot was caused by a tightening up in security during the previous 18 months. Chelmsford prison had lost its security wing but TV cameras and high wire fences had been installed. (119) There was a shortage of wardens who refused to do overtime. (120) Reformers, led by the Howard League for Prison Reform, said that "the 19th century fortress like prison should be pulled down". The Home Office admitted the prison was overcrowded but said that it couldn't be closed. (121) Five years later there were widespread reports regarding privileged prisoners who were supposed to be living the 'high life' in jail. The Weekly News thought that those who did best out of the liberal regime at Chelmsford were tough violent criminals whose notoriety afforded them respect. (122)

In March 1978 there was an inferno which swept through the prison. Initially the police thought that it was caused by a crude fire bomb but later stated that it was the result of an electrical failure. The prisoners were well behaved while the fire was being brought under control. 75 firemen were involved fighting the fire and it was estimated that repairs would cost £1,250,000. (123) Most of the money was spent on a control centre at the heart of the prison providing an advanced electronic system. (124) The basic layout of the prison remained unchanged with it remaining a 'Category B' prison with many prisoners serving sentences for violent crimes and murder. (125) While the prison was closed it was used for two weeks to shoot a number of scenes for the film version of the BBC television programme 'Porridge'. (126)

Despite the rebuilding, six years later a new governor criticised conditions at the prison due to a shortage of staff, overcrowding and a lack of facilities. The prison was regularly holding 390 prisoners although it had a supposed maximum of 238. It had reverted to being a prison for young offenders between 17 and 21 years of age, but now had few training facilities. At any one time only 80 prisoners could be employed on very basic work. (127)

The H.M. Inspector of Prisons report in 1990 was decidedly mixed but did say the atmosphere had improved. It was however extremely critical of the buildings and administrative aspects of the regime. (128) The prison had 379 prisoners who had come from the Crown courts at Chelmsford and Southend. Very little use was being made of the industrial workshops. (129) The kitchens were too small, the laundry badly laid out, the visiting area was too cramped as was the reception area. A new hospital was needed as well as a new kitchen. All these defects should have been rectified in the rebuilding after the fire. (130) The lack of integral sanitation was a great problem. Security was generally good with close liaison with the police. (131) The prison had recently changed again, back from a young offenders gaol to a local prison. A number of staff were applying for jobs in other parts of the country because of the high cost of living in the Chelmsford area. (132) Attempts were made to improve sanitation and refurbish some of the cells but in 1991 it was named the most overcrowded jail in England. (133) The arrival of payphones in 1992 did constitute a big improvement as far as the prisoners were concerned. (134) In 1995, despite most of the recommendations of the 1990 report supposedly being carried out, a new report highlighted the drug problem again as well as assaults on staff. (135)

A further H.M. Inspector of Prisons report in 1997 was even more damning. There had been a failure of senior members of the service at the prison "to recognise and eliminate too many unacceptable practices and deficiencies in the running of the prison". In all there were 143 recommendations and only 8 positive comments. The prison was severely criticised for "appalling 19th century attitudes to the treatment of young offenders". A large number of young men were lost and afraid within the prison. Specialised treatment was needed for those between the ages 17 to 21. There had been a recent suicide but the suicide awareness management team had not met for a year. (136) Bullying was still a major concern and in the two years after the report there were several suicides at the prison. (137)

The late 1980s saw a big increase in drunkenness and loutish behaviour in the town with extra police drafted in to the High Street and Moulsham Street at weekends. (138) In 1986 for example there was a gang fight involving 400 youths in Duke Street. (139) During 1993, CCTV cameras were announced for the town to combat vandalism and shoplifting. (140) The £350,000 scheme was introduced in phases but by 1996 crime in the town centre had been greatly reduced. (141) By 1998 there were 44 cameras with more on the way and shoplifting had fallen by 35%. There was a big increase in arrests for drugs, a decrease in criminal damage and a decrease in the theft of cars. (142)

The most famous recent case at the Chelmsford Crown Court involved Jeremy Bamber. He was accused of killing 5 members of his adoptive family at White House Farm. Bamber said that his father had phoned him on the night of the murders saying "Sheila has gone crazy, she has got a gun". The prosecution alleged that Jeremy tried to make it appear that his sister had committed the murders and then turned the gun on herself. Bamber's jilted girlfriend spoke about his 'plots' to kill his family and his plan to use Sheila's nervous breakdown and the possibility she would lose her children, to frame her. A gun expert stated that the silencer fitted to the gun when Sheila was shot would have made it very difficult for Sheila to shoot herself. (143) He was convicted and given five life sentences in 1986. The judge described him as "Evil beyond belief". (144) In 1989 he applied for the right to appeal against the verdict. He maintained that the judge's summing up was weighted unfairly against him but the Appeal Court supported the judge's summing up and he lost the right to appeal. (145) In 2002 he made another attempt to prove his innocence saying that new DNA evidence proved that the blood on the silencer was not Sheila's but he lost the appeal. The Appeal Court Judges said "we do not doubt the safety of the verdicts". (146) Despite this a documentary was shown on Channel 4 claiming that his lawyers had proof of his innocence. (147) In 2003 he was accused of harassing some of his extended family through the internet. (148) During 2012 Bamber took his case to the European Court of Human Rights maintaining that his whole life tariff amounted to degrading and inhuman treatment. He lost this judgement but won his appeal in July 2013. A relative of the Bamber family was quoted as saying "What about the human rights of the four people he murdered?" (149) As part of his ongoing struggle he took a lie detector test which he passed.

1991 saw an overhaul of the control centre at Essex Police headquarters. The new multi million pound information centre was surrounded by a ditch and a security fence. It employed 152 people in a three shift day; 60% of these were civilians. (150) In 2006 a merger between the Essex and the Hertfordshire and Bedfordshire force was proposed but opposition from all quarters, including Simon Burns, led to the idea being abandoned. (151) In 1992 the Chelmsford police sub division was separated from Braintree; it included Maldon and had 237 officers. (152) The County's Air Support Unit was formed in 1990 and based at Boreham airfield. Once again the county police stopped using motorcycles to save money but they were re-introduced in 2006 because of their usefulness. (153) A mounted horse section was also re-introduced in 2,000 having 9 horses in 2009. In October 2012 however it was announced that the unit was being disbanded as part of the cuts to the police force in the county. An Operational Support Group which featured in the TV series 'Police Interceptors' is based in Boreham. It responds to public order offences and violence. (154)

Essex was rated as one of the top seven safest places in the country according to an Independent Audit Report in 1996. (155) There were still concerns however particularly over drug crime. The Rettendon killings in 1995 were the result of a power struggle in the world of drugs. All three murdered men had been powerful drug dealers. (156) When two men appeared at the Chelmsford Magistrates Court charged with the killings, armed police were present at the court. The Melbourne Park area still had a significant drug problem. Leah Betts died in Broomfield hospital in 1995 after an ecstasy overdose. (157) In the 1990s crime rates rose rapidly in the new town of South Woodham Ferrers and it was claimed it was a lawless place. (158) 'Bobbies' were put back on the beat both at Chelmsford and South Woodham Ferrers. (159)

In 2001 it was finally decided to build a new court. The Shire Hall had been given a facelift in 1983 but this had done nothing to increase court space. A new Crown Court was opened in New Street. A new County Court was opened in 2005 in New London Road, dealing with civil cases. The Magistrates Court remained at the Shire Hall until 2012 when a new one opened in New Street. This has five courtrooms to compensate for the closure of Witham Magistrates Court and Harlow Court being only open three days in a week. It has 20 cells compared with 12 at Shire Hall, video rooms with a link to the prison, a jury waiting room and a deliberation room. There are also rooms for the C.P.S., Probation officers, mental health practitioners, a youth offender team and for the press. It has solar panels on the roof. (160) The historic Shire Hall is currently closed, while the council try to decide on a use for it.

The new millennium started with familiar criticism of the prison. In the third inspection in three and a half years, this time unannounced, morale was found to be low, health care inadequate and there was still a shortage of staff. (161) A year later the jail finally received a positive report but in 2003 came yet another damning indictment, this time rating the prison 132nd out of 135 in the country. After this low point there was considerable improvement with a zero tolerance approach to drug use in the jail and an increase in the number of prisoners involved in work activities. In 2005 at any one time however, 200 of 565 prisoners were still unoccupied. (162) Between 2007 and 2011 there were seven suicides in the jail. In January 2013 it was announced that the prison was to be partially closed. A proposal for a second prison in the borough at Runwell was finally dropped in 2011 after staunch local opposition; it would have housed 1,500 offenders. (163)

In the early years of the new millennium Chelmsford was still a statistically safe place in a safe county. During 2002/3 it had the third lowest burglary rate in the county and in a national survey was in the 6th safest county. (164) Whether this will continue is open to debate. In October 2012 the county constabulary was in the process of trying to save £42 million by 2014. It had already shed 807 jobs including 324 officers since April 2011. Only 11.5% of officers were on the front line in 2011. (165) There is continued debate as to whether the Police Community Support Officers are worth the cost, which was £7.4 million in Essex in 2010, when they issued just 38 fines. (166)

1) Chelmsford Prison J.G. Torry p.7
2) Torry p.16
3) Torry p.19
4) E.W.N. 17 8 1881 p.2
5) Chelmsford Prison A.J. Standley
6) A.J. Standley p.64
7) Essex Chronicle 3 12 1880 p.5
8) Essex Record Office Registers of the Chelmsford Discharged Prisoners Society D/Q 22/2 and HQ3 D62B
9) The Essex Police Force: A History Martyn Lockwood. P.10

10) Lockwood p.17
11) Lockwood p.18
12) Lockwood p.16
13) Essex Police John Woodgate p.59
14) Essex Weekly News 13 1 1881 p.5
15) E.W.N. 14 1 1884 p.5
16) Essex Chronicle 21 8 1885
17) E.C. 20 1 1888
18) E.C. 9 6 1893
19) E.W.N. 19 5 1893 p.3
20) E.W.N. 26 8 1898 p.2
21) E.C. 20 1 1905
22) E.C. 18 8 1899 p.4
23) E.W.N. 14 7 1899 p.6
24) Essex Police History Notebooks No. 8 "The Chelmsford Mystery"
25) E.C. 22 9 1905
26) E.W.N. 22 4 1892 p.7
27) E.W.N. 15 5 1896 p.5
28) E.C. 2 6 1899 p.2
29) Lockwood p.23
30) Woodgate p.100
31) E.C. 6 6 1902 p.4
32) Notebooks No. 1 'The Murder of Sergeant John Eves'
33) Notebooks No. 23 'The dogged detective, David Scott'
34) E.C. 7 7 1898
35) Notebooks No. 37 'The Moat Farm Murder'
36) Lockwood p.25
37) The Times 18 7 1881
38) Notebooks No.32 Executions and the Chelmsford prison
39) The Times 30 7 1881
40) Notebooks No. 32
41) E.C. 22 7 1898 p.5
42) Pierrepoint: A family of executioners Steve Fielding p.266
43) Notebooks No.32
44) E.C. 16 5 1889 p.5

45) E.C. 23 8 1889 p.5
46) E.W.N. 8 3 1895 p.5
47) E.C. 22 1 1897 p.5
48) E.C. 8 11 1889 p.5
49) E.C. 14 2 1902 p.4
50) Essex Record Office D/Q 22/40 Probation Officers case books
51) Standley p.82
52) Standley p.88
53) The Way We Worked: Gepp and Sons Solicitors J.B. Gilder p.39
54) Gilder p.67
55) Gilder p.70
56) Gilder p.58
57) Lockwood p.33
58) Lockwood p.36
59) Lockwood p.40
60) E.C. 16 5 1918 p.3
61) Woodgate p.125
62) Woodgate p.141
63) Woodgate p.130
64) E.W.N. 26 9 1930 p.11
65) E.C. 2 12 1927 p.6
66) E.C. 7 6 1935 p.4
67) E.C. 4 6 1937 p.3
68) Lockwood p.42
69) E.W.N. 14 11 1930 p.13
70) E.C. 1932
71) E.C. 26 8 1938 p.6
72) E.W.N. 31 12 1937 p.6
73) Torry p.84
74) Lockwood p.52
75) Woodgate p.148
76) Lockwood p.53
77) E.W.N. 8 11 1946 p.10
78) E.W.N. 18 7 1947 p.8
79) E.W.N. 2 4 1948 p.8

80) E.W.N. 10 2 1950 p.1
81) E.W.N. 14 7 1950 p.1
82) E.C. 8 1953
83) E.C. 28 8 1953
84) E.W.N. 10 11 1950 p.5
85) E.W.N. 2 11 1951 p.1
86) E.W.N. 14 6 1946
87) E.W.N. 27 6 1952 p.1
88) E.W.N. 30 11 1953 p.1
89) E.W.N. 16 7 1954 p.7
90) E.W.N. 6 5 1965 p.1
91) E.W.N. 27 5 1955 p.1
92) E.W.N. 30 10 1959 p.1
93) E.W.N. 20 11 1959 p.1
94) E.W.N. 5 2 1960 p.1
95) E.W.N. 13 4 1962 p.1
96) E.W.N. 97 1965 p.1
97) E.C. 5 9 1968 p.1
98) E.C. 7 11 1968
99) E.W.N. 1 5 1970
100) E.W.N. 7 5 1970
101) E.C. 7 6 1968 p.1
102) E.C. 21 1 1972 p.2
103) E.C. 22 4 1949 p.1
104) E.W.N. 9 11 1951 p.5
105) E.W.N. 16 11 1951 p.5
106) E.C. 13 1 1956 p.20
107) Gilder p.75
108) E.W.N. 15 2 1979 p.1
109) E.W.N. 21 7 1977 p.7
110) E.C. 4 5 1973 p.1
111) E.C. 18 1 1974
112) E.C. 19 5 1976 p.1
113) E.C. 14 5 1976 p.1
114) E.W.N. 11 2 1974 p.1

115) Lockwood p.113
116) E.W.N. 1 1 1973 p.64
117) E.W.N. 17 8 1972 p.1
118) E.W.N. 7 9 1972 p.1
119) E.C. 1 9 1972
120) E.W.N. 30 8 1973 p.1
121) E.W.N. 4 10 1973 p.1
122) E.W.N. 27 4 1978 p.1
123) E.C. 23 3 1978 p.1
124) E.W.N. 4 8 1978 p.1
125) E.C. 1 2 1979 p.88
126) E.C. 1 2 1979 p.1
127) E.W.N. 21 7 1985 p.1
128) H.M. Inspector of Prisons Report 1990 Chelmsford Prison p.1
129) Prison report p.9
130) Prison report p.10
131) Prison report p.12
132) Prison Report p.26
133) E.W.N. 20 6 1991 p.1
134) E.W.N. 8 4 1993 p.3
135) E.W.N. 23 3 1995 p.1
136) E.C. 18 7 1997 p.1
137) E.W.N. 11 3 1999 p.1
138) E.W.N 15 2 1990 p.5
139) E.C. 25 7 1986 p.1
140) E.C. 24 9 1993 p.1
141) E.C. 24 5 1996 p.1
142) E.C. 30 1 1998 p.1
143) E.C. 25 7 1986 p.1
144) E.C. 31 10 1986 p.1
145) E.C. 24 3 1989 p.9
146) E.C. 20 12 2003 p.5
147) E.C. 2 5 2003 p.7
148) E.C. 21 8 2003 p.11
149) E.C. 11 7 2013

150) E.C. 21 6 1991 p.3
151) E.W.N. 23 3 2006
152) E.C. 5 6 1992 p.3
153) Lockwood p.124
154) E.C. 19 7 2012 p.6 - 7
155) E.C. 19 4 1996 p.1
156) E.C. 8 12 1995 p.1
157) E.C. 17 11 1995 p.1
158) E.W.N. 29 10 1992 p.1
159) E.C. 2 6 2000 p.1
160) E.C. 5 4 2012 p.8
161) E.W.N. 16 11 2000 p.1
162) E.C. 13 1 2005 p.11
163) E.C. 28 10 2010
164) E.C. 8 1 2003 p.9
165) E.C. 7 4 2011 p.4 - 5
166) E.C. 2 12 2010

24

Chelmsford in the Second World War

"There came a blinding flash, a roar then chaos"

For a town of its size Chelmsford was certainly not the worst affected by the second war. It was not the subject of the Baedeker raids which so grievously affected towns such as Norwich and Exeter. Chelmsford's industrial strength however, which of course grew rapidly during the war, made it a target for predetermined German air raids. This and the fact that it was on the route of German planes on the way back from London meant that it received an amount of attention from the enemy roughly commensurate to a town like Ipswich. The area was on a likely German invasion route, resulting in very strong defences being built up around Chelmsford. In the early days of the war the biggest surprise was that Chelmsford, like Ipswich, was designated a receiving area for evacuees from London. The increasing needs of local industry meant that not only were more local women and women who were directed from towns like Bedford and Leicester, used in the big factories, but also that the war saw a big increase in their sense of independence. Chelmsford's civil defences generally worked well and there wasn't the conflict between those involved with the A.R.P. and the Home Guard which characterised towns such as Ipswich.

The early 1930s had seen recruitment for the Territorial Army in Essex at a low ebb, as people clung to the hope that the League of Nations would keep the international peace. (1) Nineteen thirty four had seen the establishment of a headquarters for the Anti Aircraft Searchlight Company in Market Road. (2) With a strong Quaker movement in the town the peace movement was well established. In 1934 a peace meeting at the Corn Exchange was so full that an overflow meeting had to be held at the Shire Hall. (3) Colonel Macnamara, the Chelmsford M.P., made a speech warning of a possible war in Abyssinia and the danger that if it started it could spread. The same week the Weekly News mentioned Churchill's rearmament speech in its editorial. (4) In Spring 1937 the first signs of a county A.R.P. scheme started with a the Chelmsford borough council holding a meeting involving all the local works, the local fire brigade as well as the voluntary organisations including the Voluntary Aid Detachment (V.A.D.), the St John's Ambulance and the British Red Cross. (5) Wing Commander Sparling, who had been appointed A.R.P. organiser for the county, spoke at the meeting. (6) In the preparations for war the town was, not unusually, behind the local rural area. Carne Rasch's son wrote a letter to the Weekly News in October bemoaning the council's tardiness. "Must we wait for another war to be caught out through a lack of timely preparations?" (7) The need for a joint scheme for the town and rural area led to a joint council conference. At this it was agreed there was a need for ambulances, first aid stations, temporary hospitals, and decontamination centres. Gas attacks were considered to be an inevitable hazard. Premises had to be found for protective clothing, bleaching materials and temporary shelters. A post of local chief A.R.P. organiser was advertised at a salary of £400 per year. An A.R.P. committee was formed with 5 representatives from each council. After a borough council meeting in October 1938 an appeal for A.R.P. volunteers was launched with large numbers needed for the Auxiliary Fire Service, first aid parties, decontamination squads, ambulance drivers and report centre staff. (8) Major H.S. Doe was appointed the head of the Chelmsford A.R.P. from 125 applications. He had 36 years service in the regular and territorial armies and was a British Legion worker and churchwarden at St. John's church, Moulsham. The initial response in the borough was disappointing and as a result an A.R.P. exhibition was held at Bonds. Even though Germany had just taken Austria many people still thought a war wouldn't happen. Jack Macnamara publicly doubted the town's preparedness for a conflict. At a public meeting on A.R.P. in June 1938 the view was expressed that shelters could minimise the effects of blasts but the government's then current strategy was to disperse large numbers of people, with shelters only being provided for those caught in a raid away from home or work. (9) Chelmsford needed 250 wardens to first issue the gas masks, but in addition 220 volunteers were needed for first aid, 300 for the fire services and 60 special constables. In all, 1,000 volunteers were needed for the town. (10) By the middle of 1938 the rural area had twice as many volunteers as the borough.

The Munich crisis of September 1938 made a war seem highly probable. Trenches were immediately dug in Admirals Park, the Recreation Ground, Oaklands and Lionmede.

The most urgent task seemed to get the 66 thousand people of the Chelmsford area fitted with gas masks. Seven lorries fitted with enough masks for most of the population arrived from Cambridge on September 27th 1938. (11) Four distribution centres were set up. Most people however stopped taking them wherever they went, during the 'phoney war' period, when the expected attacks from the air didn't materialise. Another problem was the lack of fire fighting equipment and personnel. Munich had at least the effect of rapidly increasing the number of volunteers joining within a week. The Poor Law part of St. John's hospital was converted into a decontamination centre and similar centres were set up at the Manor Road and Corporation Road council depots. First aid centres were established at Moulsham School and in the Civic Centre. At a public meeting in November 1938 the Mayor, Councillor Bellamy said that the town's A.R.P. was still 60% below what was needed. In January 1939 the Borough Engineer was making A.R.P. work the priority, to the exclusion of everything else. (12) The town was divided into 6 sections with each sections having between 9 and 17 sectors. Each sector had 6 wardens. The warden was usually a middle aged or elderly man and the warden service was under the control of the police.

The government had already ruled that Chelmsford would be a receiving area for evacuees. Its two councils were very unhappy at this decision and Jack Macnamara, the town's M.P., raised the matter with the Ministry of Health to no avail. The view in the town was "what is the point of transferring the children from one danger point to another". (13) Some of the better off Chelmsfordians were already making plans to evacuate their children. A double shift system was agreed to accommodate the likely number of children in the areas' schools. The 9,000 expected was downgraded to 7,000, but in the event considerably less arrived. (14) In the week war broke out several thousand evacuees arrived in Chelmsford and were billeted in the town and surrounding rural area. Many people were shocked by the verminous state of some of the children. In Writtle and Broomfield premises were found for unbilletable people that households had refused to take. By the week after war broke out there were 1,400 new pupils in Chelmsford. (see chapter 20) By May 1940, towards the end of the 'phoney war' period, most of the evacuees had returned to London, but there were still 610 London children in Chelmsford schools. John Marriage, the local historian, remembered starting at the newly opened Moulsham Senior School and joining pupils from Cann Hall School, Leytonstone, in otherwise empty classrooms. The number of evacuees rose again with the start of the London blitz which resulted in some of the homeless arriving in Chelmsford. By the end of October 1940 there were 466 official refugees in the borough, of which 177 had recently arrived. A further 1,107 refugees had however found a place in the town by private means. One elderly man was evacuated to Upper Bridge Road, next to the railway line. The house was then hit by a bomb!

As the war progressed the role of the billeting officer had to change, as he had to find billets for the large number of workers who were directed towards Chelmsford to work in its factories. The rapid expansion of the big firms to meet the demands of war and the call up of so many existing workers meant that sufficient employees were never going to be provided by the local workforce, even with the drafting in of many local women. It wasn't until June 1942 however that he used his compulsory billeting powers for the first time. Mayor Taylor sent a letter to the Home Office saying that the reason for the reluctance in the town to have more Irishmen in billets was the unsavoury reputation of their predecessors. (15) After this, the Government made a decision not to send any more Irishmen to the town. Towards the end of the war the council compulsorily purchased properties for billeting hostels. (16) A common complaint from those providing billets was the inadequate allowances given to them.

By the start of the war Chelmsford should have had in place three types of A.R.P. measure: these were preventative, alleviative and remedial. Preventative included the provision of public and private shelters. When the war started the first order for public shelters had only just been placed. Alleviative included the treatment of the wounded. Remedial included the communal feeding and the provision of rest centres for those whose houses were destroyed or seriously damaged after a raid. (17) News of a raid was sent first to the borough's central report centre at the Civic Centre, then to the county report centre at the County Hall and finally to the regional control centre at Cambridge. (18) During the 'phoney war' period the sirens were regularly tested. In April 1940 there was a full scale A.R.P. exercise to test the responses. (19) There was a fierce argument in the town as to whether A.R.P. workers should be paid, with many arguing that some of those in the 24 paid posts could afford to do them freely. (20) Generally the system worked well, except for odd occasions as in 1943 when a central area warden resigned over the Home Guard training on his patch. (21) A week after the war started all the A.R.P. services had their full complement, except the auxiliary fire services, which still needed 150 more men and some of the casualty services which needed just a few more men. The auxiliary firemen still needed uniforms. (22) First aid training and gas courses were proceeding apace for those who were new volunteers.

Like many other small or medium sized towns, the lack of what many townsfolk saw as sufficient protection in the form of shelters was a consistent bone of contention right up until the end of the war when the V-2s were falling. Some of the first public shelters to be built were initially built for schools. (see chapter 20) The public was allowed to use them after they had been cleaned when the schools had closed. (23) In December 1940 the shelters were declared too cold but they had to be used because several school grounds had been machine gunned during recent raids. (24)

In July 1940, just before the air raids started, the council debated the provision of household shelters. The government provided the cost of materials but the rest of the cost had to be found by the council. (25) Chelmsford's borough engineer admitted there weren't enough public shelters, particularly in the northern part of the borough, but the council maintained as it did throughout the war, that shelter provision was limited by the government's upper limit of provision for 10% of the population. (26) In January 1941 the attempted bombing of all Chelmsford's big factories pushed the government into allowing shelters to be built for all houses within 250 yards of the main works. (27) The council maintained that the cost of providing any further shelters in addition to these would be prohibitive. (28) Despite the urgency there were inevitable delays in the shelters being built, because builders were extremely busy and there was a shortage of labour and materials. In August 1940 the government said that public shelters could only be built in the shopping streets of Chelmsford and refused a request to build one on the Boarded Barns housing estate. (29) July 1940 had already seen a petition for a public shelter presented by residents of the Rainsford housing estate. (30) In the meantime, the under pressure council was reporting firms to the Home Office for slow progress on the construction of the school shelters. (31) Before the end of 1940, with the town under heavy bombing, a Chelmsford Air Raid Shelter Committee (C.A.R.S.C.) was formed. Although there was a strong Communist influence, it represented a wide range of interests in the town, but this didn't prevent some critics maintaining that its real aim was to cause discontent amongst the townsfolk and its workforce in particular. Representatives of the committee presented a petition to the council calling for the provision of many more bomb proof shelters and for alternative accommodation for those who had lost their homes. (32) It was presented by the Labour Councillor, A.E. Hodge. This petition also included the unfeasible demand for the provision of interior Haldane shelters to house all the people of Chelmsford which would have pushed the total cost up to £350,000. The Rector of Springfield signed it because there had been the awful raid on Coventry night before. Bellamy, the chair of the Council's A.R.P. committee, said that they had gone as far as the government allowed them to. Alderman Smith was at least more constructive, saying that the Air Ministry should re-grade the town in terms of the level of threat it faced from the air. (33) The council set up a new committee to consider matters raised by the C.A.R.S.C., but the general view on the council was that there were a lot of towns under more threat than Chelmsford and the town would just have to wait its turn. In January 1941 the Ministry of Homeland Security provisionally agreed to the provision of 9 public shelters for the town but the C.A.R.S.C. naturally felt this was insufficient. (34) Meanwhile the council decided against the provision of Haldane interior shelters for houses near the big works and the Borough engineer came up with a system of blast or 'baffle' walls instead. Eventually a mixture of 220 six person outside shelters and 50 blast walls was agreed. (35) Chelmsford council received 100% grants on all shelters built from 1941 onwards but there was an acute shortage of labour to actually build them. The fire brigade were regularly pumping out water from the shelters that had been completed. (36) To combat the intense level of cold in the shelters the council eventually provided a moderate level of heating whilst ensuring there was adequate ventilation. The council also strengthened the school shelters, where there was danger of collapse.

Several rural parishes complained about the absence of public shelters, when in fact the majority of bombs were falling on the rural areas. As in the town, there were endless delays in delivery and erection when they were assigned them for example in Great Baddow. (37) Bet Allen in Great Leighs said "We didn't have any shelters in the village. We'd hide under the table if we thought a bomb was coming." (38) The district council left the decision regarding the use of school shelters to the individual parishes. In 1944 there was a petition from Galleywood residents for shelters and by the end of the year domestic shelters were being distributed free in the rural area. (39)

By December 1941 there were domestic shelters provided for 7,000 people in the town, usually of the Haldane type. The C.A.R.S.C. continued to press for more shelters and in March 1943, six more public shelters were provided. They were completed in March 1944 but before this the shelters in the Recreation Ground were in a dreadful state having been vandalised. (40) (41) Chelmsford borough bid for 5 additional public shelters but the government didn't accede, still favouring domestic shelters. The council maintained that the joint domestic and public shelter provision for 15,000 people was well above the average for a town of Chelmsford's size. (42) In April 1944 further school shelters were still being built. (43)

Brian Kemp, who was at Moulsham Junior School during the war, spent a lot of time in a shelter, often visiting one three or four times a day. (44) M. Davies spent most of his time in a cellar. Colleen Yaxley lived in Great Baddow. "In our garden my granddad and uncle built an air raid shelter under what was the rockery." "During the war we spent much of our time in one or other of the brick built shelters at the village school." "There was no proper lighting so we spent the time singing or being read to." "When the siren went we went into it and when the 'all clear' was sounded we practised crawling out of the rear escape exit." "I was far more frightened of the mosquitoes flying about than the bombs." (45) In Great Leighs, Alf Quilter was an A.R.P. messenger. "When I heard there was an air warning, I had to leap on my bicycle..... blowing three short blasts and then another on my whistle." "Then I had to go all the way round again blowing a continuous blast when the 'all clear' came through." Later a siren was installed in the village. If an invasion had occurred the church bells would have been rung, so they were not rung on Sundays during the war. (46)

The Home Guard was originally formed as the Local Defence Volunteers, to deal with the perceived threat of invasion being led by a vanguard of parachutists. Some months after Bishop Wilson had floated the idea (see chapter 22), Anthony Eden announced the formation of the L.D.V. in 1940. Wilson was one of the first to join up as part of the overwhelming local response. He had said "the descent would take place where troops were not stationed but my town guards would be at hand in every district." (47) The zone headquarters for the new Home Guard was the Territorial Army offices in Market Road. The 1st parade of the 1st Chelmsford L.D.V. group took place on the 8th of June. Initial organisation was carried out by a Major Wilkes, who was a local engineer in Chelmsford, with the volunteers grouped into four companies, each with a company commander. Many volunteers were ex-servicemen from the first war. (48) They were supposed to use pillboxes but at the start of the Home Guard few had been built. There were supposed to be 58 in the Danbury area but only 17 had been constructed. (49) The Home Guard joined with police in checking identity cards, because Chelmsford was in the restricted zone. The Chelmsford battalion had few weapons at the beginning and even borrowed some rifles from K.E.G.S. that had been used for training. (50) After a year however, the local strength stood at 1,631 for all ranks, for which there were 1,378 rifles. When conscription was introduced for the Home Guard, the local numbers rose to 3,000. There were regular exercises such as those in September 1941 when the Home Guard took the role of the enemy with hand to hand 'fighting' in the street, storming the Shire Hall and the police station. (51) In May 1942 there was a tragic accident during an exercise when a 61 year old woman in Navigation Road was killed after she had stood outside her door to watch the spectacle. What was supposed to be a smoke bomb was in fact a homemade real explosive. The authorities had no idea who made it. (52) From 1942 local home guard men of the 6th battalion were transferred into the anti aircraft unit because there was a shortage of men for the AA batteries.

George Brown worked for Hoffmann and joined the Home Guard unit there and went for shooting practice on his days off. Eventually he was given a uniform. The main job was to defend Hoffmann's if it was attacked. He saw his main duties as light relief from work, learning about map reading and weaponry. Towards the end of the war he patrolled the River Chelmer railway viaduct. In the early days of the Home Guard Len Appleton was drilled in the County Hall car park with, in the early days, no uniform or weapons. (53) Peter Hebdon joined the Marconi Company of the Home Guard in May 1942, by which time the 'Dad's Army' image had virtually gone. He got to use a wide assortment of weapons including Browning automatic rifles, Sten guns, spigot mortars, hand grenades, sticky bombs and plastic explosives. Hebdon guarded the ammunition dump at the Territorial Drill Hall in pitch black conditions. He witnessed a German plane destroyed by a rocket from one of the new AA rocket batteries and was later trained to join one of the latter which was based at the Recreation Ground.

The training for the AA batteries was severe and many of the men did not stay long. For this reason the commanding officers of the AA batteries were chosen with care. The batteries shared the local air space with the R.A.F. night fighters. All the defences were used in the two big incendiary attacks on the town in 1943 (see later). There were no serious Home Guard injuries on the second raid of May 13 when 13 people were killed in the town. Hebdon slept in one of three Nissen huts when there were no enemy planes about. The flying bombs had to be left for the Mosquitos and Typhoon fighters because they "came in too fast for us to load and fire". (54)

Evidently not everybody enjoyed being in the Home Guard. In November 1942 came the first local prosecution of a person for being absent from Home Guard duty. (55) Compulsory Home Guard duty was not ended until 1944. (56) Apart from the AA battery, other specialist branches of the local Home Guard developed included a Signal section in which the main element was experts from the Marconi factory. The 6th battalion even had its own band. (57) Chelmsford's Guard worked well with the local A.R.P., particularly on the nights of the incendiary raids when Guard men were heavily involved doing rescue and salvage work.

The rural Home Guard faced similar problems to those in the town. "Uniforms and weapons were practically non-existent when the first men assembled for instruction; shotguns, pikes and pick axes served as makeshift arms and armbands with the letters LDV were the only uniform." The men paraded three times a week in Great Leighs because there were ammunition dumps around the village which needed protecting. They manned road blocks and patrolled vulnerable points. (58) In Roxwell just 40 men patrolled the village and the big surrounding area. (59)

After Operation 'Overlord' and with it the removal of the threat of invasion, absenteeism in the Guard increased, possibly made worse by petty new official instructions. The final parade for the Essex Home Guard took place at Chelmsford Cathedral on Sunday 19th of November 1944. Nine hundred members were present representing all the county's units. (60)

It was recognised from the start that the fire services would play a vital role in protecting the town. By 1941 the Essex Chronicle thought the fighting services were well organised with equipment centred on groups of shops. (61) Recruiting sufficient numbers for the Auxiliary Fire Service was always a problem however, with conscientious objectors often being offered places because it counted as a useful occupation. In 1940 there was a protest by brigade members at the inclusion of several 'conchies' in their ranks. (62) By that time the Auxiliary service had 78 members in the town with 19 trailer pumps and 19 towing vehicles. (63) There was a desperate need for mobile canteens and sleeping accommodation for both the fire brigade and the auxiliary service. A recommendation that the two forces amalgamate met with some resistance but was eventually carried out and a second fire station was erected at the police headquarters at Springfield. (64)(65)

While fire watching remained voluntary there was a big shortage of recruits in the town. (66) It meant staying on duty at night on top of a building, often in cold or freezing conditions. In February 1942 there were 56 streets without fire guards. By October of that year some women were refusing to do fire guard duty, after an element of compulsion had been introduced. The Council's Fire Guard Committee agreed saying there were sufficient men available "without forcing women to do the work". (67) Fire guarding increasingly lost out to the more attractive proposition of joining the Home Guard.

Nineteen forty three saw the headline "Fire guard boys save the Cathedral". (68) The Essex Chronicle was probably only allowed to report the incident, because it was good propaganda for fire brigade recruitment. Three boys aged 18, 17 and 15 were on fire brigade duty on the Cathedral roof during an incendiary raid when 79 1 kilo incendiaries fell in the vicinity of the Cathedral. They put out one which fell on the northern roof. According to the Chronicle, John used the stirrup pump and Albert fetched the water. "The bomb blazed away and became lodged between beams and matchboarding." One boy got a hacksaw and hacked away at the piece that was still burning. Pieces of the roof and melting lead fell into the Cathedral. "The fire was out within seconds." "These young men saved the Cathedral." The BBC was told to do a feature on the incident but actors played the three boys. Chelmsford Cathedral Chapter gave each boy £15, a lot of money then. Privately the boys regarded the incident as a laugh: it only took half a bucket of water to extinguish the fire. (69)

The local fire services were severely criticised after the two incendiary raids. This was in part due to the damage to the 5,000 gallon water carrier on the site of the old Wells and Perry building in Duke Street. The Marconi and Hoffmann factory fire brigades arrived promptly at the fire at Archer's suet factory and dealt with it efficiently. (70) There were severe delays in the Fire Service pumps getting to the bus station in the second raid however. The one hour delay was a factor in the building being gutted and 80 buses wrecked. (71) In 1944 the Regional Commissioner Sir William Spens paid a surprise visit to Chelmsford in response to an unsatisfactory report from an inspector. He had a conference with the Mayor which led to the resignation of the Chief Fire Officer. (72) The fire guard regime wasn't relaxed in the town until March 1945. (73)

For fire protection the R.D.C. divided the large area into four districts. (74) At the outbreak of the war the rural Auxiliary Fire Brigade was desperately short of equipment having only a single heavy trailer pump, 6 light trailer pumps, 20 manual pumps and 35 hand pumps. (75) In May 1940 a much needed temporary fire station was built at Great Baddow. (76) The R.D.C. negotiated a reciprocal agreement with Billericay whereby each council would help with the others fires. (77) In September 1940 three of the four district fire services went to the aid of outside areas: Great Baddow went to Tilbury and Shellhaven, Ingatestone went to Thames Haven and Great Waltham went to Purfleet. (78)

Because of the likelihood of air attacks, a curfew was imposed in all areas in and around Chelmsford from July 1940 in tandem with the strict blackout on all private and commercial premises. (79) A week before the outbreak of the war the traffic lights were masked and the kerbs painted white to aid driving in the blackout, along with lamp posts and fire hydrants. (80) In 1941 the editor of the Essex Chronicle complained that numerous shops were flouting the blackout, which was nowhere near complete. He maintained that the large amount of non essential traffic would make it more difficult for the emergency services to get to affected areas. (81) Fines were regularly imposed for breaking the blackout and were still being imposed in 1944. (92) Despite the strictures of the Chronicle the blackout does seem to have been effective enough to ensure that most bombs fell in rural areas in the early part of the war and caused little damage. (83) John Marriage remembered the disappearance of the street lights, including a number of newly installed high intensity ones in several of the main streets. Most people bought heavy curtains or constructed removable blackout frames. (84)

In terms of the defence of Eastern England, Chelmsford was just east of the General Headquarters line (GHQ). This was one of the county's four main lines, but the most formidable. "As in all parts of the GHQ line, pillboxes with interlocking fields of fire dotted the river bank (the Chelmer), sometimes in the fields and hedgerows further back." There were standard bullet proof infantry boxes which could house section of six men with light automatic weapons. The bigger shellproof artillery pillboxes could house a two pounder anti tank guns or the 6 pounder Hotchkiss gun. (85) One hundred and twenty of the pillboxes still existed in the Chelmsford area half a century later. South of Chelmsford a 12 mile anti tank trench was dug. On all the roads around Chelmsford there was a barrier of angled steel and pyramid anti tank blocks along with spigot mortar placements. Several pillboxes were sited near the big three factories. The heavy AA defences mentioned earlier were all called into action during the two heavy incendiary attacks. Headquarters of the batteries were at Lancaster House, Mildmay Road, Moulsham. Most of the men manning the batteries near the main works worked at those factories. (86)

A field near Little Baddow was used as a temporary 'starfish' decoy site. This was designed to draw German bombers away from the Chelmsford factories three miles to the west. Starfish sites were the most advanced of the various types of decoy developed and were intended to reproduce the large fires that a German bomber would expect to find after a raid on an urban area. The decoy site used a number of different fire sources "to generate the variation in brightness and colour of a full scale conflagration". Each basket would contain "a highly inflammable two and a half hundredweight package of sawdust, scrap wood and shavings all soaked in creosote". The various baskets were fired "electrically from an earth covered shelter which housed the necessary switchgear and communication". This was roughly 800 yards away. A typical starfish site could get through 25 tons of fuel in four hours. (87)The site was used on the night of the Chelmsford blitz, the 14th of May 1943, when 9 baskets were lit. It was obviously unsuccessful in deflecting the raid. (88)

Barrage balloons were important in Chelmsford and not just as part of the town's defences. Gas from the town's gasworks helped inflate over 7,000 barrage balloons. (89) The town itself didn't have any until 1942. After attacks on Marconi and Hoffmann further defence of the town was treated as an urgent matter by the authorities. "Planes would approach the town from the N.E., follow the railway line at 300 feet in a S.W. direction before swooping and dropping to make a final run on the factories." At this point they were too low for the factory defences' machine guns. Two men from the air ministry recommended 31 sites for the balloons, which was above average for a town of Chelmsford's size. They were thought to be an effective deterrent to air raids although George Brown thought otherwise. "I used to think the barrage balloons just attracted the German planes because they knew the military would only place them at important targets." (90) Occasionally loose balloons would cause damage, as in January 1943 when a trailing cable caused damage to five houses. (91) In 1943 the fire guard wanted the balloons lowered during an electrical storm because of the danger of fire. (92)

An important event during the war in the Chelmsford area was the building of Boreham airfield by the Americans. The 561st Engineer Aviation Battalion of the U.S. army arrived on the 13th of May 1943 under the command of Lieutenant Colonel Stanley H. Lomax. Five hundred and sixty men came by boat, train and truck and lived in tents until they had constructed brick built quarters. They were given 12 months to complete the work and worked shifts of 12 hours day and night seven days a week. (93) The 620 acre site had previously been orchards and a wood. In all, 130 tons of concrete were used and 50 miles of conduit and cable were laid. Two huge aviation fuel tanks with a capacity of 150 thousand gallons were submerged beneath the surface. Gigantic aircraft hangars were built as were 212 Nissen huts to house just over 2,600 men. (94) All the equipment was brought in from the U.S. In the event the airfield was finished three months early but the effort apparently caused a breakdown in Lomax's health and he died soon afterwards in hospital at Braintree.

An American soldier recalled his time helping build the airbase. He wrote of "the excitement of that first air raid (on the airbase), with its minor casualties of skinned knees and banged foreheads". The soldier also fondly remembered nights at the Shire Hall, the White Horse, the Bucket of Blood and the Royal Steamer. "Falling into ditches which appeared when no one was looking." There were the nightly farewells in the Chelmsford truck park and "the weary walk back to camp after missing the town truck". He was fed the usual lines. "I was the first 'yank' she had ever gone out with."

Another American recalled going to Chelmsford on the night of the town's worst blitz. "We were scared out of our wits." Another remembered a German plane being hit by a rocket and crashing just beyond their tent area and "those cold English fogs at 5.45 reveilles". The Battalion had a dance band which played at the Boreham Red Cross Club, the Shire Hall and the Danbury Country Club. (95)

Boreham became one of 23 operational airfields in the country, 14 used by the U.S. and 9 by the R.A.F. The first of four squadrons to be based at the airfield left the U.S. on the 29th of January 1944. There were 48 to 60 aircraft including spares. (96) They were used in the bombing offensive leading to 'D' day, attacking sites thought to be of vital importance to the defence of enemy held territory including road, rail and river bridges, airfield gun positions, railway marshalling yards and construction sites. The 394th Bomb group left Boreham the day after 'D' day. Later in 1945 the 315th Troop Carrier Group arrived at Boreham. They carried men of the British 6th Airborne Division on their way to to take part in the crossing of the River Rhine. (97)

As in the whole country, rationing was introduced much earlier in Chelmsford than it had been during the first war and an infrastructure was already in place. Food rationing was introduced on the 8th of January 1940: food could only be bought using ration books. Forty two thousand people registered for butter, 42,500 for sugar and 40,500 for ham in the town. In May 1941 rationing was started for clothing. Fish, fresh fruit and vegetables were not rationed although they were in short supply. Bread was not rationed until 1946 after the war had finished. As in the first war, a Food Control Committee was set up, in 1939 with councillors, trade unionists and two women. Eventually pressure told and women gained greater representation on the committee. Also as elsewhere, Chelmsford had by all accounts a flourishing black market. (98) In 1942 for example a farmer and a grocer were fined £5 for supplying six tins of fish without complying with the Ration Conditions Orders and in the same year a Chelmsford trader was fined £30 for selling tea and soap without receiving coupons. (99)(100) In July 1943 a cafe owner was given a 6 months jail sentence for acquiring an excess quantity of rationed goods. Of course it was much easier for people to get food in the rural area. Everybody was expected to 'Dig for Victory' and there was a big return to using allotments in both the town and the rural area. Chelmsford had less of a tradition for allotments than other Essex towns such as Colchester. Peggy Bradley's father in Beehive Lane refused to use the local milkman after a disagreement, so he bought a cow and kept it on the grass verges near the house, even building a cowshed. (101) Jean Roberts found the shopping terrible with just not enough food to buy.

Meals had to be planned and everything had to be eked out. There was no fresh fruit but lots of carrots.

Early on the war the authorities recommended that Chelmsford should have three communal feeding centres, or British Restaurants, as they became known. The first such restaurant opened in Moulsham Street in March 1941. The Mayor enjoyed beef, two vegetables, apple tart and a cup of tea. (102) 136 could be seated for a three course meal at one sitting for one shilling each and 1,450 meals were served in the first week. (103) In October 1942 the Ministry of Food told the council that their second restaurant in Rainsford Lane was the best in the country both for its menu and the quality of its food. The third restaurant was in Tunman Mead, off Victoria Road. (104) After increasing pressure the restaurants were opened for evening meals and on Saturday and Sunday. (105) In June 1942 the R.D.C. opened its first British Restaurant in Great Baddow after previously saying they were unnecessary. (106) It concentrated more on cash and carry meals. The council soon opened another in Writtle. Sybil Olive remembered eating at a British Restaurant, when she didn't eat at the Crompton Parkinson canteen, and described them as "cheap and cheerful". (107) All the British Restaurants more than broke even. With severe austerity and rationing after the war they were kept open for several years. Both VE and VJ day saw a number of parties at the restaurants.

As elsewhere women played a vital role during the war. Eventually there were over 2,000 Women's Land Army members in the whole county with many of them helping with wheat growing and other farming around Chelmsford. There was still a shortage of land girls in villages like Roxwell, with not enough of them to replace the farm workers who had left for the war. (108) Despite the opposition of the Chief Constable, the county started recruiting for the Women's Auxiliary Police in August 1941. (109) A Mrs Hurley joined the Auxiliaries during the war but was allowed only to do office work. Of course the emergency food canteens and first aid posts couldn't have been manned, without women in the town giving up a great deal of their time.

The main contribution of the women in Chelmsford during the war was in the big works, which couldn't have produced the munitions, switchgear, radios, radar equipment and ball bearings etc that are dealt with elsewhere in this book, without them. Restrictions on middle class married women working was one of the first strictures of society to be removed. Hundreds of mainly single young women were directed into the area but there were also a great many local women who had their first experience of paid work. Being at work did a great deal for their sense of independence. In March

1942 a deputation of women converged on the Shire Hall demanding 'Nurseries Now' for their children. (110) Four months later three nurseries were being prepared. (see chapter 20) Jean Roberts, later to be Mayor, was chair of the Chelmsford Women At Work Committee (C.W.A.W.C.), an effective pressure group for this and other matters, including school meals. (111) The C.W.A.W.C. had conspicuously less success when they petitioned the council to provide play centres for school children after school hours. It was argued that this would mean some mothers could evade their legitimate responsibilities. (112) The Women's Voluntary Service played an important role in the smooth running of the nurseries, providing voluntary workers, materials and equipment. (113) By 1942 there was a steady influx of women into the town. In March 1943 a further 200 were directed into the town, leaving the Billeting Officer only a few days to find them quarters. (114) These women were often blamed by the Bishop and others for the increased amount of 'boozing' and other lax behaviour by women in the town.

Working in the big Chelmsford works certainly opened the eyes of some middle class Chelmsford women. Jean Roberts was unusual in that she had taught before the war in Ealing using her maiden name, whilst married. Needless to say the arrival of her first child more than two years after she started teaching caused a bit of problem! She moved to Chelmsford when her husband got a job at Marconi. She didn't have to register for work because of the baby, but volunteered for part time work at Marconi. A friend looked after the baby. Her job was to grind down the crystals for radio sets and then test the frequency. The only training she and her fellow workers were given was a brief demonstration of a micrometer. Chatting was not encouraged. "Even the walls have ears." There were a wide range of people on her bench. Some of the working class girls tried to deliberately upset the middle class women with their coarse language and "low sexual talk". Men were only there in a supervisory capacity. Marconi's didn't have a canteen so Jean had to eat at a British Restaurant. (115) Joan Taylor worked an eleven hour day six days a week at the Hoffmann factory. (116)

Men working in Chelmsford's big factories during the war did not have an easy life either: long hours were usually followed by some kind of A.R.P. work. Kenneth Smith worked at the Crompton factory, working on lathes making components for switchgear for electric motors: he worked from 7.30. a.m. to 5. 30 p.m. during the week and on Saturday mornings. (117) Ray Knappett remembered when the whistle blew for lunch at Marconi and Hoffmann and a phalanx of cyclists would come down New Street and into the town. (118) When Bill Wilson was taken onto Hoffmann's night shift, he thought he could work as a builder during the day, as well as his 12 hour shift and a two hour journey to and from Thundersley. Not surprisingly he fell asleep at his bench several times. (119)

At the start of the conflict the treatment of conscientious objectors (C.O.s) was better than it had been during the first war but attitudes soon hardened and 'conchies' found they experienced increasingly tough conditions in the town. They had to register as a C.O. rather than enlist at the town's employment exchange and this was apparently a very unsettling experience. A C.O. such as T. Brown, who wouldn't take a life, but would carry out work to save lives in the medical services, found that he was treated reasonably tolerantly however. (120) In July a motion that the council should not employ any C.O.s was only very narrowly defeated. (121) Pressure from those inclined to persecute them persisted and in 1941 the County Council decided not to appoint any further C.O.s. (122) Twenty one cases of C.O.s already employed by the County were to be considered on their individual merits. The editor of the Essex Chronicle was firmly against them working on either Council and the local courts increasingly came down hard on C.O.s who breached the terms of their registration, for example one who refused to do ambulance work. A Salvation Army insurance agent was given three months imprisonment for refusing to be conscripted. (123) Jehovah's Witnesses were frequently jailed for refusing to co-operate with the war effort. In June 1942 one was imprisoned for three months for refusing to start work as a farm labourer, which was in the terms of his registration as a C.O. (124) Later on there was a great deal of comment about 'conchies' who received double rations to perform their farm work. "Don't class the ordinary agricultural worker with those swine" was one comment. (125) Percy Bennett was a trade unionist who had trained as a fire officer before the war. As a supporter of the peace movement he "could not take a gun to anybody". He was allowed to continue in his peaceful occupation. (126)

One area in which the people of Chelmsford did excel at during the war, was fund raising. They certainly did not agree with the Ipswich M.P. who felt that the plethora of 'War Weapons Weeks' were a gigantic swindle, because what mattered was whether the country had the materials and labour to build the aircraft, corvettes etc, not whether there was enough money. In truth, the fund raising exercises were, as much as anything, designed as morale boosting exercises.

In November 1940, a Chelmsford War Weapons Week raised a quarter of a million pounds, which according to the local papers compared well with similar sized towns elsewhere in the country. (127) A Save For Victory week in April 1941 was aimed at increasing the National Savings and encouraged the setting up of street savings groups. In February 1942 a new weapons week was designed to raise £240,000 for two corvettes but almost double, £530,000 was the outcome, the second highest in Essex. (128) During July 1943 a 'Wings For Victory' Week raised £750,000, enough to 'pay' for a Lancaster bomber. (129) A 'Salute the Soldiers' campaign raised almost a million pounds with the money earmarked for the Essex Regiment. (130) Chelmsford also contributed freely to the various salvage weeks. During a book week in April 1943, 213,000 books were collected, well over three times the 65,000 target. Two and a half thousand of these were donated to blitzed libraries, 1,000 given to children and the rest sent for recycling. (131)

As elsewhere going to the cinema was the staple form of entertainment for ordinary people. The cinemas were opened for the first time on Sundays in July 1940. (132) Towards the end of the war there was concern that children were going to the cinema too much. Dance bands like the Altona Brass Band were kept busy playing in a variety of venues, including the Corn Exchange, the hub of entertainment for soldiers. In July 1943 an all Essex dance band championship was organised at Chelmsford under the auspices of the Melody Maker. (133) Nineteen forty two saw rhythm clubs open at the Cricketers in Moulsham and the Three Cups. (134) In the same year a garrison theatre opened in the town for all members of the forces, with all the 650 seats priced at one shilling. (135) The town's big factories had visits from top ENSA entertainers. (136) In 1943 the American Red Cross set up a club for American Soldiers in the upper rooms of the Saracens Head Hotel. One hundred and fifty local women volunteered to be hostesses there! (137) When interviewed by the Essex Chronicle, 32 out of 40 American soldiers said they liked the town. (138)

Apart from concern about the amount of drinking in the town, people, including Bishop Wilson, were worried about the behaviour of young people. Wilson thought that the under 21s should be banned from pubs. Those on the bench found that they were increasingly dealing with juveniles of 17 and under. A lack of male role models at home because of the war and the disruption to education were seen as two of the causes of the increase in crime carried out by children. As in the rest of the country youth centres were being suggested as a solution by the end of the war.

As far as Chelmsford was concerned, the war started in earnest with the shooting down of a bomber which fell in Springfield on the 19th of June 1940, just before the start of the Battle of Britain. The bomber fell in Bishopscourt, the grounds of the Bishop of Chelmsford's residence. "The Heinkel bomber narrowly missed a house where there were girl evacuees, before smashing through a fence and some trees and bursting into flames." "Searchlights held the bomber continuously as he came in from the coast." "Fighter planes were up quickly and after a few bursts of machine gun fire the raider was in difficulties." "There was a momentary pause followed by a huge burst of flame, the sound of petrol tanks burning and small arms ammunition exploding in the fire." "People watching from their homes cheered loudly when the plane came down." The wounded surviving German gave himself up but the other three airmen were buried in an unmarked grave in Writtle Road cemetery. (139) For Chelmsford, this marked the end of the end of the 'phoney war' period. On the 10th of August the first bomb was dropped on the district. Eight days later a plane crashed in the Chelmsford area as a result of the Battle of Britain. When a bomb fell behind the Saracens Head causing a little damage, bombs were still a novelty and the manager raised £100 for charity by charging a shilling per head for people to see the crater. (140)

On the 19th of August the town suffered its first casualties of the war. A Heinkel appeared without warning over the town and dropped 23 small high explosives and incendiaries, probably targeting the police headquarters. They fell wide of their target but demolished or damaged a number of nearby houses. In one, a police sergeant and his family were killed. (141) The fire brigade and civil defence were quickly on the scene but it was felt there were too many 'sightseers'. Chelmsford's gasworks were targeted the day afterwards but again the bombs fell wide of the mark, one leaving a crater in Navigation road. George Brown's parents' house, where they and he had lived most of their lives, was badly damaged. The army managed to salvage some of their possessions. Three houses were destroyed in the raid and three others had to be demolished afterwards. 50 needed repairs. (142) Most bombs were still falling harmlessly in the rural area. A number of bombs, which fell near Chignall Smealy, succeeded only in shaking up a shepherd! (143) A British plane crashed in White Hart Lane, Springfield, with the pilot bailing out. A few days later a Messerschmitt was shot down at Rettendon and the crew of two were taken prisoner. In September 1940 the number of raids in the area increased greatly, with over 100 incidents being reported to the control room at the Civic Centre. On September 3rd a number of British planes were shot down and many high explosives and incendiary bombs were dropped on the outlying districts of Chelmsford. A number of unexploded bombs had to be defused by the bomb squad who were hard pressed. One hundred and fifty incendiaries were dropped in the Roxwell area and the Rural District fire brigade were kept busy as were the animal A.R.P organisation. One of the few bombs that fell inside the borough, hit

WRVS members outside Victoria Road YMCA ready to take mobile canteen out in 1940
(Courtesy of E.R.O.)

upper Mildmay Road, injuring a woman. At this stage Chelmsford was subject to only very light attacks, compared with London which was enduring the blitz.

The perception of the war by Chelmsford townsfolk was changed markedly when the seven time mayor and part owner of the Essex Chronicle, John Ockelford Thompson (see chapter 13) was killed on the 13th of October 1940 along with four members of his family. He had been recently invited to be Mayor again and would have done so had he lived. One direct hit from a lone German bomber on their house at Brierly Place, New London Road, was enough to kill the Mayor, his wife, his son (a lieutenant colonel in the army) two grand children asleep in the basement and a maid. The A.R.P. teams worked non-stop for 15 hours. Thompson's body was not removed until October the 15th. At the funeral in the cathedral the coffin was decorated by his deputy lord lieutenant's plumed hat. His son's coffin was wrapped in a union jack. Bishop Wilson, a close friend of Thompson, was apparently too upset to give the address. After the funeral the procession moved slowly down the High Street and into New London Road watched by large crowds before arriving at the Writtle Road cemetery. (144)

October 1940 saw a falling off in the number of local incidents. Curiously Roxwell received attention in three successive raids but it may have been mistaken for Willingale Aerodrome. On October the 12th a Spitfire crashed at The Cherry Tree on the New London Road killing the pilot. Unfortunately large crowds again hampered the work of the rescue services. Four people were killed when a bomb fell on Watchhouse Road, Galleywood. (145)

In November a number of German aircraft received heavy machine gunfire from the town's defences. One plane released a stick of bombs that fell across Springfield. The first fell on the police headquarters (see chapter 23) (146) On the 11th of November, German planes targeted the Crompton works. Again the bombs missed, one exploding in Upper Bridge Road. (147)

In December a landmine fell on Stock parish church causing a good deal of damage, although the steeple was left intact. The road to Ingatestone was closed for 18 hours after the attack. (148) The German News agency inaccurately claimed that the Hoffmann ball bearing factory had been hit and seriously damaged. (149) A few months later two soldiers home on leave were waiting at a bus stop at Danbury when a car pulled up and a well dressed woman put a packet containing £150 in their hands. It was her son's birthday and he had been killed on active service. (150) In January 1941 enemy aircraft machine gunned a slow moving train outside Chelmsford, killing two people. (151) During April 1941 the Eastern Commissioner warned the general public that an invasion was still likely. In the same month a large bomb aimed at the Crompton factory missed its target but shook the building. (152)

On the 17th of May 1941 there occurred the most destructive attack on the town so far. Seventeen workers at Marconi's New street factory were killed. In a daring attack two bombs were direct hits and one fell on the centre of the machine shop. The next day a 500llb UXB was found still ticking. It was exploded even though this inevitably caused more damage. Production was badly hit, falling by over a third, because over 60% of the machines were damaged and most of the factory's roof had been destroyed (See chapter 5 for the company's contribution to the war effort). The workers complained that there had been no anti aircraft fire because the machine gun on the top of the factory was only manned during the day. (153) Around the factory 250 houses were damaged with two destroyed. A few days later the cathedral was filled for a service for the Marconi victims. (154) Five months later a memorial to the workers was unveiled. (155)

The week following the Marconi raid saw a bomb caused extensive damage to Danbury church and a high explosive brought down a block of flats in Coval Lane, killing six people and seriously injuring another five. (156) After a number of quiet months, a lone raider bombed Hoffmanns and some neighbouring houses, in July 1942, killing 4 people and injuring 20. Production was limited for a while with a good deal of damage to the lapping shop and a concrete floor which collapsed. (157) Tailor made machines were difficult to replace quickly (See chapter 7). The Hoffmann Fire Brigade were summoned. Luckily no regular shift was working at the time so injuries were much fewer than they otherwise would have been. (158) The civil defence and rescue services worked well. There were two rescue squads, three ambulances, two stretcher parties, one mortuary van and the National Fire Service. A rest centre for those bombed out was opened at the local Congregational Church. Angry residents complained, however, that no sirens had warned of the attack and AA defences at Hoffmann had failed to fire.

In October 1942 the Hoffmann factory was raided again, with houses in Henry Road and Rectory Lane also damaged and four people killed. One bomb scored a direct hit on the works, penetrating the roof and exploding in the assembly shop, leaving a crater fourteen feet across and six feet deep. Of course rain fell through the roof causing further damage. Only eight machines were affected, but the cage and the assembly shop were put out of action. (159) Like the previous attack this caused a big dip in production with six weeks production lost. (160) A Luftwaffe aerial photograph of Chelmsford as early as 1940 shows Hoffmann's clearly, and the Germans obviously targeted the factory. Bernard Wren's house was destroyed in the raid and rescuers had to dig him out. It was a year before he could start his education again. Many of those in nearby houses were saved from serious injury by their Morrison shelters.

In March 1943, 60 incendiary bombs fell close to the military hospital at New Hall, Boreham. On April the 19th, during a raid by 20 German bombers, Springfield jail was seriously damaged with the governor losing all his belongings. This was the night of the first major incendiary raid on Chelmsford. At one point there were eight major fires burning in the town. All of the town's Bofors guns and other defences went into action against the raiders. One of the bombs hit Archer's Suet factory causing vast amounts of suet to fill the street. (161) Eileen Hance lived opposite the factory in New Street, next to the Cathedral school. "We were bombed one night, when fire bombs hit Archer's. That went up in flames and the fire engines dealt with that." "We had just managed to put it (the fire bomb) out when the firemen rushed in with a hose and they were covered in suet from the factory." "The firemen did more damage than the fire." (162) The bombers also targeted the Crompton factory but again missed the target.

On Friday the 14th of May 1943, Chelmsford's blitz occurred, its heaviest raid of the war. The attack lasted an hour and the barrage balloons had already been raised. One bomber alone dropped 44 high explosives, 6 parachute mines and 312 kilos of incendiaries. Once again there was little damage to the big factories. The only hit was to Marconi's new factory in Pottery Lane. This made and tested wireless components for anti submarine devices. (163) There was no shift working at the time and nobody was injured. A parachute mine caused widespread damage to surrounding houses. (164) There was a great deal of destruction in the centre of town. The bus station was destroyed and there was much destruction in and around Duke Street.(165) Chelmsford's Y.M.C.A. building, Cannons restaurant, by the station, and a coal yard were demolished.(166) In Moulsham the area between Baddow Road and Lady Lane was heavily hit. Nine bombs, intended for the gasworks, actually fell between Mildmay Road and Lynmouth Avenue. Two 500 kg bombs fell between Goldlay Road and Lynmouth Avenue, destroying a number of houses. A number of incendiaries that fell on Lady Lane did not start fires. The civil defence services were very stretched and additional rescue parties and mobile canteens etc had to be in surrounding areas. In all there were 46 deaths and 226 injured. One thousand people were made homeless but they were mainly put up by friends and relatives and did not need billets. A week later the Essex Chronicle criticised certain national newspapers for "revealing that Chelmsford was the victim of the previous weeks blitz". (167)

For a year the skies over Chelmsford were quieter. In early 1944 with an Allied invasion of the European mainland expected, the government designated the east coast of England, from the Wash to Lands End, a protected area. Visitors were banned from a zone which included Chelmsford.

On Friday the 16th of June 1944, 200 V-1 rockets were launched and Chelmsford suffered its first attacks: a great deal of damage was done to houses but there were no deaths. (168) Most of the V-1s and V-2s fell harmlessly in the rural area around Chelmsford. In October a V2 fell 40 yards from the Bell, Rettendon slightly injuring two people. A day later, one fell in a sugar beet field at Great Waltham. Other V2s fell in Danbury, Writtle and Roxwell. (169) In December 1944 a V2 caused the greatest individual loss of life in the town during the war. It came down near Hoffmann's, destroyed a large area of the factory, and demolished a number of houses in Henry Road. Thirty Hoffmann employees were killed, along with nine residents in the road. Most of those who died at the Hoffmann factory were young women who had just been to a carol service. "There was a festive spirit among the employees at Hoffmann that early morning." "There came a blinding flash, a roar then chaos. People were trapped. The screams of the dying and injured were distressing." (170) Bertie Upson, a Hoffmann worker and member of the firms A.R.P., recalled "I shouted at the girls to get out". He told them to go to the canteen that hadn't been hit. "I kept four fellows back with me and said we had to help". "We got bodies and people who had been injured and half carried them out". A nurse told them not to bring any more bodies to the surgery, only those who were injured. "We had to leave dead bodies at the surgery door." Hoffmann's gave Upson 30 shillings and seven coupons to buy new shoes because the soles of his existing pair had been burnt through. He was promised a medal but this didn't materialise. Upson said "all I wanted was for them to be alive". (171) The factory's cage and assembly department were badly damaged. Chelmsford's fire brigade sent four pumps and a number of American servicemen came to help. A food kitchen was operating in Henry Road within half an hour. Hoffmann's profits fell by three quarters. (172) One man who was slightly injured had come to live in 'nice quiet Chelmsford' after being bombed out twice in Deptford! (173)

When the war finished the Chelmsford A.R.P. area had received 1,326 high explosives, 136 oil and phosphorescent devices, 25,065 small incendiaries, 28 flying bombs and 35 rockets. (174) In January 1945 the council formed a welcome home committee for returning servicemen which was also to give early consideration to a war memorial in the town. On V.E. day crowds of people danced in Tindal Square. Morrison shelters were moved out into the streets to be used as tables for street parties. (175) Amongst Himmler's hoard of treasure found after the war was a silver cup with the words 'Chelmsford Races' under the rim of the base. To this day nobody knows how it came into his possession! (176) The R.A.F., when overrunning a field at Quedlingburg, Germany, found a scale model of Hoffmann and Marconi. It was based on a photo taken by a German reconnaissance aircraft in 1941 and the model was remarkably accurate in most details. (177) William Joyce (Lord Haw Haw) was executed for treason on the 3rd of January 1946. Before the war he lived at Chelmerton Avenue, Great Baddow and knew Chelmsford very well, which was the reason pieces of local knowledge often cropped up in his propaganda broadcasts. An apocryphal story was that a local newsagent who disliked Joyce's fascist views, refused to serve him. He maintained that the hideous scar on his face would frighten the children who came into buy sweets!

Initially there was a proposal to build a community centre as a war memorial in the town. This ran into opposition, particularly from the British Legion. (178) Fund raising proved difficult in such austere times and the memorial fund was closed with only £2,000 raised. The memorial in front of the civic centre that had been erected after the first war was adapted to pay homage to those who had lost their lives in the second conflict. (179) Chelmsford's British Restaurants were kept open while rationing continued but were closed after 1949. (180)

The start of the Cold War saw a small group of people enthusiastically joining the Civil Defence organisation but the response overall in the Chelmsford area was disappointing. (181) Despite the apparently very real threat of a nuclear war in the early post war years, the Chelmsford public remained generally apathetic to recruitment drives. Each of the big three companies had no Civil Defence organiser, despite being requested to appoint one. (182) By 1953 there were just 400 volunteers in the area as a whole. (183) In 1959 the organisation had a new headquarters next to the Eastern National Bus Garage. (184)

The town, with its longstanding Quaker and peace movement, unsurprisingly had a strong C.N.D. presence, from the 1960s to the movement's heyday in the early 1980s. In 1961 a massive C.N.D. march passed through Chelmsford, stopping on its way to Trafalgar Square. (185) Chelmsford was regularly one of the starting points for marches to the U.S. base at Wetherfield. By the 1980s there were a number of branches in the rural area including Great Waltham and Danbury. In 1981 the Friends of the Earth highlighted the nuclear waste being carried through Essex on trains on its way to Windscale."Several tons of irradiated fuel passes through Chelmsford on a monthly basis." (186) Doubtless the vast majority of Chelmsford citizens continued to sleep soundly in their beds!

1) Essex Weekly News 21 1 1931 p.11
2) E.W.N. 30 11 1934 p.9
3) E.W.N. 13 3 1936 p.8
4) E.W.N. 13 3 1936 p.8
5) War Memories E.W.N. 16 6 1979 p.6
6) Chelmsford at War : An introduction Andrew Begent
7) War memories E.W.N. 23 8 1979 p.6
8) W.M. 30 8 1979 p.6
9) W.M. 6 9 1979 p.6
10) W.M. 6 9 1979 p.6
11) W.M. 13 9 1979 p.6
12) W.M. 20 9 1979 p.6
13) W.M. 27 9 1979 p.8

14) E.W.N. 30 6 1939 p.9
15) W.M. 27 3 1980
16) Chelmsford Borough Council minutes 26 5 1943
17) E.R.O. A.R.P. Reports C/W/3/3/2
18) E.R.O. A.R.P. Reports C/W/ 1/2/20
19) Begent p.27
20) W. M. 25 10 1979
21) E.C. 15 1 1943
22) E.W.N. 15 9 1939
23) W.M. 31 1980
24) E.C. 27 12 1940
25) E.C. 2 8 1940
26) E.C. 30 8 1940
27) E.C. 3 1 1941
28) C.B.C. minutes 1940
29) E.W.N. 27 9 1940
30) E.W.N. 30 7 1940
31) C.B.C. minutes 31 7 1940
32) E.W.N. 29 11 1940 p.5
33) E.W.N. 29 11 1940 p.5
34) C.B.C. minutes 1 1 1941
35) C.B.C. minutes 10 2 1941
36) C.B.C. minutes 1 1 1941
37) Begent p.46
38) Great and Leighs Pat Watkinson.
39) Chelmsford Rural District Council minutes 18 7 1944
40) Begent p.170
41) Begent p.225
42) E.W.N. 31 3 1944 p.4
43) C.B.C. minutes 26 4 1944
44) E.R.O. SA 15/1/4/7/1
45) B.B.C. The Peoples War http://www.bbc.co.uk/ww2peopleswar/stories/93a3841193shtml
46) Pat Watkinson
47) The Essex Home Guard Peter Finch p.8

48) Finch p.193
49) Finch p.30
50) Finch p.194
51) E.C. 26 9 1941
52) E.W.N. 15 5 1942 p.5
53) Begent p.27
54) Essex Countryside Vol.44 1995
55) Begent p.163
56) Begent p.264
57) Finch p.199
58) Watkinson
59) Roxwell Revealed: An Anthology
60) Finch p.283
61) E.C. 17 1 1941
62) E.C. 9 8 1940
63) C.B.C. minutes 23 8 1940
64) C.B.C. minutes Nov. 1940
65) Begent p.83
66) E.C. 27 6 1941
67) E.C. 30 10 1942
68) E.C. 21 5 1943 p.7
69) Begent p.182
70) Begent p.176
71) Begent p.200
72) Begent p.247
73) Begent p.295
74) C.R.D.C. minutes p.349 28 9 1939
75) C.R.D.C. minutes p.338 21 11 1939
76) C.R.D.C. minutes p.27 16 4 1940
77) C.R.D.C. minutes p.63 21 5 1940
78) C.R.D.C. minutes p.181 17 9 1940
79) Begent p.43
80) E.W.N. 1 9 1939
81) E.C. 3 1 1941
82) E.C. 28 1 1944

83) Begent p.84
84) Essex Countryside Vol. 32 Dec. 1982
85) WW2 Defences in Essex E.C.C. 1998 p.20
86) Finch p.251
87) WW2 decoy Bombing sites in Essex E.C.C. Planning
88) Begent p.190
89) Begent p.122
90) Begent p.158
91) Begent p.164
92) C.B.C. minutes 24 11 1943
93) Boreham Racing Circuit p.1
94) B.R.C. p.3
95) 'History of the 861st Engineering Battalion p.42-5 (Chelmsford Museum records
96) B.R.C. p.4
97) B.R.C. p.5
98) Begent p.107
99) E.C. 9 1 1942
100) E.C. 24 4 1942
101) http://www.bbc.co.uk/ww2peopleswar/stories/64/a3841364.shtml
102) Wartime memories 14 2 1980 - 16 3 1941
103) Wartime memories 14 2 1980 – 24 9 1941
104) Begent p.112
105) C.B.C. 27 5 1942
106) W.M. 21 2 1980
107) E.R.O. Oral history records Sybil Olive
108) Roxwell Revealed p.139
109) E.C. 29 8 1941
110) E.C. 27 3 1942
111) E.C. 3 7 1942
112) E.W.N. 30 10 1942 p.5
113) E.W.N. 26 11 1943 p.2
114) E.C. 19 3 1943 p.5
115) E.R.O. SA 20/1459/1
116) Begent p.143

117) Begent p.242
118) Begent p.239
119) Begent p.146
120) E.C. 2 2 1940
121) E.C. 19 7 1940
122) E.C. 10 1 1941
123) E.C. 23 1 1942
124) E.C. 2 4 1942
125) E.C. 29 1 1943 p.2
126) E.R.O. Percy Bennett SA 31/1/6/1
127) W.M. E.W.N. 31 1 1980
128) E.W.N. 13 2 1942 p.7
129) E.C. 11 7 1943 p.5
130) E.C. 2 6 1944
131) Begent p.170
132) E.C. 26 7 1940
133) E.C. 3 7 1942
134) E.C. 3 4 1942
135) E.C. 16 10 1942
136) Begent p.142
137) E.C. 26 2 1942
138) E.C. 8 1 1943 p.5
139) W.M. E.W.N. 13 12 1979
140) W.M. E.W.N. 13 12 1979
141) http://www.essex.police.uk/museum/history 24.htm
142) W.M. E.W.N. 10 1 1980
143) W.M. E.W.N. 10 1 1980
144) W.M. E.W.N. 24 1 1980
145) W.M. E.W.N. 24 1 1980
146) http://www.essex.police.uk/museum/history 24.htm
147) Begent p.70
148) W.M. E.W.N. 31 1 1980
149) Begent p.70
150) W.M. E.W.N. 7 2 1980
151) Begent p.70

152) Begent p.84
153) Begent p.85
154) W.M. E.W.N. 7 2 1980
155) Begent p.116
156) W.M. E.W.N. 7 2 1980
157) W.M. E.W.N. 20 2 1980
158) Begent p.135
159) Begent p.150
160) Begent p.152
161) Begent p.186
162) http://www.bbc.co.uk/ww2peopleswar/stories/38/a3841238.shtml
163) Begent p.192
164) Begent p.193
165) Begent 200
166) C. Museums records
167) Begent p.222
168) Begent p.257
169) C. Museums records
170) C. Museums records
171) E.C. 19 3 2009 p.19
172) Begent p.272
173) W.M. E.W.N. 19 12 1945
174) W.M. E.W.N. 22 12 1945
175) W.M. E.W.N. 8 5 1945
176) E.W.N. 29 6 1945 p.9
177) E.W.N. 26 10 1945 p.2
178) E.W.N. 4 1 1946 p.2
179) E.W.N. 1 10 1948
180) E.W.N. 2 12 1949 p.12
181) E.C. 17 11 1949
182) E.W.N. 25 4 1952 p.1
183) C.B.C. minutes 28 10 1953
184) C.B.C. minutes 28 1 1959
185) E.W.N. 10 2 1961 p.1
186) E.C. 26 1 1981 p.

25

Sport in the Chelmsford area before 1945

"The Kaiser of Essex sport"

The quote in the title refers to Robert Cook, who bestrode Essex and Chelmsford sport like a colossus in the late Victorian and Edwardian period both as a participant and a very able administrator. He was given the nickname by the Bishop of Colchester who was a keen supporter of Essex sport. Chelmsford was the centre of much thriving county sport including athletics and cycling as well as football, cricket and other sports. These were all mainly the preserve of the well heeled upper middle class amateur. By the first war however all the big local firms had their own sports days and teams for individual sports. The inter-firm sports days had also been well established. By the incorporation, the town and surrounding villages had not only a variety football and cricket teams, but lawn tennis and cycling were well established; boxing, swimming and skating were also well followed. Quoits had also been practised in several local public houses. By the end of the century, hockey was popular with both sexes. Rugby however didn't get established in the area until after the first war. By the second war Chelmsford had a professional football club. If it hadn't been for the war this club might have gained entry to the football league. The 1930s of course saw Chelmsford City's famous cup run, which as it turned out was the apogee of its fortunes. Although Essex County Cricket Club had been formed in the county town in 1876, county cricket was not played in the county town until well after the first war. Although a Chelmsford cricket week was well established by the second war, cricket in the county town did not gain uniformly large crowds and wasn't a sound financial proposition.

Robert Cook was born in 1858; his first love was boxing but soon turned to cycling and he was riding a boneshaker at the age of 10; even a compound leg fracture couldn't dissuade him from following the sport. His organising genius at the young age of 21 saw him call together the cycle clubs of Essex for a cycle meet. This led to the first county cycling championship in the country in 1882. From 1885 meetings were held at the New Street cricket ground which belonged to the Bishop of Colchester. The organisation became the Essex County Cycling and Athletics Association. The New Street ground was known for being a very fast grass track. In addition Cook played every county football fixture from 1883 to 1889 as well as playing cricket. He was Secretary of the County Football Association for over 20 years. (1) As a Vice President of the Football Association he became a figure of national importance. In later years he took up more leisurely sporting pursuits. He won several regional billiard titles. He also became a town councillor. Cook was only 50 when he died in 1908 and was buried in the Writtle Road cemetery. On his gravestone under a tall Celtic Cross, is a bike, a cricket bat and ball and stumps, a football and two laurel leaves. Supporting the cross are two sorrowful athletes. The inscription reads

'The pioneer of Essex athletics'
'Founder of Essex County Cricket and Athletics Associations'
'A real friend An exemplary freemason'
'He ran well the race that was set before him'

The West Essex Bicycle Club had been established at the Shire Hall in 1875. It was almost exclusively upper middle class in membership because of the cost of the machines. The club included members of leading families such as the the Bolingbrokes, the Wenleys and the Wrays. Fred Spalding junior was known as one of the fastest cyclists in Essex as was Cook himself on his 'Xtraordinary Challenge'. Cook led an annual torchlight procession through the town. The club collapsed in the 1880s but was revived as the West Essex Riding Club with its headquarters at the Kings Head. (2) Cycling was marked in the town, like hockey, by the participation of women. In 1897 the Chelmer Cycling Club was formed in Springfield and by 1906 a cycling club had reformed in Chelmsford, which was also open to women. These were eventually to merge after the second war. Herbert Pash, the son of J.B. Pash, was heavily involved with the Essex Cycling and Athletics Association, first as a renowned athlete himself then as an administrator. By 1891 the 10th annual race meeting of the Essex County Cycling and Athletics Association was held on the cricket ground at New Street. Events included a two mile walk, a two mile bike ride, a one mile open bike handicap, a five mile bike handicap, a one mile flat championship race and a half mile steeple chase handicap race. (3) By the early 1900s these county championships had grown further so that according to the Chronicle the town was the sporting centre of Essex. "Marquees, sideshows and miles of bunting decorated the grounds and a uniformed ladies band supplied martial music". A crowd of ten thousand was not unknown. "After the racing the competitors, officials and notables adjourned to the Shire Hall for dinner".

A separate athletics club in the town didn't exist until 1934, even though there were a great many athletes in the town. Although they wouldn't admit to it, by this time, all the big firms employed athletes to win the inter sport championships. Ray Fullerton, for example, was head hunted by Marconi to compete in all the sports events. He clocked on and off and then went off to train. Fullerton was the instigator of the Chelmsford Athletics Club borrowing two huts that were situated by the Marconi masts, which were being dismantled. The huts were moved to a site close to Marconi's sports ground and the new club was the first in England to have its own clubhouse.

Boneshaker of the 1860s which was still popular in the 1890s (Courtesy of E.R.O.)

The lack of a separate athletics club in the town until 1934 was because of the pre-eminence of the local works sports clubs. These were essentially very different to the genteel upper middle class sporting activities elsewhere in the town. Prior to the 1880s the only firms large enough to have organised sporting and social events were Eddington's, Coleman and Morton and the local breweries particularly the one at Writtle. (4) By the end of the century however each of Chelmsford's big three firms had well established sporting and social clubs. Crompton's Arc Works club had 300 members by 1892. By this time the firm had had cricket and football teams for at least 10 years. (5) In 1891 the Arc Works held its first cross country run over 8 miles with

11 runners competing. Crompton for many years had the only squash court in the town. The Colonel himself played squash until he was 90.The firm held its first annual sports meeting and by 1894 this was well established at its Wood Street ground. (6) By 1911 Christy's, Hoffmann and Marconi had their own sports days as well as a United Works sports day. The Hoffmann sports and social club was founded in 1905 and by the second war had thirty sections. Its sports ground was opened in Rainsford Road in 1919. Marconi's sports ground was originally in Waterhouse Lane, before moving to Beehive Lane. In 1937 the Hoffmann works football team had successful runs in both the amateur and F.A. cups. Over 3,000 turned up to see Hoffmann play Ipswich Town. (7)

By the 1880s local cricket was well established in the Chelmsford area. Little Baddow, although not officially home to a cricket club until 1904, played a match against a combined team from Great Baddow and East Hanningfield in 1793 and another against Boreham in the same year. Little Baddow played Danbury in 1800 and a club was founded in the village as early as 1885 but probably folded soon afterwards. In 1881 Chelmsford Cricket Club played 14 matches. (8) The club had been playing matches as early as 1811 first in Kings Head meadow and then at Fairfield the site of the current bus station. It had however only reformed in 1879. Finances however were frequently a problem. In 1881 for example a subscription ball was held at the Shire Hall to raise money for the Club. (9) Membership however did rise from 40 in 1879 to 160 in 1892. By 1893 the club was flourishing both on the playing field and financially. In 1894 the club played 23 matches, 17 at home. (10) Matches were played at the New Street ground, later to be the site of the Marconi factory which was its home for 32 years. By 1902 there were six other cricket clubs in Chelmsford including the Chelmsford Y.M.C.A. cricket club, which had a ground on the Broomfield Road. In 1921 the Chelmsford Cricket Club, without a ground since the building of the Marconi factory, obtained a lease on the water meadow behind the Chelmsford hospital. This was of course destined to become the home of the Essex County Cricket Club. The Chelmsford Club was later to leave this venue for Chelmer Park. (11)

The Essex County Cricket Club had been founded in 1876 at a meeting in the Shire Hall in the county town. Essex wasn't admitted to the ranks of first class counties until 18 years later in 1894. (12) A famous early Essex cricketer Charles 'Korty' Kortwright was born at Ingatestone. He played 160 matches for the county between 1894 and 1907. Kortwright took 440 wickets with a best of 8 for 57 against Yorkshire at Leyton in 1900. In 1898 he took 96 wickets in a season. Kortwright captained the club in 1903.

He also scored two hundreds and caught 167 catches. Kortwright was often regarded as the fastest bowler of his era. After he retired from cricket he was a prominent member of Chelmsford Golf Club. He died at South Weald in 1952. (13)

It was several decades before county cricket was played in the town. The county's headquarters were first at Brentwood and then Leyton. (14) By 1924 a great deal of work had been done on the New Writtle Street ground. The Weekly News commented "It only required extension towards the river and county matches could be played there". (15) In 1925 the inaugural first class cricket match was played at Chelmsford, Essex v Oxford University. A year later came the first county match against Somerset. This also happened to be the first tied match in Essex County Cricket Club history. The match was initially awarded to Somerset by the umpires on first innings scores. Later however, a ruling by the M.C.C., resulted in the points being shared. The rules of the game were also changed because the umpires had not allowed the last over to be completed.(16) After the Leyton ground was sold in the 1930s, Chelmsford became the headquarters of the Club with offices in Duke Street. (17) The cricket itself remained very peripatetic in the 1930s with eight grounds including not only what became the County Ground but also Hoffmann's cricket ground at Chelmsford being used. Attendances at the Chelmsford cricket week, when a number of matches were played at the ground, were often a problem. Despite this Chelmsford gradually obtained more county matches. When Walter 'Wally' Hammond, the Gloucestershire Test cricketer, was likely to play in the Chelmsford cricket week, seating was put in place for 2,500 spectators. (18) During 1934 the town had 6 matches including one against the Australians. (19) By 1938 however despite having a fine side Essex finances were again poor with a low membership. (20) An Amateurs versus Professionals match in Chelmsford attracted only a moderate attendance. (21) Chelmsford was the only cricket ground in the county to suffer from the war when the pavilion was damaged. (22)

Horse racing was held regularly at Galleywood until the 1930s. It had started in the 1750s and a Chelmsford Race Company had been formed in 1862 enabling a grandstand to be built with various outbuilding areas including a paddock. (23) Racing was not continuous throughout the year. New rules introduced in 1879 required larger stakes than could be afforded locally. Racing was kept going by infrequent farmers races and hunters races. (24) The original course was flat over 3 miles, consisting of a one mile straight and an oval of two miles. It crossed both the Stock Road and the Margaretting Road (twice) It was the only racecourse to go around a church! In 1890 flat racing was replaced by steeple chasing until the last meeting in 1935. One major problem with the course was that too few people paid. Thousands of spectators watched for free from the common ground. Only entrants to the grandstand paid to watch. When there was a large attendance there were probably three outside to one inside and those outside probably had a better view. It was difficult for police and officials to control proceedings and on course bookies often absconded with all the winnings. The races did however attract large numbers of visitors to the Chelmsford area coming both by road and rail. "There was a constant stream of carriage and carts of every description to and from the course throughout the day". "Numerous parties of the upper sort arrived on the course in well appointed equipages and partook of luncheon before the racing began; whilst for the less wealthy sportsmen ample provision was made at the refreshment tents in the rear of the grandstand". "A large contingent of 'East End gentry' were in attendance with games of chance, the three card trick and pea and thimble rigging". (25) In the first war the grandstand was taken over by the army for billets and much of the common was used as a training area. Several syndicates tried to run the racecourse without much success before the site was eventually sold for just £1,850. (26) Greyhound racing came briefly to Chelmsford at a site on the Writtle Road near the Crompton works in the 1920s. Racing was held there three times a week in the summer and twice in the winter. (27) In 1932 a new stadium opened at Beehive Lane. (28) There was also unlicensed greyhound racing in Kings Head Meadow and at Little Waltham in the 1930s. (29)

Because of the new Chelmsford borough's cautious approach to spending, the first proper swimming pool was not built until 1906. One had been proposed as early as 1885. As far back as 1874, a pool in what is now Central Park close to the railway, was used by swimmers. Millponds at Croxton and Moulsham were also used. Parts of the River Can were used for paddling. A Chelmsford Swimming Club was established in 1899, using a bathing place in the River Chelmer but this was not for inexperienced swimmers. The club suspended its activities in 1901, until the council built a proper pool to rival the one already built in Colchester. Chelmsford's open air pool eventually opened in July 1906 in Greyhound Mead off Waterloo Lane covering five sixths of an acre. It was lined with concrete cement. On either side there was a terrace planted with trees and shrubs. There were two spring diving boards and a timber island of step platforms in the centre. On one side was a dressing shed 80 feet in length and 36 dressing boxes. There was also a cycle shed. The pool was built in nine months at a cost of £700, under the supervision of the Borough Engineer Cuthbert Brown. (30)

The Chelmsford Swimming Club was revived with Robert Cook heavily involved. The rivers were still used. M.L. Bellamy remembered swimming at Sandford Mill during the first war. By 1935 the swimming baths were in a state of considerable disrepair. An initial £20,000 scheme was rejected as too expensive. A reduced scheme costing £8,000 was put forward. One councillor said "the present one was both dangerous and poisonous" and could not be patched up. (31) A proposed site using part of the Recreation Ground was abandoned because of objections to using part of the town's public park. (32) In 1937 no agreement could be reached on the council regarding a new site in Admirals Park. (33) By July 1938 it had finally been decided to build a new pool on the site of the old one. The war of course prevented any immediate start to the building. (34)

Chelmsford Football Club played its first amateur matches in the 1870s. The club struggled in its early years and was actually disbanded in May 1883 only to be reformed later the same year. It was decided to join the new county football association and wear light and dark blue shirts. The club normally used the cricket club's ground in New Street. For a while the club used Colchester's ground. This caused friction between the two sets of supporters. In 1893 the club reached the final of the Essex Senior Cup. They beat Romford in front of a 3,000 crowd and thousands met the team off the train back at Chelmsford. (35) Well before the end of the century there were a number of other established football clubs in the town. The Anchor Works had a cricket and football club by 1882. (36) By 1896 a new club, Old Cromptonians, was playing and beating the current Anchor Arc Works team. (37) At the turn of the century both Chelmsford United and Chelmsford Swifts could field strong local teams. Chelmsford F.C. still had the strongest representation in Essex County teams however. In 1895 they had been founder members of the North Essex League. During the early 1900s they moved leagues several times, to the South Essex League, the South East Anglian League and they spent one season in the Spartan League in 1908-9. In 1912 they became one of the founder members of the Athenian League. (38) During 1922 the club was relegated and dropped into the Middlesex County League. In 1923 they entered a team in the Essex and Suffolk Border League in which they finished second. They then moved up into the London League. In the following 5 years they won the East Anglian Cup 3 times. The club had been playing at Kings Head meadow but in 1925 moved to a ground at New Writtle Street, where they didn't have to fish the ball out of the river! In 1931 the club won the London League and also reached the first round of the F.A. Cup. Surprisingly for those who think football hooliganism is a comparatively recent phenomenon, after a rough match between Grays and Chelmsford in 1932, a large number of spectators crowded round the dressing rooms and made a rush for the players. Several players were injured. The one policeman on duty was powerless to prevent the mayhem. Police reinforcements did not arrive in time.(39) In 1935 the club was one of the founder members of the Eastern Counties League, but left two years later to join the Essex County League. Chelmsford stayed in that league for just a single season.

If the club was to join the new Southern League it had to turn professional. Negotiations took place between the amateur club and the new club. Chelmsford City, the club's new unwarranted name, agreed to take over the New Writtle Street ground, with an option to buy it for £2,000. The new directors met the entire liabilities of the previous club. Facilities were brought up to the required standard. (40) The intention was eventually to provide a ground capable of holding 25 to 30,000 people. A new supporters' club reached 1,000 members as the season started. A new manager, Billy Walker, was brought in to build a new team of the required standard. Walker had scored 244 goals in 531 league games for Aston Villa and had managed Sheffield Wednesday. After Chelmsford, he managed Nottingham Forest when they won the F.A. Cup. He assembled a team capable of achieving football league status. There were several internationals with a good deal of league experience. It was not until the ninth match against Cardiff that a victory was achieved however. Walker left before three months of the season had been completed. (41) City's outstanding achievement that season was reaching the fourth round of the F.A. Cup. A home crowd of 10,200 saw Chelmsford beat Southampton 4-1. In the next round they were drawn away against Birmingham City. Chelmsford lost 6-0 in front of a crowd of 45,000, including 4,500 who had made the trip up from Essex. The club gained just over £1,000 from the game. A run of 8 wins in 9 games took City to mid table in the league by the end of the season. (42) In the next season the players were to wear numbers on their backs for the first time. All games were abandoned at the start of the war. A number of friendly games were however played during the 'phoney war' period, with Arsenal, Spurs, Chelsea, Fulham and Aston Villa all sending teams. Southend United also used the ground in the early part of the war. From 1941 Marconi used the City ground for storing supplies. (43) It also became a site for barrage balloons.

Bowling became very popular in the town during the late Victorian and Edwardian period. For this reason the Recreation Ground (now Central Park) which opened in 1894, not only had three tennis courts, an athletics track and the space for a cricket pitch, but also a bowling green. This proved so popular that a second green was added in 1906 and led to the establishment of the Chelmsford Bowling Club. Members wore slippers on the green. Bowls was also played in the large gardens of private houses. Canon Lake had his own bowling team. Another bowling green was laid down in 1908 by the Arc Works Club. Both Marconi and Hoffmann had their own bowling greens. In 1908 the Falcon Private Bowling Club was established at the rear of the Falcon public house. This was soon transferred to the gardens of the Bell Hotel on the corner of Tindal Street. The club moved to Seymour Street in 1937 where it was reckoned to have one of the finest greens in the country. John Ockelford Thompson, the seven times mayor, was a keen bowls enthusiast and had a green in the grounds of his house at Brierly Place. The Brierly Place team were given the right to use the name of Princess Mary Louise, granddaughter of Queen Victoria, for their club. (44)

The first Chelmsford Lawn Tennis Club was founded in 1878, only a year after the first Wimbledon tournament. In 1885 the club had 100 members both male and female. Its male members included doctors, solicitors, clergy and other professionals. It used land next to the cricket ground in New Street but its headquarters were at the White Hart Inn in Tindal Street. In 1892 it had 60 members and its Vice President was Beadel the local M.P. (45) A rival club, the Chelmsford Borough Lawn Tennis Club was formed in 1885 but had collapsed by 1897. A new club the Grove formed in 1893 was much more successful. By 1896 it had between 50 and 60 members. (46) In 1895 the Grove was one of two clubs which formed the Essex Lawn Tennis Association. During 1907 the two clubs were joined by the Mildmay. The Grove's original courts were in Grove Road, Moulsham, but by 1895 they were in Vicarage Road where they remained for 75 years. An early President was Frederick Wells. The ground was rented from the Mildmays until 1913 when the site was bought with interest free loans from members and donations. Membership of tennis clubs was expensive because the grass courts had to be maintained. As early as 1880 the club announced annual rates of subscription of 10 shillings for men and 5 shillings for ladies. (47) This and an extensive social side, ensured that membership was exclusively upper middle class. The original Chelmsford Lawn Tennis Club folded in the 1910s but reformed in the 1920s. (48)

The Chelmsford Golf Club was founded in May 1893. Initially it used a 9 hole golf course at Galleywood common. One of the founding members was Garrad Baker, a High Street chemist, who was Secretary of the Chelmsford Race Committee. This probably accounted for the decision to establish a 9 hole course there. The course was two miles from Chelmsford station and because of this, carriages had to be hired from the Saracens Head by members. Despite this the club proved popular at a time when the game was enjoying a boom. The Chelmsford club is the eleventh oldest in the country. One of the earliest golf course architects, Tom Dunne, laid out the course. An entrance fee was set at two guineas, with an annual subscription of one guinea for men and half a guinea for ladies. Lord Rayleigh was the first president and A.J. Balfour, the Prime Minister between 1902 and 1905, the first vice president. In 1895 the club had 89 members, 68 men and 21 ladies. By 1906 this had increased to 163, 107 men and 56 ladies. (49) In the same year a clubhouse was provided adjoining the Horse and Groom public house. Membership was increased to one pound and ten shillings for men and fifteen shillings for ladies. The local parish council complained to the lord of the manor about a place of natural beauty being destroyed. A new agreement leased the links to the club for three years at a rent of ten pounds per annum. There was to be no cutting down of trees and golf couldn't be played in July and August when members of the local Working Men's Club could use the course. This, plus the fact that gypsies often camped on the common and military rest camps also caused damage to

Chelmsford Gold Club, Widford during the 1920s
(Courtesy of E.R.O.)

the course, were probably instrumental in Sir Daniel Gooch of Hylands House offering to lease some land at Widford to the club, suitable for an eighteen hole course. The new course opened in 1911. (50) Most of the all round cost of £1,500 was raised by loans from members. Fourteen holes of the course were on the Chelmsford side of the railway line. The other four holes were on the Widford side. By 1914 membership had increased to 241. During the war the holes on the Widford side were ploughed up. When Hylands was sold after the first war, the club bought the freehold. In 1938 the club opened its extension to the course on the Chelmsford side and the Widford holes were no longer required. At the start of the war membership stood at 324. The course only suffered damage once when a stick of bombs fell on the second fairway. (51)

Hockey was another sport which was followed by women as well as men in Chelmsford. The Chelmsford Hockey Club was formed in 1898 and from the start was open to women as well as men. Photos show that there were mixed teams as well as single sex ones. Herbert Marriage, the tenant of Moulsham Lodge gave permission for the use of a field behind the tennis courts. Subscription was two shillings and sixpence for tennis players and five shillings for non tennis players. Ladies games were played during the week and men's and mixed teams played at the weekend. The ladies teams often featured well known names in the town, particularly the Whitmores, the Bodkins and the Marriages. K.E.G.S. old boys also provided a team. In 1900 the Chelmsford club moved to the New Street ground. After the News Street ground was sold in 1912, old girls of Chelmsford High School decided to form a ladies club in the town. A field behind Widford Hall was initially used but in 1924 the club transferred to Crompton's Athletics ground at Wood Street. (52) Well known town families in the team at this time included the Christys and the Cramphorns. The ladies travelled to away games by a variety of means, bicycle, pony and trap, motorcycle, car or train. Often two large cars were used. By the 1930s the club was attending Easter hockey festivals at Bournemouth, Ramsgate and Southend. During the war matches continued right up to October 1940. The men had played at New Writtle Street, sharing the ground with the Cricket Club since 1922/3. In the previous decade they had played at various venues including Springfield. (53)

Organised rugby made a surprisingly late entrance to the Chelmsford area. In 1920 six men sat down at the Saracens Head Hotel to form Chelmsford Rugby Club. The first pitch was off the Baddow Road, near the present Army and Navy roundabout and was shared with a herd of cows. The club then moved to another pitch in Wood Street. In the 1930s the club transferred to Writtle. One or two players took to arriving by plane;

they would disembark already changed, just to demoralise the opposition! (54) The club had difficulty in attracting the best local players who often preferred to go to the more prestigious London clubs.

Skating had long been popular in the Chelmsford area on frozen ponds. Just before the first war there were certainly two skating rinks in the town, one near the railway station and one on the old Coleman and Morton foundry site on New London Road. The latter ran a programme of competitions and also a fancy dress carnival. (55) The County roller skating rink was a popular meeting place for young people and, managed by Albert Duke, it probably continued until the second war, when it was used by Marconi for the assembly and testing of radio equipment. They still had a valve depot there in 1964. Skating was also allowed on the Recreation Ground lake in the Edwardian period when it froze. Harold Orrin remembered skating to work at the Arc works, when the water froze. (56)

Boxing had a long tradition in the county town. As early as 1882 the Essex Amateur Championships were held in the Shire Hall. (57) In the Edwardian period there were regular boxing evenings in the town including one at one of the skating rinks in 1913. (58) During the interwar period there were regular tournaments put on by the National Sporting Club at the Corn Exchange. Various town dignitaries including the Mayor were often present. (59) There was also a regular Scouts boxing event. In the 1930s boxing and judo exhibitions were held to raise money for carnival funds. These often featured well known current boxing celebrities. (60) The Essex Home School often gained considerable success in junior boxing tournaments. (61)

Earlier in the 19th century, quoits was popular as a game in the Chelmsford area, particularly in Springfield. In the late 19th century there was a pitch behind the Carpenters Arms on the Broomfield Road and it was also played at Link House farm, West Hanningfield. "The quoits were about the size of a ten plate with a notch for the forefinger on the underside". A hen's feather was placed in the opposite square. Players threw at the feather in the opposite square. Hoffmann had a pitch on their sports ground until about 1939. (62)

Billiards was popular in the town in the late 19th century. A billiard tournament was held at the Phoenix Coffee House in 1884. (63) The game was still regularly played after the first war, when players played for the Pretyman Cup, named after the local M.P., at the Hoffmann Athletic and Social Club in 1920. (64) Six years later the cup was played for at the Marconi Club when it was won by the Chelmsford Y.M.C.A. (65) The sport was popular at the Conservative Club. Snooker was also played at the latter and

1923 saw the first mention in the local papers of a snooker tournament held there. Of the other minority sports, netball was being played at Crompton's Wood Street ground by 1923. (66) The year before, the Weekly News reported on a badminton match played between Chelmsford and Colchester at the Drill Hall. (67)

The Boer War showed up the lack of fitness of many young people. Even before this however, gyms were being established in the area. The Chelmsford Gymnasium was formed in 1891. K.E.G.S. had its own gymnasium by 1894. The log books of the local junior schools at the turn of the century showed that increased emphasis was being placed on fitness.

Well before the second war the exclusivity of many sports in the Chelmsford area had been removed by the increase of leisure time, especially on Saturdays and the role of the big three works in making a wide variety of sports affordable to working people. These firms had also played their part in blurring the distinction between amateur and professional which had been so important to the cycling and athletics enthusiasts in Robert Cook's Day.

1) Essex Countryside 1977 Vol.25 June
2) Chelmsford Museums records
3) Essex Weekly News 24 7 1891 p.2
4) C. Museum Research material for Chelmsford Pastimes pamphlet
5) Essex Weekly News 17 2 1982
6) E.W.N. 29 6 1894 p.6
7) C. Museums records
8) E.W.N. 20 5 1881 p.5
9) E.W.N. 9 12 1881
10) E.W.N. 20 9 1894 p.4
11) Pastimes In Times Past p.15-17
12) E.W.N. 20 4 1894
13) Essex County Cricket Club William A. Powell p.15
14) Past Times In Times Past p.13
15) E.W.N. 2 1924
16) 60 Classic Essex Matches Tony Debenham etc. P.30-31
17) Essex Countryside 1982 Vol 30 April
18) E.W.N. 6 7 1928 p.8
19) Essex Chronicle 20 4 1934

20) E.C. 22 4 1938 p.12
21) E.C. 12 8 1938
22) Essex County Cricket Club Lemmon and Marshall p.207
23) Galleywood Race Course Christine Whybro
24) E.C. 4 5 1973
25) E.W.N. 20 3 1885 p.2
26) C. Museums records
27) E.C. 23 9 1927 p.8
28) E.C. 3 3 1932 p.3
29) The Essex Village Book Pusey
30) Essex Review July 1906
31) E.C. 29 11 1935 p.9
32) E.C. 31 5 1935 p.2
33) E.C. 29 10 1937 p.9
34) E.C. 1 7 1938 p.9
35) 'Wheel Em In' The Official History of Chelmsford City Club Steve Garner p 1-2
36) E.W.N. 17 2 1882
37) E.W.N. 13 3 1896
38) Garner p.3
39) E.C. 22 1 1932 p.3
40) Garner p.4
41) E.C. 19 8 1938 p.12
42) Garner p.6
43) Garner p.10
44) Pastimes in Times Past The Friends of Chelmsford Museum. P.7-8
45) E.W.N. 15 4 1892 p.5
46) E.W.N. 8 5 1896 p.5
47) E.C. 30 4 1880 p.5
48) C. Museums sports research materials
49) Chelmsford Golf Club 1893-1993 p.18-26
50) Chelmsford Golf Club p.30-31
51) Chelmsford Golf Club p. 35-54
52) Pastimes in Times Past The Friends of Chelmsford Museum
53) http://en.wikipedia.org/wiki/Chelmsford_Hockey_Club
54) C. Museums Research papers for pastimes exhibition

55) E.C. 5 10 1910, 7 10 1910, 17 2 1911
56) Essex Record Office Oral tapes Harold Orrin
57) E.W.N. 4 8 1882 p.5
58) E.W.N. 3 10 1913 p.5
59) E.W.N. 2 2 1923
60) E.W.N. 2 3 1934 p.10
61) E.W.N. 4 4 1930
62) C. Museums Research papers for Pastimes exhibition.
63) E.W.N. 26 1 1884 p.5
64) E.W.N. 19 3 1920 p.6
65) E.W.N. 26 3 1926 p.7
66) E.W.N. 2 2 1923 p.5
67) E.W.N. 3 3 1922 p.5

26

Sport in the Chelmsford area after 1945

"We are planning not just for the time when Chelmsford will be a fourth division club but when they will be one of the top clubs in the country."

It is over a century since Chelmsford was the unarguably the centre of sport in Essex. When it comes to the national game the county now has three football league clubs but although Chelmsford City made a number of applications to join the league, none of them came close to success. After a good deal of mismanagement the club is at least back in its own home town but no nearer to having its own ground. The county town is home to the Essex County Cricket Club, which was very successful towards the end of the century, but immediately after the war there were long spells when cricket wasn't played at all in Chelmsford. For a brief period in the early 1950s, Boreham had one of the fastest and most popular motor racing circuits in the country. Long held plans to re-establish horse racing in the area stalled in the new millennium, until the all-weather track opened briefly at Great Leighs in 2008. For all its early problems the county town does now house one of the best sport and leisure centres in the county, the Riverside.

After the war Chelmsford City started well, winning both the Southern League and the Southern League Cup in 1946. The manager was Arthur Rowe, later to be the successful manager of Tottenham Hotspur. (1) An early proposal to have dog racing at the New Writtle Street ground was rejected by the council after complaints from local residents. Many football clubs had followed this route in the 1930s because greyhound racing was popular and brought in much needed finance. After the war however, the Football League was against clubs holding race meetings and the club's shareholders thought racing might hurt Chelmsford's league ambition. The poor finances of the club were met by the supporters who donated £1,000 in 1947. (2) In 1948/9 City finished second in the league but was told its application for football league status had arrived too late! (3) The club continued however to attract major players, including Hong Ying 'Frank' Soo, an Anglo Chinese footballer, who had previously played for the Football League clubs Luton and Stoke City . He signed to Chelmsford for a reported fee of £2,500. After finishing his playing career at the club he went on to coach various European clubs in the 1950s and 1960s. City's leading player of the 1940s was probably Denny Foreman who scored 96 goals in 101 appearances. The club's lethal strike force of Syd Plunkett and Cecil McCormack scored an incredible 89 goals between them in the 1949/50 season. By 1949 City had three players with a combined market value of £28,000. Although 11,327 turned up for the 3rd round F.A. cup home tie against Ipswich, which City lost after a replay, managers and shareholders bemoaned the lack of big crowds to support the team. Their average crowds of 4,000 didn't match Colchester's 10,000: indeed the only guaranteed large crowd was when Chelmsford played its local rivals. In 1949 a club record 16,807 saw Chelmsford play Colchester. During the early 1950s the clubs' crowds contracted further and this was a major reason why Colchester and Gillingham were elected to the Football League ahead of City. (4) By 1952 the gates were under 3,000 and the players had to go part time. (5) The club became even more dependent on supporters' donations. By 1954 the club was losing £700 a week. (6) The following year a tax demand of over £10,000 on previous donations seriously threatened the club's future. (7) This demand was eventually dropped and this and a new supporters' pool, where all the money was given to the club as a donation, led to a big improvement in the club's financial position. (8) Both Arthur Adey and Roy Stroud were leading goal scorers in the 1950s.

The club managed to raise £10,000 to install floodlights in 1960. (9) In 1963 the club produced its first ambitious plan for expansion. This would have included a swimming pool and ten pin bowling alongside a new football ground. (10) A group of well known Football League professionals were signed by chairman John Coward but Chelmsford still failed initially to get anywhere near winning the Southern League and had to watch the likes of Oxford, Hereford and Cambridge enter the Football League. In 1967 in another application for football league status, the club received only one vote. (11) The club had gone back to full time professional status but this was again threatened by poor finances. Despite this, the club was able to win the Southern League in 1968 for the first time since 1946/7. (12) Further financial problems led to the club merging with Brentwood but the club remained at New Writtle Street. (13)

Wes Maughan scored 50 goals in 111 appearances in the 1960s.

Despite winning the southern league in 1972, the club declined to apply to the Football League. Hereford, who finished second were elected because of their F.A. Cup run and their sound financial position. Another ambitious plan to redevelop the grounds and enhance the club's bid for League status was announced in 1974. The chairman Alan Cherry said "We are planning not just for the time when Chelmsford will be a fourth division club but when they will be one of the top clubs in the country". (14) This scheme was turned down by the planners because it included office development. Another overly ambitious plan the following year was opposed by residents. (15) In 1975 Cherry was replaced by Claude Seymour when City owed £120,000 and the police were called in to look at the books. (16) Another proposal was made to bring in greyhound racing, which was again blocked by local residents. (17) Extra finance was essential because the club had been relegated from the Premier division of the Southern League. A punk rock festival at the ground was an unmitigated disaster (see chapter 28). (18) By the end of the 1970s crowds had dropped to below 400. Jimmy Greaves played for the club in the 1976-7 season. Probably the most popular player in the 1970s was Frank Peterson who scored 146 goals in 302 appearances.

In 1981 a new company, Chelmsford City 1980, was formed which bought the freehold of the New Writtle Street ground. The early 1990s saw more grandiose schemes for the ground including a hotel. City's stadium would have been improved to a 10,000 all seater. (19) Meanwhile the debts of the club had risen to £600,000! (20) In 1994 Dennis Wakeling, the chairman of a new consortium, was already maintaining that the club would have to move to become viable but later that year the Inland Revenue applied to the high Court to have the club wound up. (21) By June 1994 the debts had risen to £1.3 million, a massive total for a non league club. (22) Again there was a call for an investigation into the club's finances. A proposed merger with Braintree Town was fiercely resisted by supporters. (23) Meanwhile Chelmsford City (1980) Limited was wound up in court. (24) A development company took control of the ground, while City continued to use it for the 1994/5 season. (25) A move to possible sites in Sandon, Howe Green and North Springfield was considered and short term ground shares with Maldon, Braintree and Thurrock were discussed. (26)

In 1997 the club were finally ordered to leave their New Writtle Street ground by the administrators and played their last game there in August. (27) It is now the site of an anonymous housing estate. The ground was demolished two years later. (28) Initially City played at Maldon but then shared with Billericay. A possible site for a new ground was found at Beaulieu Park, Boreham. (29) The new stadium was to have 1,000 seats in a grandstand and standing for 3,000 but the plan was inevitably delayed by the planners in 2002. This led to calls for City to use the Melbourne athletics stadium. Initially there were plans for a temporary ground to be built opposite the athletics stadium but these were blocked by local residents and had to be abandoned altogether when a £400,000 grant from the Football Foundation didn't materialise. (30) A Council investment of a million pounds was instrumental in the club finally returning to the town in 2004 when a new pitch was placed within the Melbourne athletics track. The first game saw a 2,998 crowd watch City play against its previous landlords, Billericay. In 2006 a new 1,000 seat grandstand was built along with a supporter's clubhouse. (31) Since gaining promotion to the Conference South the club has regularly reached the playoffs without being strong enough to reach the Conference, the tier below the Football League.

From 1950 Chelmsford Ladies Football team played in the Essex Women's League. (32) In 1951 they played London Ladies at Kings Head Meadow. (33) A Chelmsford City Ladies team was established in 1986.

The Chelmsford area has produced a number of distinguished footballers. Geoff Hurst, scorer of the World Cup final hat trick in 1966, was born in Ashton Under Lyne, Lancashire, but lived in Chelmsford for 18 years after moving there at the age of six. He was the son of Charlie Hurst who was a centre half with Oldham, Bristol Rovers and Rochdale as well as Chelmsford City. Geoff went to the Kings Road and Rainsford Schools. His parents continued to live in Chelmsford after he moved to digs in East London so that he could play for West Ham United. (34) He was also a promising cricketer playing for the Essex second eleven and gaining one first class appearance for the County against Lancashire in 1962. Hurst was married at Chelmsford Cathedral in1964. Mervyn Day, the West Ham goalkeeper went to Kings Road School before attending K.E.G.S. He became a successful professional player despite the Grammar School not being football orientated at the time. (35) The City player, Tony Butcher, like Hurst and Mervyn Day went to Kings Road School and remains both the club's leading scorer with 288 goals in 13 years and the player with the most appearances. He said "It was impossible (for City) to get in the league because it was a closed shop". (36)

Although Essex took over the New Writtle Street cricket ground in 1946 the state of the wicket was a cause for concern, as was the low crowds. In 1952 only a narrow vote reprieved matches at the county town after the festival week lost money. Three thousand people paid £377 over the 6 days compared with the 29,243 who had paid

£3,005 in a record week that had just ended at Ilford. (37) After a great effort to increase the crowds, 25,000 people attended the next cricket week but attendances soon went back to being low and in 1957 there was no cricket week in the town. (38) The Weekly News commented that this was "one more indication that the people of the town are not sports minded". County cricket did not return to Chelmsford for ten years. In 1964 the club had moved its headquarters back to the town. The intention was to buy the ground from the Wenley Trust. This would enable the club to build a new pavilion and use the surrounding land to lay out a car park and eventually an indoor cricket hall. (39) The actual buying of the ground only came about because another county, Warwickshire lent the club £15,000 on an interest free loan. (40) A new pavilion was built in 1970 and 1971 saw a record seven and a half thousand crowd at the County Ground The team led by Brian 'Tonka' Taylor started doing well in one day cricket, finishing 3rd in 1969, 4th in 1970 and 3rd in 1971 in the John Player League. (41) Finances were however still tight and local prisoners painted the pavilion and tended the pitch. (42) In 1975 almost 25,000 crammed into the ground to watch the Australians for three days and Hampshire in the John Player League for one day. (43)

After a number of near misses including a second place in the County Championship and a narrow loss in the Gillette Cup semi final the county finally won its first trophy in its 103 year existence, the Benson and Hedges cup in 1979. In August of the same year Essex went on to win the county championship for the first time. (44) After three second places Essex finally won the John Player League in 1981. (45) In 1985 the county won the 60 over Nat. West. Trophy at Lords. (46) The following year the county won the County Championship for the second time. (47) When Essex won its fifth county title in 1991, victory was secured at Chelmsford as was its sixth title in thirteen years the following year. (48)(49) In 1997 the club won the 60 over trophy again at Lords and won the Benson and Hedges trophy the following year. (50)

Despite this unprecedented run of success, Essex was relegated to the second division of the County Championship in 1999, when it was split into two, because of their low finish the previous season. The last match of the following season saw them promoted back to the top tier. (51) Each of the following two seasons again saw relegation followed immediately by promotion. (52) Two thousand and five saw Essex win the one day league with three matches to spare and three years later the County won the Friends Provident final at Lords. (53)(54) After relegation again, 2009 saw promotion for the county again after a dramatic late run in. Once again this was followed by immediate relegation. Since then, the club has stayed in division two of the Championship and four unsuccessful visits to twenty-twenty finals day in 2006, 2008, 2010 and 2013 have been the county's only flirtation with success. In 1996 the club took advantage of £100,000 grant to build an indoor cricket school for young cricketers. The land was bought from Chelmsford City Football Club. (55)

In 1992 Graham Gooch, one of the cricketers most responsible for the county's success, was honoured in the form of a sculpture placed the near the ground on New London Road. The £20,000 bronze figure by John Doubleday was commissioned by property developers. Gooch, of course, unveiled the work. (56) Gooch was arguably the greatest of many outstanding Essex players during the club's halcyon period. He captained both Essex and England in a playing career spanning from 1973 to 2000 during which he became the most prolific run scorer of all time, with over 67,000 runs in all forms of the game. In 1980 he was named the Wisden cricketer of the year. His career underwent an unusual detour when he went on the 1982 rebel tour of South Africa. This resulted in him and others such as Geoffrey Boycott, Alan Knott and Bob Woolmer being banned from Test cricket for three years. In the film 'The Wilderness Years' he said that 'others' had decided he had no place in English cricket so he decided to go on the tour. After returning to the Test team in 1985 a severe loss of form led him to being dropped. By 1990 however, he was successfully leading England as captain, his position strengthened by his habit of leading from the front, his batting average being twice that of his fellow teammates. In 2001 after his retirement as a player he became head coach at Essex. During 2009 he became England's batting coach, a position which he took full time in 2012. He was one of the first sportsmen to promote hair transplants after his hair began receding in the mid 1990s.

Keith Fletcher played a vital role in the transformation of Essex into a major power in county cricket. He was nicknamed the 'Gnome' by teammate Ray East, because his winklepickers had begun to turn up at the toes because of wear. Fletcher, according to cricket writer Colin Bateman, was "a tough cookie, a shrewd man who could bluff opponents like the most disarming of poker players". He was captain of the national team when the defection of several high profile players to the previously mentioned, unofficial tour of South Africa occurred. In the mid 1990s Fletcher was manager of England, a particularly unsuccessful period for the team. He returned to coach the Essex team until 2001.

Another famous recent Essex county cricketer was Nasser Hussain, who grew up in Ilford and went to Forest School, Walthamstow. He was selected for Essex's Under 11 team as young as eight years old. At 12 he was the youngest to play for Essex's

Under 15 team. . His bowling suffered after he grew 'a foot' in a winter. Nasser felt he had let his father down and for a while he slipped behind his playing contemporaries. His batting progressed however, although he never thought he was a natural. Hussain made his Test debut in 1990 and was England's captain from 1999 to 2003. His career was by no means smooth, often responding defiantly to criticism. After he retired from cricket he immediately became a commentator for Sky Sports. Hussain, still lives locally with his family at Little Baddow, and in 2010 was coaching at New Hall School.

Peter Edwards died in 2,000. Behind the scenes, as secretary and general manager he contributed greatly to Essex's period of success. (57) In 2008, during redecoration at the County Ground, a large cache of cricketing memorabilia collected by Edwards was discovered, including a bat signed by Bradman on his last Ashes tour and a signed photo of W.G. Grace. (58)

In 2011 Trevor Bailey died. Known as 'Barnacle' Bailey because of his defensive batting qualities, Bailey was reckoned to be the leading all rounder for most of his international career. Bailey played 61 Tests for England and captained the county from 1961 to 1966. In his later playing days he was also the club's secretary. Bailey also played football to a high level, playing for Cambridge University, Clapton, Leytonstone and Walthamstow. He added to his income by advertising Brylcream, Shredded Wheat and Lucozade. He was a Test Match Special commentator for 25 years until 1999, during which time fellow commentator Brian Johnston nicknamed him the 'Boil'. Jonathan Agnew, also of Test Match Special, wrote of him "Dogged batsman, Aggressive bowler. Intelligent cricketer. Wonderfully concise pundit. Great sense of humour."

Of course the most illustrious current Essex cricketer is the present England Test and O.D.I. captain Alastair Cook. Cook went to the independent, St Pauls Cathedral School and then boarded at the Bedford School. While still at school he played for Maldon cricket club in the summer holidays. He played for Essex's Academy before making his debut for the first eleven in 2003. Cook marked his first Test match for England with a century. He went on to become the youngest English batsman to score 5,000 runs. Cook was appointed captain of the Test team in August 2012 after the retirement of Andrew Strauss. He plays piano and saxophone, contributing on the latter to Freefonix, a CBBC animated series.

Two thousand and six saw the first mention of the re-development of the County Ground. The first scheme proposed increasing seating by 2,000 and an improved cricket school. Initially 180 flats were to be built on the car park and existing cricket school to finance the rest of the scheme. (59) The financial crisis has ensured that the development has failed to go ahead despite planning permission and environmental authorisation being obtained. Concern was expressed about the danger of flooding and the lack of suitability of the proposed tower blocks for the surroundings. Early in 2013 however it appeared that the scheme was finally about to begin.

Chelmsford Cricket Club survived to reach its bicentenary in 2011. It moved to the council owned Chelmer Park in 1972. At the time of writing the club had won 7 league titles in the previous 15 years.

Rugby restarted after the war at Kings Head Meadow. The Chelmsford team consisted mainly of apprentices from the local works. The Club moved again, this time to Melbourne Park where it rented a pitch from the borough corporation. By the time of its 40th anniversary in 1961 the club had moved again to Coronation Park with a new clubhouse and purpose built changing rooms. (60)

The men's hockey club was reformed in 1946 at a meeting at the Golden Fleece in Duke Street. Fixtures started on Saturdays but from 1956/7 regular fixtures were played on Sundays. In 1971/2 the men's club moved to Chelmer Park. The club became part of Chelmsford Sports Club which included the Chelmsford Ladies Hockey Club and the Chelmsford Cricket Club. The 1989/90 season was the first season an artificial pitch was used and the club celebrated its centenary in 1997/8.

After the second war Vivienne Wiseman, a former member, reformed the Chelmsford Ladies Hockey Club. A council pitch at Admirals Park was used for home matches along with a small pavilion. The club moved to Broomfield cricket ground in 1961. Increased membership led to a return to council pitches, this time at Melbourne Park. In 1971 the Ladies joined the Men at Chelmer Park. During 1972 the Essex team which won the All England title contained seven members of the Chelmsford club. Since the 1980s Chelmsford Ladies have regularly finished in the top four of the All England Indoor Championships. In 1979, as National Outdoor Hockey champions, Chelmsford played in the European club competition. Mixed hockey continued after the war, with Chelmsford winning the Colchester Exiles tournament six years running. The Veterans Ladies team won the national title in 1998 and 1999. By 2,000 there were five outdoor ladies teams, four playing league hockey.

At the end of the 1997/8 season the separate men's and ladies' clubs were merged and this was followed by the laying of a new water based artificial pitch. The existing sand based pitch was also re-laid and the clubhouse extended and reformed. In 2003/4 the ladies won the English Hockey League for the third time in five years. The men won promotion to the Premier Division of the E.H.L. for the first time. In 2008/9 the men were East Indoor champions for the first time and were also the first winners of the national Indoor title. (61)

After the war, the Chelmsford Athletics Club continued at its ramshackle headquarters at Waterhouse Lane, but in the 1960s the club moved to Melbourne Park with a plush new £8,500 clubhouse. In a 1962 a new cinder track was opened at the park. Twenty years later the track was dilapidated and the National Athletics League deemed it not up to the standard for matches. By the 1990s the ground was only used for training. The club contested matches at Brentwood, Harlow and Ilford. Eventually National Lottery funding was raised for a new artificial track, extension of the car park and a new road. (62) The scheme also included a 600 seater grandstand and lighting. (63) The new facilities were opened by Sir Trevor Brooking. In 2000 further lottery funding was given to add further indoor facilities including a 60 metres indoor track.

After the war the Boreham airfield (See chapters 18 and 24) was rapidly becoming derelict, when the Chelmsford Auto Club started using it for motor cycle racing. The first of eight motor cycle meetings was held on the 2nd of September 1950. John Surtees, Ken Kavanagh and others rode there on the fast three mile track. There were 9,000 at a meeting in 1951. (64) Motor car testing started and the first car race was held in 1949. The meetings continued in 1951 and 1952, with the first 100 mile per hour circuits in the country achieved since the days of the Brooklands circuit before the war. With sponsorship from the Daily Mail, crowds at Boreham reached 80,000 in 1952. (65) In 1953 there was a shock end to racing on the circuit when advanced plans for racing during the Coronation year were cancelled. The Chelmsford Auto Club were organising the first British Grand Prix of Motor Cycle racing and the West Essex Car Club was to hold international meetings, after attracting some of the world's best drivers the previous year, including Mike Hawthorn and Stirling Moss. The Daily Mail gave no reason for its withdrawal of sponsorship. (66) During 1955 the Ford Motor Company bought the airfield to test trucks. In the 1970s and 1980s Fords built rally cars at the airfield. Although most of the airfield has been dismantled, part of it was still used by the Essex Police Helicopter Unit and the Essex Air Ambulance in 2012.

There had been no horse racing in the Chelmsford area for over 60 years when plans were announced in 2001 for a new racecourse on the Essex Show ground at Great Leighs. John Holmes, a local entrepreneur, announced plans for a 120 horse training facility and a one mile oval track. There was to be a covered grandstand holding 5,000 people. (67) The project was made much more expensive by the plans of the E.C.C. to route a bypass right through the new course. In 2003 the new racecourse received a licence from the British Horse Racing Board. It was to be the first new racecourse in the country for 75 years. The facilities were to include a restaurant, bars and a nightclub, a fitness centre, conference facilities, TV production facilities and a permanent 100 stall training yard. (68) By 2005 work on the grandstand and the all weather track was underway but lack of compensation for the by-pass slowed construction and brought about the postponement of the opening when race meetings had already been allocated. (69) The new racecourse finally opened in April 2008 but went into administration in 2009, after the temporary licence had been withdrawn. This was a severe disappointment after the course and the facilities had been well received but bad weather had adversely affected crowds. Holmes was left with debts of £25 million. The track was bought by a new company in 2011 which had a bid to start racing again in 2013 turned down by the B.R.B. A new application was entered in January 2013 to restart racing in 2014 but this was turned down six months later. The new owners MC Racetracks had been granted permission by the city council to use the powerful lighting despite strong opposition from local residents. In December 2013 the racecourse was taken over by Fred Done, the owner of Betfred. There will be an application for racing fixtures to take place in 2015.

By 1949 the open air swimming baths was in dire need of replacement, or at least improvement. A five year scheme to modernise the baths at a cost of £35-40,000 was delayed by financial restrictions. In 1952 another more modest scheme was proposed at a cost of just under £14,000. By this time the dressing rooms were in a disgusting condition. (70) In 1961 cutbacks delayed a new indoor pool, which was delayed again two years later when the county Council refused to give a grant of £223,000. (71)(72) Nineteen sixty five finally saw the opening of the £280,000 new pool next to the original outdoor pool off Waterloo Lane. (73) In 1975 the new pool was closed because of a collapsed ceiling. (74) The bill went up to £130,000 when severe corrosion was found. (75) A learner pool was added to the indoor pool in the 1980s. Protests prevented the closure of the outdoor pool in 1983 with 3,000 people signing a petition. (76) In 1985 the outdoor pool was included in the £5 million plans for the new Riverside Leisure complex. (77)

The Riverside Leisure Centre was opened in April 1987. Apart from the two indoor pools and the outdoor pool it included an international standard ice rink, a sports hall with room for six badminton courts, four squash courts and a health and fitness centre. The final cost was £7 million. (78) From the start design faults were obvious in the new complex. In 1989 the management pulled out of running it, at a time when there were 25 major leaks in the roof. (79) The council took over the running of the centre but one problem was that it was proving impossible to prevent people entering without paying. A £30,000 facelift started in 1989 to rectify the faults. (80) In 1991 no private company could be found to run the Riverside and the only bid from the council's own direct services was accepted. (81). After plans for a new complex fell through, the Riverside underwent a complete refurbishment in 2010. The ice rink is now reckoned to be one of the best in the country.

The ice hockey team the Chelmsford Chieftains celebrated its 25th anniversary at the Riverside in 2012. They played their first game against Peterborough in September 1987. The Chieftains spent nine seasons in the English Premier Ice Hockey League between 1998 and 2008 before deciding for financial reasons to enter the National Ice Hockey League.

After the second war the Chelmsford Golf Club's finances were in a poor state with an overdraft of over £4,000. New members in the early 1940s enabled the condition of the course to be improved. The well known amateur Michael Bonallack won the club championship ten times in fifteen years. In the 1960s overspending led to another worsening of the club's finances but a revival in the 1970s enabled the installation of a pop-up watering system and an extensive reconstruction of the course. (82) In the early 1970s work began on reclaiming gravel pits at Little Waltham and a 9 hole course was established which became Channels golf club. This was extended to an 18 hole course in the 1980s and finally 27 holes in the 1990s. A new course the Hylands was also established at Margaretting in the 1980s and a new golf centre was also opened on Regiment Way. (83)(84)

The Grove Tennis Club moved again in the 1960s to Moulsham Drive and celebrated its centenary in 1993. Its Vicarage Road site was sold to raise finance for the new development. The club now has six all weather courts and a membership approaching 350. (85) Its new courts were opened by Mrs Christine Truman Janes.

In the late 1980s Chelmsford had its own American Football team but in 1991 the Chelmsford Cherokees merged with the Colchester Gladiators. "We both realise that neither club can reach the top on its own." (86) Initially they played as the Essex Gladiators at Melbourne Park, with some games at Basildon. (87) In 1992 however, after a proposed merger between the Essex Gladiators and the Kent Mustangs fell through, the club reverted to its original name of the Colchester Gladiators. There is currently a local university team, the Anglia Ruskin Phantoms.

In 1990 ten pin bowling, which was in the middle of a nationwide expansion, came to Chelmsford. A 36 lane bowling alley was built on the Widford industrial estate. It was the tenth to be built in the country that year. (88) Chelmsford Table Tennis Club only dates from 2007, but it was previously known as Great Baddow Table Tennis Club before 1982 and Baddow Village Table Tennis Club from 1982 until 2007.

In addition to the Sports Centres at the Melbourne Stadium and the Riverside, which has recently undergone another facelift, there is also a leisure centre at South Woodham Ferrers and a small sports centre, the Dovedale in Moulsham.

At the beginning of 2013 the redevelopment at the County Ground was finally scheduled to start later in the year. As for Chelmsford City F.C., it remains very unlikely that it will have its own stadium. In October 2013 it was announced that the third stage of the Tour de France would pass through Chelmsford City in 2014. The route will take the peloton through Howe Street, Great Waltham, Chignal Smealy and Roxwell.

1) Essex Weekly News 29 3 1949 p.9
2) E.W.N. 22 8 1947 p.3
3) Official History of Chelmsford City Football Club Garner and Selby p.19
4) Garner and Selby p.24
5) E.W.N. 1 2 1952 p.3
6) E.W.N. 17 12 1954 p.1
7) E.W.N. 18 3 1955 p.1
8) E.W.N. 24 8 1956 p.8
9) Garner and Selby p.55
10) E.W.N. 15 1 1963 p.1
11) Garner and Selby p.71
12) E.W.N. 10 5 1963 p.1
13) E.W.N. 19 12 1969 p.1
14) E.W.N. 14 3 1974
15) E.W.N. 3 2 1975 p.1
16) E.W.N. 18 9 1975 p.1
17) E.W.N. 24 2 1977 p.1
18) E.W.N. 22 9 1977 p.1
19) Essex Chronicle 2 2 1990 p.1
20) E.C. 9 11 1990 p.1
21) E.C. 25 3 1994 p.6-7

22) E.W.N. 23 6 1994 p.1
23) E.W.N. 7 7 1994 p.63
24) E.C. 8 7 1994 p.1
25) E.W.N. 1 6 1995 p.7
26) E.W.N. 28 12 1995 p.1
27) E.W.N. 21 8 1997 p.71
28) E.C. 18 6 1999 p.7
29) E.C. 5 2 1999 p.7
30) E.W.N. 21 5 2003 p.7
31) E.W.N. 5 1 2006 p.1
32) E.C. 10 3 1950
33) E.C. 22 6 1951
34) E.C. 3 5 1996 p.1
35) C Museums records Chelmsford people
36) C. Museums Oral records Interview by Dot Bedenham
37) E.W.N. 30 5 1952 p.1
38) E.W.N. 7 8 1953 p.3
39) E.W.N. 10 7 1964 p.13
40) Essex County Cricket Club Lemmon and Marshall p.273
41) E.W.N. 11 5 1971
42) E.W.N. 12 12 1974 p.1
43) E.W.N. 28 8 1975 p.10
44) 60 Classic Essex Matches Tony Debenham etc p.74 - 77
45) Debenham p.78 – 79
46) Debenham p.84 - 85
47) Debenham p.86 - 87
48) E.C. 20 9 1991 p.1
49) E.C. 4 9 1992 p.1
50) Debenham p.100 – 103
51) Debenham p.106 – 107
52) Debenham p.107 – 108
53) Debenham p.110 – 111
54) Debenham p.118 - 119
55) E.W.N. 30 5 1996 p.7
56) E.W.N. 2 11 1992 p.1

57) E.W.N. 21 19 2000 p.1
58) E.C. 22 3 2002 p.7
59) E.W.N. 4 5 2006 p.1
60) E.W.N. 13 1 1961 p.9
61) http://en.wikipedia.org/wiki/ChelmsfordHockeyClub
62) C. Museums Pastimes exhibition records
63) E.W.N. 13 9 1990 p.1
64) E.W.N. 4 5 1951 p.7
65) E.W.N. 8 8 1952 p.3
66) Boreham E. Burgess p.59 – 62
67) E.W.N. 5 4 2001 p.16
68) E.W.N. 26 6 2003 p.2
69) E.W.N. 21 9 2006 p.13
70) E.W.N. 26 9 1952 p.1
71) E.W.N. 15 9 1961 p.5
72) E.W.N. 17 5 1963 p.1
73) E.W.N. 17 9 1965 p.9
74) E.C. 4 4 1975
75) E.W.N. 6 11 1975
76) E.W.N. 15 9 1983
77) E.W.N. 14 7 1984 p.1
78) E.W.N. 2 4 1987 p.1
79) E.W.N 2 2 1989 p.1
80) E.W.N. 7 7 1989 p.9
81) E.W.N. 11 10 1991 p.1
82) Chelmsford Golf Club 1893 – 1993 p.63 - 76
83) E.C. 31 5 1985
84) C. Museums Pastimes research materials
85) Grove Lawn Tennis Club website
86) E.W.N. 10 1 1991 p.1
87) E.W.N. 25 4 1991 p.51
88) E.C. 23 2 1990 p.1

27

Leisure and Entertainment in Chelmsford before 1945

"They discussed matter of common interest over a meal and minutes were deliberately not kept"

In the late Victorian and Edwardian period most of the entertainment in Chelmsford was provided for the upper class of the rural area and the middle classes in the town. These of course were in the main the only people who had both the leisure time and the income to follow the wide variety of pursuits available. Many of the concerts had a religious connection but were held at a wide variety of venues besides St Mary's parish church, with the Corn Exchange, the Shire Hall and various church halls also used. Visiting theatre companies regularly reached the town with Fred Spalding Junior promoting a variety of plays, musicals and pantomimes usually at the Corn Exchange, because Chelmsford had lacked a permanent theatre since the early Victorian period. An interesting feature of Chelmsford life was the Odde Volumes which appealed to the intellectual pretentions of a number of Chelmsford aesthetes. The ordinary Chelmsford working class man had an extraordinary number and variety of public houses in which to drink. In Tindal Street alone there were 14 drinking establishments in the late nineteenth century. Twice a year the Chelmsford worker could go to the town's fair. The cautious approach of the new municipal authority meant that Chelmsford was late in getting its public library and its first public park. The rapid expansion of the big three firms in the town saw the establishment of the works outing as a highlight in the calendar. During the inter war period the social clubs of these firms often dominated the out of work activities of their employees. By the outbreak of the second war

Chelmsford had no less than five cinemas. In their early days all of these to a greater or lesser extent combined live entertainment with the celluloid variety. At the start of our period, Hylands, as the biggest estate in the Chelmsford area, played a part in the entertainment of many people in the area, with fetes, harvest festivals etc.

In 1890 the Essex Chronicle was bemoaning the County town's lack of a public Recreation Ground, two years after the opening of one in Colchester. (1) In August a memorial signed by 44 citizens in favour of a public park was passed on to a small committee set up to investigate the matter. (2) By 1893 a number of different possible sites were being discussed including one off the Springfield Road. The Chronicle was worried that a park would add to the borough's debt, bringing it close to its allowed maximum of £71,000 when there were other things the fledgling borough needed, like an improved sanitation system. (3) It quickly became enthusiastic again when a public subscription was launched by the Mayor, Frank Whitmore: eventually over £1,500 was raised. The land covering what is now basically Central Park was acquired on a 21 year lease. It was to cost one and a half pence in the pound on the rates to maintain it. (4) The Recreation Ground was opened in July 1894. That year the Chelmsford Town Band, the West Essex band and the Industrial School band all played at the ground to large crowds. There was a discussion as to whether the park should be open before 12 p.m. on Sundays, with some thinking it would deter people from going to church. The Weekly News thought you couldn't force people to go to church. (5) It was extended in 1898 and in the same year the Council purchased the site from the trustees. (6) By 1902 walking in the park was very much part of the summer for Chelmsford citizens. "During the summer the Chelmsford Recreation ground has looked very charming for gay flower beds, the lake with its swans and ducks and the shady walks have proved most attractive." The Weekly News pointed out that a number of people had come to a concert deliberately without their purses and that because of the presence of a number of 'yahoos' in the park the caretaker had to carry a cane with him! (7) During the first war Bell Meadow was laid out as part of the Recreation Ground. (8) In the 1920s, regular dances were held in the park. (9)

During the 1880s there was a wide variety of musical entertainment available for middle class patrons in Chelmsford. In one week in 1880 for example there was a musical glee concert at St John's, Moulsham, a concert lecture and recitation at the Mechanics Institute, a concert of sacred music at the Shire Hall by the Chelmsford Town Band and a series of recitals for the Infirmary at the Shire Hall. In addition the West Essex band gave a concert at the Corn Exchange as well as one in Broomfield. The

Recreation Ground bandstand during the 1900s
(Courtesy of E.R.O.)

town band gave another concert in front of the Shire Hall. For the upper classes and the county set there were Balls held at the Shire Hall such as the County Ball held each year and a Bachelors Ball which was also popular. (10) There were also subscription balls such as the one that took place in 1884, when the Chronicle reported "a company numbering about 130 was present". "Dancing commenced shortly after 9 o'clock to the strains of Mr H. Byford's quadrille band and was kept up with spirit until between five and six in the morning." (11)

The first festival of choirs was held at St Mary's Church in 1881 and became an established part of the Chelmsford calendar. (12) In 1884 15 choirs took part at the church. (13) The festival grew into the Essex Musical Association which was formed in 1906. Their first competitions and concerts were held at the Corn Exchange but the Association's events were extended to include the Shire Hall in 1911. The Association also put on orchestral concerts. A 1913 performance of Stravinsky's 'Rite of Spring' provoked a strong response. The audience shouted, booed and whistled drowning out the music and forcing the composer to hide backstage. (14) There was an increase in the participation of Women's Institute choirs during the inter war period. The Association gave increasing prominence to contemporary British composers such as Holst, Delius, Vaughn Williams and Armstrong Gibbs from Danbury. (15)

Gibbs was born at the 'Vineyards', Great Baddow in 1889. He was brought up by five maiden aunts after his mother died when he was two. His prodigious musical gifts were evident at an early age and his aunts wanted him to obtain a musical education abroad, but his father, the soap and chemical manufacturer, insisted that he receive a public school education. After going to Winchester he read history at Cambridge, whilst also receiving composition and harmony lessons. Adrian Boult was so impressed with Gibb's music to a play 'The Crossings' that he funded Gibbs for a year he spent as a mature student at the Royal College of Music. There he studied conducting under Boult, composition under Vaughn Williams and was given a part time teaching post. Gibbs moved to Danbury in 1919 and set up a choral society which took part in the E.M.A. festivals. After one of his compositions was played at a festival in Bath he became an adjudicator and later the Vice President of the National Federation of Music Festivals. Gibbs then combined touring the country, adjudicating festivals, conducting and composing. He also conducted the Danbury Choral Society and sang with the church choir. During the second war he went to the Lake District, where he wrote his third symphony, the 'Westmorland'. He returned to Danbury after the war and reformed the choir. Gibbs was mainly known for his songs for solo voice but also wrote music for the stage, religious music and a great deal of chamber music much of which remains unpublished. He continued composing and conducting until his death in Chelmsford in 1960 and is buried with his wife in Danbury church. (16) (17)

One notable artist with close connections to Chelmsford was Alfred Bennett Bamford (1857-1939). Born and bred in Romford, Bamford went to the Camden School of Art before becoming the art master at the newly formed Chelmsford County High School for Girls, where he was the only male teacher. He was responsible for the largest collection of sketches of Essex, including a number of watercolours of Chelmsford. Bamford was also passionate about the military. He belonged to the Volunteers of the Essex Regiment and by 1897 had risen to honorary Major. Bamford retired from the regiment in 1901, but was put in charge of a prisoners of war camp during the first war. The Chelmsford Museum houses a number of his paintings including Old Houses, the Friars, Moulsham Street.

Fred Spalding promoted a wide variety of entertainments in the light nineteenth century. In 1888 for example he put on a production of 'Sleeping Beauty' for three nights at the Corn Exchange. The inmates of the workhouse came in for free. (18) In the same year he arranged for Mr Doyly Carte to bring his production of 'HMS Pinafore' to Chelmsford. (19) Each year Spalding brought a pantomime to the town. As late as 1910 the council gave permission for an 'electric theatre' to set up in Kings Head Meadow. (20) Occasionally a well known celebrity visited Chelmsford, such as Oscar Wilde in 1884, who gave a talk on 'Dress', leading to the Chronicle naturally enough to give a long description of his apparel. (22)

The strength of the town's shopkeepers' hold on the old Board of Health showed in the vote in 1884 to abolish the town's fair which was held twice a year, supposedly because of "the great nuisance caused to those living close to the market". The money such fairs brought to the town brought about a rethink and a May fair was held the following year at Bell Mead. (23)(24)

In the late nineteenth century many workers could not afford proper holidays but the work's outing was increasingly popular. In 1887 for example the Arc Works had their annual outing to Southend. Forty workers set of from the Chelmsford Post Office at 6.0. a.m. and they stopped at Battlesbridge for breakfast. There was time at Southend to take the steamer across to Rochester as well as numerous other seaside enjoyments. (25) In 1892 a much larger number of the firm's employees, 254, went to Great Yarmouth for the day. (26) During 1906 Hoffmann workers went to the same resort. (27) These outings were not restricted to the big works. In 1880 for example the Industrial School took their annual trip to Walton on the Naze and there were regular Sunday school outings. (28)

Chelmsford's big firms established social clubs with a wide variety of activities in addition to their sporting activities (see chapter 25). Smokers' concerts were popular before the war. In 1891 for example an Arc Works Smokers concert included comics and the works' band played. During 1892 a concert was put on at the Corn Exchange in aid of the Arc Works Sick Benefit Society. An orchestra played the music of Mendelssohn. (29) Promenade concerts also started to be performed at the firm's sports ground at Wood Street. In 1903 a Smokers concert was held at Wood Street to celebrate the opening of new recreation rooms. (30) The works also regularly hosted groups of minstrel players. In 1907 the Hoffmann Company launched its Athletics and Social Club. It soon had 350 members. (31) By 1910 the Club had rooms in Baddow Road where it was putting on dances. (32) In 1911 Marconi opened social club premises in New London Road.

During the inter war period 'whist drives' took over from smokers concerts as popular entertainments at the works' social clubs and elsewhere in the town. (33) By 1923 Hoffmann was attracted 500 people to their whist drives. (34) The New Year festivities at the Hoffmann club hosted 450 people in fancy dress in 1922. (35) In May 1925 the club had a big party with over 750 people present. (36)

Chelmsford's better off citizens had always had their own clubs of course. The Chelmsford Beefsteak Club was one of oldest clubs of its type in the country founded in 1768, although no books older than 1781 survive. It still existed in the 1990s. There were a set of rules to be observed by the membership when they dined first at the Black Boy and then later at the Saracen's Head. Membership was limited to 40 and consisted of an elite group of influential local people. They discussed matters of common interest over a meal and minutes were deliberately not kept. Fifteen High Sherriffs were members but other members included Carne Rasch, Edward Pretyman, Henry Marriage and George Taylor. Each new member would donate bottles of claret. (37)(38) In 1903 one of its oldest members, a Mr Kemble, died: he had been a member for over half a century. Another exclusive society in the town was the Old Town Jury Club, which also usually met at the Saracens Head and whose membership was also made up from the town's establishment. During the club's annual dinner in 1881, for example strong anti co-operative comments were made. (39) At its annual dinner in 1892 at the White Hart Hotel Alderman W.W. Duffield presided and Fred Spalding was Vice President. Edmund Durrant was present; Usborne, the local M.P. was missing but usually attended. Councillor Cramphorn proposed a toast to the Army, Navy and Auxiliary forces. By the 1930s the club was defunct. (40)

The Chelmsford Club was established in 1884 for "the benefit of the professional and business men of the town". Directors of the club included prominent local business men such as J.S. Brown, J.G. Bond and T.H.P. Dennis. (41) Buildings in Museum Terrace, New London Road were obtained. "The accommodation will comprise of a spacious and well furnished reading room, liberally supplied with leading newspapers and magazines and works of reference: a lofty and well ventilated billiard room with two tables; a commodious smoking room, a chess and card room and a refreshment buffet under the charge of responsible steward." "Arrangements will be made with one of the telegraph agencies for transmission to the club of important events." "The club will be open daily from 12 a.m. to 12 p.m." "In our opinion it will supply a want that has long been felt among the gentlemen of Chelmsford. (42) Less than six months later the club had 110 members with all the 5,000 £1 shares taken up. (43) In 1892 many of Chelmsford's 'great and good' were present at a dinner including T. Usborne, Mayor Whitmore, Chancellor, Duffield and Councillor Bodkin. The dining room was especially lighted for the occasion with three large electric lamps. (44)

A major leisure pursuit of the upper classes in the late Victorian and Edwardian period in the Chelmsford area was hunting. In 1892 a stag was captured in the town itself. It was cornered in a shed at the back of Gray and Sons Brewery on Springfield Road. (45) The Essex Beagles was a well known hunt. In 1893 they met at Writtle with several ladies riding and chased a hare to Roxwell village. A second hare was chased to Writtle Park. (46) In 1904 a stag was cornered in the Chief Constable's quarters in Springfield, resulting in stag hunting through the town being stopped. (47) As late as 1922 however there was a fox hunted through Moulsham. (48)

Chelmsford's Odde Volumes Society, whilst not unique in the country, was certainly original enough to add its particular flavour to life in late Victorian Chelmsford. Its founder was the publisher Edmund Durrant. He was born in 1843 in Chelmsford and was educated at K.E.G.S.. Durrant spent some years at a publishing firm in London. He then succeeded the late D. Burrell the bookseller at 90, the High Street, Chelmsford. Bookselling had already been established in the County for well over 100 years. Durrant added a new department to the business, which published many works of local interest. "He held it as an axiom that every person of intelligence should strive to obtain a full knowledge of the history and literature of the county in which he resides." In 1892 he founded the Essex Review and was also heavily involved with the museum and its fight for survival (see later). For many years he was its honorary secretary. Durrant was prominent in the campaign for a public library. He also arranged and was secretary for the Cambridge lectures at the museum (see later). Durrant was an active churchman and one of the managers of the National Schools in Chelmsford. (49)

Durrant founded his Sette of Odde Volumes in 1888, "a bookish club of genial eccentrics". Its members had to give a talk on their own specific subject. Each member had his own unique volume number and would only answer to this. Durrant was volume 1, Chancellor was volume 8. Meetings were held above Durrant's shop. (50) In 1894 the Odde Volumes "held a special meeting to present a handsome silver tea service to Vol. 1 and his appendix, Mr and Mrs Durrant, in recognition of the hospitality they have shown the Odde Volumes since the formation of the society". (51) There was also a Ladies' Sette of the Odde Volumes which was organised by Mrs Durrant and its meetings were sometimes held at the house of the Mayoress, Lady Cramphorn.

(52) It may have been the oldest such society in the British Empire. The Ladies' Sette was particularly fond of outings especially cycle rides to Danbury and Maldon and by 1895 was already in its sixth season. (53)(54) In 1900 Durrant died and was buried in the borough cemetery in Writtle Road. The Odde Volumes disappeared a few years after his death.

A scheme for a public library was floated several times before the borough was formed. In 1887 the editor of the Essex Chronicle expressed his support for the idea. (55) The need was made all the greater because the Mechanics Institute, which had the town's best collection of books, was in serious decline. A public library was one of the schemes put forward when ways of celebrating the Queen's Diamond Jubilee were discussed before 1897. The council's cautious approach to spending meant that this was never a serious possibility. In 1899 an appeal for subscriptions for a joint museum and library fund was launched. (56) Books for a free library started arriving in 1903 but there was still a significant shortage of funds. In 1904 Frederic Chancellor wrote to Andrew Carnegie, the American millionaire and philanthropist. He agreed to give the town £2,500 but this was to be used purely for the library part of the scheme, which now included a new museum and a new art school. The total cost of the new buildings in Market Road was £8,000 and their upkeep was found from an extra rate of half a penny in the pound. (57) The library was opened in 1906 by Lord Rayleigh after 1,000 applications for tickets. (58)

From the start it was felt that the space allocated to the library and reading rooms would soon prove too small. By 1930 the need for a new building was urgent. A competition was held for the best design but the council couldn't get sanction for the necessary loan. (59)(60) Eventually finance was found and the new building was opened in April 1935 in Duke Street by the Mayor Sidney Tayor. (61)

Chelmsford Museum in common with many others in the country came about as a result of a Philosophical Society in this case formed in 1828. The Museum was first housed in the Old Chelmsford Gaol buildings in 1835 in Moulsham Street, when its founder Thomas Clarkson Neale was governor of that prison. In 1843 the collection had been moved to buildings in the then New Bridge Street (now New London Road). By the 1880s the Museum had moved to more emphasis on lectures rather than purely displays of exhibits. Many of these were held at the Shire Hall as well as evening soirees. In 1884 the lectures included one by Colonel Crompton. (62) From 1888 the museum started to put on the Cambridge University Lectures with up to half the members attending. They ended in 1893. Many of the members of the Museum obtained University Certificates, particularly women. Edmund Durrant featured in many of the Museum's own lectures. In the late 1880s the Museum started to give free admission on some evenings with great success. (63)

The Museum was however struggling financially. Because of this the Essex Field Club was asked to consider joining with the Chelmsford and Essex Museum, in the hope that a new and better museum could be established. Initially there was very little opposition from within the Committee and subscribers. A public meeting in March 1891 at the Shire Hall gave unanimous support to the merger. The aim was for the new Museum to cover natural history, archaeology and geology more than it had previously done. William Cole, the secretary of the Field Club, took up possession of the Museum premises and its contents and the museum was closed to the public in 1893. It became known as the Essex Field Club Central Museum. £2,000 was needed for a new building but an appeal for funds from the public raised very little money. The Field Club wanted the Council to provide accommodation and financial support for the Museum, whilst the Club managed it, but the Council was not prepared to give financial support without running the museum itself. Chelmsford Museum remained closed while the Field Club opened negotiations with Passmore Edwards for the opening of a museum in West Ham. Edwards was prepared to contribute £2,500 for the opening of a museum there. Frederic Chancellor was immediately opposed to moving the Museum. He complained that a meeting had been held out of the way at Loughton. It was alleged that some of the Museum's exhibits had gone missing and others were chaotically boxed. The long delay had alienated opinion in the town. At the Loughton meeting both Durrant and Chancellor strongly opposed the removal of the Museum from Chelmsford. A committee was set up to determine what elements of the collection belonged to Chelmsford and should remain there. The committee proved unworkable with both Cole and Chancellor on it. (64)(65)

The Field Club exhibits were removed from Chelmsford in September 1898, after the Club had signed an agreement with West Ham for its new museum. Chelmsford Museum's problems continued when the owners of Museum Terrace wanted to extend the Chelmsford Club's accommodation into the Museum's premises. The Museum moved into the empty Mechanics Institute building in 1899. The Passmore Edwards Museum opened in 1900. Chelmsford and Essex Museum's fortunes were at a low ebb but were to quickly revive under the ownership on the Council. In 1901 the trustees of the Museum offered to hand over its collection of objects to the corporation. (66) Chancellor designed the new Museum, Library and Art School, but sharing meant that space for the Museum was limited. Initially after the first war it was intended to build a new library and museum at Fairfield Lodge but after the Council took over the Oaklands estate in 1929 it decided to move the Museum to Oaklands House.

The Hylands estate has played a significant part in the lives of people in Chelmsford throughout our period. Arthur Prior had bought the estate in 1858 for £43,000. He had been born in Hertfordshire in 1816 and was a partner in Truman Breweries. (67) Prior had several rooms in the house redecorated and in the 1880s he approached Great Eastern Railways about the construction of a railway siding specifically for the use of the estate. When built, this ran parallel to the main Chelmsford to London line. He "used to bring his guests from London in a railway carriage which was then shunted on to the siding and then his guests would disembark to waiting carriages and horses to the house". (68) Pryor periodically extended the estate, by buying up nearby properties and farms including Widford Hall. (69) Game was strictly preserved on the estate because Prior was a keen hunter until illness forced him to give up. (70) In 1884 for example the Weekly News reported "Mr Arthur Prior had been entertaining a distinguished party of guests during which some of the well stocked preserves were shot over, six guns in two days bagging over 800 head of game". (71) Prior was generous in allowing the estate to be used for fetes and other occasions. The Mechanics' Institute fete was regularly held there. In 1890 Prior threw open Hylands for three nights entertainment when up to 1,000 attended. (72) During 1892 the grounds were again opened to the public. (73) Prior regularly held dinners for his tenants. During the years of the agricultural depression he commonly gave significant rent reductions. (74) Prior's wife Elizabeth died in 1894 after which he was an invalid. On his death in September 1904 his body was carried from Hylands to Widford church in one of the estate's farm wagons. (75)

His son, also named Arthur Prior, decided not to live at Hylands and rented out the estate for a few years. The next owner Sir Daniel Fulthorpe Gooch came from Beccles in Suffolk and was closely associated with the Great Western Railway. He was the grandson of his namesake, Sir Daniel Gooch who designed over 60 classes of steam locomotive and was responsible for laying the first ever transatlantic cable. Gooch employed Chancellor to prepare plans and carry out improvements to Hylands House. A new arched side entrance was built and an oak secondary staircase. The banqueting room was renovated including a wall panel by Wenley and Son. (76) Like Prior, Gooch bought several neighbouring farms. At the time between 16 and 20 gardeners were employed on the estate. For the Coronation fete in June 1911 there were 700 guests, who were mainly Widford parishioners and estate tenants. (77) On the 24th of June 1912 there occurred a wedding at Hylands which made both the national and international papers. Dorothy Taylor from New York married Claude Graham White, the well known aviator. It became known as the first air wedding because White arrived by plane and there was a great gathering of the finest air pilots. By this time the Hylands' stables were being used to house the new 'horseless carriages', mainly Rolls Royces and Daimlers. (78) A Crompton dynamo provided the electricity for the house and telephone poles were soon erected across the park. Gooch's staff included a butler, a housekeeper, a cook, a ladies maid, an odd man and a hall boy. There were also three chauffeurs, a coalman, a groom and a number of gamekeepers and gardeners as well as an engineer.

Gooch was a notable sportsman and accompanied Shackleton on his trip to the South Pole. He went as a last minute substitute on the 'Endurance' because of his expertise with dogs. Unfortunately one of Gooch's legs became infected and he had to return. The leg had to be amputated and he was fitted with an artificial one. Lady Gooch played a leading role in organising the hospital at Hylands House during the first war (see chapter 15). (79) King George inspected the Territorials on the estate in 1915, as did Lord Kitchener later the same year. After the war the estate was briefly put up for sale when Gooch moved to Hampshire but it was soon withdrawn. Lady Gooch died in 1921 and Daniel Gooch followed five years later.

After being bought by a syndicate of local gentlemen led by David Hodge of Widford Hall, the estate was bought for £17,000 by the Hanbury family from Chigwell. (80) John Hanbury died soon afterwards but his widow continued to live at the house. (81) A group of herons moved onto trees at Hylands when their trees at Boreham were felled. Mrs Hanbury allowed voluntary organisations such as the Red Cross to hold rallies on the estate. Before the second war the house was considered as a possible home for the Agricultural College. (82) During the war the estate was used as a home for prisoners of war and the recently formed S.A.S. (83) During their stay, Major Paddy Blair Mayne succeeded in driving a jeep up the main staircase which woke up a startled Mrs Hanbury! The vehicle had to be dismantled to get it down the stairs.

H. Fairbank was a gardener at Hylands before the first war. He went there as an apprentice, having undergone a period of training at the Essex Institute of Agriculture, which was then based at the Technical School in Chelmsford with classes at Rainsford End. His main practical experience was obtained at Hylands. The garden had two main sections. A large walled garden was to be found close to the London to Chelmsford

Road. This enclosed a number of glass houses, including vineries, peach houses, various plant houses and a pine pit. Auxiliary buildings included a fruit store, a mushroom house and a potting shed. The glass houses were demolished after the war. The other section was the pleasure gardens around the house. These also had glass houses, including a large palm house or conservatory, a tropical house, a cool house for display purposes and several carnation houses. There were a number of 'bothies' on the estate for single gardeners. The garden workers included the head gardener, two foremen, one for each section, five inside gardeners, three kitchen gardeners and four on the pleasure grounds, plus four youths of which Fairbank was one. Hylands' head gardener had a bungalow on the grounds but most of the others had a fair journey to work, including Fairbank who rode his bike from Rainsford End. His wages were just six shillings a week. The experienced gardeners averaged 14 shillings a week. There was a free joint of meat at Christmas. Fairbank was occasionally allowed to 'beat' for the hunting parties. One of his regular jobs was to mow the lawn with a pony drawing the mower. "We used to put shoes on the pony's feet so that the lawn was not marked by their footsteps." There was a daily display of flowers. (84)

Maurice Abbott worked at Hylands, as a gardener, later after the war. Wages had increased substantially; he was paid 32 shillings and 6 pence. Workers were dismissed arbitrarily. The presents at Christmas depended on the number of years of service. Abbott remembered tramps on their way to the workhouse constantly calling at the front lodge to get a cup of tea or 'tuppence', for a meal. The 'roadster' left stones outside to show the lodge was a 'soft touch'. Abbott left Hylands when Mrs Hanbury had a clear out of staff. He was summoned and told "I want you out of my house by Saturday". Abbott and his family by now had a house on the estate. "But madam I've worked for you for six years and I've a child of five." "I don't care where you go but I want you out of your house." Abbott, luckily for his family, obtained a good gardening job in Kent. (85)

Bob Cannon and his wife Trudy met on a bus travelling from Chelmsford to Hylands. They couldn't marry until after they had left the estate. Bob was a pleasure gardener and Trudy looked after the nursery. The owner was generous at Christmas but there were no contracts of employment. Cannon left after Mrs Hanbury had given all her outside staff three months notice. "I suspect that she had lost some money on the Stock Exchange." (86)

During the inter war period the main entertainment for working people was the cinema. By the time of the second war the town boasted five cinemas. The first of these was the Chelmsford Picture House, later the Select cinema, which opened in 1910. Initially it was owned by A.R.P. Hickley. Six hundred people could be seated on one floor. Early animated pictures were shown with the help of one of the most foremost film pioneers, Sir William Jury. (87) The cinema had a number of different owners during the inter war period, firstly S. Singer, then R.H. Etchells and finally Sidney Harris. (88)

The Empire cinema on the Springfield Road was opened in 1912, mixing cinema with live entertainment. During 1913 for example, Miss Diana Hope who had recently sung in front of the King and Queen, performed there. (89) In 1921 the cinema was owned by the Chelmsford Empire and Hippodrome Company Limited, but by 1928 the Eastern Counties Cinema Group controlled it. The Empire was badly gutted by fire in 1940 and never re-opened as a cinema. (90) It was however used during the second war as a repertory theatre.

The Regent was opened in 1913 initially as a theatre. Its site was on that of the old Cross Keys public house in Moulsham Street. The building was designed by Francis Burdett Ward. It had steel based foundations and was a large building with 1,126 seats. Seven hundred and twelve were on the ground floor and three hundred and fifty four in the balcony. There were four boxes each seating 15 people each. (91) Carpets and draperies cost £1,500 and the theatre had good off stage facilities with four dressing rooms. There was a large foyer and an anteroom. The scenery was treated with non flammable materials and the safety curtain came down before a film started. After the war, cinema was very much mixed with variety. By 1925 the Regent was showing only films. (92) The owners were still however allowing the Chelmsford Amateur and Operatic Society to perform there. By 1928 it had also become part of the Eastern Counties Cinema Limited circuit and was regularly showing talking films. (93)(94) In 1930 there was a serious fire at the Regent despite the safety precautions, whilst 1,100 people were present. (95)

Another cinema was the Pavilion on Rainsford Road which opened in 1920 and seated 500. (96) Like the Select, there were several different owners before the second war when Mr C.A. James owned the cinema. (97)

In 1933 plans were announced for a new super cinema at Chelmsford by Ritz (Chelmsford) Limited. The site was originally to be on the corner of Moulsham Street and Baddow Road. (98) It was actually built on the site of the old tannery in Baddow Road and was opened in 1935 by Mayor Taylor. (98) The cinema was the 49th to be opened in the chain of County cinemas. With a capacity of 1,748 people it was easily the largest cinema in Chelmsford. "The architect Mr Robert Crowle is recognised as the greatest authority on acoustics in the world and the very wide range Western Electric projection and sound apparatus has been installed." "A feature of the cinema is the concealed lighting which with green, red, gold and silver speckled effects on the ceiling and walls looks most attractive." "Special ventilating apparatus has been installed to ensure the air is changed every fifteen minutes." Forty five people were employed at the cinema. The first film shown was 'The 39 Steps'. Balcony seats were two shillings and one shilling and sixpence. Prices in the stalls were one shilling and sixpence, nine pence and sixpence. The car park had 200 places and the restaurant was designed to hold dinner dances. (99) County Cinemas were taken over by the Odeon chain in 1939. (100)

The first Chelmsford Carnival was held in 1923. It was designed to raise funds for the Chelmsford and Essex Hospital which was increasingly short of funds. Fred Spalding was in charge of the carnival committee. The Mayor and the members of the Corporation took part in the procession through the principal streets of the town. There was an evening fete at the Hoffmann Athletic ground at Rainsford End. All the big firms decorated lorries including the Marconi entry, the 'Bolshevic Beaver Bandski'. A gas lorry was fitted up as a kitchen. The Essex Industrial School Band, the Boy Scouts and the Boy's Brigade all took part. Fred Munnion gave a concert in the evening. Music for dancing was provided by Crompton's band. Net receipts were £350 but the following year twice that amount was raised. (101) In 1924 carnival events lasted all week with the procession on the Friday. "Many thousands enjoy revelry on the longest day." "There was also a procession of illuminated and decorated boats on the river." (102) In 1925 the procession started at the market and took two hours to return. Eleven thousand four hundred people paid for admission to the Recreation Ground in the evening. (103) By 1927 the carnival was raising £1,500. (104) In 1933, the year of the first carnival queen, there were over 17,000 at the carnival fete. The following year the fete was held at the Chelmsford City football ground and featured the Dagenham Girl Pipers, a cabaret, boxing and a wrestling tournament. There was a grand cabaret show at the Regent. The procession started at 3.0. p.m. and finished with a fete with 11 bands, a fair and side shows. (105) Although crowds continued to increase in the 1930s the money raised was nowhere near the level the hospital increasingly needed but the carnival had become a major event in the life of the town.

The second war, of course, made the following of leisure pursuits more difficult but by no means prevented them (see chapter 24). War also saw the removal of the archives of the recently formed Essex Record Office to Wales for safety reasons. The documents had been classified at County Hall by the archivist F.G. Emmison. Before the war 400 people a year were visiting the E.R.O.

1) Essex Chronicle 12 7 1890
2) Essex weekly News 8 8 1890 p.5
3) E.W.N. p.5
4) E.W.N. 28 8 1893 p.4
5) E.W.N. 27 7 1894 p.4
6) Chelmsford Borough Council minutes 25 11 1898
7) E.W.N. 29 8 1902 p.5
8) C.B. C. minutes 27 6 1917
9) C.B.C. minutes 30 9 1925
10) E.W.N. 181 1884 p.4
11) E.C. 8 2 1894 p.4
12) E.W.N. 10 6 1881 p.5
13) E.W.N. 20 6 1884 p.5
14) Essex Musical Association 1906 – 2006 p.2 – 6
15) E.M.A. p.6 - 12
16) Chelmsford Museums records Chelmsford People
17) Life of C. Armstrong Gibbs Blue Plaque pamphlet
18) E.W.N. 20 7 1888 p.5
19) E.W.N. 27 4 1888
20) E.W.N. 7 1 1887 p.5
21) E.W.N. 2 9 1910
22) E.W.N. 17 10 1884 p.5
23) E.W.N. 1 2 1884 p.6
24) E.W.N. 15 5 1885 p.5
25) E.W.N. 30 9 1880
26) E.W.N. 22 7 1892 p.5
27) E.W.N. 25 7 1906 p.8
28) E.W.N. 3 9 1880
29) E.W.N. 26 2 1892
30) E.W.N. 13 3 1903 p.4
31) E.W.N. 14 12 1906 p.6

32) E.W.N. 4 3 1910 p.8
33) E.W.N. 8 10 1920 p.5
34) E.W.N. 23 11 1925 p.7
35) E.W.N. 6 1 1922 p.5
36) E.W.N. 8 5 1925 p.7
37) Pastimes in Times Past Friends of Chelmsford Museum pamphlet
38) Chelmsford Beef Steak Club Thomas Kemble
39) E.W.N. 26 11 1881
40) E.W.N. 9 12 1892 p.5
41) E.C. 8 2 1884 p.5
42) E.W.N. 1 8 1884 p.5
43) E.W.N. 20 3 1885 p.3
44) E.W.N. 2 2 1892 p.5
45) E.W.N. 1 4 1892 p.5
46) E.W.N. 10 11 1893 p.7
47) Springfield I. Clark
48) E.W.N. 27 1 1922 p.5
49) Essex Review 1900 Vol. 9 p.228 – 231
50) Pastimes in Times Past
51) E.W.N. 31 5 1894 p.2
52) E.W.N. 21 7 1898 p.5
53) E.W.N. 20 5 1898 p.5
54) E.W.N. 27 1 1895 p.5
55) E.C. 8 87
56) E.W.N. 24 1 1899
57) C. Museums records
58) E.C. 12 6 1906
59) E.W.N. 25 7 1930 p.9
60) E.W.N. 2 5 1930 p.14
61) E.W.N. 12 4 1935 p.6
62) E.W.N. 20 6 1884 p.5
63) C. Museums records
64) The Vicious Circle The Case of the Essex and Chelmsford Museum v the Essex field Club 1893 – 1899 Peter A Boyd
65) C. Museums records

66) E.W.N. 27 9 1901 p.2
67) Hylands Stephen Foreman
68) Hylands p.68
69) Hylands p.69
70) C. Museums records
71) E.W.N. 10 1884 p.5
72) E.W.N. 5 5 1890 p.5
73) E.W.N. 12 8 1892 p.5
74) E.W.N. 20 7 1894 p.5
75) Hylands p.71
76) Hylands p.72
77) Hylands p.74
78) Hylands p.79
79) C. Museums records
80) Hylands p.84
81) Hylands p.86
82) Hylands p. 88
83) Hylands p.92
84) 'Happy days at Hylands Park, Chelmsford Essex Countryside No. 160 1970
85) C. Museums records 'Memories of Hylands' Maurice Abbott
86) C. Museums 'Halcyon days for some at Hylands." Bob Abott
87) E.C. Obituary of A.R.P. Hickley 23 11 1945
88) Chelmsford Cinemas Bob Grimwood p.18
89) E.W.N. 22 8 1913 p.5
90) Grimwood p.17
91) 'The Life and Death of the Regent Theatre 1911 – 1975 Kevin Bush
92) E.W.N. 7 8 1925 p.7
93) Grimwood p.19
94) E.W.N. 6 12 1929 p.7
95) E.W.N. 2 5 1930 p.2
96) E.C. 8 10 1920 p.5
97) Grimwood p.18
98) E.W.N. 20 10 1933 p.7
99) E.W.N. 1 11 1935 p.3
100) Grimwood p.19

101) C. Museums records
102) E.W.N. 27 6 1924 p.2
103) C. Museums records
104) E.W.N. 17 6 1927
105) E.W.N. 14 7 1933

28

Leisure and Entertainment in Chelmsford since the war

"Young people should not be allowed to enjoy themselves"

In the new millennium it could be said that Chelmsford is starved of the variety of large scale live entertainment that a new city should provide. Since the second war there have been a number of occasions when Chelmsford's lack of a sizeable theatre, in addition to art galleries and music venues, have been shown up in comparison with Colchester. There have however been periods when the town has had a vibrant music scene. In the 1940s and early 1950s dances could be found in eight or nine regular venues. The Cathedral Festival was strong enough for a few years towards the end of the century to briefly boast its own fringe. In the late 1960s and early 1970s live rock, folk, jazz and even reggae could all be found in medium and small sized venues. The town was a centre in the county for a succession of cultural phenomenon: 'Teddy Boys', 'Mods', 'Skinheads', and 'Punks' all found a significant base in Chelmsford. During the 1990s the county town had a thriving 'indie music scene'. The second half of the century saw the gradual decline of the works' clubs which had been at the heart of so many people's social lives; the Marconi Club however, unlike the Company itself, still survives in Chelmsford. Immediately after the war the cinema remained for a while most people's major form of entertainment with four surviving cinemas. The rise of television and other forms of entertainment meant that by the end of the 1970s the town had no permanent cinema. Chelmsford finally had a permanent theatre by the 1960s but had to share the premises. Despite the onset of the N.H.S., the carnival survived and actually flourished in the early post was years before declining and finally disappearing due to council and public apathy. It had been a major event in many local people's lives. Throughout much of the later part of the twentieth century Hylands House was under threat, but in the new millennium it survives in much of its former glory.

Despite the continuing effects of post war austerity the town tried to make a real effort both with the Festival of Britain in 1951 and the Coronation of 1953. The council's version of the Festival made an attempt to include things that the townsfolk would not see if they visited the Festival in London. (1) Although the final events were more restricted than those originally planned there were still a variety of activities from wrestling to a swimming gala, an industrial exhibition and a literary exhibition. There were also open air performances of ballet, football matches and an athletics meeting. A souvenir programme was produced for the occasion. (2)(3)

In 1953 the council did its best to improve the town's longstanding reputation for doing as little as possible to celebrate royal events which dated back to the 1897 jubilee. Seven days of events were planned for the Coronation, starting with a civic service at the cathedral followed by a band concert in Central Park and a variety concert at the Regent. The second day had a variety of children's events. On the Tuesday large screen T.V. sets were placed in the Corn Exchange, Rainsford School, London Road School, Trinity School and the Drill Hall. There were to be two Coronation Balls, one at the Shire Hall and one at the casino. In the event only 100 tickets were sold for the former and it was cancelled, perhaps reflecting people changing attitudes to entertainment. The Wednesday following the Coronation featured various events in Central Park, including boxing and wrestling displays as well as a concert for old people in the evening. A historical pageant was to be feature of Friday with a swimming gala held in the evening. The Saturday featured a variety of events including a procession, illuminated boats on the rivers, golf and bowls tournaments, a bonfire and community singing. Seven thousand medals were produced to commemorate the occasion. Street parties were held and prizes were given for the best decorated streets. (4) As with the Festival of Britain, the actual activities fell somewhat short of what had been promised, with the Chronicle decrying the town's shabby flags. Only 15 traders decorated their shop windows when 350 had been invited to do so. (5) The historical pageant did not go ahead. Many of the street parties had to be transferred indoors because of the weather. (6) Two brochures were produced, one to advertise events and one as a souvenir of the local celebrations. (7) Coronation Park was opened in Springfield in May 1953 to celebrate the occasion. (8)

Despite the threat of the creation of the N.H.S. hanging over the town's carnival, record crowds attended the first one after the war in 1946 with 20,000 people at the evening. (9) The carnival of 1951 attracted 50,000 people, including 30,000 at a fair in the Kings Head Meadow. (10) A Ministry directive stating that "participation by hospital members or officers in the collection of money for hospital purposes" was not allowed appeared to have put an end to what had become a major event in Chelmsford life. (11) As a fund raiser the carnival was never a big contributor to hospital funds. In 1953 a new committee was formed without the participation of hospital staff. Despite the drabness of much of town life the carnival was often a lively affair. In 1953 the maids of honour resigned in a dispute over the new voting system for the selection of the beauty queen. After she was crowned fighting broke out in the crowd! (12) In 1955 Marconi students had to apologise to the Melbourne Park Flower Queen after drenching her with water. The previous year they had ruined the winning Crompton float. By 1961 the carnival was beginning to encounter difficulties, with the editor of the Weekly News criticising the preponderance of commercial floats, which were little more than advertising, and bemoaning the lack of private entries. (13) Poor weather in 1963 caused the committee to fall back on previously invested funds. (14) Despite large crowds turning up to the evening fete, the carnival was suffering from a lack of financial support from local traders, and according to the Weekly News, from the local council. (15) In 1968 although 20,000 people attended the fete in Admirals Park only £34 was collected in the streets. (16) During the 1970s the carnival was generally on a better financial footing. In 1982 it raised £3,000 for various local charities including the League of Friends of the three local hospitals and the local branch of Age Concern. (17) By 1987 the number on the organising committee had shrunk and sponsorship was again difficult to find. Just enough members were recruited to keep the event afloat. (18) The early 1990s saw another revival with 50 floats at the 1996 procession but two years later this had fallen again to 20, with the decline of Chelmsford's big firms playing a part. (19) In 1999 the Essex Chronicle reported "The Carnival is over" after it made only £450 for charities the previous year. (21) Changes in the route, which no longer included Moulsham Street, were thought to be a cause, as was the lack of street collectors. There had also been a major problem with the floats which were badly rusted. (22) An attempt to revive the event in 2000 came to nothing. (23) Lack of sponsorship from local firms was the main reason for the new venture failing to get off the ground, even though a few carnivals survive elsewhere in the county.

Interior of the Golden Fleece, Duke Street during the 1940s
(Courtesy of E.R.O.)

In the immediate post war years Chelmsford still hadn't been provided with a permanent civic theatre. The Chelmsford Amateur Operatic and Dramatic Society continued to use the Regent and a repertory company used the previously disused Empire cinema on the Springfield Road. Today the C.A.O.D.S. uses the Civic Theatre and celebrated its 90th anniversary in 2010. It now has a thriving independent junior section. By the mid 1950s pressure for a theatre in the county town was slowly building up. Seventy people turned up to a first meeting at the Cathedral Hall where a Chelmsford Theatre Association was formed. "We want a nice little 500 seater theatre." (24) By 1958 the petition for a theatre had reached 10,000 signatures. (25) The Empire cinema was considered first, but by 1960 a new theatre was being built in Fairfield Road as part of a Civic Centre, which was to include the council's assembly rooms. (260 Its facilities were limited but better than the local papers had expected, with seats for 600. Its green room and two large dressing rooms could accommodate a cast of 50 – 60. There was a projector room for showing films and a room for a buffet and bar. (27) Amateur productions were encouraged from the start by the council. In 1961 it gave £2,000 to the Chelmsford Theatre Association which had been so influential in finally obtaining a theatre for the town. It was also given three months rent free use of the theatre. (28) The Civic Centre finally opened in May 1962. Initially there was just a thirteen week season of plays and there was immediate pressure to extend it. (29) Its most expensive seats were seven shillings and sixpence and the cheapest one shilling and sixpence. During the following year there were two 12 week seasons each given to a different repertory company. (30) Despite audiences initially being high, the theatre soon had difficulty in attracting sufficient people because of having to compete with television, now in most homes, and bingo. A drop in audiences in 1965 caused the season to be reduced to four months. (31) In 1966 plays were being performed to a half empty auditorium. By 1968 the new director of the theatre, John Ridley was asking the council for a higher subsidy to support the theatre and enable an extension of the season (32) It was seriously thought that the theatre might have to close, which of course led to a short lived rush to go to the theatre. (33) In 1972 the council finally gave the go ahead to convert the existing facilities, which included the assembly rooms, to a purpose built permanent theatre. The alterations included an extension to the orchestra pit and the establishment of two theatres, the Civic and next to it the smaller Cramphorn, which opened in 1981. (34) In 1991 the two theatres were making a profit when many were struggling to survive. This was undoubtedly due to good management by New Palm productions. (35) In 1996 a short lived repertory theatre, the Rainsford opened in Fox Crescent with a lottery grant for lighting and other equipment. By the new millennium it was increasingly clear that the Civic was not big enough to support expensive productions and attract well known acts but it survived to celebrate its 50th anniversary in 2012.

Today the Chelmsford Museum is a major attraction for visitors to the town, especially since its extension opened in 2010. In the 1960s however it had been criticised for "being Victorian in every way". Its curator had replied that the council were now spending more on the museum and attempts were being made to reduce the vandalism which had played a part in the fall in the number of visitors. Its collection had been changed in the 1950s to concentrate more on exhibits from Chelmsford and Essex. Exhibits from outside the county were removed. In 1973 Princess Margaret opened the Essex Regimental Museum, which was an extension to the existing museum and was built to house the military collection from Warley barracks, where it had previously been displayed. (37) During 1986 there was discussion about moving the museum exhibits to the library buildings at the Civic Centre. Oaklands would then have become a centre for the visual arts. The Essex Regimental Museum would have transferred to Hylands House and a new Industrial Museum would have been provided. (38) After this came to nothing, in 1991 it was decided to tell the story of Chelmsford's history in a £75,000 permanent display. (39) Later, permanent displays of a Victorian kitchen and the later history of Chelmsford, 'including the town's music and leisure scene', were added. Oaklands also has displays of pottery and glassware as well as natural science display rooms featuring local birds and geology. As early as 1982, the council were discussing a big extension to Oaklands house. By 1988 Sandford Mill had been acquired by the council and was being used to store surplus museum artefacts. (40) Gradually the Mill was developed to house large industrial exhibits and today is used primarily for educational purposes. In 2006 plans were announced for a £3.5 million extension to the museum which it was hoped would see the return of some of the Marconi Archive to the town. (41) Despite some opposition from the Victorian Society to the plans when it opened in 2010, the new extension doubled the size of the museum. It houses the permanent 'Bright Sparks' exhibition, which shows how the rise of the big three firms transformed the small market town, which was Chelmsford in the late nineteenth century. The extension also houses the updated Essex Regiment Museum. Its new interactive displays are a far cry from the dusty old museum of 50 years ago. In 2011 – 2012 there were 60,000 visitors to the museum a big increase on previous figures.

The museum's display of ceramics and pottery now includes 'Chelmsford Cissies' by the Turner Prize winner Grayson Perry, which the Museum bought for £8,000 in 2004. Perry was born in Chelmsford and grew up in a town which he later described as 'soulless' (see later). Although he was untrained he remains the only current potter you will see displayed in art galleries. Perry was added to Who's Who in 2007, along with Anthony Marwood, the K.E.G.S educated violinist. In 2013 he delivered the Reith lectures.

Chelmsford's Museum also contains some of the work of Lynton Lamb, the illustrator and painter who lived the later part of his life at Sandon before dying in 1977. It also houses some of the work of Edward Bawden a leading light in the group of Great Bardfield artists until his death in 1989. Early in 2013 the museum presented a joint exhibition of two artists who were both born in Chelmsford in 1956, Wladyslaw Mirecki and Paul Rumsey. Mirecki has painted a large number of watercolours of Essex and Suffolk. Rumsey's drawings cover dark subject matter, often inspired by folktales and mythology using charcoal and ink.

Despite improvements to the public library at the Civic Centre in 1974, it was obvious that the premises were too small for a central county library. (42) A site in Fairfield Road next to the Cramphorn was deemed not suitable by the council. When the new county library was opened as part of the new County Hall complex in 1988 it was the third biggest in the U.K. (43)

After the second war the Hylands estate quickly returned to normality, after the excesses of the S.A.S. in the house and the presence of German P.O.W.s on the estate. The 1946 Essex Show was held in the grounds and 20,000 people turned up. Before she died in 1962 Christine Hanbury was keen on Hylands being the site of the new Essex University. (see chapter 21) The estate was already deteriorating before her death. Hanbury's three nieces who inherited the property all had substantial property of their own. While the former butler and his wife remained there as caretakers they showed around various organisations with a view to take over the house. In May 1963 a serious fire broke out. Fire engines came from the surrounding rural parishes and as far afield as Basildon.

Several institutions, including the E.C.C., were interested in buying the estate until finally the Chelmsford Borough Council obtained sanction for a loan to buy Hylands at a price of £150,000. (44) In 1966 an estimate of £3,000 was obtained for repairs to the dry rot that was now rife and repairs to the roof. At this time the work could be done fairly cheaply. The borough's gardeners worked hard to restore the gardens that were already overgrown. In 1967 the house was made a Grade 2 listed building. Already a variety of possible uses were being put forward for both the house and the estate including horse racing, but the serious proposal that caused most controversy was for a 18 hole golf course. The council eventually scrapped the plans being considered after a stormy council meeting. (45) Meanwhile estimates for repairs to the house had already risen to £100,000 by 1968. In 1969 the lead was stripped off the roof and rain started to penetrate the building. The grants available then were very limited and the council said it couldn't afford the now very expensive repairs. Chelmsford borough council wanted to demolish the house in 1971 but this was blocked by the E.C.C. planners. The golf course idea was brought up again with part of the house to be used for conferences but this was again defeated in what the Essex Chronicle called "A decision of indecision." (46) A property company put in an offer to restore the house but this was dependent on a 75% grant from the E.C.C. which was not forthcoming. A move for a demolition order was defeated in the council by 17 votes to 12. (47) Further plans in the early 1970s, included a sports complex and an industrial museum. A scheme to demolish the wings was dropped in favour of demolishing the entire house. After the council voted for demolition they needed the approval of the Ministry of the Environment to actually carry it out, (48) The E.C.C. opposed demolition because they now wanted to use it for their offices. After the borough council received a 'booby' prize from an Architectural Heritage Year body, the borough had to make the case for demolition at an inquiry. (49) The chairman of the Parks committee said "Hylands was bought as a park. The house just happens to be on it. It has no historical or architectural value. We cannot ask the ratepayers to fork out half a million pounds just because it is there." These remarks are redolent of the attitude which had already led to the desecration of Tindal Street. It was said that the mansion might collapse at any time with infestation so rife that no timbers were safe: of 53 ceilings, 20 had already collapsed. In the event the Department of the Environment refused permission for the demolition to go ahead. (50)

The Chelmsford Society was pleased with the decision and by a report which said the house was far from being beyond repair. During following year a private company resurrected the golf course idea, planning to use the central part of the house as a clubhouse. The public would still have access to the estate. (51) E.C.C. pressed again to use the building for its offices but in 1979 the council accepted an offer from a property company to convert the house in to private offices. (52) (53) The Chelmsford Society pressed for the house to be used as an Arts Centre. (54) Chelmsford borough council was split again over the issue, but it looked like it would go back to the government again to get permission for demolition, after the agreement with the property company fell through. (55) In 1982 a six months deadline was given to get a private buyer. (56)

Changes in the control of the borough council meant that demolition didn't happen. Two years later a grant of a quarter of a million pounds ensured that some restoration work could finally take place although this was well short of the one million pounds needed in total. Negotiations started with Period and Country Homes to convert part of the house into luxury flats with the State rooms being opened to the public 60 days a year. (57) Meanwhile a new plan to convert part of the public park to a municipal golf house divided the public. (58) The Chelmsford Society maintained that the plan would ruin "a uniquely landscaped area of great natural beauty." They supported an alternative course on adjoining farmland. (59) Half a million pounds was spent on restoring the outside of the house but at least as much again was needed for internal restoration. The house was put up for sale again in 1987 so that private owners could bear that cost. An action Committee tried to stop the golf course on the estate. (60) County planners turned down submissions to use the house as a golf clubhouse, restaurant, hotel and offices. They did recommend that it be used as a conference and function centre with exhibitions and galleries, with the stables used for crafts or conservation workrooms that would allow a degree of public access to the house. The county planners would allow a golf course on the estate only if the clubhouse and car park were near the A12. (61) After a 13,000 signature petition and a public inquiry the golf course did go ahead; it is now the Hylands golf complex. (62)

By now the public park was being used for music events (see later). In 1991 the public were allowed into the house for the first time in 20 years, to see the extent of the interior neglect. (63) During 1994 work finally began on restoring the interior of the house. (64) The aim was to restore it to the way it looked in the early nineteenth century, including the gardens landscaped by Repton. Visitors would be able to see the entrance hall looking very much as it did in Labouchere's day. (65) In 1996, after English Heritage could give no more money the council applied to the National Lottery Fund. (66) By now the total cost of restoration was estimated to be £5 million. "Hylands will soon have gobbled up £3 million of Chelmsford's council tax in order to get it back to its nineteenth century grandeur." "There is no doubt it will be an architectural gem." "It will be a beehive of creative and social activity run for the benefit of the public." (67) In 1999, a Hylands war plaque was unveiled which made reference to the use of the house as HQ. for the S.A.S., late in the war (see chapter 27). (68) During the same year the East wing was opened to the public. By 2001 work was ready to start on the last stage of the restoration work. "When we have completed phase four by Easter 2003 there will be a banquet room, another reception area and a full size kitchen". (69) Plans were put on display for the restoration of Repton's parkland pedestrian approach, the grand staircase in the house, gardens, farm buildings and a visitor's centre, craft studios and a tea room. (70) In 2003 the West wing was opened showing the banqueting room and the basement; at the same time a new bid for a grant of £3million to complete the restoration work was put in. (71) This was obtained from English Heritage but the council still had to find another £2 million for the refurbishment work. Landscaping continued with a mass clearance of trees and the recreation of Repton's Lake. New trees were planted so as not to interfere with the views. Work on the estate itself was duly finished in 2007, with the restored Parkland providing beautiful views of the estate and the house itself. The lake can be seen from the Repton room. The fully restored house had already been opened to the public in September 2005 almost 30 years after the council had tried to get it demolished.

In the immediate post war years Chelmsford had four thriving cinemas. The Empire was never used as a cinema after the war and was eventually demolished in 1961. The Pavilion on the Rainsford Road was improved in both its exterior and interior in the 1950s. Before it closed in 1988 it was no longer screening the best films. (72) The Select cinema in New Writtle Street was refurbished after the war with a state of the art sound system and a 'wrap around screen' but as early as 1967 it was being used for Bingo, after getting a reputation as a 'flea pit'. (73) Although it briefly reverted to being a cinema in 1988 it closed permanently in 1992. The Regent, apart from occasional amateur productions and pantomimes, operated solely as a cinema after the second war. It was popular, with queues for entrance often joining up with those for the Odeon, in the immediate post war years. After passing to E.M.I., the Regent ceased being a cinema in 1975 initially also being used for bingo. The Regent is a grade 2 listed building and the current owners cannot alter the facade at the front. (74) Chelmsford's Odeon reopened in 1947 but was taken over by the Rank Organisation in 1948. The cinema was used for variety shows, dances and live music as well as films until it closed in 1981. Unusually for a cinema of its size it had no organ. Despite suggestions for its conversion it was never made into a multi screen cinema. By the 1980s Chelmsford was in danger of being without a permanent cinema, although films were regularly being shown at the Cramphorn. In 1987 a new twin screen cinema was planned on the old site. A multi screen complex was finally opened in 1993 just a few yards from the original site. (76)

As early as 1978 a scheme to establish a local commercial radio station in Chelmsford faltered when the mast was not ready. (77) BBC Radio Essex was also set to be established but by 1983 there was still no progress, by which time Colchester was also being mentioned as a possible home town for the new station. The old Hawker Siddeley site in New London Road was found, but the refusal of a planning application for a radio mast again put the plans for a BBC station in Chelmsford in doubt. (78) (79) BBC Essex finally started broadcasting from the town in November 1986. It now broadcasts from its studios in New London Road. Current radio presenters include Ray Clark, Dave Monk, Sadie Nine, Mark Punter and Ian Puckey. Well known presenters who have passed through Radio Essex include Jonathan Overend, Mark Pougatch, Dermot O'Leary and Eric 'Monster' Hall. To commemorate the fortieth anniversary of the launching of offshore radio in Britain in April 2004, BBC Essex launched their own ship-based radio station. The station transmitted 60s music and memories all week. Another broadcast in August 2007 marked the anniversary of the closing of the pirate stations by the Marine Offences Act. BBC Essex celebrated 25 years broadcasting in 2011.The commercial station Heart FM now broadcasts from Glebe Road, Chelmsford, having transferred from Southend. In 2013 plans were announced to start a new Chelmsford community radio station.

In 1959 Chelmsford started its own arts festival week. This included performances by the Chelmsford Ballet Company, the St Cecilia's Choral Society, the Essex Symphony Orchestra, the Moulsham Dramatic society and the Kelvedon players. (80) Chelmsford borough council continued to back the festival in succeeding years and by the time of the fifth festival in 1964 it included operas at the Civic and exhibitions at the Corn Exchange. (81) The 10th festival in 1969 featured events across Chelmsford in Mildmay Hall, the Cathedral, the Odeon and the Civic theatres. (82) By 1973 the festival was experiencing both artistic and financial problems. (83) In 1975 however there was the biggest response to the festival with 23 full houses and more than 10,000 people attending the 25 events. (84) During the 1978 festival events ranged from an opera to poetry in a pub. (85) Despite often shaky finances the festival, now called the Cathedral Festival, involved 3,000 performers. (86) After 2007 the festival ceased, when it failed to find sponsorship.

Joan Weston and the Chelmsford Ballet Company had been heavily involved in setting up the original Arts festival. She had founded the Chelmsford Ballet Company in 1949 after two years as the Broomfield Y.M.C.A. Ballet Company. Early performances were often at the Shire Hall. In the 1960s a scholarship fund was started and the number of dancing members rose to above one hundred. Weston retired in 1969 and died in 1991. Patrons of the company have included Dame Beryl Grey and Lady Sutherland. The Company continues to put on high class productions at the Civic Theatre.

Apart from Armstrong Gibbs, another famous local classical composer was Elizabeth Maconchy. She was a socialist and after being born in Hertfordshire and growing up in Ireland, spent the last 40 years of her life in Boreham. She came to Essex in the 1950s. Before the second war she had studied at the Royal College of Music and her suite 'The Land' was premiered at the 1930 season of Promenade Concerts. After the war Maconchy wrote for the leading ensembles, orchestras and soloists of the day. She chaired the Composers Guild of Great Britain and was president of the

Society for the Promotion of New Music. Over 50 years she wrote 13 string quartets and many other chamber and instrumental works. Maconchy also wrote for single voice, piano and chamber orchestra. (87) In 1987 she was made a Dame of the British Empire. Maconchy died in 1994 and in February 2007 a blue plaque was unveiled to her by her daughter. (88)

Although a survey in the 1950s showed up the lack of live entertainment in Chelmsford compared with Colchester, there was however a considerable amount of live music, particularly for dances. One of a number of popular local ballroom dance bands were the Blue Ramblers. One of the eight members, Johnny Alliston, remembered "Everybody had a function especially at Christmas including factories, shops, as well as hunt balls that were sometimes a fair distance from Chelmsford such as Saffron Walden". They didn't have an agent after the band started as a hobby and then became semi professional. The Ramblers sometimes had to play for five hours at one gig. Occasionally champion dancers were also hired for example at the Shire Hall. They were the relief band for the Ted Heath Orchestra several times, because the latter would only play one and a half hour sets. Alliston found the functions at Crompton's and Hoffmann's very smart with nice dance rooms. (89) Other local dance bands included the Chelma Five, the Embassy Orchestra and Bill Bateman's Orchestra.

Clive Beattie worked at Marconi in the 1950s. He remembered Chelmsford having a lively social scene. Before the arrival of 'teddy boys' he would wear a gabardine suit, dark and sombre, but he might sport a waistcoat and 'brothel creeper' shoes. Beattie said the Shire Hall had all the best big bands including Kenny Baker, Cyril Stapleton, Joe Loss and Ted Heath. The Corn Exchange also got the biggest bands but in 'rough and ready' surroundings. He also remembered several coffee bars including the Orpheus on the New London Road, which was underground, and the Amber which was close to the Cathedral. (90)

Pete Searles, who lived in Danbury in the 1950s, played in various skiffle groups, including Mark Shelley and the Deans, which were pushing out the dance bands by the end of the decade. His various bands played the Odeon, the Marconi Club, the Lion and Lamb and the County Hotel. They often played five nights a week. In the 1960s his band played the 'Saturday Scene' concerts supporting acts like Joe Brown, Screaming Lord Sutch and The Who (see later) (91)

The 'teddy boys' divided opinion in the town. Despite occasional disturbances the manager of Chelmsford's casino supported them and organised a dance for the teddy boys and their girlfriends. "I find them perfect gentlemen." "Teddy boys dress immaculately and are always spotlessly clean, though I don't like their shoes." (92) Despite this support, brawls outside the Odeon were quite common.

By the early 1960s well known rhythm and blues groups were the order of the day at the Corn Exchange. Although the Rolling Stones and the Beatles never played in the town, Georgie Fame, Zoot Money, the Small Faces and the Animals all played there. The Who played an early date. There were sometimes fights when 'mods' came from Basildon. They met in the Steamer and would meet skinheads from Brentwood off the train. There was a Scooter club called the 'Prize Guys' which met at the Golden Fleece. Later in the decade one of the most memorable nights was when the Corn Exchange was packed for Jimi Hendrix just after his first single had been released. Footage of the gig can still be found on 'You Tube'. All the local groups including the Mooche, the Coletrane Union and the RBQ played the Corn Exchange regularly to support the headliners. In 1967, apart from Jimi Hendrix, the venue hosted Shotgun Express, featuring Rod Stewart, the Small Faces, Graham Bond, Arthur Brown, Pink Floyd, Fleetwood Mac and John Mayall. To see Pink Floyd would have cost you 8 shillings and 6 pence in advance or 10 shillings on the door. Besides the rock acts at the Corn Exchange there was a thriving folk scene with two clubs, one at the White Hart and one at the Saracen's Head. Well known acts such as the Strawbs, the Incredible String Band and Martin Carthy played the town. Nic Jones, who became well known in the 1970s before a bad car accident in 1982, grew up in Chelmsford and was a swimming lifeguard in the town. Dave Moran, who also went on to be a nationally known musician, ran the Chelmsford folk club. Paul Simon, who lived for a while at Brentwood, played at the club. Folk singers booked for the Civic Theatre included Buffy Saint Marie, Bert Yansch and Julie Felix. For a while there was even a reggae club in the town. (93)

One of the most controversial events at the end of the decade, which was to have a great effect on live music in the town, was the demolition of the Corn Exchange (see chapter 12) and its replacement after several years by the Chancellor Hall, named after Frederic Chancellor. There was considerable opposition to the removal of what was by now a much loved music venue. What made matters worse was that the new hall was scheduled to house only 300 people, although when it opened its capacity was 500. (94) The local papers expressed concern that the new building might become a 'white elephant' even before it had opened. (95) Chancellor Hall opened in 1974 to capacity audiences but four years later it was already in trouble after stewards walked out and a cashier resigned over working conditions. (96) The Hall had trouble attracting well known acts. It did however book some of the biggest 'punk' acts including the Clash and Siouxie and the Banshees. The former caused problems when there was a violent skirmish between punk rockers and teddy boys. (97)

Chelmsford was quite a centre for 'punk' activity. Seven months after the trouble outside the Chancellor Hall there was a serious clash between punks and skinheads in Anchor Street, where the latter were squatting in two houses. Grayson Perry, mentioned earlier in this chapter, said "Chelmsford was quite a hot bed of punk." "I ripped the sleeves of a grey school shirt then stencilled HATE all over it with a home-made stencil." "I bought plastic sandals wore the school blazer and put Vaseline in my hair." "My piece de resistance was from a bag of horse tacks." "It was a huge dog collar with whopping great horse studs, very brutal looking that I wore round my neck very proudly." The great metal chain links used to smack him in the teeth when he danced. Bob Geldof hauled him onto the stage when the Boomtown Rats played the Chancellor Hall. (98) Chelmsford's thriving punk scene resulted in several well known local bands such as Anorexia and Nasty Habits. Besides the Chancellor Hall, gigs were played at 'Deejay's', the only nightclub at the time, the Odeon, the Y club and the Prince of Orange (now O'Connors).

A punk festival at the Chelmsford City football ground was a disaster when only 1,500 fans turned up after the Clash didn't materialise, the Jam pulled out a week before the event and the Damned refused to play after it became obvious they weren't going to get paid. Bands that did turn up included Eddie and the Hot Rods, Chelsea, Slaughter and the Dogs and the reggae band Aswad. John Peel was the compere and he had bottles and cans thrown at him for his trouble. "Fans pelt the stage as punk show flops" reported the Weekly News (99) The promoter, Bob Mardon, lost £14,000. It was a sorry end to what was the first, and probably the only punk festival.

In the 1990s the Y Club at the Y.M.C.A. put on a number of top Indie acts before they became well known including the Cranberries, Radiohead and Teenage Fanclub. Liam Howlett, later in the Prodigy, worked at the club. At the same time the Army and Navy pub became the "bastion of grunge, metal and indie pop bands". (100) In 1994 Oasis played the venue when they were starting to get attention from the national press. Trevor Holds, a local record shop owner, said "It was a brilliant gig just before they released anything. It was the final date of the tour and the last chance to see them in a venue of that size". In 2002 a letter in the Weekly News said "Where are young music lovers to go now the Army and Navy has closed for refurbishment?" (101) After being used for mainstream entertainment the Army and Navy was finally demolished in 2007.

Hylands had had live music events before the V festival. Back in 1970 a proposed pop concert on the estate caused much local alarm. The council decided however that it was not a suitable venue. (102) In 1989 the Chelmsford Spectacular started after the success of the centenary celebrations in Hylands Park. They had been organised by the council, the Friends of the Samaritans and BBC Essex. (103) The 1989 event lost money because of rain but put on a wide variety of music events including the D'Oyly Carte Opera and the Joe Loss Orchestra. (104) Chelmsford's Spectacular in 1990 was however a great success with 40,000 people in the park. Fifteen thousand people saw a collection of 60s groups. The 1993 Spectacular saw 65,000 people watch a line up that included Take That. (105) In 1994 it was voted the best organised outdoor event in Britain. (106) During 1995 however the event was called off because of the risk of a £70,000 loss. (107) The Spectacular was revived in 1996 but it gained the lowest audience in four years and had to be bailed out with money received from the V festival. (108) It carried on until 2001 when the council felt it could no longer subsidize it. The Spectacular was revived again in 2003 but a big loss of £65,000 due to poor weather meant the end of the event. (109) August 2008 saw the holding of the world Scouting Jamboree in the park. Interestingly the event saw 11 children disappear, presumably to become asylum seekers. (110)

In August 1996 a large Rock Festival took place at Hylands with 70,000 attending the two days. (111) Richard Branson's Virgin group took control of what became a largely 'Brit. Pop' festival. (112) The original idea had come from the lead singer of Pulp, Jarvis Cocker. In 1997 100,000 attended and Branson said "We will keep coming back as long as the people of Chelmsford want us." (113) In the early years there were frequent complaints, chiefly about litter and traffic problems, but these have diminished in recent years. An early letter said "what is considered by everybody except Chelmsford Borough Council to be a public park looks like a refuse tip and in places smells like a sewage farm". (114) A tongue in cheek reply to this and other letters included "Young people should not be allowed to enjoy themselves. They should stay out of public places until they have learnt to dress in respectable clothing ('hush puppies' and beige slacks) and are proficient in the art of intolerance and bigotry, while remaining anonymous at all times." (115) The V festival continues to be commercially successful and it brings in much needed revenue for both the council and the city. Many critics maintain that it plays safe musically, sticking to tried and trusted stadium fillers, and bookers lack the imagination of those at Glastonbury. Headliners in 2012 included the Stone Roses, Noel Gallagher, the Killers, Snow Patrol and Tom Jones. In 2013 major acts included Beyonce, the Script, Jessie J, The Kings of Leon, the Stereophonics and Emeli Sande. The festival now shares its line up with a site at Stafford. Since 2006 a much smaller festival, Brownstock, has been established near South Woodham Ferrers. The audience for the first festival consisted of 100 friends of the organisers and featured ten straw bales, 2 BBQs and a trailer for a stage. Although it had grown by 2013 so that it featured well known headliners such as the Fratellis and Tom Odell, it still featured a great many unsigned bands.

For several decades it has been obvious that the county town, now a city, lacks the major entertainment venue it deserves. By 1978 the Chancellor Hall was only being used at a rate of 50% on Saturday nights. Even the Essex Musical Association found it too small for their festival. After being used as a dance centre in the 1990s, it was empty for a long period until it reopened in 2012 as a nightclub, Evoke, with occasional live performances.

The demand for an Arts Centre goes back four decades. Hylands was often suggested as a venue particularly by the Chelmsford Society. In 1978 a project involving an art gallery and a theatre at a new civic complex was proposed but there was a dispute whether money from the Cramphorn Trust Fund could be used. (116) A decade later there was a serious plan for a self financing Art Centre which came to nothing. In 1996 a £30 million millennium centre incorporating a 1,600 seat regional theatre, a new museum and an art gallery, a science and technology discovery centre, commercial cinemas and restaurants was put forward jointly by the County Council and the Borough Council. This scheme would have also included the Essex Record Office. (117) The refusal of lottery funding the following year meant that the scheme was 'dead in the water'. (118) A new Record Office was built as a separate building in Wharf Road which opened in 2000. It now has over 7 miles of documents as well as oral records. A successful Arts trail around the town which involved 70 artists has been running for four years. (119)

The Chelmsford Club still survives (see chapter 27); some would say a relic of a bygone age. In 2012, in an effort to revive its flagging fortunes, it asked ladies to join for the first time at an annual subscription of £395. They have to be invited by a current member and sponsored by two others. There was some opposition to the change. The Club is still at Staple Grove, on the corner of New London Road. (120)

The Essex Chronicle, which this book has used intensively as a major resource, has won a number of awards in recent years particularly as best newspaper in the East of England. It was originally launched from a shop in Chelmsford High Street in

1764; then it was printed at the back of the Royal Oak public house in Tindal Street. In 1820 it moved to 98 the High Street, the premises that were Jessops in the late 20th century. During 1892 extra premises were bought in Tindal Street. In 1964 the newspaper celebrated 200 years of continuous production. During 1967 Northcliffe Newspapers bought a new press for the paper. In 2002 its Westway presses closed and production moved to Gloucestershire. The paper is now printed in Broxbourne, Hertfordshire. During 2012 the paper's offices moved to the Hedgerows Business Park in Springfield. (121)

At a time when the new city is about to become an even bigger magnet for shoppers, it is very disappointing that Chelmsford is a good distance behind other Essex towns when it comes to the provision of large scale live entertainment, although a new scheme for a 1,500 seater concert venue as a part of a new revamped Riverside complex was mooted in 2013. Panic magazine, a local independent music magazine that has existed since 2005, continues however to highlight the large number of pubs and other small venues such as the Golden Fleece, the Bassment and Asylum that do put on live music. The Panic awards that have been held annually since 2008 give prizes for best local band, best local venue, and best local contribution to the local independent scene. To be fair to the city council it does sponsor and put on a variety of leisure and entertainment events. In 2013 the '3 foot festival' returned for the eighth time, catering for 12,800 pre-school children. The council also organises the Fling festival for adults held in Central Park. This mixes music with comedy, dance, circus and literature. As is the case in other Essex towns Chelmsford has seen a recent rise in the popularity of stand up comedy, with a regular Comedy Club operating at Chelmsford City Football Club.

1) Chelmsford Borough Council minutes 22 2 1950
2) C.B.C. minutes 23 5 1951
3) Essex Chronicle 2 2 1951
4) E.C. 26 9 1952
5) E.C. 29 5 1953 p.1
6) E.C. 5 6 1953 p.1
7) C.B.C. minutes 24 9 1952
8) C.B.C. minutes 20 5 1953
9) Essex Weekly News 9 7 1948 p.2
10) E.W.N. 6 7 1951 p.8

11) E.W.N. 27 10 1950 p.1
12) E.C. 20 3 1953
13) E.W.N. 17 3 1961 p.6
14) E.W.N. 16 8 1963 p.5
15) E.W.N. 27 11 1964 p.1
16) E.W.N. 12 7 1968 p.9
17) E.C. 1 7 1983 p.5
18) E.C. 13 11 1987 p.1
19) E.C. 5 7 1996 p.5
20) E.W.N. 17 4 1997 p.3
21) E.C. 30 4 1999 p.1
22) E.C. 6 8 1999
23) E.W.N. 18 5 2000 p.15
24) E.W.N. 17 5 1957 p.7
25) E.W.N. 31 10 1958 p.5
26) E.W.N. 24 6 1960 p.6
27) E.W.N. 4 11 1960 p.6
28) E.W.N. 1 12 1961 p.1
29) E.W.N. 10 5 1962 p.1
30) E.W.N. 29 11 1963 p.1
31) E.W.N. 20 8 1965
32) E.W.N. 1 11 1968 p.8
33) E.C. 1 11 1968
34) E.C. 26 4 1972 p.1
35) E.W.N. 27 6 1991 p.3
36) E.W.N. 23 3 1966 p.4
37) E.C. 19 4 1973 p.5
38) E.C. 15 5 1986 p.1
39) E.W.N. 2 5 1991 p.7
40) C.B.C. minutes 8 9 1988
41) E.W.N. 15 6 2006 p.1
42) E.C. 19 4 1974 p.3
43) E.C. 13 8 1999 p.7
44) Hylands Foreman p.96
45) Hylands Foreman p.100

46) E.C. 27 10 1972 p.6
47) E.C. 2 2 1973 p.3
48) E.W.N. 8 5 1975 p.9
49) E.W.N. 26 12 1975 p.1
50) E.W.N. 29 7 1976 p.1
51) E.W.N. 19 5 1977 p.1
52) E.C. 19 5 1978 p.4
53) E.W.N. 2 8 1979 p.3
54) E.C. 6 4 1979 p.5
55) E.C. 1 5 1981 p.3
56) E.C. 14 5 1982 p.1
57) E.W.N. 5 7 1984 p.1
58) E.C. 6 3 1984 p.5
59) E.W.N. 16 1 1986 p.1
60) E.W.N. 25 5 1988 p.7
61) E.W.N. 9 6 1988 p.1
62) E.C. 20 10 1988 p.1
63) E.W.N. 4 7 1991 p.1
64) E.C. 11 11 1994 p.1
65) E.W.N. 9 3 1995 p.12
66) E.W.N. 29 8 1996
67) E.W.N. 26 6 1998 p.1
68) E.W.N. 4 3 1999 p.8
69) E.W.N. 5 4 2001 p.3
70) E.W.N. 12 12 2992 p.11
71) E.W.N. 27 3 2003 p.1
72) Grimwood p.18
73) E.C. 23 5 2003 Times past Cinemas John Marriage
74) Grimwood p.19
75) E.C. 6 3 1987 p.1
76) E.C. 8 10 1993 p.3
77) E.C. 28 3 1980 p.2
78) E.C. 22 7 1983 p.1
79) E.C. 18 3 1985 p.1
80) E.W.N. 1 5 1959 p.5

81) E.W.N. 21 2 1964 p.1
82) E.W.N. 31 1 1969 p.9
83) E.W.N. 5 7 1973
84) E.W.N. 22 5 1975 p.1
85) E.W.N. 6 4 1978
86) E.W.N. 22 2 1990 p.1
87) Chester Novello. Com – Anthony Burton 2006
88) C. Museums Chelmsford people records
89) C. Museums Oral history records – J. Alliston
90) C. Museums Oral history records – Clive Beattie
91) C. Museums Oral history records –Peter Searles
92) E.W.N. 1 7 1955 p.1
93) C. Museum - Musicians
94) E.W.N. 31 5 1968 p.1
95) E.C. 5 2 1971 p.9
96) E.W.N. 18 11 1976 p.32
97) E.W.N. 9 11 1979
98) C. Museums records Music memories
99) E.W.N. 22 9 1977
100) E.C. 28 1 2005 p.3
101) E.W.N. 24 10 2002
102) E.W.N. 3 4 1970
103) E.C. 26 8 1988 p.1
104) E.C. 1 9 1989 p.1
105) E.C. 21 5 1993 p.1
106) E.C. 28 1 1994 p.1
107) E.C. 17 2 1995 p.1
108) E.C. 8 10 1996
109) E.W.N. 20 11 2003 p.1
110) E.C. 8 8 2007
111) E.C. 10 5 1996 p.1
112) E.C. 23 8 1996 p.1
113) E.C. 22 8 1997 p.1
114) E.C. 28 9 1998
115) E.C. 24 11 1998

116) E.C. 1 9 1978 p.1
117) E.C. 1 9 1978 p.1
118) E.C. 20 6 1997 p.3
119) E.C. 15 9 2011 p.3
120) E.C. 3 5 2012 p.15
121) E.C. 26 7 2012 p.2

Conclusion

In 2014, with the one remaining industrial site, Marconi at New Street being developed little remains, apart from the excellent display at the museum and e2v, to remind people of the city's great industrial heritage. In terms of the city itself it is possible to think of a parallel Chelmsford universe, where quaint yards and courts lie off a Tindal Street, with its restored old buildings, which itself is matched by a Moulsham Street with more buildings of Tudor origin and the city is not cut into two by an inner ring road. It would be good to think that the new city will give due attention to the need to develop itself as a cultural centre as well as the endless desire for more shops and houses.

Index

1

15 to 1 145
1834 Poor Law Amendment Act 349
1866 Industrial Schools Act 372
1870 Forster Education Act 353, 366
1876 Health Act 329
1881 Census 191
1888 Electric Lighting Act 69
1890 Housing of the Working Classes Act 156
1891 Education Act 368
1899 Small Dwellings Act 331
1902 Education Act 370
1904 Wireless Telegraphy Act 86
1907 Probation of Offenders Act 439
1918 Fisher Education Act 376
1918 Representation of the People Act 242
1919 Addison Housing Act 334
1924 Wheatley Act 335
1935 Ribbon Development Act 207
1944 Butler Education Act 383
1944 Education Act 389
1952 Development Plan for Essex 213
1970 Elementary Schools Act 367
1976 Education Act 396
1988 Education Act 398
1998 School Standards and Framework Act 399

2

2MT Writtle 93, 94

3

3 foot festival 548
3D map of the galaxy 147
315th Troop Carrier Group 468
3rd Special Reserve Battalion 279

4

4 Sevens patent 88
40 thieves 260
4th and 5th standards 373

5

561st Engineer Aviation Battalion of the U.S. army 467
5th Territorial Force 279

A

A12 176, 178, 179, 181
A12 bypass 181
AA batteries 463
AA defences 466, 476
AA guns 131
AA rocket batteries 463
Abberton reservoir 325
Abbey Well 141
Able bodied pauper 349, 356
Able bodied paupers 356
Abolition of the Poor Law 361
Abortion Bill 263
Abyssinia 457
AD712 108
Adam Hewitt 54
Admiral H.W. Grant 105
Admiral Park 200

Admiral Rous Inn, Galleywood 435
Admirals Park 236, 298, 317, 320, 457, 491, 507, 534
Admirals Park water tower 320
Adrian Boult 517
Adult Education Learning Centre 400
Adulteration of food 152
Adulteration of milk 432
A.E. Dean and Marconi Wireless and Telegraph Co. Ltd 304
A.E.Hodge 259
A.E.I. 112
AEI Valve 144
Aeroplane week 283
A.E.U. 159, 160
AEU 145
A.Garton 134
Age Concern 534
A.G.E. Morton 196
Agreements Book 12
Agricultural College 24, 524
Agricultural College at Writtle 262
Agricultural depression 5, 7
Agricultural Institute 17
Agricultural labourer 12
Agricultural Labourers Union 15
Agricultural Show 69
Airborne Telephony Research Department 91
Air Chief Marshall Harris 256
Airey houses 339, 342
Airships 287
Air Support Unit 449
Airy Neave 411
A.J. Balfour 494
Alan Bond 141
Alan Cherry 502
Alan Stephens 396
Alastair Cook 506
Albert Place 195
Albert William Hawkes 44
Albright 70, 73
Alderman Richardson 340
Alderman Smith 461
Alderney 57
A level students 395
Alexandra Palace 97, 109, 110
Alf Quilter 462
Alfred Bennett Bamford 517
Alfred Conybeare 205

Alfred Green 13
Alfred Harmsworth, Lord Northcliffe 90
Alfred Morton 37
Algar 350
All England title 507
Alliance 267, 268, 269
Allied Breweries 140
Allied-Lyons 141
Allotments 468
All Saints Church at Springfield 422
All Saints Church at Writtle 412
All Saints Church in Chelmsford 412
All Saints Church in Springfield 411
All weather track 500
Altona Brass Band 472
Alum Bay 85
Aluminium houses 337
Alyn and Deeside (North Wales) 268
Amalgamated Society of Engineers 75, 155
Amalgamated Society of House Decorators and Painters 156
Amateurs versus Professionals 489
Amber 543
Ambulance train 287
Ame 141
American Centurion tank 132
American Football 510
American Red Cross 472
Amphetamines 444
Amy Johnson charity fund 369
Amy Johnson funds 367
Anchor Inn 205
Anchor Ironworks 66
Anchor Street 65, 67, 70, 200, 545
Anchor Works 38, 40, 296, 491
Andover 349
Andrew Carnegie 521
Andrew Clark 13, 127, 281, 415
Andrew Southgate 31
Andrew Strauss 506
Aneurin Bevan 258
Angel yard 199
Anglia Higher Education College 400
Anglia Polytechnic 135, 400
Anglia Ruskin 217
Anglia Ruskin Medical Technology campus 149
Anglia Ruskin Phantoms 510
Anglia Ruskin University 115, 149, 400
Anglicans 366

Anglo American 171
Anglo American Company 320
Animal feed mill 21
Animal feeds 17
Animals 544
Anne Knight 236, 422
Ann Knight building 217
Anorexia 545
Antarctic 284
Anthony Eden 462
Anthony Marwood 537
Anti Aircraft Searchlight Company 456
Anti-compulsory vaccination league 297
Anti German riots 280
Anti tank trench 466
A. Piska 338
A.P. Lundberg 66
Appeal Court 448
Apprentices 55, 153
Apprenticeship scheme 68
Approved School 382
Aqua Libra 141
Arbour Lane 89, 98, 111, 115, 153, 205, 434
Archbishop of Canterbury 289
Archdeacon Mildmay 409
Archer's Suet factory 476
Architectural Heritage Year 539
Arc lamps 201
Arcon 337
Arc Works 64, 66, 69, 77, 228, 376, 518
Arc Works Club 493
Arc Works Sick Benefit Society 518
Arc Works Smokers concert 518
Argus 4 147
Armistice Day 378
Armstrong Gibbs 517, 542
Armstrong Whitworth Apollo 108
Armstrong Whitworth Company 75
Army and Navy 176, 178, 179, 180, 212, 545
Army and Navy roundabout 178, 179, 495
Arnold Weinstock 112
A.R.P. 456, 457, 458, 459, 463, 470, 474, 478
ARP 442
A.R.P. Hickley 154, 157, 240, 245, 351, 376, 526
A.R.P. messenger 462
Arsenal 492
Arthur Adey 501
Arthur Brittain 45
Arthur Brown 544

Arthur Burrows 90, 91, 93
Arthur Lunney 156, 233, 331, 355
Arthur Prior 31, 230, 412, 523
Arthur Rowe 500
Artificial pitch 507
Artillery pillboxes 466
Arts Centre 539, 547
Arts trail 547
Ascension Islands 112
A.S. Duffield 234, 353
Ashton 261
Asparagus 21
Asquith 243
Assize Court 428, 445
A.S.T.M.S. 163
Aston Villa 492
Aswad 545
Asylum 548
Athenian League. 491
Athletics 485
Athletics club 487
Athol steel houses 334
Atmel 147
Atmel Corporation 147
Atomic bomb 416
Attendance committee 368
Attendance officer 368
Austin Seven 200
Australia 71
Australians 489, 504
Austria 408, 457
Austrians 286
Automatic vending machines 140
Automobile Show 39
Auxiliary Fire Brigade 465
Auxiliary firemen 459
Auxiliary Fire Service 457, 464
Auxiliary Units 100
Aylmer Maude 41, 240

B

Baby bulge 395
Babycham 140
Bachelors Ball 516
Baddow 299, 358
Baddow laboratories 111
Baddow Road 170, 175, 176, 194, 199, 319, 372, 408, 477, 495, 518

Baddows 7
Badger Line 183
Badminton 497
Badminton courts 509
BAE 116
Baedeker raids 456
BAE Insyte (Integrated System Technologies) 116
BAE Systems 147
Baker Smith 257
Balfour Education Act of 1902 366
Ball and roller bearings 120
Ball bearing mountain 135
Ball journal bearing 123
Bancroft 379
Bancroft wing 380
Band of Hope 373, 378, 406
Banking 47
Baptist chapel 422
Baptists 419
Barbara Castle 163
Barbican 121
Barclays 48, 197
Barclays Bank 13, 197
Barclay, Tritton, Bevan and Co 13
Barking 413
Barley, 7
Barnes Mill 336
Barn Murder trial 445
Barr 142
Barrack Square 203
Barrage balloons 467
Barrett cousins 51
Barretts 156
Basildon 111, 165, 216, 323, 392, 438, 444, 538
Basque Children's Committee 245
Bass 141
Bass group 141
Bassment 548
Battlebridge 518
Battle of Britain 473
Battle of Jutland 89
Bay Horse Inn 194
B.B.C. 100, 109
BBC 465
BBC Essex 546
BBC Radio Essex 541
Beadel 231, 493
Beatles 544
Beaulieu Park 183, 219, 401

Beaulieu Park. 343
Beaulieu Park Development 219
Beaullieu Park 502
Beccles 523
Bedales School 92
Bedford 456
Bedford School 506
Beeches Road 341
Beech Report 233, 318
Beedy 236
Beef 7
Beefsteak Club 197, 232
Beehive Lane 468, 488, 490
Bee keeping 10
Begging 354
Belgian refugees 283
Bellamy 202, 205, 460
Bellefield 195, 242, 284
Bell Hotel 198, 493
Bell Mead 518
Bell Meadow 515
Bell, Rettendon 477
Bellway homes 117
Benfleet 144
Benson and Hedges 504
Bent aerial 86
Bentall-Simplex of Scunthorpe 61
Berechurch Hall 67
Berkshire Territorial's 281
Bernard White 437
Bernard Wren 476
Bertie Upson 478
Bert Smith 40
Bert Yansch 544
Beryl Dean 410
Bet Allen 461
Bethnal Green 413
Beveridge 256
Beyonce 547
Bicknacre 304
Bill Bateman's Orchestra 543
Billericay 270, 382, 502
Billet 458
Billeting hostels 459
Billeting officer 459
Billeting Officer 470
Billets 333
Billiard 486, 496
Billington Craig 238

Bill Lambert 116
Bill Pigram 116
Bill Ward 78
Bill Wilson 470
Billy Walker 492
Bilton 32
Binacre 219, 394
Bird, Hawkes and Woodcock 31
Bird in Hand 33
Birmingham 71
B.I.S.F. 337
B.I.S.F. houses 341
Bishop Hall Mills 12
Bishop John Perry 411
Bishop John Trillo 410, 417
Bishop of Colchester 486
Bishop of Manchester 415
Bishop of St Albans 409, 412
Bishop of St Albans, Edgar Jacob 413
Bishop of Truro 415
Bishoprics bill 413
Bishopscourt 416, 417, 472
Bishops Hall 121, 205
Bishops Hall mill 11
Bishops Road 202
Bishop Watts Ditchfield 283, 409
Bishop Wilson 462, 472, 474
BL8 homes 343
Black boxes 108
Black Boy 519
Black Boy Inn 32, 156, 197
Black Boy public house 406
Blackfriars Place 194
Black market 468
Blackout 465
Blackshirt 246
Blacksmith 10
Blacksmiths 17
Blackwater estuary 175
Blackwater valley 6
Blondel electric lights 202
Bluebell 65
Blue plaque 135, 242
Blue Ramblers 543
Bluetongue disease 24
Blue trains 99
Bluewater 217
B. Mair 125
BMI (Black and ethnic minority) 210

Boarded Barns 205, 333, 334, 343, 460
Boarded Barns estate 154, 262, 322, 329, 341, 377, 408, 412, 419
Board of Education 377
Board of Guardians 158, 234
Board of Health 47, 68, 226, 227, 228, 234, 295, 317, 319, 320, 329, 518
Board of Trade 70
Board school 369
Boards of Guardians 361
Bob Battey 394
Bob Cannon 525
Bob Geldof 545
Bob Mardon 545
Bob's Full House 145
Bodkin 229, 495, 520
Boer War 74, 85, 89, 93, 95, 204, 232, 277, 286, 375, 497
Bofors guns 476
Bolinbroke and Wenley 220
Bolingbroke 204, 217, 227, 229, 258, 486
Bomb armer 131
Bond 204
Bonds 442, 457
Boneshaker 485
Boomtown Rats 545
Bootle constituency 245
Boreham 19, 154, 181, 193, 219, 257, 264, 298, 329, 335, 338, 343, 350, 392, 449, 488, 500, 508, 542
Boreham airfield 22, 442, 449, 467, 508
Boreham bypass 180, 219
Boreham Conservation Society 219
Boreham House 18, 219
Boreham Red Cross Club 468
Boreham School 338
Borough Council 176
Borough Engineer 161, 458
Boswells School 393, 394, 399
Boundaries Commission 267
Boundary Commissioners 230
Bournemouth 375, 495
Bouverie Road 204
Bowers farm 174
Bowling 492
Boxing 382, 485, 496, 527, 533
Boy's home 359
Bradford Street 202, 372
Bradford Street site 377

Bradman 506
Bradwell 340, 410
Braemar Avenue 204
Braintree 181, 467, 502
Braintree Town 502
Brentwood 17, 489, 501, 544
Brentwood and Ongar 270
Brentwood Catholic Cathedral 417
Brentwood College 399
Brewery House 205
Brew house 14
Brian Clapham 261
Brian Johnston 506
Brian Kemp 461
Brian Taylor 504
Brierly Place 16, 195, 205, 249, 474, 493
Brightlingsea 174
Bright Sparks 537
Bristol Rovers 261
Britain's first spaceship 110
Britannia Soft Drinks 141
British 6th Airborne Division 468
British Admiralty 89
British Aerospace 115
British Broadcasting Company 93
British Broadcasting Corporation 93
British Coal 57
British Electricity Authority 56
British Electric Transformer Company 76
British Expeditionary Force 89
British Grand Prix of Motor Cycle racing 508
British Horse Racing Board 509
British Iron and Steel Federation (B.I.S.F.) 336
British Legion 457, 478
British Museum 276
British Rail 78, 182
British Red Cross 457
British Restaurant 470
British Restaurants 469, 479
British School 194, 370
British Schools 366, 367, 368
British Steel 57
British Union of Fascists 246
British Vitamin Products 139
British Westinghouse 73
Brit. Pop 546
Brittain Pash 196, 198
Brittons Hall 11
Britvic 48, 138, 139, 140, 141, 198

Britvic 55 140
Britvic Corona 141
Britvic Soft Drinks Limited 141
Brockley Road, Springfield 320
Brompton Hospital 148
Brook End 325
Brook End sewage farm 317
Brookes Crompton 79
Brooklands 508
Brooklands hostel 111
Brooklands house 418
Broomfield 7, 11, 51, 52, 98, 172, 174, 177, 193, 235, 247, 318, 321, 343, 350, 392, 393, 442
Broomfield Court 61
Broomfield hospital 308, 309, 310
Broomfield Hospital 306
Broomfield Ironworks 52, 200
Broomfield Road 53, 141, 161, 180, 190, 200, 374, 379, 395, 488, 496
Broomfield School 394
Broomfield Secondary Modern School 397
Broomfield Secondary School 392
Broomfield Y.M.C.A. Ballet Company 542
Brown and Son 34, 175, 182, 205
Brown and Son Limited 36, 181, 322
Brown Bayley 133
Browning automatic rifles 463
Browning Avenue 343
Browning's farm 52
Brownstock 547
Brunel University 147
Brush Electric Co 68
Bucket of Blood 467
Buffy Saint Marie 544
Burgess Well 317
Burgin generator 66
Burnham pay scales 377
Bus station 184, 216
Butler Act 390, 395, 397
Butler Education Act 390
Butter 7, 468
Buttsbury 350
Buxton 297
Bypass 173, 177, 178, 179, 180
Byrne Brothers 60
Byrne Investment Management 60

C

Cable and Wireless 105
Cable and Wireless Limited 94, 105
Cadbury 383
Cadbury Science block 399
Caesaromagus 220
C.A. James 526
Calcutta 74
Californian 88
Callender's Cables and Construction Co. Limited 76
Camberwell Green 41
Cambrai 279
Cambridge 458, 459, 501
Cambridge University extension classes 379
Cambridge University Lectures 521
Camille Holland 436
Campbell's Thunderbolt 127
Can 31, 169, 177, 180, 212
Canada 372, 436
Canada Dry Rawlings 141
Canadians 284
Canberra 108
Cancer 360
Cancer cases 298
Cancer treatment 147
C. and E. Martin 377
Cann Hall School 458
Cannons restaurant 44, 477
Canteen 131
Captain and Mrs Pollard 353
Captain Brewster 407
Captain Drummond 41
Captain H.J. Round 244
Captain Peter Eckersley 92
Captain Showers 431, 440
Captain Wenley 41
Cardiff 492
Cardinal Bourne 418
Cardwell reforms 277
Carne Rasch 231, 408, 457, 519
Carnival 258, 527, 532, 534
Carnival Committee 302
Carpenters Arms 496
Carrots 21
C.A.R.S.C. 461
Casino 533
Castlemain Tooley 141

Casuals 354, 355
Cater's supermarket 203
Cathedral 205, 289, 418, 464, 542
Cathedral Festival 532, 542
Cathedral roof 464
Catholic Church 418
Catholic Radcliffe College, Leicester 262
Catholic School 368, 377
Cattle 9
Cattle drovers 22
Cavity magnetron 96, 112
C. Cockerell 108
C. Conybeare 240
CCTV cameras 448
CDD sensors 147
C.D. Rackman 242
Cecil McCormack 501
Celery 21
Cemetery 300
Central Criminal Court 432
Central Essex Town Planning Scheme 206
Central Park 176, 204, 443, 444, 490, 492, 515, 533, 548
Cerebro-meningitis 282
C.E. Ridley 229, 300
Chain Home Stations 96
Chairman of the Royal Art Commission 265
Champ 197
Champagne sales 331
Champions estate 331
Chancellor 227, 228, 296, 301, 317, 320, 331, 352, 367, 368, 379, 411, 520, 522
Chancellor Hall 544, 547
Chancellor of the Duchy of Lancaster 264
Chancel screen 409
Channels golf club 510
Chantry farm 19
Chaplain 429
Chapman 140
Charity Commissioners 367, 374, 395, 411
Charity Organisation Society 350
Charity school 367
Charity School Commissioners 374
Charles and Geoffrey Barrett 121
Charles Fremd 438
Charles Gepp 437
Charles Hawkes 44
Charles 'Korty' Kortwright 488
Charles Nicholson 409

Charles Pertwee 9
Charles Russell 34
Charles Sales 434
Charles Samuel Franklin 95
Charles Wells 31
Charlie Hurst 503
Charlie Kray 446
Charlie Osborne 78
Charter 227
Chartist movement 160, 236
Chateau Chelmsford 24
C.H. Blacker 247
Cheetah engine 130
Chelma Five 543
Chelmer 11, 31, 168, 177, 180, 182, 321, 322, 466
Chelmer and Blackwater 182
Chelmer and Blackwater canal 11
Chelmer and Blackwater Navigation 31, 34, 45, 46
Chelmer Cycling Club 486
Chelmer Institute 400
Chelmer Institute of Further Education 399
Chelmer Mill 12, 21
Chelmer Park 488, 507
Chelmerton Avenue, Great Baddow 478
Chelmer valley 7
Chelmer Valley 181
Chelmer Valley High School 397, 398, 399
Chelmer Valley Route 179
Chelmer Village 325, 342
Chelmsford Adult School 280
Chelmsford Against the Poll Tax 269
Chelmsford Air Raid Shelter Committee 460
Chelmsford Amateur and Operatic Society 526
Chelmsford Amateur Operatic and Dramatic Society 535
Chelmsford and Dengie Savings Bank 439
Chelmsford and District Flying Club 174
Chelmsford and District Liberal Association 230
Chelmsford and District Trades Union Council 156
Chelmsford and Essex 304, 306, 308
Chelmsford and Essex Hospital 54, 128, 195, 284, 300, 527
Chelmsford and Essex Museum 182, 522, 536
Chelmsford and West Essex Infirmary 299
Chelmsford and West Essex Liberal Association 230

Chelmsford Area Planning Group 211
Chelmsford Assize 436, 437
Chelmsford Assize Court 434
Chelmsford Athletics Club 487, 508
Chelmsford Auto Club 508
Chelmsford Ballet Company 542
Chelmsford Bank 197
Chelmsford Bankruptcy Court 6
Chelmsford Beef Steak Club 519
Chelmsford blitz 466
Chelmsford Borough Council 178, 218, 221, 236, 339
Chelmsford Borough Lawn Tennis Club 493
Chelmsford Bowling Club 493
Chelmsford Business Park 149
Chelmsford Carnival 527
Chelmsford Cathedral 414, 464
Chelmsford Cemetery 196
Chelmsford Charity School 439
Chelmsford Cherokees 510
Chelmsford Chieftains 510
Chelmsford Cissies 537
Chelmsford Citizens Air Raid Committee 154
Chelmsford City 57, 104, 485, 492, 500, 545
Chelmsford City 1980 502
Chelmsford City F.C. 511
Chelmsford City Ladies team 503
Chelmsford Club 195, 488, 519, 547
Chelmsford Coal Club 152
Chelmsford College 193, 399
Chelmsford Communist party 246
Chelmsford Company 195, 211
Chelmsford Co-operative Party 154
Chelmsford County High School for Girls 241, 517
Chelmsford Cricket Club 488, 507
Chelmsford cricket week 485
Chelmsford Crown Court 448
Chelmsford Discussion Society 237
Chelmsford Education Committee 370, 384, 401
Chelmsford Electric Lighting Company 70
Chelmsford Empire and Hippodrome Company Limited 526
Chelmsford Environment Partnership 221
Chelmsford Excavation Committee 220
Chelmsford F.C. 491
Chelmsford Festival 418
Chelmsford Football Club 491
Chelmsford Gas Company 46, 234

Chelmsford Golf Club 489, 493, 510
Chelmsford Group Hospital Managing Committee 307
Chelmsford guardians 355
Chelmsford guardians committee 361
Chelmsford Gymnasium 497
Chelmsford High Street 547
Chelmsford Hockey Club 495
Chelmsfordian magazine 375
Chelmsford Ladies Football team 503
Chelmsford Ladies Hockey Club 507
Chelmsford Lawn Tennis Club 493
Chelmsford Lighting Company 71
Chelmsford Magistrates Court 449
Chelmsford Museum 521
Chelmsford mystery 433
Chelmsford Philosophical Society 193
Chelmsford Picture House 525
Chelmsford Poor Law Guardians 54
Chelmsford Poor Law Union 158, 349, 350
Chelmsford Poor Law Union guardians 6
Chelmsford prison 191, 434, 436, 444
Chelmsford Quarter Sessions 432
Chelmsford Race Company 489
Chelmsford Railway Clerk Association 157
Chelmsford railway station 299
Chelmsford R.D.C. 206
Chelmsford Red Cross hospital 283
Chelmsford Rugby Club 495
Chelmsford Rural District 210
Chelmsford Rural District Council 54
Chelmsford Rural Sanitary Authority 170
Chelmsford's attendance committee 368
Chelmsford's blitz 477
Chelmsford's S.D.L.P. 269
Chelmsford's Food Control Committee 289
Chelmsford Society 183, 214, 216, 539
Chelmsford Society of Carpenters 155
Chelmsford Spectacular 546
Chelmsford Sports Club 507
Chelmsford Star Co-operative 151, 152, 194, 284
Chelmsford Star Co-operative Society 421
Chelmsford station 182
Chelmsford Swifts 491
Chelmsford Swimming Club 490
Chelmsford Technical College 399
Chelmsford Theatre Association 535
Chelmsford Town Band 228, 515
Chelmsford Traders Association 153
Chelmsford Trades Council 153, 157, 161, 162, 164
Chelmsford Union 192
Chelmsford United 491
Chelmsford War Weapons Week 471
Chelmsford Wastewater Treatment Works 325
Chelmsford water bill 322
Chelmsford Women At Work Committee (C.W.A.W.C.) 470
Chelmsford Women's Aid Group 342
Chelmsford Women's Liberal Association 54
Chelmsford Y.M.C.A. 237, 496
Chelmsford Y.M.C.A. cricket club 488
Chelsea 492, 545
Cherry Garden villas 196
Cherry Tree 475
Chestnutt Villas 195
Chicken pox 281
Chief Constable 171, 200, 430, 433, 434, 440
Chief Constable Francis Peel 440
Chief Constable John McHardy 430
Chief Constable John Unett 440
Chief Fire Officer 286, 465
Chignal 17, 270, 350, 392, 416
Chignall 336, 337
Chignalls 7, 288
Chignall Smealy 473
Chignals 296
Chignal St James 11, 422
Chigwell Row 437
Chindits 99
Chingford 286
Choat and Saltmarsh 296
Christ Church 421
Christine Hanbury 538
Christopher Kingsley 271
Christy 422, 488
Christy and Norris 58, 155
Christy and Norris' disintegrator 51
Christy and Norris hammer mill 21
Christy Brothers 56, 57, 59
Christy Brothers and Company Limited 54
Christy Brothers (Chelmsford) Limited 56
Christy Company 121
Christy disintegrator 53
Christy Electrical 60
Christy Group 148
Christy Hunt Engineering Ltd at Earls Colne 61
Christy News 60

Christy's 48, 495
Christy Sports and Social Club 60
Church Commissioners 416
Church Evangelical Council 417
Churchill 457
Church League for Women's Suffrage 241, 242
Church of England 395, 405, 406
Church of England School, Springfield 378
Church of England senior school 377
Church of Holy Name 419
Church of the Immaculate Conception 195
Cinder track 508
Cinema 532
Cinemas 515, 525
City and South London line 72
City Imperial Volunteers 277, 278
City Technology Colleges 398
Civic 536, 542
Civic Centre 183, 536, 538
Civic Society 213, 214
Civic Trust 214
Civil defence 473
Civil Defence organisation 479
Civil radar 144
C. Langton 246
Clapton Orient 261
Claremont villas 205
Claremont Villas 196, 418
Clarence Clamp 129
Clark 285
Clarkson 40, 41, 42
Clarkson and Capel Steam Car Syndicate 38
Clarkson Limited 39
Clash 544
Claude Graham White 524
Claude Seymour 502
Claydon 129
Cliff Bohannon 76
Clive Beattie 543
Clive Jenkins 163
Closing order 319
Clothing 468
Clover 11
C.N.D. 479
Coach and Horses Inn 202
Coal 31
Coates 45
Coates wharf 205
Coates' yard 34

Coca Cola 140
Cock Inn 203
Coco Cola 142
Coggleshall 45, 194
Coke 42
Colchester 8, 54, 68, 169, 172, 196, 209, 213, 232, 263, 285, 370, 397, 412, 437, 468, 490, 501, 515, 532
Colchester Gladiators 510
Colchester's Jumbo tower 317
Coldham Farm 436
Cold War 103, 107, 113, 114, 139, 144, 146
Coleman and Morton 37, 52, 68, 169, 195, 487, 496
Coleman and Morton Ironworks 152
Coletrane Union 544
Colleen Yaxley 462
Collins 202
Colonel Charles Kenneth Howard-Bury 244
Colonel Crompton 38, 155, 278, 433, 521
Colonel John Robert Macnamara 245
Colonel Macnamara 250, 255, 456
Colonel R.E.B. Crompton 64
Colonel Travers 279
Colonel Tufnell 13, 331
Colour television 110
Columbus Special School 401
Combines 21
Comedy Club 548
Commonwealth Party 255, 256, 258
Communist 460
Communist Party 247
Community Card 155
Community Health Council 308
Composers Guild of Great Britain 542
Compressors 131
Computer 108
Concilliation Bill 240
Conduit 172
Conduit 207
Conference South 503
Congregational Chapel 203, 420, 422
Congregational Church 155, 196, 419, 476
Conscientious objectors 280, 464, 471
Conscription 280, 285
Conservative 257, 341
Conservative Club 195, 496
Conservative government 393
Conservative party 260

Conservative Regional Association 230
Conservatives 234, 240, 261, 262, 267, 268, 269, 270, 271, 396
Conservative Working Men's Club 230
Control room at the Civic Centre 473
Conybeare 361
Cookery 371
Cooking appliances 71
Cooper 238
Co-operative Insurance Society 153
Co-operative Permanent Building Society 153
Co-operative Wholesale Society (CWS) 152
Copford 437
Copland 195, 229, 237
Corbusier 340
Corder 350
Corinthians 261
Corn Exchange 6, 9, 15, 46, 171, 198, 202, 203, 212, 227, 230, 231, 237, 242, 243, 244, 245, 246, 247, 260, 263, 283, 304, 406, 408, 419, 456, 472, 496, 514, 516, 518, 533, 542, 543, 544
Coronation 533
Coronation Ball 533
Coronation of 1953 533
Coronation Park 507, 533
Coroner 443
Coroner's service 196
Corporation Road 205, 390
Corsham 56
Cottage Place 139
Council Chamber 248
Council houses 334, 335, 336, 340, 343
Councillor A.E. Hodge 460
Councillor Bellamy 214, 458
Councillor Brown 161
Councillor Cramphorn 519
Councillor Gepp 408
Councillor Lander 217
Councillor Roberts 214
Councillor Wells 370
County Ball 516
County Championship 504
County Cinemas 527
County Council 170, 205, 233, 304, 375, 379, 392, 396, 471
County Council's Technical Instruction committee 376
County Court 449

County Football Association 486
County Ground 489, 504, 506
County Hall 202, 268, 459, 528
County High 399
County Hotel 179, 543
County Linen 45
County lunatic asylum 350, 359
County medical officer of health 316
County Police headquarters 200, 445
County Police station 200
Courtaulds 48
Courts of Assize 443
Coval Lane 174, 176, 179, 299, 475
Coventry 460
Crabb, Veley and Smee 34
Cramphorn 17, 495, 536, 538, 541
Cramphorn Road 202
Cramphorns 17
Cramphorn Trust Fund 547
Cranberries 545
Crane Court 199, 376, 419
Cricket 485
Cricketers 472
Crickitt and Co 47
Crickitt, Menish and Crickitt 47
Crimean War 65
Cristabel Pankhurst 237
Crompton 30, 39, 46, 48, 68, 71, 76, 77, 148, 158, 193, 221, 277, 334, 527, 543
Crompton and Co 228
Crompton Arc Lamp 79
Crompton Arc Works 202, 432
Crompton-Burghin engine 68
Crompton - Burgin 67
Crompton Company 155
Crompton Controls 79
Crompton dynamo 524
Crompton dynamos 69
Crompton factory 470, 475, 476
Crompton float 534
Crompton Greaves 79
Crompton lamp 67
Crompton Lighting 79
Crompton locomotive 72
Crompton Parkinson 64, 77, 78, 110, 144, 163
Crompton Parkinson canteen 469
Crompton's Arc Works 53, 200
Crompton's Arc Works club 487
Crompton sports ground 68

Crompton's searchlight 69
Crompton Street 205
Crompton's Wood Street ground 497
Cropping Book 11, 12
Cross Keys inn 194
Cross Keys public house 526
Crossrail 183
Crown Court 204, 445, 449
Crown Windley Bros Limited 47
Croxton 490
Croxtons Mill 21
Croxton Water Mill 12
Croydon 110
Croydon Review 226
Crystal Palace 143
Crystal Palace exhibition 67
Crystal Palace station 110
Crystals 99
C.S. Henry 231
Cucumber 8
Cultivation of Land Act of 1917 284
Cuthbert Brown 490
Cycling 485
Cyrano de Berjerac 93
Cyril Frost 171
Cyril Stapleton 543
Czechoslovakia 143

D

Dagenham Girl Pipers 527
Daily Mail 375, 508
Daily Mirror 257
Daimler 524
Dairying 7
Dalston 38, 86
Dame Beryl Grey 542
Dame Nellie Melba 90
Damned 545
Damp courses 319
Danbury 7, 24, 172, 181, 193, 270, 305, 324, 332, 350, 356, 377, 422, 475, 477, 479, 488, 517, 521, 543
Danbury Choral Society 517
Danbury church spire 69
Danbury common 318
Danbury Park 394
Daniel Gooch 284, 495, 523, 524
Darby 229

Darby Digger 14
Darby Land Digger Syndicate 14
Dardanelles 284
D.A.T.A 134
Dave Monk 541
Dave Moran 544
Daventry 96
David Bowie 268
David Ennals 307
David Hodge 524
David Houghton 10
David Johnson 45
David Rackham 420
D. Burrell 520
Debenham 199
Debenhams 180
Decca 145
Decontamination squads 457
Deejay's 545
De Havilland Comet 108
Delius 517
Dence 232, 235, 237, 238, 240
Dengie Hundred 230
Denise Wiffen 308
Dennis Wakeling 502
Denny Foreman 501
Dental CCDs 146
Department of the Environment 179, 539
Depression 357
Deptford 478
Derby 409
Derby Cables 76
Derby Cable Works 76
Derbyshire 66
Despard 238
Dewar trophy 42
D.F.C. 257
D.F.C. ribbon 257
Diarrhoea 301
Dig for Victory 20, 468
Dilly Miller 198
Diocesan Sustentation Fund 415
Diocese of Rochester 408
Diocese of St Albans 408
Diphtheria 296, 301, 376, 378
Discharged Prisoners Society 439, 440
Dispensary 296
Distressed Areas 161
District Valuer 335

Ditcham 90
Divorce Act 415
Dixon 232
D.J. Horner and E.C. Wells 148
Doctor George M. Brett 143
Doctor Gibson 197
Doctor Pepper 141
Doctor Thresh 301, 330
Dole 161
Dolphin Inn 198
Dolphin Yard 17
Doppler effect 108
Doppler radar 144
Dordogne 259
Dorothea and Madeleine Rook 240
Dorothea Rook 241
Dorothy Taylor 524
Dorset Avenue, Great Baddow 341
Dorset house 205
Dot com boom 115, 146
Double decker electric tram car 72
Dovedale 511
Dovedale House 122, 193, 397
Doyly Carte 518
Doyly Carte Opera 546
Dr Bodkin 368
Dr Crippen 88
Dr E. Eastwood 106
Dr F.S.G. Warman 415
Dr Grigsby 231
Drill Hall 285, 463, 497, 533
Dr John Thresh 297, 316
Dr Newton 298
Dr Reid 235
Dr Thresh 282, 298, 299, 302, 318, 321, 331
Drummond 238
Dublin 436
Duffield 228, 520
Duke of Edinburgh 116
Duke of Kent 411
Dukes Head Inn 197
Duke Street 44, 155, 170, 172, 173, 174, 180, 181, 198, 202, 203, 205, 228, 249, 296, 374, 419, 448, 465, 477, 489, 507
Dull and defective children 371
Dunmow 321, 390
Duplex houses 337
Durrant 228, 367, 522
Durrant's 32

Durrant's field 198
Dykes 46
Dymond 11

E

E2v 48, 109, 138, 146
Earthquake 169
Easiform houses 337
East and West Hanningfield 192
East Anglian Cup 491
East Anglian Division of Territorial's 281
East Anglian Institute of Agriculture 11
Eastbourne Company 39
East Dagenham 263
Easter hockey festivals 495
Eastern Area Milk Organisation 16
Eastern Commissioner 475
Eastern Counties 355
Eastern Counties Cinema Group 526
Eastern Counties Cinema Limited 526
Eastern Counties League 492
Eastern Gas Board 444
Eastern National 133, 165, 175, 183, 339
Eastern National Company 174
East Hanningfield 305, 325, 336, 350, 442, 488
East, West and South Hanningfield Voluntary Schools 391
Ebenezer 419
Ebenezer Chapel 195, 296, 419
Ebenezer Howard 333
E.C.C. 178, 180, 248, 261, 306, 308, 372, 376, 377, 390, 394, 395, 508, 538
E.C.C. Education Committee 370
Ecclesiastical Commissioners 414
E.C.C. Technical Instruction Committee 10
Echometer 98
Eckersley 83, 94
Economist 263
E. Corder 359
Eddie and the Hot Rods 545
Eddington 52, 199, 487
Eddingtons 14
Edisbury 257
Edison 71
Edmund Durrant 226, 519, 520, 521
Education committee 371
Education Committee 285, 382
Edward Bawden 537

Edward Craggs 281
Edward Gepp 412
Edward Heath 264
Edward Joliffe 370
Edward Pretyman 519
E.E. 112
EEV 100, 138, 163, 179
EEV Company 111
EEV valves 109
E.F.U. 21, 24
E.G. Brown 128
Eggs 302
E.H. Carter 295, 297
Eileen Hance 476
Electrical engineers 74
Electrical Engineers 277
Electrical Trades Union 75
Electric domestic appliances 71
Electric furnaces 72
Electricity 336
Electricity generation 64
Electric lighting 64, 248, 249
Electric oven 54
Electric trains 177
Electric welding equipment 72
Electrification 177
Elettra 95
Eley Metrology (Sales Services) Ltd 47
Elim 423
Elim Evangelical Church 417
Elizabeth Maconchy 542
Elm Road 196
E.M. Bancroft 241
Emeli Sande 547
E.M. Gardiner 240
E.M.I. 541
Emile Burghin 66
Emmy 110
Empire 541
Empire cinema 526
Empire day 378
Empire theatre 203
Employment Exchange 163
Employment Register 123
Endowed Schools Act of 1869 374
Engineers Standardisation Association 75
English Defence League 266, 423
English Electric 143
English Electric Canberra 108

English Electric Company 105
English Electric Valve Company 109, 143
English Electric Valves Limited 143
English Hockey League 507
English Premier Ice Hockey League 510
Enumerators 191
Epping 171
Eriksson 116
Ernest George Pretyman 234
Ernest J Miles 322
Ernest Ridley 374
Ernst Hoffmann 121, 193
Essex Agricultural Labourers Union 6
Essex Agricultural Show 9
Essex Agricultural Society 10, 22, 23, 54
Essex Air Ambulance 310, 508
Essex Amateur Championships 496
Essex and Suffolk Border League 491
Essex and Suffolk Water 325
Essex Archaeological Society 54
Essex Assize 443
Essex Beagles 520
Essex Chronicle 39, 42, 47, 52, 56, 57, 67, 85, 125, 155, 157, 168, 169, 172, 227, 230, 232, 236, 240, 249, 258, 259, 263, 276, 279, 283, 287, 305, 318, 355, 356, 369, 372, 374, 407, 408, 432, 433, 438, 464, 465, 471, 472, 477, 515, 521, 534, 538, 547
Essex County Council 10, 47, 168, 213, 216, 232, 321
Essex County Cricket Club 261, 485, 488, 500
Essex County Cycle Association 260
Essex County Cycling and Athletics Association 486
Essex County League 492
Essex County Medical Officer of Health 297
Essex County Police Force 430
Essex County Public Assistance Committee 361
Essex County Treasurer 439
Essex Cycling and Athletics Association 486
Essex dance band championship 472
Essex Diocese 405, 413
Essex Education Committee 394
Essex Farmers Union 15
Essex Field Club 54, 522
Essex Field Club Central Museum 522
Essex Gladiators 510
Essex Home School 381, 496

Essex Industrial School 205, 228
Essex Industrial School Band 527
Essex Institute of Higher Education 400
Essex Joint Standing Committee 432
Essex Lawn Tennis Association 493
Essex Mill 55
Essex Monday Club 266
Essex Musical Association 516, 547
Essex National Ice Hockey League 510
Essex Police 440, 443
Essex Police headquarters 449
Essex Police Helicopter Unit 508
Essex Police Training School 445
Essex Quarter Sessions 372
Essex Record Office 260, 434, 527, 547
Essex Regiment 228, 277, 279, 472
Essex Regimental Museum 536
Essex Regiment Way 181
Essex Review 330, 421, 520
Essex River Board 177
Essex Senior Cup 491
Essex Show 18, 22, 538
Essex Show ground 508
Essex Symphony Orchestra 542
Essex Territorial Association 249
Essex University 538
Essex Waterways Limited 182
Essex Wildlife Trust 182, 323
Essex Women's League 503
Eurofighter 147
European Court of Human Rights 448
Evacuees 382, 456
Everest 146
Excess profits tax 286
Execution 438
Executions 434, 436
Exeter 456
Exocet missiles 115

F

F.A. Cup 492
Faheem Ahtar 117
Fair 514, 518
Fairfield House 200, 289
Fairfield Lodge 523
Fairfield Road 535, 538
Falcon Private Bowling Club 493
Falklands 114

Falklands war 145
Family Fortunes 145
F. And A. Parkinson 75
Farleigh Hospice 297, 308
Farm labourer 8
Fascism 225, 246
Fascist 162
F.B. Wiseman 55
F.C. Floud 261
F.C. Langton 262
Fell Christy 51, 52, 55
Felsted 321
Fenton 316
Fertiliser industry 53
Festival of Britain in 1952 533
F.F. Christy 56, 84
F.G. Emmison 528
F.G. Kellaway 94
Field Club 522
Filtration tanks 316
Finchley Avenue 206, 336
Finmeccanica 116
Fire brigade 286, 287, 351, 461, 473
Fire fighters 145
Fire Guard Committee 464
Fire services 457
First aid 457
First aid training 459
Fitters 124
Fitzwilliam College, Cambridge 263
Flag days 283
Flat racing 489
Fleece, Duke Street 435
Fleetwood Mac 544
Fling festival 548
Floodlights 501
Flood prevention scheme 176
Flood Relief Committee 176
Florence Balgarnie 236
Florence Fenwick Miller 236
Florrie Kantner 241
Flour mills 53
Flushing cisterns 320
Flyover 179
F.M. transmitter 109
F.N. Sutherland 106
Food Control Committee 157, 468
Food kitchen 478
Food rationing 468

Foot and mouth 6
Football 485
Football League 501
Ford Motor Company 508
Fordson Estate Limited 220
Forli War cemetery 245
Foundation Schools 399
France 147
Frances Chancellor 241
Francis Burdett Ward 526
Francis Peel 440
Frank Christy 51, 53, 54, 153
Frank Cooper 397
Frank Fell Christy 60
Franklin 83
Franklin Beam Aerial 96
Frank Rogers 374
Frank Searle 40
Frank Soo 501
Frank Whitmore 198, 227, 381
Fratellis 547
Fred Chancellor 370
Frederic Chancellor 171, 195, 197, 220, 227, 234, 242, 284, 412, 521
Frederick Binyon 276
Frederick Greenwood 37
Frederick Wells 196, 493
Fred Foreham 438
Fred Marriage 159, 350, 361
Fred Munnion 283, 527
Fred Spalding 43, 173, 248, 249, 259, 441, 514, 518, 519, 527
Fred Spalding junior 191, 197, 486
Fred Spalding senior 14, 406
Fred Taylor 433
Fred Tyrell Smith 157
Fred Warner 378
Fred Willett 218
Freefonix 506
Freestons 198
Free Trade 244
Friars Infants 391
Friars Place 176, 194, 204
Friars Road 194
Friars School 370, 371, 382, 395
Friendly Societies 152
Friendly society 155
Friendly Society of Skinners 155
Friends Meeting house 200

Friends Meeting House 31, 280, 305
Friends of Marconi Nature Reserve 221
Friends of the Earth 479
Friends of the Samaritans 546
Friends Provident final at Lords 504
Friends School in Croydon 53
Frinton 85
Fruit culture 10
Fruit growing 18
Fryerning 206, 319, 322, 350
Fulham 492
Fund raising 471
Funnions 90, 283
Furbank 228
F.W. Warner 129

G

Gaia satellite 147
Galleywood 15, 24, 213, 247, 266, 299, 322, 354, 461, 489, 493
Galleywood racecourse 412
Galleywood Road 206
Gallipoli 279
Gaol 428
Gaol Lane 170, 434
Garden City 333
Garrod Baker 493
Gas 249, 336
Gas Act 46
Gas mains 335
Gas manufacture 45
Gas masks 457, 458
Gasometers 46
Gasworks 45
Gate porter 352
Gaza 279
G. Chalcroft 233
G.C.H.Q. 100
G.E.C. 115, 146, 164, 179
Geddes Axe 159, 334, 376, 379
General Booth 408
General Electric Company. (G.E.C.) 112
General Headquarters line (GHQ) 466
General Moller 244
General Strike 75
General Strike of 1926 160
General Union of Operative Carpenters and Joiners 156

Generator 71
Geoff Hurst 503
George 199
George Bernard Shaw 237
George Bolingbroke 199
George Brown 263, 463, 467, 473
George Clare 42
George E Clare 434
George Kemp 84
George Knowles 18
George Newton 438
George Patience 446
George Sargent 437
George Street 342
George Taylor 248, 519
George Young 153
Georgie Fame 544
Georgina Brackenbury 241
Gepp 229, 367
Gepp and Sons 434, 439, 445
Gepp's, the solicitors 45
G.E.R. 8, 125, 172, 287
German bomb 445
German prisoners of war 127, 286, 439
German rearmament 96
Germans 286
Germany 147
G.H. Coleman and A.R. Morton 38
G.H. Nelson 105
Gibcracks 339
Gibcracks, Danbury 338
Gilbey 362
Gillette Cup 504
Gillingham 501
Girls High School 393, 395, 398, 400
Gisbert Kapp 66
Gladys and Neville Harding 343
Glasgow Tradeston 245
Glaxo Smith Kline 399
Glebe Road 542
Global Marine Systems 149
Gloucester 132
Gloucestershire 548
G. Mansfield 17
G.M.S. 398
Goat Hall, Galleywood 343
Godfrey Isaacs 83, 86, 88, 94
Godfrey Mews 194, 221
Golden Fleece 199, 266, 507, 544, 548

Goldlay House 10
Goldlay Road 153, 201, 332, 477
Good Easter 7, 17, 332, 335, 350
Good Easter County School 391
Gordon Reece 262
Gotha aircraft 289
Government Wages Board 15
Governor 438
G.P. Gepp 440
Grace Bartlett 307
Grace Chapelow 240
Graham Bond 544
Graham Gooch 505
Graham Ramsey 310
Grammar school 296, 375, 379
Grammar school 10, 200, 228
Gramme generator 66
Gramme Generators 66
Grand Jury Room 230
Grandstand 489
Grantham 256
Grant maintained schools 398
Gray and Sons 31, 32
Gray and Sons Brewery 520
Gray and Sons (Chelmsford) Limited 32
Grays 492
Gray's brewery 216
Grayson Perry 537, 545
Great and Little Leighs 20
Great and Little Leighs Protection Society 216
Great Baddow 13, 24, 34, 44, 60, 99, 115, 143,
    172, 193, 210, 214, 216, 235, 247, 266,
    270, 321, 335, 340, 350, 392, 393, 394,
    406, 432, 461, 465, 469, 488
Great Baddow bypass 176
Great Baddow comprehensive 394
Great Baddow High School 399
Great Baddow Laboratories 114
Great Baddow parish council 179
Great Baddow Research Laboratory 98
Great Barfield artists 537
Great Crash 249
Great Eastern Railway 171, 234
Great Eastern Railways 7, 523
Great Ejection 419
Greater London 210
Greater London Plan 210, 212
Great Leighs 7, 13, 19, 23, 181, 192, 285, 286,
    289, 350, 422, 461, 462, 500, 508

Great Leighs School 391
Great Leighs village 280
Great Waltham 7, 124, 172, 192, 219, 235, 305, 331, 350, 370, 465, 479
Great War 333, 336, 358, 360
Great Western 40
Great Western Railway 523
Great Yarmouth 518
Green belt 214, 219
Green pea 8
Greens 21
Grenoble 147
Gresham Scientific Instruments 147
Greyhound Mead 490
Greyhound racing 490, 500
Griggs Yard 334
Grove 493
Grove Road 194
Grove Tennis Club 510
Guardian 221, 412
Guardians 350, 352, 354, 356, 358
Guglielmo Marconi 83
Guisely, Yorkshire 75
Gulf War 114
Gustav Binswanger 112
Guy Harlings 410, 411
G.W. Gepp 226
Gymnasiums 379

H

Hadow Report 377, 415
Haldane interior shelters 461
Haldane shelters 460
Half Moon Inn 197
Hall Street 83, 85, 86, 194, 297, 317
Halstead 23
Ham 468
Hamlet House 193
Hamlet Road 204, 238, 281
Hammond 489
Hanbury 524
Hanbury family 524
Hand grenades 463
H. and T. Godfrey 43, 194
Handy women' 305
Hanningfield 323, 333
Hanningfield Reservoir 325
Hanningfields 7, 270

Hansen's Disease 304, 308
Harley Jones 409
Harlow 392
Harold Hill 323
Harold Orrin 9, 44, 496
Harrison 202
Hartford End 34
Hatfield Peverel 240
Hawker Siddeley 78, 343, 541
Hawkes 44
Hawksley 42, 174
Hayward 407
H. Bailey 379
H.B. Norris 55
H. Byford's quadrille band 516
Health and fitness centre 509
Heart 542
Heather Case 45
Hedgerows Business Park 548
Heinkel 473
Heinkel bomber 472
Helena Downing 236
Helen Ogston 238
Helipad 310
Hemp Cottage 194
Henry Collings Wells 229, 296
Henry Curtis-Bennett 244
Henry Ford 220
Henry Ford Institute of Agriculture at Boreham 18
Henry George Ince 446
Henry Guy 193
Henry Marriage 21, 519
Henry Mildmay 374
Henry Newton 200
Henry Pierrepoint 437
Henry Road 476, 477
Henry Round 86
Henry Wilson 415
Herald's College 228
Herbert C. Capel 38
Herbert Marriage 356, 495
Herbert Pash 240, 486
Herbert Rolley 13
Herbert Samuel 88
Herbert Tritton 13
Hereford 501
Hertfordshire 542
Hertz 84

Heybridge 175
Heybridge Basin 31, 35
H. Fairbank 524
H.H. Gepp 445
HH Wills Physics Lab 143
High Chelmer 215
High Easter 350
Higher Education Committee 377
Higher School Certificate 379
High Farming 5
High Sherriff 439, 442, 445, 519
High Street 43, 44, 169, 170, 174, 175, 176, 180, 181, 197, 199, 204, 211, 212, 220, 228, 288, 316, 421, 422, 448
High Street site 218
Highways Board 169, 234
Highwood 181, 331
Hilda Grieve 316
Hillary Clinton 271
Himmler 478
Historical pageant 533
H.J. Round 89
H.J. Selwyn Ibbetson 229
H.M.I. 375
H.M. Inspector of Prisons report in 1990 447
H.M. Inspector of Prisons report in 1997 447
HMS Pinafore 518
Hoare banking family 219
Hoffmann 21, 30, 48, 76, 90, 125, 130, 148, 155, 158, 198, 202, 205, 277, 282, 284, 300, 330, 338, 358, 383, 442, 463, 465, 467, 470, 475, 476, 477, 488, 493, 496, 518, 543
Hoffmann Athletic and Social Club 496
Hoffmann Athletic ground 527
Hoffmann bearings 110
Hoffmann club 519
Hoffmann Company 12, 51, 98, 120, 156, 285, 332, 518
Hoffmann factory 476
Hoffmann Fire Brigade 476
Hoffmann Housing Association 337
Hoffmann Manufacturing Company 121
Hoffmann memorial 196
Hoffmann's cricket ground 489
Hoffmann works football team 488
Holst 517
Holy Trinity at South Woodham Ferrers 412
Home Guard 416, 456, 459, 462, 463

Homeless 342
Home Office 437, 460
Home of Radio 94
Home Rule 231
Home School 396
Homes Fit For Heroes 333
Horner and Wells 148
Horse and Groom public house 494
Horse racing 489, 508
Horses 7, 21
Horticulture 10
Hospital and Benevolent Fund 128
House Committee 300
House of Commons 236
House of Correction 428
House of Lords 225
Housing associations 343
Housing Commissioner 335
Housing of the Working Classes Act of 1890 330
Hove 73
Howard League for Prison Reform 446
Howe Green 331, 422, 502
Howe Street 13
H. Sergeant 280
H.T. Veley 296
Hubble space telescope 147
Hubert Ashton 23, 257, 258, 260
Huguenot 11
Hungarians 286
Hunting 520
Hurley 469
H. Whitehead and Partners 57
H.W. Thornton 287
Hydro electric power 56
Hylands 18, 22, 24, 31, 281, 284, 397, 399, 400, 495, 510, 515, 523, 524, 540, 546
Hylands comprehensive school 394
Hylands estate 523, 538
Hylands hospital 283
Hylands House 18, 412, 523, 533, 537
Hylands' stables 524
Hylands war plaque 540

I

Ian Puckey 541
Ilford 256
Ilford Workers' Association 256
Image orthicon 109, 143, 144

Imperial Airways 98
Imperial network of radio stations 105
Imperial stations 106
Incandescent filament lamp 66
Incendiary attacks 466
Incendiary bombs 476
Incendiary raid 464, 476
Incredible String Band 544
Independent Labour League 232
Independent Labour Party (I.L.P.) 225
Independent Television Authority 110
India 71
Indie scene 532
Indoor cricket school 505
Indoor pool 509
Industrial banks 73
Industrial Reorganisation Corporation 120, 133
Industrial school 372
Industrial School 284, 373, 381, 431, 518
Industrial School band 515
Infantry boxes 466
Infirmary 295, 296, 360
Influenza 289
Ingatestone 32, 176, 206, 235, 240, 321, 322, 324, 350, 465, 475, 488
Ingatestone Secondary School 394
Inland Waterways Association 182
Inner relief road 213
Inspector Hodges 442
Inspector of Nuisances 320
Inspector Peagram 431
Inspector Simmons 437
Instant X rays 146
Institute of Electrical Engineers 72
Institute of Mechanical Engineers 40
Inter-firm sports 485
International Radio Conference 87
Ionosphere Forecast System 147
Ipswich 68, 225, 232, 246, 335, 381, 456
I.R.A. 411
I.R.A. bomb 266
Iraq 60
Ireland 52, 542
Irishmen 459
Irn Bru 142
Iron foundry 55
Isaacs 94
Isolation hospital 299, 378

J

Jack Macnamara 457, 458
J. Alliston 543
James Alfred Norris 52
James Berry 437
James Christy 51
James Christy junior 54
James Dace 196
James Fenton 195, 196, 419
James Frost 406
James Lee 437
James Morley 437
James Norris 55
James Pertwee 237
James Ramsey 435
James Tomlinson 139
Jamieson 84
Japanese 133
Jarvis Cocker 546
J.A. Sparks 245
J.B. Priestley 256
Jean Hunwick 338
Jean Roberts 262, 390, 468, 470
J.E. Grant 214
Jehovah's Witnesses 471
Jeremy Bamber 448
Jessie Craigen 236
Jessie J 547
Jessops 548
J.F. Mayall 56
J. Furbank 228
J.Furbank 226
J.G. Bond 199, 519
J. Hirst 439
J.H.S. Coleman and G.E.M. Morton 38
J.H. Tritton 280
Jim Dyer 61
Jimi Hendrix 544
Jim Young 143, 144, 146
Joan Bliss 342
Joan Taylor 470
Joan Weston 542
Joe Brown 543
Joe Loss 543
Joe Loss Orchestra 546
John Bateman 434
John Bercow 271
John Bewley 65

John Copland Abstemers Army 406
John Copland Temperance Association 406
John Coward 501
John Davis 434
John Doubleday 505
John George Bond 204
John Gladwin 418
John Hall 194
John Hanbury 524
John Holmes 23, 508
John Janker 201
John Johnson 194
John Kempster 230
John Lewis 217
John Logie Baird 96
John Marriage 177, 210, 215, 458, 466
John Mayall 544
John Moses 267
John Ockelford Thompson 195, 240, 249, 421, 474, 493
John Payne 399
John Payne School 393
John Perry 417
John Player League 504
John Randall and Harry Boot 96
John Ridley 536
John Ruskin School of Art 400
John Saltmarsh 195
John Strachey 258
John Surtees 508
John Tiarks 416
John Tindall 266
John Trillo 417
John Waine 417
John Watts Ditchfield 413
John Wittingale 270
John Woods 36
Joint isolation hospital 298
Joint sewage farm 321
Jonathan Overend 541
Joseph Billio 213
Joseph Brittain Pash 9, 15, 372, 381
Joseph Ellis 205
Joseph Francis 317
Joseph Wilson Swan 66
Journal bearings 131
J.S. Brown 35, 519
J's hospice 308
J. Tomlinson 233

Judge Tindal 198
Judge Tindal Statue 202
Judo 496
Julie Felix 544
Juvenile crime 441
J.W. Davidson 41
J.W. Garton 132, 134
J.W. Trusler 338

K

Kaiser of Essex sport 485
K. Attwood 267
K.E.G.S. 240, 276, 374, 375, 379, 389, 393, 395, 396, 398, 399, 400, 462, 497, 520
K.E.G.S. old boys 495
Keith Fletcher 505
Kellaway 97
Kelly's Directory 139
Kelvedon 8, 374
Kelvedon Hatch 287
Kemble 519
Ken Kavanagh 508
Kennedy family 271
Kenneth Smith 470
Kenny Baker 543
Kensington Court Company 71
Kent Mustangs 510
Kerb Drill 442
Killers 546
Kimberley 277
King Edward the Sixth school 373
King George 524
King of Siam 68
Kings Arms 194
King School, Accra, Ghana 268
Kings College 38
Kings College London 263
Kings Cross station 67
Kings Head 197, 321, 486
Kings Head Meadow 174, 176, 180, 203, 205, 217, 316, 322, 490, 503, 507, 518, 534
Kings of Leon 547
Kings Road 154, 205, 339, 503
Kings Road School 94, 377
Kings Road Store 155
King's Royal Rifle Corps 244
Kingsway Housing Association 337, 341
Klystron 143, 144, 146

L

L3 Vision 147
L32 288
L33 288
Labouchere 540
Labour 259, 260, 261, 262, 264, 266, 270, 337
Labour council 337
Labour Exchanges 371
Labour government 394, 399
Labour Party 257, 258, 261, 267
Labour Party League of Youth 256
Labour Test 349
Ladies Sette of the Odde Volumes 520
Lady Cramphorn 520
Lady Gooch 284, 524
Lady Lane 194, 204, 206, 316, 329, 332, 377, 477
Lady Rayleigh 240, 241, 299
Lady Sutherland 542
Lake District 517
La Mooche 544
Lancashire 503
Lancaster bomber 130
Lancaster House, Mildmay Road 466
Land Army girls 18
Langford treatment works 325
Langford works 324
Langley 219
Laurel Grove house 195
Lawrence Binyon 276
Leader of the House of Commons 264
League of Friends 534
League of Nations 456
Learning difficulties 371
Le Cateau 279
Lee brothers 44
Leeds 68
Leeds Corporation 68
Leez Priory 220
Legg Street 199
Legg Yard 199
Leicester 456
Leighs 7, 19
Le Mans 24 hour race 127
Len Appleton 463
Leo Abse's Divorce Bill 263
Leonard Fell Christy 53, 54
Lesley Plummer 261
Leslie Leaver 213

Less eligibility 349
Les Sparrow 14
Leyton 489
Leytonstone 438
L.G.B. 298, 332, 333, 353, 354, 357, 359, 361
Liam Howlett 545
Liberal 262, 268
Liberal Democrats 269, 270
Liberals 235, 266, 267
Lieutenant-Colonel Sir Vivian Leonard Henderson 244
Lieutenant Colonel Stanley H. Lomax 467
Lime 31
Limerick 231
Link House farm, West Hanningfield 496
Lion and the Lamb 543
Lionmede 457
Liptonice 141
Liptons 204, 362
Little Baddow 14, 331, 332, 343, 350, 466, 488, 506
Little Leighs 235, 350
Little Oxney Green 181
Little Waltham 7, 11, 14, 21, 192, 332, 350, 490
Little Wigborough 287
Liverpool Street 41
Liverpool Street station 287
Livestock 22
Lloyd George 88
Local cricket 488
Local Defence Volunteers 462
Local Food Control Committee 285
Local Government Board 170, 171, 235
Local Government Board Commissioner 227
Local Management of Schools 398
Lodge- Muirhead system 92
Lodging houses 319
London Airport 107, 108
London and North Eastern Railway Line 172
London and Westminster Bank 197
London blitz 458
London General Omnibus Company (L.G.O.C.) 39
London Road Car Company (L.R.C.) 39
London Road Congregational church 289
London Road nurseries 390
Longstomp reservoir 282
Longstomps 319, 320, 322
Longstomps Avenue 206
Longstomps Road 195, 200

Loos 279
Lord Derby 280
Lord Emlyn 73
Lord Eustace Cecil 229
Lord Lieutenant of Essex 174, 374, 381
Lord Rayleigh 53, 374, 494, 521
Lord Roberts 279
Lordship farm 16, 18
Lord Torrington 69
Lord Tweedmouth 237
Loughton meeting 522
Lovedays 229
Lower Anchor Street 202
Loyal North Lancashire Regiment 244
L.S.D. 444
Lucking and Son 196
Luckin Smith 204
Luftwaffe aerial photograph 476
Lunney 320, 332, 357, 360
Lydia Bridges 145
Lydia Wells 33
Lynmouth Avenue 477
Lynton Lamb 537
Lyons Hall 220, 280
Lyons Hall barracks 285

M

M12 181
M25 181
Mace 229
Mackintosh 45
Macnamara 257
Mad cow disease 22
Magic eyes 175
Magistrate 356
Magistrates 354
Magnetron 143
Magnetron 'blocks' 96
Magnetrons 144, 146
Maidstone Motor Omnibus Company 39
Major Carne Rasch 6, 7, 231, 278, 369
Major H.S. Doe 457
Majority and Minority Reports of the Royal Commission into the Poor Laws 361
Major Jack Brinson 220
Major Paddy Blair Mayne 524
Major Rasch 232
Major Wilkes 462

Malay 71
Malcolm Stamp 310
Malcolm Wallace 164
Maldon 144, 213, 263, 352, 389, 443, 502, 521
Maldon and East Chelmsford 270
Maldon cricket club 506
Malnutrition 305
Malta 259
Maltings 31, 33, 194
Manchester 38
M and G 149
Mangold 11
Manning 338
Manor Road 329
Mansio 220
Mansion House 67, 241
Maplin 178
Marconi 30, 48, 95, 145, 148, 155, 158, 163, 164, 165, 194, 202, 238, 329, 334, 337, 338, 340, 381, 444, 465, 467, 470, 475, 488, 492, 493
Marconi/Adcock HF D/F stations 100
Marconi Applied Technologies (M.A.T.) 146
Marconi Archive 537
Marconi Club 496, 532, 543
Marconi College 83, 115, 205
Marconi Communication Systems Limited 113
Marconi Company 83
Marconi Company of the Home Guard 463
Marconi doppler 108
Marconi – E.M.I. 109
Marconi – E.M.I. Company 97
Marconi – E.M.I. system 97
Marconi House 87, 93
Marconi Instruments 21
Marconi Instruments Limited 105
Marconi International Marine Communications Limited 105
Marconi International Marine Communications Ltd 111
Marconi International Marine Company 85
Marconi laboratories 115
Marconi Marine 113
Marconi masts 487
Marconi Osram Valve Company 144
Marconiphone 95
Marconi P.L.C. 115
Marconi Ponds Nature Reserve 221
Marconi radar 108, 114

Marconi Radar 103, 113, 114, 115, 116, 221
Marconi radios 88
Marconi Road 202
Marconi Scandal 84, 88
Marconi's New street factory 475
Marconi Square 216
Marconi's sports ground 487
Marconi Statue 216
Marconi Strategic Communications 116
Marconi Telegraphy Company Limited 84
Margaret Thatcher 262, 264, 265, 270
Margaretting 125, 219, 270, 335, 350
Margaretting Hall 18
Margaretting Road 489
Marine Offences Act 542
Mark Cazalet 411
Market 9, 22, 197
Market garden course 18
Market gardening 7
Market House 198
Market road 200
Market Road 203, 246, 374, 419, 521
Mark Pougatch 541
Mark Punter 541
Marks and Spencer 197, 220
Mark Shelley and the Deans 543
Marriage 10, 11, 17, 215, 422, 495
Marriage family 31
Marriages 21
Marriage Square 199
Marshall Aid 259
Marshall and Snellgrove 199
Marshall tractor 17
Martello system 113
Martin Carthy 544
Mary Scott 45
Mashbury 350
Mason Arms 194
Mason's Villa 195
Massey Harris 15
Master of Emmanuel College 265
Maternity and Child Welfare Centre 305
Maternity Unit 310
Maternity ward 304
Maurice Abbott 525
Maurice Esterson 143
Mayor Arthur Andrews 260
Mayor Bellamy 249
Mayor Con Johnson 267

Mayoress Mrs F.A. Wells 373
Mayor George Taylor 280
Mayor J.O. Thompson 283
Mayor Sidney Tayor 521
Mayor Taylor 459, 526
Mayor Thompson 158
M.C.C. 262, 489
MC Racetracks 509
M.C.S. 114
M. Davies 462
Meadgate 401
Meadgate farm 14, 260
Means test 161, 361
Measles 281, 298
Mechanics Institute 152, 196, 236, 375, 515, 521, 522, 523
Medlicott's 197
Melbourne 218, 343
Melbourne athletics stadium 503
Melbourne Court 340
Melbourne estate 212, 336, 337, 378
Melbourne Park 390, 392, 443, 449, 507, 508, 510
Melbourne Park estate 338
Melbourne Park Flower Queen 534
Melchior 91
Melford Villas 195
Melody Maker 472
Memorial 289
MENTOR system 108
Merit Star 430
Merlin engine 130
Mervyn Day 503
Mesopotamia 177, 210
Mesopotamia Island 196, 203, 215, 406
Messerschmitt 473
Methodist chapel 422
Meyer 238
Michael Ashcroft 400
Michael Bonallack 510
Microprocessor 108
Microwave tubes 145
Middle Class Union 245
Middlesex County League 491
Mid Essex Conservative Association 231
Mid Essex constituency 225
Mid Essex education executive 392
Mid Essex Education Executive Committee 389
Mid Essex Plan 212

Mid Essex Technical College 111, 381
Mid Essex Technical School 394
Midford on Sea 54
Midwives 305
Mike Hawthorn 508
Mildmay 17
Mildmay family 11
Mildmay Hall 542
Mildmay Road 125, 194, 221, 296, 297, 317, 318, 320, 329, 331, 477
Military Cross 261
Military Service Bill 280
Military Traffic Scheme 282
Milk 7, 285, 296
Milk float 9
Milk Marketing Board 16
Milky Way galaxy 147
Millenium Wheel 265
Miller Christy 54, 288
Millington 255, 256, 305
Minister for Transport 271
Ministry of Education 392
Ministry of Food 391, 469
Ministry of Health 333, 334, 336, 355, 390, 458
Ministry of Transport 74, 158, 159, 176, 178
Ministry of Transport and Civil Aviation 107
Minnie Pallister 246
Minoprio 209, 212, 213
Minoprio Plan 175, 210, 410
Minster of State for Health 271
Miss Ann Rope 368
Miss B.S. White 246
Miss Chancellor 240
Miss Diana Hope 526
Miss Joseph 238
Miss Louisa Crabb 34
Miss Maloney 238
Miss Ridley 240
Mixed hockey 507
M.L. Bellamy 491
M.M. Davies 262
Moat Farm 436
Mobile phone 103
Model and Kettle lodging houses 408
Model and the Kettle 201
Model shop 83, 97
Mods 444, 544
Mods 532
Monopolies Commission 141

Moonie cult 417
Moores family 45
Morrison shelters 476, 478
Mosley 247
Mosquito 130, 463
Motor cars 123
Motor car testing 508
Motor cycle racing 508
Motor generators 131
Motorised taxi cab rank 54
Motor racing circuits 500
Motor show 74
Moulsham 52, 122, 179, 190, 193, 204, 281, 301, 305, 316, 329, 330, 336, 367, 391, 397, 400, 490, 520
Moulsham barracks 198
Moulsham Dramatic society 542
Moulsham Drive 206, 510
Moulsham Hall 194
Moulsham Junior School 461
Moulsham Lodge 194, 340, 416, 495
Moulsham Mill 12, 21, 22
Moulsham School 394, 399
Moulsham schools 339
Moulsham Schools 206, 378, 393
Moulsham secondary schools 392
Moulsham Senior School 458
Moulsham Street 153, 175, 176, 194, 201, 215, 228, 295, 332, 342, 399, 448, 469, 521, 534
Moulsham Teetotal Army 406
Mounted horse section 449
Mount Everest 244
Mountnessing 446
Mousham Drive 339
Mousham Mill 17
Mousham Mills 17
Moving sculpture 148
Mr and Mrs Martin 353
Mrs Bird's school 377
Mrs Conybeare 355, 358
Mrs Drummond 239
Mrs Durrant 520
Mrs Fenwick Miller 237
Mrs Pash 373
Mrs Tidboald 368
MTE Rayleigh 135
Mundella Act of 1880 367
Munich crisis 457

Munitions 42, 286
Munitions of War Act 75
Muriel Carston 44
Muriel Patience 446
Museum 379, 443
Museum, Library and Art School 522
Museum Terrace 199
Museum Terrace, New London Road 519
Muslim 196
Mussolini 95
MYRIAD 108

N

Nasser Hussain 505
Nasty Habits 545
National 42
National Association of Operative Plasterers 157
National Athletics League 508
National Curriculum 398
National Defence Committee 278
National Employers Federation 75
National Federation of Discharged and Demobilised Prisoners 334
National Federation of Engineers 159
National Federation of Music Festivals 517
National Fire Service 476
National Front 266
National Government 245, 246
National Health Service 162, 305
National Heritage 209, 215
National insurance 158
National Insurance 243, 358
Nationalisation of the electricity supply industry 56
National Lottery Fund 540
National Lottery funding 508
National Omnibus and Transport Company 174
National Omnibus Company 43, 172
National Outdoor Hockey champions 507
National Physical Laboratories 100
National Registration Act of 1915 280
National River Authority 182
National School 367
National Schools 367, 520
National Society of Child Nurseries 390
National Sporting Club 496
National Steam Car Co 41
National Telephone Company 172

National Trade Defence League 239
National Union of Agricultural Labourers 12
National Union of Police 440
National Union of Women's Suffrage Societies 54
National Union of Women's Suffrage Societies (N.U.W.S.S.) 237
N.A.T.O. 107, 113
Nat. West. Trophy 504
Nave organ 411
Navigation Road 36, 170, 463
Naysmyth 52
Negative pressure unit for premature babies 148
Nelion Ridley 34
Nelson Road 202
N.E. of Springfield 343
N.E.R. 40
Netball 497
Neville Chamberlain 244
Newark 134
Newark, Notts 135
New Bridge Street 197, 199, 521
Newfoundland 85
New Hall 219, 376, 399, 400, 401, 418, 476
New Hall School 298
New Labour 259
New London Road 170, 176, 190, 195, 196, 203, 228, 248, 297, 420, 449, 496, 521, 541
New London Road estate 419
New River Water Supply Company 317
New Street 30, 44, 83, 86, 88, 92, 95, 97, 98, 111, 115, 121, 143, 170, 199, 200, 202, 205, 434, 444, 449, 493
New Street cricket ground 486
New Street factory 83, 105
New Street ground 488
New Street works 89
New Writtle Street 174, 195, 200, 205, 334, 351, 489, 491, 495, 501, 541
New Writtle Street cricket ground 503
New Writtle Street ground 500, 502
New York 144
New Zealand 71, 107
N.H.S. 295, 300, 532
Nic Jones 544
Nick Simmons Smith 408
Nigel Fanshawe 395
Nikolaus Pevsner 205
Nissen hut 463, 467
Nite-Watch 146

Noakes End 341
Noel Gallagher 546
Nonconformism 419
Nonconformist Cemetery 195
Nonconformists 369, 373
Nonconformists 366
Nonconformity 405
Non contributory pension scheme 55
Norman Hadden 261
Norman Lamont 265
Norman Squier 379, 395
Norman St John Stevas 262
Norman St Stevas 393
Northampton 71
North Avenue 205, 333
Northcliffe Newspapers 548
North Eastern Railway Company 39
North Essex League 491
North Melbourne 342
North Sea Oil 110
North Somerset 56
North Springfield 218, 502
Norwich 67, 225, 277, 335, 456
Norwich school board 370
Norwich Union 234
Nottingham Forest 492
Nuisance 319
Nuisance Inspectors 318, 324
N.U.P.E. 162
Nursery Road 195
Nursery Street 200
N.U.T. 157
N.U.W.S.S. 238, 240, 241
NXEA 183
Nyad 198
Nye Bevan 305

O

Oaklands 193, 194, 200, 204, 206, 282, 284, 457, 537
Oaklands hospital 283
Oaklands House 32, 523
Oaklands Lodge 193
Oaklands Park 250, 443
Oakum 356
Oakum picking 354, 429
Oasis 545
Obscenity and the Law 263

Odde Volumes 514
Odde Volumes Society 520
Odeon 527, 541, 543, 545
Odeon cinema 176
Office of Fair Trading 141, 142
Old Age Pensions 359
Old Bailey 437
Old Chelmsford Gaol 521
Old Contemptibles Association 290
Old Cromptonians 491
Old Friary 204
Old Houses, the Friars 517
Old Kent Road 38
Old Oak 197
Old Town Jury Club 197, 519
Old White Hart Inn 194
Olivia Hale 338
Ongar 171, 390
Onions 21
Ontario Museum 79
Open air pool 490
Open air swimming baths 509
Operational Support Group 449
Operation 'Gadfly' 114
Operation 'Overlord' 464
Operatives Bricklayers Society 156
Orams 202
Orange Tree 277
Orchard Lodge 196
Orchards 7
Orchard Street 305
Orchid Drinks 141
Orpheus 543
Orpington 262
Osborne House 85
Oscar Wilde 518
Osea Island 175
Oswald Mosley 246, 266
Ottawa agreement 16
Our Lady Immaculate Church 418
Outdoor relief 356, 357
Outdoor relief stations 357
Overcrowding 319
Owen College 297
Oxbridge entrance exams 395
Oxford 501
Oxford and Buckinghamshire Light Infantry 283
Oxford University 116
Oxford University Conservative Association 268

Oxney Green 422

P

Paardeberg 277
Paddington station 69
Padoga 198
Palmer and Harvey 45
Panic magazine 548
Paraffin 42
Pargetting 218
Parkeston Quay, Harwich 60
Parkway 179, 180, 194, 216, 218, 220
Passmore Edwards 522
Passmore Edwards Museum 182, 522
Patching Hall estate 337
Patents 100
Patrick Abercrombe 211
Pattern makers 124
Paul Rumsey 537
Paul Simon 544
Pavilion 526, 541
P.C. Henry Baker 204
Peace meeting 456
Pearl Assurance building 203
Peas 7
Peckham 41
Pedestrianisation 181
Peggy Bradley 468
Pendeen 204
Penny farthings 171
Pepsi 140, 141
Percy Bennett 471
Percy Rainbird 129, 289
Period and Country Homes 539
Pertwee 198, 296, 317, 352
Peter Edwards 506
Peter Hebdon 463
Pete Searles 543
Petrol 320
Petroleum Act 431
Petroleum inspectors 171
Petrol rationing 175
Petty Sessions 431, 443
Pevsner 219
Philip Bartlett 76, 130
Philosophical Society 521
Phoenix 32
Phoenix Coffee House 496

Phoenix Dynamo Company Ltd 143
Phoney war 458, 459
Piers Aubyn 412
Pig rearing 21
Pillar Limited 47
Pillboxes 462, 466
Pink Floyd 544
Pinkham 45
Piquets 287
Planning act 206
Plastic explosives 463
Playle Company 57
Pleshey 7, 14, 350, 414
Plessey 7
Plessey Company 112
Plough 200
Pneumonia 282
Poldhu 85, 87
Police 354
Police Commissioners 439
Police Community Support Officers 450
Police Federation 440
Police Headquarters 442
Police motorcyclists 443
Police Museum 436
Police station 287
Polio 306
Polish Broadcasting Corporation 97
Pollard Ball Bearings Limited 134
Pollards garages 200
Poll Tax 269
Pollution 321
Pool 198
Poole Harbour 85
Poor law 358
Poor Law 349, 354, 356
Poor law guardians 158
Poor Law guardians 232, 233, 349
Poor Law Inspector 355
Porridge 447
Postmaster General 91
Potatoes 17, 21
Pottery Lane 477
Poultry 10, 18
Power valves 145
Prefab 336, 337
Prefabs 339, 341
Premier Division of the E.H.L. 507
Preparatory School 375, 381

President of the Association of Poor Law Unions 361
President of the Institute of Automobile Engineers 74
President of the Union 263
Presto 203
Presyterian Church 421
Pretoria, South Africa 71
Pretyman 16, 157, 238, 242
Pretyman Cup 496
Primary schools 391
Primers for shells 131
Primitive Methodist church 283
Primrose Hill 202
Primrose League 230, 237
Prince 92
Prince of Orange 545
Prince of Wales 10
Princes Road 339, 378, 400
Princess Anne 271
Princess Margaret 411, 536
Princess Mary Louise 493
Prison 169, 428, 446
Prison school 429
Prittlewell 437
Private finance initiative 309
Private W. Rawlinson 277
Privatisation 165
Privy midden 316
Prize Guys 544
Prodigy 545
Proms 542
Provost Moses 410
Pro wave 147
Public Assistance Committee 161
Public Health Act of 1876 321
Public library 521
Public Library, Museum and School of Art 204
Public Loans Board 318
Public shelters 460
Public works schemes 151
Pulp 546
Pump Lane 183, 218, 342
Punch and Judy show 233
Punk festival 545
Punk rock festival 502
Punks 532
Pupil teacher 368
Pupil teacher system 371

Purdey's 141
Purfleet 465
Purleigh 434

Q

Quadrant 152, 155
Quaker 11, 51, 479
Quaker movement 456
Quakers 422
Quarter Sessions 443
Quasi voucher 398
Quedlingburg 478
Queens Award for Exports 113
Queens Award for Industry 113, 114, 144, 147
Queens Award for Technical Achievement 113
Queen's Diamond Jubilee 521
Queen's Head Inn 197
Queensland 373
Queensland Crescent 339
Queen's Road 195
Queen Street 175, 200, 228
Queen Victoria 67, 493
Queer as Folk 417
Quoits 496
Quoits 485

R

Rab Butler 392
R.A. Butler 261, 263
Racecourse 508
Radar 83, 100, 103, 107, 108, 143
Radio beacons 111
Radiohead 545
Radio Society of Great Britain 92
Radio telephones 94
Radiotherapy machines 147
Radishes 21
R.A.F 259
R.A.F. 113, 256
Ragged school 366
Ragged Trousered Philanthropists 260
Railway 177
Railways 168
Railway station 182
Railway Street 153, 154
Railway strike 127
Railway Tavern 228

Rainbow trout 323
Rainsford 190
Rainsford End 10, 332, 524
Rainsford End houses 334
Rainsford House 247
Rainsford housing estate 460
Rainsford Lane 174, 177, 179, 200, 316, 332, 336, 372, 469
Rainsford Road 170, 174, 179, 200, 236, 334, 368, 372, 422, 488, 526, 541
Rainsford School 391, 393, 398, 399, 401, 503, 533
Rainsford Senior 382
Rainsford windmill 31
Ralph Chapman 138, 139
Ramsden Heath 264
Ramsgate 495
Rank Organisation 541
Ransome and Marle 134
Ransome, Hoffmann and Pollard 120
Ransome, Hoffmann, Pollard 134
Ransome, Hoffmann, Pollard site 400
Rasch 279
Ration Conditions Orders 468
Raven Thompson 246
Ray Clark 541
Ray East 505
Ray Fullerton 487
Ray Knappett 470
Raymond Unwin 211, 333
RBQ 544
R.D.C. 191, 214, 235, 236, 282, 298, 319, 321, 322, 324, 335, 336, 339, 350, 353, 390, 465, 469
Reading 268
Rebel tour of South Africa 505
Receiver sets 99
Recreation Ground 200, 212, 247, 283, 284, 337, 457, 463, 491, 492, 496, 515
Rectory Lane 121, 179, 476
Rectory Lane Churchyard 196
Rectory Lane Youth Centre 395
Rectory Road 202
Red Cow 406
Red Cross 419, 524
Red Cross hospital 284
Red Cross Society 284
Red Devil 141
Red Flag 171

Redgates 414
Redistribution of Seats Act 1885 229
Red Lion pub 195
Refrigeration business 59
Refugees 459
Regent 194, 526, 527, 533, 535, 541
Regent Street 41
Regent Theatre 283, 289
Reggae club 544
Regiment Way 510
Registrar of the Archdeacon of St Albans 439
Registrar of the Chelmsford County Court 439
Reliance Life Assurance Company 234
Relief fund 72
Remembrance Day 276
Repeal of the Combination Acts in 1824 - 1825 155
Repton 541
Rettendon 7, 264, 318, 324, 338, 350, 473
Rettendon killings 449
Reverend Andrew Clark 279
Reverend Barnyard 357
Reverend Canon Lake 240
Reverend Claud Hinchcliffe 241
Reverend E.P. Gibson 357
Reverend Falkner Allison 416
Reverend F.W. Atkin 237
Reverend G.C. Postans 236
Reverend Gibson 358, 359
Reverend J.A. Kershaw 374
Reverend John Morgan Whiteman 297
Reverend J.W. Crompton 236
Reverend Pearson 369
Reverend Stanley Gibson 236
Reverend Thurlow 378
Reverend T. Macdougal Mundle 240
Revised Code 367
R. Hadley 266
R. Harrington 159
R.H. Etchells 526
R.H.P. 134, 163, 164
R. Hunt and Co 61
Ribbon development 205
Richard Ackland 256
Richard Branson 546
Richard Buickham 438
Richard Coates 35
Richard Coleman 37
Richard Crabb 34

Richard Davis 434
Richard Francis 198
Richard Wenley 218
Richenda Christy 52, 54, 240
Rich family 220
Richmond Park 38
Ridley 31
Ridley's 53
Rifle Brigade 65
Rignals Lane 32
Rio Tinto Zinc Corporation 47
Ripley 47
Ritz (Chelmsford) Limited 526
Rivenall 112
River Authority 215
River Can 490
River Chelmer 6, 33, 121, 197
River Chelmer railway viaduct 463
River Crouch 216
Rivermead 400
Rivermead campus 400
River Rhine 468
Riverside Leisure Centre 509
River Stour 324
River Wid 31, 184
R.J. Kemp 106
R.J. Smith 56
Road widening schemes 158
Robert Cook 485, 497
Robert Crowle 526
Robert Greenwood 207
Robert Telford 116
Robert Tressell 260
Robinson Fruit Shoot 142
Robinson King and Company (Chelmsford) Ltd 47
Robinsons 141
Rochdale Pioneers 152
Rochford 206, 265
Rochford constituency 264
Rochford Road 153, 201, 221
Rockers 444
Rod Stewart 544
Rogers 374, 375
Roller milling 17
Rolling Stones 544
Rolls Royce 524
Romano – Celtic temple 221
Roman Road 331
Roman Road Mission room 406

Roman settlements 190
Rontgen Ray 300
Rook 241
Rookes Evelyn Crompton 65
Rope Walk 194
Roseberry Hotel 406
Roseberry Road 204
Roseberry Yard 44
Rosemary Rutherwood 412
Rothesay 206
Rothesay Avenue 193, 336
Round 83, 90
Rowntrees 45
Roxwell 154, 192, 332, 338, 350, 464, 469, 473, 477, 520
Roxwell Labour Camp 339
Royal Academy 248
Royal Artillery 234, 256, 282
Royal Automobile Club 74
Royal College of Music 542
Royal College of Sciences 38
Royal Field Artillery 261
Royal Flying Corp 92
Royal Military Academy, Greenwich 234
Royal National Lifeboat Institution 95
Royal Navy 85
Royal Show 10, 14
Royal Signals Unit, 99
Royal Steamer 467
Royal Warrant 142
Royal Yacht 85
Roy Stroud 501
R. Pertwee 370
R. Telford 106
Rufus Isaacs 88
Rugby 485
Runner beans 21
Runwell 7, 206, 318, 332, 350, 450
Rural council 175
Rural District Council 170, 248, 318, 333
Rural Sanitary Authority 234, 318, 332
Russian gun 198
Rutland and Stamford Young Conservatives 268
R. Whites 141
R.W. Thompson 65

S

Sadie Nine 541

Saffron Walden 390, 543
Saint Augustine of Canterbury 419
Saltmarsh 330
Saltmarsh's nursery 194
Salute the Soldiers 472
Salvage weeks 472
Salvation Army 407, 408
Sam Crozier 435
Sam Dougal 437
Samuel Courtauld 84
Samuel Dougal 436
Sanctuary 410
Sandford Mill 247, 322, 324, 491, 537
Sandford Mill Industrial Museum 116
Sandford Mill Museum 94, 125
Sandford Road 434
Sandhurst 244
Sandon 13, 125, 177, 181, 221, 332, 335, 350, 377, 392, 393, 400, 443, 502, 537
Sandon Parish Council 178
Sandon School 394
Sanitary Committee 317, 319
Sanitary inspector 319
Saracens Head 163, 197, 198, 207, 473, 494, 519
Saracens Head Hotel 15, 197, 472, 495
S.A.S. 524, 540
Saturday Scene 543
Save For Victory 471
Scarlet fever 298, 299
Scavenging 319
School board 366, 368, 369, 370
School Certificate 379
School for wardens 438
School Medical Officers of Health 305
School of Agriculture 376
School of Art and Technology 381
School shelters 461
Science Museum 79
Scimitar 115
Scooter club 544
Scotland Yard 40
Scottish farmers 8, 16
Scouting Jamboree 546
Screaming Lord Sutch 543
Script 547
S.D.P. 267, 269
Seabrooks 19
Seachart' echo finder 113
Sea Dart missiles 115

Searchlight magazine 162
Searchlights 69, 74, 277
Sea Wolf 115
Sebastapol cannon 198, 202
Sebastopol 65
Select cinema 246, 351, 525, 541
Select Committees 264
Senator George McGovern 268
Senta and Remoh 443
Sergeant John Eves 434
Sergeant Peters 433
Sergeant Scott 435
Serrin Arc Lamps 66
Service industries 47
Sette of Odde Volumes 520
Settlement Laws 355
Seven Up 141
Sexual Offences Act of 1967 263
Seymour Street 200, 493
Shackleton 284, 524
Sheep rot 6
Sheffield Wednesday 492
Shellhaven 465
Shell Haven 47
Shenfield 177
Shepherds Bush 41
Sherriff's Office 437
Shire Hall 21, 47, 160, 161, 198, 199, 204, 230, 235, 239, 250, 266, 279, 280, 284, 354, 355, 361, 369, 393, 406, 411, 428, 431, 434, 443, 445, 449, 450, 456, 462, 467, 486, 487, 488, 496, 514, 515, 516, 521, 522, 533, 542, 543
Shire Passage 198
Shirley Williams 265, 396
Shoeburyness 174
Shop stewards 78
Shotgun Express 544
Showerings and Waterways 140
Sick Benefit club 154
Sick club 53
Sidney Harris 526
Sidney Taylor 259
Sidney Walter Robinson 242
Silver End 329
Silvertown 68
Simon Aseinstein 144
Simon Burns 181, 268, 269, 270, 310
Simon Heffer 268

Siouxie and the Banshees 545
Sir Alec Douglas Home 263
Sir Daniel Gooch 523
Skating 496
Skating rinks 496
Skeletal army 407, 408
Skiffle 543
Skinheads 544
Skinheads 532
Skipton 257
Skreens Park, Roxwell 284
Slaughter and the Dogs 545
Sleeping Beauty 518
Slimsta 140
Small Faces 544
Smallpox 297, 299
Smash and grab 443
S.M.O. 305, 376, 382
Smokers' concerts 518
Snooker 496
Snow Patrol 546
Social Democrats 265
Society for the Essex Female Discharged Prisoners 429
Society for the Prevention of Cruelty to Children 432
Society for the Promotion of New Music 543
Society of Friends 283
Society of Operative Bricklayers 156
Soft fruit 7
Somme 279
South Africa 278
South African Government 113
Southampton 71
Southbank Sinfonia 418
South East Anglian League 491
Southend 180, 373, 444, 495, 518, 542
Southend pier 72
Southend United 492
Southend Water Company 324
Southern League 500, 501
Southern League Cup 500
South Essex League 491
South Essex Waterworks Company 324
Southhampton University 263
South Hanningfield 323, 350
South Lodge Hotel 196
South porch 410
South Wales 68

South Weald 262, 489
South Woodham Ferrers 164, 216, 218, 264, 449, 511, 547
Soviet farms 78
Space cameras 146
Spaghetti junction 184
Spalding 190, 196, 197, 198, 202, 213
Spalding Junior's 207
Spalding Senior 260
Spanish Civil War 245
Sparrow and Co 47
Sparrow and Tufnell Bank 48
Sparrow, Tufnell and Co 197
Spartan League 491
Special Chief Constable 440
Special constables 286, 440, 442, 457
Special Constabulary 441
Spectator 375
Speed cameras 446
Spigot mortars 463
Spitfire 475
Spotted Dog 198, 199, 202
Springboard 342
Springfield 7, 11, 22, 46, 174, 176, 177, 182, 190, 193, 200, 210, 212, 216, 227, 235, 247, 264, 266, 333, 336, 342, 350, 370, 486, 495, 533
Springfield Green 200
Springfield jail 476
Springfield Lyon 205
Springfield Lyon site 149
Springfield Medical Centre 308
Springfield parish council 262
Springfield Park 390
Springfield Place 308
Springfield Place. 10
Springfield prison 319
Springfield Road 153, 173, 180, 198, 205, 407, 421, 526
Springfield schools 369
Springfield wharf 31
Spurs 492, 500
Squash court 488
Squash courts 509
Squire 13
S. Singer 526
Stabilovolt 99, 143
Stag hunting 520
Stamford School 268

Stan Brown 290
Standardisation 64
Standardisation 99
St Andrews 416
St Annes 377
Stansted 181
Staple Grove 547
Starfish decoy site 466
Starvision 145
St Cecilia's Choral Society 542
St Cedd 410
Steam driven lorries 43
Steamer 544
Steam fire engine 233
Steam ploughs 17
Steam road engine 65
Steam roller 169, 170
Steamship 'Chelmsford' 172
Steeple chasing 490
Stellar satellite communication amplifier 146
Sten gun 130
Sten guns 463
Stephen Cottrell 418
Stephen Robinson 271
Stereophonics 547
Stevas 64, 78, 112, 134, 177, 180, 182, 263, 264, 309, 394, 446
St Giles 304, 308
Stirling Moss 508
St John Payne Roman Catholic School 400
St John Payne School 399
St John's 283, 361, 376, 378, 411
St John's Ambulance 260, 457
St John's church 193, 287, 457
St John's church at Danbury 412
St John's Churchyard, Moulsham Street 196
St John's hospital 304, 458
St John's Hospital 307
St John's maternity ward 308
St John's, Moulsham 515
St John's Road 175
St John's school 193, 368, 371, 377
St John's Terrace 368
St John's Vicarage 195
St Joseph's Salesians School 262
St Leonards on Sea 43
St Martin's at Little Waltham 411
St Mary's 409
St Mary's at Fryerning 411

St Mary's at Widford 412
St Mary's Church 296, 516
St Mary's churchyard 196
St Mary's churchyard, Great Baddow 196
St Mary's parish church 198, 406, 514
St Mary the Virgin at High Easter 412
St Michael and All Angels at Galleywood 412
St Neots 56
Stock 53, 241, 270, 282, 322, 324, 333, 350
Stock Exchange 146
Stock parish church 475
Stock Road 489
Stone 31
Stone bridge 194
Stone ground flour 17
Stonehouse 130
Stone masons 36
Stone Roses 546
St Peter 410
St Peters 368, 391, 410
St Peters College 401
St Peter's School 283
St Philip's Priory 196, 418
St Philip's Priory site 377
St Pius 419
Stravinsky's Rite of Spring 516
Strawbs 544
Stroud 60
S.T. Shipman 406
Stuart Mole 264, 268, 341
Studio E at Lime Grove 144
Stump Lane 205
Submarine 144
Subscription ball 488
Subscription balls 516
Suez 259, 261
Suez crisis 132
Suffolk Hussars 228
Suffragettes 41, 237
Suffragists Church Women Protest Committee 241
Sugar 468
Sugar beet 21, 284
Sunday school 405, 419, 421
Sunday Times 399
Sunderland 267
Susan 182
Sussex Road Motor Company 39
Sutherland 106

Sutherland Lodge 368
Swan Company 67
Swan United Electric Co 66
Sweden 107
Swimming baths 233, 491
Swimming pool 382
Switchgear 78
Switzerland 177
Sybil Olive 77, 162, 257, 469
Syd Plunkett 501
Sylvia Pankhurst 238

T

Tabor 241
Taiwan's Keeling Harbour 61
Take That 546
Tameside decision 394
Tanks 131
Tank week 284
Tar 31
Tariff Reform League 239
Taunton Commission 374
Taylor Walker 32
T. Brown 471
T.D. Ridley 33
Technical High School 397
Teddy Boys 443, 532, 543
Ted Heath 264, 266, 543
Ted Heath Orchestra 543
Teenage Fanclub 545
Teenage gangs 442
Teenagers 443
Telefunken 84, 86
Telephone 175
Telephone installation 65
Telephony transmitter 90
Television 83, 96
Telstar 110
Temperance Council 52
Temperance hotel 406
Temperance movement 405
Temperance societies 378
Tenant farmers 6
Tennyson Road 341
Ten pin bowling 510
Territorial Army 41, 256, 456, 462
Territorials 524
T.G.W.U 77

Thames Haven 465
Thatcher government 398
Thaxted 44, 413
Theatre 382
The Lynmouth 69
The Meadows 217
The Price Is Right 145
Thermal imaging 146
Thermal imaging camera 145, 147
The 'Yards' 202, 214
Thimble boilers 42
Thomas Chapman 152
Thomas Churchman Darby 14
Thomas Clarkson 30, 38, 172, 239
Thomas Clarkson Neale 193, 521
Thomas Dixon Ridley 32
Thomas Hay 375
Thomas Sadler 437
Thomas Tidboald 193
Thomas Usborne 231
Thomas Webb 411
Thornwoods 195
T.H.P. Dennis 39, 48, 65, 153, 193, 234, 317, 519
Threadneedle Street 247
Thrust bearing 123
Thundersley 471
Thurrock 502
Thyratron 143
Tied cottages 20
Tilbury 465
Tilekiln Road 206
Timber 31, 175
Times 437
Time Team 401
Tina 265
Tindal Square 43, 48, 198, 202, 212, 215, 239, 263, 334, 478
Tindal Street 17, 152, 198, 199, 204, 212, 215, 228, 330, 493, 514
Tiptree Heath 6
Titanic 87, 88
T.M. Gepp 439
Tolly Cobbold 34
Tom Dunne 494
Tom Dyckoff 221
Tom Dymond 10
Tom Jones 546
Tom Odell 547
Tom Turner 139, 201

Tony Butcher 503
Tony Tuckwell 398
Toronto 144
Torquay Bus Company 39
Tottenham Grammar School 383
Tour De France 146
Tower Gardens 207
Townfield Street 33
Town Planning Committee 246
Traction engines 169
Tractors 16, 21
Trade cycle 151, 357
Trades Council 151, 157, 158, 160, 162, 246, 284, 333, 390
Trades Disputes and Trades Unions Act of 1927 160
Trafalgar Square 479
Tramps 354, 355
Transistor 108
Transvaal 278, 413
Travellers Rest lodging house 319
Treadmill 428, 429
Tree of Life 411
Trenches 383
Trevor Bailey 506
Trevor Brooking 508
Trevor Holds 545
Tribunals 281
Triffolium 11
Trinity College, Cambridge 261
Trinity Road logbook 378
Trinity Road Primary school 401
Trinity Road School 371, 372
Trinity School 378, 533
Tritton 220, 286
Tritton family 13, 280, 415
True Temperance Association 407
Truman Breweries 523
Tudor almshouses 193
Tunman Mead 469
Turkey 60
Turret ring 131
T. Usborne 520
T.V. advertising 140
Twenty twenty finals day 504
Tyco Electronics 79
Tyndal Street 278
Typhoon 463

U

U boats 100
Underground tube train 72
Under Sheriff 439
Under Sherriff 437, 445
Under water cameras 144
Unemployed 357, 376
Unemployment 174, 357
Unemployment relief 358
Unemployment Relief Committee 161
Unemployment Relief Fund 154, 158
Unilever 60
Union Court 199
Union Yard 330
United Builders Labourers Union 156
United Cordwainers 155
United Nations 144, 258
United Reform Church 421
United Works sports day 488
United Works Sports days 68
Upper Bridge Road 200, 277, 336, 475
Upper Holloway 413
Upper middle class 486
Utility furniture 338
UXB 475

V

V1 rockets 477
V-2s 460, 477
Vaccination 306
Vacuum laboratory 143
Vagrants 354, 434
Valve diathermy apparatus 303
Van Dieman's Road 173, 204
Van Diemans Road 201, 206
Vaughn Williams 517
V.E. day 478
Veley 367
Veterans Ladies team 507
V festival 546
Vicarage Road 195, 204, 493, 510
Vic Hales 378
Victoria National School 199, 228, 367
Victoria National Schools 368
Victoria Road 44, 139, 169, 217, 444
Victoria school 372
Victoria schools 377

Victoria Street 41
Victoria Tube 79
Vietnam 264
Vine Products 140
Vineyard 24
Vineyards 200
Vineyards, Great Baddow 517
Vivienne Wiseman 507
Voluntary Aid Detachment 457
Voluntary aided status 395
Voluntary hospitals 295
Voluntary schools 366
V.P. Wines 140

W

Wage Committee for Essex 242
Waitrose 217
Wakefield 297
Walter Bagehot 263
Waltham 413
Walthams 7, 13, 321
Walton on the Naze 518
W. and H. Marriage 12
W. and S. Eddington 37
Wandsworth 42
War Agricultural Committee 15, 18
War Agricultural Executive 20
War Agricultural Executive Committee 20
War Bonds 283
War Cry 407
Warden 459
Wardens 457
War Department 41
Warley 437
War memorial 478
War Office 278
War Savings Committee 283
War Weapons Weeks 471
Watchhouse Road, Galleywood 475
Watching posts 287
Waterhouse Lane 144, 145, 146, 174, 488, 508
Waterhouse Lane factory 144, 145
Waterhouse Street 205
Waterloo Lane 199, 203, 248, 390, 490
Waterloo Lane pool 371
Water mains 324
Watts Ditchfield 409, 414
W. Cole 522

We Also Helped 130
Weekly News 8, 9, 43, 53, 70, 84, 93, 95, 97, 159, 162, 169, 171, 206, 213, 227, 229, 230, 231, 233, 238, 244, 245, 249, 260, 267, 278, 280, 286, 296, 297, 321, 322, 332, 340, 352, 354, 357, 359, 373, 374, 391, 442, 444, 446, 457, 489, 497, 504, 515, 534, 545
Weinstock 114, 115, 144
Welfare State 362
Wells and Perry 31, 174, 203, 333, 465
Wells Street 153, 154
Wenley 84, 199, 204, 217, 227, 258, 486
Wenley and Son 523
Wenley Trust 504
Wesleyan chapel 420
Wesleyan school room 283
Wes Maughan 501
West Bromwich Albion 261
West Chelmsford 270
West Devon Electric Supply Company 56
West End 180, 183
West Essex band 515
West Essex Car Club 508
West Essex Cycling Club 486
West Essex Militia 194, 197
West Essex Riding Club 486
West Ham 192, 412, 444, 522
West Ham United 503
West Hanningfield 176, 350
Westlands 340, 343, 393
Westlands Aircraft Limited 145
Westlands estate 416
Westlands School 394
Westmoreland 517
West ward 247
Westway 111, 548
Wetherfield 479
W.F. Toynbee 242
W.G. Grace 506
Wheat 7, 8, 11, 16
Wheatsheaf 33
Wheatsheaf at Rettendon 33
Wheelwright 17
Whisky money 10, 376
Whist drives 414, 519
White Hart 32, 282, 544
White Hart Hotel 9, 170, 198, 202, 230, 519
White Hart Inn 493

White Hart Lane 342
White Hart Lane, Springfield 473
White Horse 467
White House Farm 448
Whitmore 52, 228, 229, 352, 495, 520
Whitmore and Bunyon 52
Who 543
Whooping cough 281
Wickford 318
Wid 6
Widford 46, 140, 142, 177, 181, 227, 235, 247, 336, 350, 495, 511, 523
Widford Bridge 173
Widford business park 45, 140
Widford church 297, 523
Widford Church of England school 378
Widford Hall 523, 524
Widford Industrial Estate 148
Widford school 378
Widford War Memorial 378
William Augustus Lucking 195
William Beadel 230
William Beal 438
William Booth 407
William Burnett 437
William Christy 53, 55
William Joyce (Lord Haw Haw) 478
William Jury 526
William Lewis Gray 41
William Mildmay 193
William Perry Newport Ridley 31
William Poyntz 430
William Preece 92
William Ridley 33
William Seabrook 19
William Spens 465
William Ward Duffield 234
William Waters 116
William Wenley 199
William Wilkes 437
Willingale 181
Willingale Aerodrome 475
Wilshere sisters 368
Wimbledon 493
Winchester 517
Winchester College 261
Windmill 53
Windmill Arms 194
Windmill Inn 205

Windscale 479
Windsor Castle 67
Wing Commander Millington 257
Wing Command Sparling 457
Wings For Victory 472
Winnifred Sayer. 90
Wireless operators 85
Wireless telegraphy 85, 89
Wireless Telegraphy and Signal Company 84
Wisden 261, 505
Witham 8, 10, 130, 145, 391
Witham depot 391
Witham magistrates court 449
W.J. Courtauld 248
W.J. Iden 43
W.J. Morrison 40
Wladyslaw Mirecki 537
W.M. Tufnell 48
Wolsey Road 200
Women at Work Committee 390
Women's Auxiliary Police 469
Women's Freedom League 238
Women's Institute 517
Women's Land Army 20, 285, 469
Women's Liberal Association 237
Women's Peace Corp 442
Women's Police Department 446
Women's Primrose League 230
Women's refuge 342
Women's Social and Political Union (W.S.P.U.) 237
Women's suffrage 225, 232, 237
Women's Total Abstinence Union 406
Women's Volunteer Service 390
Women Volunteers Service 470
Woodford 412
Woodford villas 194
Woodhall 340, 341, 416
Woodham Ferrers 7, 174, 192, 216, 324
Woodham Ferris 297, 318, 331, 350, 431
Woodhill 232
Wood Street 68, 170, 206, 301, 351, 354, 359, 495, 518
Wood Street workhouse 159
Woodwork 378
Woolpack Inn 283
Woolwich 68
Woolworths 197, 204
Worcester College, Oxford 268

Workers Union 12, 15, 156, 157, 160, 246
Workhouse 191, 281, 354, 355, 356
Workhouse children 358
Working Men's Compensation Act 232
World War One 171, 302
W.P. Gepp 440
Wray 486
Wray and Fullers 36
Wray Bolingbroke 218
Wray family 36
Wren chapel 265
Wrestling 527, 533
Wright 205
W. Rimmer 393
Writtle 23, 24, 31, 91, 92, 98, 111, 172, 181, 193, 214, 216, 218, 219, 221, 235, 247, 270, 283, 318, 321, 324, 335, 336, 350, 359, 366, 469, 477, 487, 495, 520
Writtle and Widford Nursing Association 283
Writtle boys home 362
Writtle brewery 34
Writtle Green 422
Writtle Institute 20
Writtle junior boys and girls 391
Writtle parish church 54
Writtle Park 520
Writtle Road 64, 72, 111, 115, 196, 200, 205, 301, 490, 521
Writtle Road Arc Works 74
Writtle Road cemetery 473, 474, 486
Writtle sewage 321
W.S.P.U. 238, 239, 241
W.T. Ditcham 90
W.W. Duffield 46, 191, 226, 230, 236, 353, 519
Wykham Chancellor 409

X

X mill 58
X ray 143
X-ray equipment 300

Y

Yale University 263
Yards 212
Yarmouth 54
Y club 545
Yehudi Menuhin 418

Y.M.C.A. 284, 477, 545
Young Liberals 240
Youth centre 382
You Tube 544
Ypres 279

Z

Zambia 61
Zeppelin 277, 287, 288
Zoot Money 544

Lightning Source UK Ltd.
Milton Keynes UK
UKOW03f1647191114

241867UK00013B/970/P